[redacted]

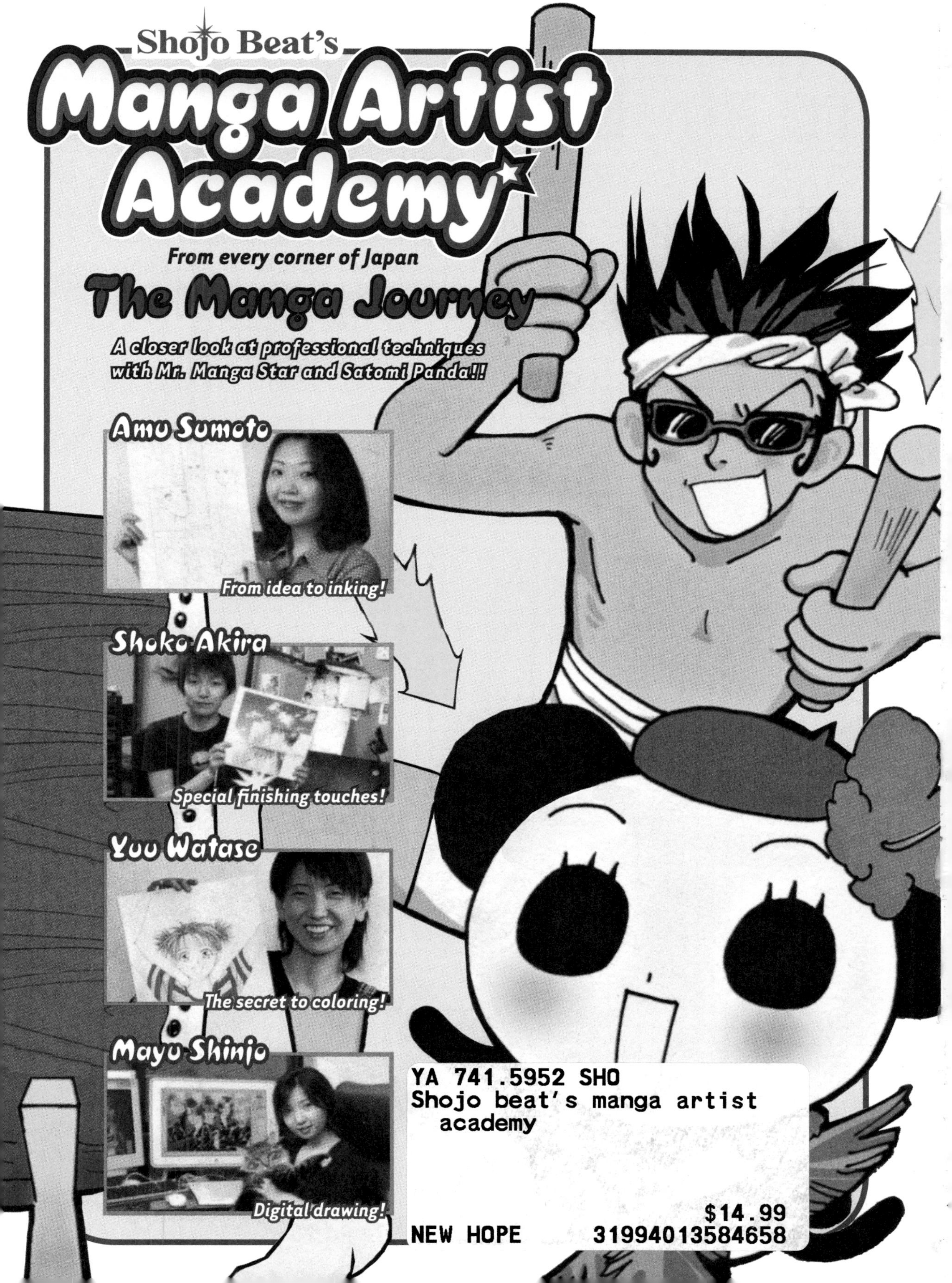
Shojo Beat's
Manga Artist Academy
From every corner of Japan
The Manga Journey
A closer look at professional techniques with Mr. Manga Star and Satomi Panda!!
Amu Sumoto
From idea to inking!
Shoko Akira
Special finishing touches!
Yuu Watase
The secret to coloring!
Mayu Shinjo
Digital drawing!

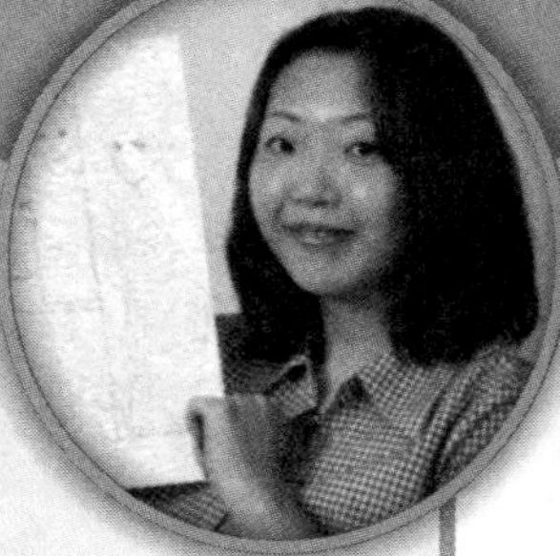

FROM IDEA TO ROUGH DRAFT.

Here's a look into the initial process of creating a manga and a day in the life of Amu Sumoto, currently featured in *Cheese!* magazine.

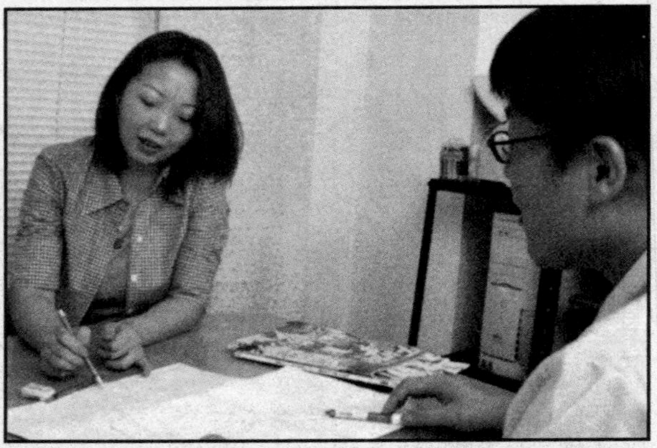

Amu Sumoto in a meeting with her editor. A manga artist also needs to be open to other people's opinions!

A storyboard meeting, otherwise known as a manga blueprint!

The most rigorous work for a manga artist isn't the script, it's creating the storyboard. If you've got a good storyboard, then that in itself makes your product a lot more interesting! First, pull together a rough story flow of the plot and create a storyboard by splitting the story into frames. We have meetings with editors based on that storyboard!

A SHINES.

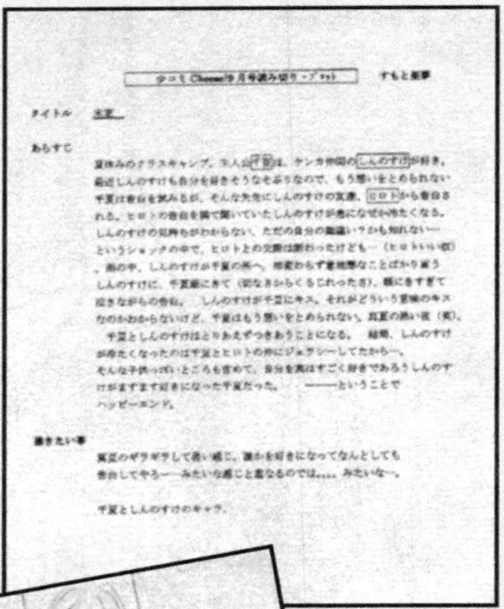

THE PLOT

A plot synopsis breaks down the story. It makes it easier to visualize the scene if you incorporate key graphics and lines!

←

THE STORYBOARD

The storyboard roughly outlines the structure, composition, and lines. Try to incorporate detailed graphics so other people can understand it!

↓

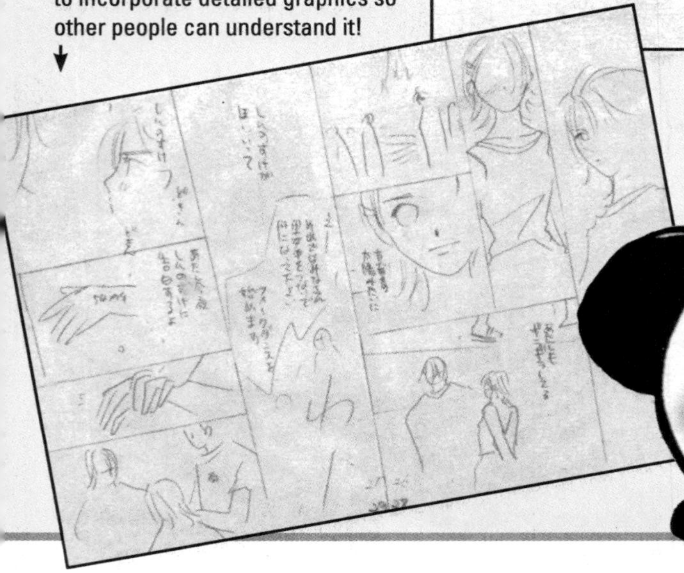

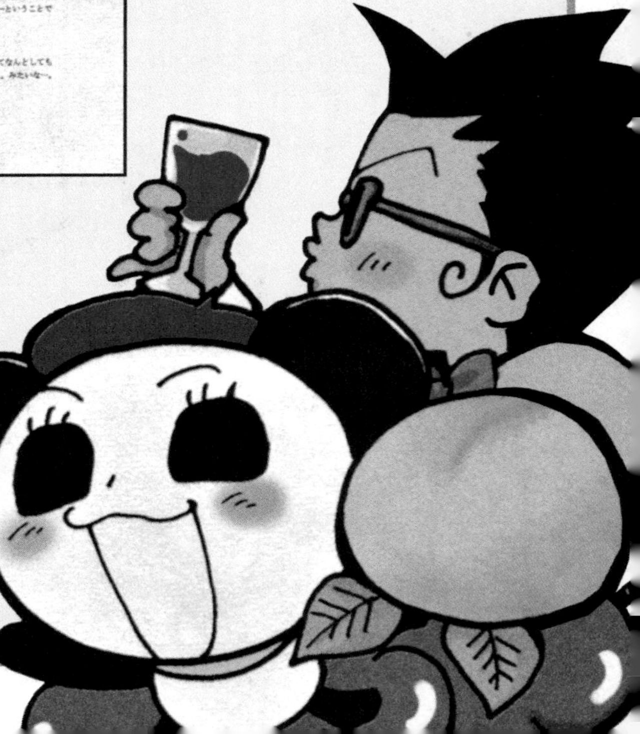

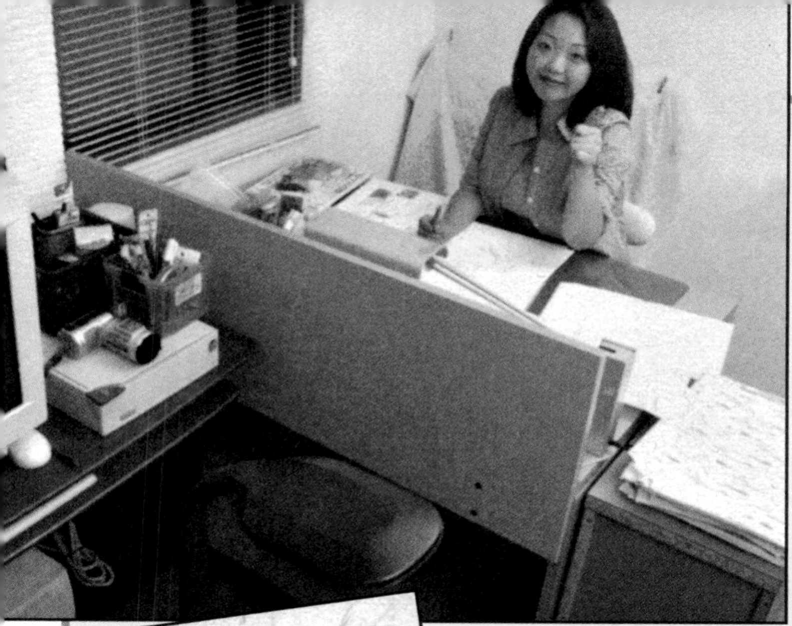

Use a soft pencil for a soft touch in the rough draft!

After you're done with the storyboard, on to the rough draft! If you apply a lot of pressure when you're doing your rough draft, you may not be able to erase it, or you may even damage the draft. You should use a soft pencil and draw gently!

Your mantra should be "simple is best" when working on the rough draft. Too many lines make inking more difficult, so keep it neat with few lines! Consider the rough draft a milestone on the way to actually inking!

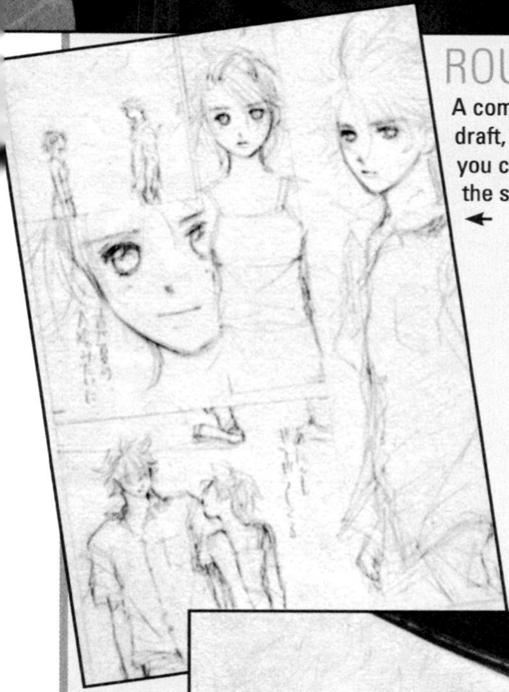

ROUGH DRAFT COMPLETED

A completed rough draft. It's a very rough rough draft, but this is only the beginning! This is where you check if the whole page looks sharp. Evaluating the size of the drawings is a good start. ←

THIS IS WHERE PROFESSIONAL

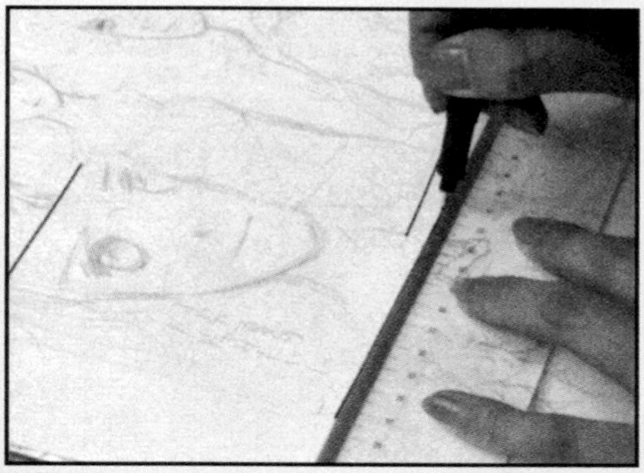

↑ Check out how the ruler is flipped over. This minimizes stains on the draft! A glimpse of professional wisdom in action.

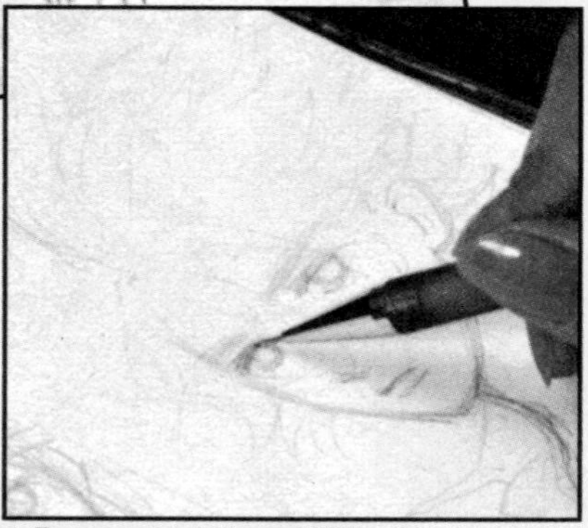

↑ Try not to touch the draft!! The oil from your hands can sometimes interfere with the ink!!

Flip your ruler over to draw a line!

After you're done with the rough draft, the first step in inking is adding the panel borders. When using a ruler to draw lines, it's standard protocol to flip the ruler over to avoid getting ink in between your manuscript and the ruler. If your ruler doesn't have a beveled edge, you can stick a penny on the backside so there's a little space between the ruler and your draft. Sumoto is using a 0.8mm water-based marker to draw the panel border.

INKING MUST BE DONE CAREFULLY YET DARINGLY!

The moment everything's been building up to… Let's start inking!
Put your heart and soul into each line and remember that practice makes perfect.

For the profile lines, use a G-pen, which will enable you to draw strong lines. Check out how she has tissue under her right hand so that the oil from her hand won't get on the draft. There are manga artists who place tissue under their left hands, too!

Why ink from the left side?

A right-handed person should start inking from the left. This is to keep your hand from smudging ink that hasn't dried yet.

Use a G-pen for the main lines that need to stand out and give your illustrations depth. Conversely, use a crow quill nib (also called round nib) pen to more easily draw fine lines for the smaller details. Some professionals use older pens to draw the thicker profile lines. You should have at least two pen sizes to be able to distinguish between the thick and fine lines.

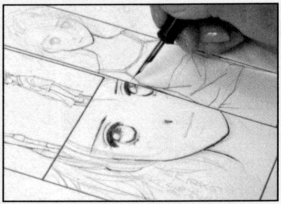

Use a crow quill nib pen for details like inside the eyes, where you need finer touches. But not every nib works for every person, so if you find a pen nib difficult to use, make sure you change it.

Use a crow quill nib pen when drawing hair, too. The fresher the ink, the easier it is to use. So keep drawing and try to use it up as quickly as possible.

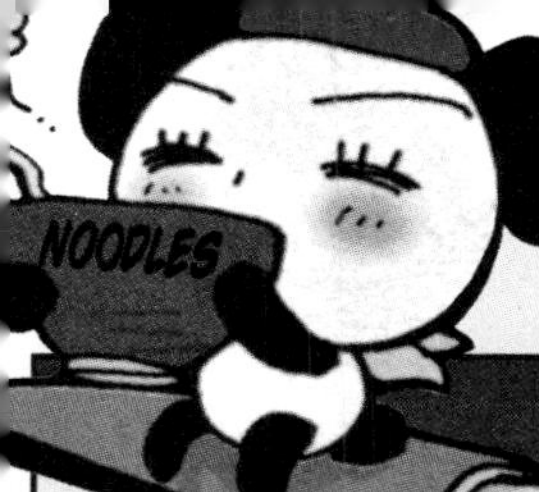
NOODLES

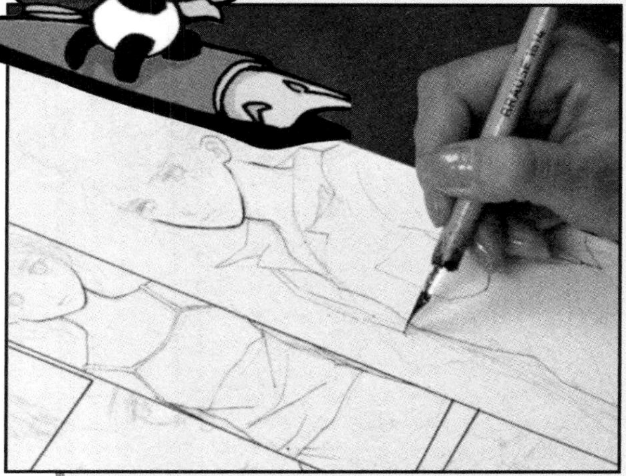

Practice makes perfect with the pen!

You may think that you can draw with a pencil but not with a pen. All that means is that you need to get used to your pen! There's a lot of practice that goes into being able to draw exactly how you want with a pen.

Swing your entire forearm from your elbow when drawing long curves. There're always angles that are hard to draw, so rotate the paper or even turn it upside down.

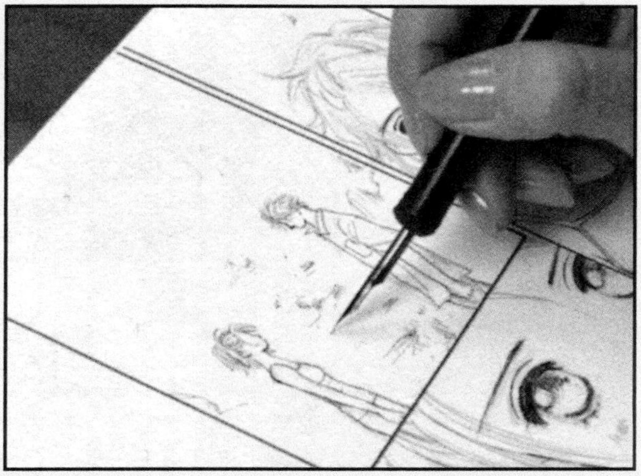

Use the fine touch of the crow quill nib pen when drawing the background and effects. Make sure you really push the pen nib into its holder, because the more the nib is exposed, the harder it is to draw.

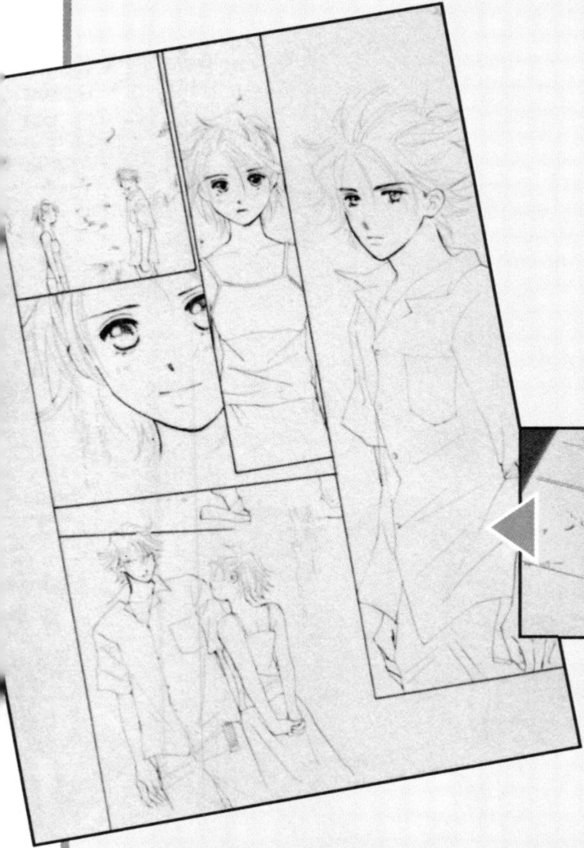

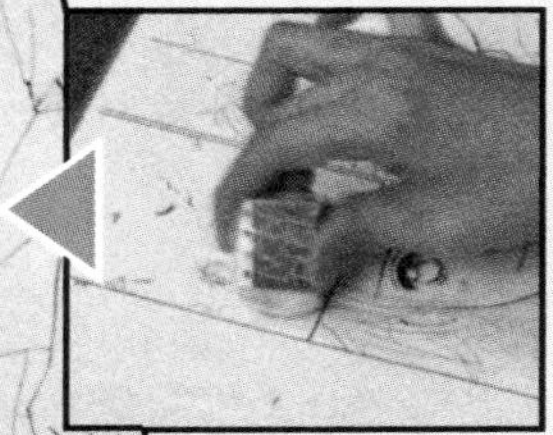

INKING COMPLETED!

When you're done inking and the ink has dried, make sure you erase all remaining pencil marks. Sumoto uses the Indust eraser by MONO.

Even pros can get visibly rusty if they haven't used a pen for a while. As an amateur, you should try to use a pen at least once a day.

GETTING USED TO THE PEN IS THE MOST IMPORTANT STEP!

THE FINAL TOUCHES ARE THE SOUL OF A BEAUTIFUL DRAFT!

After Amu Sumoto, the ever-popular *Betsucomi* manga artist Shoko Akira showed us the secret to the finishing touches.

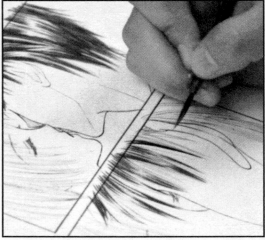

▲ Large areas should be blacked in with a pigment ink marker like a PROCKEY, but create dynamic lines using a thin, long brush when coloring your characters' hair. Just go for it without worrying about staying in the frame.

The three main ingredients to the finishing touches are blacks, whites, and tones.

You're not done just because you finished inking! You could even say that the finishing touches make or break your product. The finishing touches mainly consist of the blacks, whites, and tone process.

They all seem easy, but a pretty finish takes practice. Check out the pictures of Akira's techniques and master them yourself through practice!

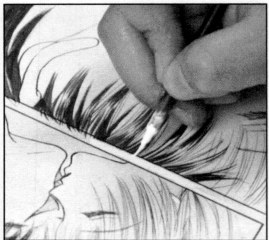

There are two ways to use white ink. One is for correction and the other is outlining against a colored background. This picture shows Akira correcting the black ink that didn't stay in the frame. →

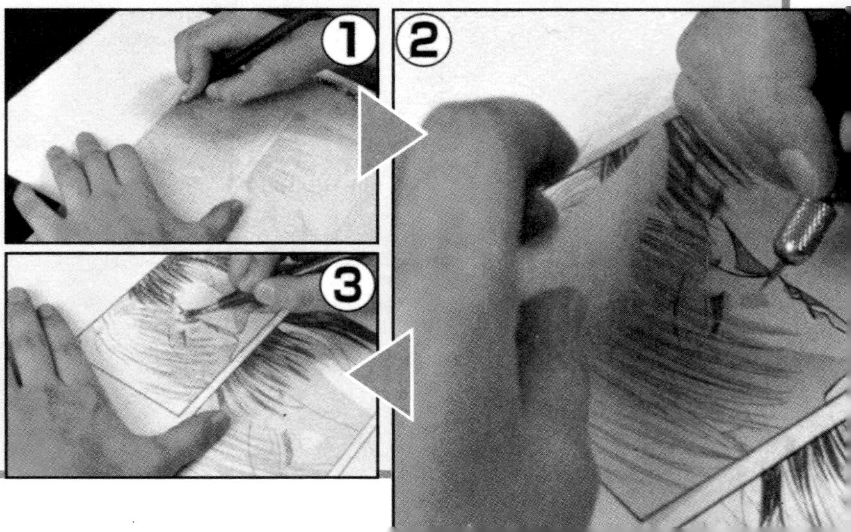

When using screen tones, place the entire sheet on your draft and roughly cut it. Then lightly glue it to the draft and cut it in more detail. Finally, apply adequate pressure when rubbing to make sure it sticks. Be careful not to rub on scraps of screen tone. →

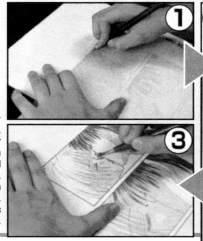

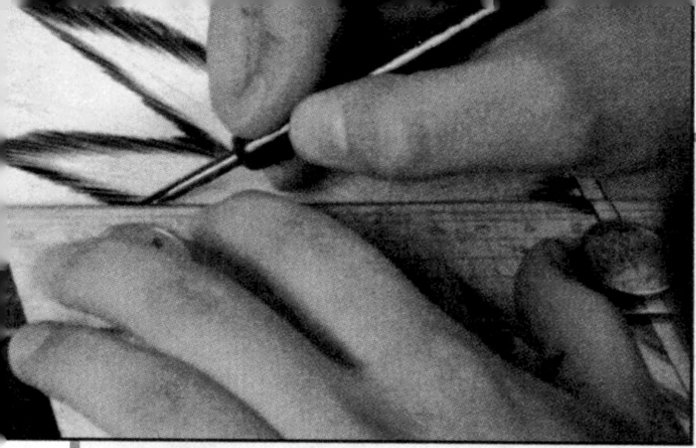

Akira uses a light blue pencil to draw a rough outline of the shape and starts drawing the flash with a pen accordingly. When you're starting off, you should begin by touching the previous line and quickly bring your pen towards the center. ←

GET COMFORTABLE USING SPECIAL TECHNIQUES RATHER THAN JUST READING ABOUT THEM!

Master special techniques and enhance the ambience of your image.

Now we're dealing with some advanced techniques! They're difficult until you get used to them, but they're all effective ways of enhancing the ambience of your images, so it's well worth your while to practice and master them.

Let's start with solid flashes. You can buy screen tones, but as a beginner you should draw them yourself. Just think of it as practice! Scraping screen tones is also a must-have technique for blurry expressions.

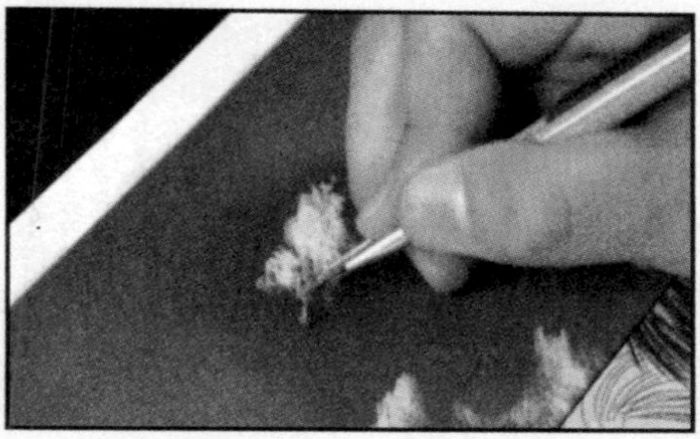

You can erase screen tone patterns with an eraser! Akira is using a sand eraser here to get a cloud effect. She's using MONO's typewriter eraser. ↓

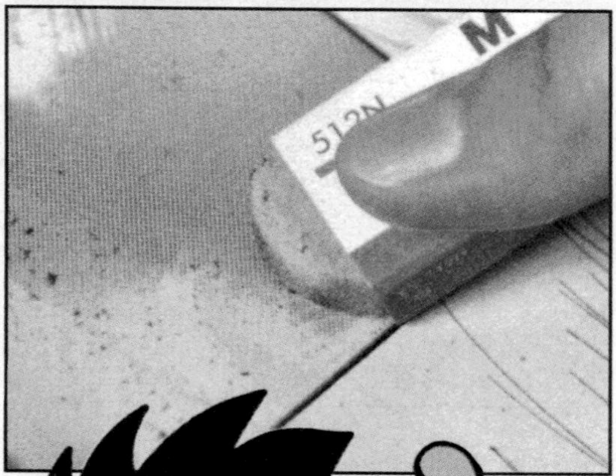

COMPLETED PAGE

Screen tone knives are great for cutting the screen tone, but a lot of pros use normal utility knives for scraping. Try exploring different angles.

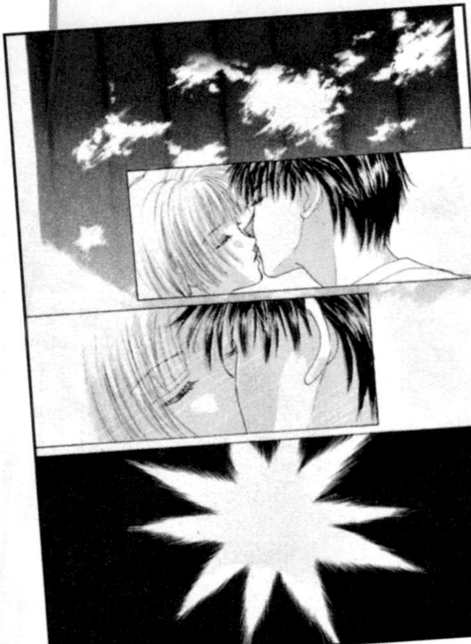

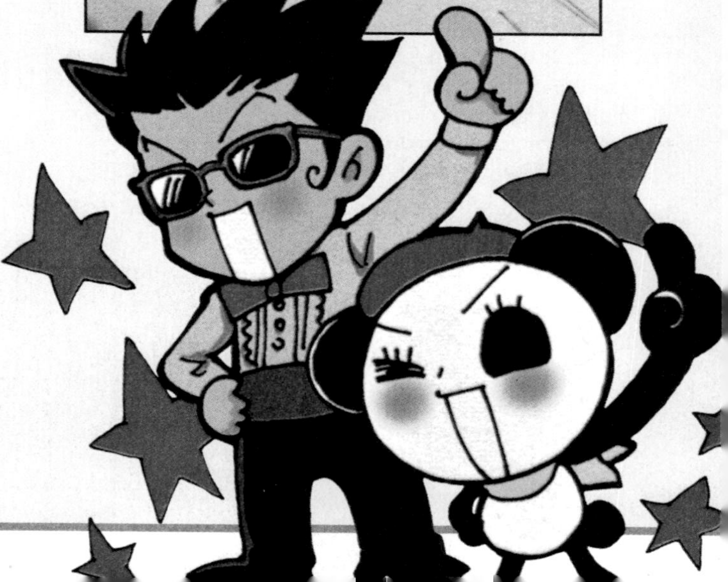

The Yuu Watase Edition
(Hometown: Osaka Prefecture, Kishiwada)

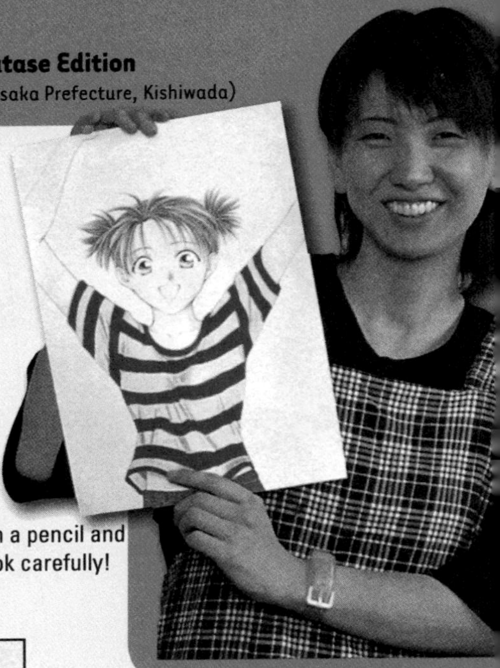

HOW TO DRAW COLOR PAGES, WATASE-STYLE!

A beautiful color page! Learn how to draw color pages from Yuu Watase, whose *Imadoki!* is currently running in *Shojo Comics*!

Do your inking in water-resistant color ink!

The first few steps are the same, even for color pages. Do a rough draft with a pencil and then carefully start adding color. Make sure you use water-resistant ink. Look carefully! Why is Watase not directly adding ink to her rough draft?

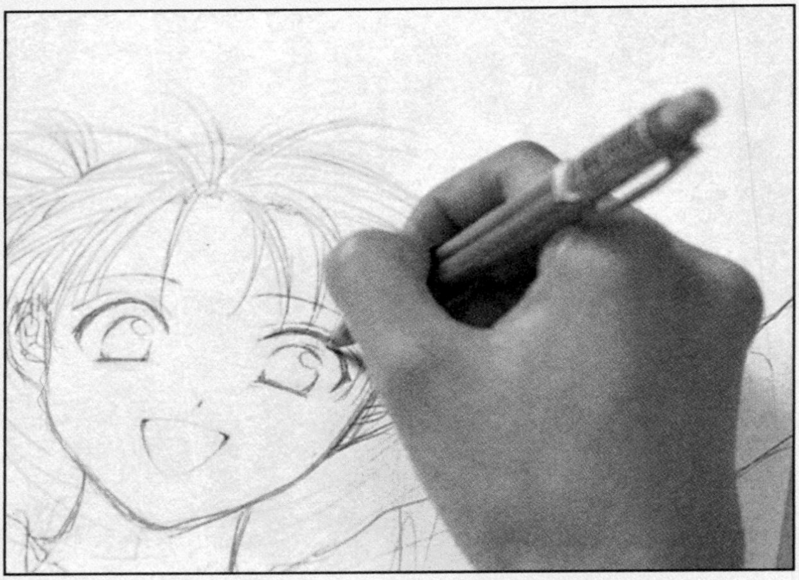

← Do a rough draft as always. Watase is using both 0.5mm and 0.3mm mechanical pencils. She uses 2B lead to avoid damaging the paper.

Pay attention to little details so you don't damage the page!

Check out how she adds ink by placing the rough draft on a light box so it's transparent. This is so erasing the pencil marks doesn't damage the final page. Another technique we should all try mimicking.

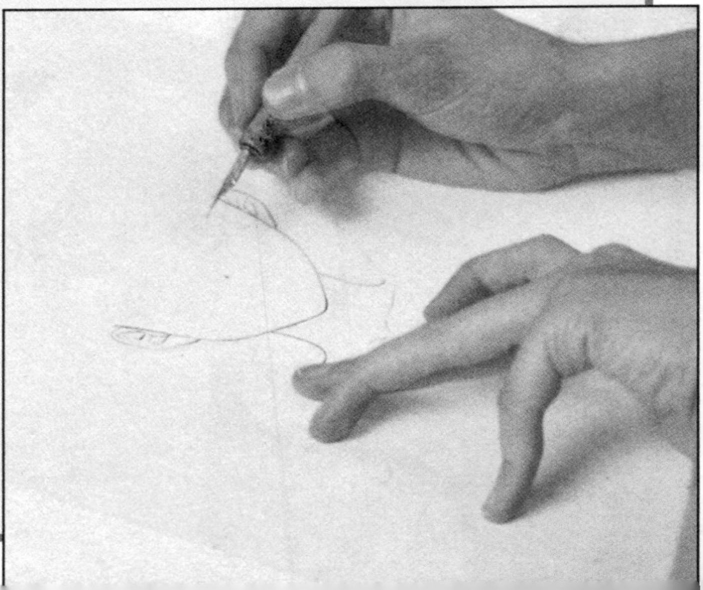

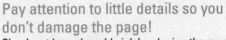

→ She uses HOLBEIN water-resistant sepia ink. Look closely at Watase's left hand. She's holding the paper down by touching as little surface as possible, to avoid transferring the oil from her hand.

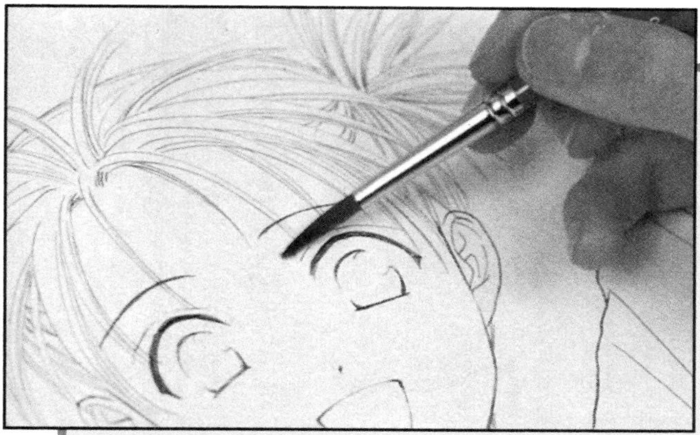

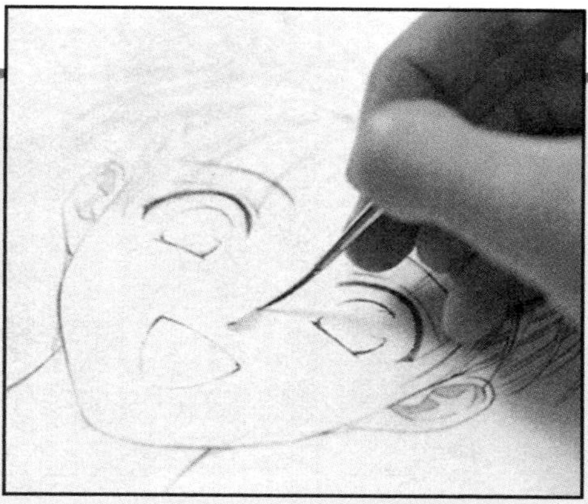

LIGHTLY LAYER THE INK.

Apply the ink as if you're putting makeup on your characters!

You can tell from the picture that when adding light colors like the character's skin tone, you should layer the ink lightly. The ink should be so light you can't even tell if it's there! Directly adding dark color can make it uneven, and the final product often ends up looking unnatural.

And there's nothing you can do when you screw up with dark colors—just another reason to keep layering light colors. Be thorough with this process, and pretend like you're putting makeup on your characters.

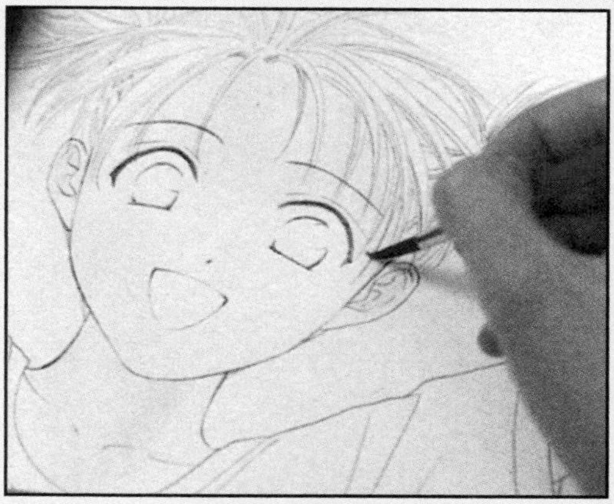

↑ Before you start adding ink, brush water on the parts you'll be coloring. This will make it less likely that the ink will go on unevenly. Even when you want to blur the profile, dampening the area prior to coloring will reduce the chances of uneven ink.

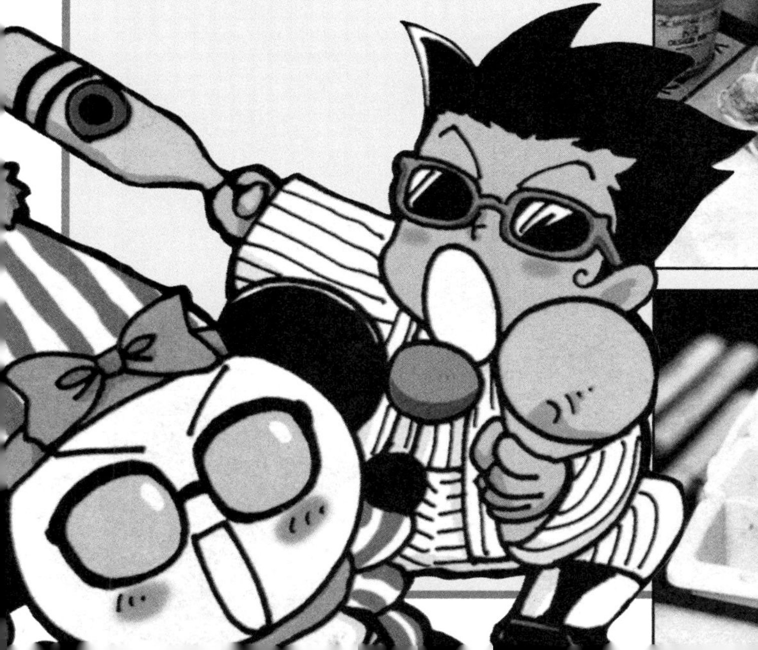

Make sure the brush is completely damp before dipping it in ink. Use the side of the your wash container or tissues to adjust the amount of ink on your brush as you work.

← ↓

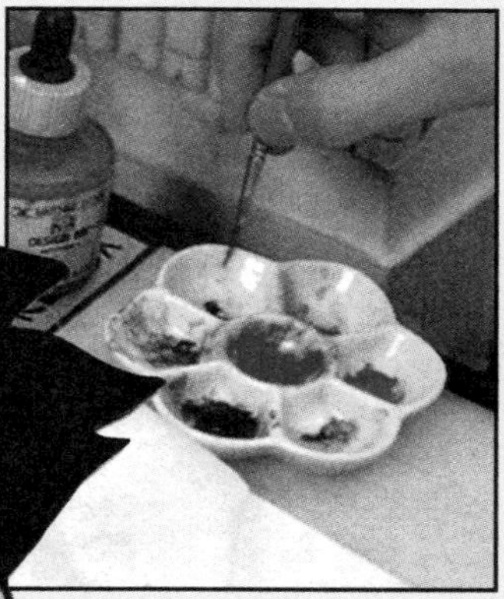

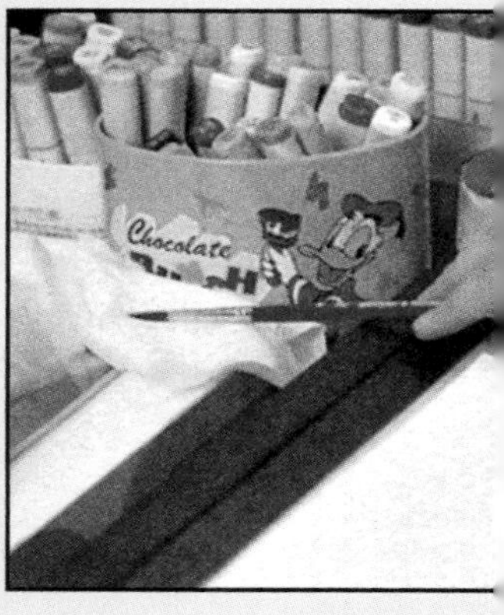
Chocolate

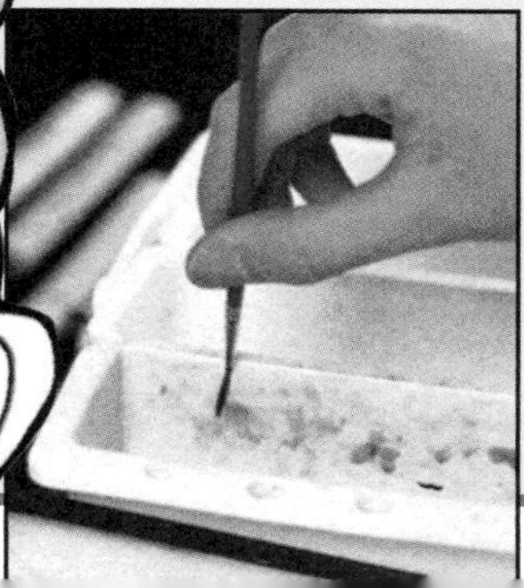

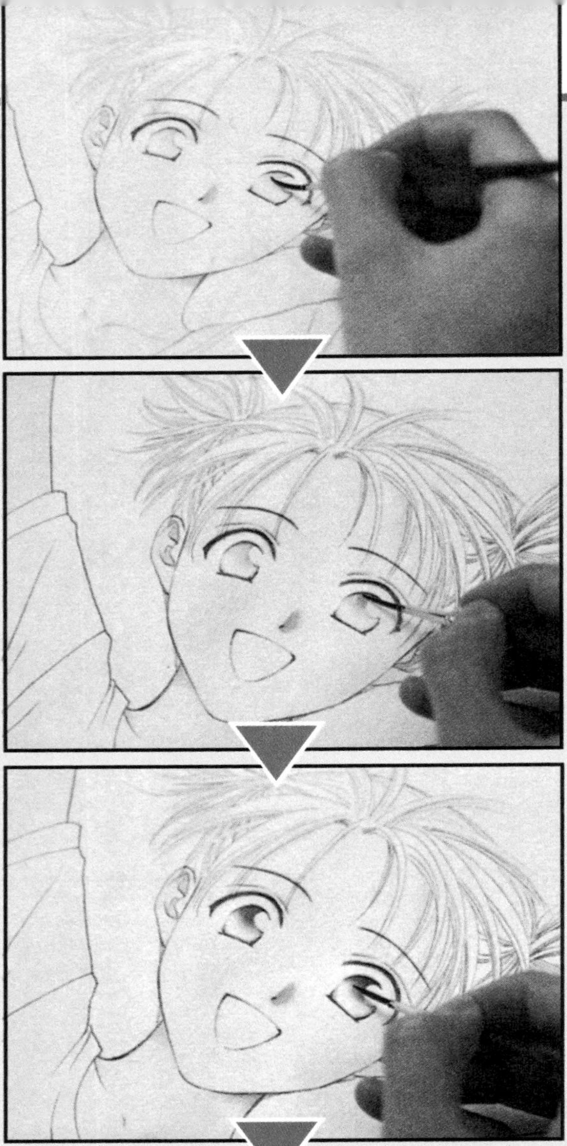

PAY SPECIAL ATTENTION TO THE DETAILS!

When you're done with the skin tone, start adding the details. Even a small mistake stands out with the detailed areas, so proceed with caution.

Even the brightness of your character's eyes should be achieved by layering ink!

Some professionals color in the eyes last, but Watase does the eyes right after she finishes the character's skin. Create a darker color by layering light colors, and switch colors only when you want a darker color than what you're able to achieve through layering. Dark colors stand out when you don't stay in the lines, so be careful. Make sure you wait until the surrounding ink dries before proceeding.

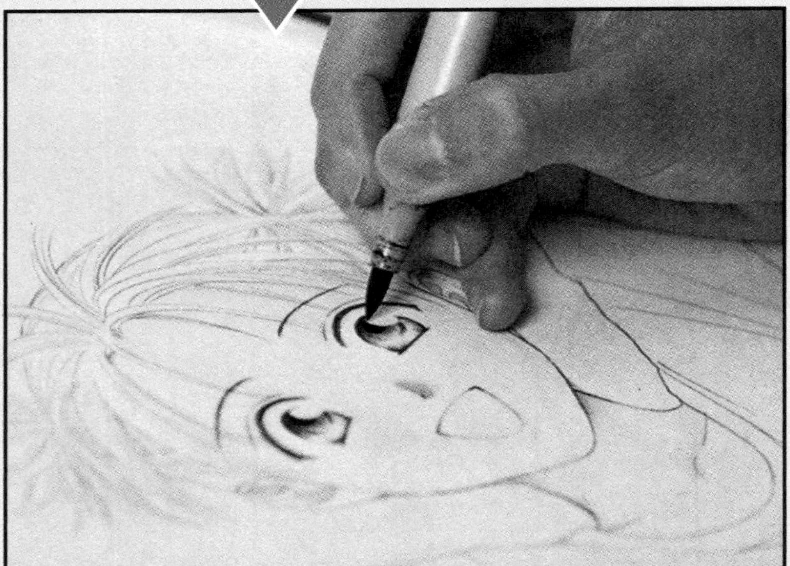

← Layering allows you to see the color progress. The brightness of this character's eyes is the product of patiently layering colors. The final touches are done with a COPiC marker with a brush-like tip. The key to success is in the character's eyes!

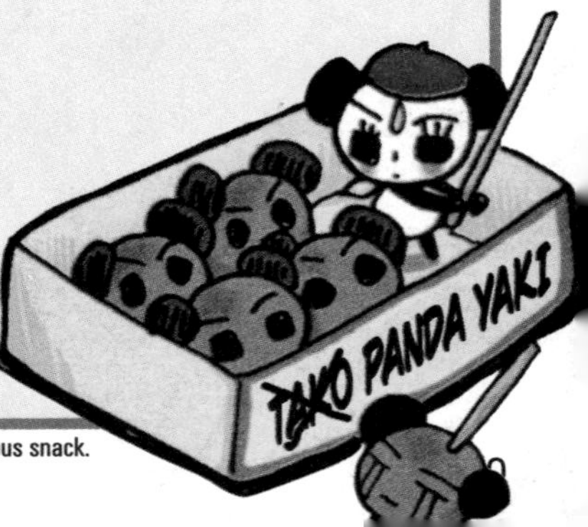
TAKO PANDA YAKI

*Tako-yaki is a famous Osakan octopus snack.

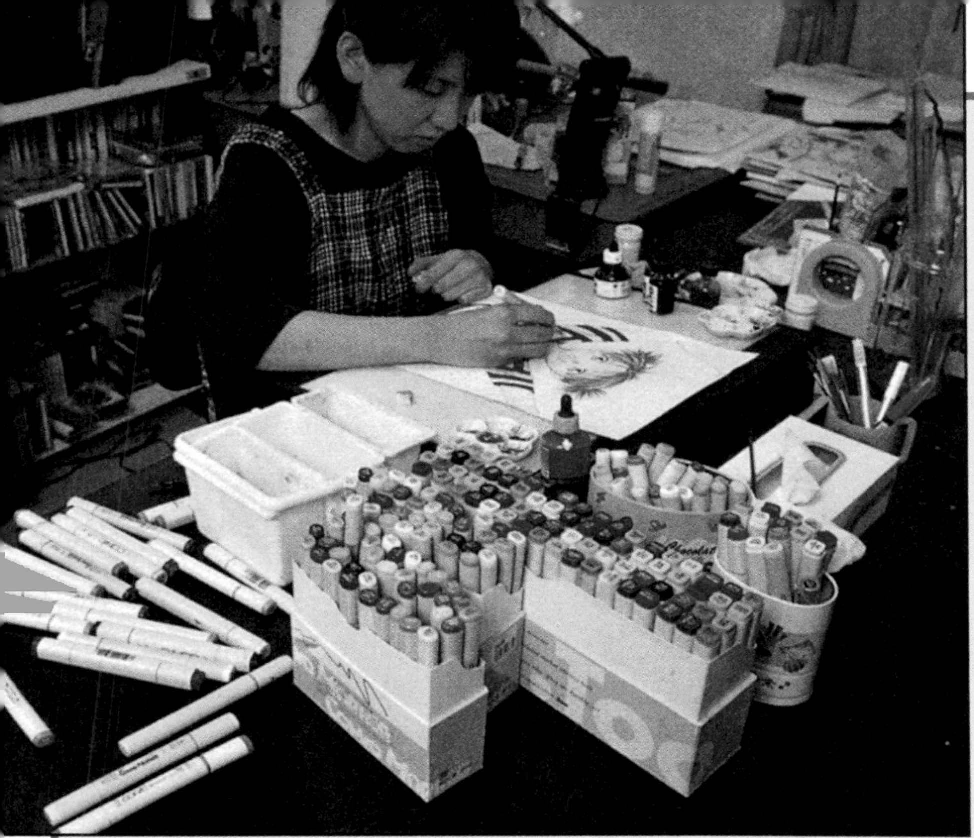

Speed is the key to avoiding unevenness when coloring!

Use a COPiC marker for coloring hair, too. Be careful and stay in the lines for the finer portions, but do it quickly and efficiently. Changing the speed of application makes the ink go on unevenly, so maintain speed. Practice makes perfect! Giving the color depth also comes back to the basics of layering. Check out the pictures in order to see the process of layering first hand. As you can see from the picture above, COPiC markers come in an extensive array of colors. It's unreasonable to try to buy all of them in the beginning, so we recommend choosing the colors you think you'll use and gradually expanding your collection. By the way, Watase is using colors CM21, CM68 and CM70 on the character's hair here. "CM" represents similar colors and the higher the number, the darker the color.

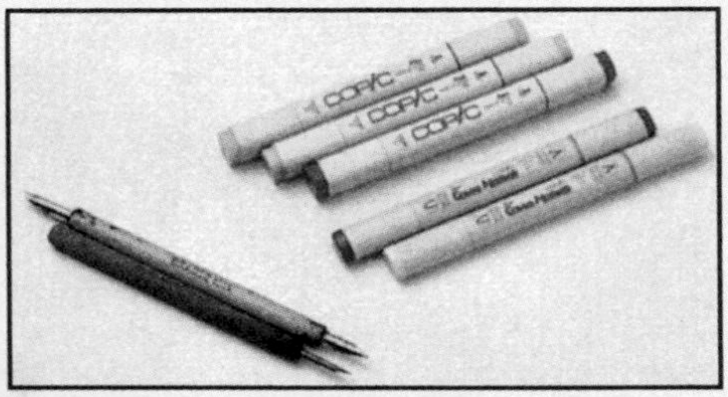
COPIC
COPIC
COPIC

↑ COPiC pens and inking pens that Watase uses. COPiC pens are sold at most art stores for about $6.

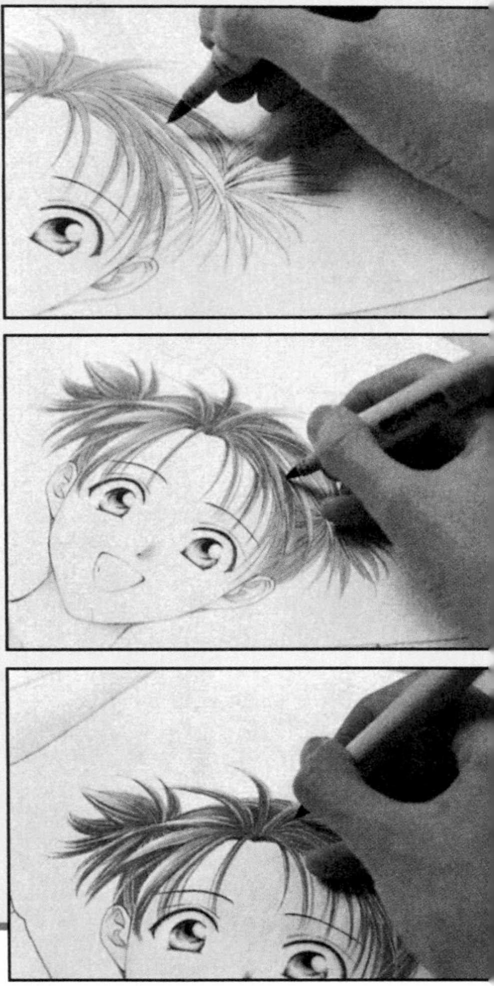

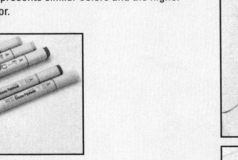

→ When coloring hair, move your marker or your pen along the lines. This makes the touch and unevenness look like natural hair flow, contributing to a good-looking finish. It's difficult to maintain tension without rushing yourself, though.

LINES, ESPECIALLY WITH

When you're done with the human parts, like skin tone, it's time to complete your work by coloring the clothes! Use the white ink for accents this time, not corrections!

Create a rough guide for where the ink will be added with a discreet color pencil.

Before actually coloring in the stripe pattern on the character's shirt, Watase maps out the pattern with a red pencil, taking into consideration how the shirt drapes. If you do this with a normal pencil, you will see it through the ink when you're done coloring. By doing this with a color pencil, you can create a rough guide that won't stand out later.

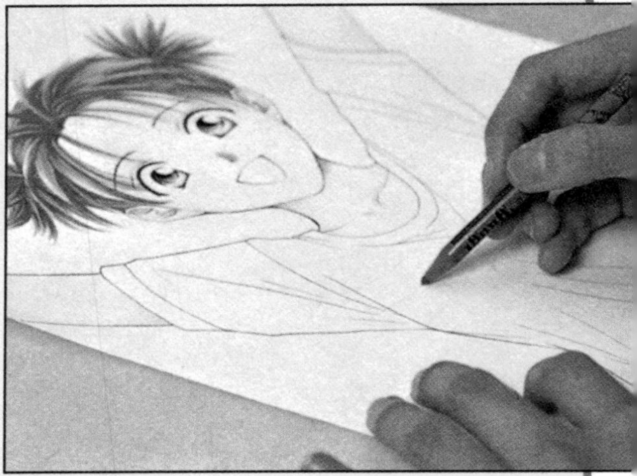

↑ A rough draft of the shirt's stripe pattern with a red pencil. Think about how to make the final draft look as natural as possible, and consider how the shirt drapes. This is where you can really show off your manga artist sense!

Remember, the pencil draft is just a rough guide. In this case, it's best to add the color just outside the lines. Make sure you hide the pencil marks. ↓

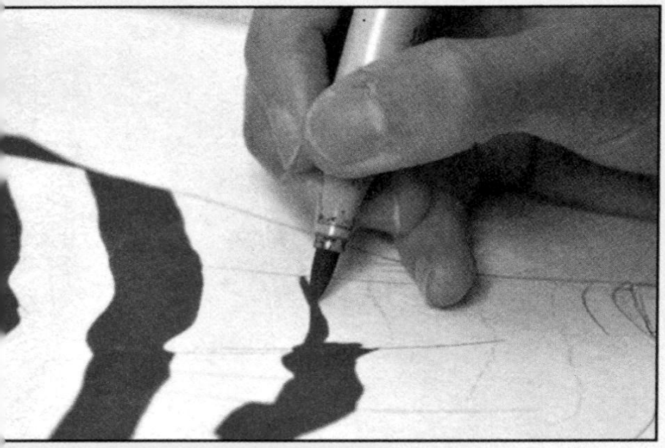

Add shadows by layering ink according to the drape of the clothes!

Color the areas that have been mapped out with the red pencil so that you can't see the guidelines anymore. Make sure you add shadows according to the stripes for the striped pattern. The shadow should go across both red and white areas! Sometimes the areas where the light hits the clothes are left alone, and the highlights done later. Don't just slap on the same color, but think about the material and texture of the clothes you're coloring.

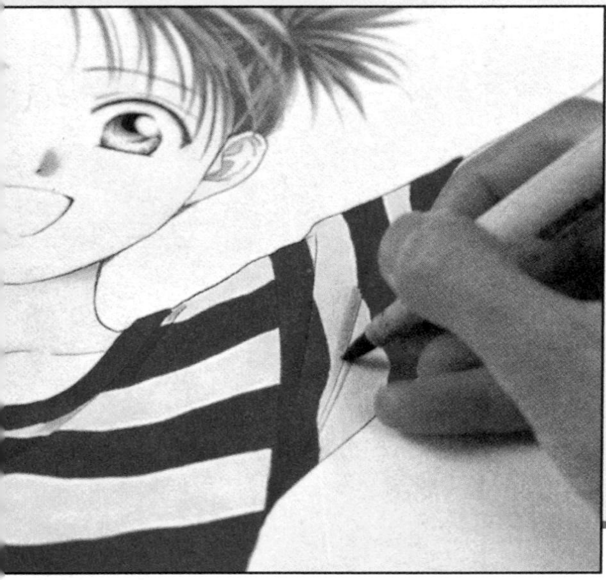

← Add some grey to the white borders, too. Don't forget to layer when adding shadows, so it doesn't get too dark.

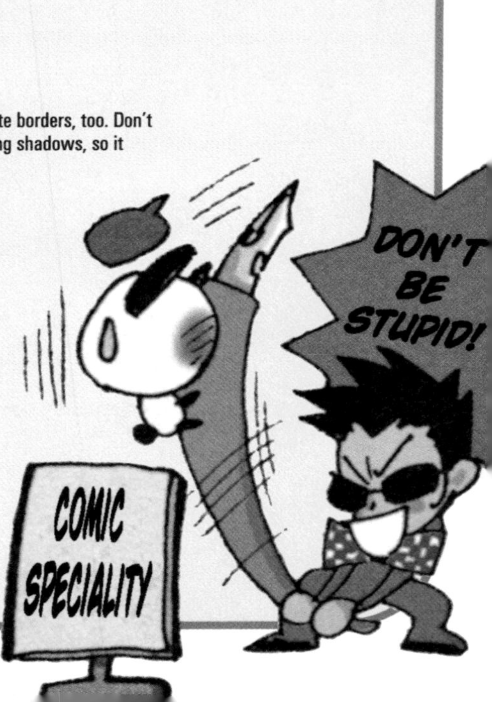
DON'T BE STUPID!
COMIC SPECIALITY

BE CAREFUL TO STAY IN THE THE DARK COLORS!

Use white ink to highlight the eyes and hair!

The last step of coloring is adding the white ink. You should think of this as "painting with white" instead of correcting your work. Add luster (highlights) to the eyes and hair with white ink.

▲ See how much energy you add to your character by highlighting the eyes with some white ink!

See how effective white ink is in adding luster to hair! You can enhance the spatial effect by being conscious of the illuminated area and the shadow area when adding the white ink. ←

The ink she's using is Dr. Martin's Bleed Proof White. Controlling the thickness of the ink is an important point. ➤

FINISHED!

▲ Use white ink for the stitches on the jeans, too. Yet another detail that can only be done with this ink! Use a fine, thin brush.

White ink is all about the thickness. Play around with different dilutions.

Stitches and buttons should be done with white ink. If it's too thick, it'll peel when it dries. But on the other hand, if it's too thin, you can see through it. So play around with different dilutions and see what works best for you.

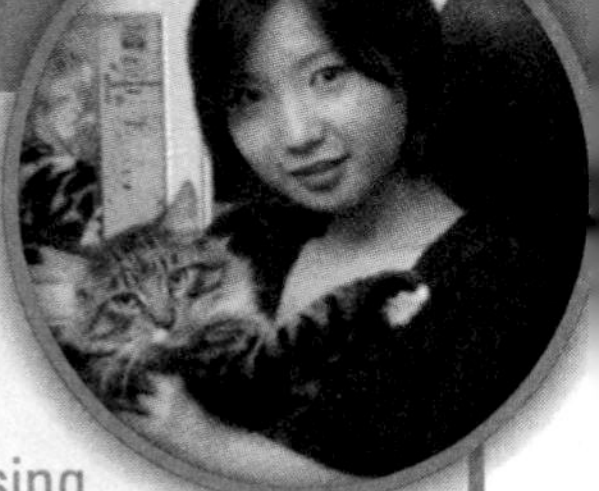

DIGITAL DRAWING!

These days, there are manga artists who use computers for the drawing process. We had *Sho-Comi's* Mayu Shinjo show us firsthand!

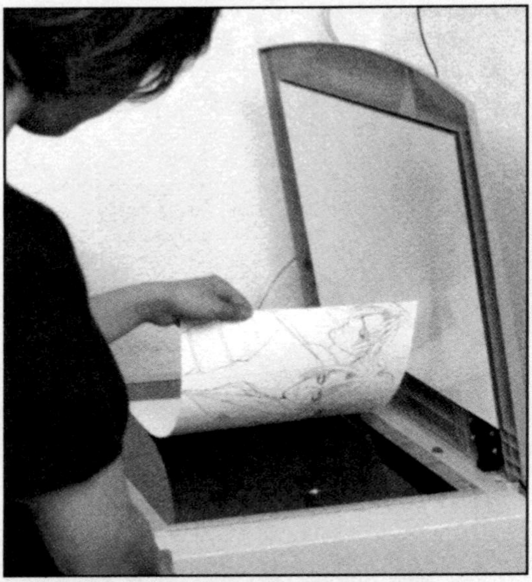

You can upload the original drawing by using a scanner. Shinjo uses 600dpi resolution when scanning images.

Create beautiful color pages using your computer!

It can get a little expensive, but there are more and more manga artists who use computers to do their illustrations. There're two main types of computer systems used—Windows and Macintosh (Mac).

Windows may be more common, but manga artists tend to use Macs! Macs are slightly more convenient for illustrations. Let's follow Mayu Shinjo as she takes us through the drawing steps using the Mac.

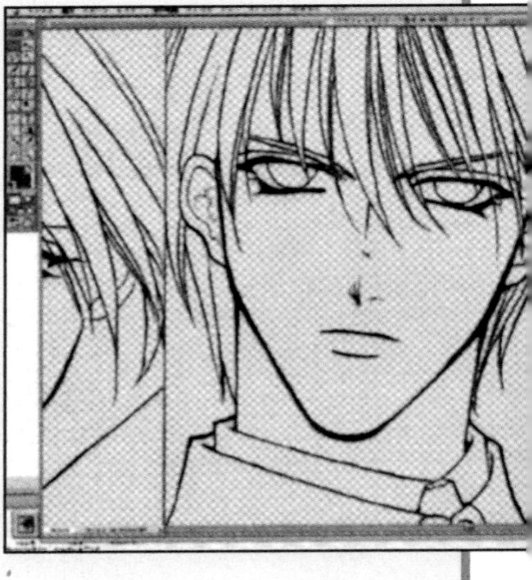

Everything other than the lines made transparent. The grid pattern represents the transparency. This is saved as a separate layer (kind of like an anime cel) and combined later.

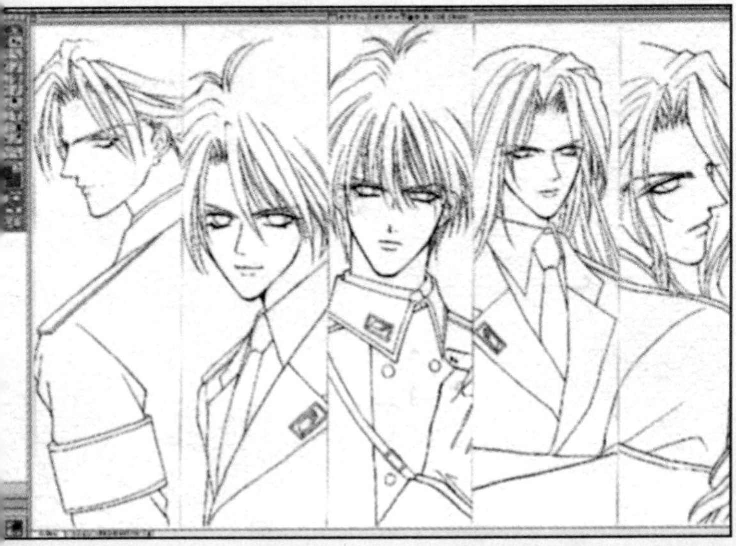

This is the scanned image. The image is monochrome now, but this is where color is going to be added. Make sure you take care of any unwanted spots from the scanning process.

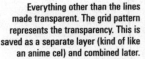

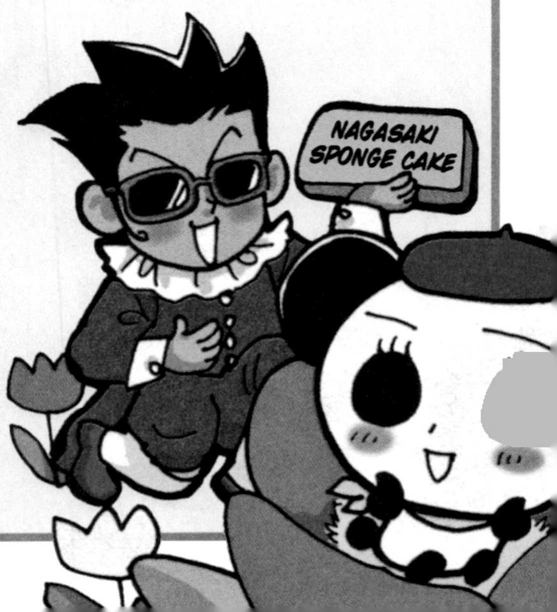
NAGASAKI SPONGE CAKE

Shinjo's system is a 500 MHz Power Mac G4 with 1G of memory. She uses an EPSON ES-8500 scanner. In all, her high-tech equipment cost about 2.5 million yen ($22,000). The software she's using here is Adobe Photoshop.

◄

Masking is key with digital coloring.

We're finally going to start coloring, but masking is a huge part of the digital coloring process. This is the same as masking in airbrushing. You protect the parts that shouldn't be colored so that the ink stays in the lines where it should be.

After you're done with the masking settings, it's time to start coloring. There are brushes that will help give the drawing special touches, and airbrush-like effects are just as easy! You can even use a pattern like a stamp! And you can redo your work if you mess up, so the quality of work improves too.

Not to say that computer illustrations are easier than using actual paints, but the fact that you can redo areas as many times as you want, and some special effects can only be done on a computer, are definite advantages!

▲ The top picture is the original scanned image. The middle picture is what it looks like after it's been masked. The red portions are the parts that are protected. The bottom picture shows the process of adding color to the skin. You can see how the masked parts didn't get colored.

▲ Here's a completed page! Its brilliance and perfection are a sight to behold. It's been drawn in layers—from the background to the line work— and each layer can be touched up and/or corrected.

THE MANY COMPUTER EFFECTS!

Digitized data allows for special effects that aren't possible by hand. We're going to experiment with different effects that can only be done on the computer.

Mosaic effects and blurring are just a few effects that can be done instantaneously!

The advantage of computer illustration is that it allows effects that can't be done by hand to be done instantaneously! Here're a few of the many effects that can be done with the software that's being used here, Photoshop. You can apply the effects on the entire screen or specify the area through masking, or apply the effects layer by layer.

▲ Specify the area and apply the mosaic effect inside the circle. You can even specify the mosaic size. You can blur a designated portion of facial lines as well.

This is an illustration that's been put through a filter that blurs it in a radial pattern, then processed through a zoom setting.

←

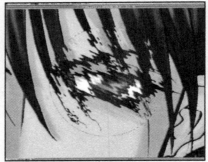

This is a different effect that can be achieved through a "ripple" filter. By putting the background through this filter, you can finish an underwater scene in the blink of an eye!!

←

The journey to becoming a manga artist begins with the first step. Manga artists aren't made in a day!

We've seen a lot of professional techniques from different artists, and they're all fabulous! But even a professional isn't born that way. No matter who you are, you start off as a beginner. These artists all thought about what they needed to do to express their own images, and worked hard at it to develop their skills. Don't forget the importance of curiosity and persistence! With those two things in mind, let's enter the *Manga Artist Academy*!

Shojo Beat's Manga Artist Academy

Table of Contents

From Every Corner of Japan,
the Manga Journey

The Amu Sumoto Edition   1

The Shoko Akira Edition   2

The Yuu Watase Edition   6

The Mayu Shinjo Edition   8
   14

Prologue: I Like Manga   18

Chapter 1: The Emiko Sugi Edition   20
"Let's Start with Drawing!"

Chapter 2: The Shoko Akira Edition   38
"Let's Create the Characters!"

Chapter 3: The Masami Takeuchi Edition   56
"Let's Create a Story!"

Chapter 4: The Chie Shinohara Edition   74
"Let's Organize the Panels!"

Chapter 5: The Yuu Watase Edition   96
"Let's Draw a Draft!"

Chapter 6: The Miyuki Kitagawa Edition   116
"Let's Draw the Background!"

Chapter 7: The Rie Takada Edition   134
"Let's Add Color!"

Chapter 8: The Yukako Iisaka Edition   150
"Advanced Techniques"

Chapter 9: The Mayu Shinjo Edition   164
"The Importance of the Final Touches!"

Chapter 10: Aim for the Manga Stars   180

Satomi's Submission Diaries   184

Invaluable Data for Shojo Manga Artists   187

Index   196

PROLOGUE: I LIKE MANGA.

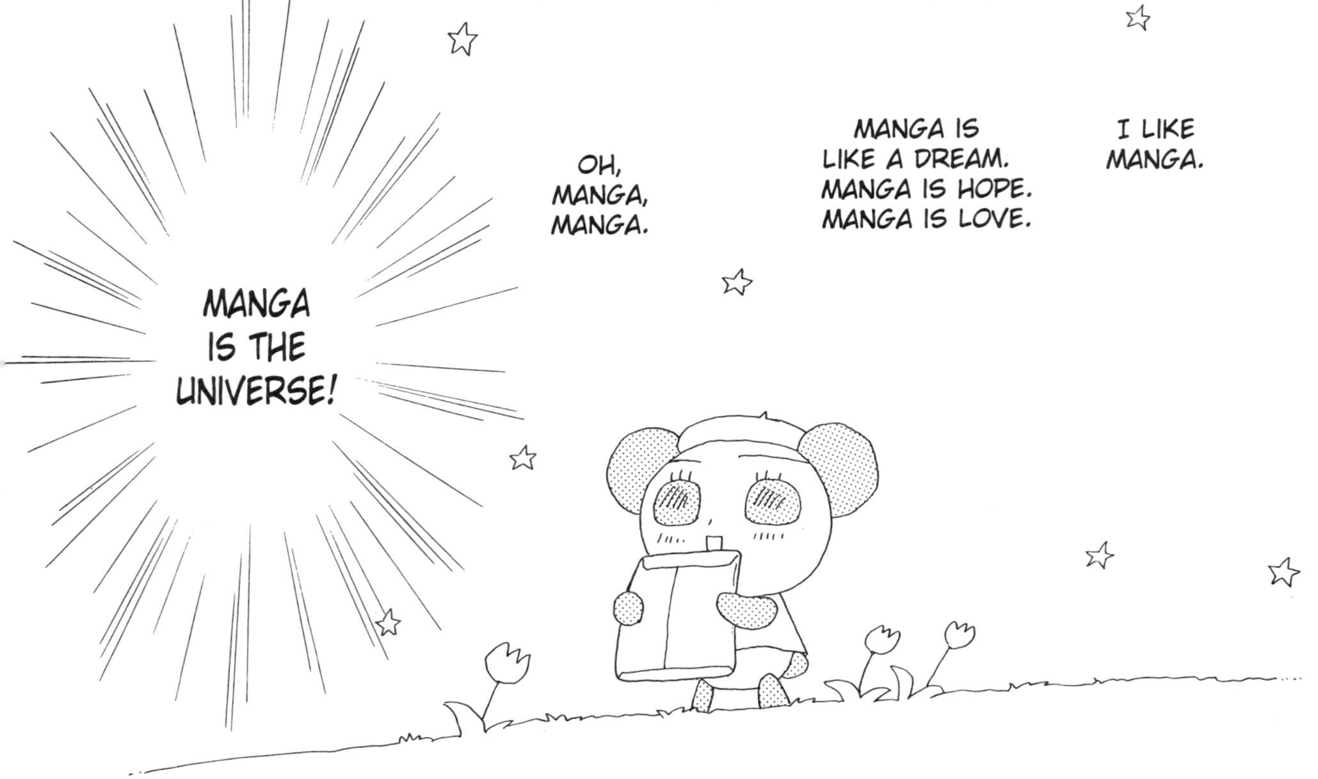
I LIKE MANGA.
MANGA IS LIKE A DREAM. MANGA IS HOPE. MANGA IS LOVE.
OH, MANGA, MANGA.
MANGA IS THE UNIVERSE!

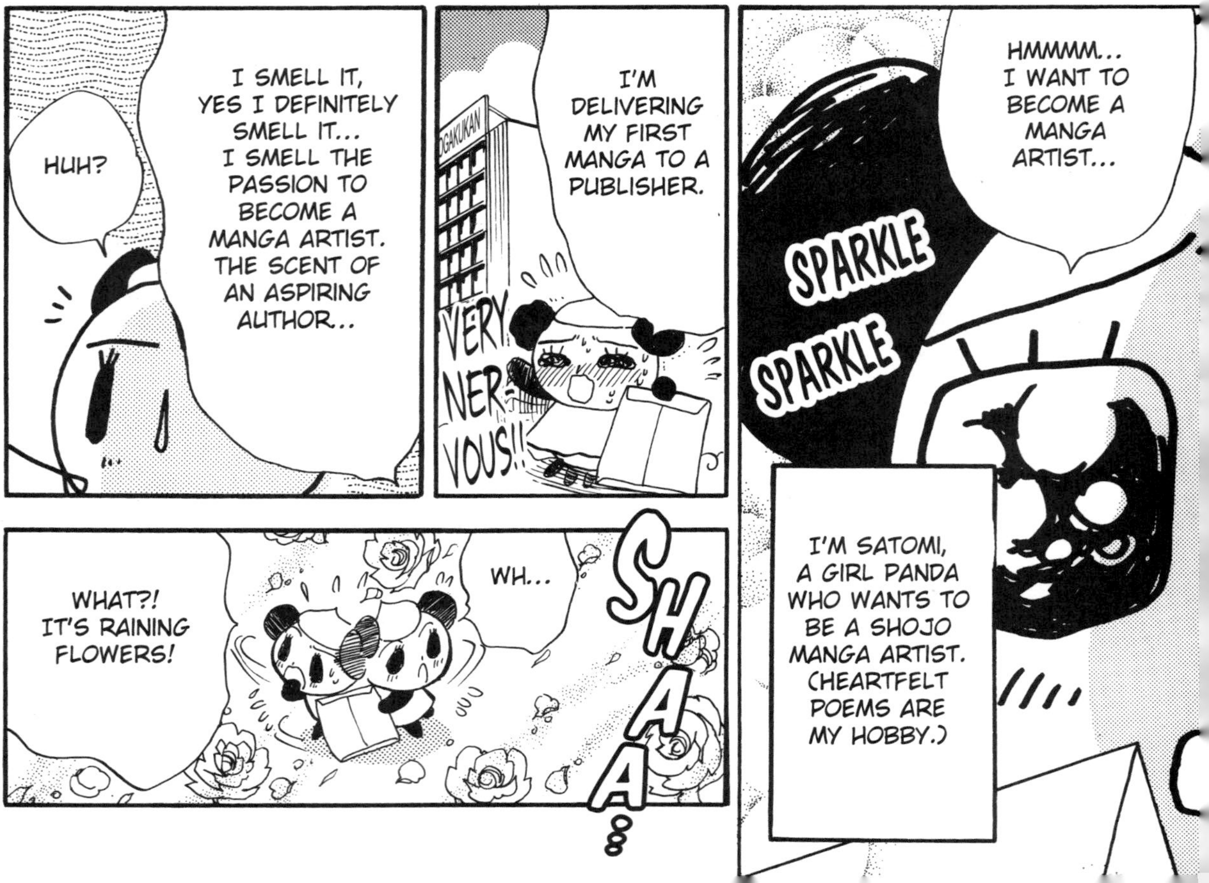
HMMMM... I WANT TO BECOME A MANGA ARTIST...
SPARKLE
SPARKLE
I'M SATOMI, A GIRL PANDA WHO WANTS TO BE A SHOJO MANGA ARTIST. (HEARTFELT POEMS ARE MY HOBBY.)
I'M DELIVERING MY FIRST MANGA TO A PUBLISHER.
VERY NER-VOUS!!
I SMELL IT, YES I DEFINITELY SMELL IT... I SMELL THE PASSION TO BECOME A MANGA ARTIST. THE SCENT OF AN ASPIRING AUTHOR...
HUH?
SHAAA...
WH...
WHAT?! IT'S RAINING FLOWERS!

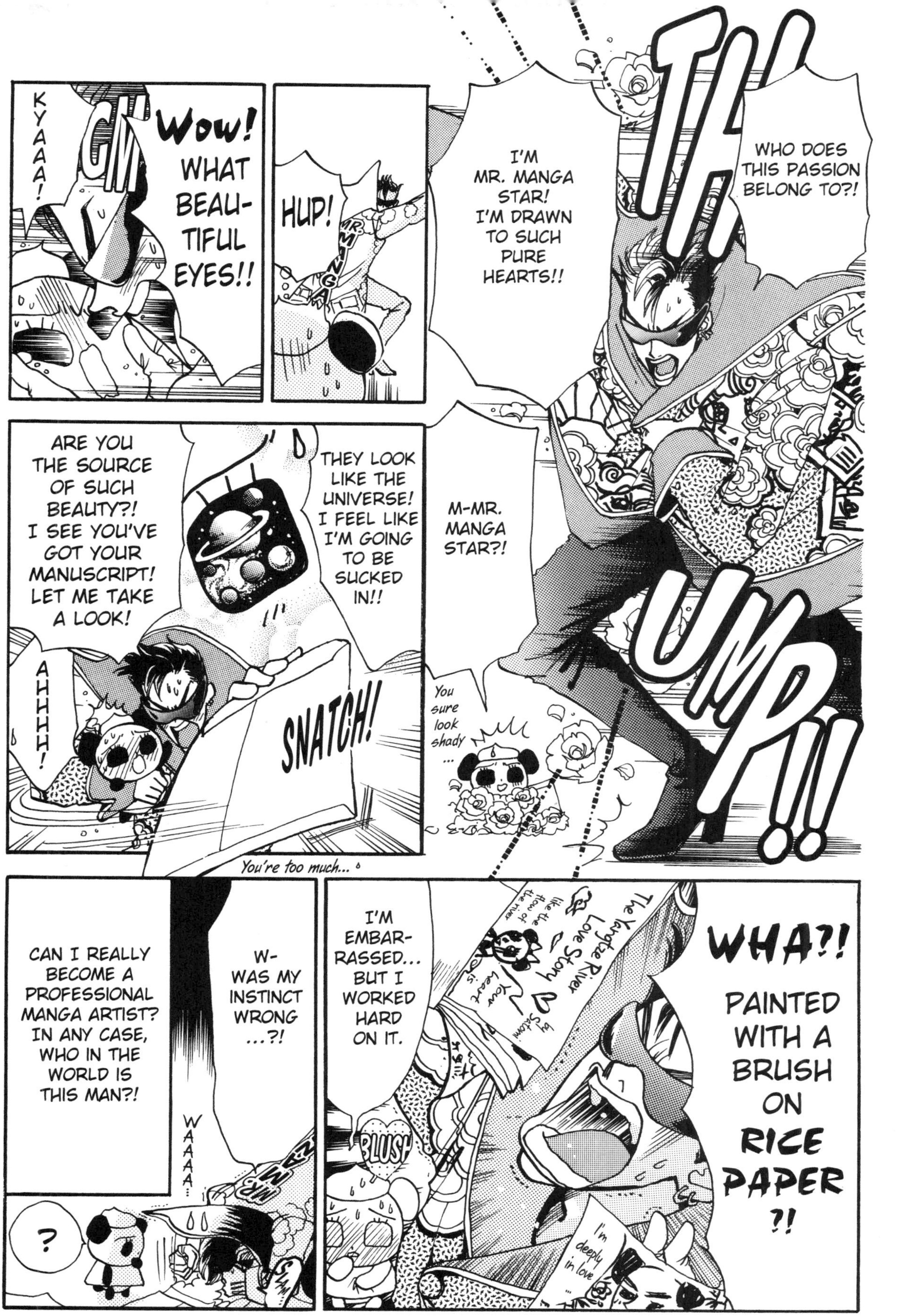
THUMP!!
WHO DOES THIS PASSION BELONG TO?!
I'M MR. MANGA STAR! I'M DRAWN TO SUCH PURE HEARTS!!
M-MR. MANGA STAR?!
You sure look shady...
HUP!
MR. MANGA
Wow! WHAT BEAUTIFUL EYES!!
KYAAA!
THEY LOOK LIKE THE UNIVERSE! I FEEL LIKE I'M GOING TO BE SUCKED IN!!
ARE YOU THE SOURCE OF SUCH BEAUTY?! I SEE YOU'VE GOT YOUR MANUSCRIPT! LET ME TAKE A LOOK!
AHHHH!
SNATCH!
You're too much...
WHA?!
PAINTED WITH A BRUSH ON RICE PAPER?!
The Yangtze River Love Story
by Satomi
like the flow of the river
Your heart is
I'm deeply in love
I'M EMBARRASSED... BUT I WORKED HARD ON IT.
BLUSH
W-WAS MY INSTINCT WRONG...?!
CAN I REALLY BECOME A PROFESSIONAL MANGA ARTIST? IN ANY CASE, WHO IN THE WORLD IS THIS MAN?!
WAAAA...
?

CHAPTER 1: THE EMIKO SUGI EDITION

LET'S START WITH DRAWING!

The first step in becoming a manga artist is to start drawing! Here to start you off is a segment by Emiko Sugi, whose popular series is being featured in *Cheese!* magazine.

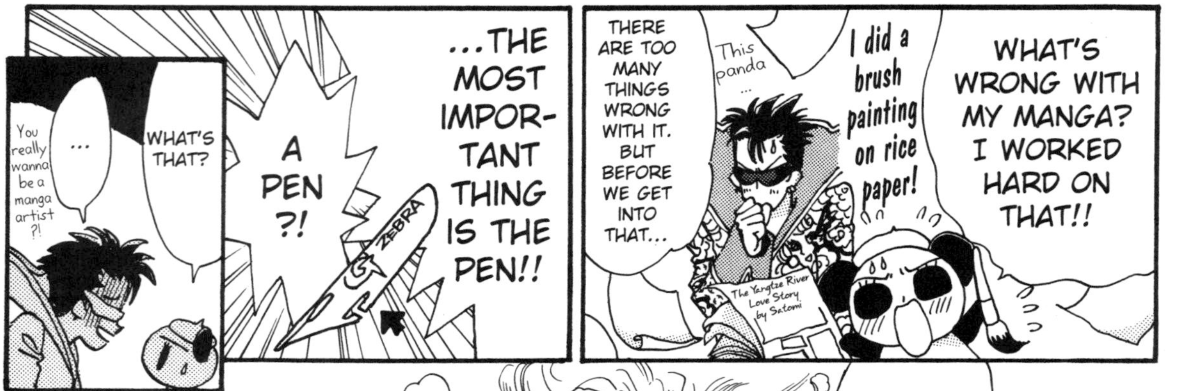

WHAT'S WRONG WITH MY MANGA? I WORKED HARD ON THAT!!
I did a brush painting on rice paper!
This panda ...
THERE ARE TOO MANY THINGS WRONG WITH IT. BUT BEFORE WE GET INTO THAT...
The Yangtze River Love Story by Satomi
...THE MOST IMPORTANT THING IS THE PEN!!
ZEBRA
A PEN?!
WHAT'S THAT?
...
You really wanna be a manga artist?!

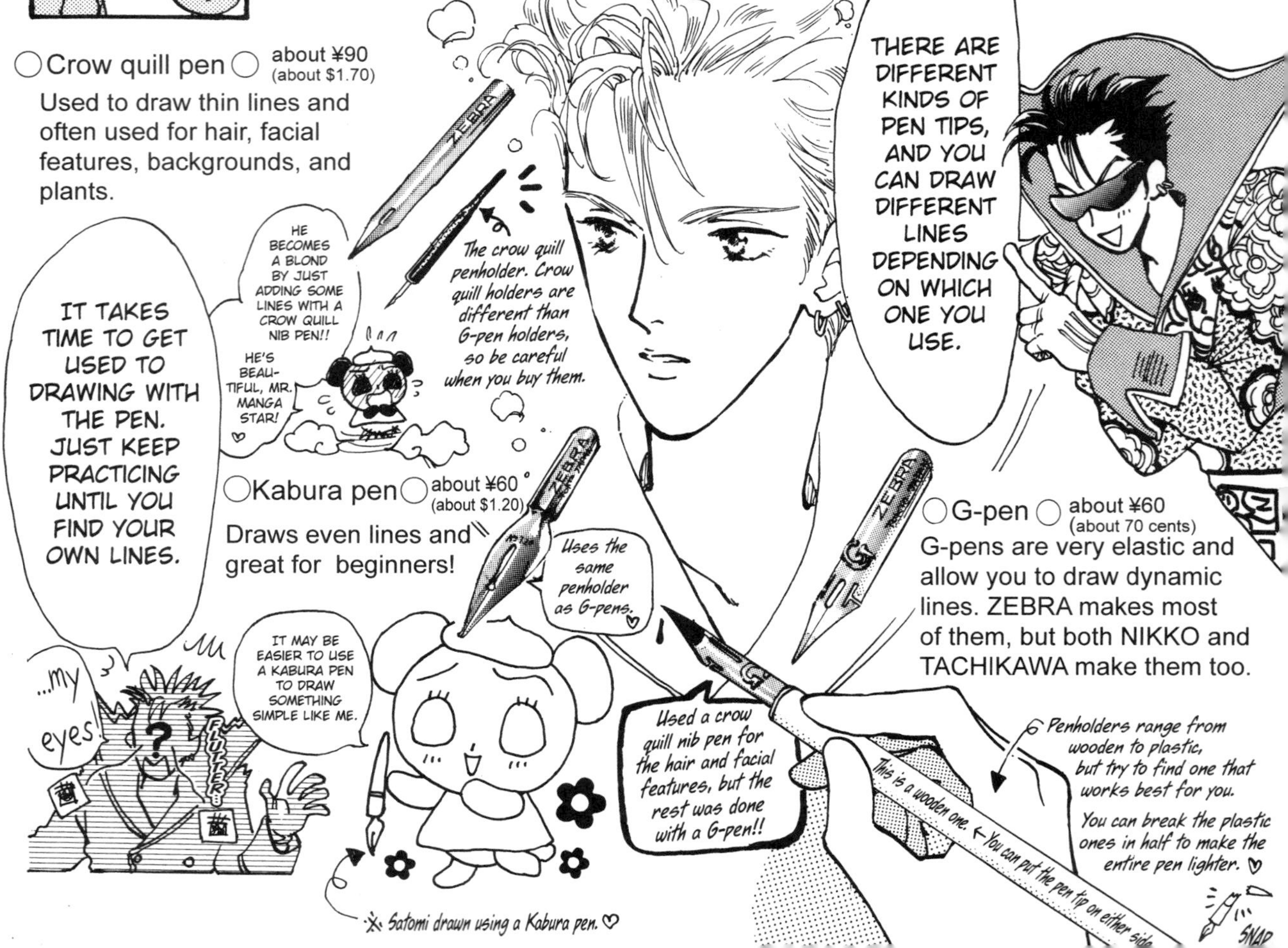

THERE ARE DIFFERENT KINDS OF PEN TIPS, AND YOU CAN DRAW DIFFERENT LINES DEPENDING ON WHICH ONE YOU USE.
The crow quill penholder. Crow quill holders are different than G-pen holders, so be careful when you buy them.
HE BECOMES A BLOND BY JUST ADDING SOME LINES WITH A CROW QUILL NIB PEN!!
HE'S BEAUTIFUL, MR. MANGA STAR!
IT TAKES TIME TO GET USED TO DRAWING WITH THE PEN. JUST KEEP PRACTICING UNTIL YOU FIND YOUR OWN LINES.
Uses the same penholder as G-pens.
Used a crow quill nib pen for the hair and facial features, but the rest was done with a G-pen!!
IT MAY BE EASIER TO USE A KABURA PEN TO DRAW SOMETHING SIMPLE LIKE ME.
...my eyes!
FLUTTER
Penholders range from wooden to plastic, but try to find one that works best for you.
You can break the plastic ones in half to make the entire pen lighter. ♡
This is a wooden one. ← You can put the pen tip on either side.
SNAP
※ Satomi drawn using a Kabura pen. ♡

◯Crow quill pen◯ about ¥90 (about $1.70)
Used to draw thin lines and often used for hair, facial features, backgrounds, and plants.

◯Kabura pen◯ about ¥60 (about $1.20)
Draws even lines and great for beginners!

◯G-pen◯ about ¥60 (about 70 cents)
G-pens are very elastic and allow you to draw dynamic lines. ZEBRA makes most of them, but both NIKKO and TACHIKAWA make them too.

◯The Paper◯

KENT paper or high quality paper is best fit for manga.
Try to pick thick, high quality paper.
(80-100lb. Paper is classified by weight.)

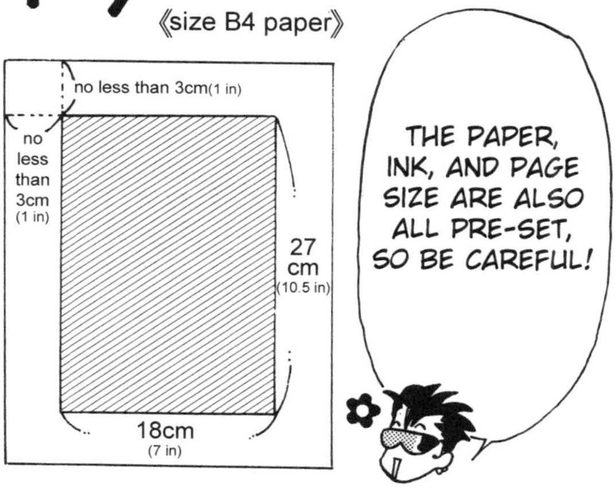
《size B4 paper》
no less than 3cm(1 in)
no less than 3cm (1 in)
27 cm (10.5 in)
18cm (7 in)
THE PAPER, INK, AND PAGE SIZE ARE ALSO ALL PRE-SET, SO BE CAREFUL!

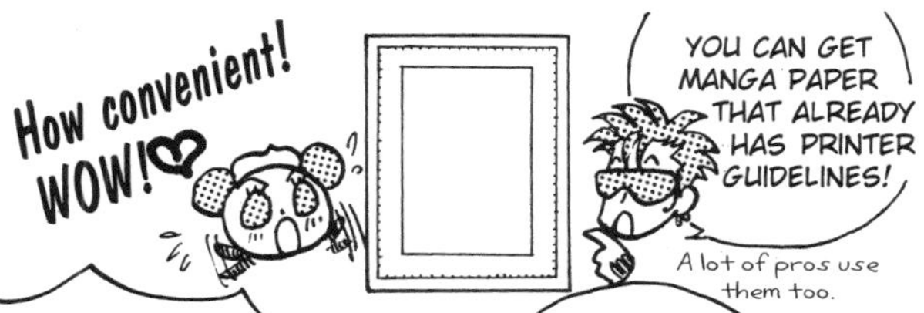
YOU CAN GET MANGA PAPER THAT ALREADY HAS PRINTER GUIDELINES!
A lot of pros use them too.
How convenient! WOW!

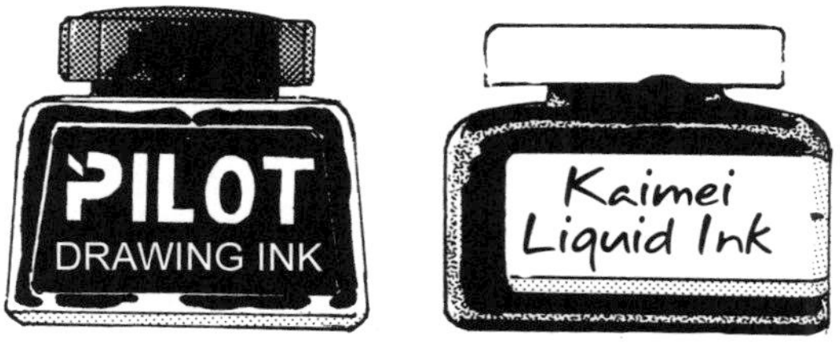
PILOT
DRAWING INK
Kaimei Liquid Ink

◯Drawing ink◯ ◯Liquid Ink◯

They're both black and let you draw neat lines. Choose which one you like using best. The liquid ink tends to be better for filling in blacks.

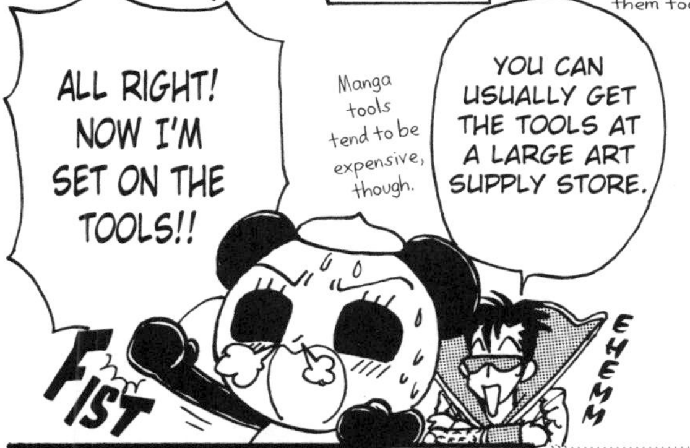
YOU CAN USUALLY GET THE TOOLS AT A LARGE ART SUPPLY STORE.
Manga tools tend to be expensive, though.
ALL RIGHT! NOW I'M SET ON THE TOOLS!!
FIST
EHEMM

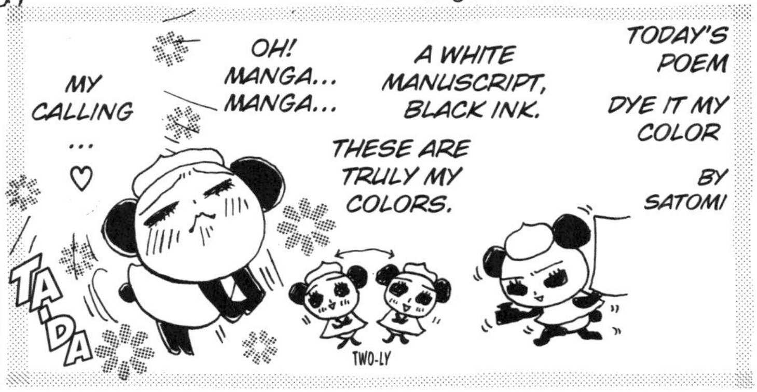
TODAY'S POEM
DYE IT MY COLOR
BY SATOMI
A WHITE MANUSCRIPT, BLACK INK.
THESE ARE TRULY MY COLORS.
OH! MANGA... MANGA...
MY CALLING... ♡
TA-DA
TWO-LY

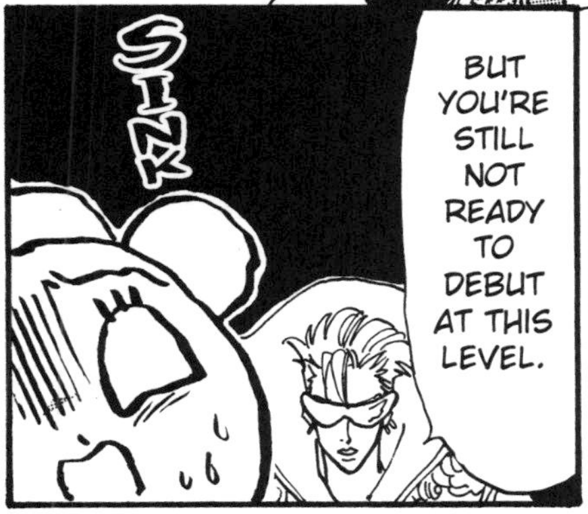
BUT YOU'RE STILL NOT READY TO DEBUT AT THIS LEVEL.
SINK

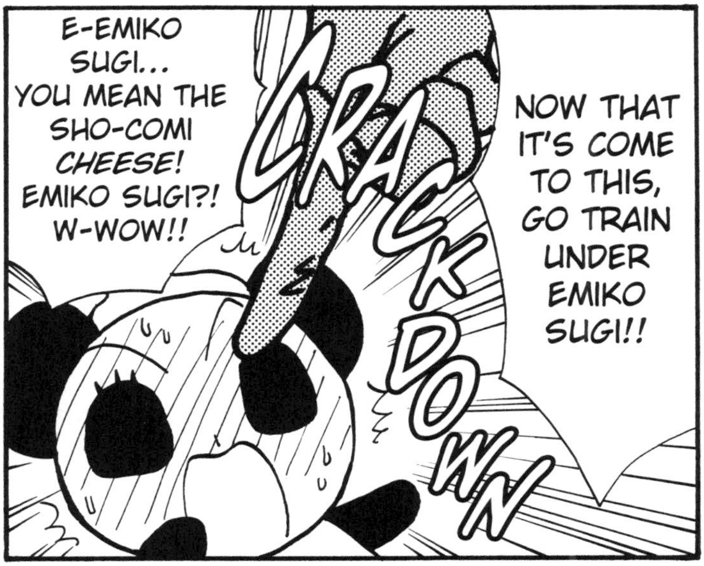
NOW THAT IT'S COME TO THIS, GO TRAIN UNDER EMIKO SUGI!!
E-EMIKO SUGI... YOU MEAN THE SHO-COMI CHEESE! EMIKO SUGI?! W-WOW!!
CRACKDOWN

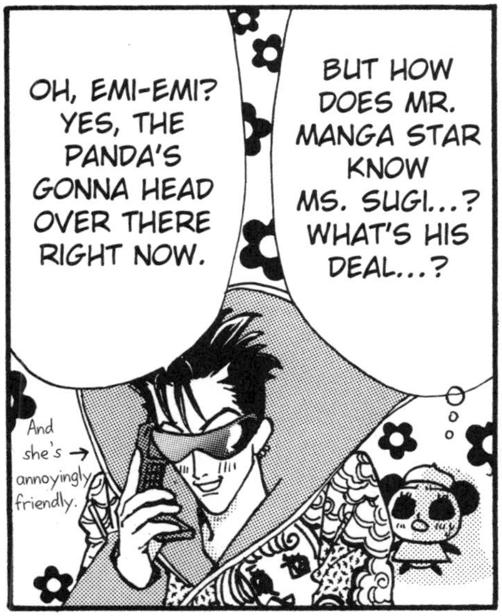
BUT HOW DOES MR. MANGA STAR KNOW MS. SUGI...? WHAT'S HIS DEAL...?
OH, EMI-EMI? YES, THE PANDA'S GONNA HEAD OVER THERE RIGHT NOW.
And she's annoyingly friendly.

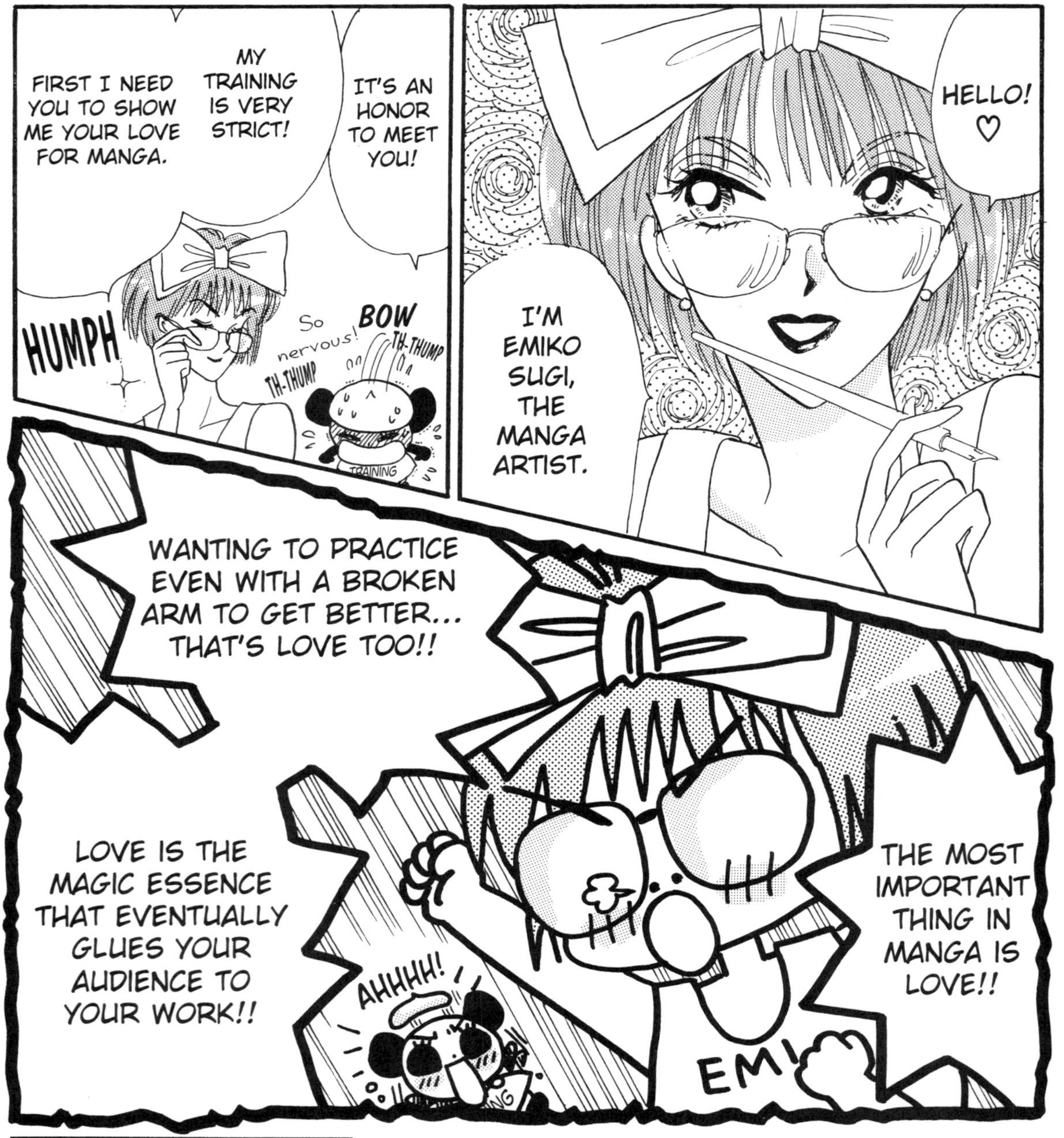
HELLO! ♡
I'M EMIKO SUGI, THE MANGA ARTIST.
IT'S AN HONOR TO MEET YOU!
MY TRAINING IS VERY STRICT!
FIRST I NEED YOU TO SHOW ME YOUR LOVE FOR MANGA.
BOW
TH-THUMP
So nervous!
TH-THUMP
HUMPH
TRAINING
THE MOST IMPORTANT THING IN MANGA IS LOVE!!
WANTING TO PRACTICE EVEN WITH A BROKEN ARM TO GET BETTER... THAT'S LOVE TOO!!
LOVE IS THE MAGIC ESSENCE THAT EVENTUALLY GLUES YOUR AUDIENCE TO YOUR WORK!!
EMI
AHHHH!

COPYING PROFESSIONAL DRAWINGS IS THE FIRST STEP TO BECOMING A PRO.

Anyone who wants to be a manga artist probably has a favorite artist or piece of work— someone or something that you aspire to. Such feelings are the first step in becoming a manga artist! It's difficult to just jump in and start drawing original work, so start by copying your favorite pro. There's a long career of know-how packed in their work!! Copying is the quickest way to become a pro. The more you draw, the more you improve, so the importance of practice can't be stressed enough!

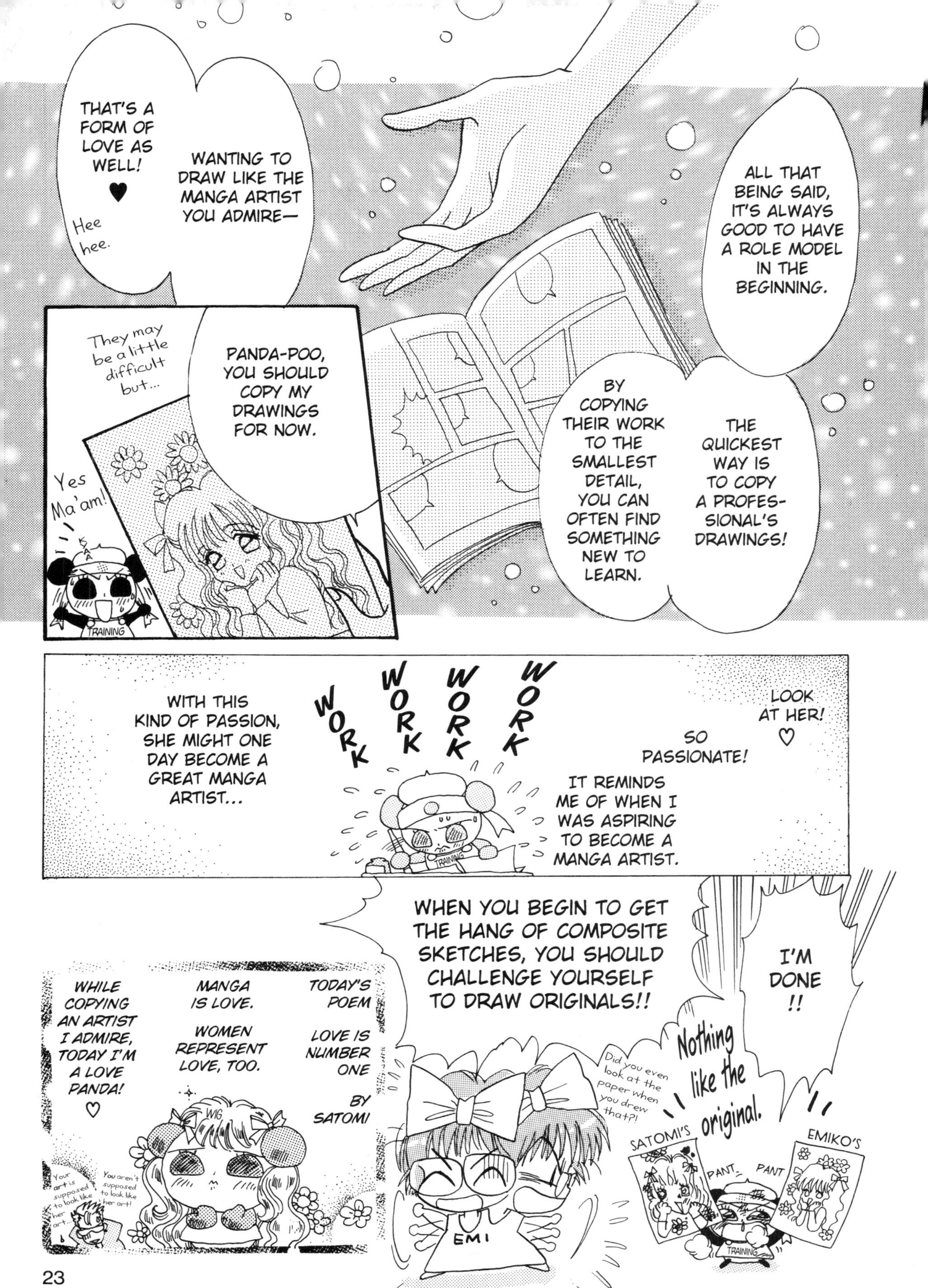
ALL THAT BEING SAID, IT'S ALWAYS GOOD TO HAVE A ROLE MODEL IN THE BEGINNING.
WANTING TO DRAW LIKE THE MANGA ARTIST YOU ADMIRE—
THAT'S A FORM OF LOVE AS WELL! ♥
Hee hee.
THE QUICKEST WAY IS TO COPY A PROFES-SIONAL'S DRAWINGS!
BY COPYING THEIR WORK TO THE SMALLEST DETAIL, YOU CAN OFTEN FIND SOMETHING NEW TO LEARN.
PANDA-POO, YOU SHOULD COPY MY DRAWINGS FOR NOW.
They may be a little difficult but...
Yes Ma'am!
KYAA
TRAINING
LOOK AT HER! ♡
SO PASSIONATE!
IT REMINDS ME OF WHEN I WAS ASPIRING TO BECOME A MANGA ARTIST.
WORK WORK WORK WORK
WITH THIS KIND OF PASSION, SHE MIGHT ONE DAY BECOME A GREAT MANGA ARTIST...
TRAINING
WHEN YOU BEGIN TO GET THE HANG OF COMPOSITE SKETCHES, YOU SHOULD CHALLENGE YOURSELF TO DRAW ORIGINALS!!
I'M DONE !!
Nothing like the original.
Did you even look at the paper when you drew that?!
SATOMI'S
EMIKO'S
PANT PANT
TRAINING
EMI
TODAY'S POEM
LOVE IS NUMBER ONE
BY SATOMI
MANGA IS LOVE.
WOMEN REPRESENT LOVE, TOO.
WHILE COPYING AN ARTIST I ADMIRE, TODAY I'M A LOVE PANDA! ♡
WIG
You aren't supposed to look like her art!
Your art is supposed to look like her art...

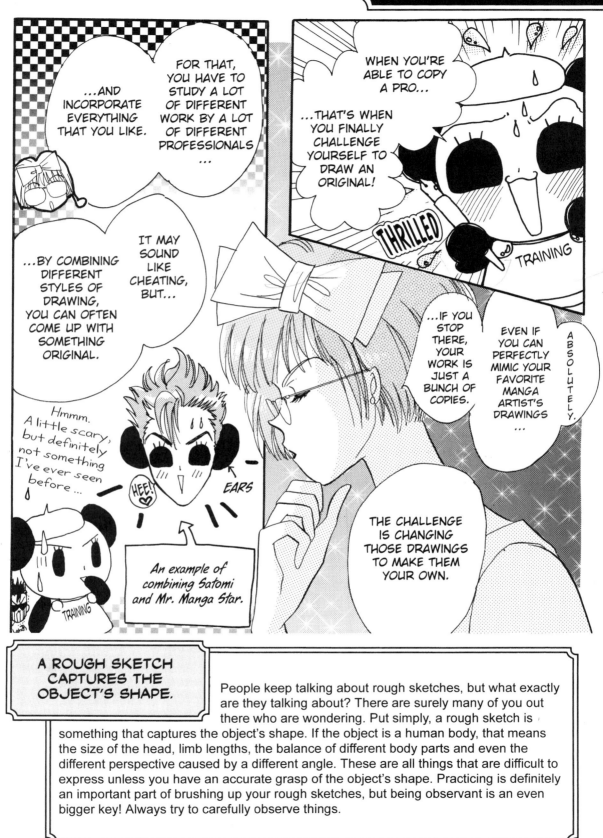

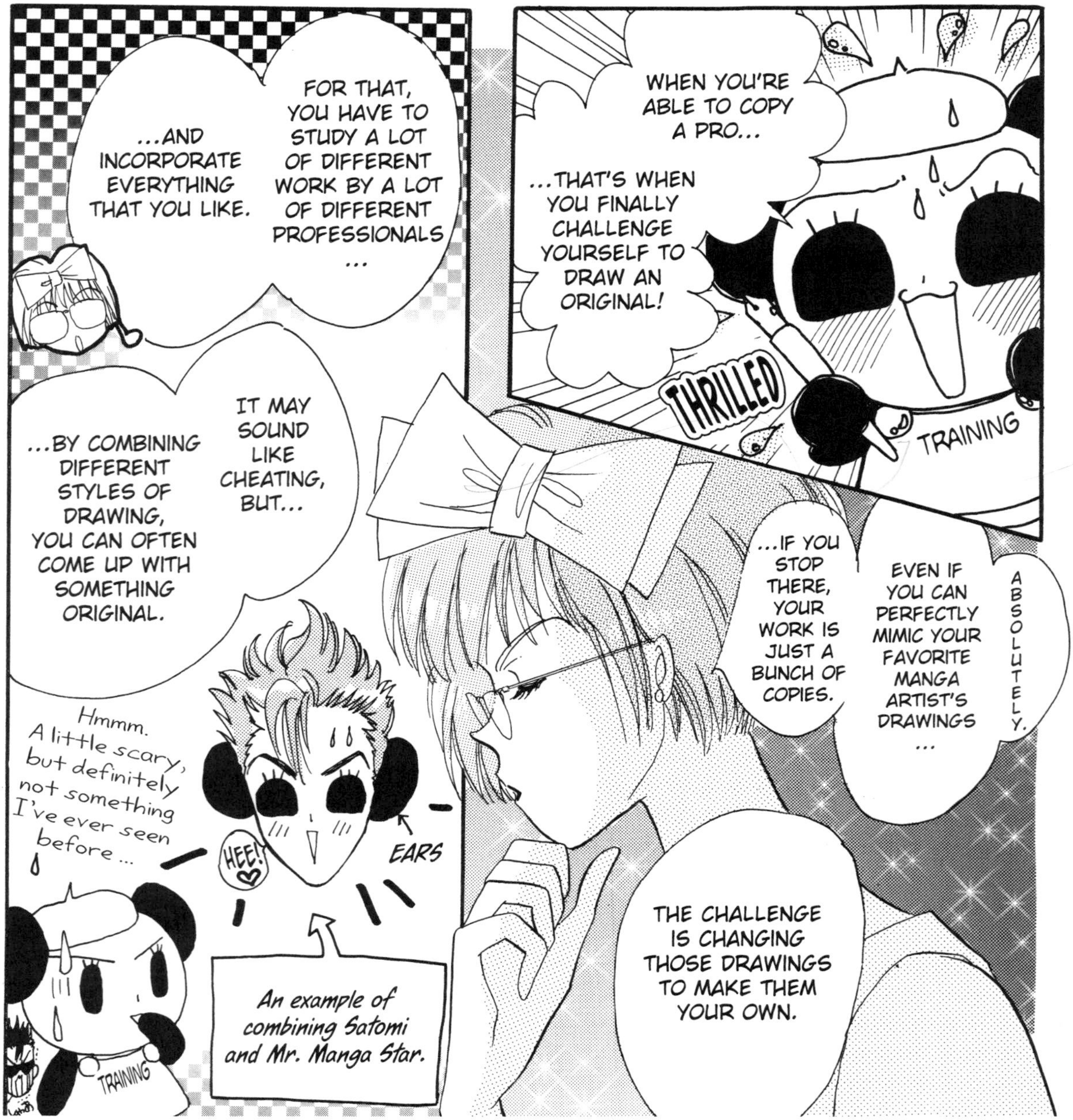
WHEN YOU'RE ABLE TO COPY A PRO...
...THAT'S WHEN YOU FINALLY CHALLENGE YOURSELF TO DRAW AN ORIGINAL!
THRILLED
TRAINING
EVEN IF YOU CAN PERFECTLY MIMIC YOUR FAVORITE MANGA ARTIST'S DRAWINGS...
ABSOLUTELY.
...IF YOU STOP THERE, YOUR WORK IS JUST A BUNCH OF COPIES.
THE CHALLENGE IS CHANGING THOSE DRAWINGS TO MAKE THEM YOUR OWN.
FOR THAT, YOU HAVE TO STUDY A LOT OF DIFFERENT WORK BY A LOT OF DIFFERENT PROFESSIONALS...
...AND INCORPORATE EVERYTHING THAT YOU LIKE.
IT MAY SOUND LIKE CHEATING, BUT...
...BY COMBINING DIFFERENT STYLES OF DRAWING, YOU CAN OFTEN COME UP WITH SOMETHING ORIGINAL.
HEE!
EARS
Hmmm. A little scary, but definitely not something I've ever seen before...
An example of combining Satomi and Mr. Manga Star.
TRAINING

A ROUGH SKETCH CAPTURES THE OBJECT'S SHAPE.

People keep talking about rough sketches, but what exactly are they talking about? There are surely many of you out there who are wondering. Put simply, a rough sketch is something that captures the object's shape. If the object is a human body, that means the size of the head, limb lengths, the balance of different body parts and even the different perspective caused by a different angle. These are all things that are difficult to express unless you have an accurate grasp of the object's shape. Practicing is definitely an important part of brushing up your rough sketches, but being observant is an even bigger key! Always try to carefully observe things.

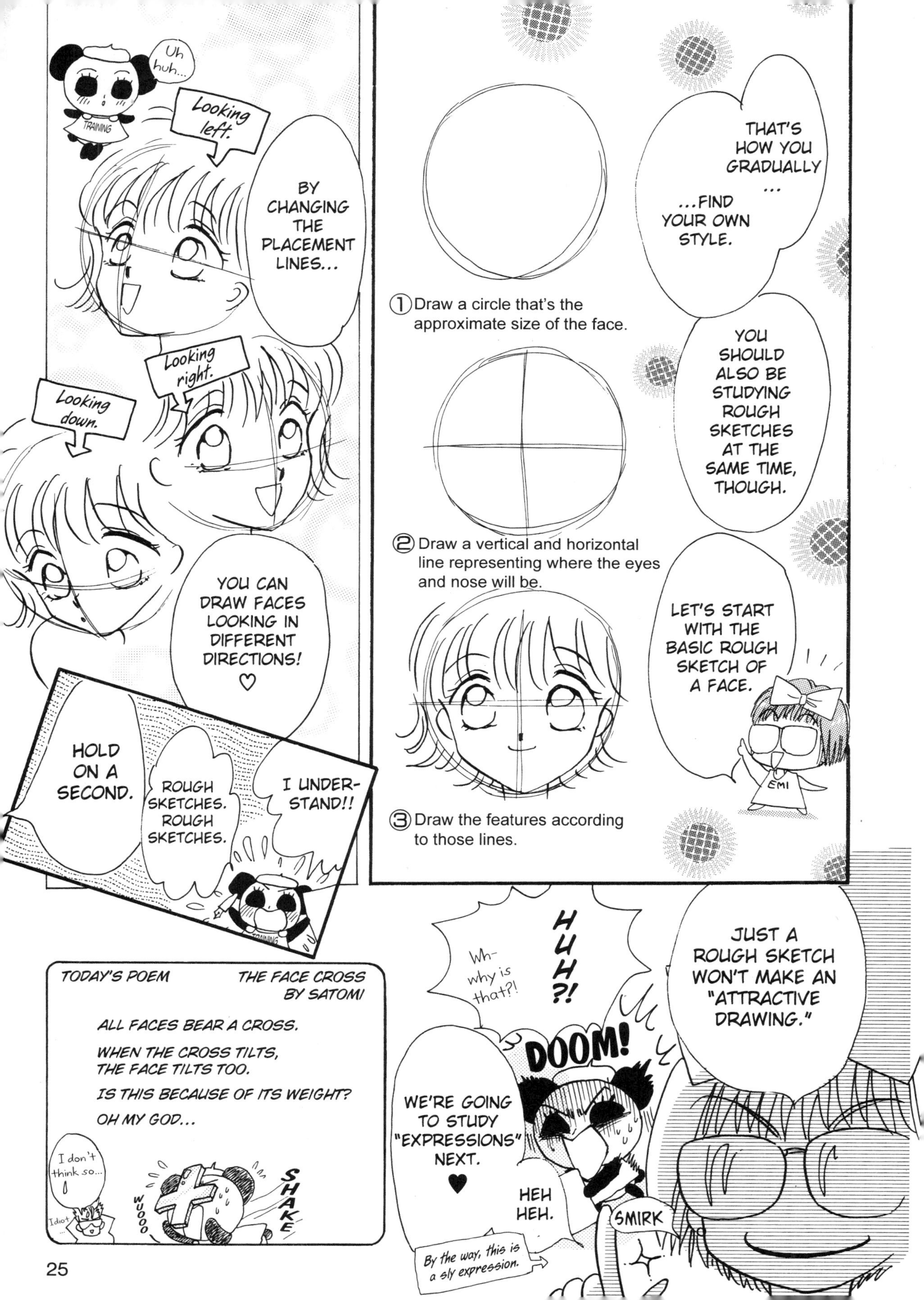
THAT'S HOW YOU GRADUALLY...
...FIND YOUR OWN STYLE.
① Draw a circle that's the approximate size of the face.
YOU SHOULD ALSO BE STUDYING ROUGH SKETCHES AT THE SAME TIME, THOUGH.
② Draw a vertical and horizontal line representing where the eyes and nose will be.
LET'S START WITH THE BASIC ROUGH SKETCH OF A FACE.
EMI
③ Draw the features according to those lines.
Uh huh...
TRAINING
Looking left.
BY CHANGING THE PLACEMENT LINES...
Looking right.
Looking down.
YOU CAN DRAW FACES LOOKING IN DIFFERENT DIRECTIONS! ♡
I UNDER-STAND!!
ROUGH SKETCHES. ROUGH SKETCHES.
HOLD ON A SECOND.
JUST A ROUGH SKETCH WON'T MAKE AN "ATTRACTIVE DRAWING."
HUH?!
Wh- why is that?!
DOOM!
WE'RE GOING TO STUDY "EXPRESSIONS" NEXT. ♥
HEH HEH.
SMIRK
By the way, this is a sly expression.
TODAY'S POEM
THE FACE CROSS
BY SATOMI
ALL FACES BEAR A CROSS.
WHEN THE CROSS TILTS, THE FACE TILTS TOO.
IS THIS BECAUSE OF ITS WEIGHT?
OH MY GOD...
I don't think so...
Idiot...
WUOOO
SHAKE

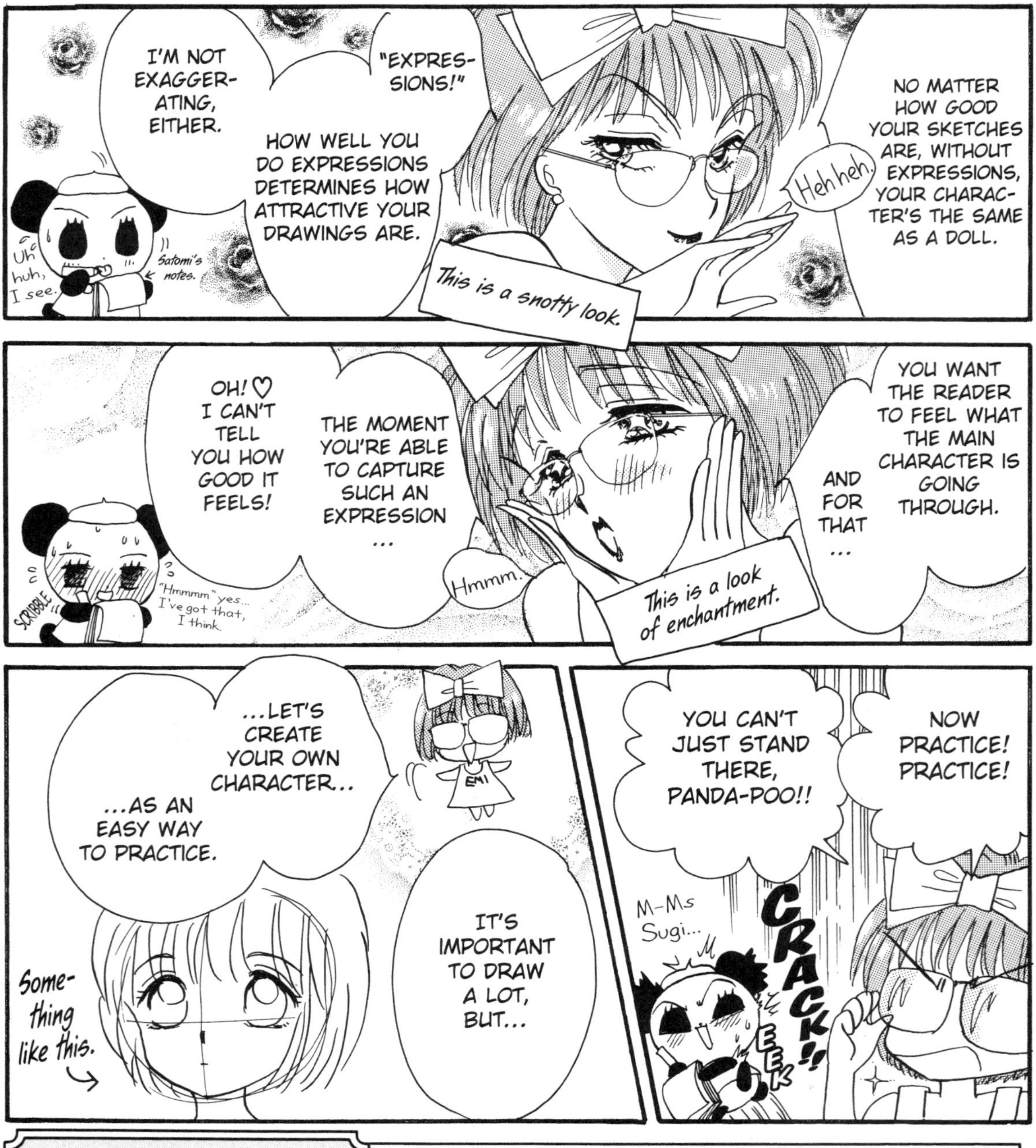
NO MATTER HOW GOOD YOUR SKETCHES ARE, WITHOUT EXPRESSIONS, YOUR CHARACTER'S THE SAME AS A DOLL.
Heh heh.
HOW WELL YOU DO EXPRESSIONS DETERMINES HOW ATTRACTIVE YOUR DRAWINGS ARE.
"EXPRES-SIONS!"
I'M NOT EXAGGER-ATING, EITHER.
This is a snotty look.
Satomi's notes.
Uh huh, I see.
YOU WANT THE READER TO FEEL WHAT THE MAIN CHARACTER IS GOING THROUGH.
AND FOR THAT...
THE MOMENT YOU'RE ABLE TO CAPTURE SUCH AN EXPRESSION...
OH! ♡ I CAN'T TELL YOU HOW GOOD IT FEELS!
Hmmm.
This is a look of enchantment.
"Hmmmm" yes... I've got that, I think.
SCRIBBLE
NOW PRACTICE! PRACTICE!
YOU CAN'T JUST STAND THERE, PANDA-POO!!
CRACK!!
M-Ms Sugi...
EEK
IT'S IMPORTANT TO DRAW A LOT, BUT...
...LET'S CREATE YOUR OWN CHARACTER...
...AS AN EASY WAY TO PRACTICE.
EMI
Some-thing like this.

PRACTICE DIFFERENT EXPRESSIONS ON A REGULAR BASIS!

Do you find yourself drawing adorable girls even when you're doodling? Practice is practice, so of course your drawings will improve. But just because your drawings improve doesn't necessarily mean that your manga skills are getting better! No matter how well you draw a character looking prim, it's not an expression that comes up often in manga. It's important to convey the characters' emotions in manga, so you've got to be able to draw a variety of expressions. Try incorporating different expressions in your everyday doodling.

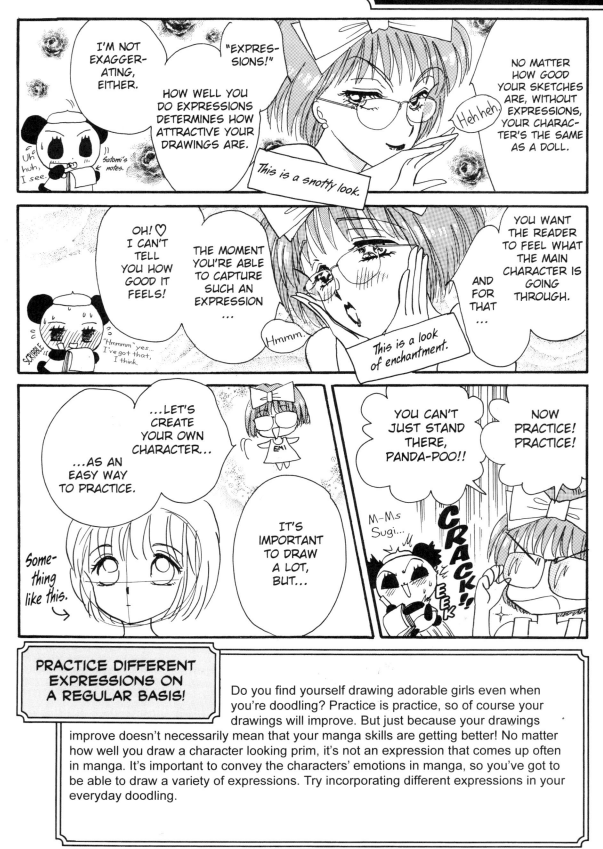

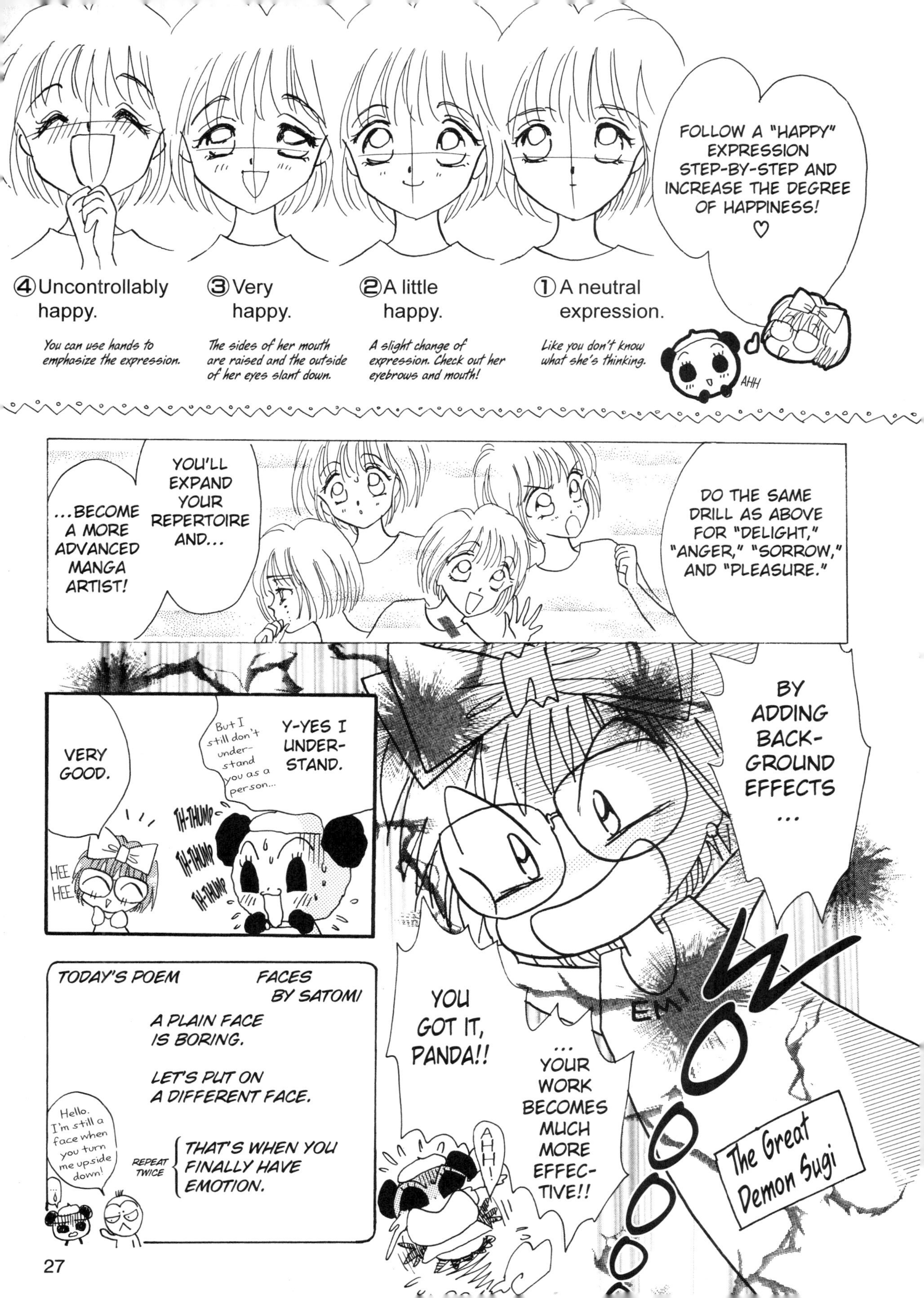
FOLLOW A "HAPPY" EXPRESSION STEP-BY-STEP AND INCREASE THE DEGREE OF HAPPINESS! ♡
AHH
①A neutral expression.
Like you don't know what she's thinking.
②A little happy.
A slight change of expression. Check out her eyebrows and mouth!
③Very happy.
The sides of her mouth are raised and the outside of her eyes slant down.
④Uncontrollably happy.
You can use hands to emphasize the expression.
DO THE SAME DRILL AS ABOVE FOR "DELIGHT," "ANGER," "SORROW," AND "PLEASURE."
YOU'LL EXPAND YOUR REPERTOIRE AND...
...BECOME A MORE ADVANCED MANGA ARTIST!
BY ADDING BACK-GROUND EFFECTS ...
... YOUR WORK BECOMES MUCH MORE EFFEC-TIVE!!
YOU GOT IT, PANDA!!
AHH!
EM
WOOOOO
The Great Demon Sugi
Y-YES I UNDER-STAND.
But I still don't under-stand you as a person...
VERY GOOD.
TH-THUMP
TH-THUMP
TH-THUMP
HEE HEE
TODAY'S POEM
FACES BY SATOMI
A PLAIN FACE IS BORING.
LET'S PUT ON A DIFFERENT FACE.
REPEAT TWICE
THAT'S WHEN YOU FINALLY HAVE EMOTION.
Hello. I'm still a face when you turn me upside down!
...

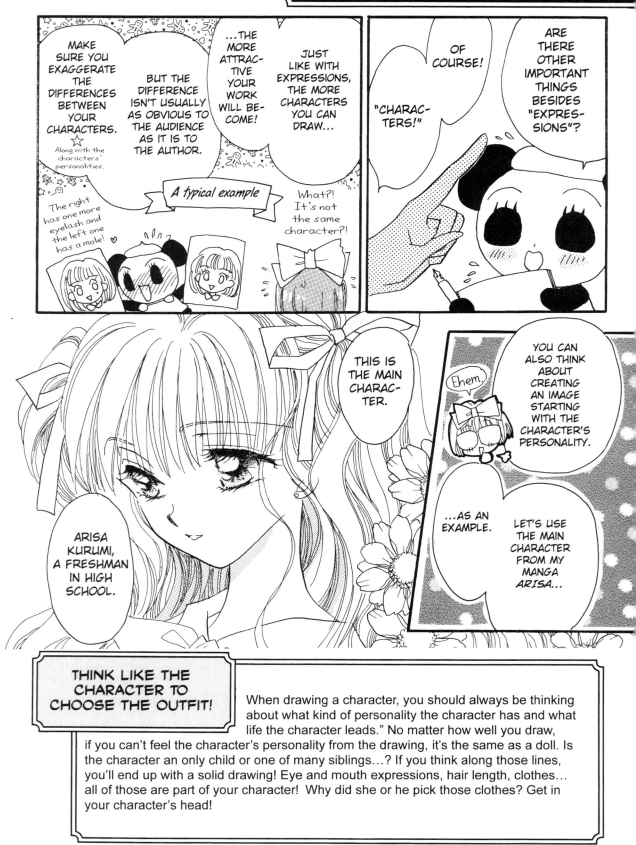

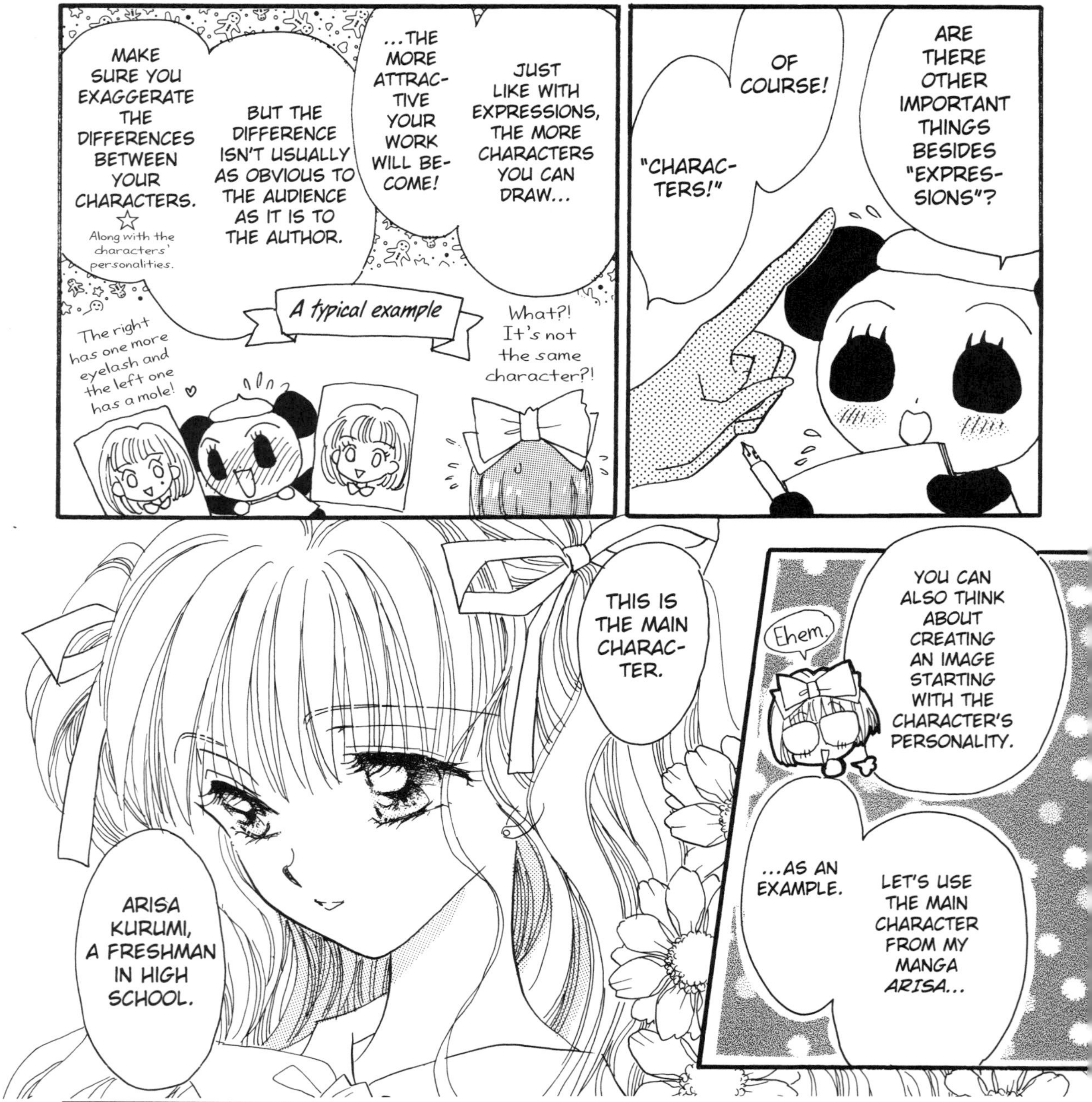
ARE THERE OTHER IMPORTANT THINGS BESIDES "EXPRESSIONS"?
OF COURSE!
"CHARACTERS!"
JUST LIKE WITH EXPRESSIONS, THE MORE CHARACTERS YOU CAN DRAW...
...THE MORE ATTRACTIVE YOUR WORK WILL BECOME!
BUT THE DIFFERENCE ISN'T USUALLY AS OBVIOUS TO THE AUDIENCE AS IT IS TO THE AUTHOR.
MAKE SURE YOU EXAGGERATE THE DIFFERENCES BETWEEN YOUR CHARACTERS. ☆
Along with the characters' personalities.
A typical example
What?! It's not the same character?!
The right has one more eyelash and the left one has a mole! ♡
YOU CAN ALSO THINK ABOUT CREATING AN IMAGE STARTING WITH THE CHARACTER'S PERSONALITY.
Ehem.
LET'S USE THE MAIN CHARACTER FROM MY MANGA *ARISA*...
...AS AN EXAMPLE.
THIS IS THE MAIN CHARACTER.
ARISA KURUMI, A FRESHMAN IN HIGH SCHOOL.

THINK LIKE THE CHARACTER TO CHOOSE THE OUTFIT!

When drawing a character, you should always be thinking about what kind of personality the character has and what life the character leads.” No matter how well you draw, if you can’t feel the character’s personality from the drawing, it’s the same as a doll. Is the character an only child or one of many siblings…? If you think along those lines, you’ll end up with a solid drawing! Eye and mouth expressions, hair length, clothes… all of those are part of your character! Why did she or he pick those clothes? Get in your character’s head!

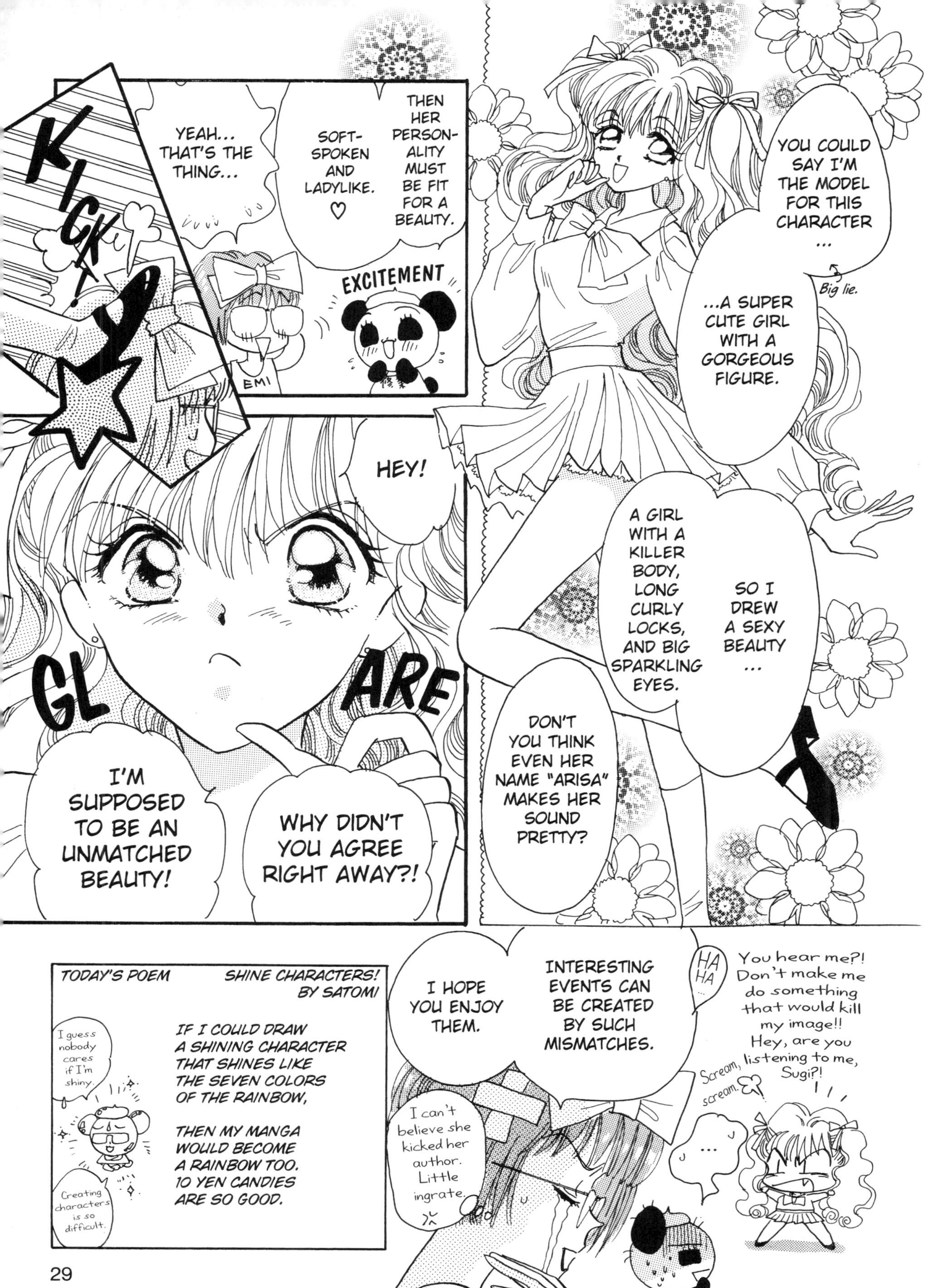
YOU COULD SAY I'M THE MODEL FOR THIS CHARACTER...
Big lie.
...A SUPER CUTE GIRL WITH A GORGEOUS FIGURE.
SO I DREW A SEXY BEAUTY...
A GIRL WITH A KILLER BODY, LONG CURLY LOCKS, AND BIG SPARKLING EYES.
DON'T YOU THINK EVEN HER NAME "ARISA" MAKES HER SOUND PRETTY?
THEN HER PERSONALITY MUST BE FIT FOR A BEAUTY.
SOFT-SPOKEN AND LADYLIKE. ♡
YEAH... THAT'S THE THING...
EXCITEMENT
EMI
KICK!
HEY!
GLARE
WHY DIDN'T YOU AGREE RIGHT AWAY?!
I'M SUPPOSED TO BE AN UNMATCHED BEAUTY!
You hear me?! Don't make me do something that would kill my image!! Hey, are you listening to me, Sugi?!
HA HA
INTERESTING EVENTS CAN BE CREATED BY SUCH MISMATCHES.
I HOPE YOU ENJOY THEM.
Scream, scream.
...
I can't believe she kicked her author. Little ingrate.
TODAY'S POEM
SHINE CHARACTERS! BY SATOMI
IF I COULD DRAW A SHINING CHARACTER THAT SHINES LIKE THE SEVEN COLORS OF THE RAINBOW,
THEN MY MANGA WOULD BECOME A RAINBOW TOO.
10 YEN CANDIES ARE SO GOOD.
I guess nobody cares if I'm shiny.
Creating characters is so difficult.

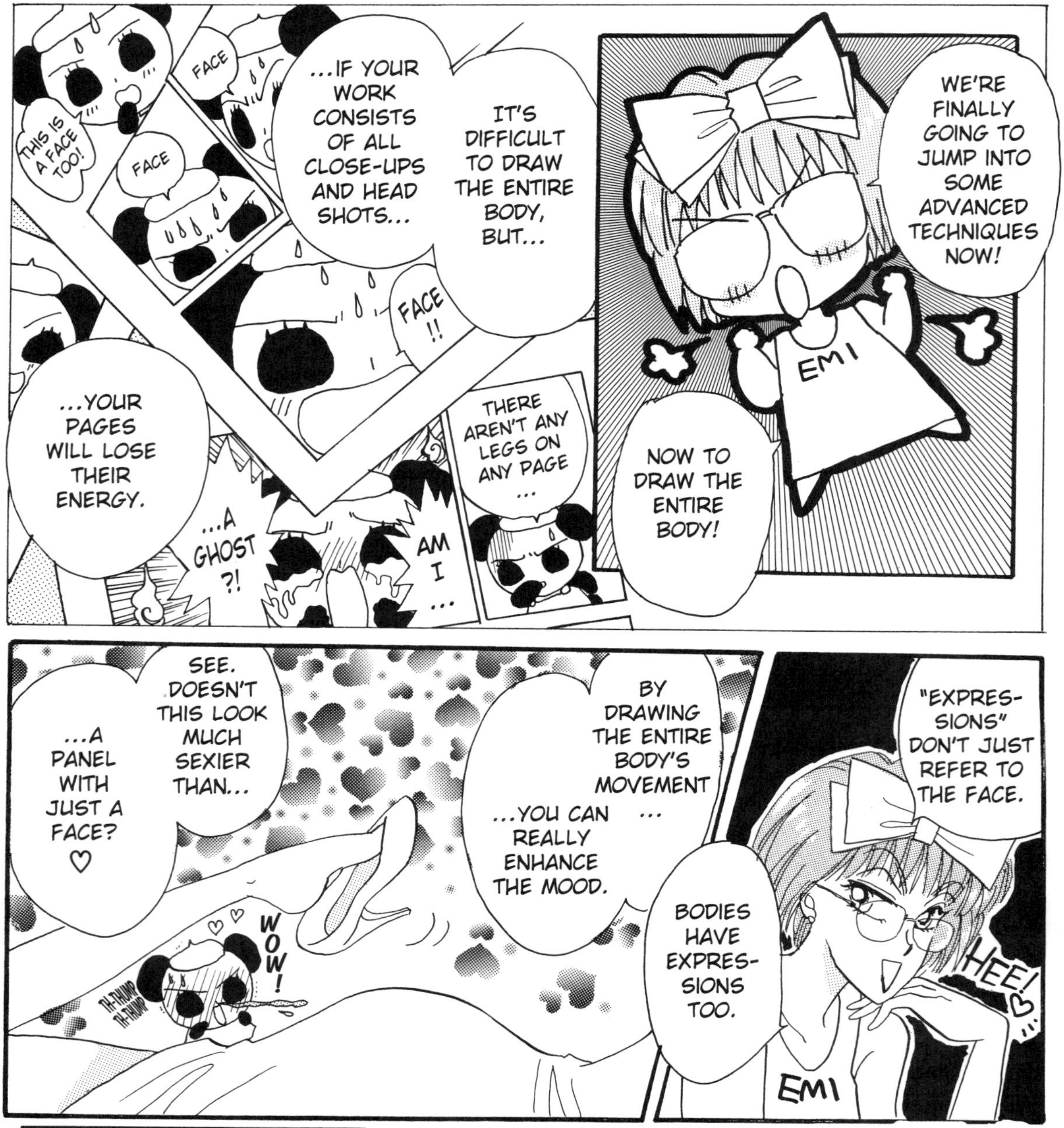

WE'RE FINALLY GOING TO JUMP INTO SOME ADVANCED TECHNIQUES NOW!
EMI
NOW TO DRAW THE ENTIRE BODY!
IT'S DIFFICULT TO DRAW THE ENTIRE BODY, BUT...
...IF YOUR WORK CONSISTS OF ALL CLOSE-UPS AND HEAD SHOTS...
FACE
THIS IS A FACE TOO!
FACE
FACE !!
...YOUR PAGES WILL LOSE THEIR ENERGY.
THERE AREN'T ANY LEGS ON ANY PAGE ...
AM I ...
...A GHOST ?!
"EXPRESSIONS" DON'T JUST REFER TO THE FACE.
BODIES HAVE EXPRESSIONS TOO.
HEE! ♡
EMI
BY DRAWING THE ENTIRE BODY'S MOVEMENT ...
...YOU CAN REALLY ENHANCE THE MOOD.
SEE. DOESN'T THIS LOOK MUCH SEXIER THAN...
...A PANEL WITH JUST A FACE? ♡
WOW!
TH-THUMP TH-THUMP

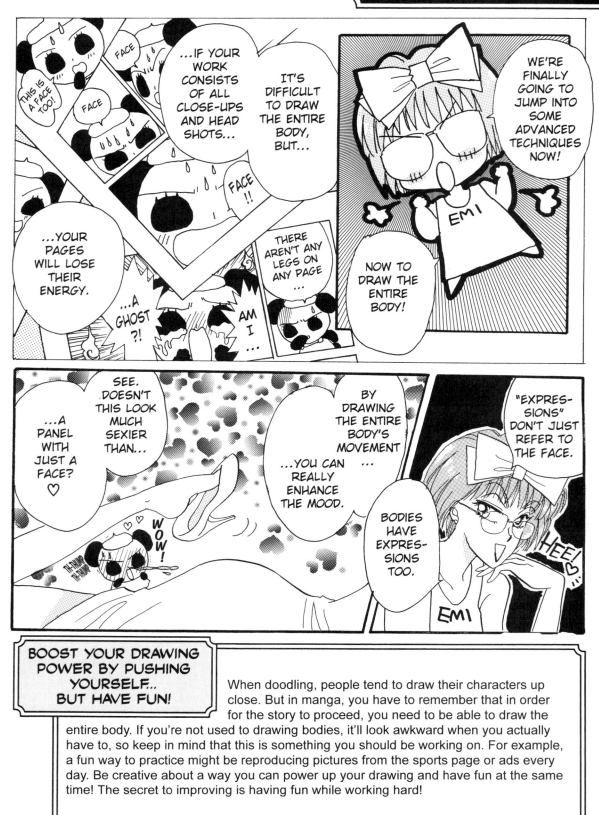

BOOST YOUR DRAWING POWER BY PUSHING YOURSELF.. BUT HAVE FUN!

When doodling, people tend to draw their characters up close. But in manga, you have to remember that in order for the story to proceed, you need to be able to draw the entire body. If you're not used to drawing bodies, it'll look awkward when you actually have to, so keep in mind that this is something you should be working on. For example, a fun way to practice might be reproducing pictures from the sports page or ads every day. Be creative about a way you can power up your drawing and have fun at the same time! The secret to improving is having fun while working hard!

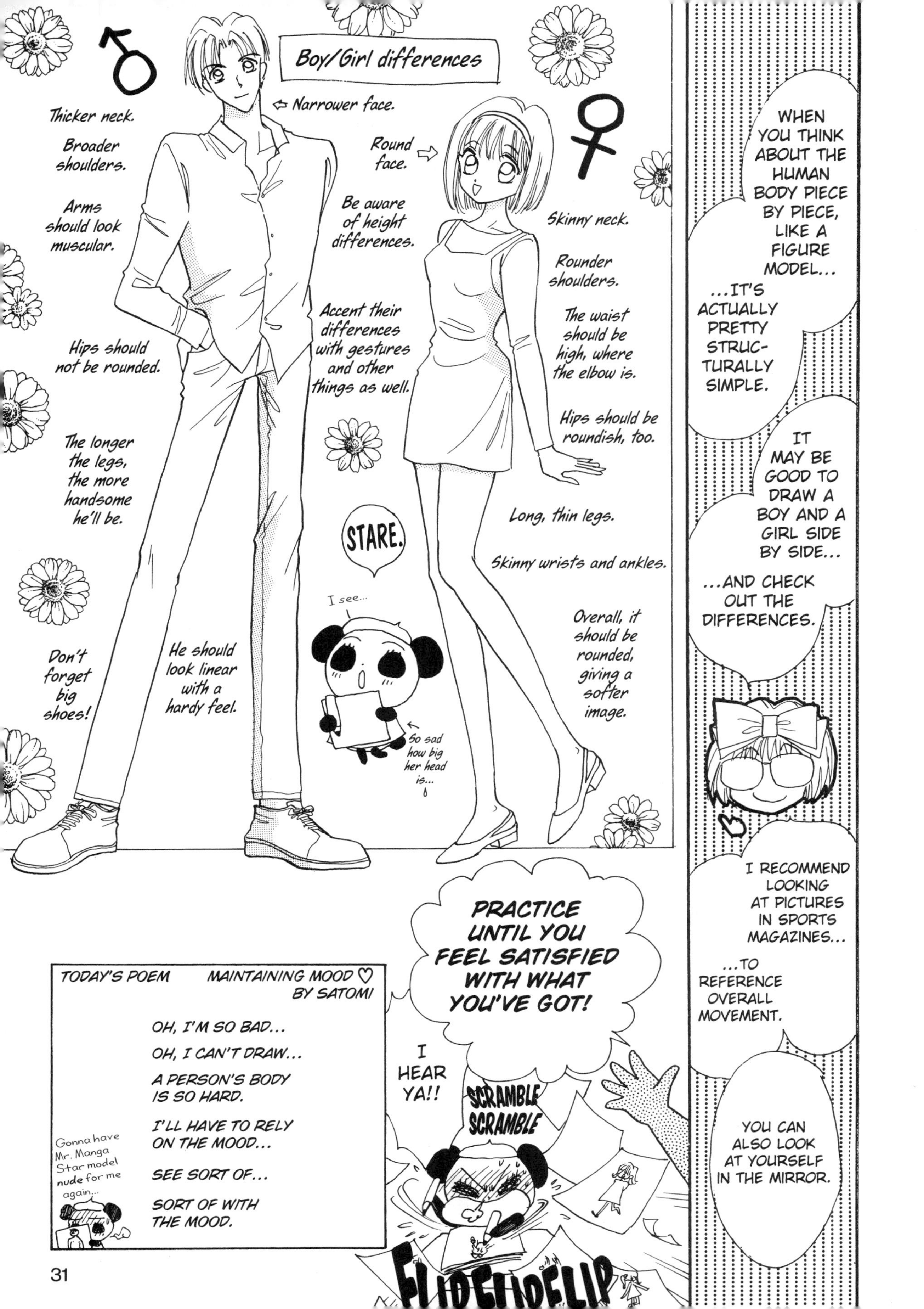
WHEN YOU THINK ABOUT THE HUMAN BODY PIECE BY PIECE, LIKE A FIGURE MODEL...
...IT'S ACTUALLY PRETTY STRUC-TURALLY SIMPLE.
IT MAY BE GOOD TO DRAW A BOY AND A GIRL SIDE BY SIDE...
...AND CHECK OUT THE DIFFERENCES.
I RECOMMEND LOOKING AT PICTURES IN SPORTS MAGAZINES...
...TO REFERENCE OVERALL MOVEMENT.
YOU CAN ALSO LOOK AT YOURSELF IN THE MIRROR.
Boy/Girl differences
Narrower face.
Thicker neck.
Broader shoulders.
Arms should look muscular.
Hips should not be rounded.
The longer the legs, the more handsome he'll be.
Don't forget big shoes!
He should look linear with a hardy feel.
Be aware of height differences.
Accent their differences with gestures and other things as well.
Round face.
Skinny neck.
Rounder shoulders.
The waist should be high, where the elbow is.
Hips should be roundish, too.
Long, thin legs.
Skinny wrists and ankles.
Overall, it should be rounded, giving a softer image.
STARE.
I see...
So sad how big her head is...
PRACTICE UNTIL YOU FEEL SATISFIED WITH WHAT YOU'VE GOT!
I HEAR YA!!
SCRAMBLE SCRAMBLE
FLIDFLIDFLIP
TODAY'S POEM MAINTAINING MOOD ♡ BY SATOMI
OH, I'M SO BAD...
OH, I CAN'T DRAW...
A PERSON'S BODY IS SO HARD.
I'LL HAVE TO RELY ON THE MOOD...
SEE SORT OF...
SORT OF WITH THE MOOD.
Gonna have Mr. Manga Star model nude for me again...

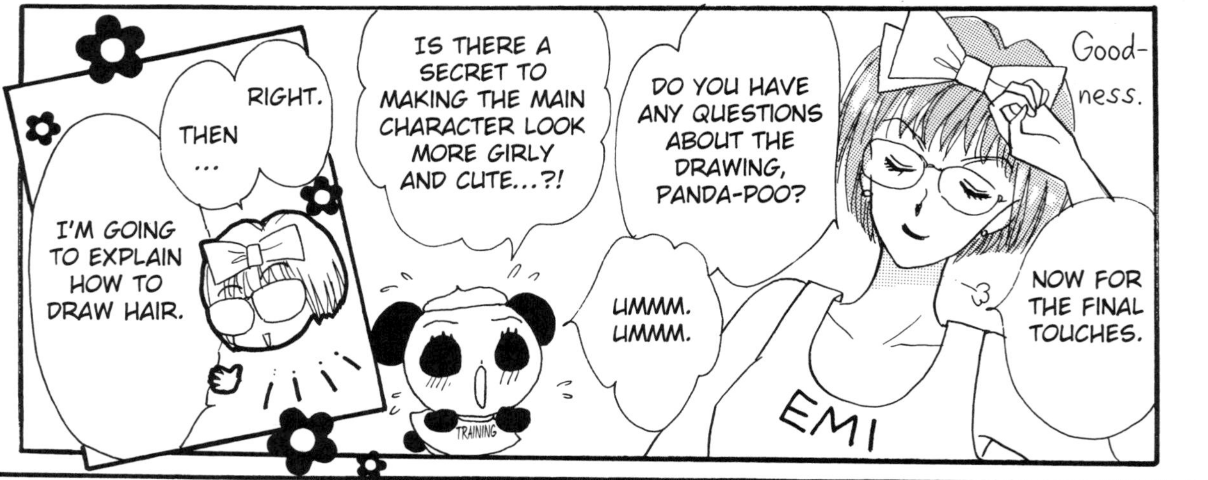
Good-ness.
NOW FOR THE FINAL TOUCHES.
EMI
DO YOU HAVE ANY QUESTIONS ABOUT THE DRAWING, PANDA-POO?
UMMM. UMMM.
IS THERE A SECRET TO MAKING THE MAIN CHARACTER LOOK MORE GIRLY AND CUTE...?!
TRAINING
RIGHT.
THEN ...
I'M GOING TO EXPLAIN HOW TO DRAW HAIR.

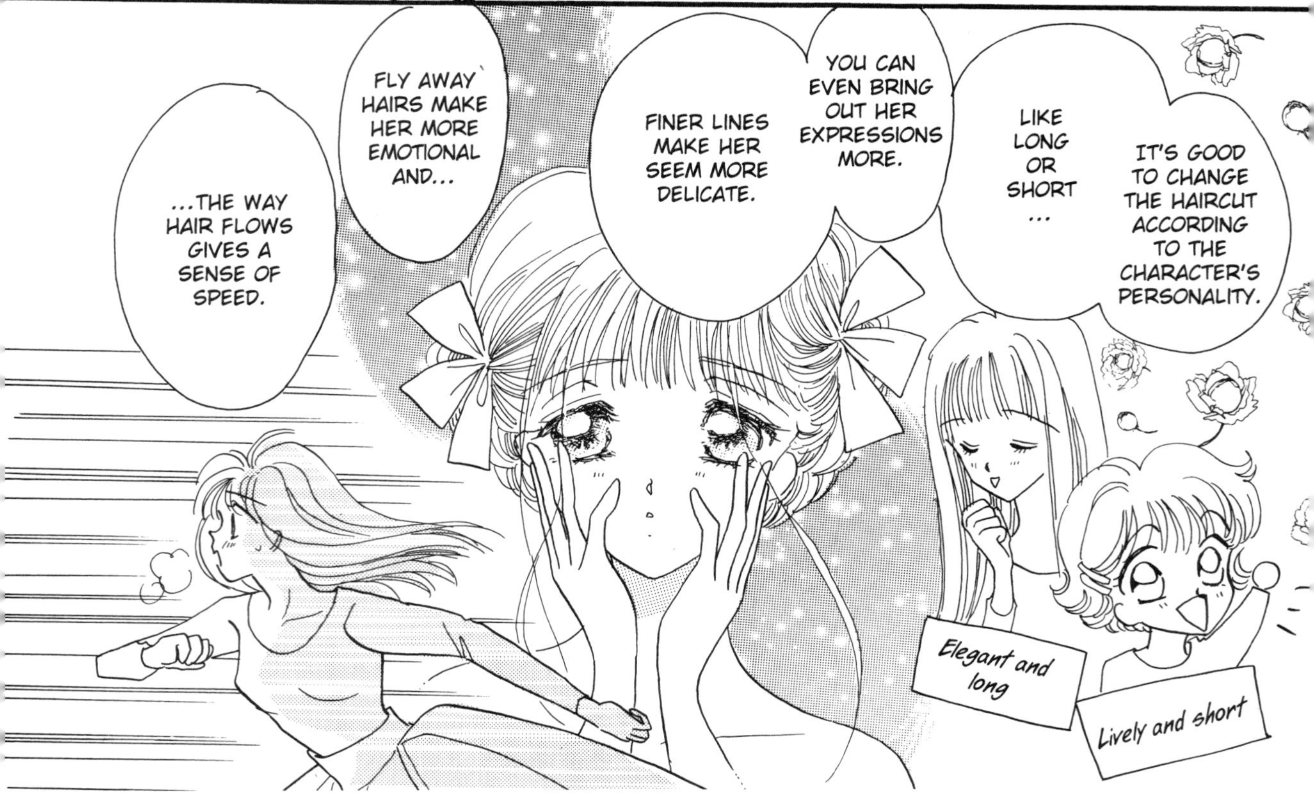
IT'S GOOD TO CHANGE THE HAIRCUT ACCORDING TO THE CHARACTER'S PERSONALITY.
LIKE LONG OR SHORT ...
Lively and short
Elegant and long
YOU CAN EVEN BRING OUT HER EXPRESSIONS MORE.
FINER LINES MAKE HER SEEM MORE DELICATE.
FLY AWAY HAIRS MAKE HER MORE EMOTIONAL AND...
...THE WAY HAIR FLOWS GIVES A SENSE OF SPEED.

IT'S IMPORTANT TO START DRAWING BEFORE YOU THINK ABOUT IT TOO MUCH!

Whether it's hair or the hands, observation is key to drawing well. Another important factor is just going for it. No matter how much you observe and have it in your head, it's hard to get that image on paper. As long as you get it on paper once, it makes it easier next time to draw based on your imagination. Don't stop at just one, and remember that the more you draw, the more it'll become your own. So keep drawing until your body "memorizes" the process. That's how you increase your repertoire.

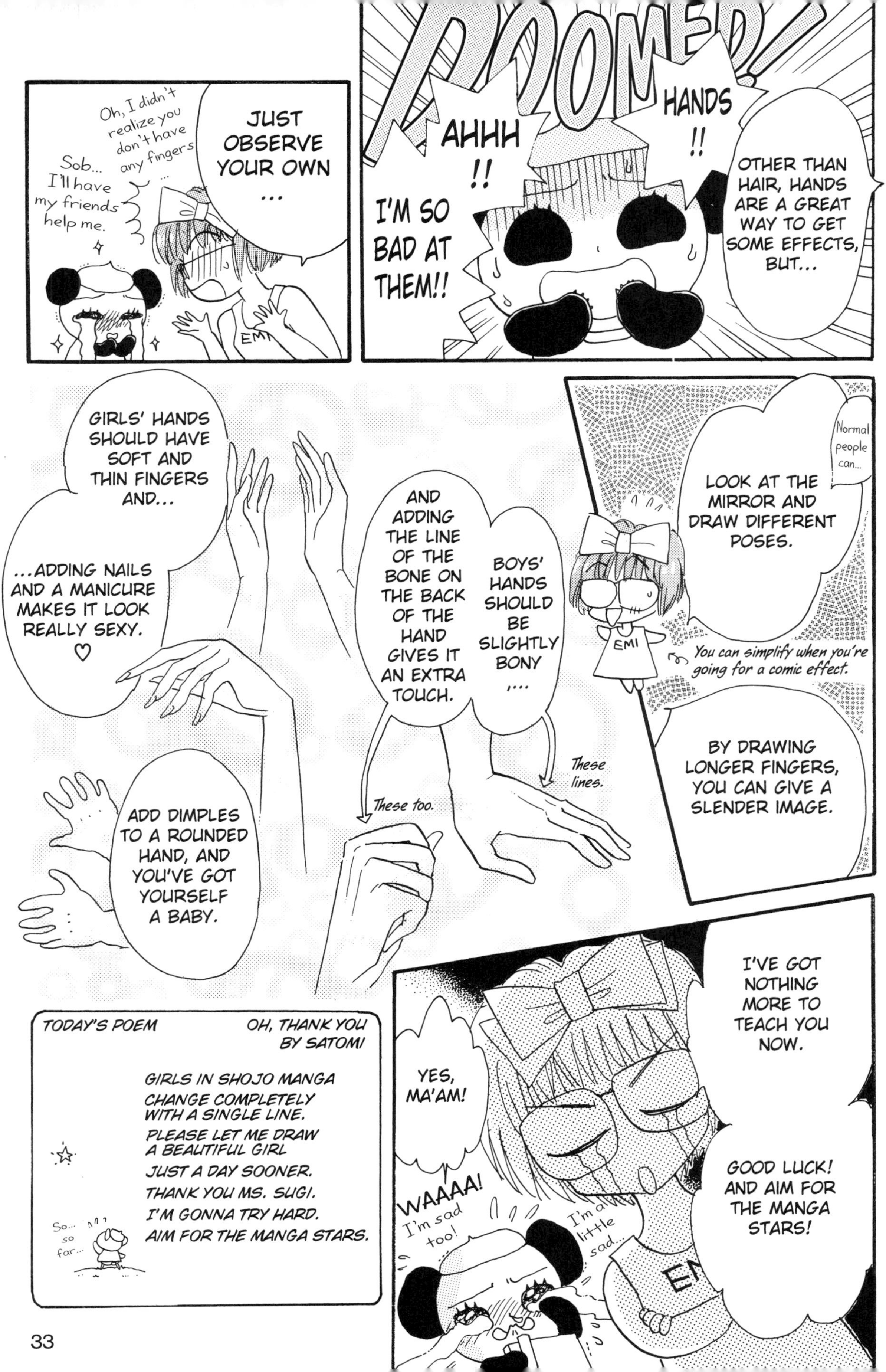
POOMED!
OTHER THAN HAIR, HANDS ARE A GREAT WAY TO GET SOME EFFECTS, BUT...
HANDS !!
AHHH !!
I'M SO BAD AT THEM!!
JUST OBSERVE YOUR OWN ...
Oh, I didn't realize you don't have any fingers ...
Sob... I'll have my friends help me.
Normal people can...
LOOK AT THE MIRROR AND DRAW DIFFERENT POSES.
You can simplify when you're going for a comic effect.
BY DRAWING LONGER FINGERS, YOU CAN GIVE A SLENDER IMAGE.
BOYS' HANDS SHOULD BE SLIGHTLY BONY ....
AND ADDING THE LINE OF THE BONE ON THE BACK OF THE HAND GIVES IT AN EXTRA TOUCH.
These lines.
These too.
GIRLS' HANDS SHOULD HAVE SOFT AND THIN FINGERS AND...
...ADDING NAILS AND A MANICURE MAKES IT LOOK REALLY SEXY. ♡
ADD DIMPLES TO A ROUNDED HAND, AND YOU'VE GOT YOURSELF A BABY.
I'VE GOT NOTHING MORE TO TEACH YOU NOW.
GOOD LUCK! AND AIM FOR THE MANGA STARS!
YES, MA'AM!
I'm a little sad...
WAAAA!
I'm sad too!

TODAY'S POEM

OH, THANK YOU
BY SATOMI

GIRLS IN SHOJO MANGA
CHANGE COMPLETELY
WITH A SINGLE LINE.
PLEASE LET ME DRAW
A BEAUTIFUL GIRL
JUST A DAY SOONER.
THANK YOU MS. SUGI.
I'M GONNA TRY HARD.
AIM FOR THE MANGA STARS.

So... so far...

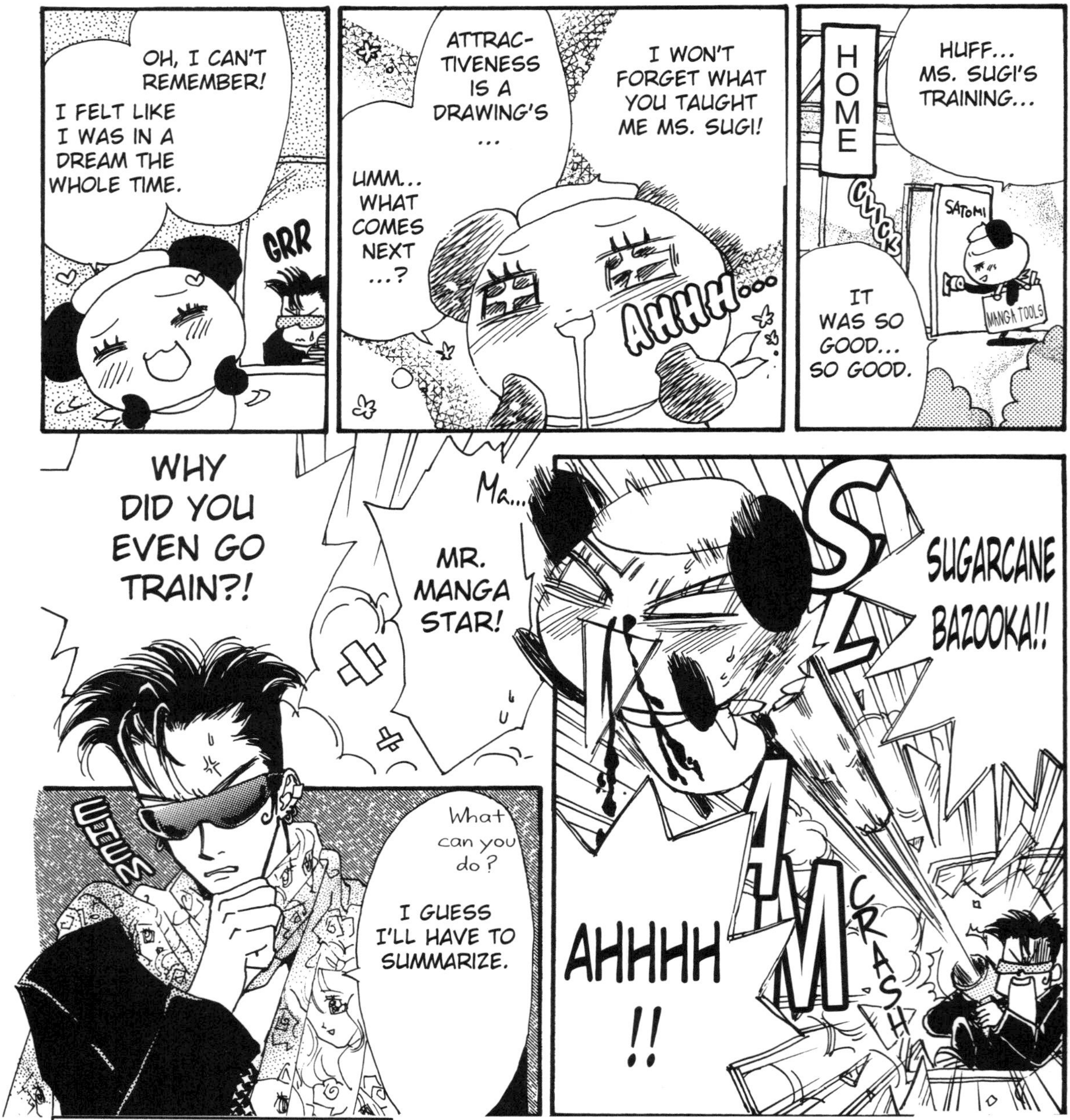
HOME
HUFF... MS. SUGI'S TRAINING...
CLICK
SATOMI
MANGA TOOLS
IT WAS SO GOOD... SO GOOD.
I WON'T FORGET WHAT YOU TAUGHT ME MS. SUGI!
ATTRACTIVENESS IS A DRAWING'S ...
UMM... WHAT COMES NEXT ...?
AHHH...
OH, I CAN'T REMEMBER!
I FELT LIKE I WAS IN A DREAM THE WHOLE TIME.
GRR
SUGARCANE BAZOOKA!!
SLAM
CRASH
AHHHH !!
Ma...
MR. MANGA STAR!
WHY DID YOU EVEN GO TRAIN?!
What can you do?
I GUESS I'LL HAVE TO SUMMARIZE.

TO BECOME A PROFESSIONAL, YOU HAVE TO WORK HARDER THAN A PROFESSIONAL!

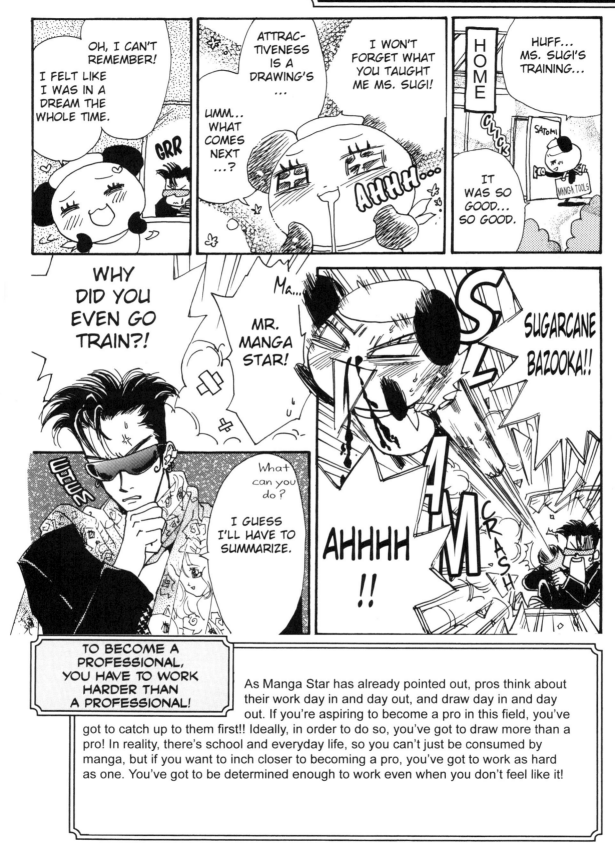

As Manga Star has already pointed out, pros think about their work day in and day out, and draw day in and day out. If you're aspiring to become a pro in this field, you've got to catch up to them first!! Ideally, in order to do so, you've got to draw more than a pro! In reality, there's school and everyday life, so you can't just be consumed by manga, but if you want to inch closer to becoming a pro, you've got to work as hard as one. You've got to be determined enough to work even when you don't feel like it!

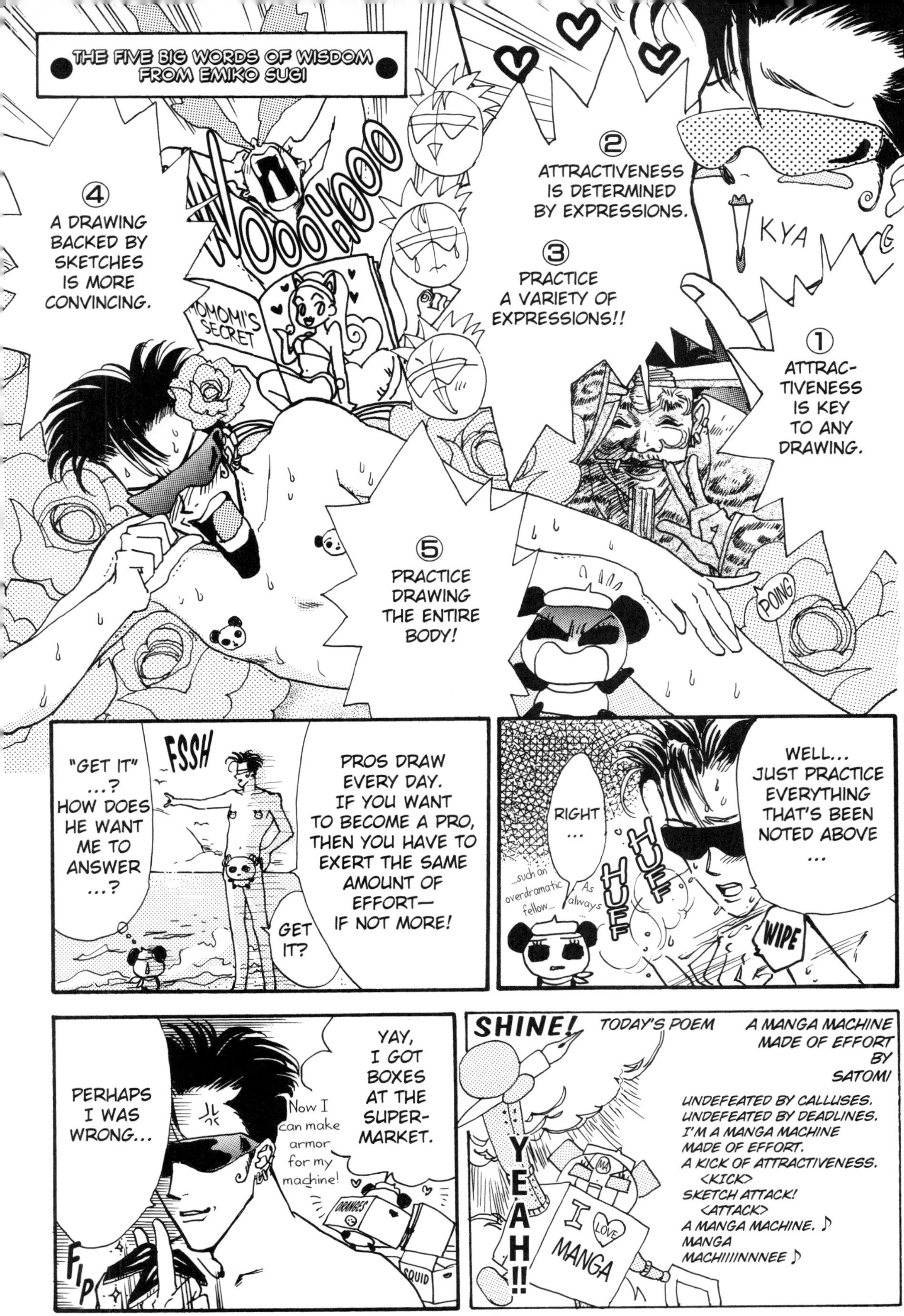
THE FIVE BIG WORDS OF WISDOM FROM EMIKO SUGI
KYA
① ATTRACTIVENESS IS KEY TO ANY DRAWING.
② ATTRACTIVENESS IS DETERMINED BY EXPRESSIONS.
③ PRACTICE A VARIETY OF EXPRESSIONS!!
WOOOHOOO
MOMOMI'S SECRET
④ A DRAWING BACKED BY SKETCHES IS MORE CONVINCING.
POING
⑤ PRACTICE DRAWING THE ENTIRE BODY!
WELL... JUST PRACTICE EVERYTHING THAT'S BEEN NOTED ABOVE ...
HUFF HUFF
WIPE
RIGHT ...
As always ...
...such an overdramatic fellow...
PROS DRAW EVERY DAY. IF YOU WANT TO BECOME A PRO, THEN YOU HAVE TO EXERT THE SAME AMOUNT OF EFFORT— IF NOT MORE!
FSSH
GET IT?
"GET IT" ...? HOW DOES HE WANT ME TO ANSWER ...?
A MANGA MACHINE MADE OF EFFORT BY SATOMI
TODAY'S POEM
SHINE!
UNDEFEATED BY CALLUSES.
UNDEFEATED BY DEADLINES.
I'M A MANGA MACHINE
MADE OF EFFORT.
A KICK OF ATTRACTIVENESS.
<KICK>
SKETCH ATTACK!
<ATTACK>
A MANGA MACHINE. ♪
MANGA
MACHIIIINNNEE ♪
YEAH!!
MA
I LOVE MANGA
YAY, I GOT BOXES AT THE SUPER-MARKET.
Now I can make armor for my machine!
ORANGES
SQUID
PERHAPS I WAS WRONG...
FLIP

You can get great techniques from a professional manga! Let's check out Emiko Sugi's professional techniques!

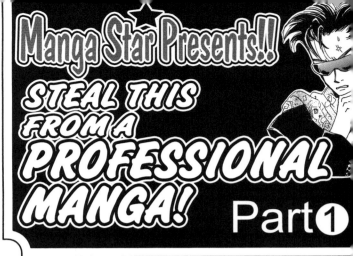

Manga Star Presents!! STEAL THIS FROM A PROFESSIONAL MANGA! Part 1

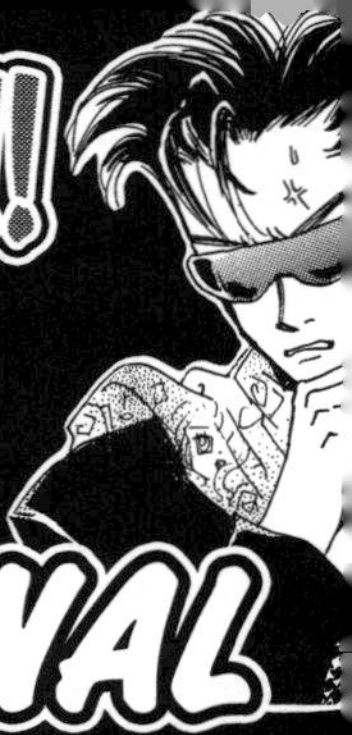

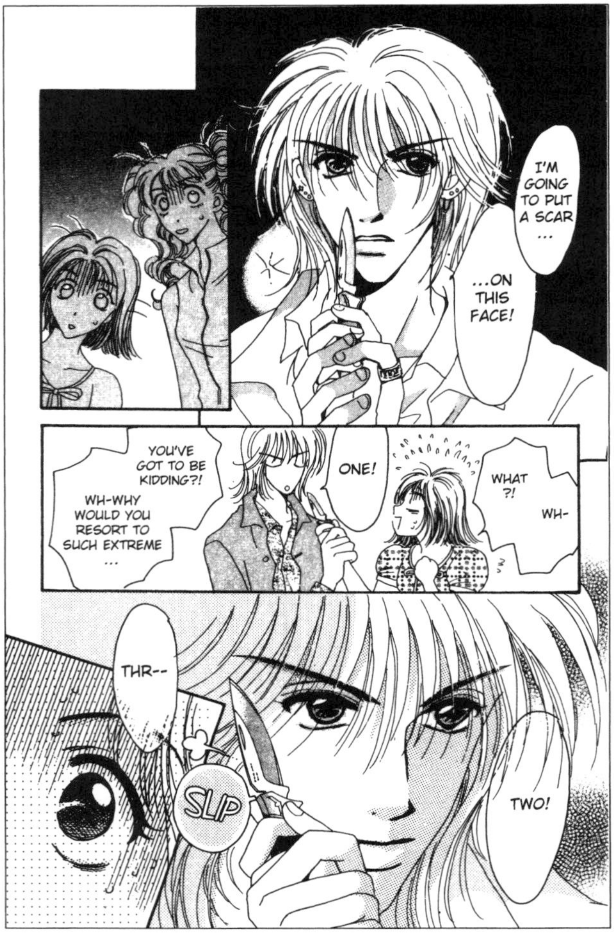

I'M GOING TO PUT A SCAR ...
...ON THIS FACE!
WHAT ?!
WH-
ONE!
YOU'VE GOT TO BE KIDDING?!
WH-WHY WOULD YOU RESORT TO SUCH EXTREME ...
TWO!
SLIP
THR--

3rd PANEL

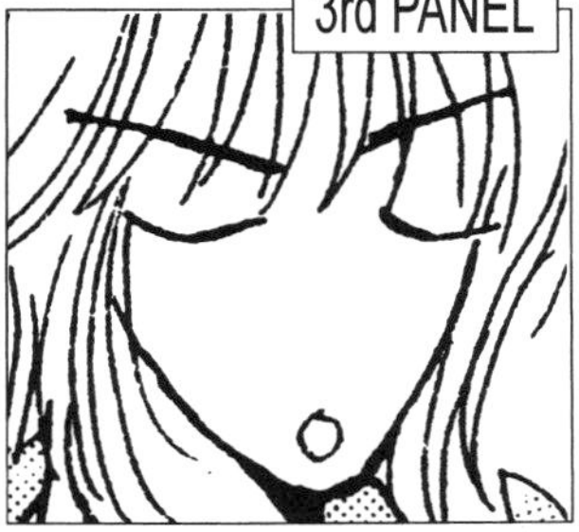

4th PANEL

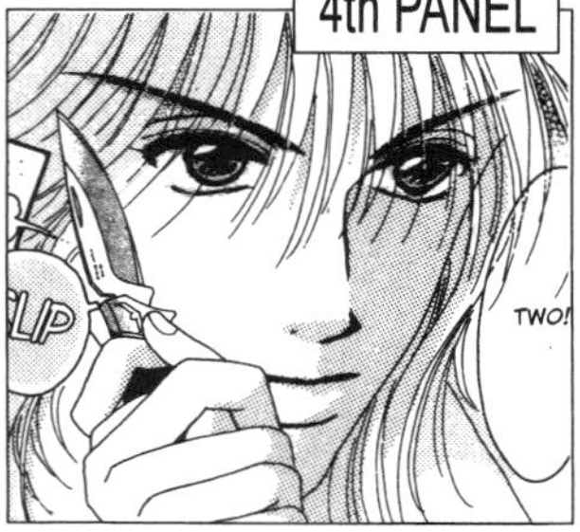

TWO!
SLIP

WHAT'S THE CORRELATION BETWEEN THE SIZE OF THE DRAWING AND THE DRAWING'S DENSITY?

Let's conduct a fun experiment here! The drawing on the left is a page from the manga, and the bottom two panels are close-ups of the third and fourth panel from that page! What can be discovered from comparing those two panels?!
By the way, the bottom two pictures are shown so they're the same size, but note how different the drawings' densities are! Yep, this means that you should change the density depending on the size of the drawing.

Large drawings need details, or it looks like something's missing and conversely, unless you simplify small drawings, the page will end up looking messy.

THERE IS A WAY TO DRAW BIG PICTURES!

On the other hand, there are different ways to draw small and big pictures. Try drawing a close-up using an entire page. You'll see how you put in different touches and draw differently than when doing a small drawing.

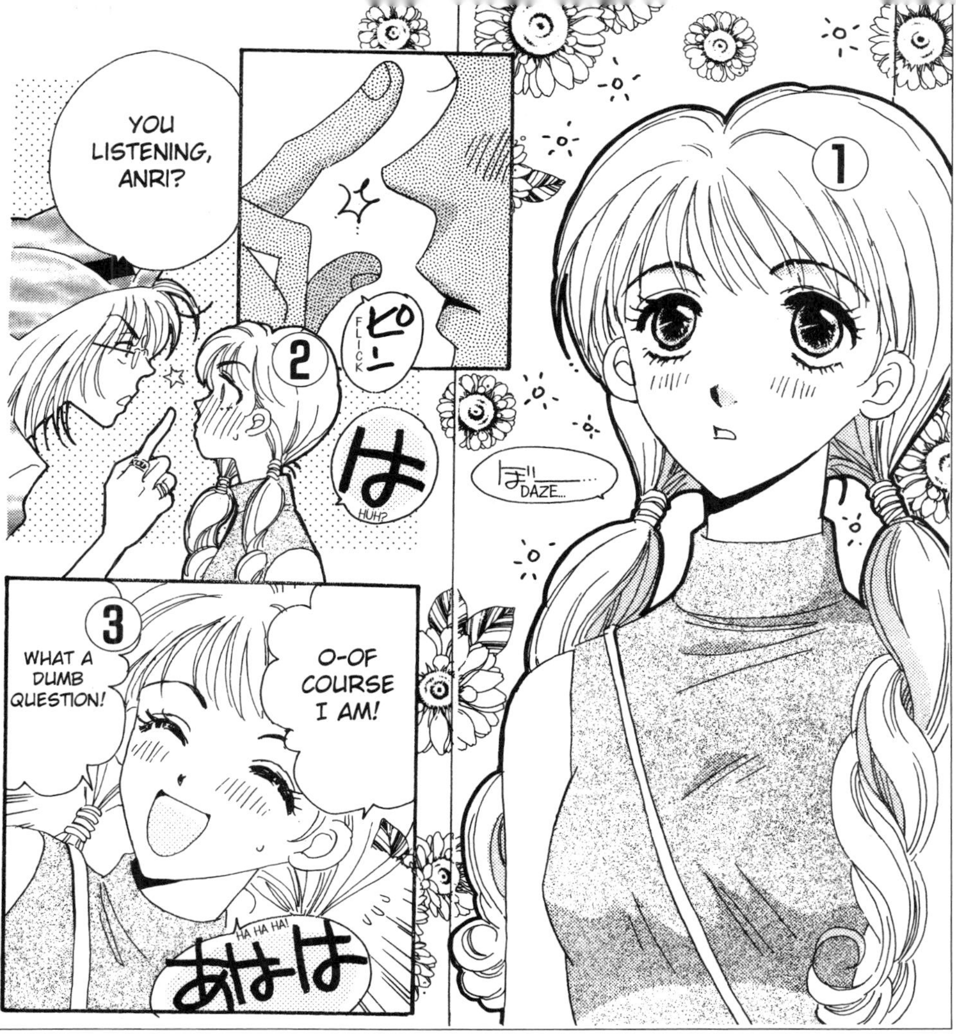
DAZE...
YOU LISTENING, ANRI?
FLICK
は
HUH?
O-OF COURSE I AM!
WHAT A DUMB QUESTION!
HA HA HA!
あはは

CONDUCT RESEARCH TO DRAW YOUR CHARACTER'S APPEAL.

You probably understand from Emiko Sugi that a character's appeal is her vivacious expressions. Now, let's take a look at how different expressions are drawn within a body of work.

FOCUS ON THE VIVACIOUS EXPRESSION AND THE OUTLINES.

The main character's in a daze in ①, She's alarmed in ②, and laughing in ③. Her changing expression is both cute and appealing. Each expression is also exaggerated, so unless you practice, you won't be able to maintain her vivaciousness. Keep practicing so you can relax for the real thing and really capture a great expression. You should also note points other than the character's expression! For example, the outline in ①! Did you notice that it's thicker than normal? By making the outline bolder, you can enhance the character's presence. When the background is detailed, you can make your character stand out by accenting his/her outline! You can also line the character with white ink! The drawing may look simple, but there're a lot of techniques involved.

WHY PUT HANDWRITTEN EFFECTS IN BALLOONS?

Lastly, look close at the mimetic words and onomatopoeias (handwritten FX).
Sugi's handwritten FX are not only carefully written, but they're also all put in balloons. This makes them stand out to the reader and eliminates the possibility of them getting passed over. On top of everything, they're very cute from a design standpoint. Another point we can incorporate in our own work.

CHAPTER 2: THE SHOKO AKIRA EDITION

LET'S CREATE THE CHARACTERS!

The next instructor is Shoko Akira,
who's currently featured in *Betsucomi*!
Now you can get character creation under your belt, too!

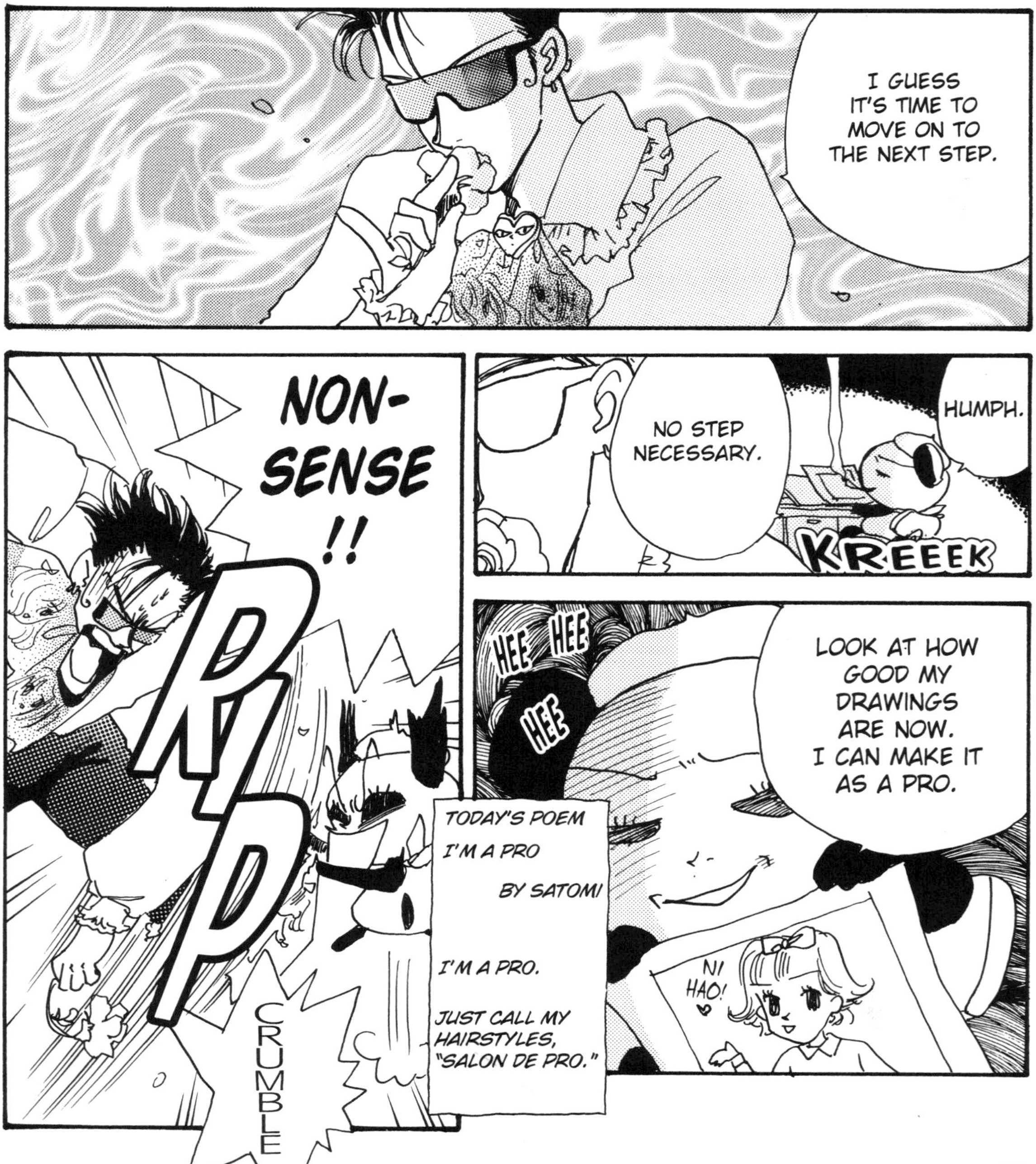

I GUESS IT'S TIME TO MOVE ON TO THE NEXT STEP.
HUMPH.
NO STEP NECESSARY.
KREEEK
LOOK AT HOW GOOD MY DRAWINGS ARE NOW. I CAN MAKE IT AS A PRO.
HEE HEE
HEE
NI HAO!
TODAY'S POEM
I'M A PRO
BY SATOMI
I'M A PRO.
JUST CALL MY HAIRSTYLES, "SALON DE PRO."
NON-SENSE!!
RIP
CRUMBLE

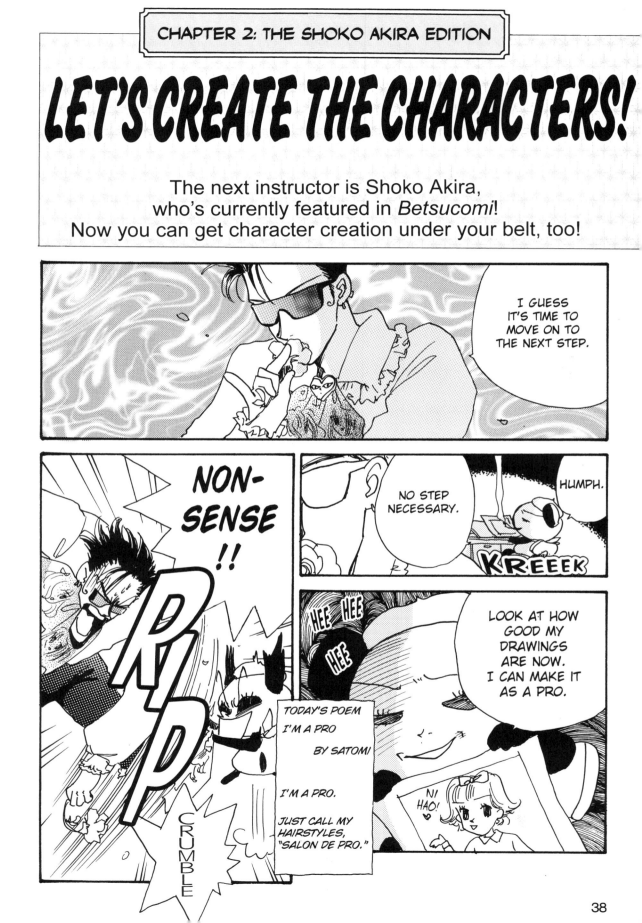

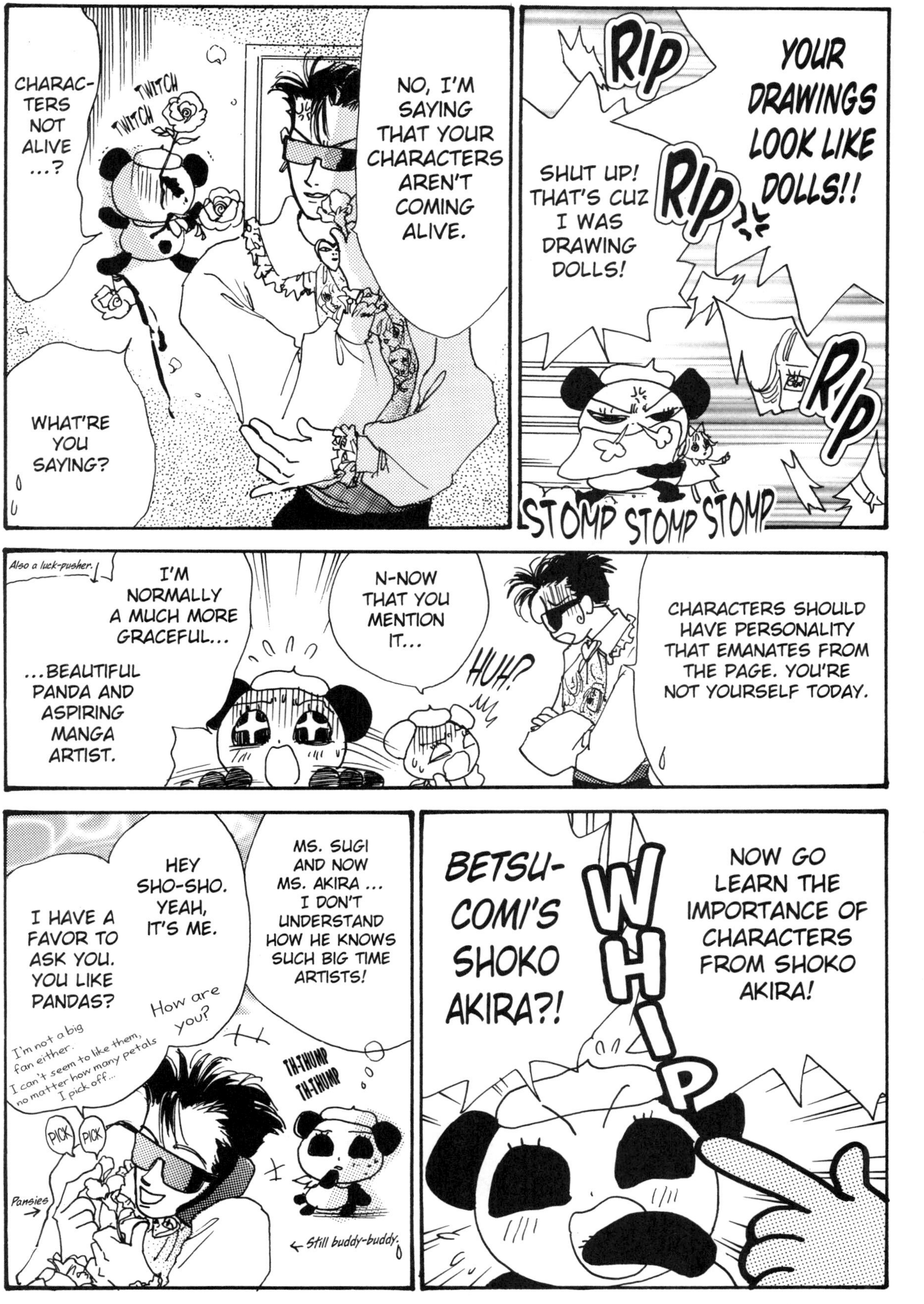
YOUR DRAWINGS LOOK LIKE DOLLS!!
RIP
RIP
SHUT UP! THAT'S CUZ I WAS DRAWING DOLLS!
RIP
STOMP STOMP STOMP
NO, I'M SAYING THAT YOUR CHARACTERS AREN'T COMING ALIVE.
CHARAC-TERS NOT ALIVE ...?
TWITCH TWITCH
WHAT'RE YOU SAYING?
CHARACTERS SHOULD HAVE PERSONALITY THAT EMANATES FROM THE PAGE. YOU'RE NOT YOURSELF TODAY.
HUH?
N-NOW THAT YOU MENTION IT...
I'M NORMALLY A MUCH MORE GRACEFUL...
...BEAUTIFUL PANDA AND ASPIRING MANGA ARTIST.
Also a luck-pusher.
NOW GO LEARN THE IMPORTANCE OF CHARACTERS FROM SHOKO AKIRA!
WHIP
BETSU-COMI'S SHOKO AKIRA?!
MS. SUGI AND NOW MS. AKIRA ... I DON'T UNDERSTAND HOW HE KNOWS SUCH BIG TIME ARTISTS!
HEY SHO-SHO. YEAH, IT'S ME.
I HAVE A FAVOR TO ASK YOU. YOU LIKE PANDAS?
How are you?
I'm not a big fan either. I can't seem to like them, no matter how many petals I pick off...
TH-THUMP TH-THUMP
PICK
PICK
Pansies
Still buddy-buddy.

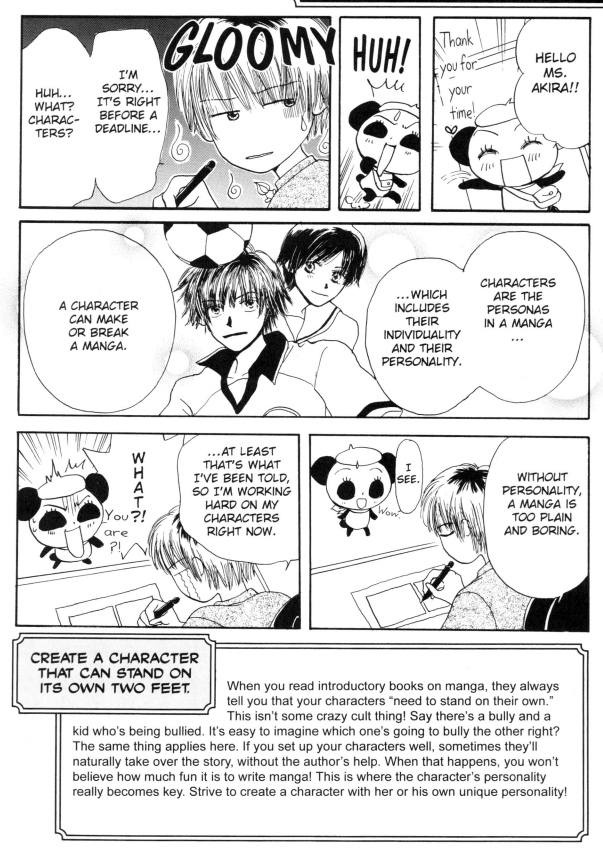

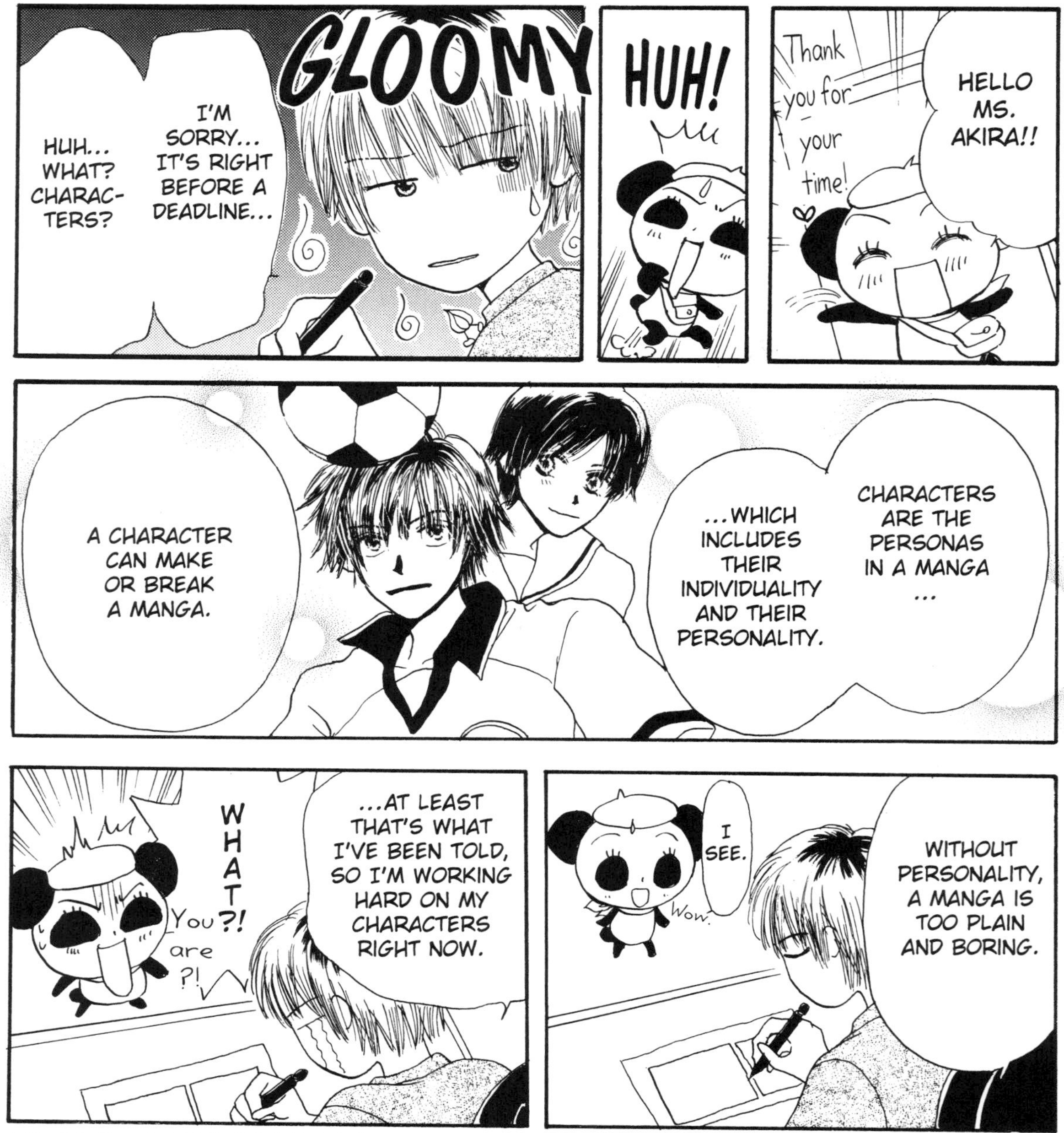
HELLO MS. AKIRA!!
Thank you for your time!
HUH!
GLOOMY
I'M SORRY... IT'S RIGHT BEFORE A DEADLINE...
HUH... WHAT? CHARAC-TERS?
CHARACTERS ARE THE PERSONAS IN A MANGA ...
...WHICH INCLUDES THEIR INDIVIDUALITY AND THEIR PERSONALITY.
A CHARACTER CAN MAKE OR BREAK A MANGA.
WITHOUT PERSONALITY, A MANGA IS TOO PLAIN AND BORING.
I SEE.
Wow.
...AT LEAST THAT'S WHAT I'VE BEEN TOLD, SO I'M WORKING HARD ON MY CHARACTERS RIGHT NOW.
WHAT?!
You are?!

CREATE A CHARACTER THAT CAN STAND ON ITS OWN TWO FEET.

When you read introductory books on manga, they always tell you that your characters "need to stand on their own." This isn't some crazy cult thing! Say there's a bully and a kid who's being bullied. It's easy to imagine which one's going to bully the other right? The same thing applies here. If you set up your characters well, sometimes they'll naturally take over the story, without the author's help. When that happens, you won't believe how much fun it is to write manga! This is where the character's personality really becomes key. Strive to create a character with her or his own unique personality!

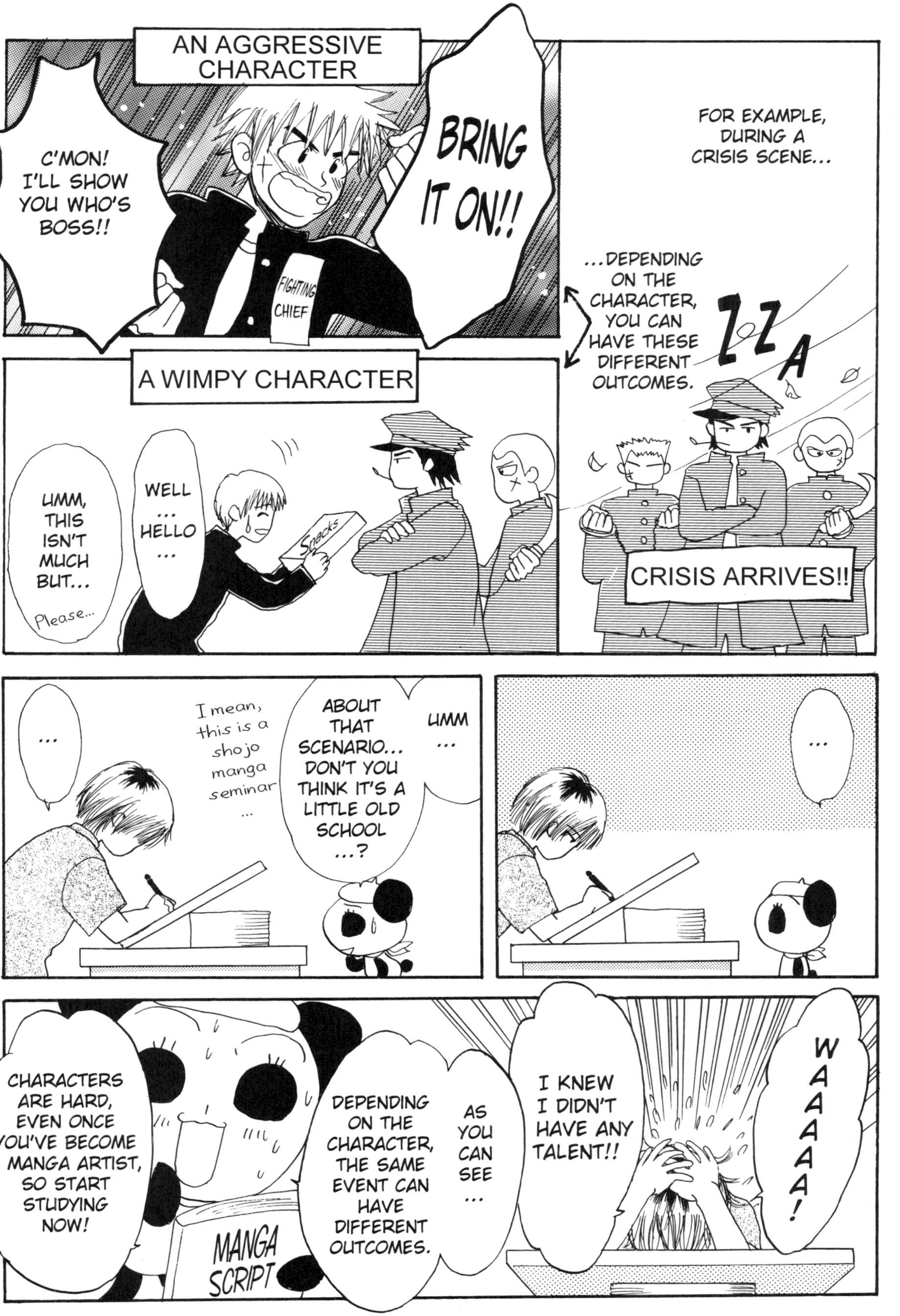
FOR EXAMPLE, DURING A CRISIS SCENE...
...DEPENDING ON THE CHARACTER, YOU CAN HAVE THESE DIFFERENT OUTCOMES.
ZZA
CRISIS ARRIVES!!
AN AGGRESSIVE CHARACTER
BRING IT ON!!
C'MON! I'LL SHOW YOU WHO'S BOSS!!
FIGHTING CHIEF
A WIMPY CHARACTER
WELL ... HELLO ...
Snacks
UMM, THIS ISN'T MUCH BUT...
Please...
...
UMM ...
ABOUT THAT SCENARIO... DON'T YOU THINK IT'S A LITTLE OLD SCHOOL ...?
I mean, this is a shojo manga seminar ...
...
WAAAAAA!
I KNEW I DIDN'T HAVE ANY TALENT!!
AS YOU CAN SEE ...
DEPENDING ON THE CHARACTER, THE SAME EVENT CAN HAVE DIFFERENT OUTCOMES.
CHARACTERS ARE HARD, EVEN ONCE YOU'VE BECOME A MANGA ARTIST, SO START STUDYING NOW!
MANGA SCRIPT

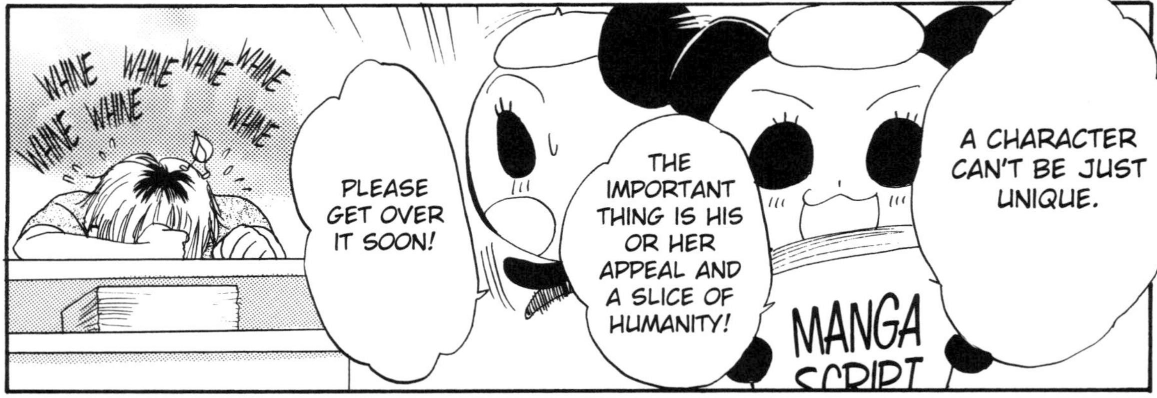
A CHARACTER CAN'T BE JUST UNIQUE.
MANGA SCRIPT
THE IMPORTANT THING IS HIS OR HER APPEAL AND A SLICE OF HUMANITY!
PLEASE GET OVER IT SOON!
WHINE WHINE WHINE WHINE WHINE WHINE WHINE

TRICKS TO CREATING A CHARACTER.

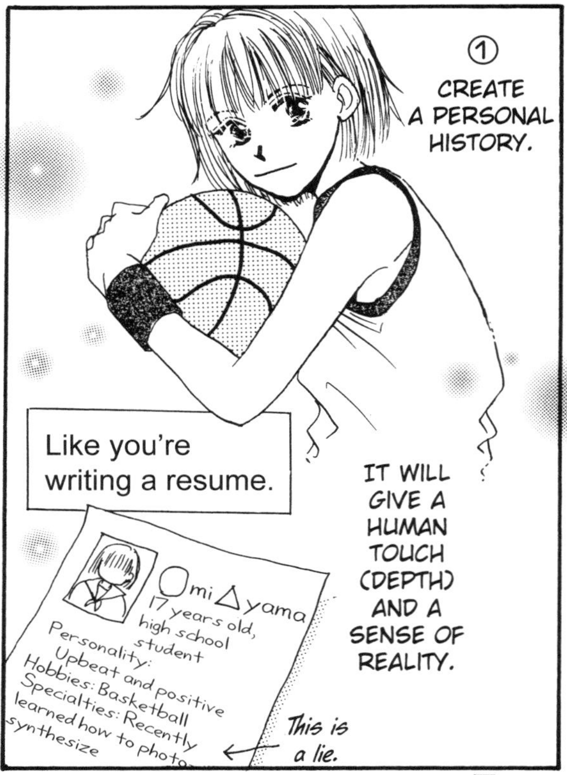
①
CREATE A PERSONAL HISTORY.
Like you're writing a resume.
IT WILL GIVE A HUMAN TOUCH (DEPTH) AND A SENSE OF REALITY.
○mi △yama
17 years old, high school student
Personality: Upbeat and positive
Hobbies: Basketball
Specialties: Recently learned how to photosynthesize
This is a lie.

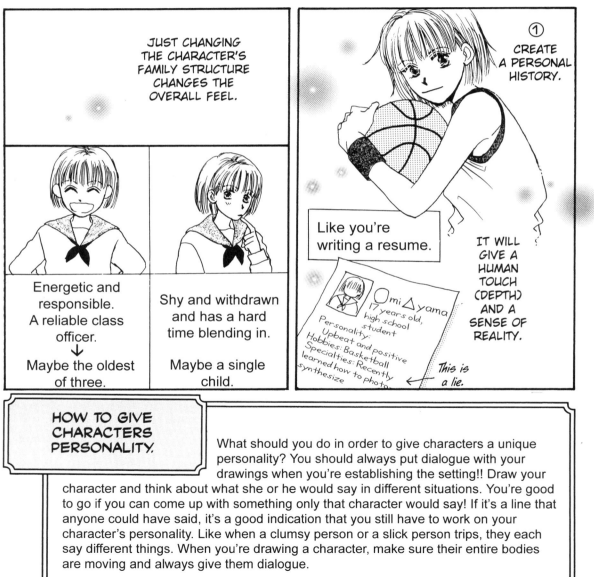

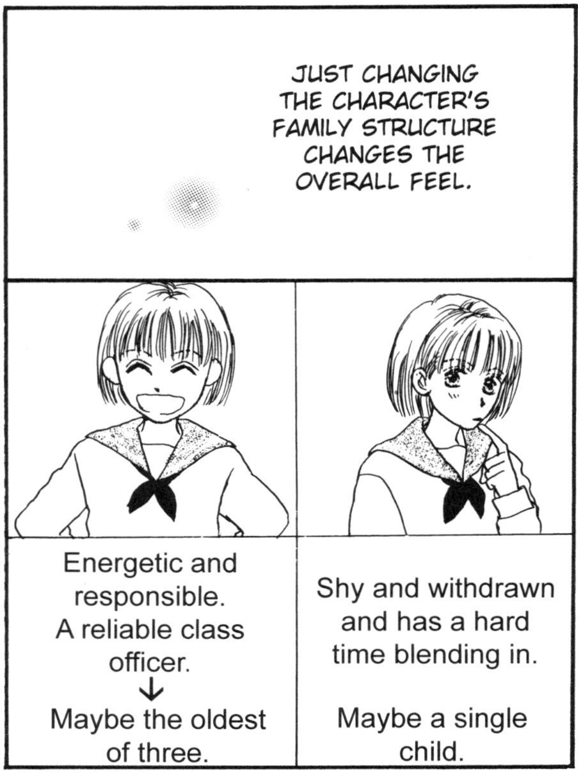
JUST CHANGING THE CHARACTER'S FAMILY STRUCTURE CHANGES THE OVERALL FEEL.
Shy and withdrawn and has a hard time blending in.
Maybe a single child.
Energetic and responsible. A reliable class officer.
↓
Maybe the oldest of three.

HOW TO GIVE CHARACTERS PERSONALITY.

What should you do in order to give characters a unique personality? You should always put dialogue with your drawings when you're establishing the setting!! Draw your character and think about what she or he would say in different situations. You're good to go if you can come up with something only that character would say! If it's a line that anyone could have said, it's a good indication that you still have to work on your character's personality. Like when a clumsy person or a slick person trips, they each say different things. When you're drawing a character, make sure their entire bodies are moving and always give them dialogue.

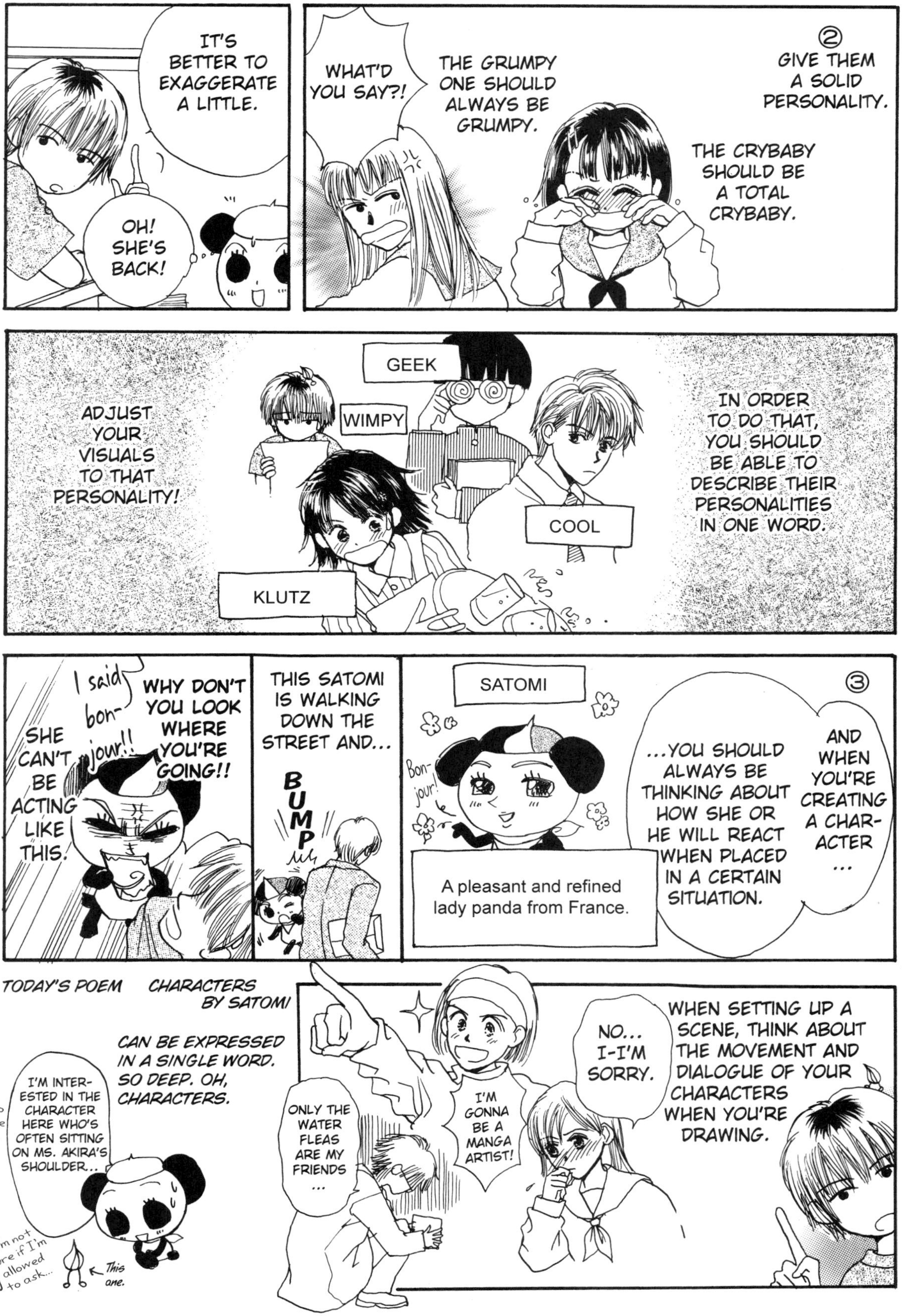
②
GIVE THEM A SOLID PERSONALITY.
THE CRYBABY SHOULD BE A TOTAL CRYBABY.
THE GRUMPY ONE SHOULD ALWAYS BE GRUMPY.
WHAT'D YOU SAY?!
IT'S BETTER TO EXAGGERATE A LITTLE.
OH! SHE'S BACK!
IN ORDER TO DO THAT, YOU SHOULD BE ABLE TO DESCRIBE THEIR PERSONALITIES IN ONE WORD.
GEEK
COOL
WIMPY
KLUTZ
ADJUST YOUR VISUALS TO THAT PERSONALITY!
③
AND WHEN YOU'RE CREATING A CHARACTER ...
...YOU SHOULD ALWAYS BE THINKING ABOUT HOW SHE OR HE WILL REACT WHEN PLACED IN A CERTAIN SITUATION.
SATOMI
Bonjour!
A pleasant and refined lady panda from France.
THIS SATOMI IS WALKING DOWN THE STREET AND...
BUMP
WHY DON'T YOU LOOK WHERE YOU'RE GOING!!
I said bonjour!!
SHE CAN'T BE ACTING LIKE THIS.
WHEN SETTING UP A SCENE, THINK ABOUT THE MOVEMENT AND DIALOGUE OF YOUR CHARACTERS WHEN YOU'RE DRAWING.
NO... I-I'M SORRY.
I'M GONNA BE A MANGA ARTIST!
ONLY THE WATER FLEAS ARE MY FRIENDS ...
TODAY'S POEM CHARACTERS BY SATOMI
CAN BE EXPRESSED IN A SINGLE WORD. SO DEEP. OH, CHARACTERS.
I'M INTERESTED IN THE CHARACTER HERE WHO'S OFTEN SITTING ON MS. AKIRA'S SHOULDER...
So cute ...
I'm not sure if I'm allowed to ask...
This one.

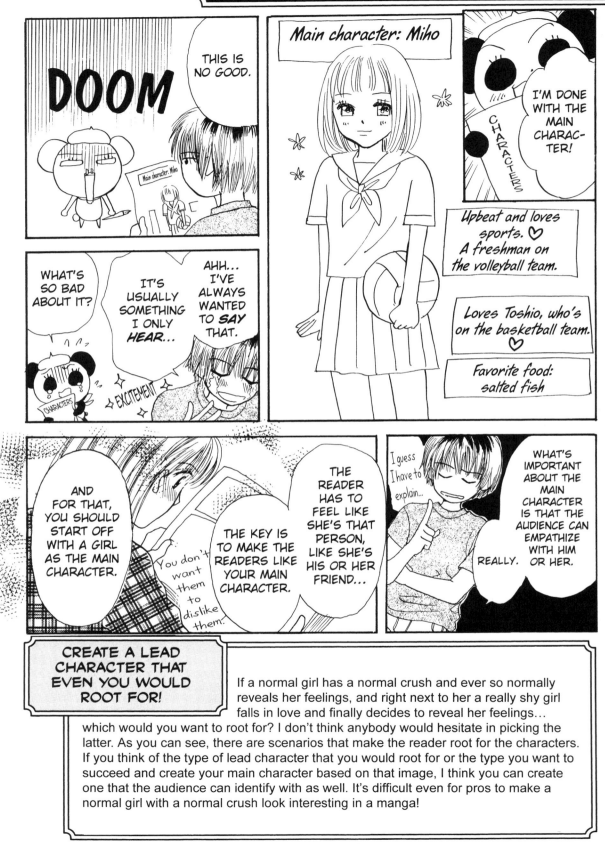

CREATING THE MAIN CHARACTER

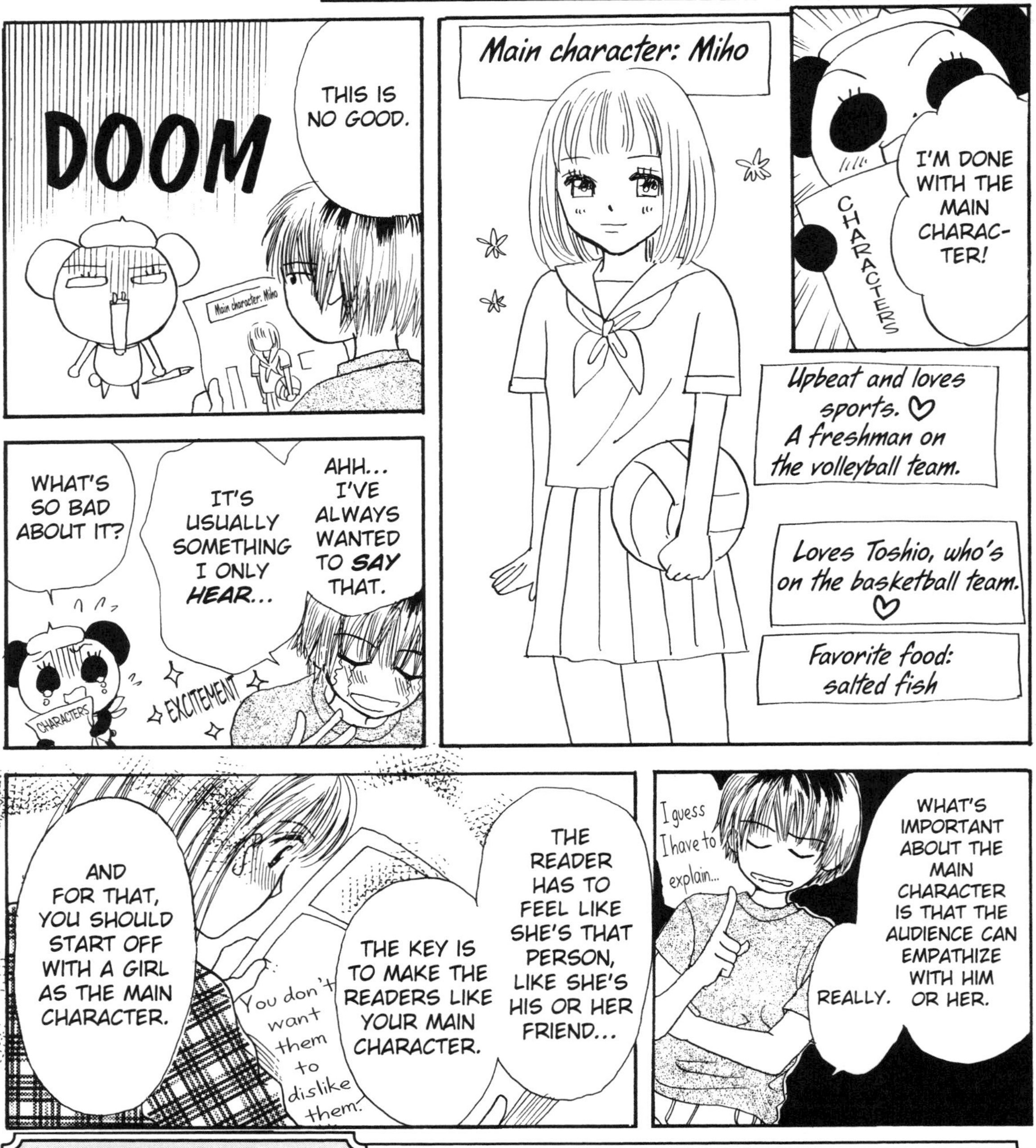
CHARACTERS
I'M DONE WITH THE MAIN CHARAC-TER!
Main character: Miho
Upbeat and loves sports. ♡ A freshman on the volleyball team.
Loves Toshio, who's on the basketball team. ♡
Favorite food: salted fish
THIS IS NO GOOD.
DOOM
Main character: Miho
AHH... I'VE ALWAYS WANTED TO *SAY* THAT.
IT'S USUALLY SOMETHING I ONLY *HEAR*...
WHAT'S SO BAD ABOUT IT?
EXCITEMENT
CHARACTERS
I guess I have to explain...
WHAT'S IMPORTANT ABOUT THE MAIN CHARACTER IS THAT THE AUDIENCE CAN EMPATHIZE WITH HIM OR HER.
REALLY.
THE READER HAS TO FEEL LIKE SHE'S THAT PERSON, LIKE SHE'S HIS OR HER FRIEND...
THE KEY IS TO MAKE THE READERS LIKE YOUR MAIN CHARACTER.
You don't want them to dislike them.
AND FOR THAT, YOU SHOULD START OFF WITH A GIRL AS THE MAIN CHARACTER.

CREATE A LEAD CHARACTER THAT EVEN YOU WOULD ROOT FOR!

If a normal girl has a normal crush and ever so normally reveals her feelings, and right next to her a really shy girl falls in love and finally decides to reveal her feelings… which would you want to root for? I don't think anybody would hesitate in picking the latter. As you can see, there are scenarios that make the reader root for the characters. If you think of the type of lead character that you would root for or the type you want to succeed and create your main character based on that image, I think you can create one that the audience can identify with as well. It's difficult even for pros to make a normal girl with a normal crush look interesting in a manga!

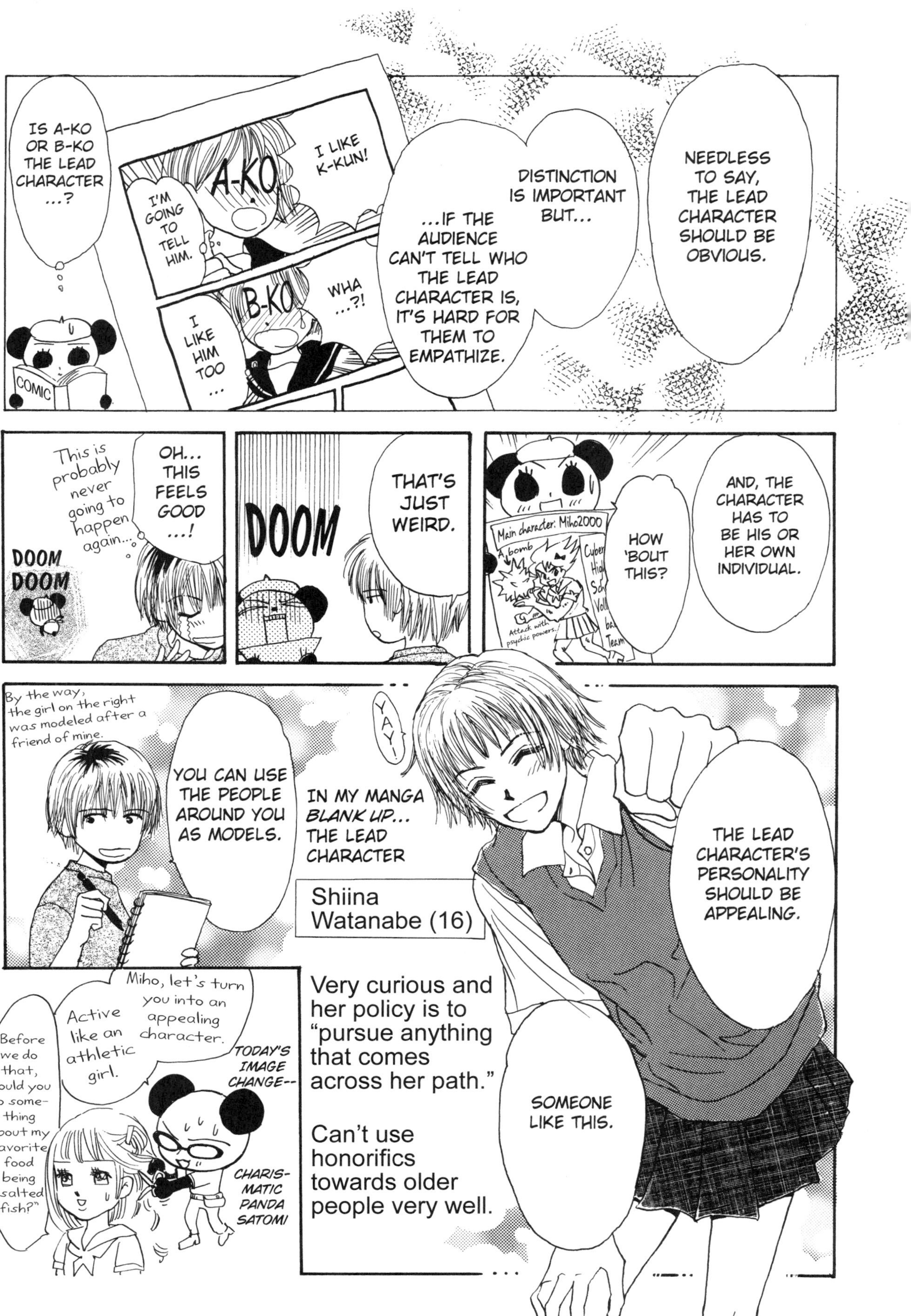
NEEDLESS TO SAY, THE LEAD CHARACTER SHOULD BE OBVIOUS.
DISTINCTION IS IMPORTANT BUT...
...IF THE AUDIENCE CAN'T TELL WHO THE LEAD CHARACTER IS, IT'S HARD FOR THEM TO EMPATHIZE.
I LIKE K-KUN!
A-KO
I'M GOING TO TELL HIM.
WHA ...?!
B-KO
I LIKE HIM TOO ...
IS A-KO OR B-KO THE LEAD CHARACTER ...?
COMIC
AND, THE CHARACTER HAS TO BE HIS OR HER OWN INDIVIDUAL.
HOW 'BOUT THIS?
Main character: Miho2000
A bomb
Attack with psychic powers!
THAT'S JUST WEIRD.
DOOM
OH... THIS FEELS GOOD ...!
This is probably never going to happen again...
DOOM DOOM
THE LEAD CHARACTER'S PERSONALITY SHOULD BE APPEALING.
YAY!
IN MY MANGA *BLANK UP*... THE LEAD CHARACTER
Shiina Watanabe (16)
YOU CAN USE THE PEOPLE AROUND YOU AS MODELS.
By the way, the girl on the right was modeled after a friend of mine.
SOMEONE LIKE THIS.
Very curious and her policy is to "pursue anything that comes across her path."
Can't use honorifics towards older people very well.
Miho, let's turn you into an appealing character.
Active like an athletic girl.
TODAY'S IMAGE CHANGE--
Before we do that, could you do some-thing about my favorite food being "salted fish?"
CHARIS-MATIC PANDA SATOMI

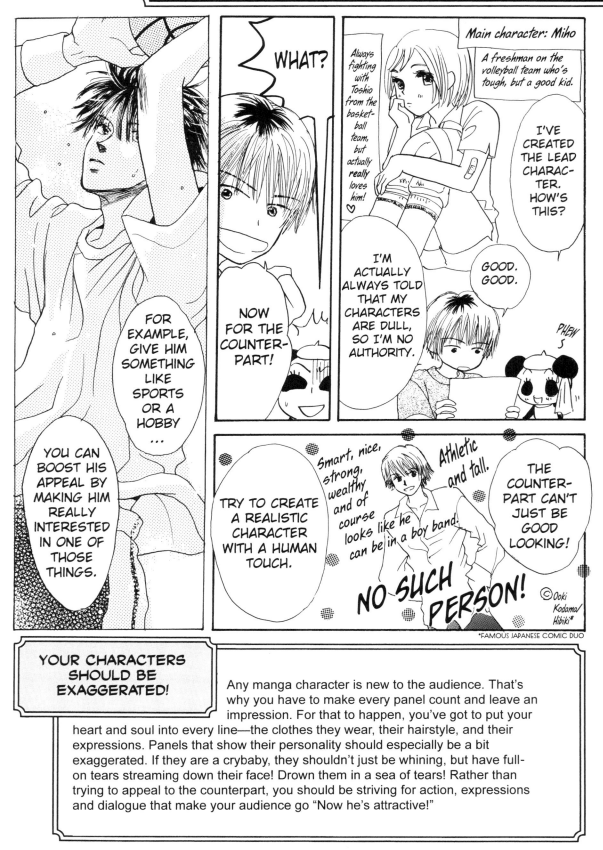

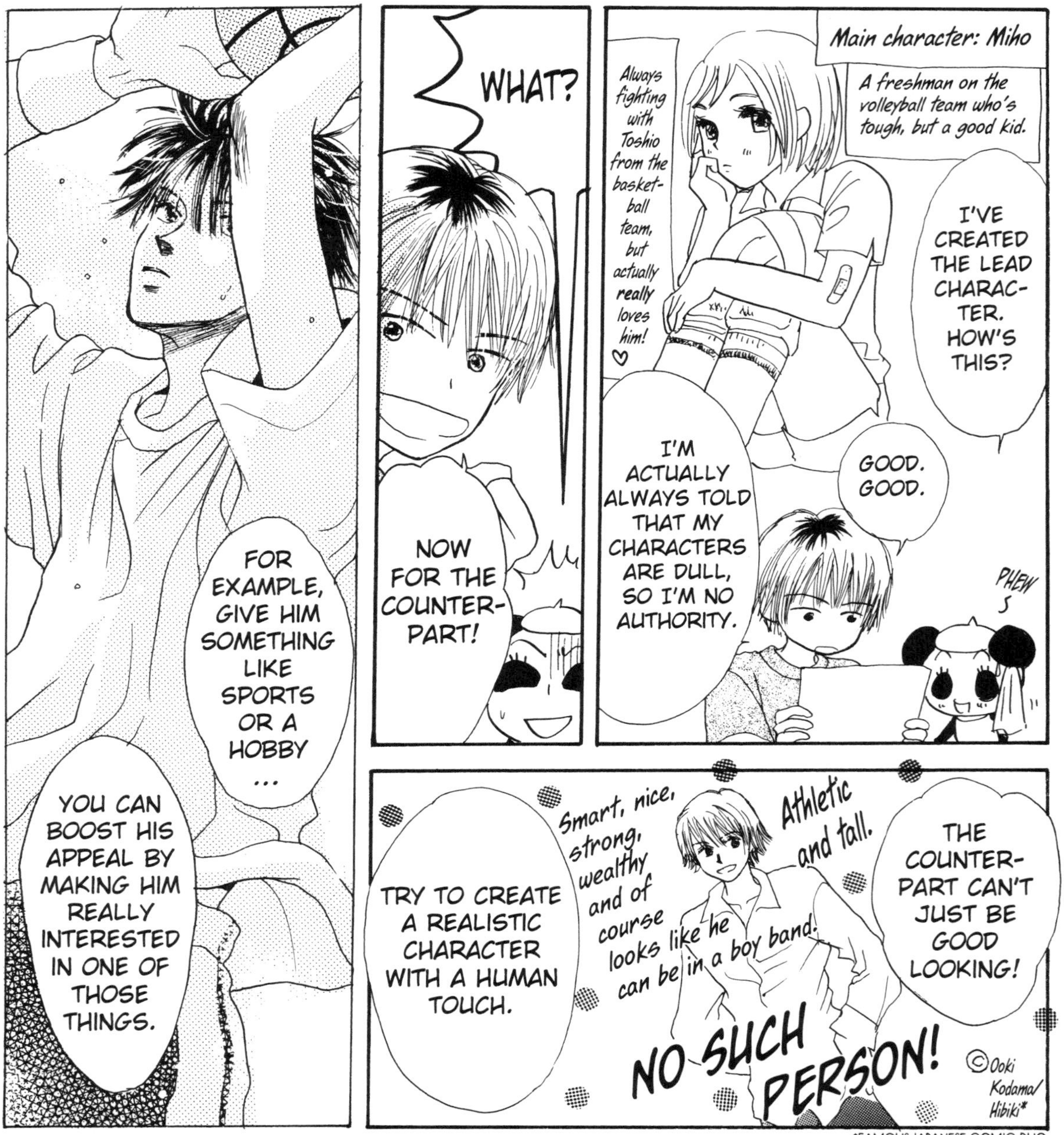
Main character: Miho
A freshman on the volleyball team who's tough, but a good kid.
Always fighting with Toshio from the basketball team, but actually really loves him! ♡
I'VE CREATED THE LEAD CHARACTER. HOW'S THIS?
GOOD. GOOD.
I'M ACTUALLY ALWAYS TOLD THAT MY CHARACTERS ARE DULL, SO I'M NO AUTHORITY.
PHEW
WHAT?
NOW FOR THE COUNTERPART!
THE COUNTERPART CAN'T JUST BE GOOD LOOKING!
Athletic and tall.
Smart, nice, strong, wealthy and of course looks like he can be in a boy band.
TRY TO CREATE A REALISTIC CHARACTER WITH A HUMAN TOUCH.
NO SUCH PERSON!
©Ooki Kodama/Hibiki*
FOR EXAMPLE, GIVE HIM SOMETHING LIKE SPORTS OR A HOBBY ...
YOU CAN BOOST HIS APPEAL BY MAKING HIM REALLY INTERESTED IN ONE OF THOSE THINGS.

*FAMOUS JAPANESE COMIC DUO

YOUR CHARACTERS SHOULD BE EXAGGERATED!

Any manga character is new to the audience. That's why you have to make every panel count and leave an impression. For that to happen, you've got to put your heart and soul into every line—the clothes they wear, their hairstyle, and their expressions. Panels that show their personality should especially be a bit exaggerated. If they are a crybaby, they shouldn't just be whining, but have full-on tears streaming down their face! Drown them in a sea of tears! Rather than trying to appeal to the counterpart, you should be striving for action, expressions and dialogue that make your audience go "Now he's attractive!"

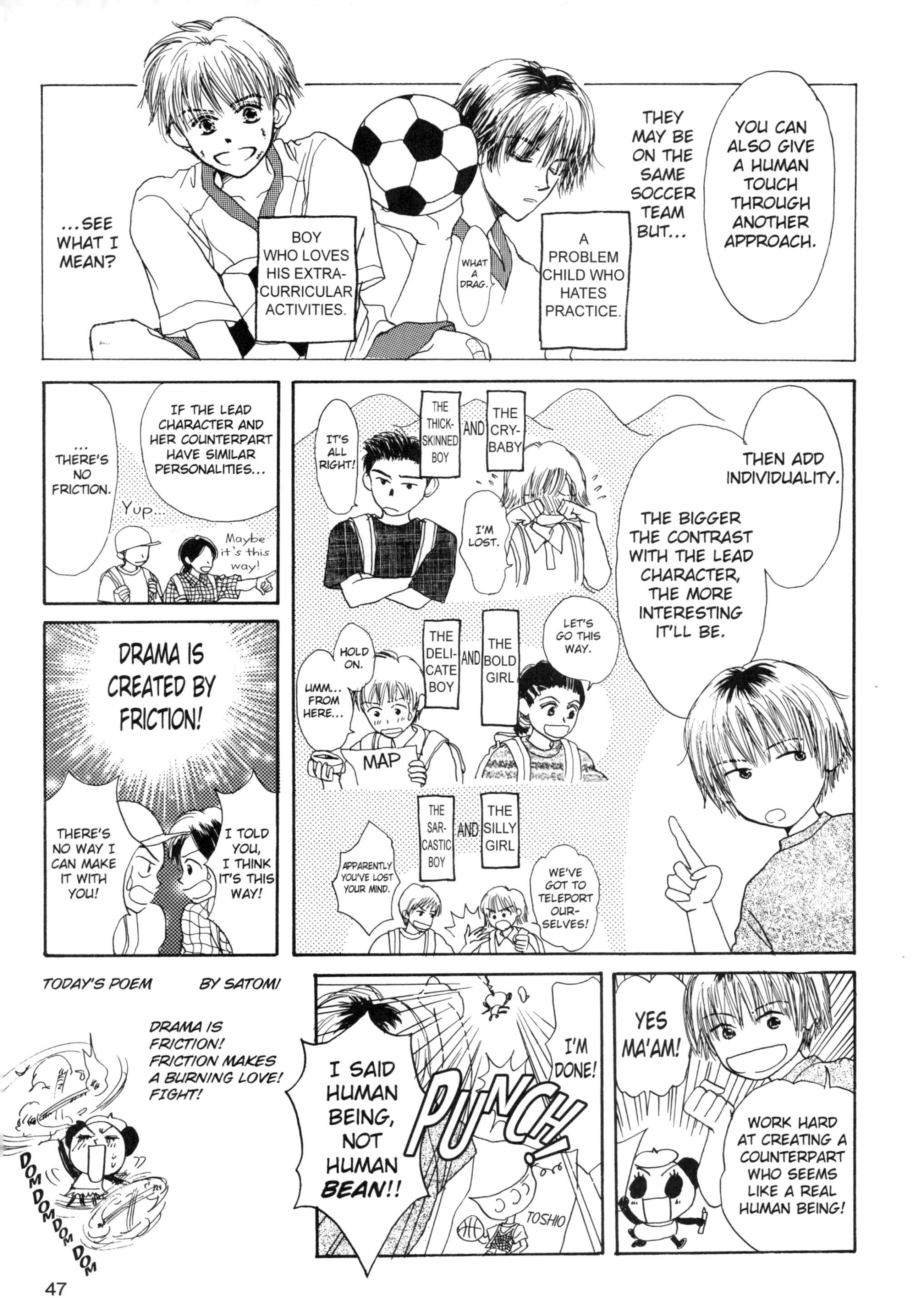
YOU CAN ALSO GIVE A HUMAN TOUCH THROUGH ANOTHER APPROACH.
THEY MAY BE ON THE SAME SOCCER TEAM BUT...
A PROBLEM CHILD WHO HATES PRACTICE.
WHAT A DRAG.
BOY WHO LOVES HIS EXTRA-CURRICULAR ACTIVITIES.
...SEE WHAT I MEAN?
THEN ADD INDIVIDUALITY.
THE BIGGER THE CONTRAST WITH THE LEAD CHARACTER, THE MORE INTERESTING IT'LL BE.
THE CRY-BABY
AND
THE THICK-SKINNED BOY
I'M LOST.
IT'S ALL RIGHT!
THE BOLD GIRL
AND
THE DELICATE BOY
LET'S GO THIS WAY.
HOLD ON.
UMM... FROM HERE...
MAP
THE SILLY GIRL
AND
THE SARCASTIC BOY
WE'VE GOT TO TELEPORT OURSELVES!
APPARENTLY YOU'VE LOST YOUR MIND.
IF THE LEAD CHARACTER AND HER COUNTERPART HAVE SIMILAR PERSONALITIES...
...THERE'S NO FRICTION.
Yup...
Maybe it's this way!
DRAMA IS CREATED BY FRICTION!
I TOLD YOU, I THINK IT'S THIS WAY!
THERE'S NO WAY I CAN MAKE IT WITH YOU!
YES MA'AM!
WORK HARD AT CREATING A COUNTERPART WHO SEEMS LIKE A REAL HUMAN BEING!
I'M DONE!
I SAID HUMAN BEING, NOT HUMAN BEAN!!
PUNCH!
TOSHIO
TODAY'S POEM BY SATOMI
DRAMA IS FRICTION! FRICTION MAKES A BURNING LOVE! FIGHT!
DOM DOM DOM DOM DOM

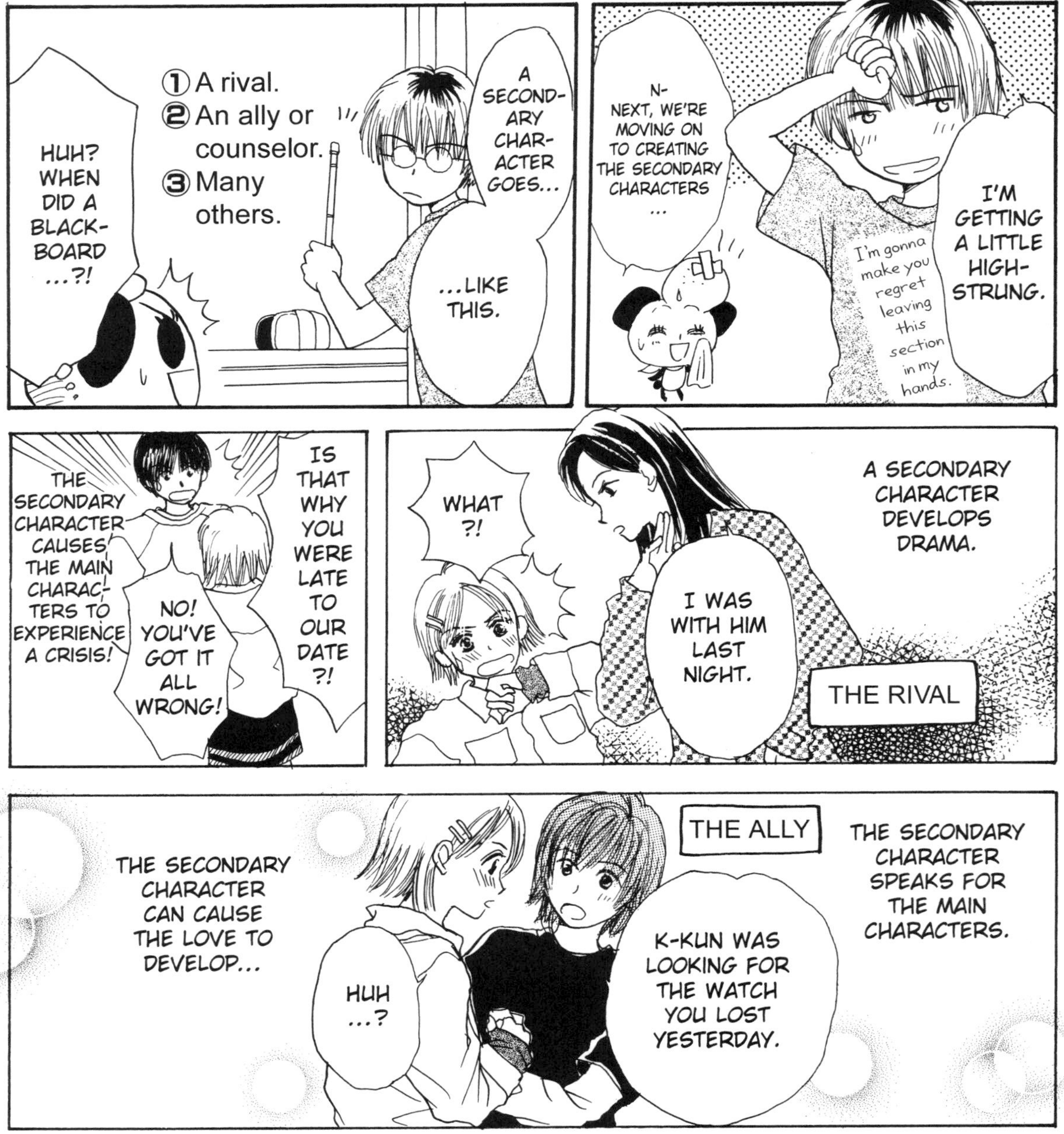
N- NEXT, WE'RE MOVING ON TO CREATING THE SECONDARY CHARACTERS ...
I'M GETTING A LITTLE HIGH-STRUNG.
I'm gonna make you regret leaving this section in my hands.
A SECOND-ARY CHAR-ACTER GOES...
① A rival.
② An ally or counselor.
③ Many others.
...LIKE THIS.
HUH? WHEN DID A BLACK-BOARD ...?!
A SECONDARY CHARACTER DEVELOPS DRAMA.
I WAS WITH HIM LAST NIGHT.
WHAT ?!
THE RIVAL
IS THAT WHY YOU WERE LATE TO OUR DATE ?!
NO! YOU'VE GOT IT ALL WRONG!
THE SECONDARY CHARACTER CAUSES THE MAIN CHARAC-TERS TO EXPERIENCE A CRISIS!
THE SECONDARY CHARACTER SPEAKS FOR THE MAIN CHARACTERS.
THE ALLY
K-KUN WAS LOOKING FOR THE WATCH YOU LOST YESTERDAY.
HUH ...?
THE SECONDARY CHARACTER CAN CAUSE THE LOVE TO DEVELOP...

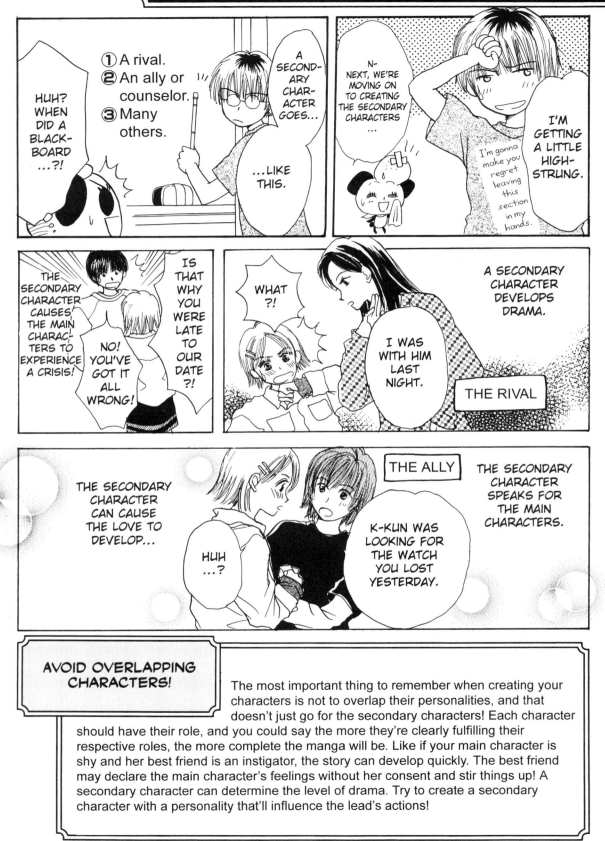

AVOID OVERLAPPING CHARACTERS!

The most important thing to remember when creating your characters is not to overlap their personalities, and that doesn't just go for the secondary characters! Each character should have their role, and you could say the more they're clearly fulfilling their respective roles, the more complete the manga will be. Like if your main character is shy and her best friend is an instigator, the story can develop quickly. The best friend may declare the main character's feelings without her consent and stir things up! A secondary character can determine the level of drama. Try to create a secondary character with a personality that'll influence the lead's actions!

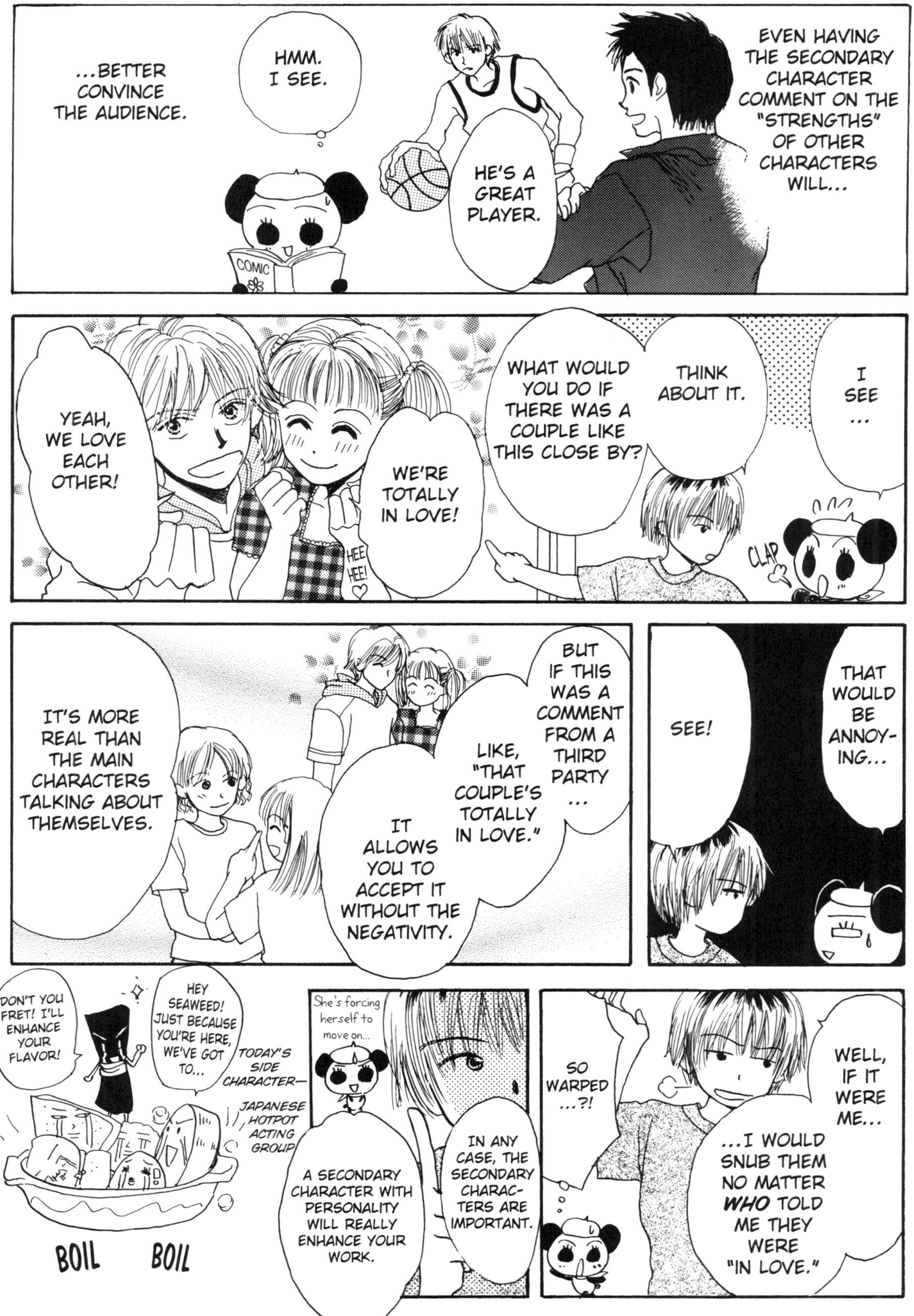
EVEN HAVING THE SECONDARY CHARACTER COMMENT ON THE "STRENGTHS" OF OTHER CHARACTERS WILL...
HE'S A GREAT PLAYER.
HMM. I SEE.
...BETTER CONVINCE THE AUDIENCE.
COMIC
I SEE ...
THINK ABOUT IT.
WHAT WOULD YOU DO IF THERE WAS A COUPLE LIKE THIS CLOSE BY?
CLAP
WE'RE TOTALLY IN LOVE!
HEE HEE!
YEAH, WE LOVE EACH OTHER!
THAT WOULD BE ANNOY-ING...
SEE!
BUT IF THIS WAS A COMMENT FROM A THIRD PARTY ...
LIKE, "THAT COUPLE'S TOTALLY IN LOVE."
IT ALLOWS YOU TO ACCEPT IT WITHOUT THE NEGATIVITY.
IT'S MORE REAL THAN THE MAIN CHARACTERS TALKING ABOUT THEMSELVES.
WELL, IF IT WERE ME...
...I WOULD SNUB THEM NO MATTER *WHO* TOLD ME THEY WERE "IN LOVE."
SO WARPED ...?!
IN ANY CASE, THE SECONDARY CHARAC-TERS ARE IMPORTANT.
A SECONDARY CHARACTER WITH PERSONALITY WILL REALLY ENHANCE YOUR WORK.
She's forcing herself to move on...
HEY SEAWEED! JUST BECAUSE YOU'RE HERE, WE'VE GOT TO...
DON'T YOU FRET! I'LL ENHANCE YOUR FLAVOR!
TODAY'S SIDE CHARACTER— JAPANESE HOTPOT ACTING GROUP
BOIL BOIL

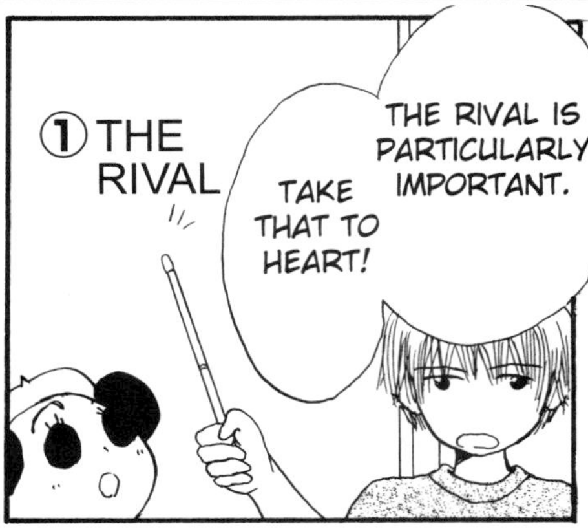
THE RIVAL IS PARTICULARLY IMPORTANT.
TAKE THAT TO HEART!
① THE RIVAL

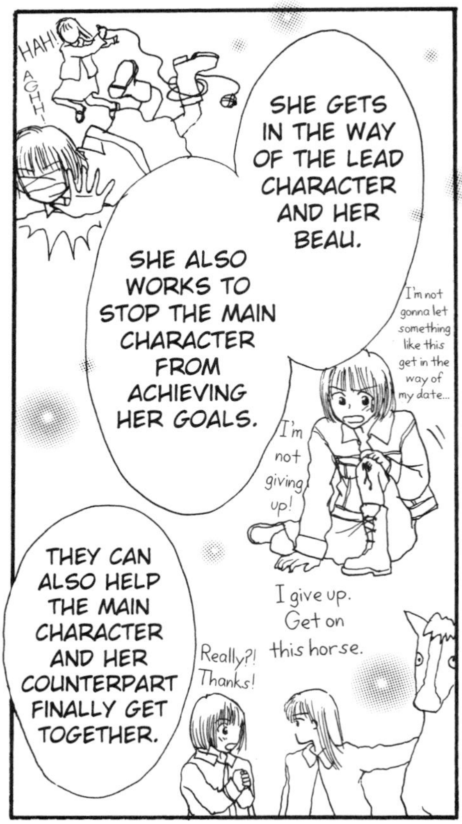
SHE GETS IN THE WAY OF THE LEAD CHARACTER AND HER BEAU.
HAH!
AGHH!
I'm not gonna let something like this get in the way of my date...
SHE ALSO WORKS TO STOP THE MAIN CHARACTER FROM ACHIEVING HER GOALS.
I'm not giving up!
I give up. Get on this horse.
Really?! Thanks!
THEY CAN ALSO HELP THE MAIN CHARACTER AND HER COUNTERPART FINALLY GET TOGETHER.

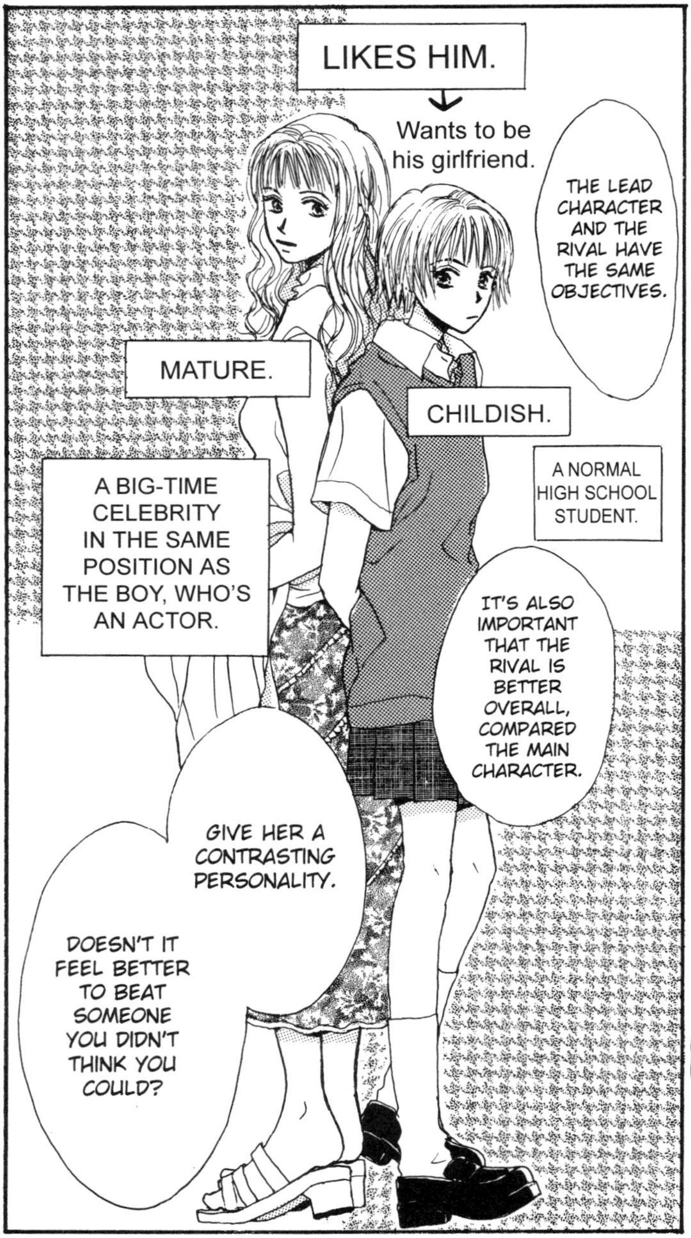
LIKES HIM.
Wants to be his girlfriend.
THE LEAD CHARACTER AND THE RIVAL HAVE THE SAME OBJECTIVES.
MATURE.
CHILDISH.
A NORMAL HIGH SCHOOL STUDENT.
A BIG-TIME CELEBRITY IN THE SAME POSITION AS THE BOY, WHO'S AN ACTOR.
IT'S ALSO IMPORTANT THAT THE RIVAL IS BETTER OVERALL, COMPARED THE MAIN CHARACTER.
GIVE HER A CONTRASTING PERSONALITY.
DOESN'T IT FEEL BETTER TO BEAT SOMEONE YOU DIDN'T THINK YOU COULD?

YOUR CHARACTERS MUST HAVE FLAWS TO COMPLETE THE STORY!

All characters should have a flaw! You can think of this as something they're not good at. For example, she doesn't like dogs, she's tone deaf, she doesn't like men, she's shy, she's a crybaby, or maybe she gets stage fright… Setting up a flaw makes it easier to create drama, and the reader can sort of anticipate what's to come, so they can relax and enjoy the manga! Just because they can anticipate doesn't make the manga any less interesting! If you're creative in how the characters overcome their flaws, you can still surprise your audience!!

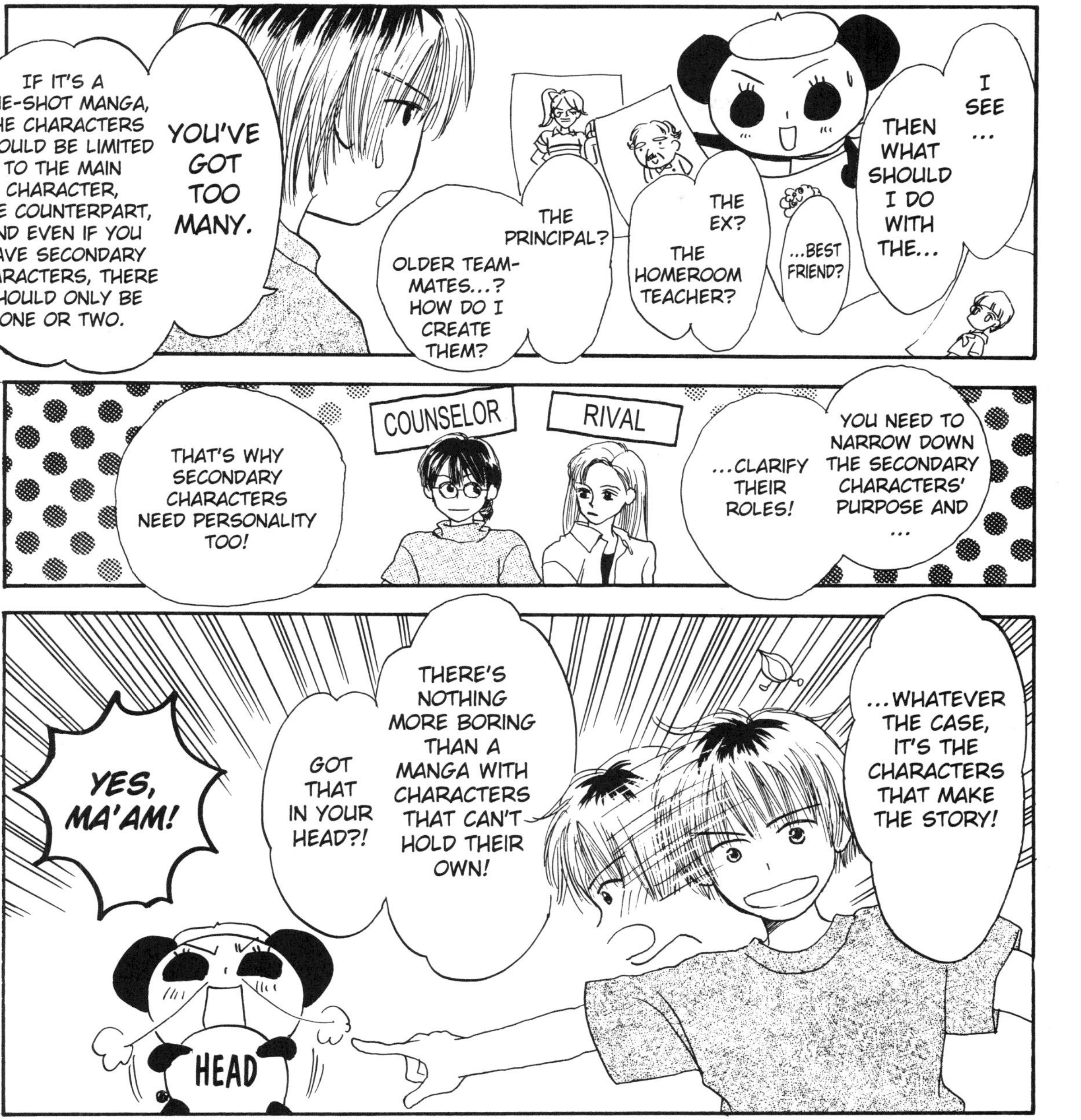
I SEE ...
THEN WHAT SHOULD I DO WITH THE...
...BEST FRIEND?
THE EX?
THE HOMEROOM TEACHER?
THE PRINCIPAL?
OLDER TEAM-MATES...? HOW DO I CREATE THEM?
YOU'VE GOT TOO MANY.
IF IT'S A ONE-SHOT MANGA, THE CHARACTERS SHOULD BE LIMITED TO THE MAIN CHARACTER, THE COUNTERPART, AND EVEN IF YOU HAVE SECONDARY CHARACTERS, THERE SHOULD ONLY BE ONE OR TWO.
YOU NEED TO NARROW DOWN THE SECONDARY CHARACTERS' PURPOSE AND ...
...CLARIFY THEIR ROLES!
RIVAL
COUNSELOR
THAT'S WHY SECONDARY CHARACTERS NEED PERSONALITY TOO!
...WHATEVER THE CASE, IT'S THE CHARACTERS THAT MAKE THE STORY!
THERE'S NOTHING MORE BORING THAN A MANGA WITH CHARACTERS THAT CAN'T HOLD THEIR OWN!
GOT THAT IN YOUR HEAD?!
YES, MA'AM!
HEAD

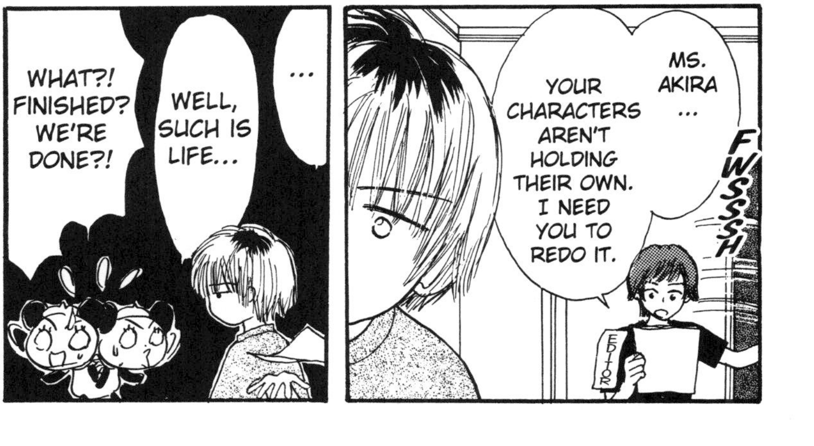
MS. AKIRA ...
YOUR CHARACTERS AREN'T HOLDING THEIR OWN. I NEED YOU TO REDO IT.
FWSSSH
EDITOR
...
WELL, SUCH IS LIFE...
WHAT?! FINISHED? WE'RE DONE?!

TODAY'S POEM *CHARACTERS BY SATOMI*

CHARACTERS ARE
A MANGA'S LIFELINE.
AIM FOR APPEALING
CHARACTERS AND
I'LL BEAR IN MIND
WHAT MS. AKIRA TAUGHT ME,
AND SATOMI
WILL NOT GIVE UP!!

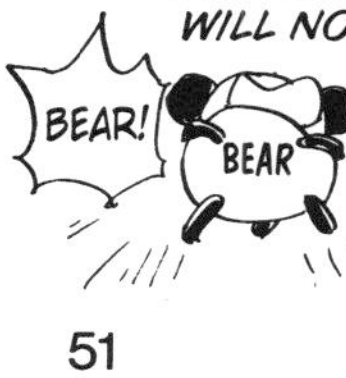
BEAR!
BEAR

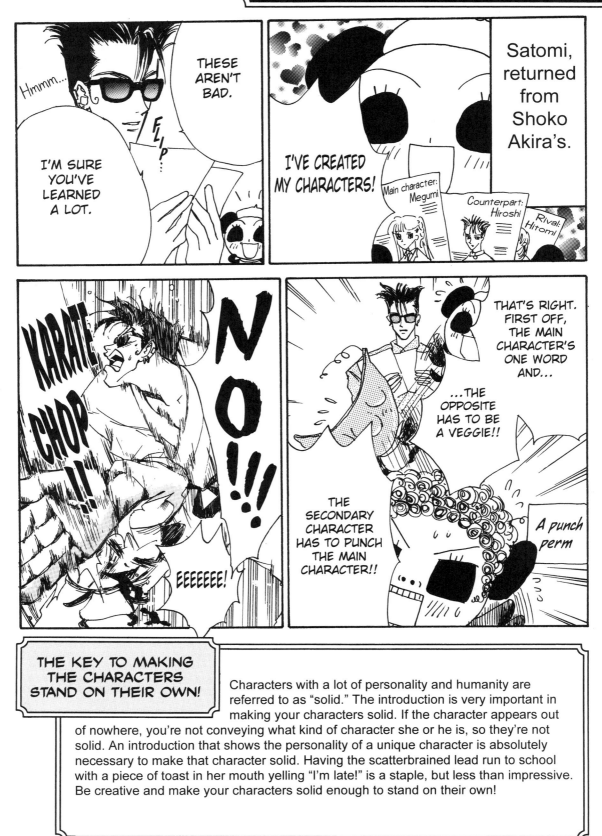

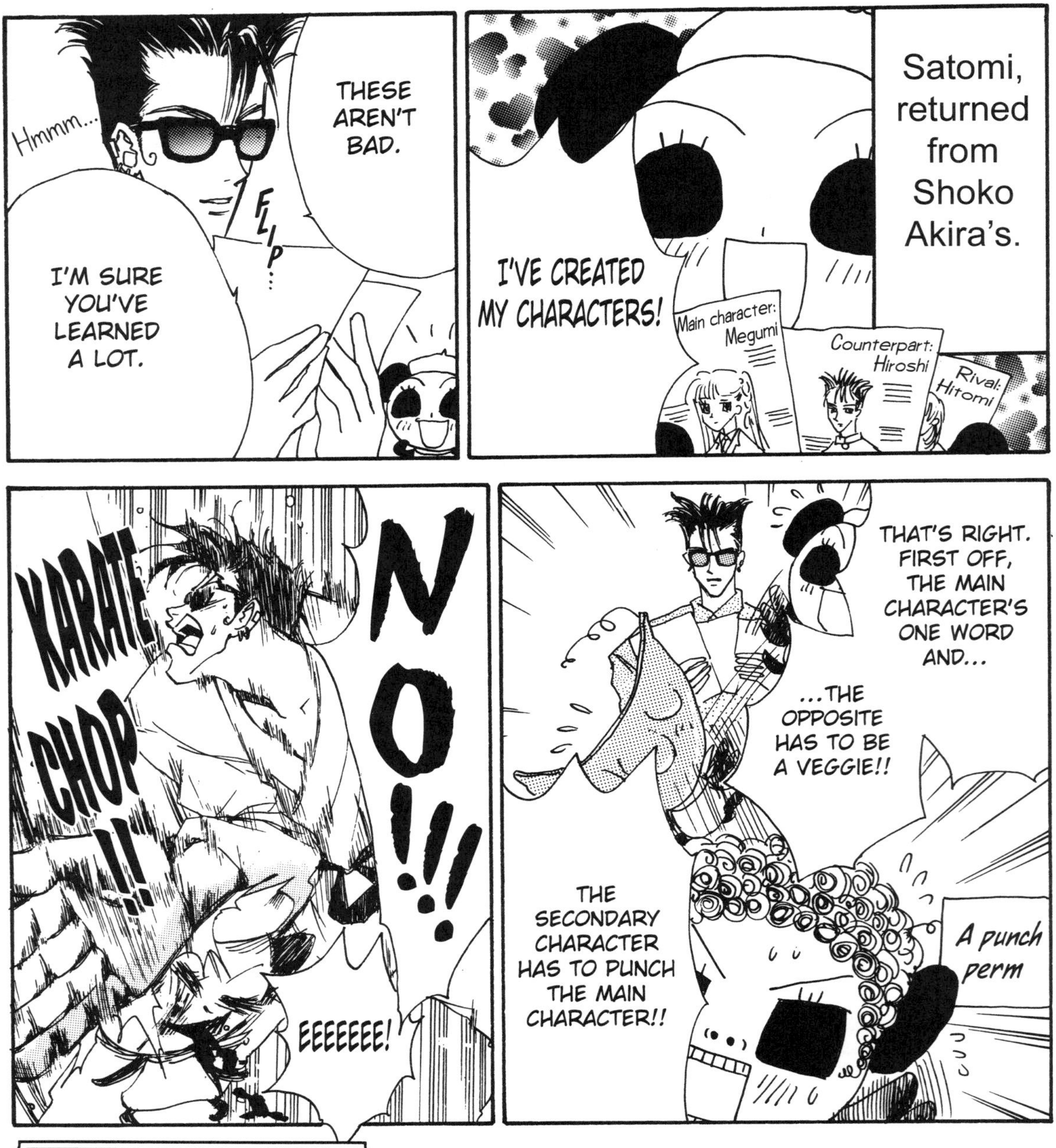
Satomi, returned from Shoko Akira's.
I'VE CREATED MY CHARACTERS!
Main character: Megumi
Counterpart: Hiroshi
Rival: Hitomi
THESE AREN'T BAD.
Hmmm...
FLIP...
I'M SURE YOU'VE LEARNED A LOT.
THAT'S RIGHT. FIRST OFF, THE MAIN CHARACTER'S ONE WORD AND...
...THE OPPOSITE HAS TO BE A VEGGIE!!
THE SECONDARY CHARACTER HAS TO PUNCH THE MAIN CHARACTER!!
A punch perm
NO!!!
KARATE CHOP!!
EEEEEEE!

THE KEY TO MAKING THE CHARACTERS STAND ON THEIR OWN!

Characters with a lot of personality and humanity are referred to as "solid." The introduction is very important in making your characters solid. If the character appears out of nowhere, you're not conveying what kind of character she or he is, so they're not solid. An introduction that shows the personality of a unique character is absolutely necessary to make that character solid. Having the scatterbrained lead run to school with a piece of toast in her mouth yelling "I'm late!" is a staple, but less than impressive. Be creative and make your characters solid enough to stand on their own!

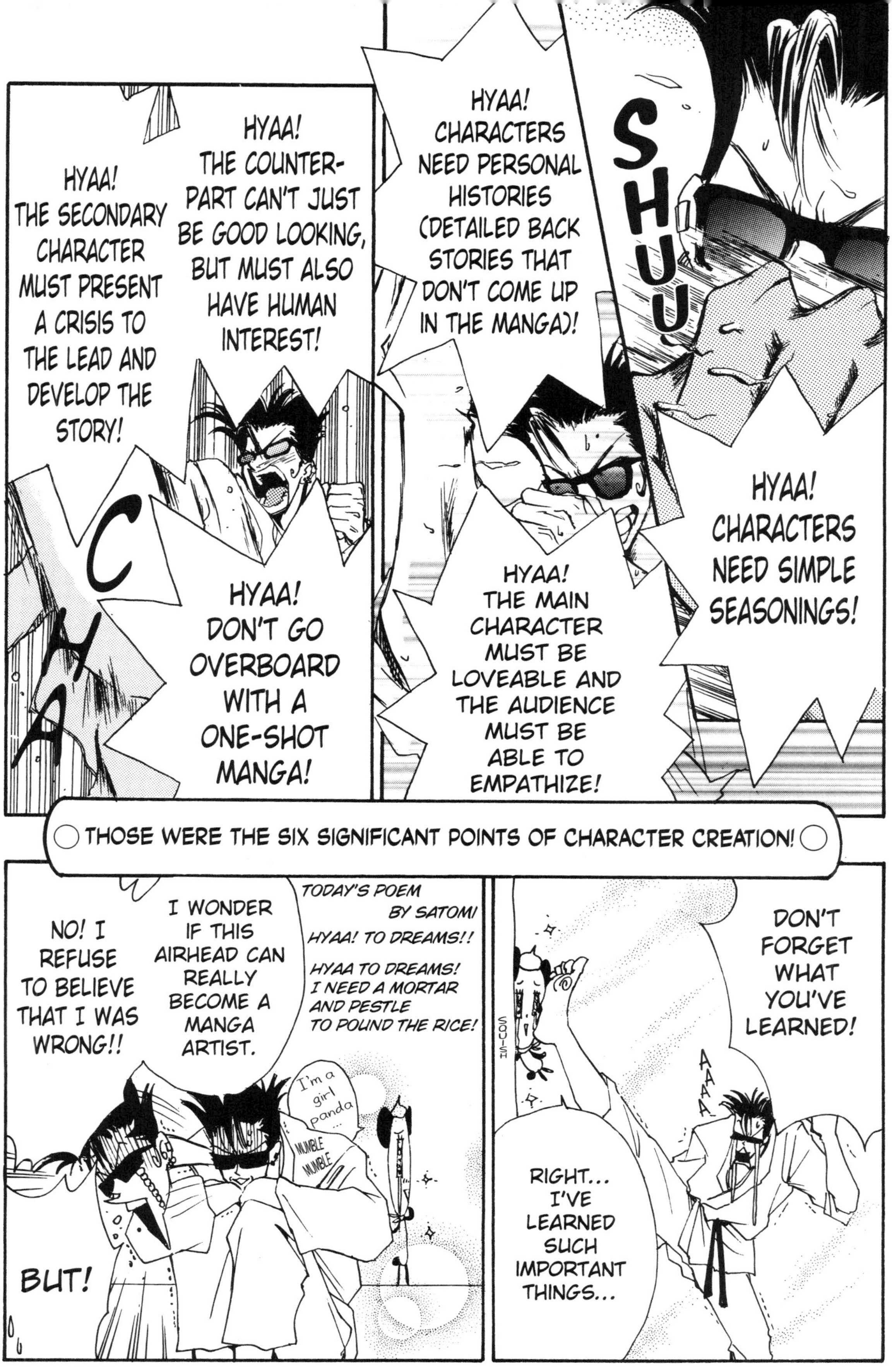
SHUUU
HYAA! CHARACTERS NEED SIMPLE SEASONINGS!
HYAA! CHARACTERS NEED PERSONAL HISTORIES (DETAILED BACK STORIES THAT DON'T COME UP IN THE MANGA)!
HYAA! THE MAIN CHARACTER MUST BE LOVEABLE AND THE AUDIENCE MUST BE ABLE TO EMPATHIZE!
HYAA! THE COUNTER-PART CAN'T JUST BE GOOD LOOKING, BUT MUST ALSO HAVE HUMAN INTEREST!
HYAA! THE SECONDARY CHARACTER MUST PRESENT A CRISIS TO THE LEAD AND DEVELOP THE STORY!
CHA
HYAA! DON'T GO OVERBOARD WITH A ONE-SHOT MANGA!
THOSE WERE THE SIX SIGNIFICANT POINTS OF CHARACTER CREATION!
DON'T FORGET WHAT YOU'VE LEARNED!
SQUISH
AAAA
RIGHT... I'VE LEARNED SUCH IMPORTANT THINGS...
TODAY'S POEM BY SATOMI
HYAA! TO DREAMS!!
HYAA TO DREAMS! I NEED A MORTAR AND PESTLE TO POUND THE RICE!
I WONDER IF THIS AIRHEAD CAN REALLY BECOME A MANGA ARTIST.
NO! I REFUSE TO BELIEVE THAT I WAS WRONG!!
I'm a girl panda...
MUMBLE MUMBLE
BUT!

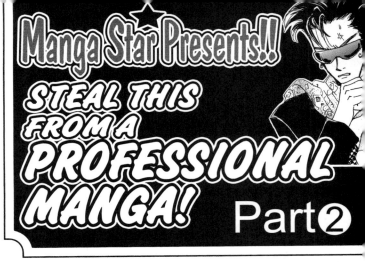

Manga Star Presents!! STEAL THIS FROM A PROFESSIONAL MANGA! Part 2

An entry from *Betsucomi's* Shoko Akira!! Let's check out her sensitive and emotional presentation and try to master it ourselves!

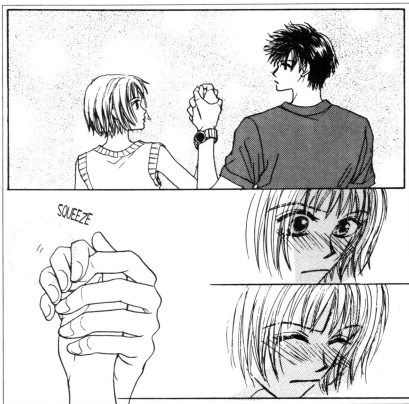

SQUEEZE

SHOW THE CHANGE IN EXPRESSION IN CONSECUTIVE FRAMES.

This is a great example of not having to use dialogue to show the character's emotion.

By maintaining the same format for the second and third frame, the change in the main character's emotion is easier to grasp. At the same time, her expression emanates emotions that can't be verbalized.

THE FACE ISN'T THE ONLY PART THAT CAN BE EXPRESSIVE.

People tend to equate expressions with the face, but there are other parts that can be just as expressive! Check out the hands in the last frame.

By showing them holding hands tightly, you can almost feel their affection. The screen tone also gives us a peek into the characters' hearts!

Aside from this example, you can draw a hand shaking in anger up close or a shoulder from the back to express emotion. If you've been reading manga carefully, I'm sure you know exactly what I'm talking about!

Expressing emotion doesn't need to be limited to the face!

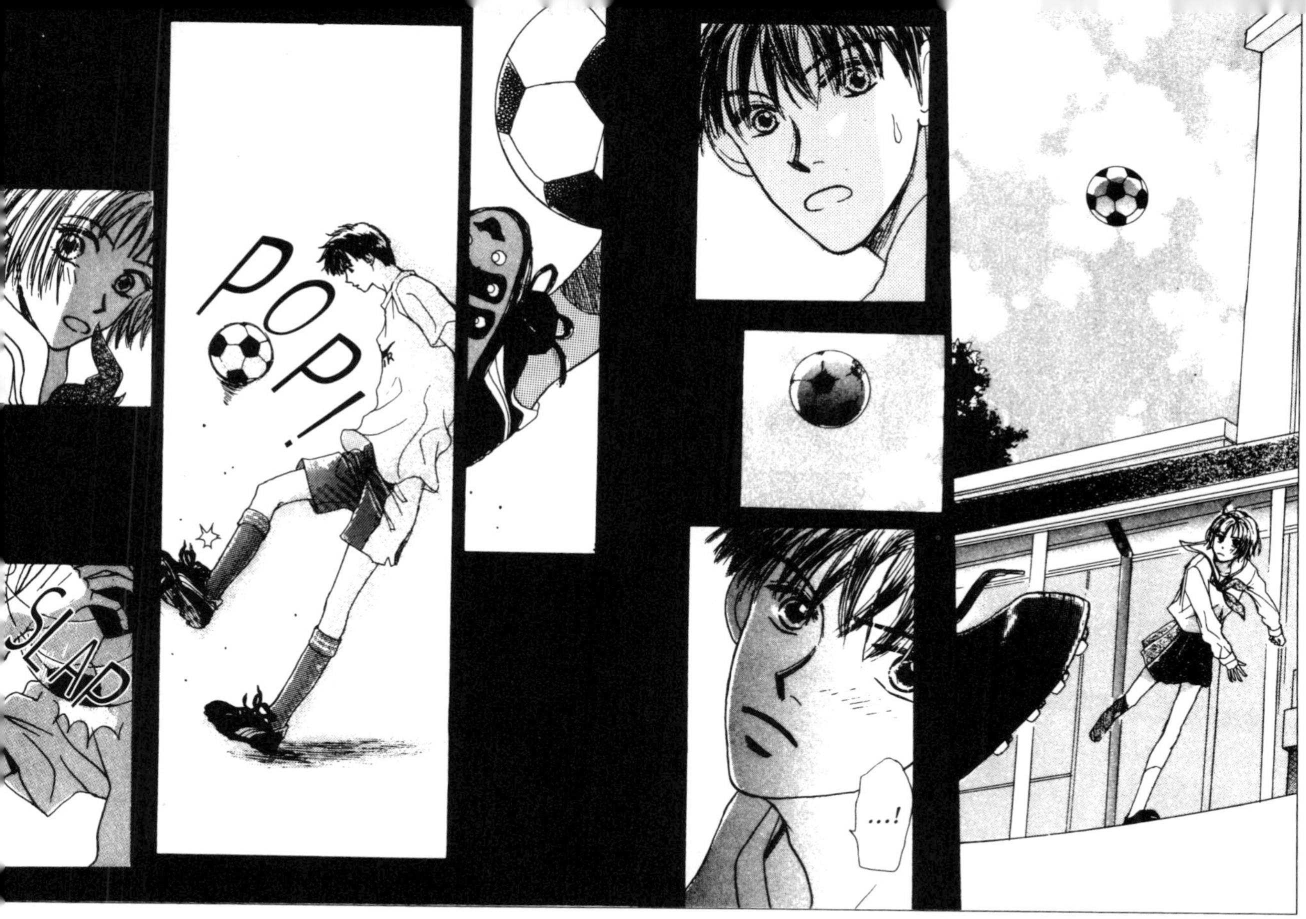
...!
POP!
SLAP

TIMING CAN SINGLE-HANDEDLY CHANGE THE MOOD!

First compare the spread above and the bottom single panel. They're both just a boy kicking a ball, but the difference in timing makes them so different!

The format above alternates between the ball and the boy's visual line. Furthermore, in order for the reader to focus on the moment as the boy kicks the ball, there's a cushion of time before and after that moment. It's like watching it in slow motion where the layout makes it so that a moment's event seems like it's taking place over an extended period of time!

Conversely, the bottom frame speeds up the process by putting the impact moment and the line afterwards in the same frame. It makes for a comical scene!

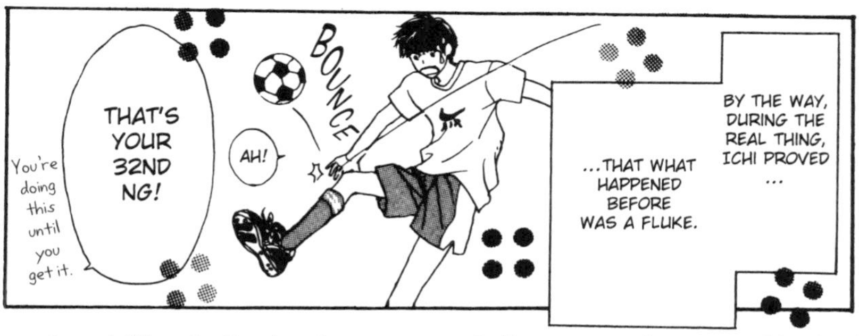
BY THE WAY, DURING THE REAL THING, ICHI PROVED ...
...THAT WHAT HAPPENED BEFORE WAS A FLUKE.
BOUNCE
AH!
THAT'S YOUR 32ND NG!
You're doing this until you get it.

Even if they're doing the same thing, the layout can make it seem serious or comical! Everything is tempo... in other words, it's timing. If you master this, you can easily build towards a climax!

In addition to the boy's movement, the screen tone used in the background enhances the comic effect. Create an effective scene by combining different elements.

CHAPTER 3: THE MASAMI TAKEUCHI EDITION

LET'S CREATE A STORY!

Now that you're done creating the characters, it's time to create a story! Let's have Masami Takeuchi describe the trick to creating stories!

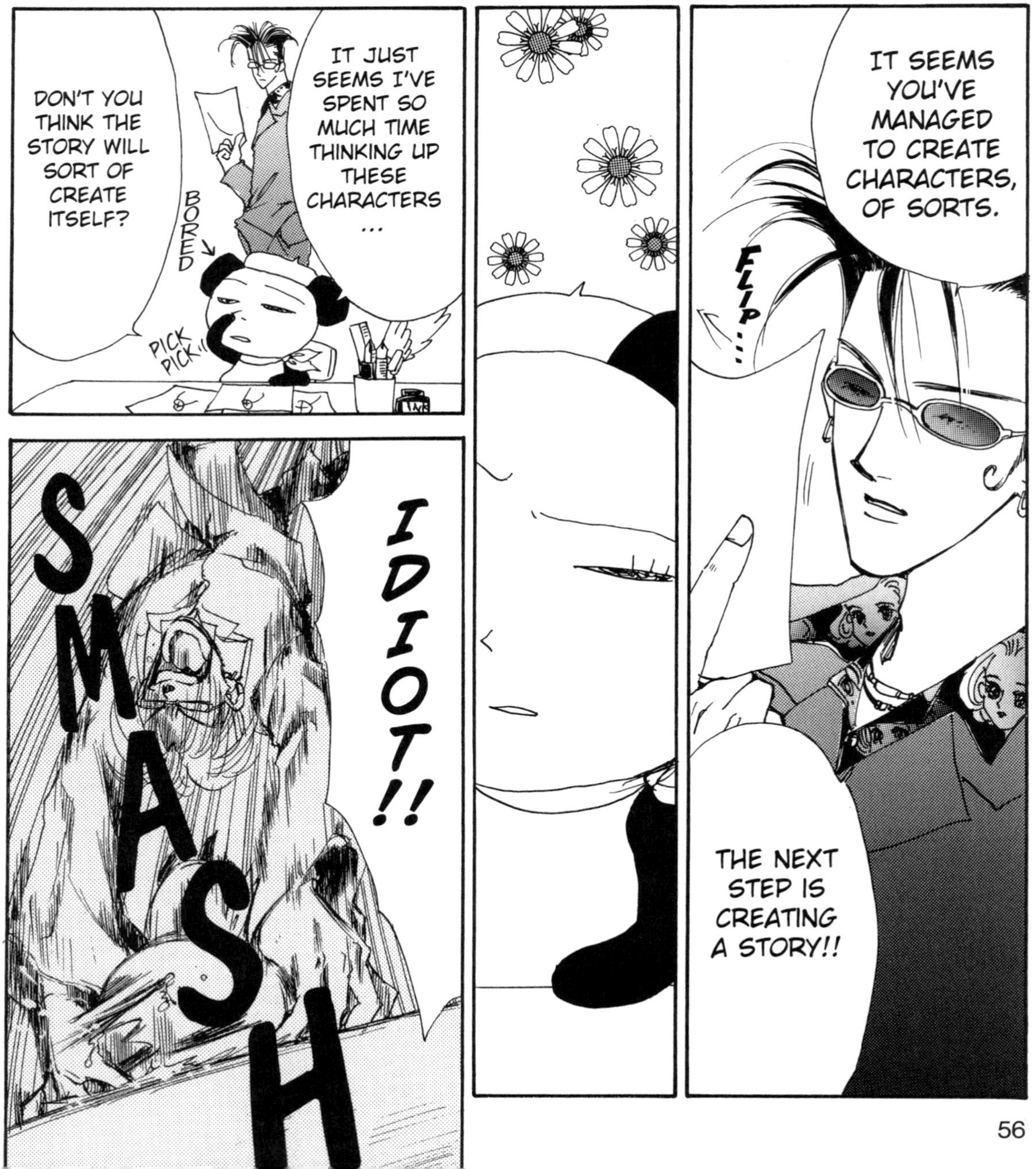
IT SEEMS YOU'VE MANAGED TO CREATE CHARACTERS, OF SORTS.
FLIP...
THE NEXT STEP IS CREATING A STORY!!
IT JUST SEEMS I'VE SPENT SO MUCH TIME THINKING UP THESE CHARACTERS...
DON'T YOU THINK THE STORY WILL SORT OF CREATE ITSELF?
BORED
PICK PICK
IDIOT!!
SMASH

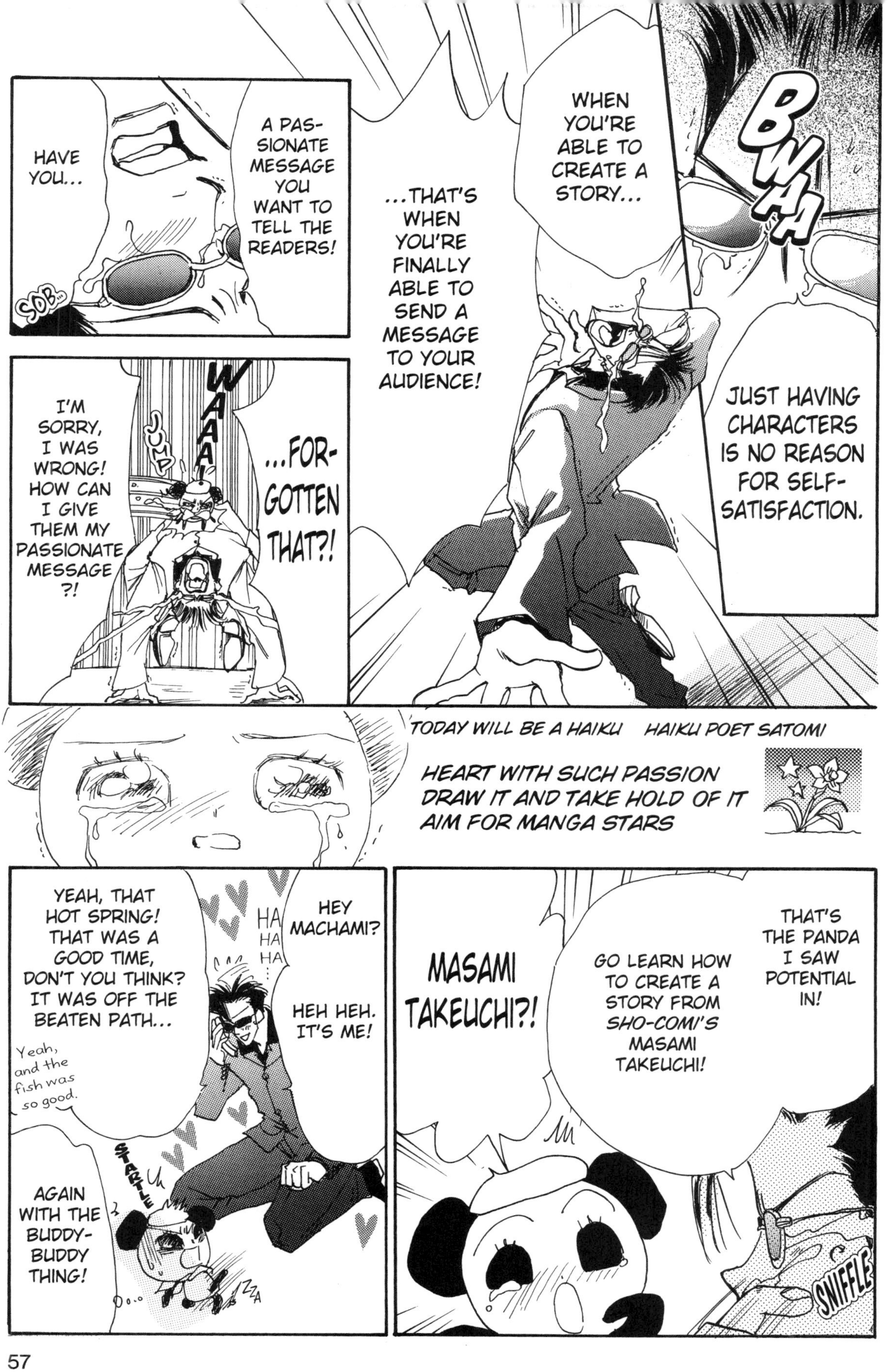

WHEN YOU'RE ABLE TO CREATE A STORY...
BWAA
...THAT'S WHEN YOU'RE FINALLY ABLE TO SEND A MESSAGE TO YOUR AUDIENCE!
JUST HAVING CHARACTERS IS NO REASON FOR SELF-SATISFACTION.
A PAS-SIONATE MESSAGE YOU WANT TO TELL THE READERS!
HAVE YOU...
SOB...
...FOR-GOTTEN THAT?!
WAAA!
JUMP
I'M SORRY, I WAS WRONG! HOW CAN I GIVE THEM MY PASSIONATE MESSAGE ?!
TODAY WILL BE A HAIKU HAIKU POET SATOMI
HEART WITH SUCH PASSION
DRAW IT AND TAKE HOLD OF IT
AIM FOR MANGA STARS
THAT'S THE PANDA I SAW POTENTIAL IN!
GO LEARN HOW TO CREATE A STORY FROM SHO-COMI'S MASAMI TAKEUCHI!
MASAMI TAKEUCHI?!
SNIFFLE
HEY MACHAMI?
HA HA HA
HEH HEH. IT'S ME!
YEAH, THAT HOT SPRING! THAT WAS A GOOD TIME, DON'T YOU THINK? IT WAS OFF THE BEATEN PATH...
Yeah, and the fish was so good.
STARTLE
AGAIN WITH THE BUDDY-BUDDY THING!

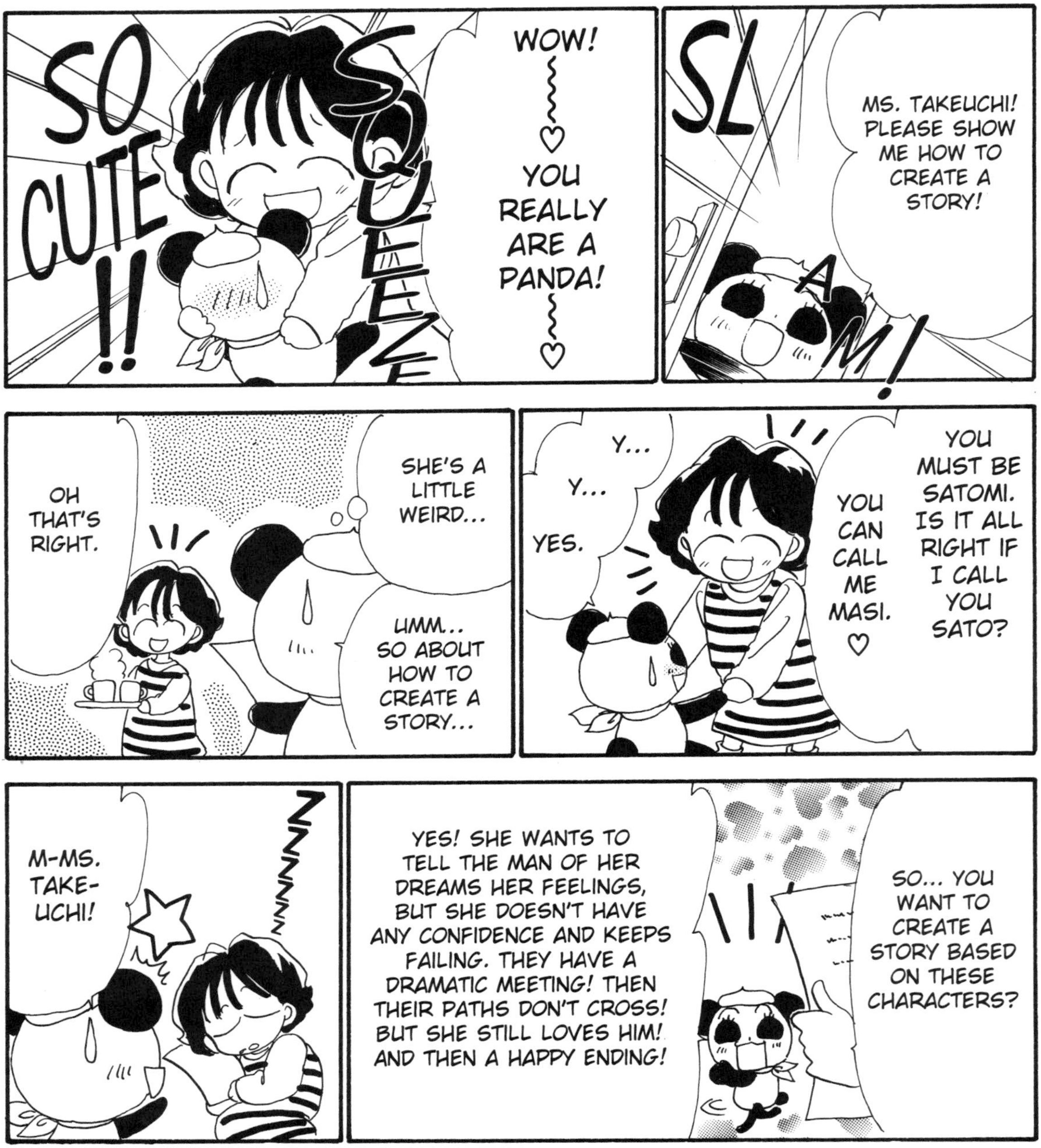
SL
MS. TAKEUCHI! PLEASE SHOW ME HOW TO CREATE A STORY!
AM!
WOW! ♡ YOU REALLY ARE A PANDA! ♡
SQUEEZE
SO CUTE!!
YOU MUST BE SATOMI. IS IT ALL RIGHT IF I CALL YOU SATO?
YOU CAN CALL ME MASI. ♡
Y...
Y...
YES.
SHE'S A LITTLE WEIRD...
UMM... SO ABOUT HOW TO CREATE A STORY...
OH THAT'S RIGHT.
SO... YOU WANT TO CREATE A STORY BASED ON THESE CHARACTERS?
YES! SHE WANTS TO TELL THE MAN OF HER DREAMS HER FEELINGS, BUT SHE DOESN'T HAVE ANY CONFIDENCE AND KEEPS FAILING. THEY HAVE A DRAMATIC MEETING! THEN THEIR PATHS DON'T CROSS! BUT SHE STILL LOVES HIM! AND THEN A HAPPY ENDING!
ZZZZZZ
M-MS. TAKE-UCHI!

WHAT THE AUTHOR WANTS TO WRITE *IS* THE THEME!

We say theme, but really you don't need to be bogged down by that word! The story you want to draw is essentially your theme! When you're writing a love story, whether it ends happily or tragically, the romance becomes the basic structure of the story and what the author wanted to say and what the main character felt becomes the theme. If you hear a story of love fulfilled from a friend, that's merely a list of facts. But if that friend seems truly happy, doesn't that warm your heart? Think of a theme that'll warm the hearts of your readers!

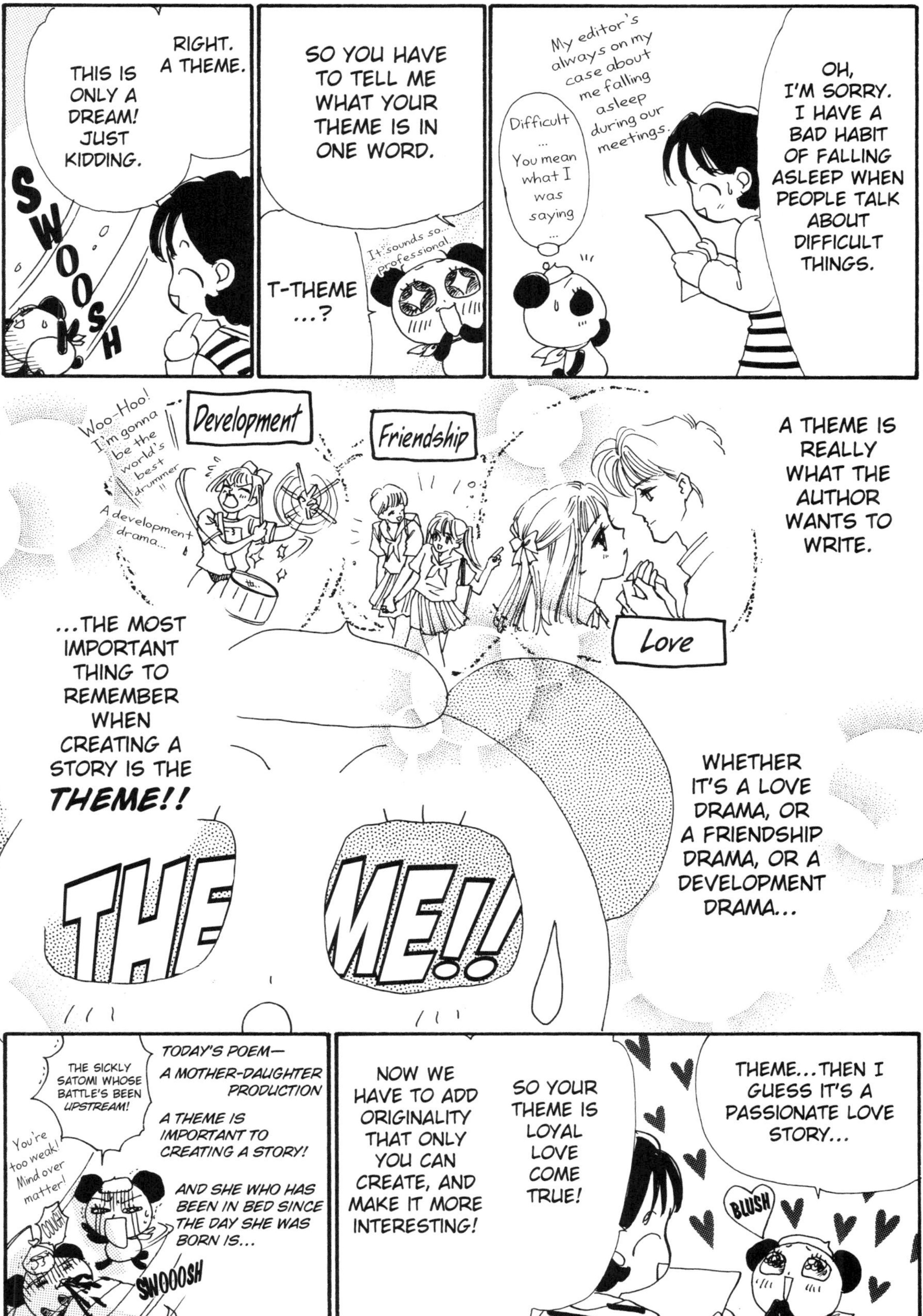
OH, I'M SORRY. I HAVE A BAD HABIT OF FALLING ASLEEP WHEN PEOPLE TALK ABOUT DIFFICULT THINGS.
Difficult... You mean what I was saying...
My editor's always on my case about me falling asleep during our meetings.
SO YOU HAVE TO TELL ME WHAT YOUR THEME IS IN ONE WORD.
T-THEME ...?
It sounds so... professional.
RIGHT. A THEME.
THIS IS ONLY A DREAM! JUST KIDDING.
SWOOSH
A THEME IS REALLY WHAT THE AUTHOR WANTS TO WRITE.
Love
Friendship
Development
Woo-Hoo! I'm gonna be the world's best drummer!!
A development drama...
WHETHER IT'S A LOVE DRAMA, OR A FRIENDSHIP DRAMA, OR A DEVELOPMENT DRAMA...
...THE MOST IMPORTANT THING TO REMEMBER WHEN CREATING A STORY IS THE THEME!!
THEME!!
THEME...THEN I GUESS IT'S A PASSIONATE LOVE STORY...
BLUSH
SO YOUR THEME IS LOYAL LOVE COME TRUE!
NOW WE HAVE TO ADD ORIGINALITY THAT ONLY YOU CAN CREATE, AND MAKE IT MORE INTERESTING!
TODAY'S POEM— A MOTHER-DAUGHTER PRODUCTION
A THEME IS IMPORTANT TO CREATING A STORY!
AND SHE WHO HAS BEEN IN BED SINCE THE DAY SHE WAS BORN IS...
THE SICKLY SATOMI WHOSE BATTLE'S BEEN UPSTREAM!
You're too weak! Mind over matter!
COUGH
SWOOOSH

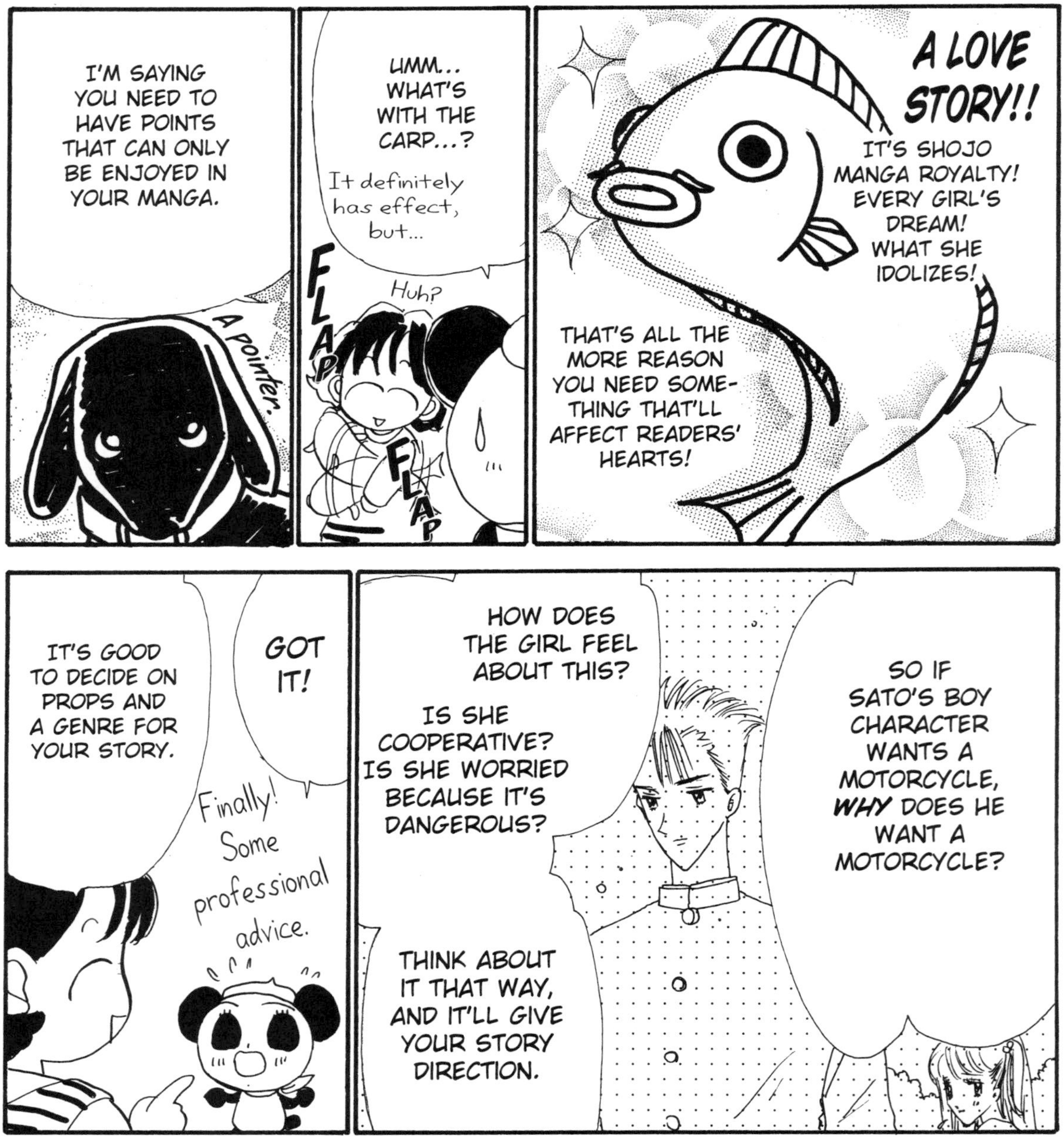
A LOVE STORY!!
IT'S SHOJO MANGA ROYALTY! EVERY GIRL'S DREAM! WHAT SHE IDOLIZES!
THAT'S ALL THE MORE REASON YOU NEED SOME-THING THAT'LL AFFECT READERS' HEARTS!
UMM... WHAT'S WITH THE CARP...?
It definitely has effect, but...
FLAP
Huh?
FLAP
I'M SAYING YOU NEED TO HAVE POINTS THAT CAN ONLY BE ENJOYED IN YOUR MANGA.
A pointer.
SO IF SATO'S BOY CHARACTER WANTS A MOTORCYCLE, *WHY* DOES HE WANT A MOTORCYCLE?
HOW DOES THE GIRL FEEL ABOUT THIS?
IS SHE COOPERATIVE? IS SHE WORRIED BECAUSE IT'S DANGEROUS?
THINK ABOUT IT THAT WAY, AND IT'LL GIVE YOUR STORY DIRECTION.
GOT IT!
IT'S GOOD TO DECIDE ON PROPS AND A GENRE FOR YOUR STORY.
Finally! Some professional advice.

SETTING THE GENRE GIVES YOUR WORK AN EXTRA APPEAL.

You could say that just by belonging to a certain genre, the manga has something that appeals to the reader! For example, if you write about a band, it increases the possibility that people in a band or who are curious about bands will read it. This can also provide an opportunity to the readers who aren't familiar with bands to realize their appeal! Just belonging to a single genre gives your work that much more appeal, so it would be a shame not to have one. High school manga are familiar and good, but try to find a little extra kick to go with it!

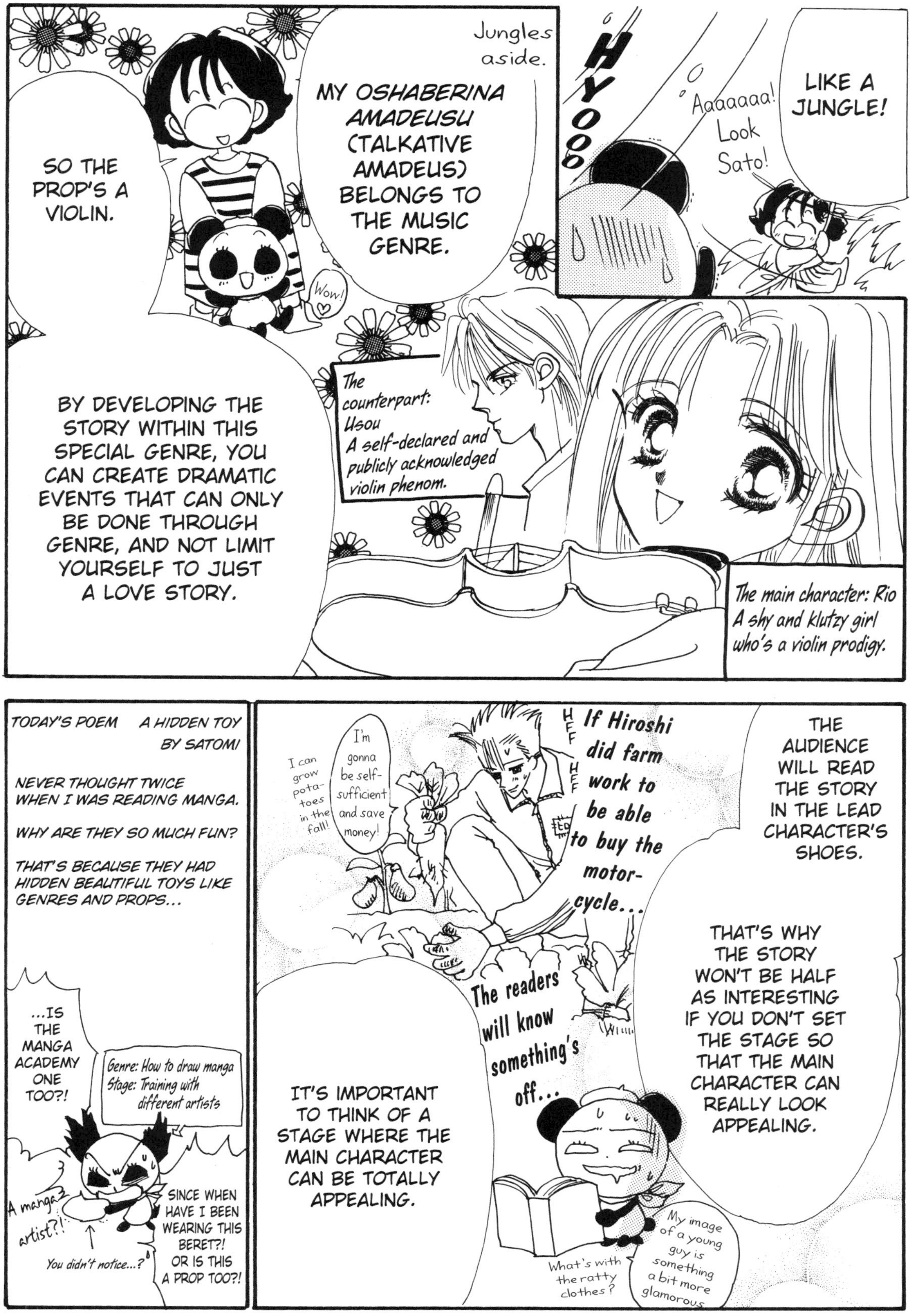
LIKE A JUNGLE!
Aaaaaaa! Look Sato!
HYOOOO
Jungles aside.
MY OSHABERINA AMADEUSU (TALKATIVE AMADEUS) BELONGS TO THE MUSIC GENRE.
SO THE PROP'S A VIOLIN.
Wow! ♡
The main character: Rio A shy and klutzy girl who's a violin prodigy.
The counterpart: Usou A self-declared and publicly acknowledged violin phenom.
BY DEVELOPING THE STORY WITHIN THIS SPECIAL GENRE, YOU CAN CREATE DRAMATIC EVENTS THAT CAN ONLY BE DONE THROUGH GENRE, AND NOT LIMIT YOURSELF TO JUST A LOVE STORY.
THE AUDIENCE WILL READ THE STORY IN THE LEAD CHARACTER'S SHOES.
If Hiroshi did farm work to be able to buy the motor-cycle...
HFF HFF
I'm gonna be self-sufficient and save money!
I can grow pota-toes in the fall!
THAT'S WHY THE STORY WON'T BE HALF AS INTERESTING IF YOU DON'T SET THE STAGE SO THAT THE MAIN CHARACTER CAN REALLY LOOK APPEALING.
The readers will know something's off...
IT'S IMPORTANT TO THINK OF A STAGE WHERE THE MAIN CHARACTER CAN BE TOTALLY APPEALING.
My image of a young guy is something a bit more glamorous
What's with the ratty clothes?
TODAY'S POEM A HIDDEN TOY BY SATOMI
NEVER THOUGHT TWICE WHEN I WAS READING MANGA.
WHY ARE THEY SO MUCH FUN?
THAT'S BECAUSE THEY HAD HIDDEN BEAUTIFUL TOYS LIKE GENRES AND PROPS...
...IS THE MANGA ACADEMY ONE TOO?!
Genre: How to draw manga Stage: Training with different artists
A manga artist?!
SINCE WHEN HAVE I BEEN WEARING THIS BERET?! OR IS THIS A PROP TOO?!
You didn't notice...?

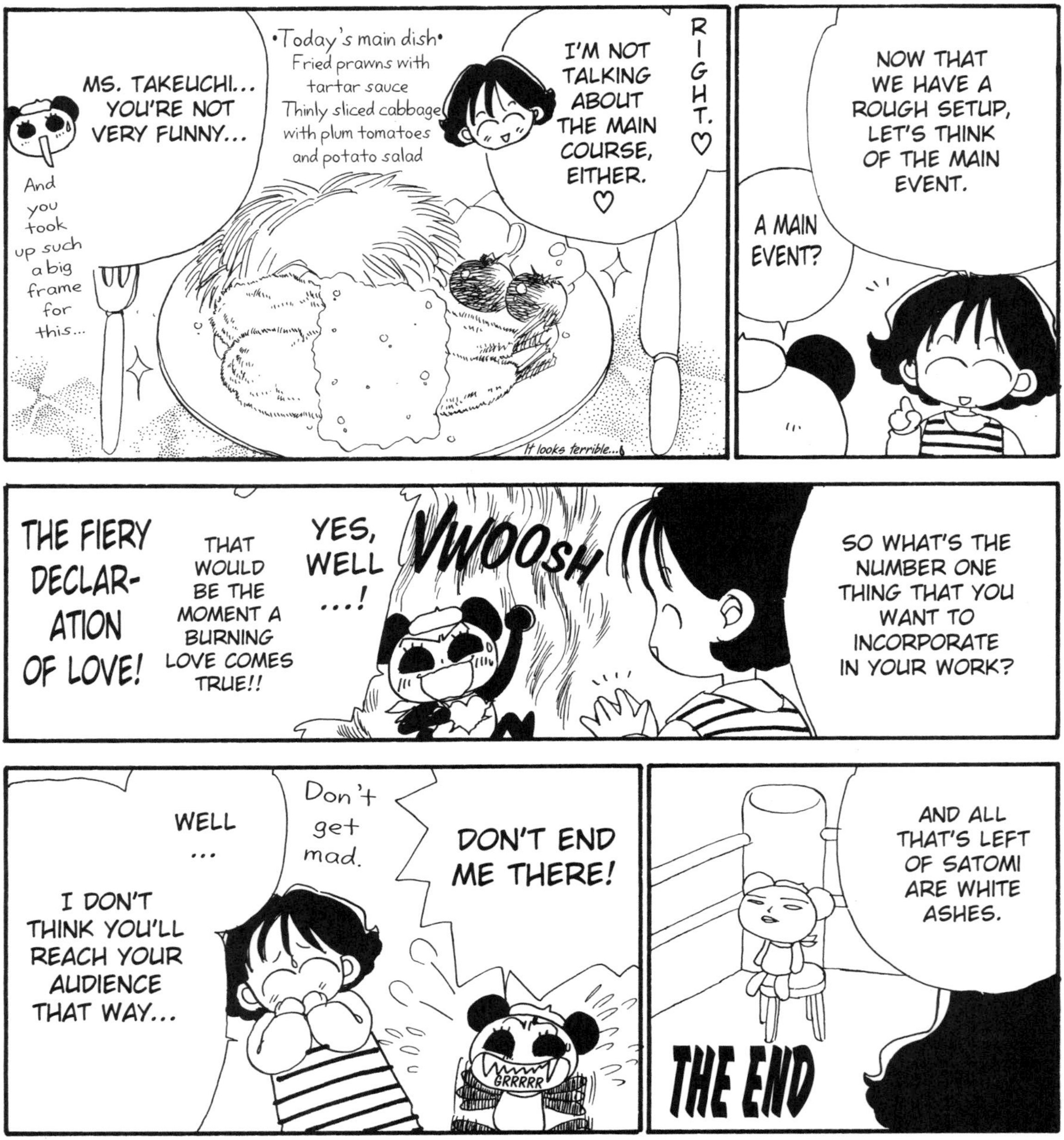
NOW THAT WE HAVE A ROUGH SETUP, LET'S THINK OF THE MAIN EVENT.
A MAIN EVENT?
RIGHT. ♡
I'M NOT TALKING ABOUT THE MAIN COURSE, EITHER. ♡
•Today's main dish• Fried prawns with tartar sauce Thinly sliced cabbage with plum tomatoes and potato salad
MS. TAKEUCHI... YOU'RE NOT VERY FUNNY...
And you took up such a big frame for this...
It looks terrible...
SO WHAT'S THE NUMBER ONE THING THAT YOU WANT TO INCORPORATE IN YOUR WORK?
VWOOSH
YES, WELL ...!
THAT WOULD BE THE MOMENT A BURNING LOVE COMES TRUE!!
THE FIERY DECLAR-ATION OF LOVE!
AND ALL THAT'S LEFT OF SATOMI ARE WHITE ASHES.
THE END
DON'T END ME THERE!
Don't get mad.
WELL ...
I DON'T THINK YOU'LL REACH YOUR AUDIENCE THAT WAY...
GRRRRR

PAGE COUNT MATTERS IN THE MAIN EVENT!

Something that you should always keep in mind when drawing manga is the distribution of pages. No matter how good your main event is, if you only give it a few pages, it won't leave a lasting impression on your audience. To put it in extreme terms, you could even think of dedicating half of the total number of pages to the main event. An event that only requires a small number of pages probably isn't worthy of "main event" status. What do you want to depict? What kind of event do you need to express that?! Create a storyboard after carefully considering all of that.

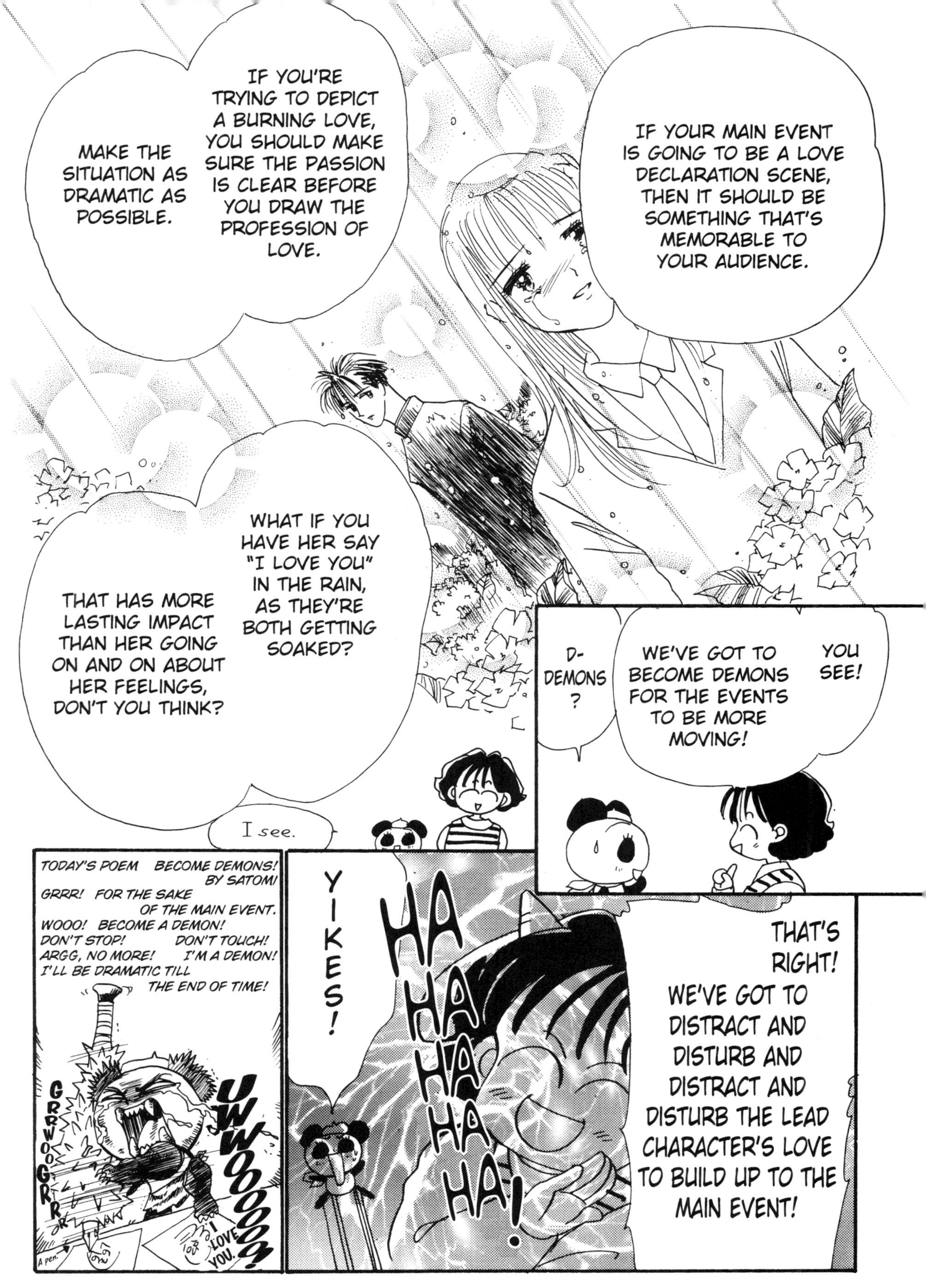
IF YOUR MAIN EVENT IS GOING TO BE A LOVE DECLARATION SCENE, THEN IT SHOULD BE SOMETHING THAT'S MEMORABLE TO YOUR AUDIENCE.
IF YOU'RE TRYING TO DEPICT A BURNING LOVE, YOU SHOULD MAKE SURE THE PASSION IS CLEAR BEFORE YOU DRAW THE PROFESSION OF LOVE.
MAKE THE SITUATION AS DRAMATIC AS POSSIBLE.
WHAT IF YOU HAVE HER SAY "I LOVE YOU" IN THE RAIN, AS THEY'RE BOTH GETTING SOAKED?
THAT HAS MORE LASTING IMPACT THAN HER GOING ON AND ON ABOUT HER FEELINGS, DON'T YOU THINK?
I see.
YOU SEE!
WE'VE GOT TO BECOME DEMONS FOR THE EVENTS TO BE MORE MOVING!
D-DEMONS?
THAT'S RIGHT! WE'VE GOT TO DISTRACT AND DISTURB AND DISTRACT AND DISTURB THE LEAD CHARACTER'S LOVE TO BUILD UP TO THE MAIN EVENT!
HA HA HA HA HA HA!
YIKES!
TODAY'S POEM BECOME DEMONS! BY SATOMI
GRRR! FOR THE SAKE OF THE MAIN EVENT.
WOOO! BECOME A DEMON!
DON'T STOP! DON'T TOUCH!
ARGG, NO MORE! I'M A DEMON!
I'LL BE DRAMATIC TILL THE END OF TIME!
UWWOOOOOM!
GRRWOOGRRRR
I LOVE YOU.
A pen.

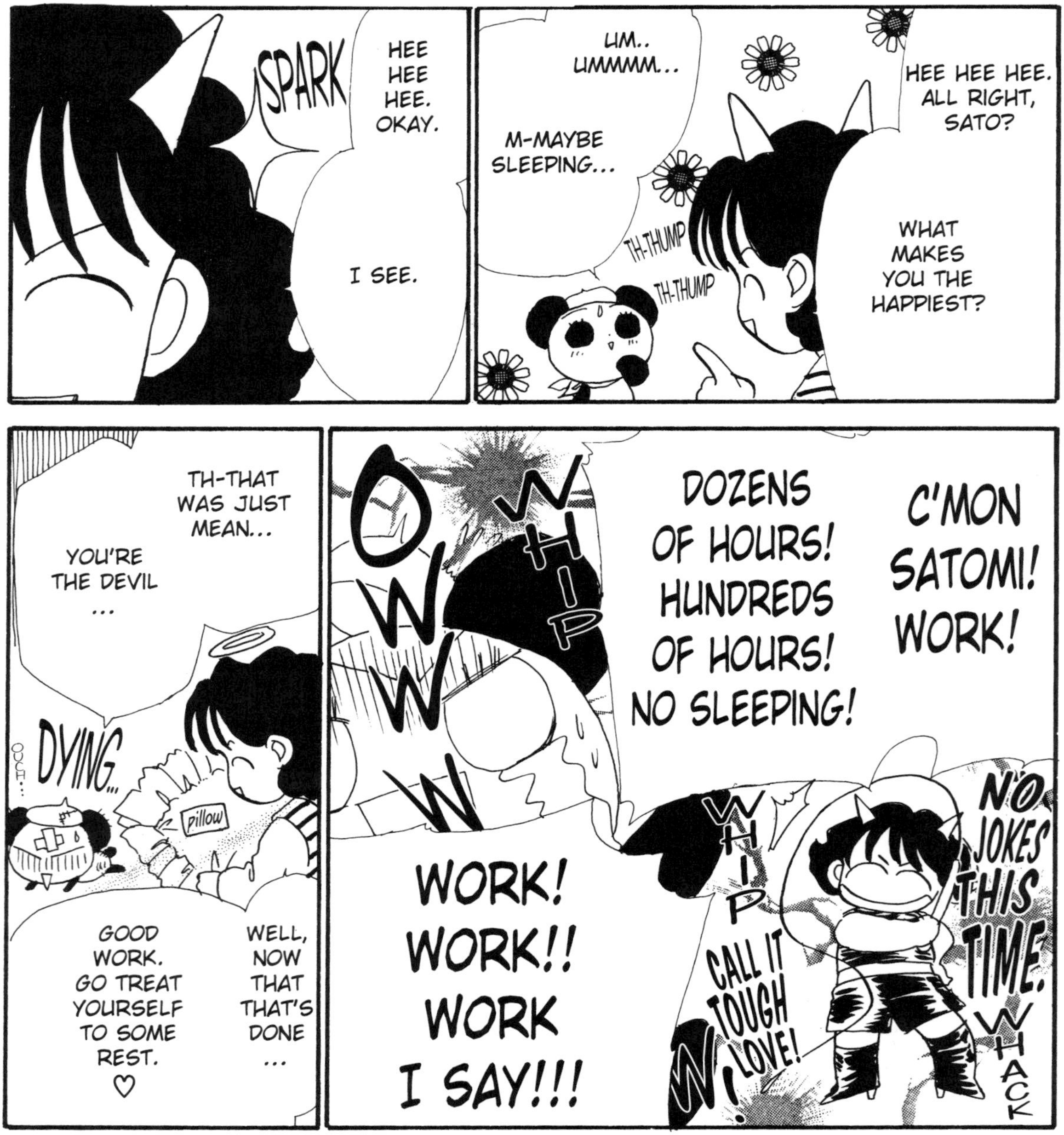
HEE HEE HEE. ALL RIGHT, SATO?
WHAT MAKES YOU THE HAPPIEST?
UM.. UMMMM...
M-MAYBE SLEEPING...
TH-THUMP
TH-THUMP
HEE HEE HEE. OKAY.
SPARK
I SEE.
C'MON SATOMI! WORK!
DOZENS OF HOURS! HUNDREDS OF HOURS! NO SLEEPING!
WHIP
OWWWW
NO JOKES THIS TIME.
WHACK
WHIP
CALL IT TOUGH LOVE!
WORK! WORK!! WORK I SAY!!!
TH-THAT WAS JUST MEAN...
YOU'RE THE DEVIL ...
DYING...
OUCH...
pillow
WELL, NOW THAT THAT'S DONE ...
GOOD WORK. GO TREAT YOURSELF TO SOME REST. ♡

YOU NEED A JUMP TO BUILD UP THE STORY.

All non-main events only exist to build up the main event. Just like Ms. Takeuchi is saying, the key is to build up from the previous events to the main event in order to really create some excitement. If there's a main character that's going to ultimately be happy, you have to spend just as much time thinking about how she'll be unhappy. The main character falls into a pit of unhappiness and, lo and behold, she's able to crawl out of it, and there's your happy ending! With a build-up like that, you'll be able to move your audience more.

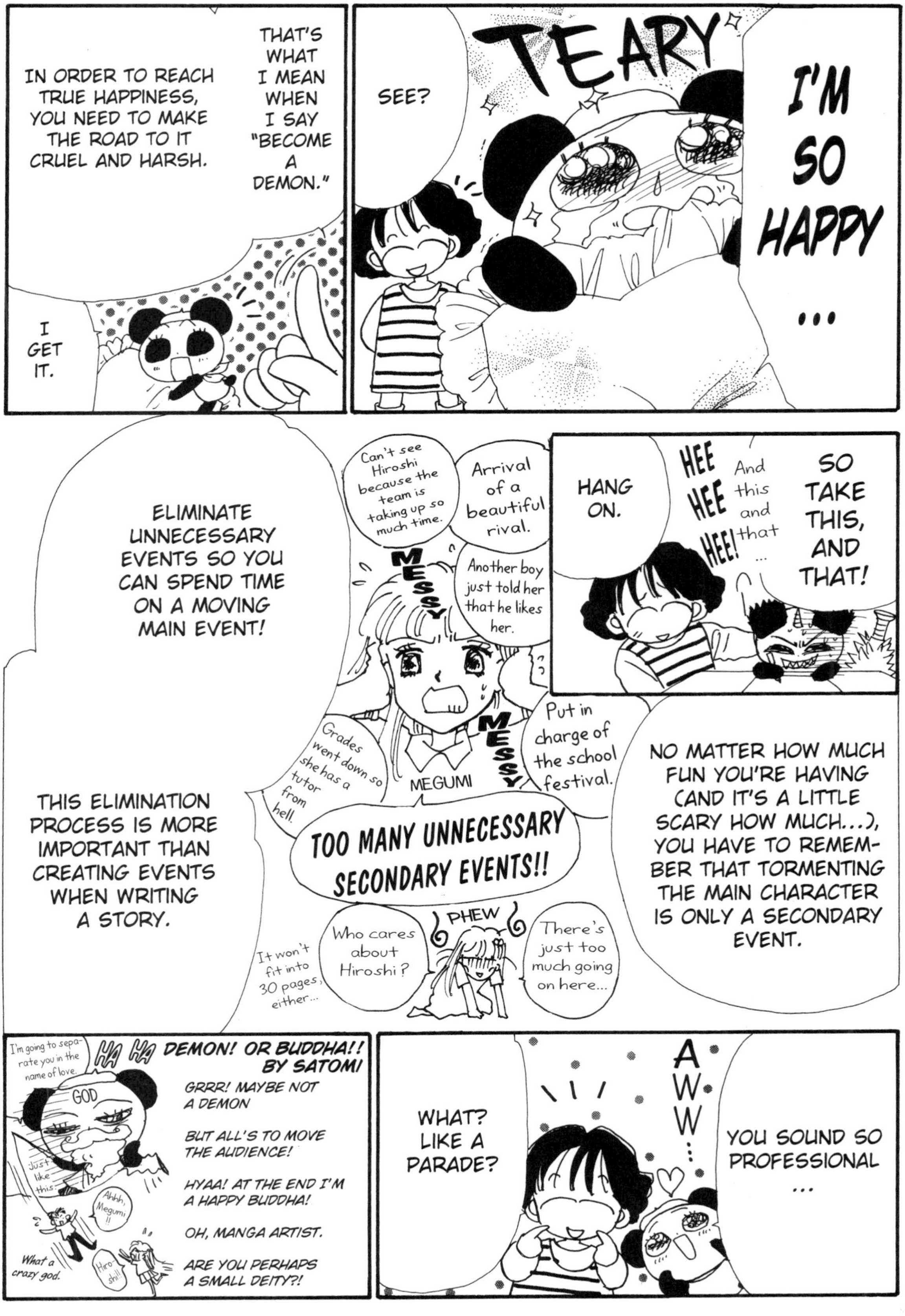
I'M SO HAPPY...
TEARY
SEE?
THAT'S WHAT I MEAN WHEN I SAY "BECOME A DEMON."
IN ORDER TO REACH TRUE HAPPINESS, YOU NEED TO MAKE THE ROAD TO IT CRUEL AND HARSH.
I GET IT.
SO TAKE THIS, AND THAT!
And this and that...
HEE HEE HEE!
HANG ON.
NO MATTER HOW MUCH FUN YOU'RE HAVING (AND IT'S A LITTLE SCARY HOW MUCH...), YOU HAVE TO REMEMBER THAT TORMENTING THE MAIN CHARACTER IS ONLY A SECONDARY EVENT.
Arrival of a beautiful rival.
Can't see Hiroshi because the team is taking up so much time.
Another boy just told her that he likes her.
MESSY
MESSY
Put in charge of the school festival.
Grades went down so she has a tutor from hell.
MEGUMI
TOO MANY UNNECESSARY SECONDARY EVENTS!!
PHEW
There's just too much going on here...
Who cares about Hiroshi?
It won't fit into 30 pages, either...
ELIMINATE UNNECESSARY EVENTS SO YOU CAN SPEND TIME ON A MOVING MAIN EVENT!
THIS ELIMINATION PROCESS IS MORE IMPORTANT THAN CREATING EVENTS WHEN WRITING A STORY.
YOU SOUND SO PROFESSIONAL...
AWW...
WHAT? LIKE A PARADE?
DEMON! OR BUDDHA!! BY SATOMI
GRRR! MAYBE NOT A DEMON
BUT ALL'S TO MOVE THE AUDIENCE!
HYAA! AT THE END I'M A HAPPY BUDDHA!
OH, MANGA ARTIST.
ARE YOU PERHAPS A SMALL DEITY?!
HA HA
I'm going to separate you in the name of love.
GOD
Just like this.
Ahhh, Megumi!!
Hiroshi!!
What a crazy god.

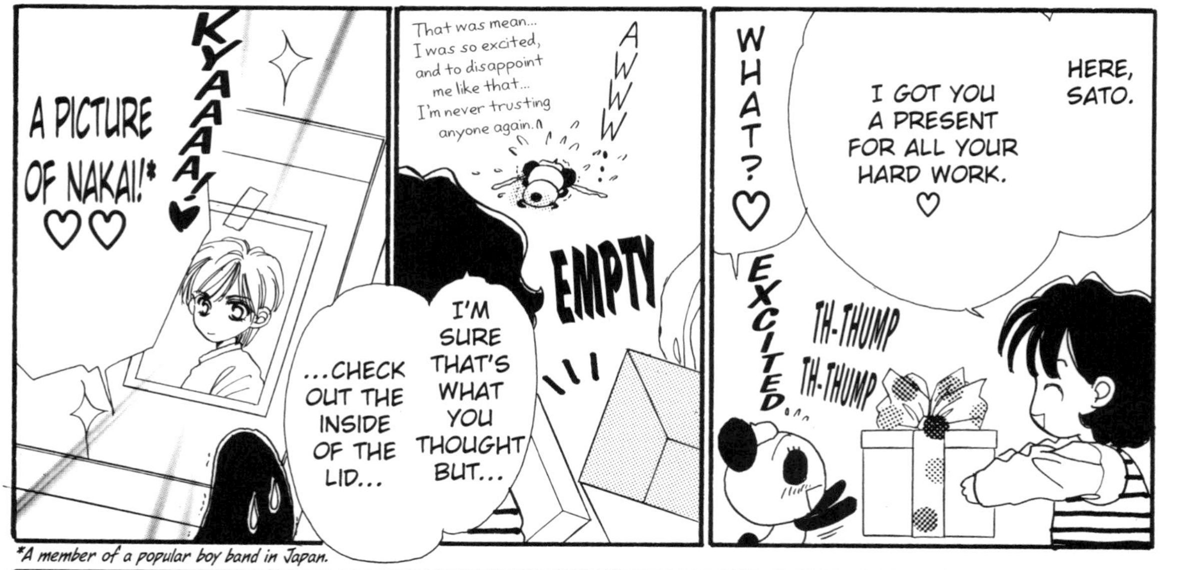
HERE, SATO.
I GOT YOU A PRESENT FOR ALL YOUR HARD WORK. ♡
WHAT?♡
EXCITED
TH-THUMP
TH-THUMP
AWWW
That was mean... I was so excited, and to disappoint me like that... I'm never trusting anyone again.
EMPTY
I'M SURE THAT'S WHAT YOU THOUGHT BUT...
...CHECK OUT THE INSIDE OF THE LID...
KYAAAA!
A PICTURE OF NAKAI!* ♡♡

*A member of a popular boy band in Japan.

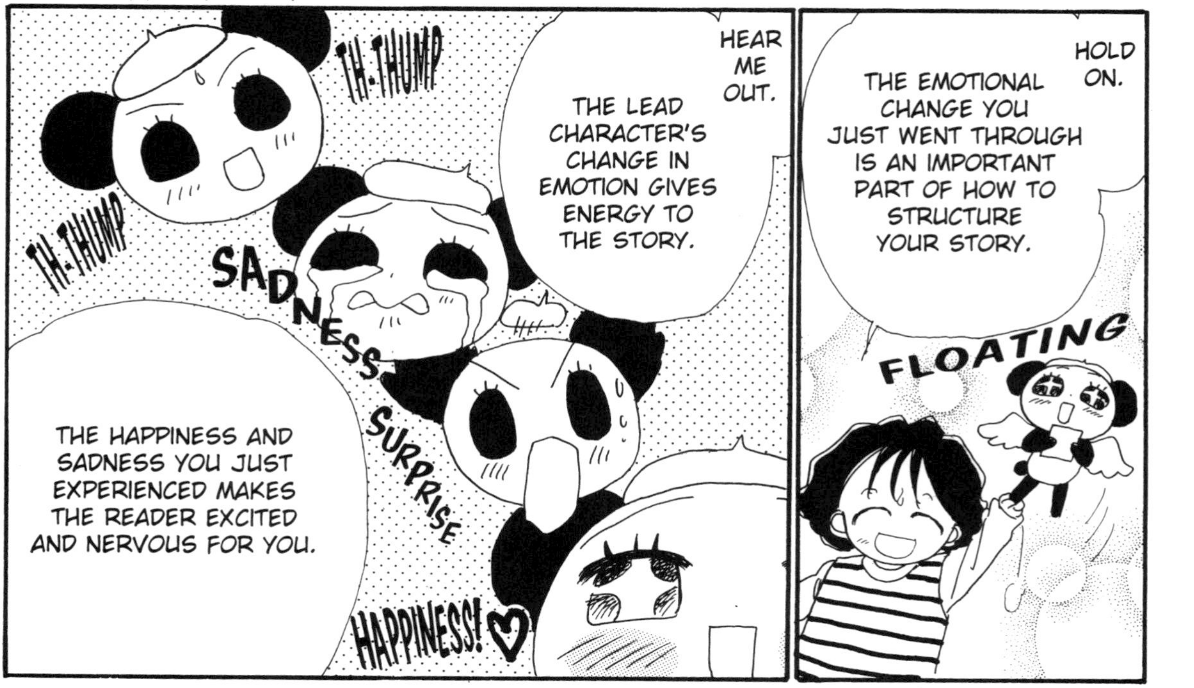
HOLD ON.
THE EMOTIONAL CHANGE YOU JUST WENT THROUGH IS AN IMPORTANT PART OF HOW TO STRUCTURE YOUR STORY.
FLOATING
HEAR ME OUT.
THE LEAD CHARACTER'S CHANGE IN EMOTION GIVES ENERGY TO THE STORY.
TH-THUMP
TH-THUMP
SADNESS
SURPRISE
HAPPINESS!♡
THE HAPPINESS AND SADNESS YOU JUST EXPERIENCED MAKES THE READER EXCITED AND NERVOUS FOR YOU.

STORY ORGANIZATION IS THE BASIC ELEMENT IN THE CREATION PROCESS!

The story's flow is its backbone. Of course, there are successful unconventional story structures. One such example is starting off with the "climax" and then going to the "introduction" and "development." This captures the audience in the beginning, giving you time to explain what has happened up until then, and it definitely leaves an impression. The same goes for sketches, but the importance of basics can't be stressed enough in realizing an original idea. In the beginning, you should stick to more conventional story structures so that you can master the basic form!!

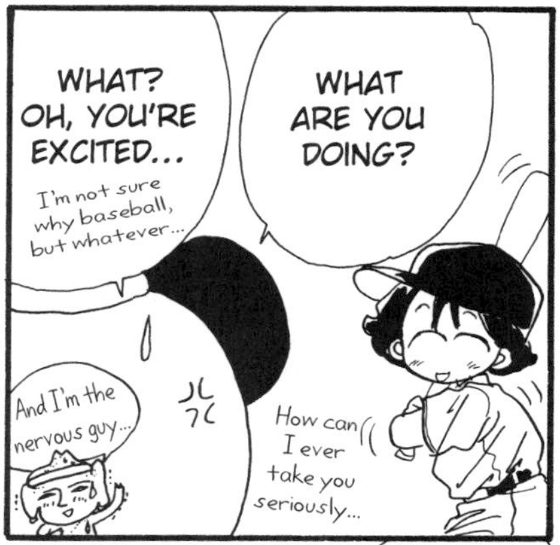
WHAT ARE YOU DOING?
WHAT? OH, YOU'RE EXCITED...
I'm not sure why baseball, but whatever...
How can I ever take you seriously...
And I'm the nervous guy...

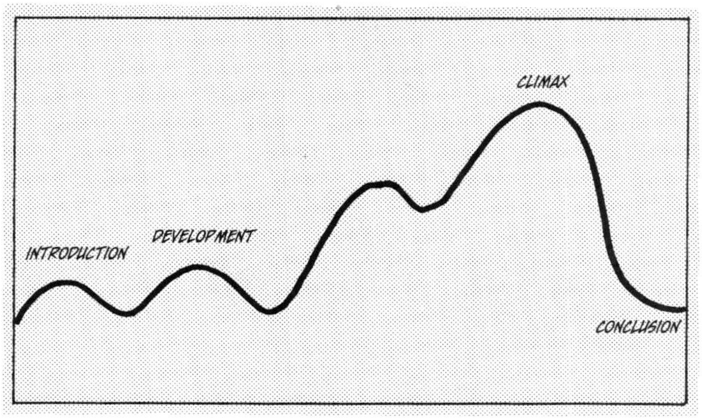
CLIMAX
INTRODUCTION
DEVELOPMENT
CONCLUSION

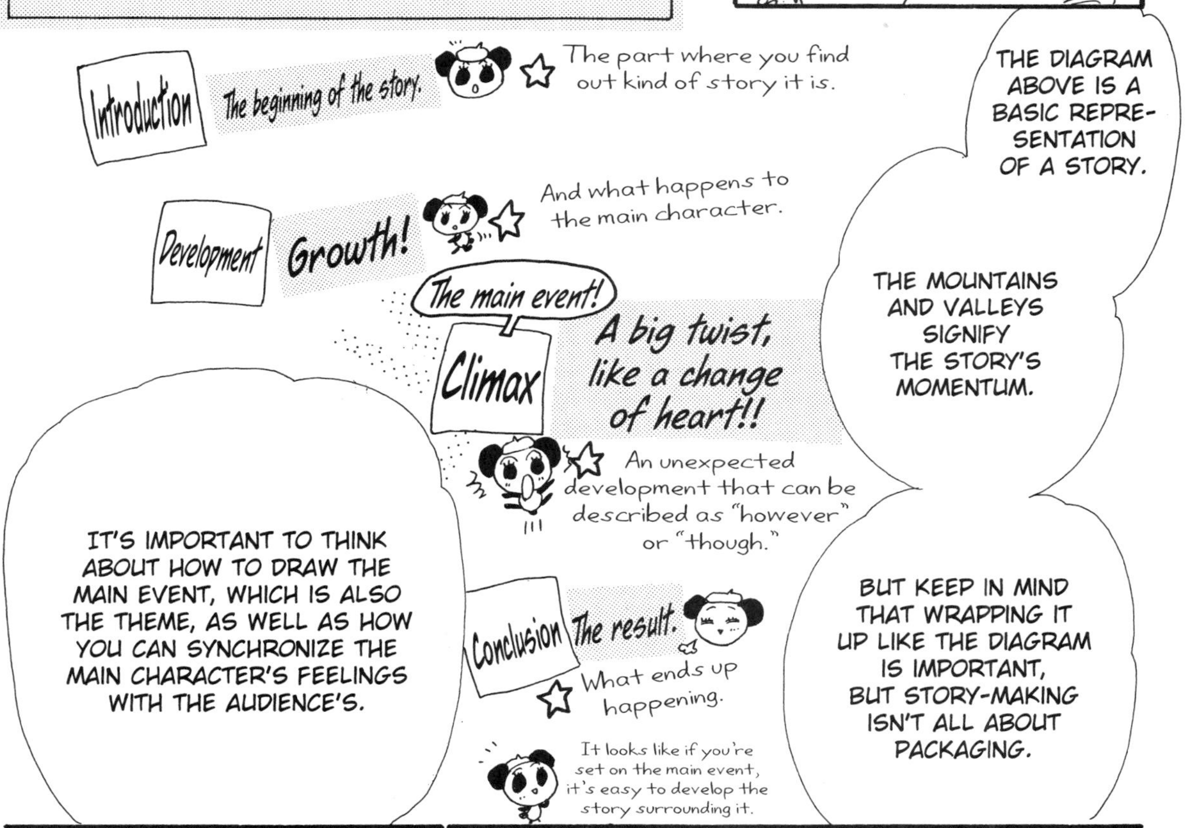
THE DIAGRAM ABOVE IS A BASIC REPRESENTATION OF A STORY.
THE MOUNTAINS AND VALLEYS SIGNIFY THE STORY'S MOMENTUM.
BUT KEEP IN MIND THAT WRAPPING IT UP LIKE THE DIAGRAM IS IMPORTANT, BUT STORY-MAKING ISN'T ALL ABOUT PACKAGING.
Introduction
The beginning of the story.
The part where you find out kind of story it is.
Development
Growth!
And what happens to the main character.
The main event!
Climax
A big twist, like a change of heart!!
An unexpected development that can be described as "however" or "though."
Conclusion
The result.
What ends up happening.
It looks like if you're set on the main event, it's easy to develop the story surrounding it.
IT'S IMPORTANT TO THINK ABOUT HOW TO DRAW THE MAIN EVENT, WHICH IS ALSO THE THEME, AS WELL AS HOW YOU CAN SYNCHRONIZE THE MAIN CHARACTER'S FEELINGS WITH THE AUDIENCE'S.

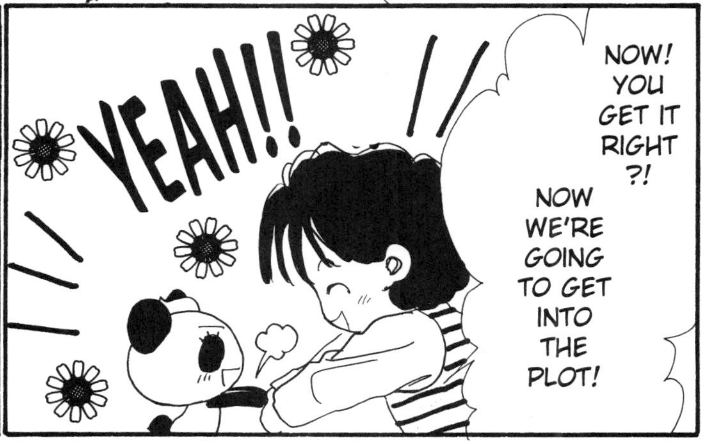
NOW! YOU GET IT RIGHT?!
NOW WE'RE GOING TO GET INTO THE PLOT!
YEAH!!

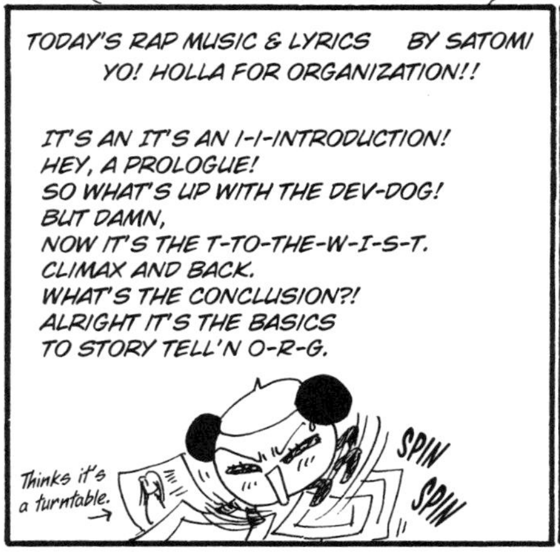
TODAY'S RAP MUSIC & LYRICS BY SATOMI
YO! HOLLA FOR ORGANIZATION!!
IT'S AN IT'S AN I-I-INTRODUCTION!
HEY, A PROLOGUE!
SO WHAT'S UP WITH THE DEV-DOG!
BUT DAMN,
NOW IT'S THE T-TO-THE-W-I-S-T.
CLIMAX AND BACK.
WHAT'S THE CONCLUSION?!
ALRIGHT IT'S THE BASICS
TO STORY TELL'N O-R-G.
Thinks it's a turntable.
SPIN
SPIN

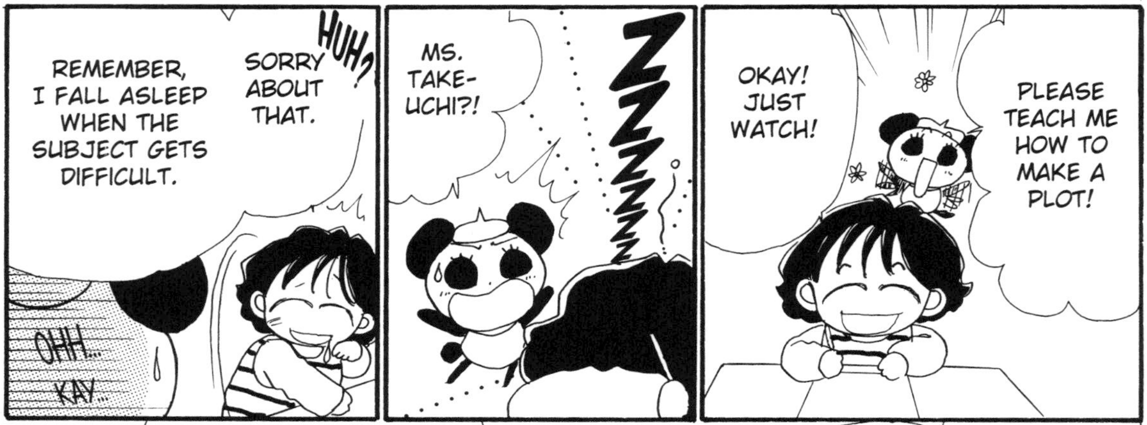
PLEASE TEACH ME HOW TO MAKE A PLOT!
OKAY! JUST WATCH!
ZZZZZZ
MS. TAKE-UCHI?!
HUH?
SORRY ABOUT THAT.
REMEMBER, I FALL ASLEEP WHEN THE SUBJECT GETS DIFFICULT.
OHH... KAY...

IT'S A LITTLE DIFFICULT TO JUST DIVE INTO CREATING A PLOT.

YOU SHOULD START BY NOTING THE DIFFERENT EVENTS YOU HAVE IN MIND.

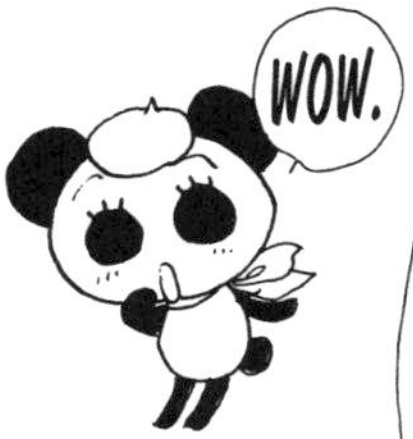
WOW.

USE THOSE NOTES AS A BASIS TO START CREATING THE STORY FLOW.

SEE, YOU'VE GOT A PLOT BEFORE YOU KNOW IT!

Example

Notes

Theme: Go on a date at the beach with a new boyfriend!

A-kun, a classmate — He looks just like my favorite celebrity.

Aggressively pursues him so the many rivals don't take him.

But she trips in front of him and her underwear is exposed! Humiliated!!

The underwear was a polka dot pattern— he thinks it's cute and this leads to the couple's first date.

- *M-mi wants to go on a date at the beach with a new boyfriend this summer. She starts dating A-kun, who she's had a crush on, after a small incident.*
- *Their first date: She sees an entirely different side of A-kun but begins to like him even more. They kiss on the way home. She's ecstatic.*
- *At school: M-mi's on cloud nine thinking they're official. However, a rumor goes around that M-mi only likes A-kun because he looks like her favorite celebrity and it hurts his feelings. He begins to ignore her.*
- *She tries to clarify the misunderstanding and asks him to meet her. But A-kun doesn't show up. She waits for hours even when it starts raining. M-mi starts crying when she thinks he's not going to show up.*
- *It stops raining and M-mi starts to go home when A-kun shows up on his motorcycle. He borrowed it from a friend so he could take M-mi to the beach. He tells her that as long as they're together he doesn't care if she likes him because he looks like her favorite celebrity. They take off on their date at the beach.*

It'll be easier when you make a storyboard later if you think about page distribution here.

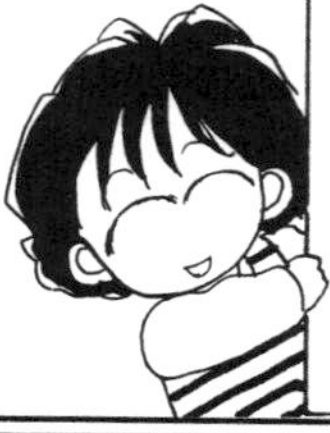

THERE'S NO ONE RIGHT WAY TO WRITE A PLOT.

A plot is also referred to as a synopsis and simply put, it's an overview of the story. There's no one right way to write a plot, so if you can incorporate the characters' dialogue and some drawings, it'll probably turn out to be a tool to visualize the story. Even professionals have different ways of writing their plots. For example, Takeuchi makes a list, others may chunk together descriptions for events and draw lines to represent the overall page layout. Since there aren't any rules, make sure to write in a way that best helps you grasp the flow. Don't forget that it's important to find a way that best fits your needs!

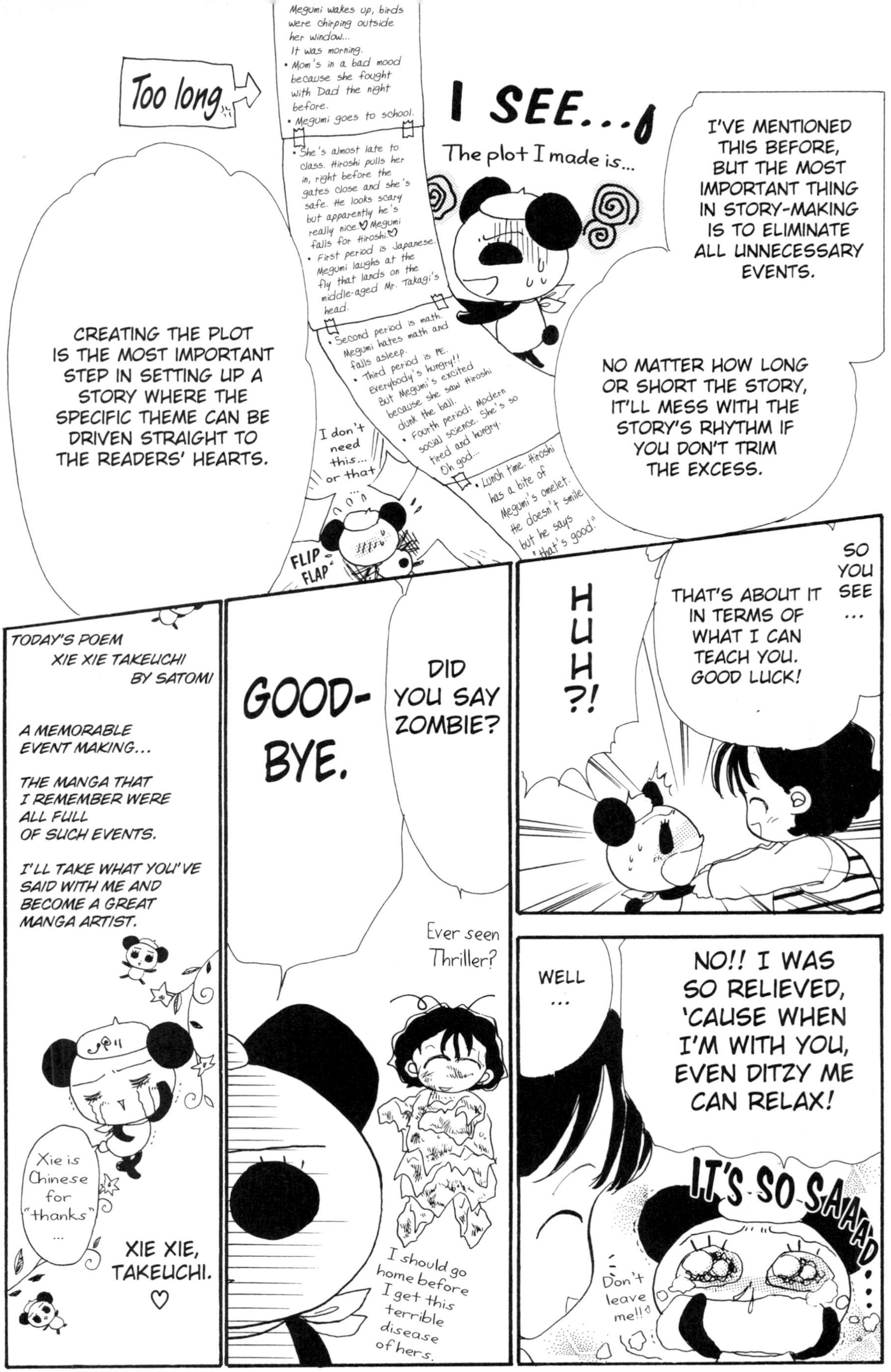
I'VE MENTIONED THIS BEFORE, BUT THE MOST IMPORTANT THING IN STORY-MAKING IS TO ELIMINATE ALL UNNECESSARY EVENTS.
I SEE...
The plot I made is...
Megumi wakes up, birds were chirping outside her window... It was morning.
• Mom's in a bad mood because she fought with Dad the night before.
• Megumi goes to school.
• She's almost late to class. Hiroshi pulls her in, right before the gates close and she's safe. He looks scary but apparently he's really nice.♡ Megumi falls for Hiroshi.♡
• First period is Japanese. Megumi laughs at the fly that lands on the middle-aged Mr. Takagi's head.
• Second period is math. Megumi hates math and falls asleep.
• Third period is PE. Everybody's hungry!! But Megumi's excited because she saw Hiroshi dunk the ball.
• Fourth period: Modern social science. She's so tired and hungry. Oh god...
• Lunch time. Hiroshi has a bite of Megumi's omelet. He doesn't smile but he says "that's good."
Too long
NO MATTER HOW LONG OR SHORT THE STORY, IT'LL MESS WITH THE STORY'S RHYTHM IF YOU DON'T TRIM THE EXCESS.
I don't need this... or that...
FLIP FLAP
CREATING THE PLOT IS THE MOST IMPORTANT STEP IN SETTING UP A STORY WHERE THE SPECIFIC THEME CAN BE DRIVEN STRAIGHT TO THE READERS' HEARTS.
SO YOU SEE...
THAT'S ABOUT IT IN TERMS OF WHAT I CAN TEACH YOU. GOOD LUCK!
HUH?!
NO!! I WAS SO RELIEVED, 'CAUSE WHEN I'M WITH YOU, EVEN DITZY ME CAN RELAX!
WELL...
IT'S SO SAAAAD...
Don't leave me!!
DID YOU SAY ZOMBIE?
GOOD-BYE.
Ever seen Thriller?
I should go home before I get this terrible disease of hers.
TODAY'S POEM
XIE XIE TAKEUCHI
BY SATOMI
A MEMORABLE EVENT MAKING...
THE MANGA THAT I REMEMBER WERE ALL FULL OF SUCH EVENTS.
I'LL TAKE WHAT YOU'VE SAID WITH ME AND BECOME A GREAT MANGA ARTIST.
Xie is Chinese for "thanks"...
XIE XIE, TAKEUCHI. ♡

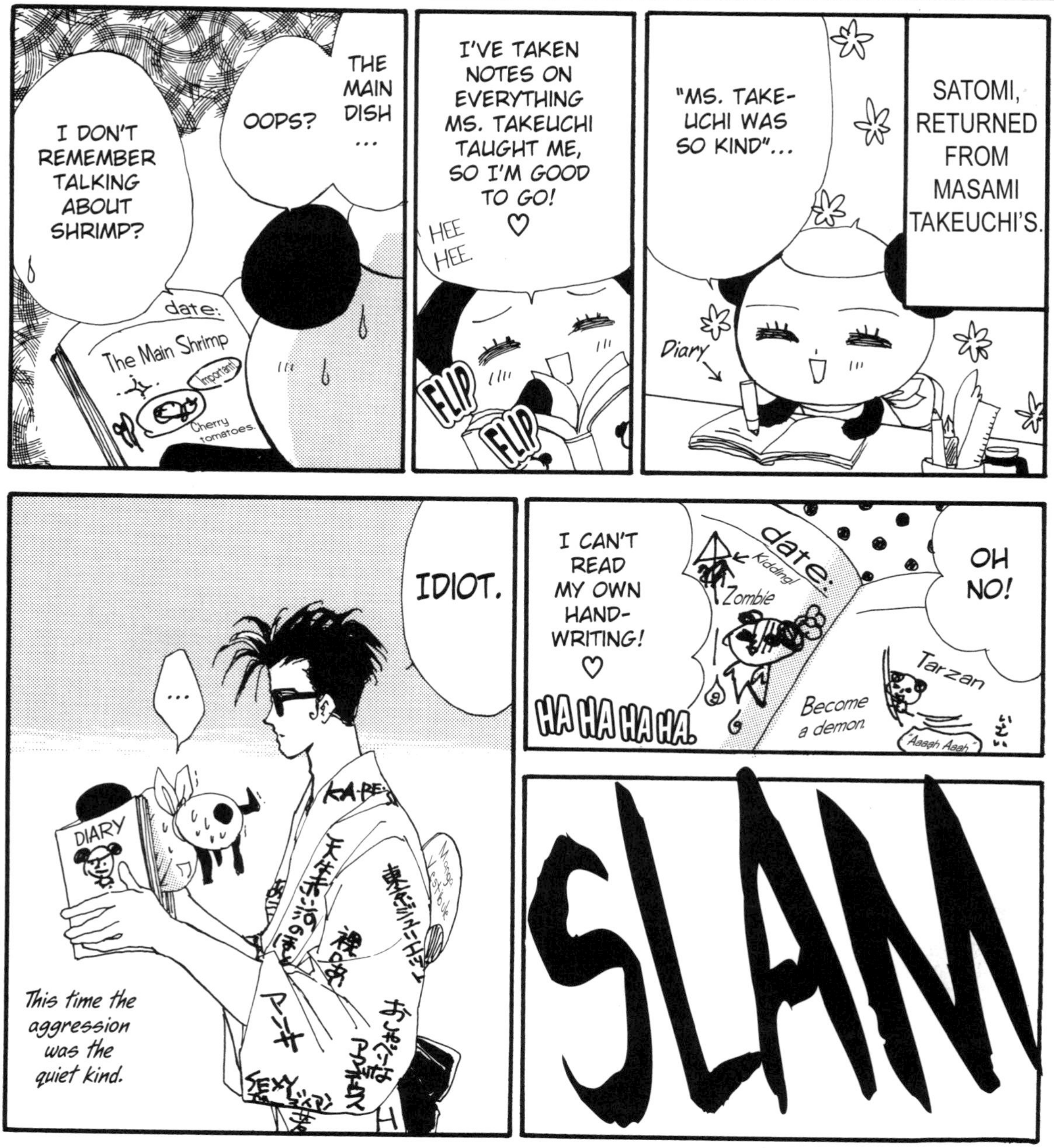
SATOMI, RETURNED FROM MASAMI TAKEUCHI'S.
"MS. TAKEUCHI WAS SO KIND"...
Diary
I'VE TAKEN NOTES ON EVERYTHING MS. TAKEUCHI TAUGHT ME, SO I'M GOOD TO GO! ♡
HEE HEE.
FLIP
FLIP
THE MAIN DISH ...
OOPS?
I DON'T REMEMBER TALKING ABOUT SHRIMP?
date:
The Main Shrimp
Important!
Cherry tomatoes.
OH NO!
date:
Kidding!
Zombie
Tarzan
Become a demon.
"Aaagh Aaah"
I CAN'T READ MY OWN HANDWRITING! ♡
HA HA HA HA.
SLAM
IDIOT.
...
DIARY
This time the aggression was the quiet kind.

AIM TO CREATE MANGA THAT IS BOTH INTERESTING AND EASY TO UNDERSTAND!

You can't forget the importance of the manga being amusing, much less understandable. The same story can be easy or difficult to understand depending on the order in which it's presented. Really think about what structure will be the easiest for the audience to understand during the plot and storyboard phase. Even if you've got a fun story, if it's hard to digest, that's enough reason for people not to read it. What a waste! Think of the order, don't rely too much on the dialogue, and maintain a good tempo. It's easier said than done, though!

MASAMI TAKEUCHI'S SEVEN MAIN POINTS OF STORY WRITING

SUMMARY

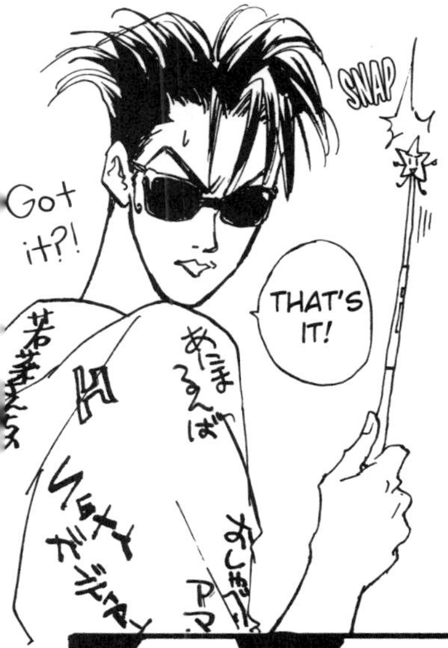
SNAP
THAT'S IT!
Got it?!

1. Create a theme: a simple one that can be summed up in one word!
2. Add some flavor through props and a genre.
3. Create a stage where the main character can really showcase her appeal!
4. The thing you want to write about most is the main event!
5. You must create obstacles for the main character to make things more interesting!
6. Create a lively story through an introduction, development, twist, and conclusion.
7. Create the backbone of the story through a plot.

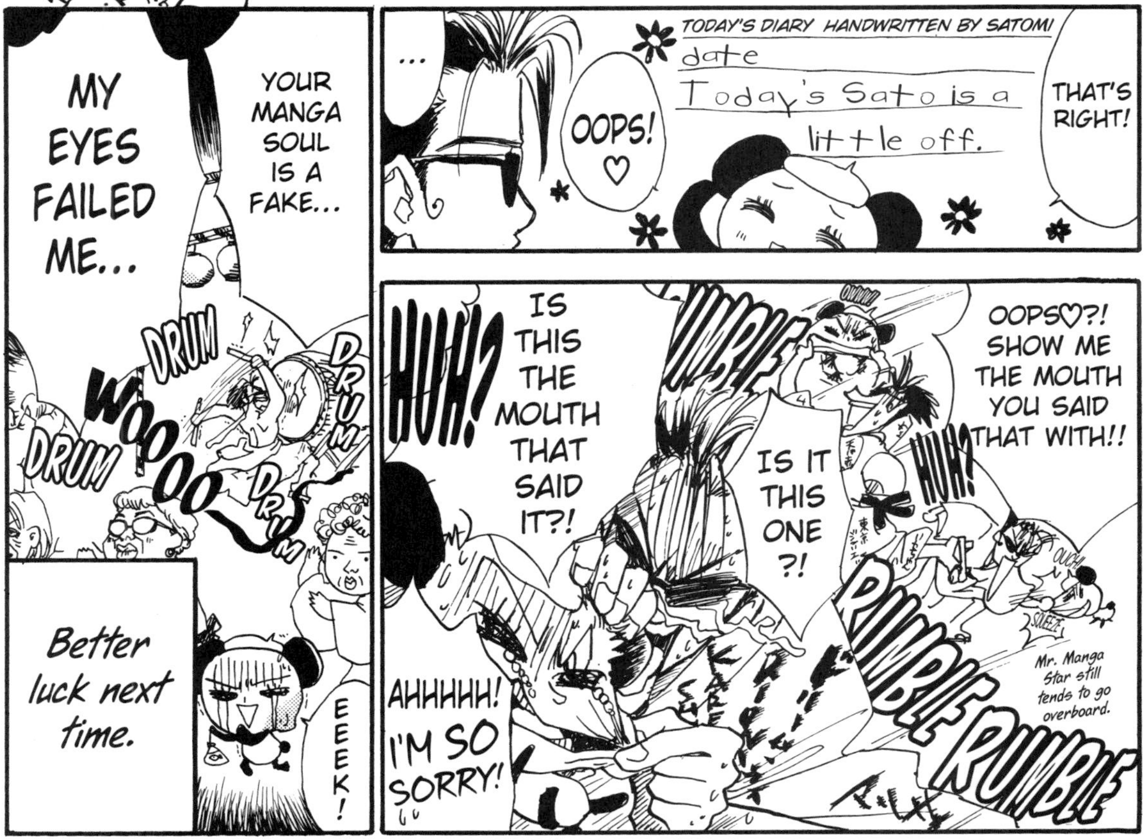
THAT'S RIGHT!
TODAY'S DIARY HANDWRITTEN BY SATOMI
date
Today's Sato is a little off.
OOPS! ♡
...
OOPS♡?! SHOW ME THE MOUTH YOU SAID THAT WITH!!
HUH?!
RUMBLE
IS THIS THE MOUTH THAT SAID IT?!
HUH?!
IS IT THIS ONE?!
OUCH
SQUEEZE
Mr. Manga Star still tends to go overboard.
RUMBLE RUMBLE
AHHHHH! I'M SO SORRY!
YOUR MANGA SOUL IS A FAKE...
MY EYES FAILED ME...
DRUM
DRUM
WOOOOO
DRUM
DRUM
Better luck next time.
EEEEK!

Check out Masami Takeuchi's manga to learn more about different background effects and how make your work more lively.

Manga Star Presents!! STEAL THIS FROM A PROFESSIONAL MANGA! Part 3

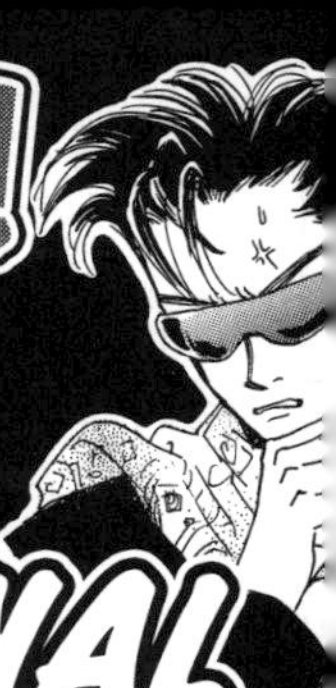

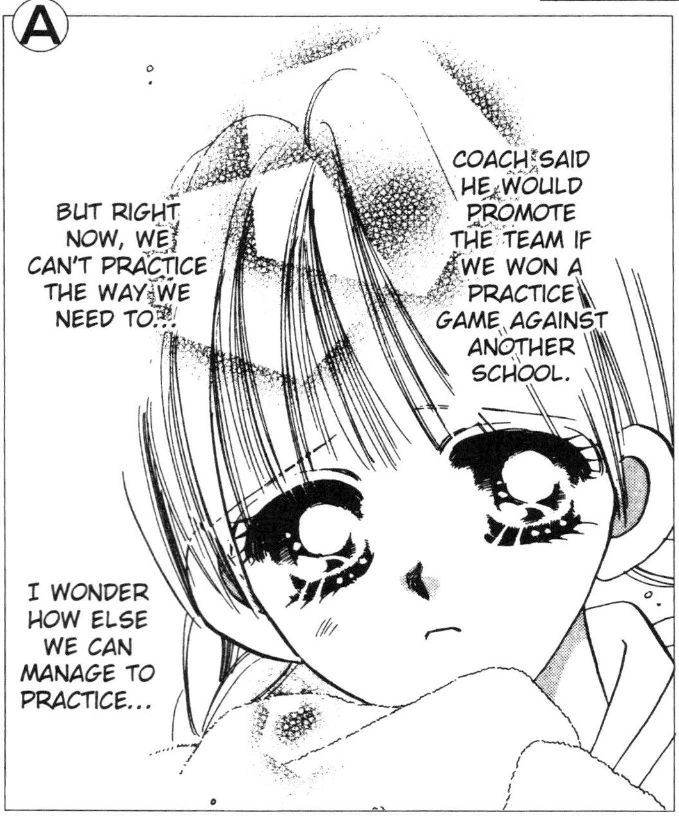
A
COACH SAID HE WOULD PROMOTE THE TEAM IF WE WON A PRACTICE GAME AGAINST ANOTHER SCHOOL.
BUT RIGHT NOW, WE CAN'T PRACTICE THE WAY WE NEED TO...
I WONDER HOW ELSE WE CAN MANAGE TO PRACTICE...

EFFECTS WITH A SCREEN TONE VERSUS EFFECTS BY HAND.

In terms of using screen tones, it's all about a good match. Can you see how the effects in the three panels are drawn differently?

The effects in "A" are from an existing screen tone, "B" was hand-stippled, and "C" was created by scraping a screen tone. If there's an appropriate screen tone, use it. If not, do it by hand. The perfect screen tone isn't always going to be around, so you have to learn how to do it by hand.

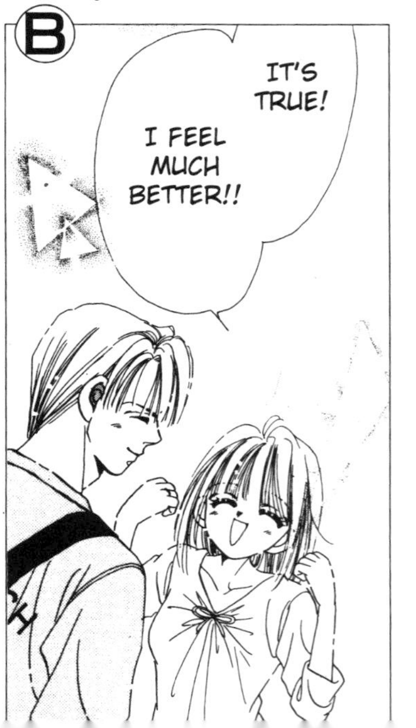
B
IT'S TRUE!
I FEEL MUCH BETTER!!

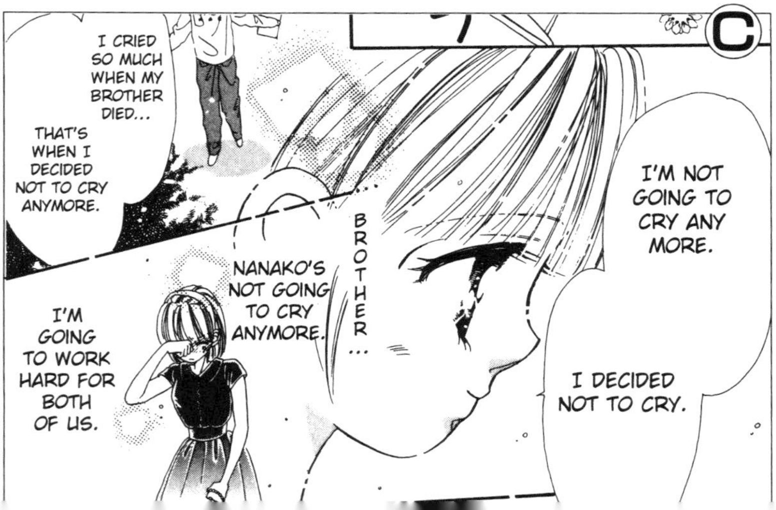
C
I'M NOT GOING TO CRY ANY MORE.
I CRIED SO MUCH WHEN MY BROTHER DIED...
THAT'S WHEN I DECIDED NOT TO CRY ANYMORE.
BROTHER...
NANAKO'S NOT GOING TO CRY ANYMORE.
I DECIDED NOT TO CRY.
I'M GOING TO WORK HARD FOR BOTH OF US.

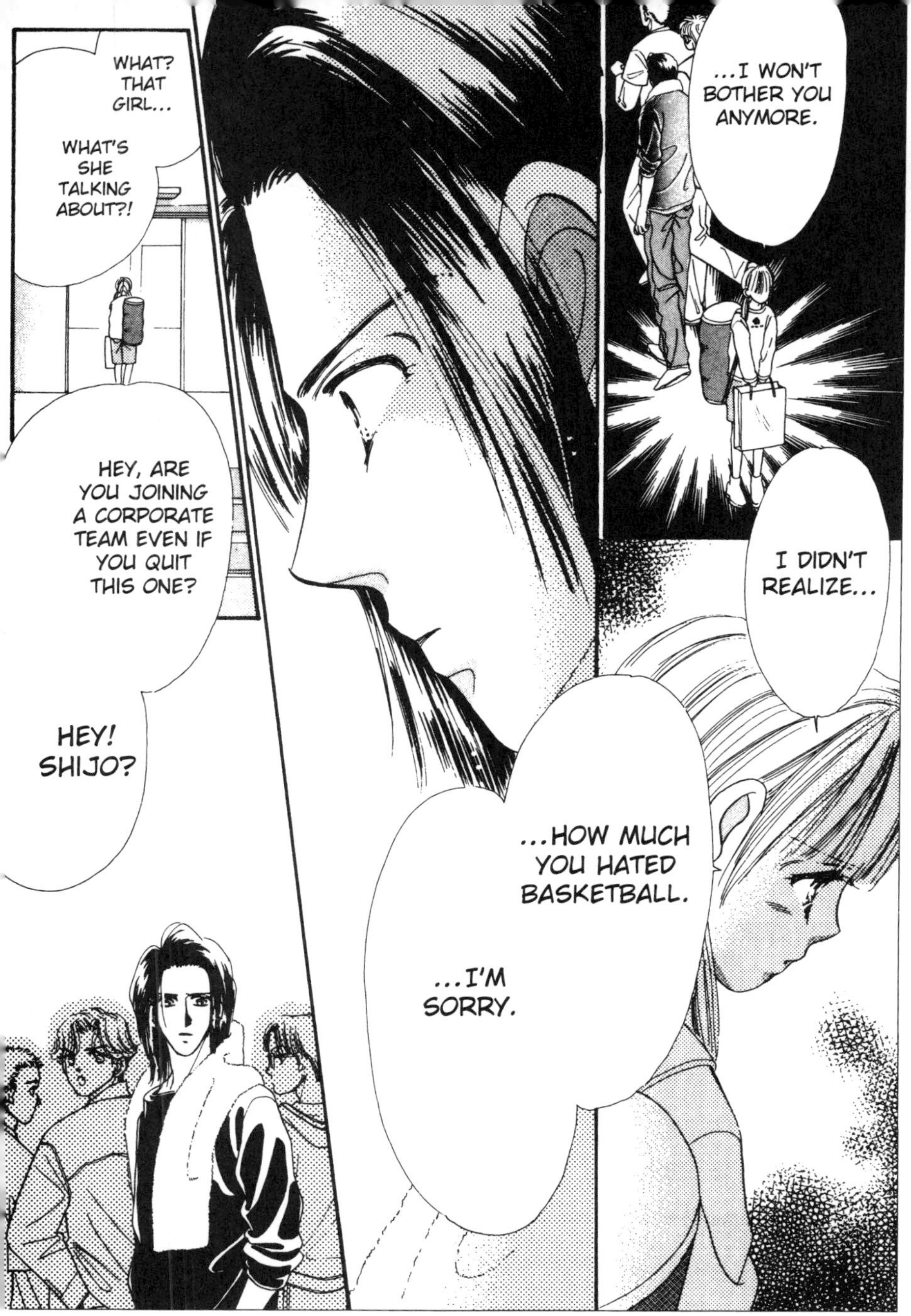
...I WON'T BOTHER YOU ANYMORE.
I DIDN'T REALIZE...
...HOW MUCH YOU HATED BASKETBALL.
...I'M SORRY.
WHAT? THAT GIRL...
WHAT'S SHE TALKING ABOUT?!
HEY, ARE YOU JOINING A CORPORATE TEAM EVEN IF YOU QUIT THIS ONE?
HEY! SHIJO?

THE EXTREME DIFFERENCE BETWEEN CLOSE-UPS AND LONG SHOTS IS GOOD.

This page may not seem like much, but there's a lot we can learn about the power of a page through it. When a close-up and a long shot coexist on the page, the close-up's power is accentuated, giving the scene some depth. But this depth is usually put on the backburner with new work. This is just an example of how pros take advantage of their works' spirit.

The audience knows the characters' positioning from the first panel, and the second and third panels close in on the characters' expressions. The third panel is the closest shot, and beginning with the fourth panel, the lens withdraws and emphasizes the character's sense of isolation.

CAREFULLY READ A PROFESSIONAL MANGA.

You may not notice when just reading a manga, but when you carefully look at a professional manga, there's a lot more depth than what first meets the eye. It's difficult to do this well when you're finally ready to draw your own, but this is the secret to a beautiful setting!

Also, check out how the lines are abbreviated in the smaller drawings compared to the big ones. The big drawings need to have screen tone effects or other considerations, or it'll look like something's missing!

CHAPTER 4: THE CHIE SHINOHARA EDITION

LET'S ORGANIZE THE PANELS!

Now that you're done with the story, let's start dividing it up into panels! We'll have Chie Shinohara fill us in on the art of panel formatting.

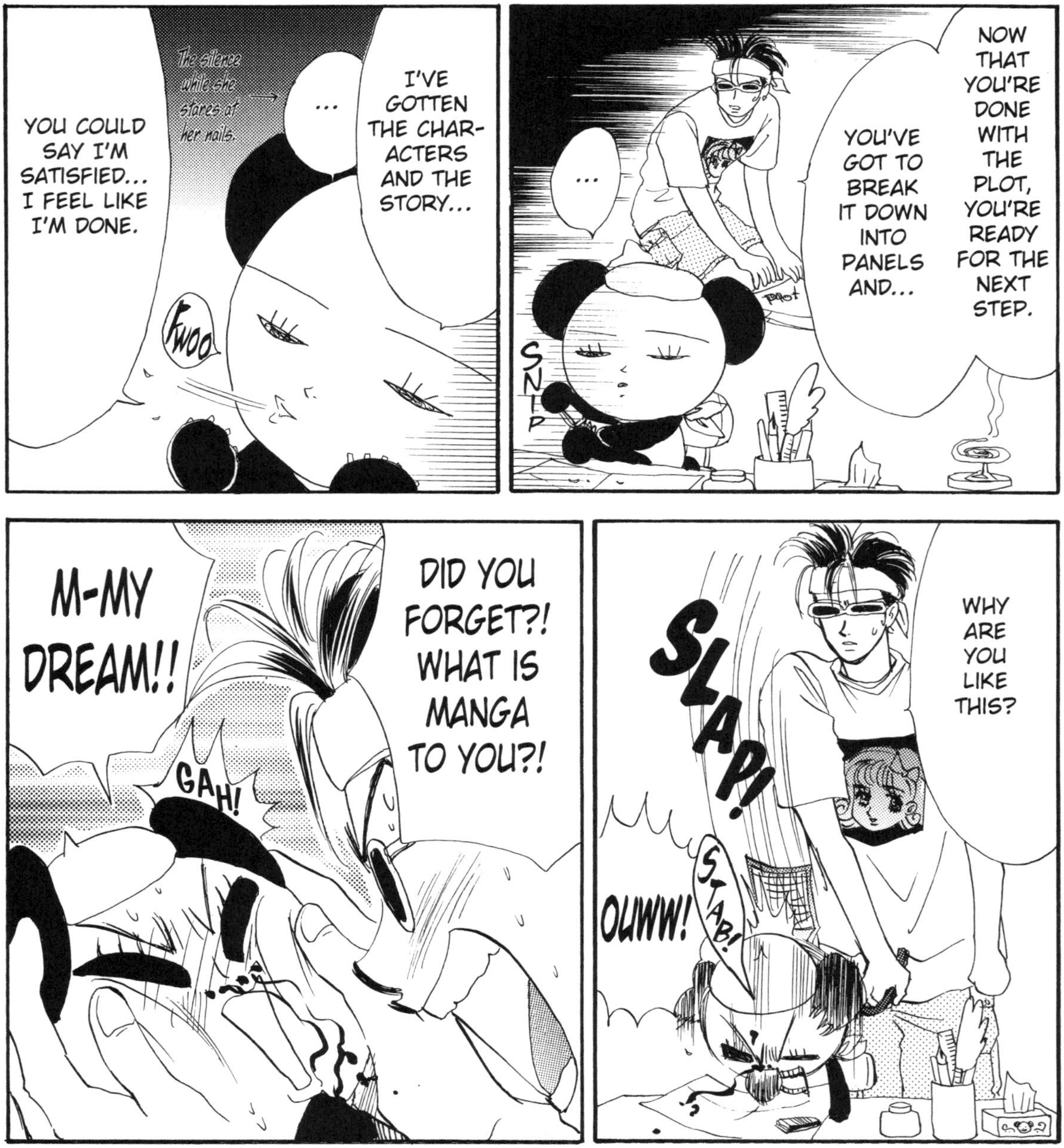
NOW THAT YOU'RE DONE WITH THE PLOT, YOU'RE READY FOR THE NEXT STEP.
YOU'VE GOT TO BREAK IT DOWN INTO PANELS AND...
...
Plot
SNIP
I'VE GOTTEN THE CHARACTERS AND THE STORY...
...
The silence while she stares at her nails.
YOU COULD SAY I'M SATISFIED... I FEEL LIKE I'M DONE.
FWOO
WHY ARE YOU LIKE THIS?
SLAP!
STAB!
OUWW!
DID YOU FORGET?! WHAT IS MANGA TO YOU?!
M-MY DREAM!!
GAH!

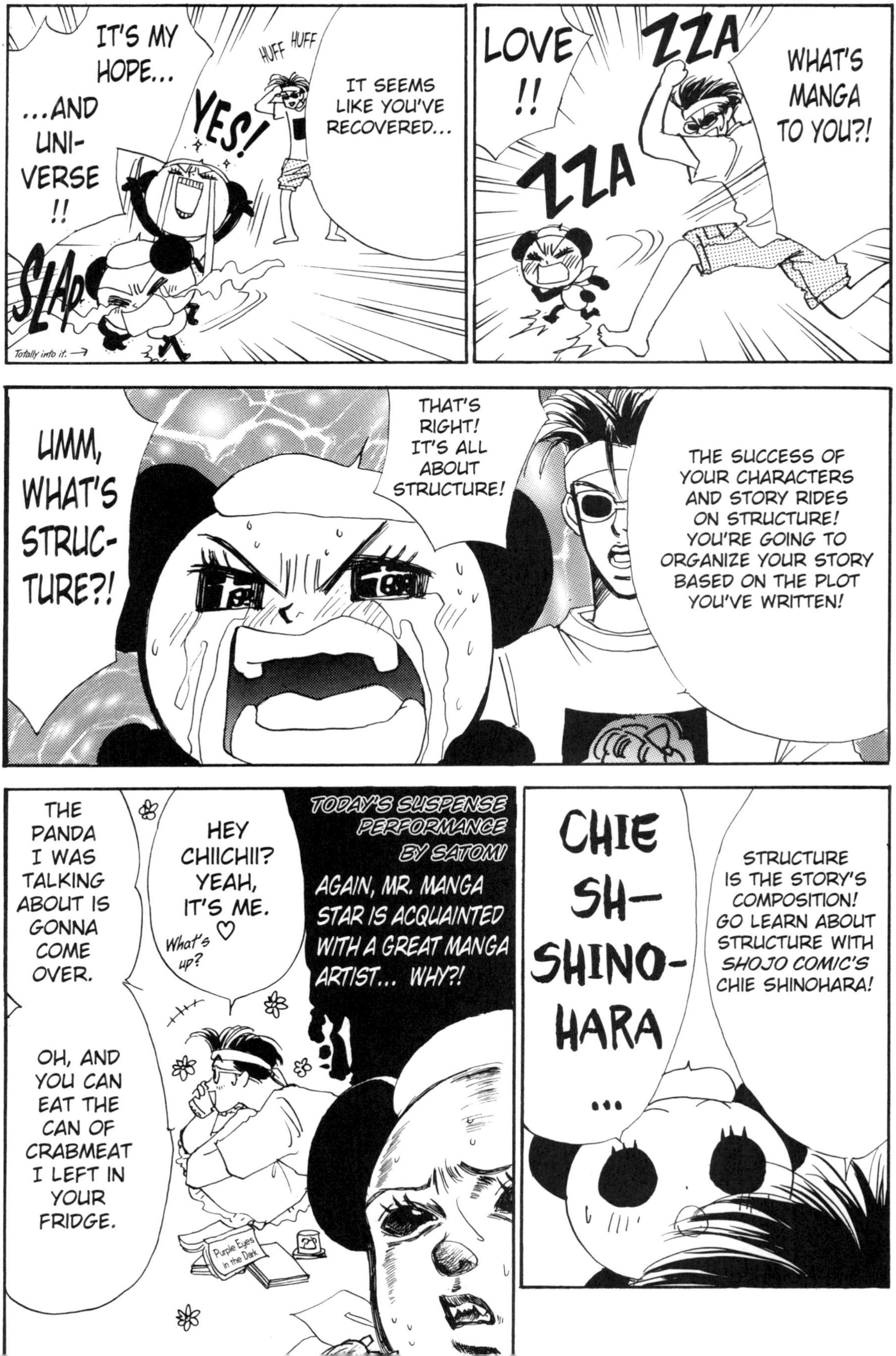
WHAT'S MANGA TO YOU?!
ZZA
LOVE !!
ZZA
IT SEEMS LIKE YOU'VE RECOVERED...
HUFF HUFF
IT'S MY HOPE...
YES!
...AND UNI-VERSE !!
SLAP
Totally into it.
THE SUCCESS OF YOUR CHARACTERS AND STORY RIDES ON STRUCTURE! YOU'RE GOING TO ORGANIZE YOUR STORY BASED ON THE PLOT YOU'VE WRITTEN!
THAT'S RIGHT! IT'S ALL ABOUT STRUCTURE!
UMM, WHAT'S STRUC-TURE?!
STRUCTURE IS THE STORY'S COMPOSITION! GO LEARN ABOUT STRUCTURE WITH SHOJO COMIC'S CHIE SHINOHARA!
CHIE SH-SHINO-HARA ...
TODAY'S SUSPENSE PERFORMANCE BY SATOMI
AGAIN, MR. MANGA STAR IS ACQUAINTED WITH A GREAT MANGA ARTIST... WHY?!
HEY CHIICHII? YEAH, IT'S ME.
What's up?
THE PANDA I WAS TALKING ABOUT IS GONNA COME OVER.
OH, AND YOU CAN EAT THE CAN OF CRABMEAT I LEFT IN YOUR FRIDGE.
Purple Eyes in the Dark

WHAT'S A STORYBOARD?!

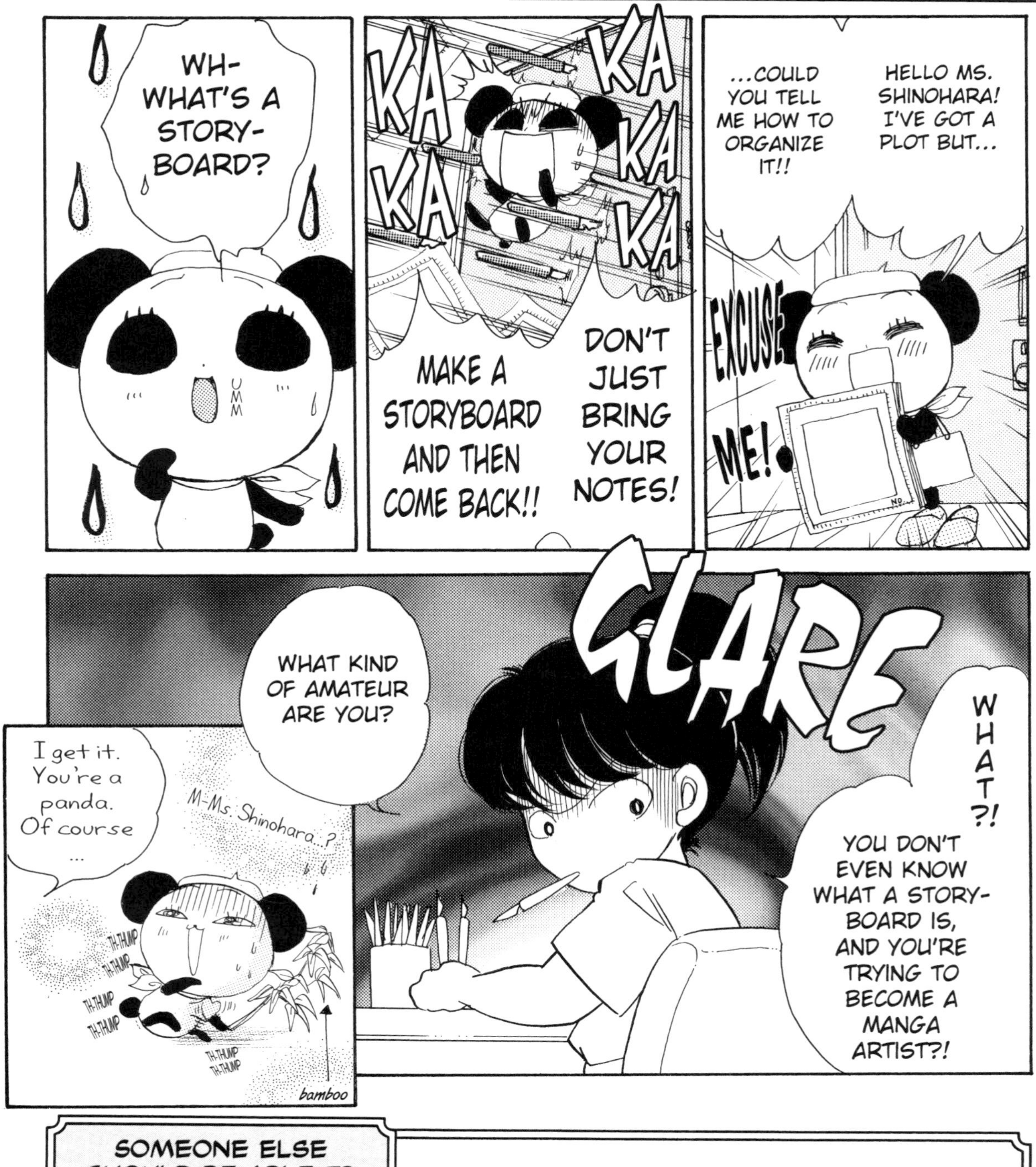
HELLO MS. SHINOHARA! I'VE GOT A PLOT BUT...
...COULD YOU TELL ME HOW TO ORGANIZE IT!!
EXCUSE ME!
KA KA KA
KA KA KA
DON'T JUST BRING YOUR NOTES!
MAKE A STORYBOARD AND THEN COME BACK!!
WH-WHAT'S A STORY-BOARD?
UMM
GLARE
WHAT?!
YOU DON'T EVEN KNOW WHAT A STORY-BOARD IS, AND YOU'RE TRYING TO BECOME A MANGA ARTIST?!
WHAT KIND OF AMATEUR ARE YOU?
M-Ms. Shinohara...?
I get it. You're a panda. Of course ...
TH-THUMP TH-THUMP
TH-THUMP TH-THUMP
TH-THUMP TH-THUMP
bamboo

SOMEONE ELSE SHOULD BE ABLE TO UNDERSTAND YOUR STORYBOARD.

A storyboard is a rough, rough draft. You think that as long as ***you*** understand it, it's okay, right? But when you become a professional, you'll have meetings with your editor based on this storyboard. So it needs to be something that clearly shows the flow of the story, no matter who reads it! Some professionals write the name of the character on the character's face, so the rough outlines can be differentiated, but while you're still a newbie, you should try to draw a complete picture. The more you draw, the better you'll get—so think about it as practice, and don't give up!

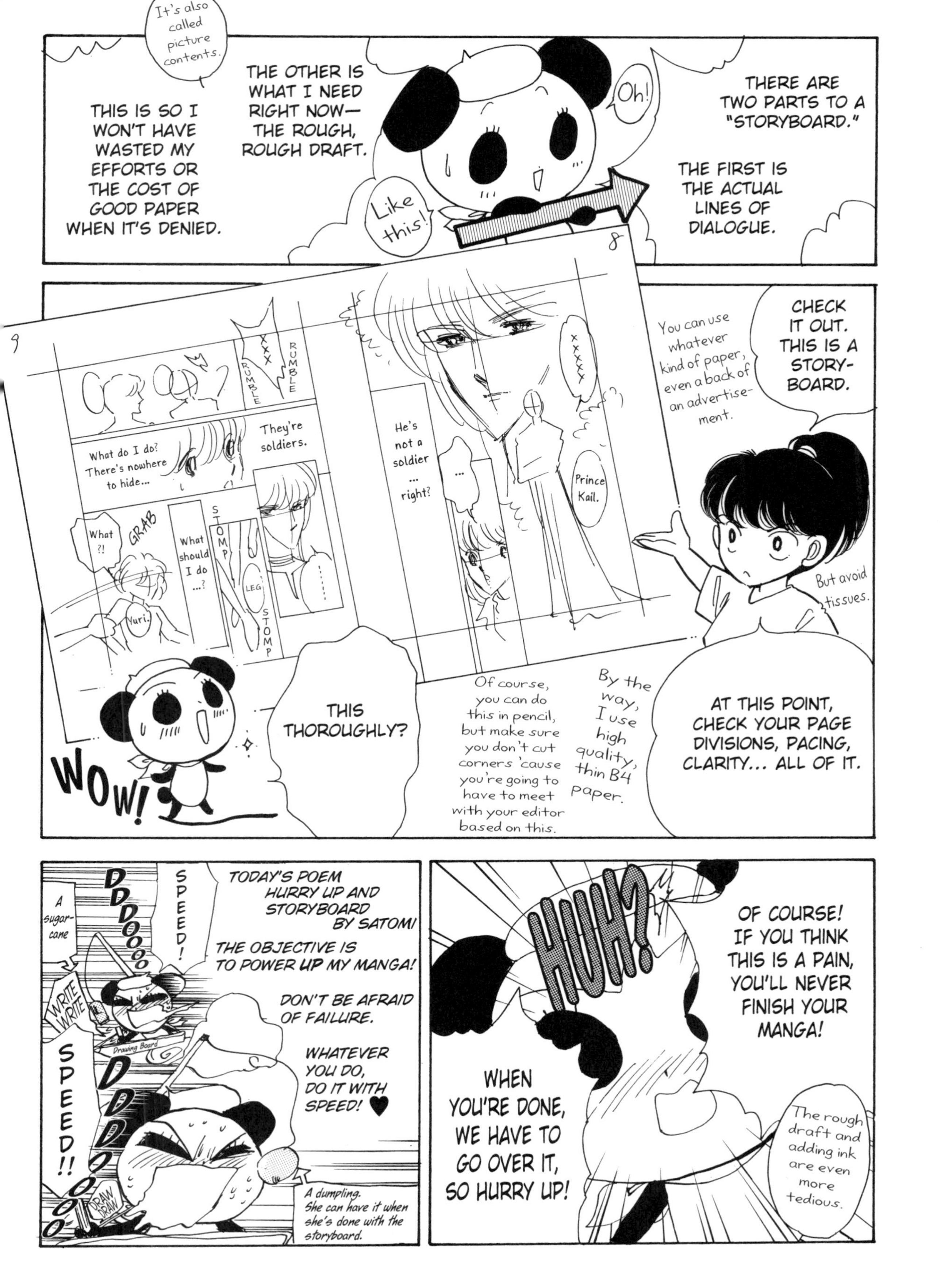
THERE ARE TWO PARTS TO A "STORYBOARD."
THE FIRST IS THE ACTUAL LINES OF DIALOGUE.
Oh!
Like this!
THE OTHER IS WHAT I NEED RIGHT NOW— THE ROUGH, ROUGH DRAFT.
It's also called picture contents.
THIS IS SO I WON'T HAVE WASTED MY EFFORTS OR THE COST OF GOOD PAPER WHEN IT'S DENIED.
CHECK IT OUT. THIS IS A STORY-BOARD.
You can use whatever kind of paper, even a back of an advertise-ment.
But avoid tissues.
8
XXXXX
Prince Kail.
He's not a soldier ... right?
...
9
RUMBLE
XXX
RUMBLE
They're soldiers.
What do I do? There's nowhere to hide...
What ?!
GRAB
What should I do ...?
STOMP
LEG
STOMP
Yuri.
AT THIS POINT, CHECK YOUR PAGE DIVISIONS, PACING, CLARITY... ALL OF IT.
By the way, I use high quality, thin B4 paper.
Of course, you can do this in pencil, but make sure you don't cut corners 'cause you're going to have to meet with your editor based on this.
THIS THOROUGHLY?
WOW!
OF COURSE! IF YOU THINK THIS IS A PAIN, YOU'LL NEVER FINISH YOUR MANGA!
HUH?
WHEN YOU'RE DONE, WE HAVE TO GO OVER IT, SO HURRY UP!
The rough draft and adding ink are even more tedious.
TODAY'S POEM HURRY UP AND STORYBOARD BY SATOMI
THE OBJECTIVE IS TO POWER UP MY MANGA!
DON'T BE AFRAID OF FAILURE.
WHATEVER YOU DO, DO IT WITH SPEED! ♥
SPEED!
DDDOOOOO
A sugar-cane
WRITE WRITE
Drawing Board
SPEED!!
DDDDOOOOO
DRAW DRAW
A dumpling. She can have it when she's done with the storyboard.

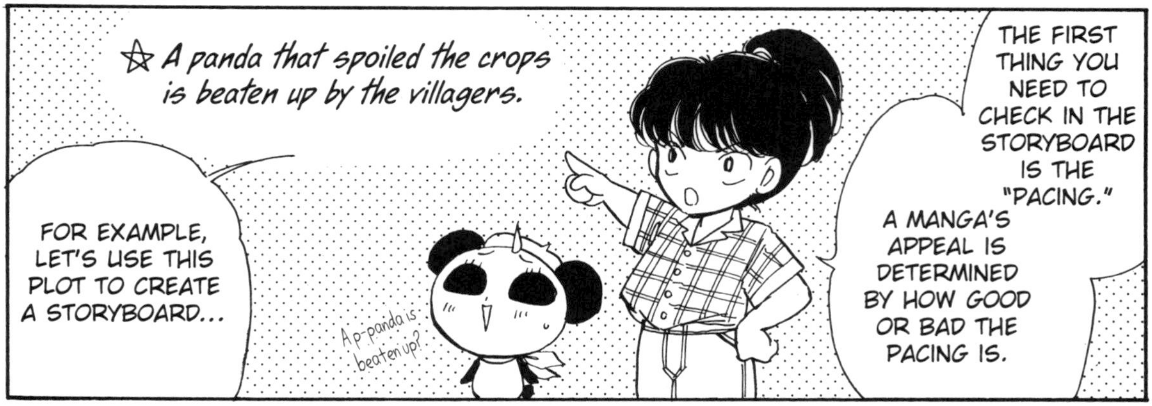
THE FIRST THING YOU NEED TO CHECK IN THE STORYBOARD IS THE "PACING."
A MANGA'S APPEAL IS DETERMINED BY HOW GOOD OR BAD THE PACING IS.
☆ A panda that spoiled the crops is beaten up by the villagers.
A p-panda is beaten up?
FOR EXAMPLE, LET'S USE THIS PLOT TO CREATE A STORYBOARD...

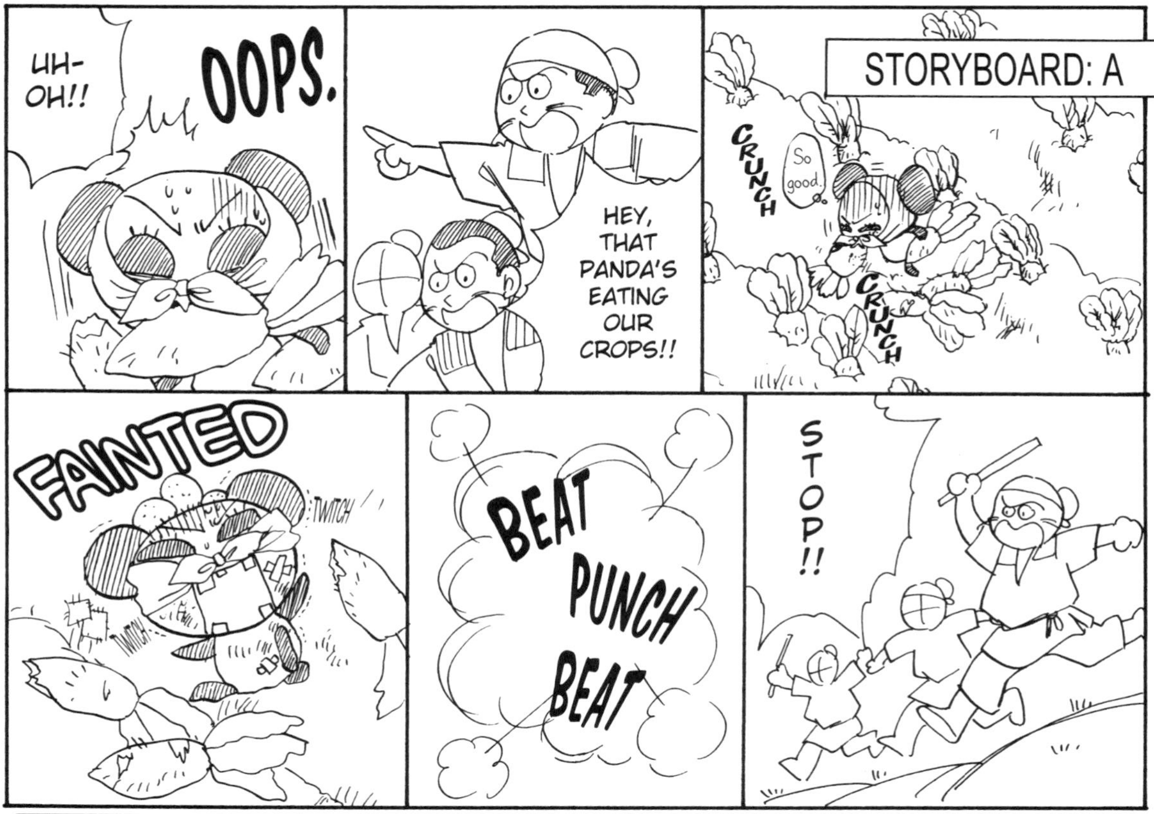
STORYBOARD: A
CRUNCH
So good.
CRUNCH
HEY, THAT PANDA'S EATING OUR CROPS!!
OOPS.
UH-OH!!
STOP!!
BEAT
PUNCH
BEAT
FAINTED
TWITCH
TWITCH

DON'T SPEND TIME ON THE CONVERSATION INSTEAD OF IMPROVING THE PACING.

I'll teach you a trick to improve the pacing. It's to "not answer what the other is asking!" For example...

A: "Wanna go to a concert?"
B: "Yeah."
A: "I forgot that ************'s concert's coming up!"
B: "I wanna go!!"

This conversation can easily be...

A: "Wanna go to a concert?"
B: "Let's go to ************'s concert!!"

By eliminating agreeable responses when engaged in a conversation, you can shave off lines and improve the pacing. The point is not to mold the conversation to the person you're conversing with.

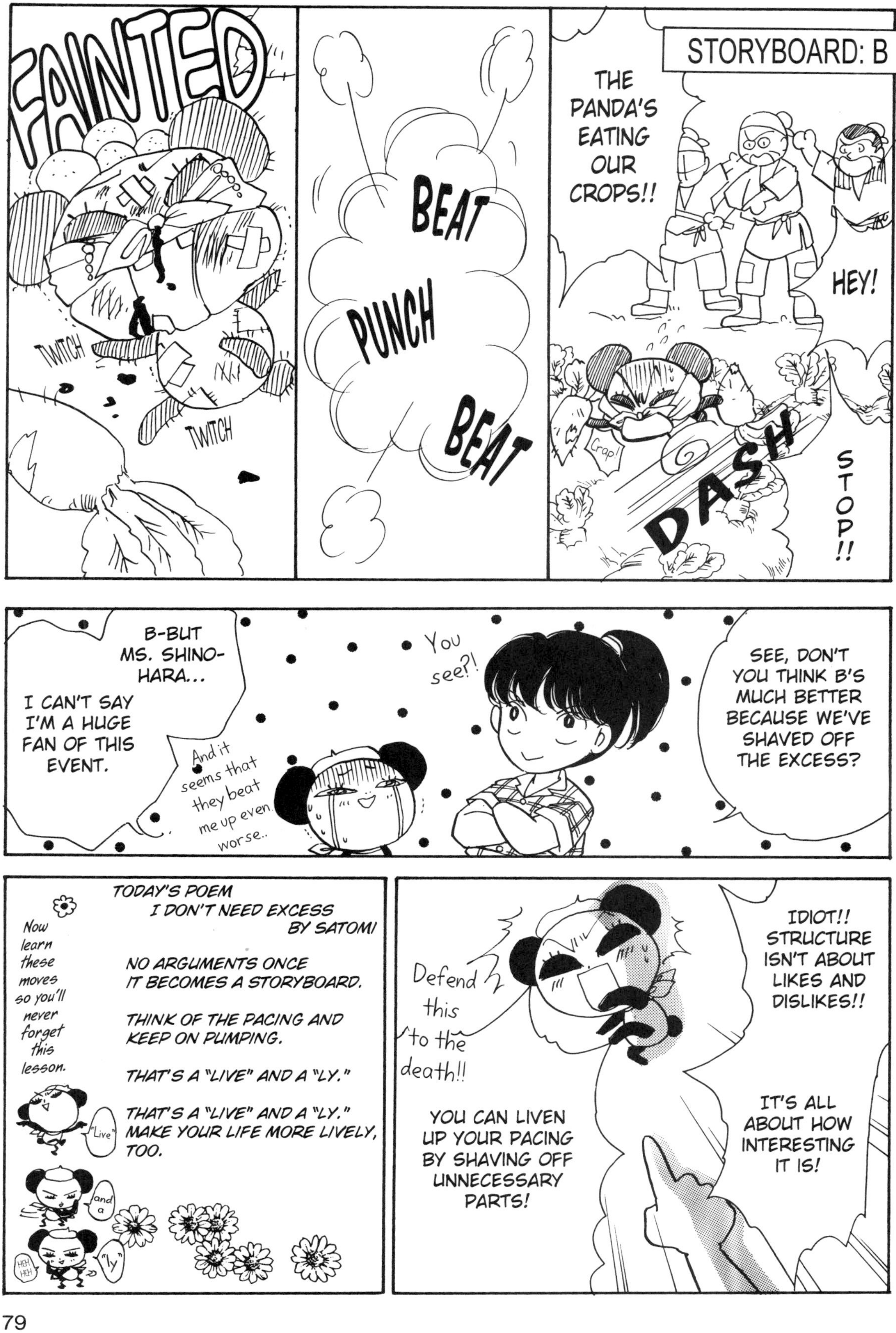
STORYBOARD: B
THE PANDA'S EATING OUR CROPS!!
HEY!
Crap!
DASH
STOP!!
BEAT
PUNCH
BEAT
FAINTED
TWITCH
TWITCH
SEE, DON'T YOU THINK B'S MUCH BETTER BECAUSE WE'VE SHAVED OFF THE EXCESS?
You see?!
B-BUT MS. SHINO-HARA...
I CAN'T SAY I'M A HUGE FAN OF THIS EVENT.
And it seems that they beat me up even worse..
IDIOT!! STRUCTURE ISN'T ABOUT LIKES AND DISLIKES!!
IT'S ALL ABOUT HOW INTERESTING IT IS!
Defend this to the death!!
YOU CAN LIVEN UP YOUR PACING BY SHAVING OFF UNNECESSARY PARTS!
TODAY'S POEM
I DON'T NEED EXCESS
BY SATOMI
NO ARGUMENTS ONCE IT BECOMES A STORYBOARD.
THINK OF THE PACING AND KEEP ON PUMPING.
THAT'S A "LIVE" AND A "LY."
THAT'S A "LIVE" AND A "LY." MAKE YOUR LIFE MORE LIVELY, TOO.
Now learn these moves so you'll never forget this lesson.
"Live"
and a
"ly"
HEH HEH

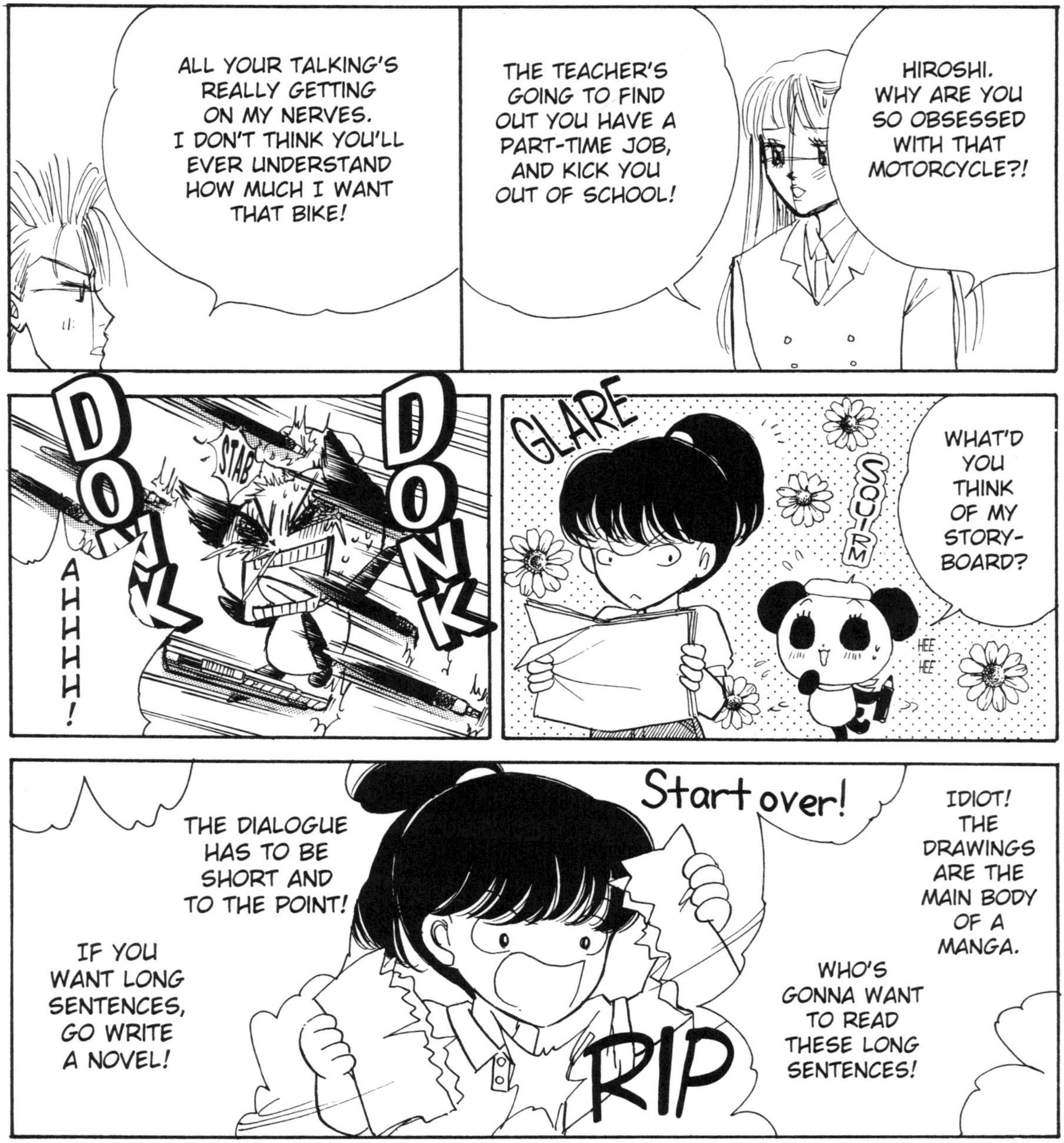
HIROSHI. WHY ARE YOU SO OBSESSED WITH THAT MOTORCYCLE?!
THE TEACHER'S GOING TO FIND OUT YOU HAVE A PART-TIME JOB, AND KICK YOU OUT OF SCHOOL!
ALL YOUR TALKING'S REALLY GETTING ON MY NERVES. I DON'T THINK YOU'LL EVER UNDERSTAND HOW MUCH I WANT THAT BIKE!
WHAT'D YOU THINK OF MY STORY-BOARD?
GLARE
SQUIRM
HEE HEE
DONK
STAB
DONK
AHHHH!
IDIOT! THE DRAWINGS ARE THE MAIN BODY OF A MANGA.
Start over!
WHO'S GONNA WANT TO READ THESE LONG SENTENCES!
RIP
THE DIALOGUE HAS TO BE SHORT AND TO THE POINT!
IF YOU WANT LONG SENTENCES, GO WRITE A NOVEL!

SHOW, DON'T TELL.

One of the biggest obstacles for newcomers is relying too much on dialogue. They tend to explain the characters' feelings and situations through dialogue. Of course, there are situations where this is necessary, but take an extra minute when you're creating the storyboard to think whether it's something you can express through your drawings instead. Like if it's a scene where the character is about to be surprised, try not to express that through dialogue. Instead, you can even make the character drop something to express it through action. It sounds old-fashioned, but it can be really effective.

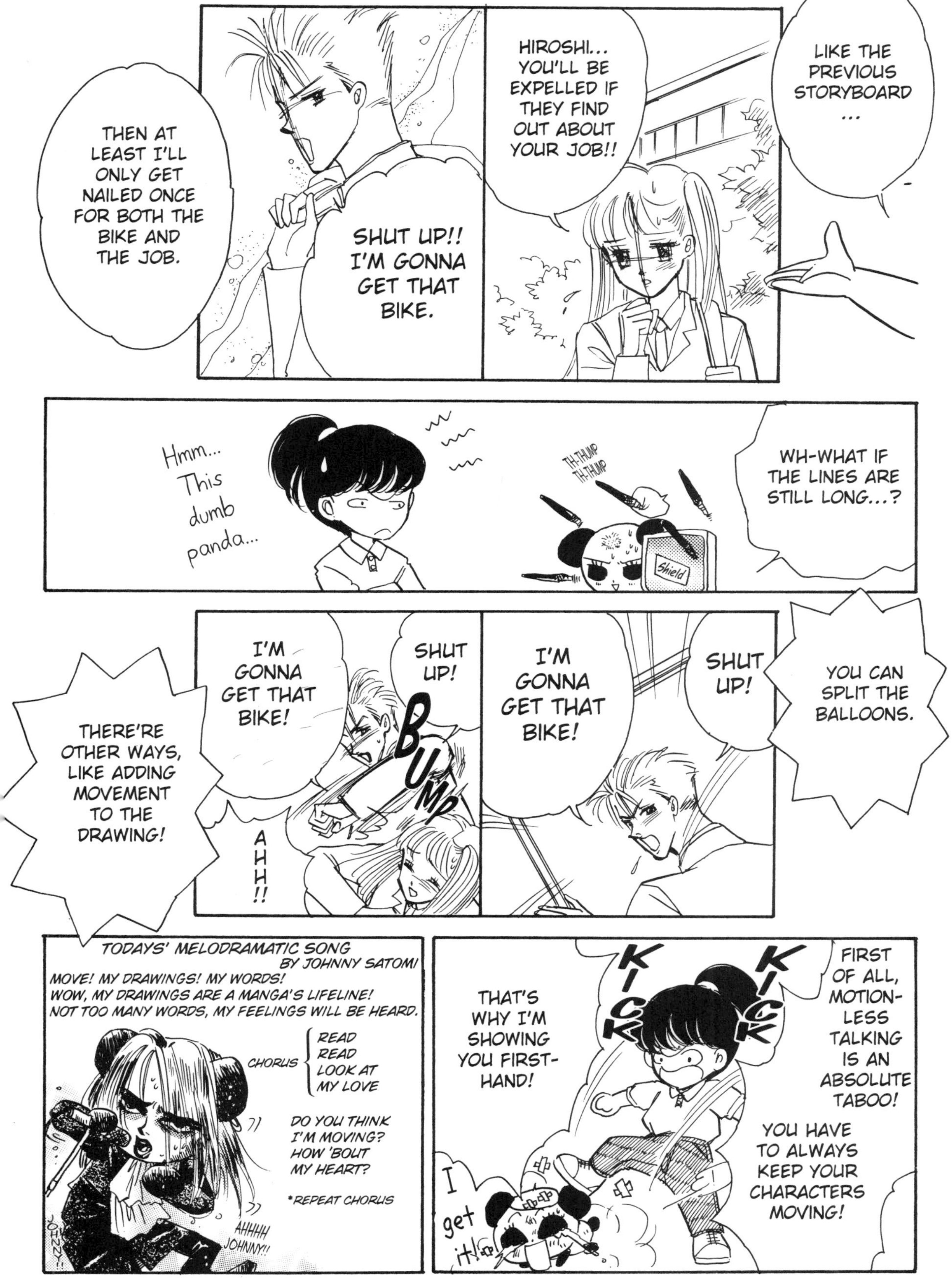
LIKE THE PREVIOUS STORYBOARD ...
HIROSHI... YOU'LL BE EXPELLED IF THEY FIND OUT ABOUT YOUR JOB!!
SHUT UP!! I'M GONNA GET THAT BIKE.
THEN AT LEAST I'LL ONLY GET NAILED ONCE FOR BOTH THE BIKE AND THE JOB.
WH-WHAT IF THE LINES ARE STILL LONG...?
TH-THUMP TH-THUMP
Shield
Hmm... This dumb panda...
YOU CAN SPLIT THE BALLOONS.
SHUT UP!
I'M GONNA GET THAT BIKE!
SHUT UP!
I'M GONNA GET THAT BIKE!
BUMP
AHH!!
THERE'RE OTHER WAYS, LIKE ADDING MOVEMENT TO THE DRAWING!
FIRST OF ALL, MOTION-LESS TALKING IS AN ABSOLUTE TABOO!
KICK
KICK
THAT'S WHY I'M SHOWING YOU FIRST-HAND!
YOU HAVE TO ALWAYS KEEP YOUR CHARACTERS MOVING!
I get it!
TODAYS' MELODRAMATIC SONG
BY JOHNNY SATOMI
MOVE! MY DRAWINGS! MY WORDS!
WOW, MY DRAWINGS ARE A MANGA'S LIFELINE!
NOT TOO MANY WORDS, MY FEELINGS WILL BE HEARD.
CHORUS { READ READ LOOK AT MY LOVE
DO YOU THINK I'M MOVING? HOW 'BOUT MY HEART?
*REPEAT CHORUS
AHHHH JOHNNY!!
JOHNNY!!

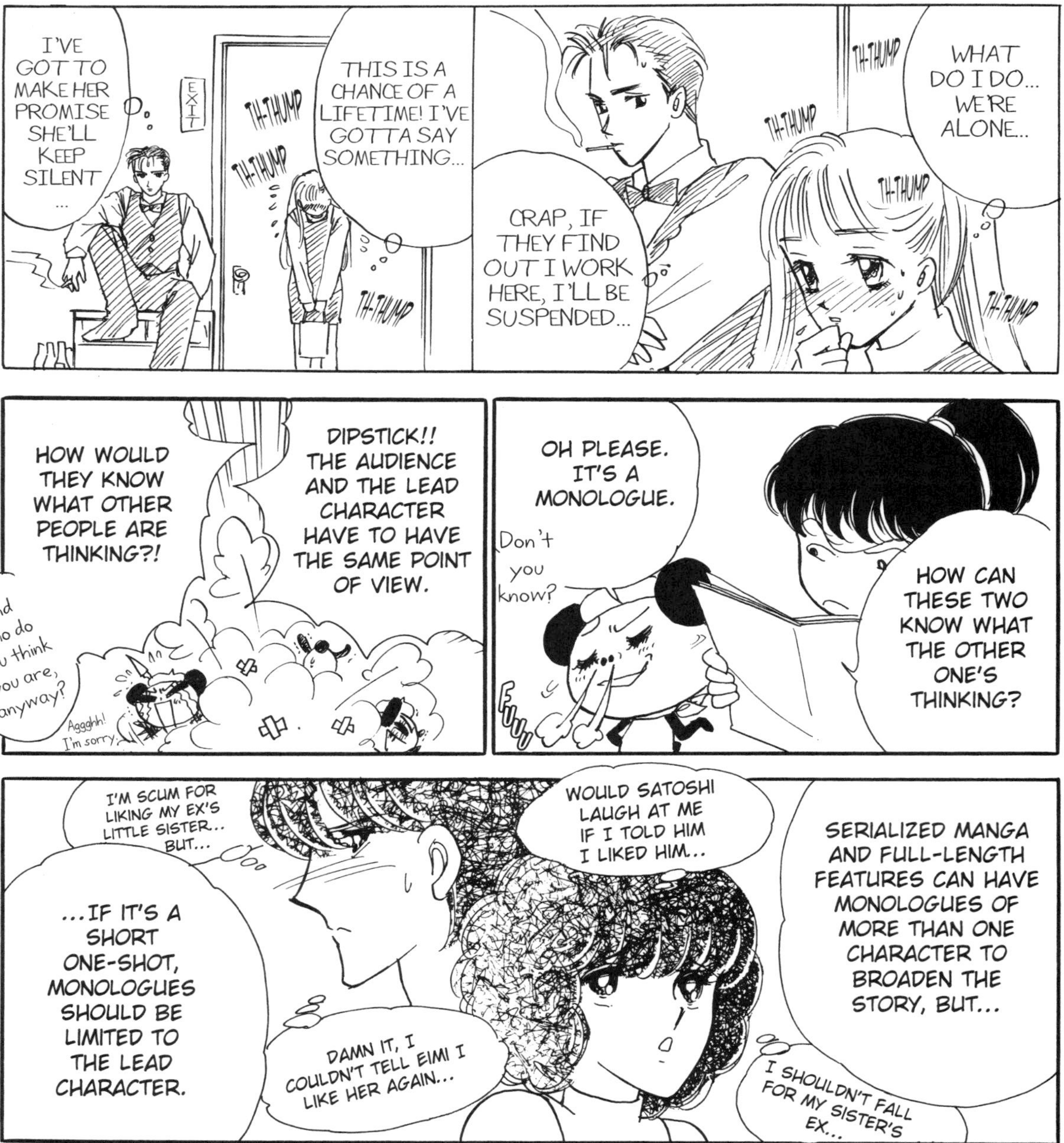
WHAT DO I DO... WE'RE ALONE...
TH-THUMP
CRAP, IF THEY FIND OUT I WORK HERE, I'LL BE SUSPENDED...
THIS IS A CHANCE OF A LIFETIME! I'VE GOTTA SAY SOMETHING...
TH-THUMP
EXIT
I'VE GOT TO MAKE HER PROMISE SHE'LL KEEP SILENT...
HOW CAN THESE TWO KNOW WHAT THE OTHER ONE'S THINKING?
OH PLEASE. IT'S A MONOLOGUE.
Don't you know?
FUUU
HOW WOULD THEY KNOW WHAT OTHER PEOPLE ARE THINKING?!
DIPSTICK!! THE AUDIENCE AND THE LEAD CHARACTER HAVE TO HAVE THE SAME POINT OF VIEW.
And who do you think you are, anyway?
Aggghh! I'm sorry.
SERIALIZED MANGA AND FULL-LENGTH FEATURES CAN HAVE MONOLOGUES OF MORE THAN ONE CHARACTER TO BROADEN THE STORY, BUT...
WOULD SATOSHI LAUGH AT ME IF I TOLD HIM I LIKED HIM...
I'M SCUM FOR LIKING MY EX'S LITTLE SISTER... BUT...
I SHOULDN'T FALL FOR MY SISTER'S EX...
DAMN IT, I COULDN'T TELL EIMI I LIKE HER AGAIN...
...IF IT'S A SHORT ONE-SHOT, MONOLOGUES SHOULD BE LIMITED TO THE LEAD CHARACTER.

LONG LINES SHOULD BE DIVIDED INTO SHORT, EASY-TO-READ SECTIONS.

Long lines are nothing but a pain for the readers, and that doesn't just go for the monologues. But if there are lines that you just can't cut, you should divide them into smaller parts with different balloons. If it's a scene that requires a lot of explaining, you should have extra pages and panels using both words and action. That should prevent at least a little boredom. It's slightly advanced, but another effective way of maintaining the readers' attention is to split the explanation into different scenes. You should do your best to avoid long subtitles and lines of dialogue.

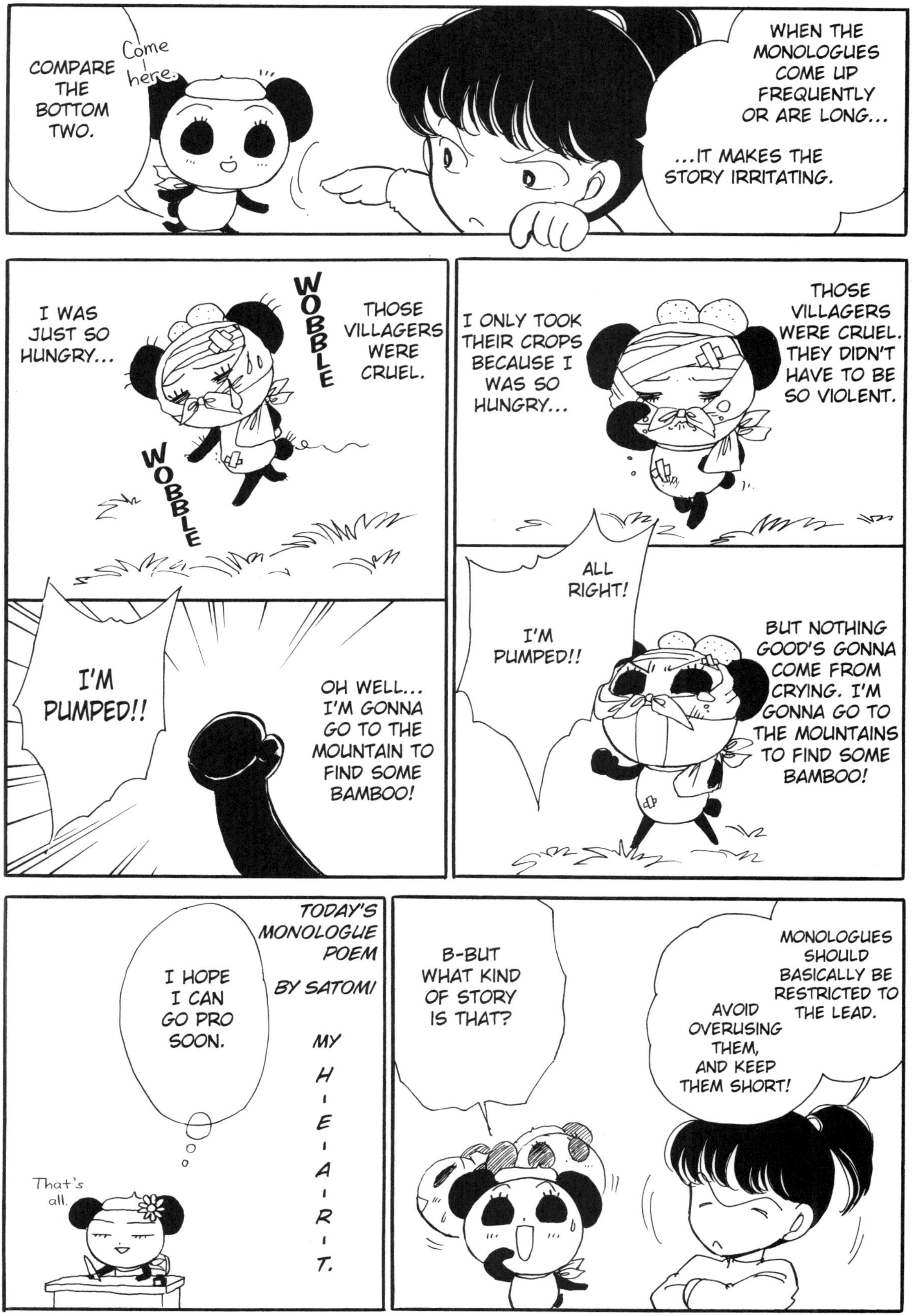

WHEN THE MONOLOGUES COME UP FREQUENTLY OR ARE LONG...
...IT MAKES THE STORY IRRITATING.
COMPARE THE BOTTOM TWO.
Come here.
THOSE VILLAGERS WERE CRUEL. THEY DIDN'T HAVE TO BE SO VIOLENT.
I ONLY TOOK THEIR CROPS BECAUSE I WAS SO HUNGRY...
BUT NOTHING GOOD'S GONNA COME FROM CRYING. I'M GONNA GO TO THE MOUNTAINS TO FIND SOME BAMBOO!
ALL RIGHT!
I'M PUMPED!!
THOSE VILLAGERS WERE CRUEL.
WOBBLE
I WAS JUST SO HUNGRY...
WOBBLE
OH WELL... I'M GONNA GO TO THE MOUNTAIN TO FIND SOME BAMBOO!
I'M PUMPED!!
MONOLOGUES SHOULD BASICALLY BE RESTRICTED TO THE LEAD.
AVOID OVERUSING THEM, AND KEEP THEM SHORT!
B-BUT WHAT KIND OF STORY IS THAT?
TODAY'S MONOLOGUE POEM BY SATOMI
MY H-E-A-R-T.
I HOPE I CAN GO PRO SOON.
That's all.

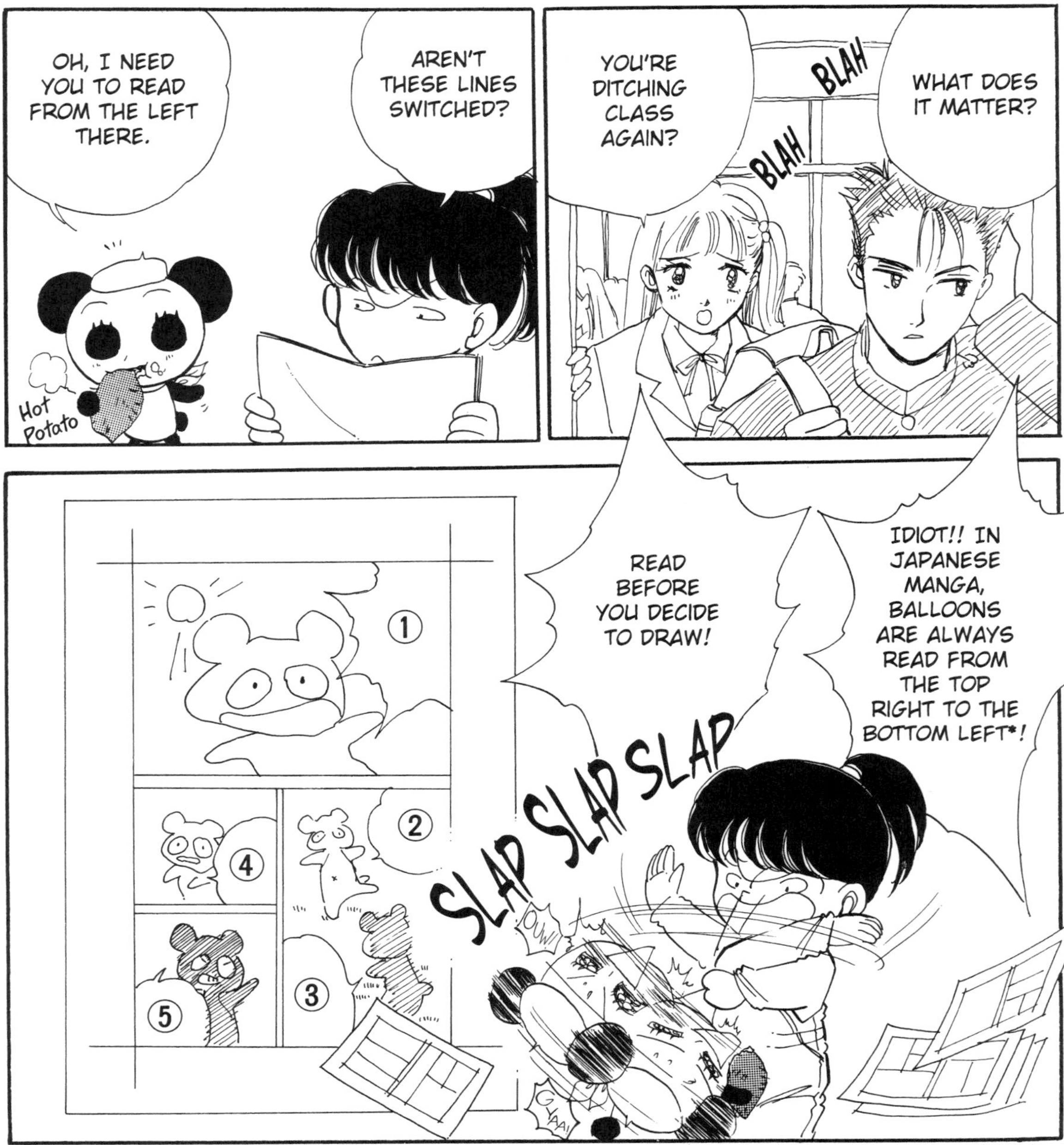
YOU'RE DITCHING CLASS AGAIN?
BLAH
BLAH
WHAT DOES IT MATTER?
AREN'T THESE LINES SWITCHED?
OH, I NEED YOU TO READ FROM THE LEFT THERE.
Hot Potato
IDIOT!! IN JAPANESE MANGA, BALLOONS ARE ALWAYS READ FROM THE TOP RIGHT TO THE BOTTOM LEFT*!
READ BEFORE YOU DECIDE TO DRAW!
SLAP SLAP SLAP SLAP
OUW!
GYAAI
1
2
3
4
5

*This is because Japanese is read right-to-left. In English, the balloons and panels are read left-to-right.

USE A PEN FOR THE BALLOON AND A PENCIL FOR THE DIALOGUE.

Entry requirements for manga contests always say that "dialogue must be written in pencil," but I've seen submissions where even the balloons were drawn using a pencil. I don't want anyone to take offense, but the balloons should be considered part of the illustration, and therefore be done in pen. Only the dialogue should be done in pencil. And the balloon shape here is just one example! Try to develop an original balloon that fits both the page and the scene's mood. Creativity is needed for drawing manga…not just for the balloons.

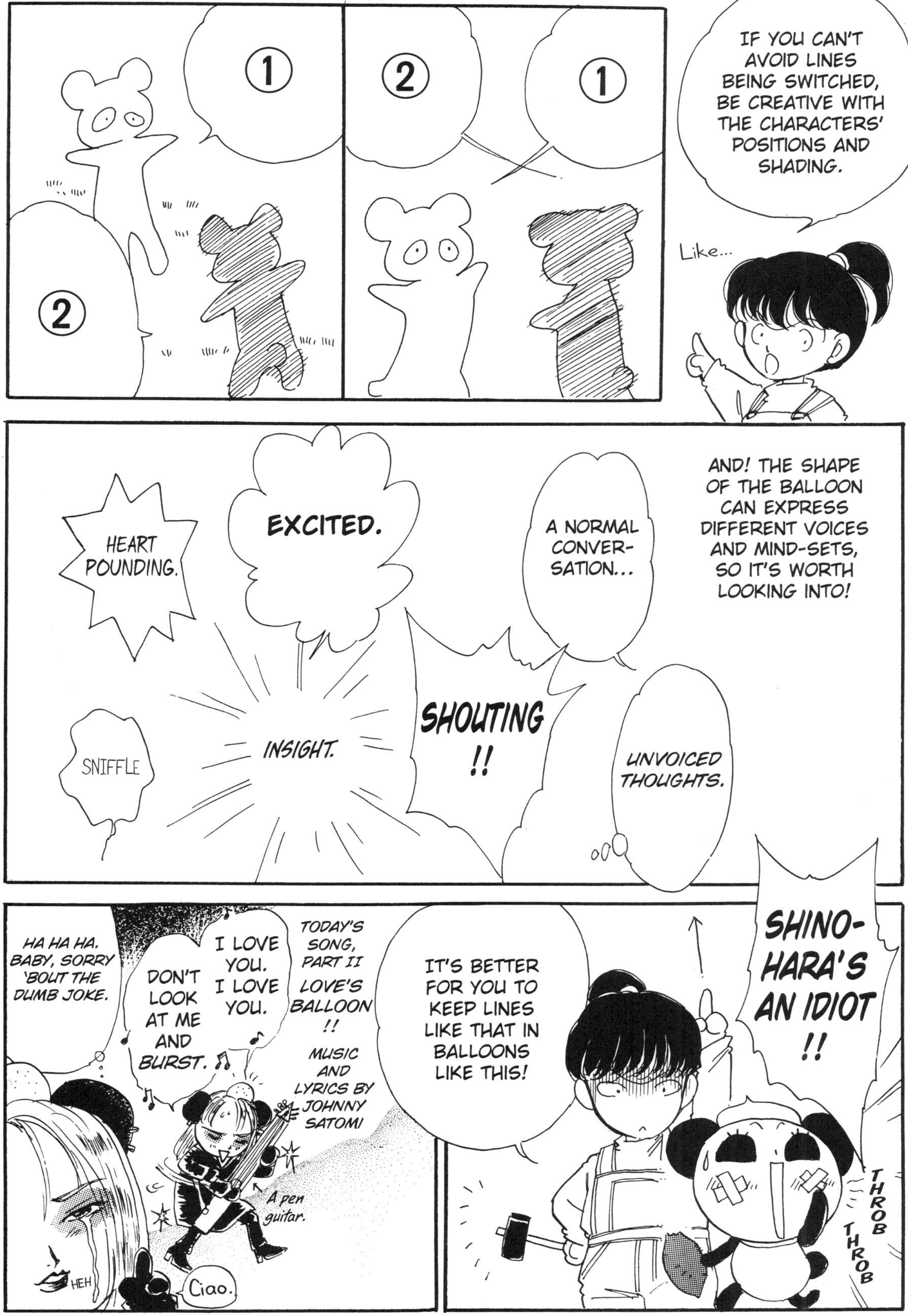
IF YOU CAN'T AVOID LINES BEING SWITCHED, BE CREATIVE WITH THE CHARACTERS' POSITIONS AND SHADING.
Like...
①
②
①
②
AND! THE SHAPE OF THE BALLOON CAN EXPRESS DIFFERENT VOICES AND MIND-SETS, SO IT'S WORTH LOOKING INTO!
A NORMAL CONVER-SATION...
EXCITED.
HEART POUNDING.
UNVOICED THOUGHTS.
SHOUTING !!
INSIGHT.
SNIFFLE
SHINO-HARA'S AN IDIOT !!
IT'S BETTER FOR YOU TO KEEP LINES LIKE THAT IN BALLOONS LIKE THIS!
THROB
THROB
TODAY'S SONG, PART II LOVE'S BALLOON !! MUSIC AND LYRICS BY JOHNNY SATOMI
I LOVE YOU. I LOVE YOU.
DON'T LOOK AT ME AND BURST.
HA HA HA. BABY, SORRY 'BOUT THE DUMB JOKE.
A pen guitar.
HEH
Ciao.

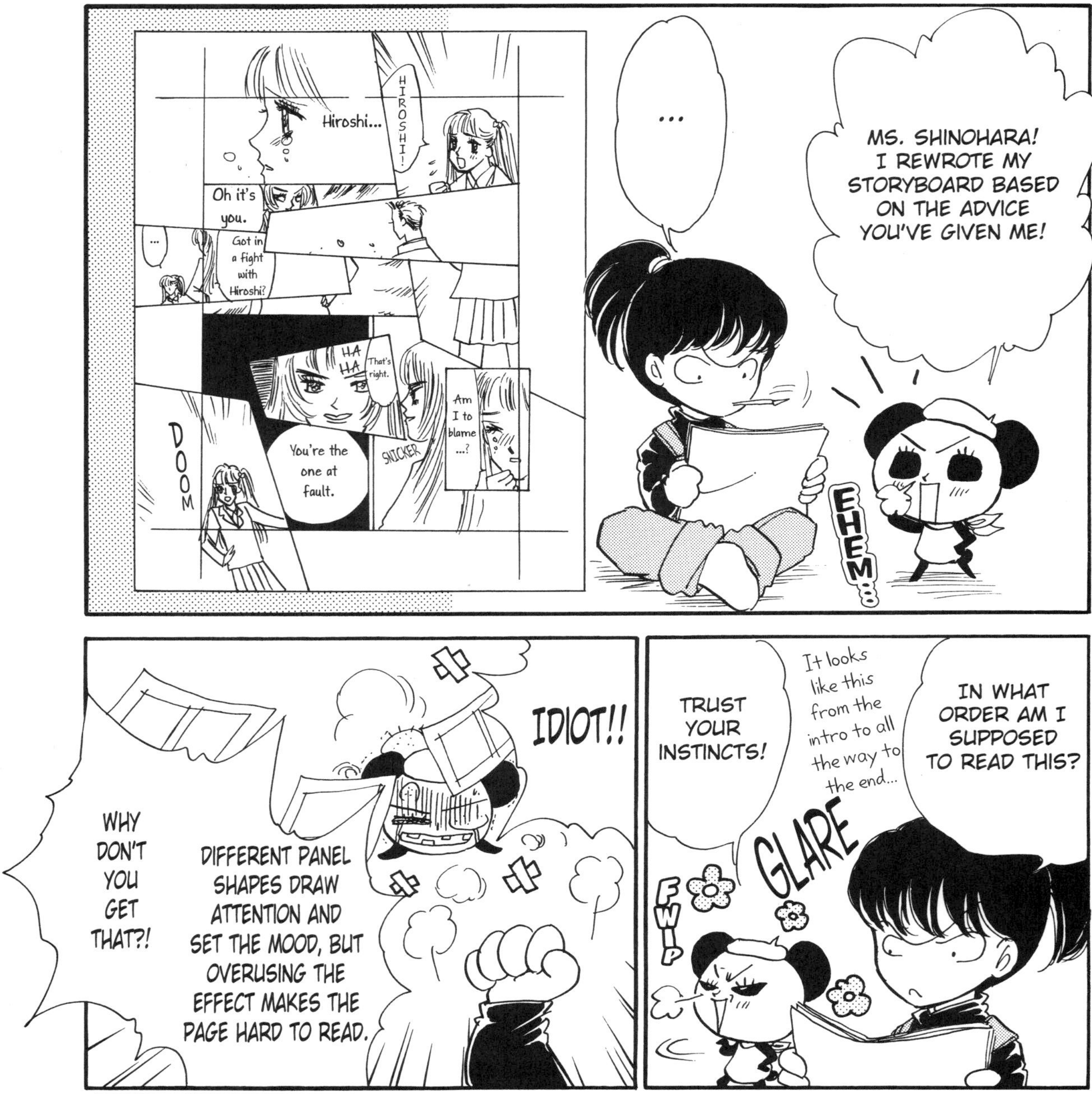
MS. SHINOHARA! I REWROTE MY STORYBOARD BASED ON THE ADVICE YOU'VE GIVEN ME!
...
EHEM...
HIROSHI!
Hiroshi...
Oh it's you.
Got in a fight with Hiroshi?
...
HA HA
That's right.
Am I to blame ...?
SNICKER
You're the one at fault.
DOOM
IN WHAT ORDER AM I SUPPOSED TO READ THIS?
It looks like this from the intro to all the way to the end...
TRUST YOUR INSTINCTS!
GLARE
FWIP
IDIOT!!
DIFFERENT PANEL SHAPES DRAW ATTENTION AND SET THE MOOD, BUT OVERUSING THE EFFECT MAKES THE PAGE HARD TO READ.
WHY DON'T YOU GET THAT?!

ONLY USE DIFFERENT PANEL SHAPES FOR SPECIAL OCCASIONS.

Just like Shinohara says, the simpler the balloon, the better. Although in shojo manga it may seem like they use a lot of different panel shapes, look closely and you'll see that a basic square panel is a fundamental. Newcomers tend to use panel shapes randomly, making the entire page difficult to read, so be careful! Even when you come across the perfect scene to use a different panel shape, think about the page's balance and aesthetics when placing it. Remember, it's all about balance and energy.

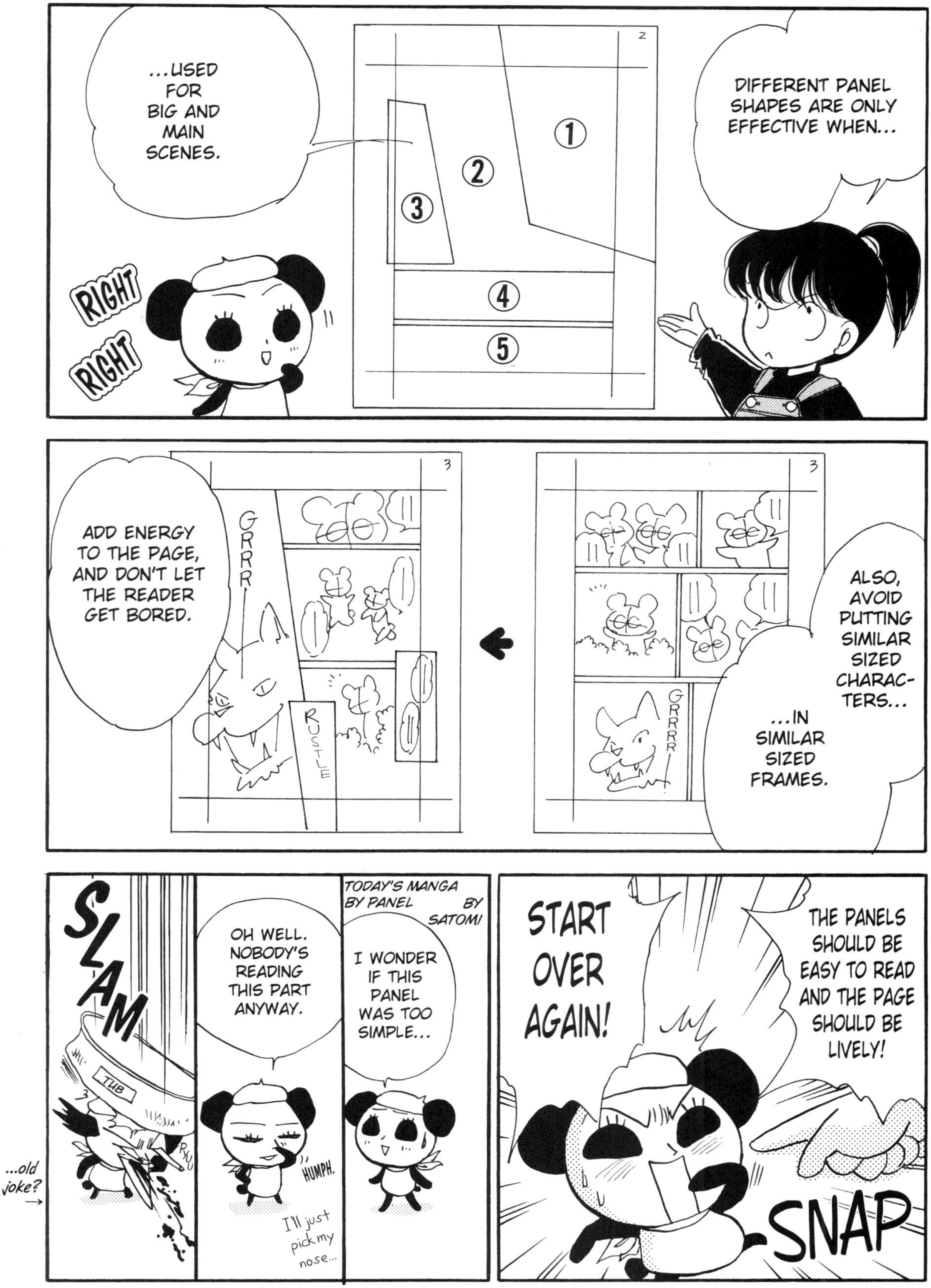
DIFFERENT PANEL SHAPES ARE ONLY EFFECTIVE WHEN...
...USED FOR BIG AND MAIN SCENES.
RIGHT RIGHT
ALSO, AVOID PUTTING SIMILAR SIZED CHARAC-TERS...
...IN SIMILAR SIZED FRAMES.
GRRRR
ADD ENERGY TO THE PAGE, AND DON'T LET THE READER GET BORED.
GRRR
RUSTLE
THE PANELS SHOULD BE EASY TO READ AND THE PAGE SHOULD BE LIVELY!
START OVER AGAIN!
SNAP
TODAY'S MANGA BY PANEL BY SATOMI
I WONDER IF THIS PANEL WAS TOO SIMPLE...
OH WELL. NOBODY'S READING THIS PART ANYWAY.
HUMPH.
I'll just pick my nose...
SLAM
TUB
...old joke?

HOW TO DRAW SPREADS AND BLEEDS

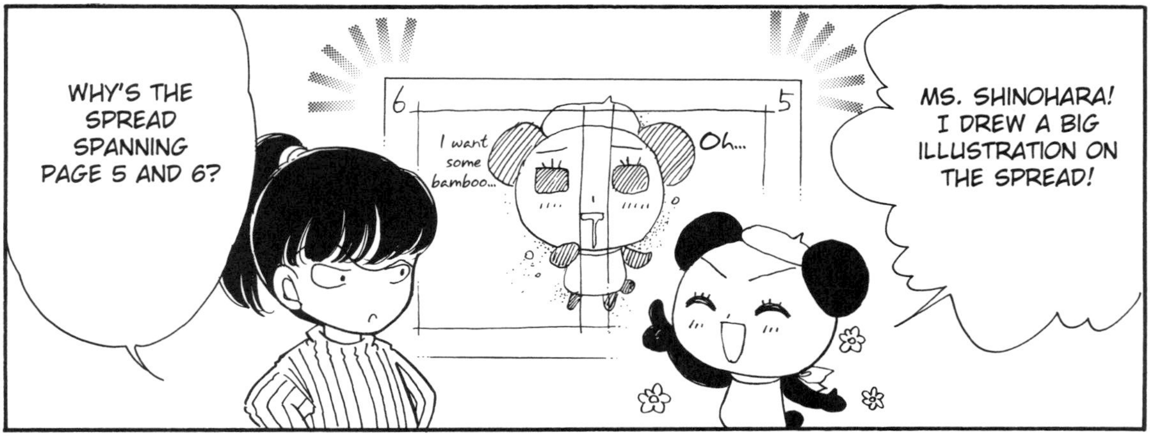
MS. SHINOHARA! I DREW A BIG ILLUSTRATION ON THE SPREAD!
5
Oh...
6
I want some bamboo...
WHY'S THE SPREAD SPANNING PAGE 5 AND 6?

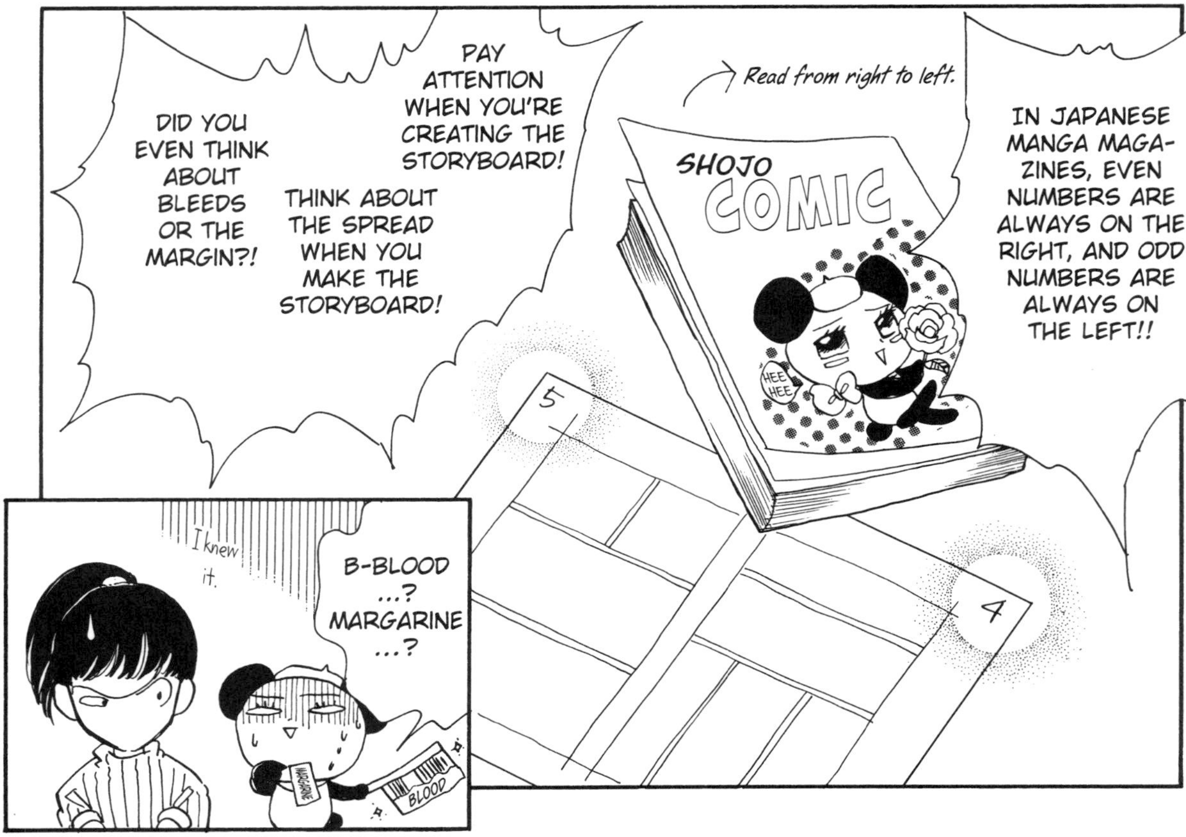
IN JAPANESE MANGA MAGAZINES, EVEN NUMBERS ARE ALWAYS ON THE RIGHT, AND ODD NUMBERS ARE ALWAYS ON THE LEFT!!
Read from right to left.
SHOJO COMIC
HEE HEE
4
5
PAY ATTENTION WHEN YOU'RE CREATING THE STORYBOARD!
DID YOU EVEN THINK ABOUT BLEEDS OR THE MARGIN?!
THINK ABOUT THE SPREAD WHEN YOU MAKE THE STORYBOARD!
B-BLOOD ...? MARGARINE ...?
I knew it.
MARGARINE
BLOOD

STRUCTURE'S ON YOUR SIDE. THINK OF THE READER WHEN DIVIDING THE PANELS.

Always think about the overall spread when you're writing your manga, especially the storyboard! When the reader sees stories in a magazine, they always look at the entire spread. How will their eye move?! Where should your illustrations be positioned to make the drawings jump out at the readers?! If you think about those things when you arrange your panels, you'll be able to come up with a nice clean page. Read your work as if you're a member of the audience! You'll master the art of page-turning before you know it!

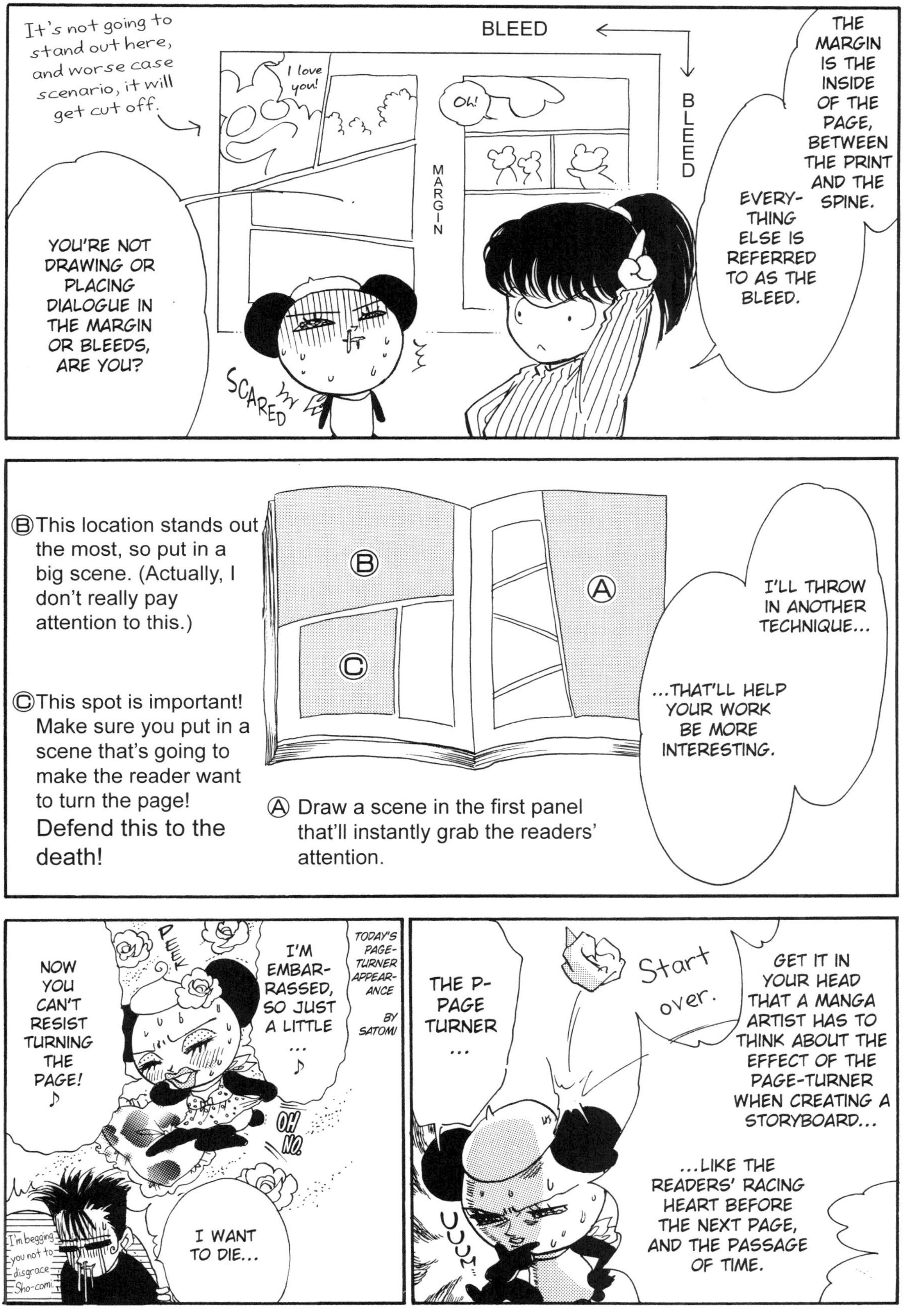
THE MARGIN IS THE INSIDE OF THE PAGE, BETWEEN THE PRINT AND THE SPINE.
EVERYTHING ELSE IS REFERRED TO AS THE BLEED.
BLEED
BLEED
Oh!
MARGIN
I love you!
It's not going to stand out here, and worse case scenario, it will get cut off.
YOU'RE NOT DRAWING OR PLACING DIALOGUE IN THE MARGIN OR BLEEDS, ARE YOU?
SCARED
I'LL THROW IN ANOTHER TECHNIQUE...
...THAT'LL HELP YOUR WORK BE MORE INTERESTING.
Ⓐ Draw a scene in the first panel that'll instantly grab the readers' attention.
Ⓑ This location stands out the most, so put in a big scene. (Actually, I don't really pay attention to this.)
Ⓒ This spot is important! Make sure you put in a scene that's going to make the reader want to turn the page! Defend this to the death!
Ⓐ
Ⓑ
Ⓒ
GET IT IN YOUR HEAD THAT A MANGA ARTIST HAS TO THINK ABOUT THE EFFECT OF THE PAGE-TURNER WHEN CREATING A STORYBOARD...
Start over.
THE P-PAGE TURNER...
...LIKE THE READERS' RACING HEART BEFORE THE NEXT PAGE, AND THE PASSAGE OF TIME.
UUUM
TODAY'S PAGE-TURNER APPEARANCE BY SATOMI
I'M EMBARRASSED, SO JUST A LITTLE... ♪
NOW YOU CAN'T RESIST TURNING THE PAGE! ♪
PEEK
OH NO
I WANT TO DIE...
I'm begging you not to disgrace Sho-comi.

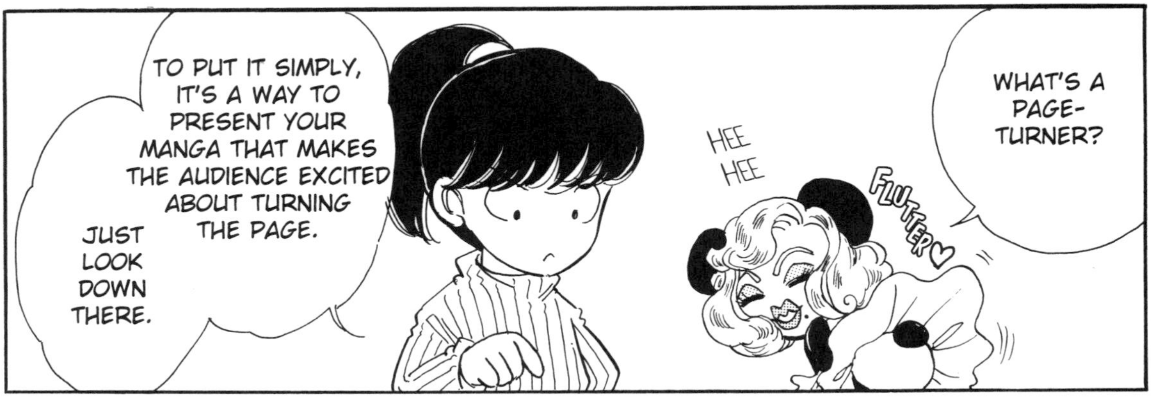
WHAT'S A PAGE-TURNER?
FLUTTER♡
HEE HEE
TO PUT IT SIMPLY, IT'S A WAY TO PRESENT YOUR MANGA THAT MAKES THE AUDIENCE EXCITED ABOUT TURNING THE PAGE.
JUST LOOK DOWN THERE.

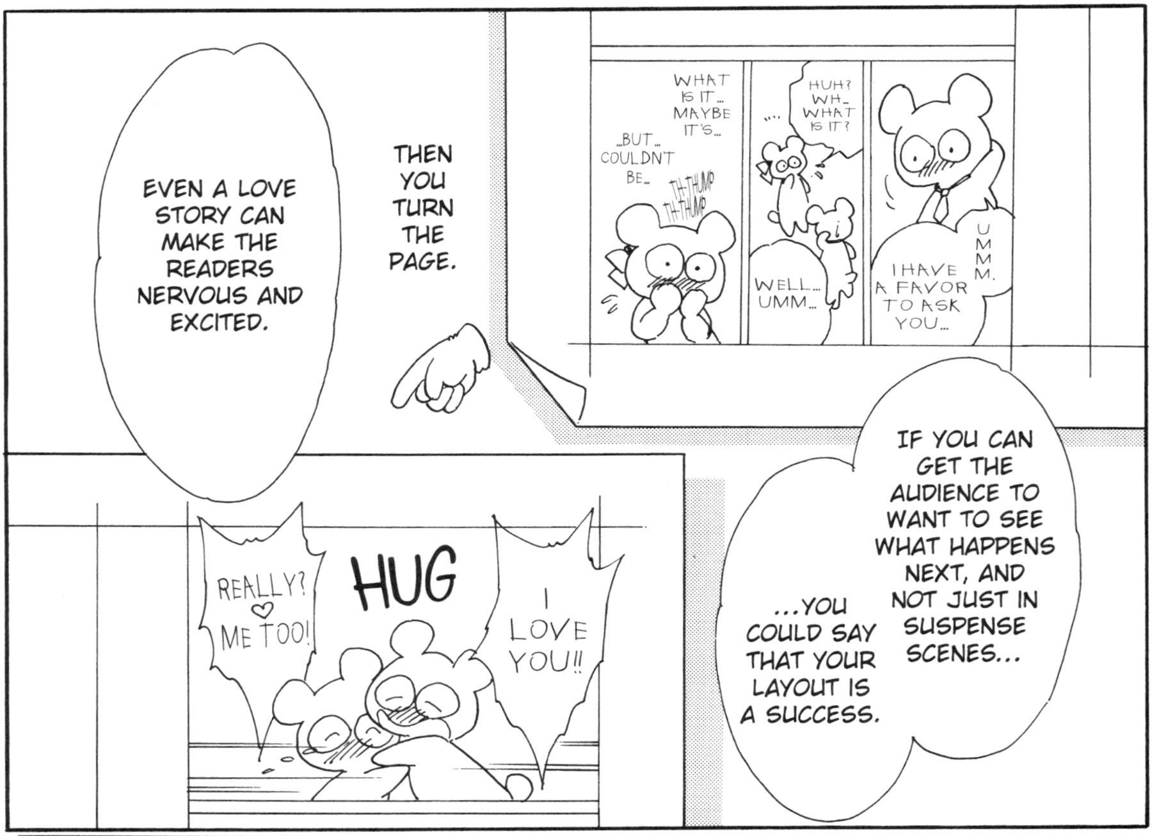
UMMM.
I HAVE A FAVOR TO ASK YOU...
HUH? WH- WHAT IS IT?
...
WELL... UMM...
WHAT IS IT... MAYBE IT'S...
...BUT... COULDN'T BE...
TH-THUMP TH-THUMP
THEN YOU TURN THE PAGE.
EVEN A LOVE STORY CAN MAKE THE READERS NERVOUS AND EXCITED.
IF YOU CAN GET THE AUDIENCE TO WANT TO SEE WHAT HAPPENS NEXT, AND NOT JUST IN SUSPENSE SCENES...
...YOU COULD SAY THAT YOUR LAYOUT IS A SUCCESS.
I LOVE YOU!!
HUG
REALLY? ♡ ME TOO!

PAY ATTENTION TO THE READERS' POINT OF VIEW.

Even if you read a lot of manga, there're probably a lot of you who were shocked to hear about the "page-turner." Any given manga is full of know-how, but pros structure it in an easy-to-read way that that's not obvious! So don't just go through the motions when you read a manga. Really try to absorb what kind of mechanisms are working to make it interesting! It doesn't cost that much to buy a manga or a manga magazine, and there're so many professional techniques packed into them. You couldn't be getting a better deal on a great textbook!

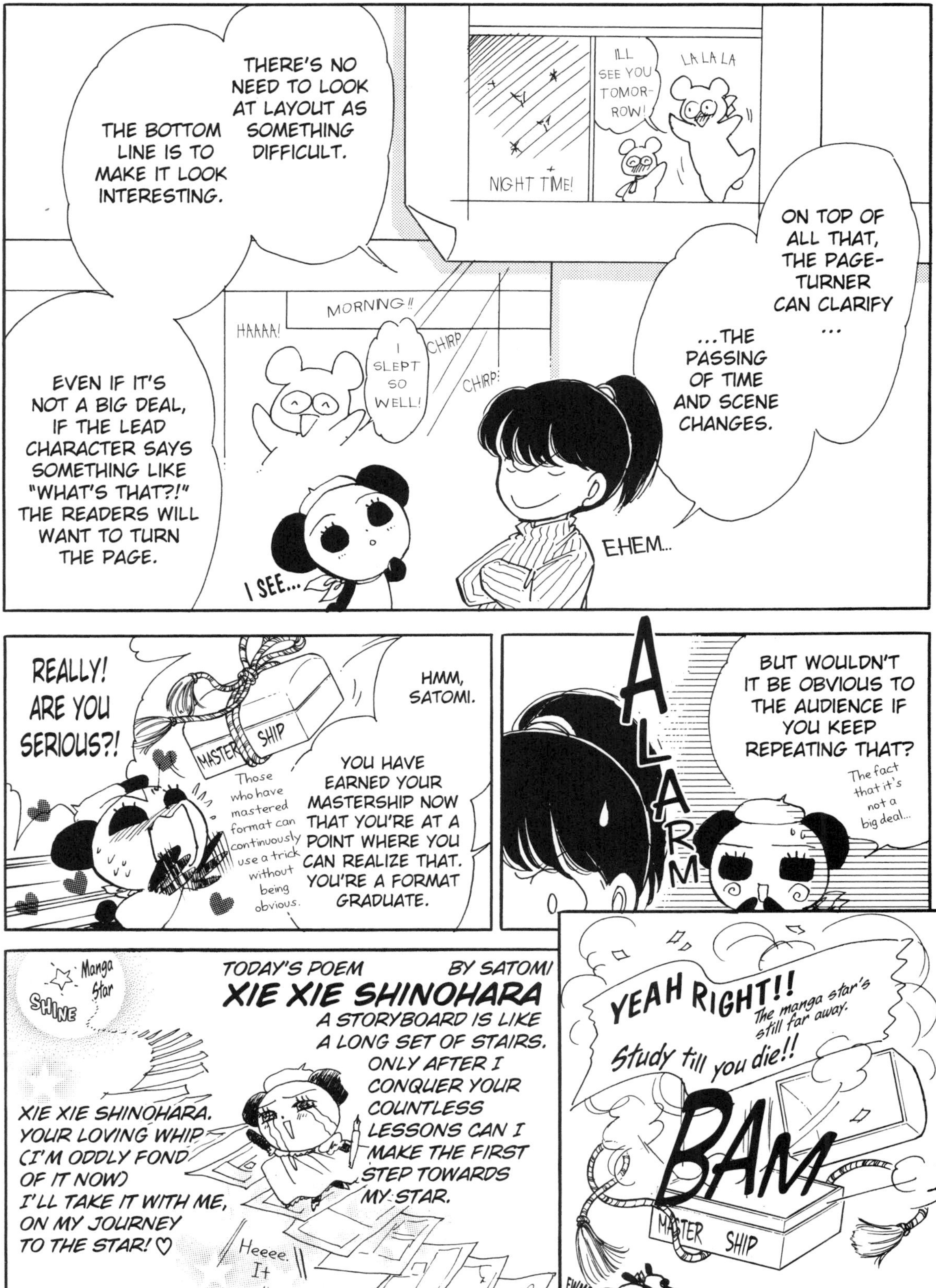
LA LA LA
ILL SEE YOU TOMOR-ROW!
NIGHT TIME!
THERE'S NO NEED TO LOOK AT LAYOUT AS SOMETHING DIFFICULT.
THE BOTTOM LINE IS TO MAKE IT LOOK INTERESTING.
ON TOP OF ALL THAT, THE PAGE-TURNER CAN CLARIFY ...
...THE PASSING OF TIME AND SCENE CHANGES.
MORNING!!
CHIRP
CHIRP!
I SLEPT SO WELL!
HAAAA!
EVEN IF IT'S NOT A BIG DEAL, IF THE LEAD CHARACTER SAYS SOMETHING LIKE "WHAT'S THAT?!" THE READERS WILL WANT TO TURN THE PAGE.
EHEM...
I SEE...
BUT WOULDN'T IT BE OBVIOUS TO THE AUDIENCE IF YOU KEEP REPEATING THAT?
ALARM
The fact that it's not a big deal...
HMM, SATOMI.
MASTER SHIP
REALLY! ARE YOU SERIOUS?!
YOU HAVE EARNED YOUR MASTERSHIP NOW THAT YOU'RE AT A POINT WHERE YOU CAN REALIZE THAT. YOU'RE A FORMAT GRADUATE.
Those who have mastered format can continuously use a trick without being obvious.
YEAH RIGHT!!
The manga star's still far away.
Study till you die!!
BAM
MASTER SHIP
FWMP
TODAY'S POEM BY SATOMI
XIE XIE SHINOHARA
A STORYBOARD IS LIKE A LONG SET OF STAIRS.
ONLY AFTER I CONQUER YOUR COUNTLESS LESSONS CAN I MAKE THE FIRST STEP TOWARDS MY STAR.
XIE XIE SHINOHARA. YOUR LOVING WHIP (I'M ODDLY FOND OF IT NOW) I'LL TAKE IT WITH ME, ON MY JOURNEY TO THE STAR! ♡
Manga Star
SHINE
Heeee. It really is far.

SUMMARY OF FORMAT

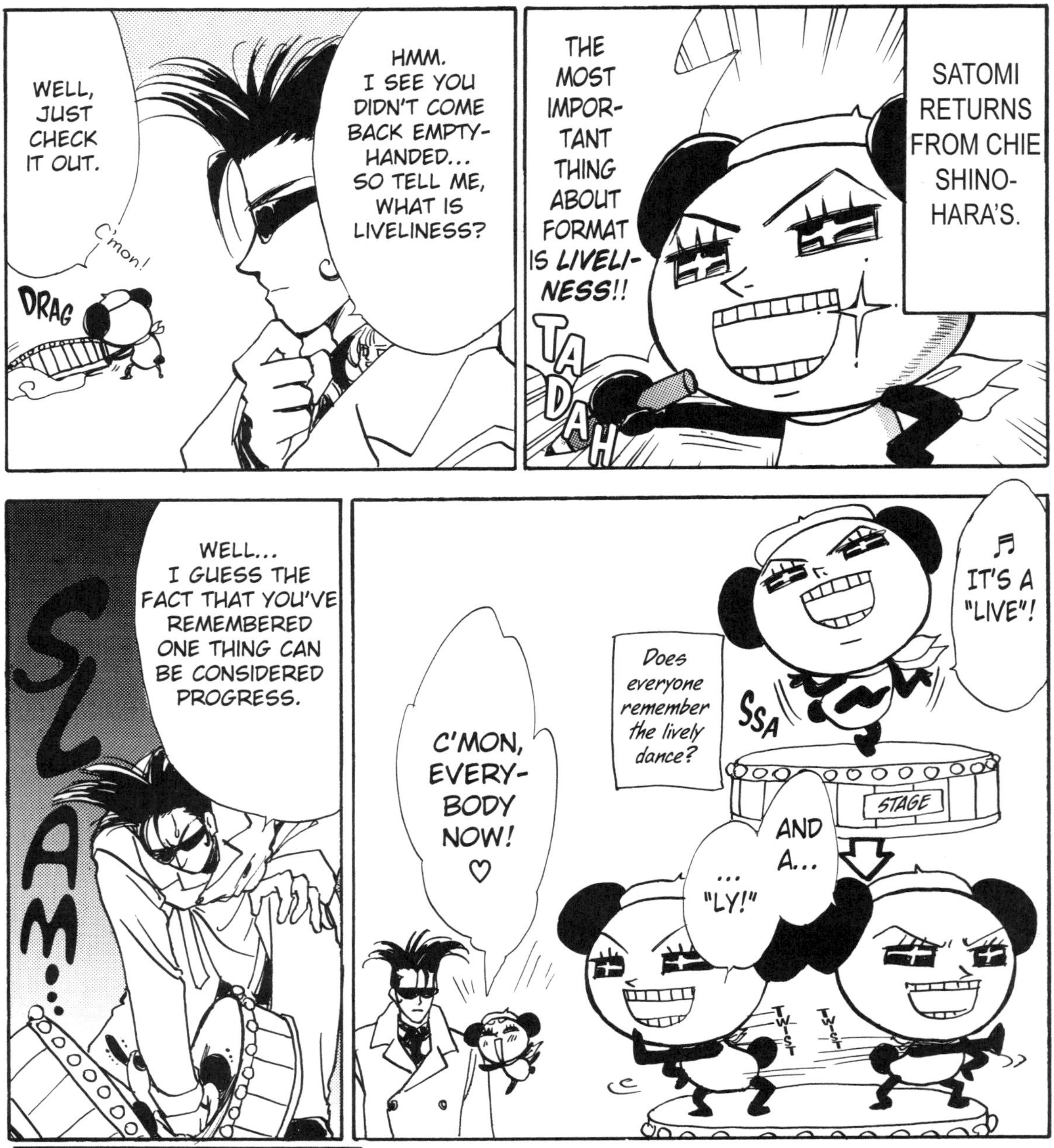
SATOMI RETURNS FROM CHIE SHINOHARA'S.
THE MOST IMPORTANT THING ABOUT FORMAT IS LIVELINESS!!
TA DAH
HMM. I SEE YOU DIDN'T COME BACK EMPTY-HANDED... SO TELL ME, WHAT IS LIVELINESS?
WELL, JUST CHECK IT OUT.
C'mon!
DRAG
♫ IT'S A "LIVE"!
Does everyone remember the lively dance?
SSA
STAGE
AND A...
... "LY!"
TWIST
TWIST
C'MON, EVERYBODY NOW! ♡
WELL... I GUESS THE FACT THAT YOU'VE REMEMBERED ONE THING CAN BE CONSIDERED PROGRESS.
SLAM...

CHECK OUT DIFFERENT WAYS TO IMPROVE LAYOUT DESIGN.

In order to improve your drawing, you just have to draw a lot. But how can you improve the format? You can gain strength by getting exposed to lots of different format types! Manga, movies, novels… anything that has a story format! What kind of sequence should the story have to make it easy to read? What needs to be drawn in order to make a reader-friendly presentation? Checking out different works, whether good examples or bad examples, is a great way to learn. So don't just glue yourself to your desk and draw manga all day. Make sure you're exposed to a variety of work!

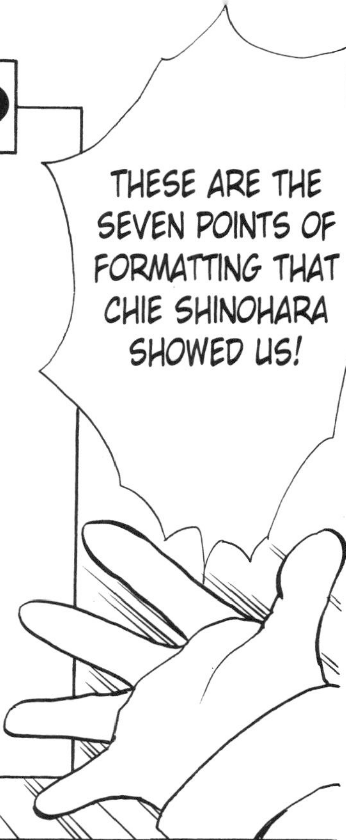
THESE ARE THE SEVEN POINTS OF FORMATTING THAT CHIE SHINOHARA SHOWED US!

● THE SEVEN FORMAT COMMANDMENTS ●

1. Always make a storyboard!
2. Eliminate excess panels and liven up the pacing!
3. Make the dialogue short and easy to digest!
4. Do NOT overuse monologues!
5. Pay attention to balloon shapes and reading sequence!
6. Make sure the panels are divided in a lively way!
7. Always think of the spread when writing the storyboard and think of a page-turner presentation!

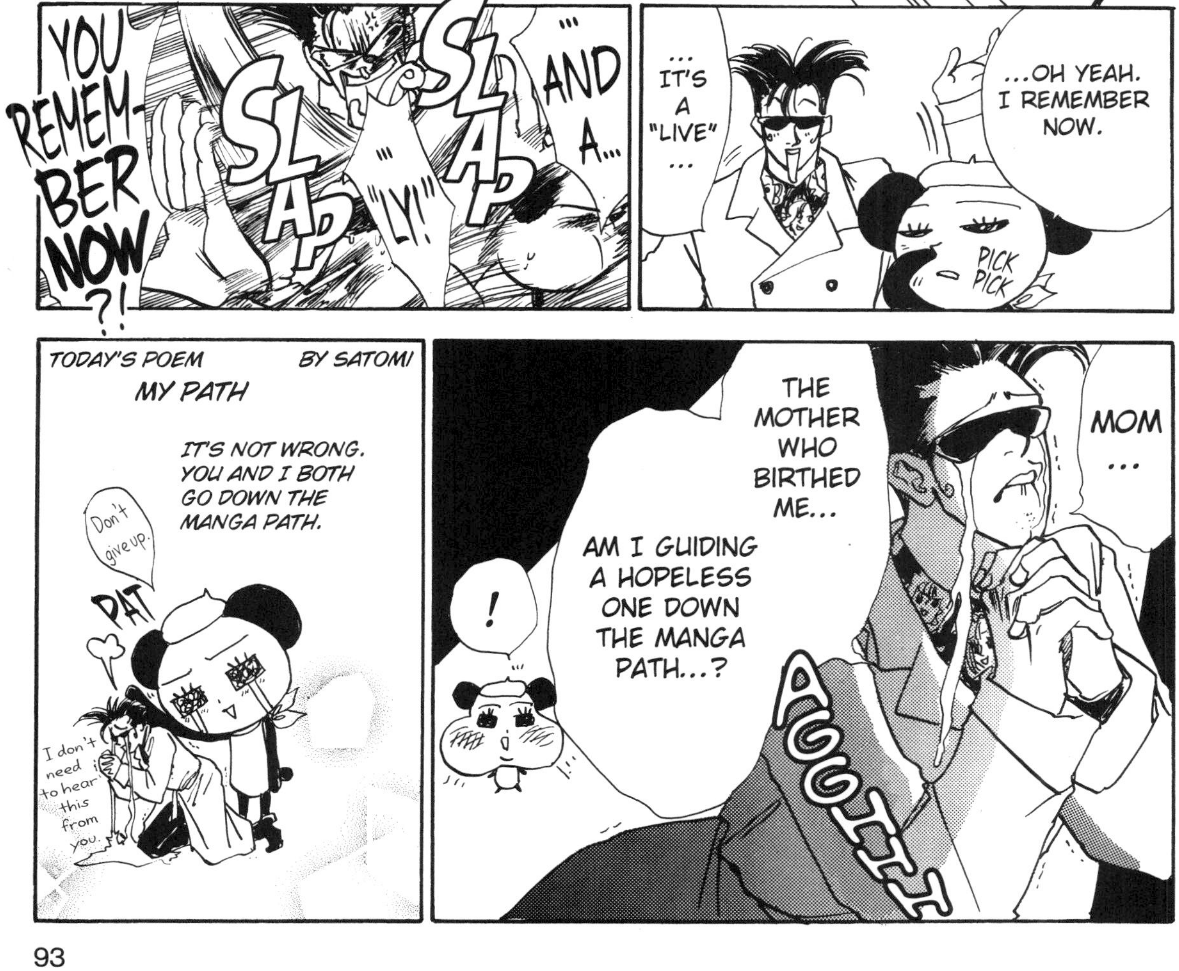
...OH YEAH. I REMEMBER NOW.
...IT'S A "LIVE"...
PICK PICK
"...
AND A...
SLAP
"LY!"
SLAP
YOU REMEMBER NOW?!
MOM...
THE MOTHER WHO BIRTHED ME...
AM I GUIDING A HOPELESS ONE DOWN THE MANGA PATH...?
AGGIII
!
TODAY'S POEM BY SATOMI
MY PATH
IT'S NOT WRONG. YOU AND I BOTH GO DOWN THE MANGA PATH.
Don't give up.
PAT
I don't need to hear this from you.

Chie Shinohara manga are superior in their clarity! Why are they so easy to read?! Closing in on Shinohara's format secret!

Manga Star Presents!! STEAL THIS FROM A PROFESSIONAL MANGA! Part 4

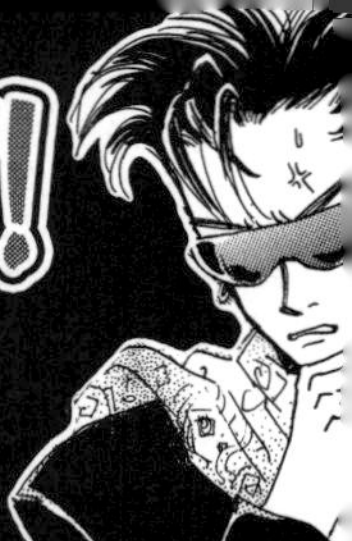

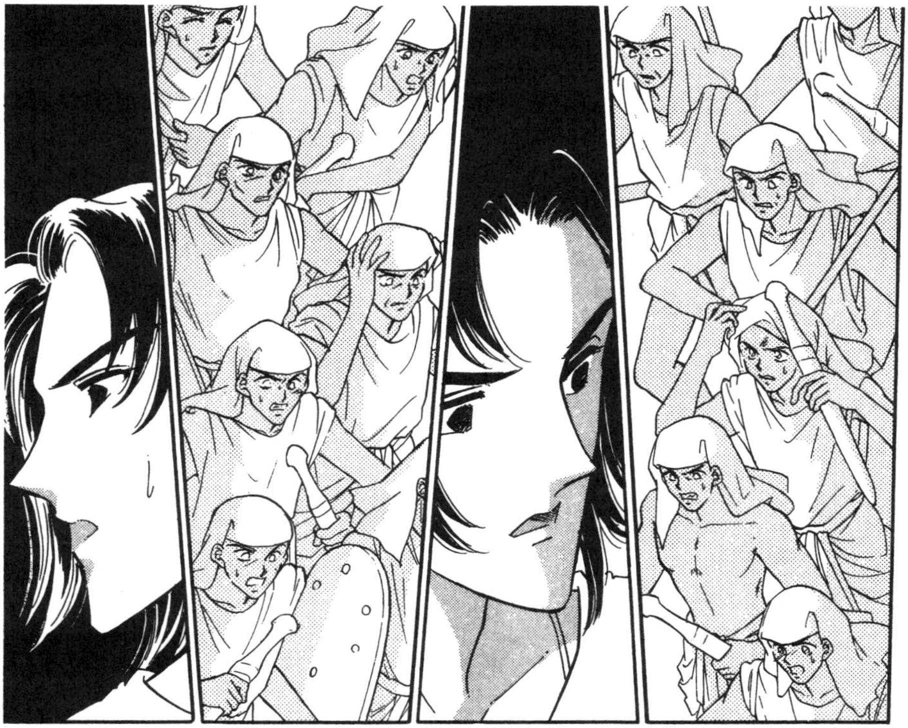

CAMERA WORK THAT COORDINATES WITH THE CHARACTER'S POINT OF VIEW.

The two examples here are basically formatted using the same method. The method is switching between the character's point of view and the scenery that she or he sees. When the scenery is presented like this, the audience (already empathetic to with character) can easily grasp the character's situation.

▲ When you look at it as one big illustration, it just looks like the crowd and the man's close-up are placed next to each other. But, if you look at it in sequence, you can tell that the man is looking at the crowd. How cool!

If you put the background and the character in the same panel, the character's size is always compromised. With this format, you can draw a close-up and maintain a sense of immediacy.

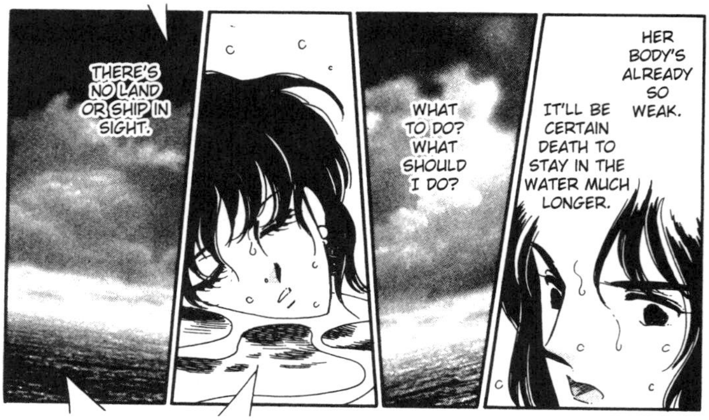
HER BODY'S ALREADY SO WEAK.
IT'LL BE CERTAIN DEATH TO STAY IN THE WATER MUCH LONGER.
WHAT TO DO? WHAT SHOULD I DO?
THERE'S NO LAND OR SHIP IN SIGHT.

WHAT'S THE REASON BEHIND THE RIGHT-TO-LEFT ATTACKS?

We're going to disclose Shinohara's subtle technique here. During Shinohara's battle scenes, the main character's allied troops always attack from right-to-left. There's actually a reason for this.

A manga page is always read right-to-left. Therefore, the reader's line of vision moves from right-to-left. By coordinating the allied troops with this visual direction, you can add some vigor to advances.

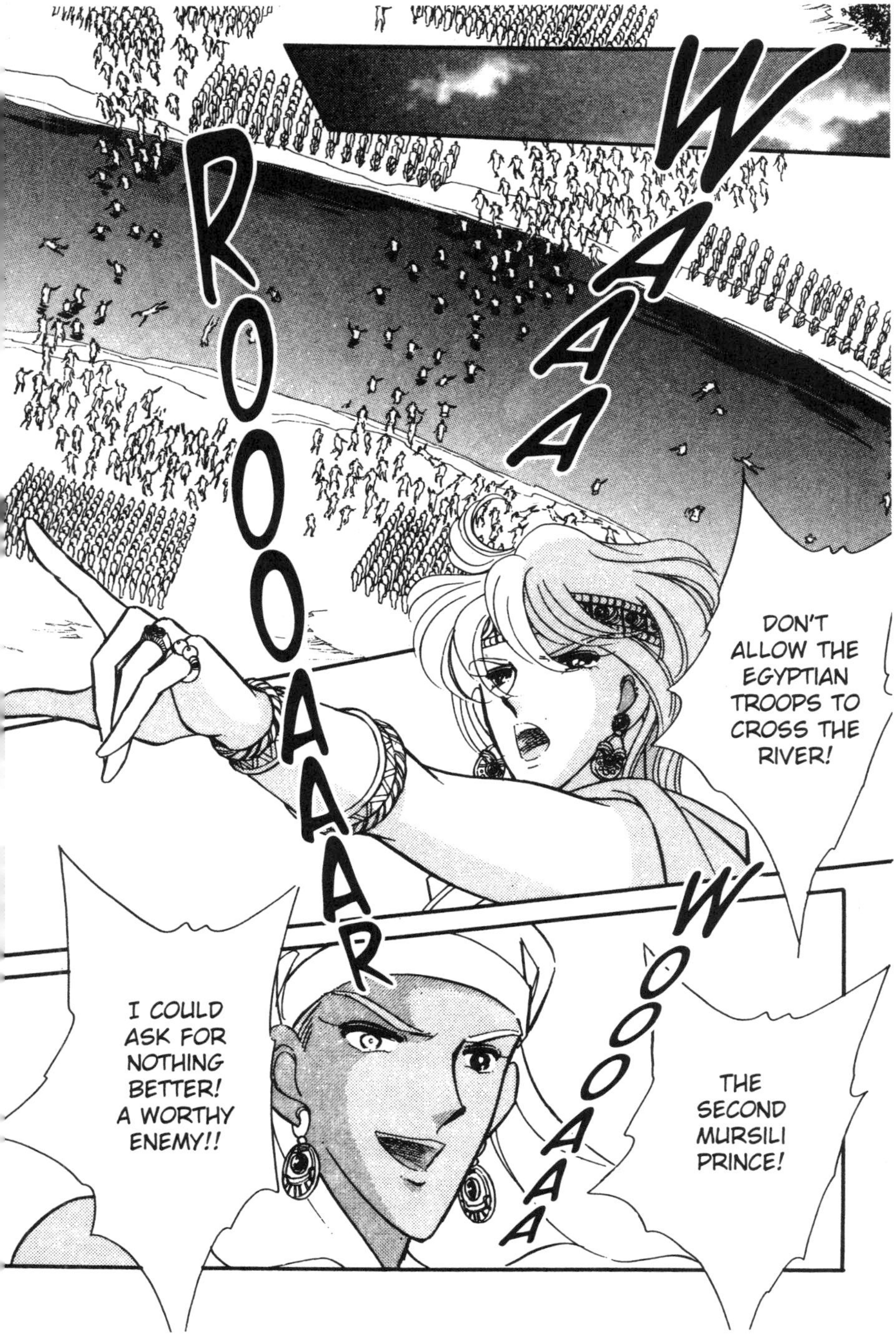
WAAA
ROOOAAAR
DON'T ALLOW THE EGYPTIAN TROOPS TO CROSS THE RIVER!
WOOOOAAAA
THE SECOND MURSILI PRINCE!
I COULD ASK FOR NOTHING BETTER! A WORTHY ENEMY!!

And when the allied troops are under attack, placing the allied troops on the left gives an extra sense of urgency.

This is true for any scene involving the main character. Many of the lead characters' scenes involve a right-to-left pattern. Even when she or he runs, it's from right-to-left! This is another rule for energizing the format!

This rule is second nature to almost all professionals, so they probably format their manga this way without even realizing it. But when you analyze it, you can see the reason.

Now that you've been let in on the secret, try incorporating this in your work.

CHAPTER 5: THE YUU WATASE EDITION

LET'S DRAW A DRAFT!

Now let's get into an actual draft!
Sho-Comi's Yuu Watase will show us how!

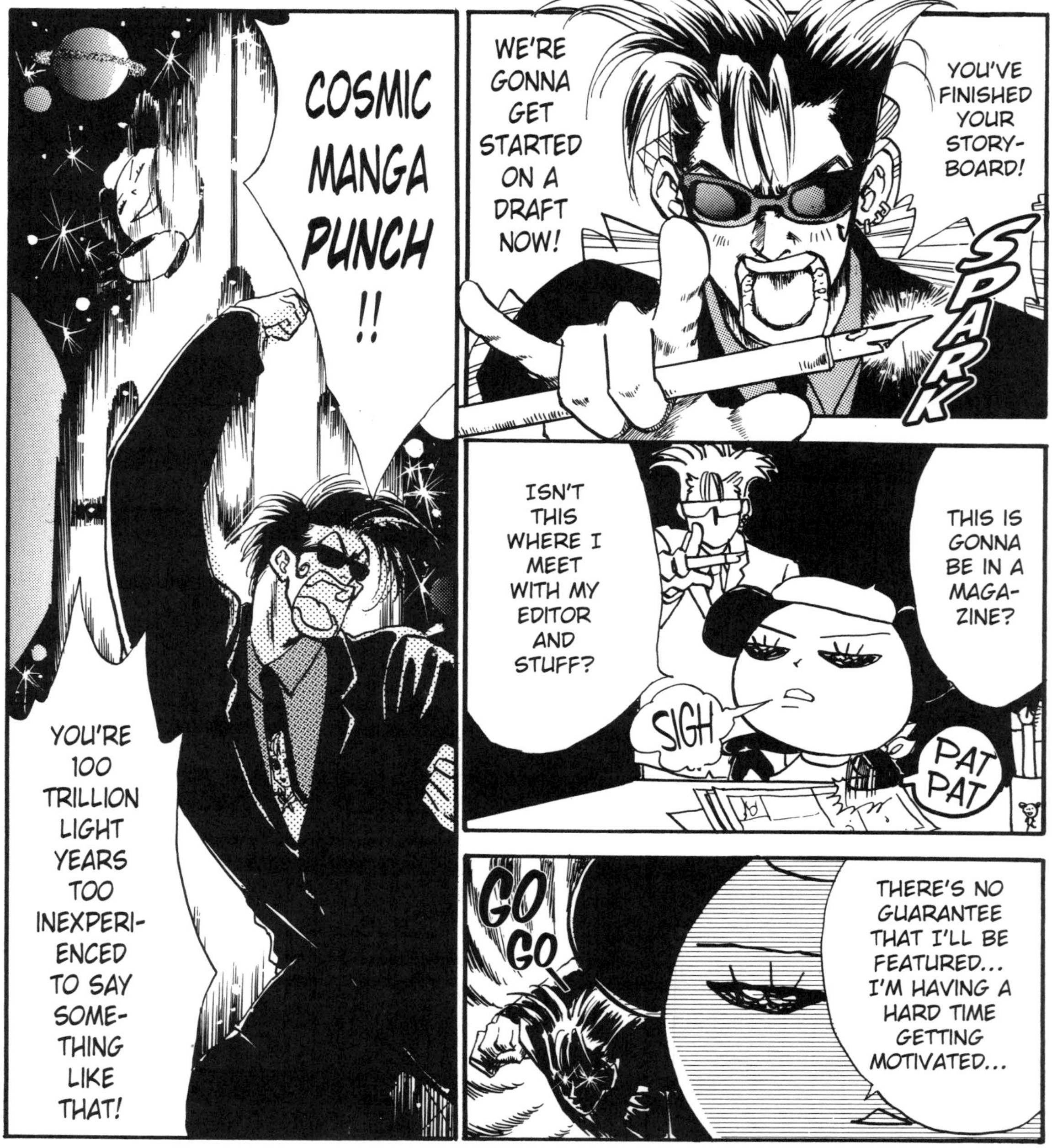
YOU'VE FINISHED YOUR STORY-BOARD!
WE'RE GONNA GET STARTED ON A DRAFT NOW!
SPARK
THIS IS GONNA BE IN A MAGA-ZINE?
ISN'T THIS WHERE I MEET WITH MY EDITOR AND STUFF?
PAT PAT
SIGH
THERE'S NO GUARANTEE THAT I'LL BE FEATURED... I'M HAVING A HARD TIME GETTING MOTIVATED...
GO GO
COSMIC MANGA PUNCH !!
YOU'RE 100 TRILLION LIGHT YEARS TOO INEXPERI-ENCED TO SAY SOME-THING LIKE THAT!

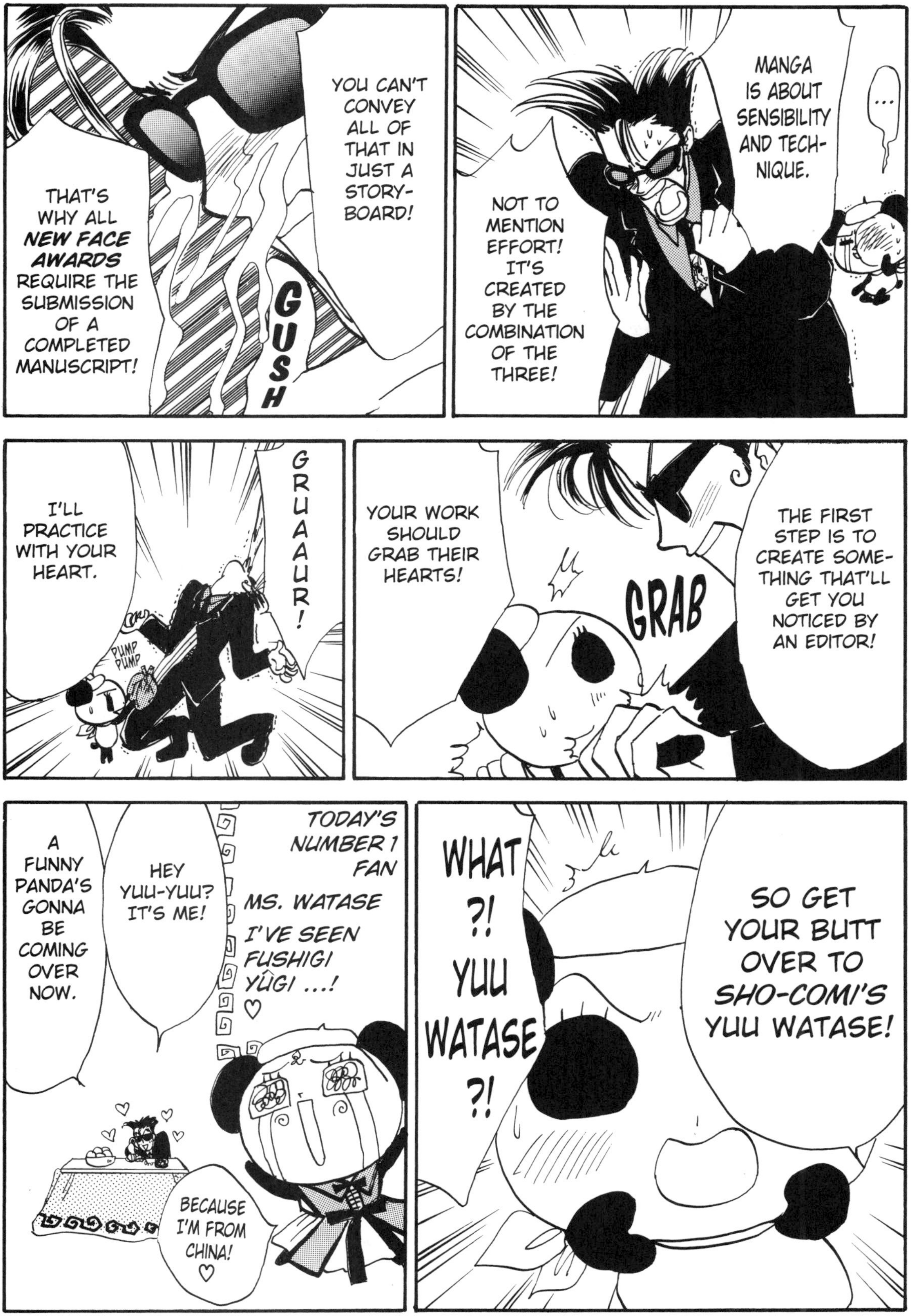
MANGA IS ABOUT SENSIBILITY AND TECH-NIQUE.
...
NOT TO MENTION EFFORT! IT'S CREATED BY THE COMBINATION OF THE THREE!
YOU CAN'T CONVEY ALL OF THAT IN JUST A STORY-BOARD!
GUSH
THAT'S WHY ALL *NEW FACE AWARDS* REQUIRE THE SUBMISSION OF A COMPLETED MANUSCRIPT!
THE FIRST STEP IS TO CREATE SOME-THING THAT'LL GET YOU NOTICED BY AN EDITOR!
GRAB
YOUR WORK SHOULD GRAB THEIR HEARTS!
GRUAAAUR!
I'LL PRACTICE WITH YOUR HEART.
PUMP PUMP
SO GET YOUR BUTT OVER TO *SHO-COMI'S* YUU WATASE!
WHAT ?! YUU WATASE ?!
TODAY'S NUMBER 1 FAN
MS. WATASE
I'VE SEEN FUSHIGI YÛGI ...! ♡
HEY YUU-YUU? IT'S ME!
A FUNNY PANDA'S GONNA BE COMING OVER NOW.
BECAUSE I'M FROM CHINA! ♡

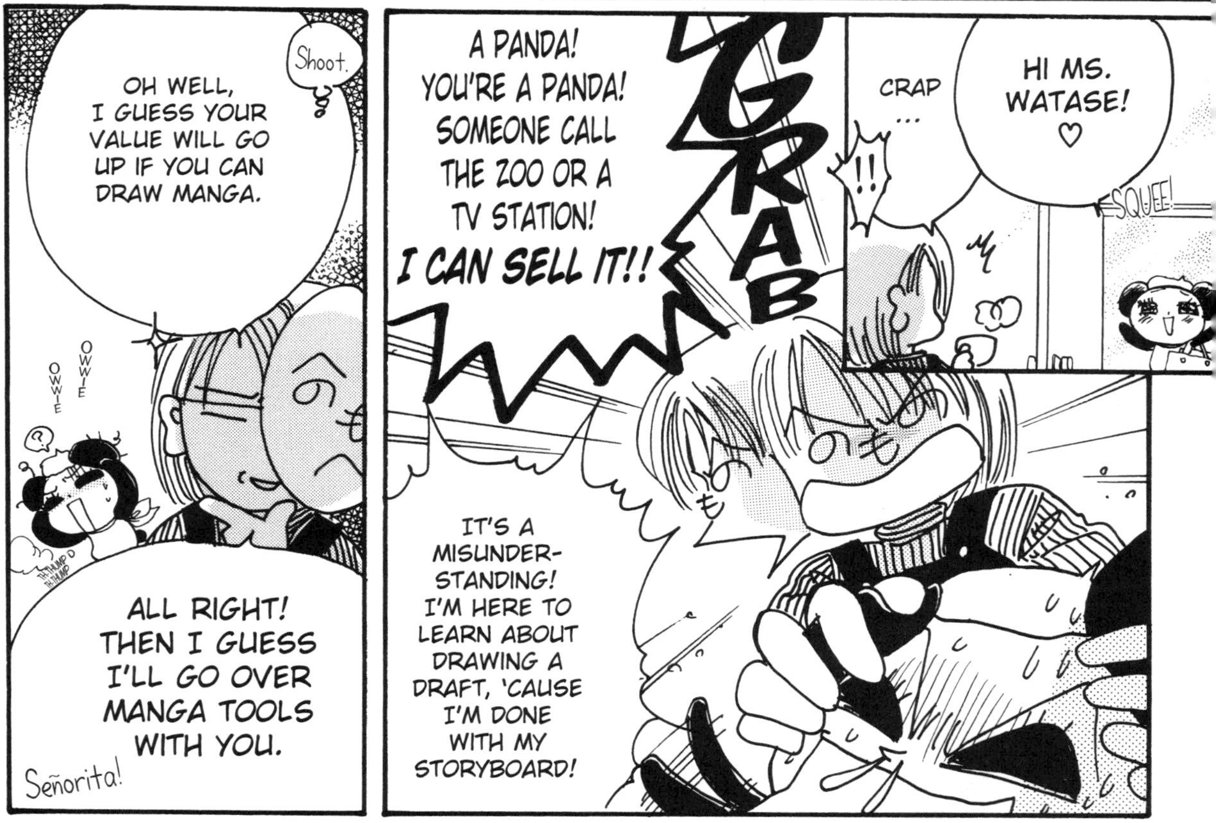
HI MS. WATASE! ♡
SQUEE!
CRAP ...
!!
A PANDA! YOU'RE A PANDA! SOMEONE CALL THE ZOO OR A TV STATION! I CAN SELL IT!!
GRAB
IT'S A MISUNDERSTANDING! I'M HERE TO LEARN ABOUT DRAWING A DRAFT, 'CAUSE I'M DONE WITH MY STORYBOARD!
OH WELL, I GUESS YOUR VALUE WILL GO UP IF YOU CAN DRAW MANGA.
Shoot.
OWWIE
OWWIE
ALL RIGHT! THEN I GUESS I'LL GO OVER MANGA TOOLS WITH YOU.
Señorita!

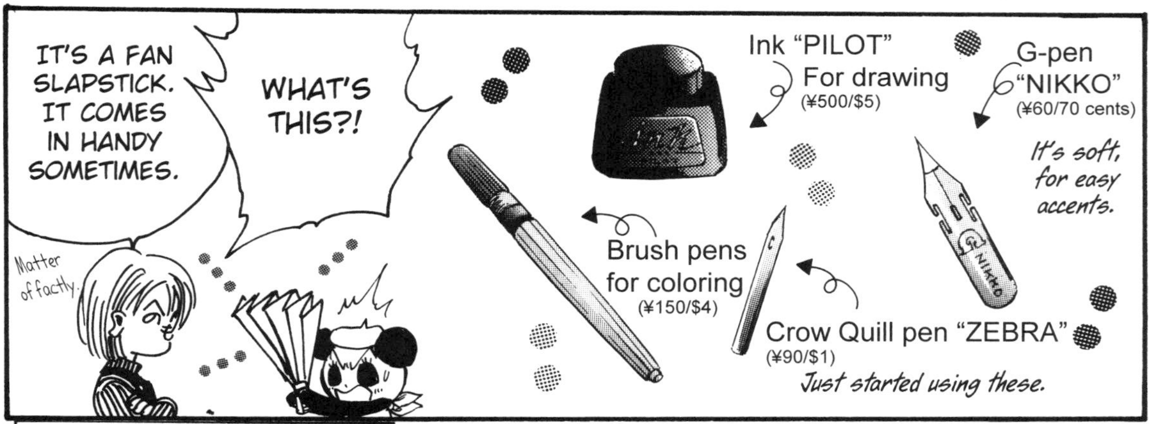
G-pen "NIKKO" (¥60/70 cents)
It's soft, for easy accents.
Ink "PILOT" For drawing (¥500/$5)
Crow Quill pen "ZEBRA" (¥90/$1)
Just started using these.
Brush pens for coloring (¥150/$4)
WHAT'S THIS?!
IT'S A FAN SLAPSTICK. IT COMES IN HANDY SOMETIMES.
Matter of factly.

SELECT PAPER BY HOW WELL IT TAKES INK.

The primary tools for drawing manga are generally pens, ink, and paper. If you have a G-pen and drawing ink, you're good to go! But the most difficult decision as a beginner is what kind of paper to get. The submission requirements in *New Face Awards* usually say to use KENT or high quality paper, but really any paper is okay! KENT and high quality paper are smooth and the ink goes on really nicely. There are different thicknesses within high quality paper, but 80-100lb (paper thickness is shown by pound) is what's used for manga. There are different qualities of paper for manga, so be careful.

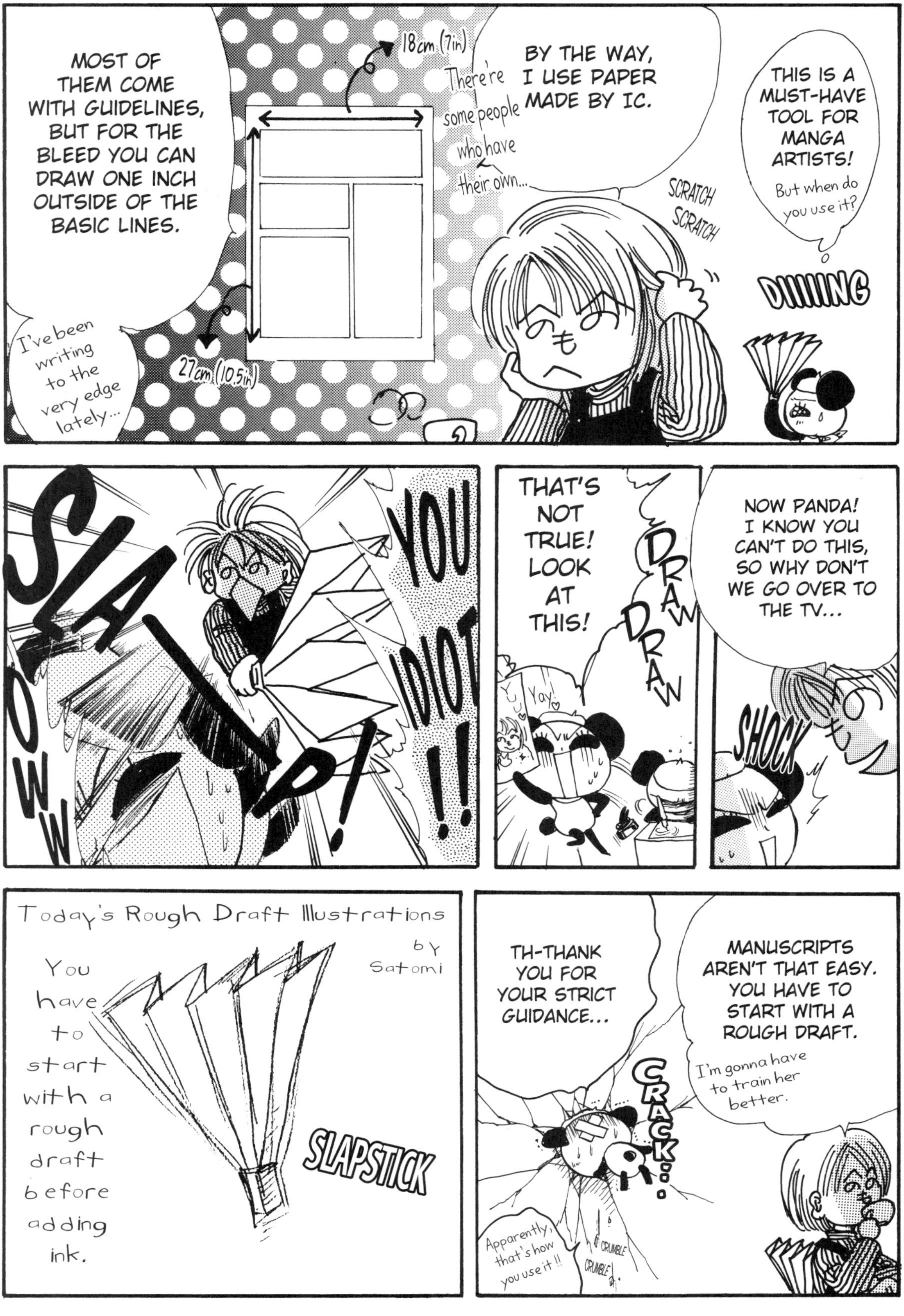

THIS IS A MUST-HAVE TOOL FOR MANGA ARTISTS!
But when do you use it?
DIIIIING
SCRATCH SCRATCH
BY THE WAY, I USE PAPER MADE BY IC.
There're some people who have their own...
18cm (7in)
MOST OF THEM COME WITH GUIDELINES, BUT FOR THE BLEED YOU CAN DRAW ONE INCH OUTSIDE OF THE BASIC LINES.
27cm (10.5in)
I've been writing to the very edge lately...
NOW PANDA! I KNOW YOU CAN'T DO THIS, SO WHY DON'T WE GO OVER TO THE TV...
SHOCK
THAT'S NOT TRUE! LOOK AT THIS!
DRAW DRAW DRAW
Yay!
YOU IDIOT!!
SLAP!
OWWW
MANUSCRIPTS AREN'T THAT EASY. YOU HAVE TO START WITH A ROUGH DRAFT.
I'm gonna have to train her better.
TH-THANK YOU FOR YOUR STRICT GUIDANCE...
CRACK!!
Apparently, that's how you use it!!
CRUMBLE CRUMBLE
Today's Rough Draft Illustrations
by Satomi
You have to start with a rough draft before adding ink.
SLAPSTICK

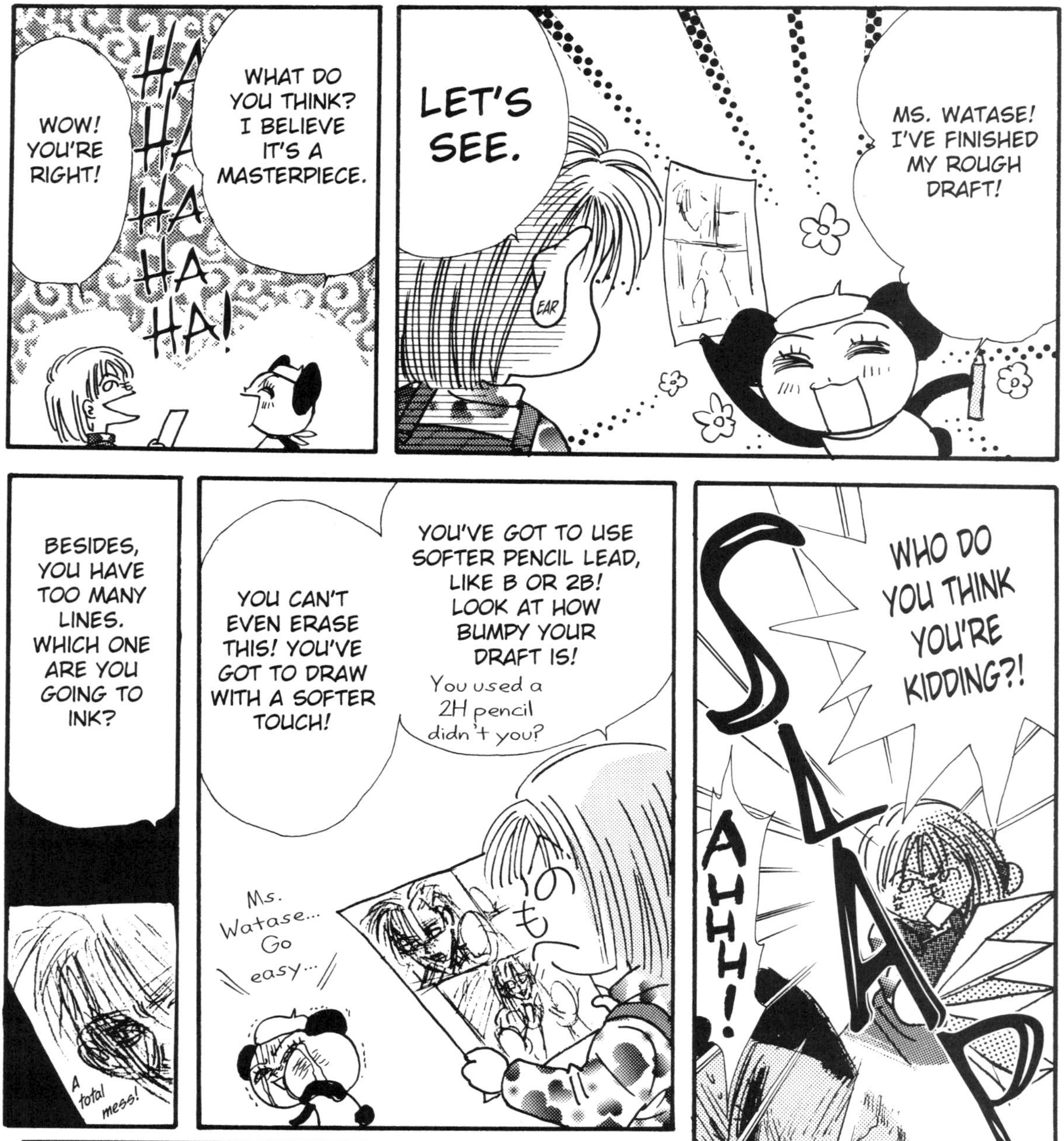
MS. WATASE! I'VE FINISHED MY ROUGH DRAFT!
LET'S SEE.
EAR
WHAT DO YOU THINK? I BELIEVE IT'S A MASTERPIECE.
HA HA HA HA HA!
WOW! YOU'RE RIGHT!
WHO DO YOU THINK YOU'RE KIDDING?!
SLAP
AHHH!
YOU'VE GOT TO USE SOFTER PENCIL LEAD, LIKE B OR 2B! LOOK AT HOW BUMPY YOUR DRAFT IS!
You used a 2H pencil didn't you?
YOU CAN'T EVEN ERASE THIS! YOU'VE GOT TO DRAW WITH A SOFTER TOUCH!
Ms. Watase... Go easy...
BESIDES, YOU HAVE TOO MANY LINES. WHICH ONE ARE YOU GOING TO INK?
A total mess!

USE THE PEN TO GET USED TO IT.

Those of you who have a good rough draft but find your page going south when you put pen to paper… Rest assured, it's a common woe! Even for professionals! It just means that you're used to the pencil you've been using since childhood, and not to the pen you just added to your collection. Your skill with the pen is similar to that of a child who breaks the lead on a fat pencil. The only solution is to accustom yourself to the pen. Use a pen even when you're doodling, and make it your own!

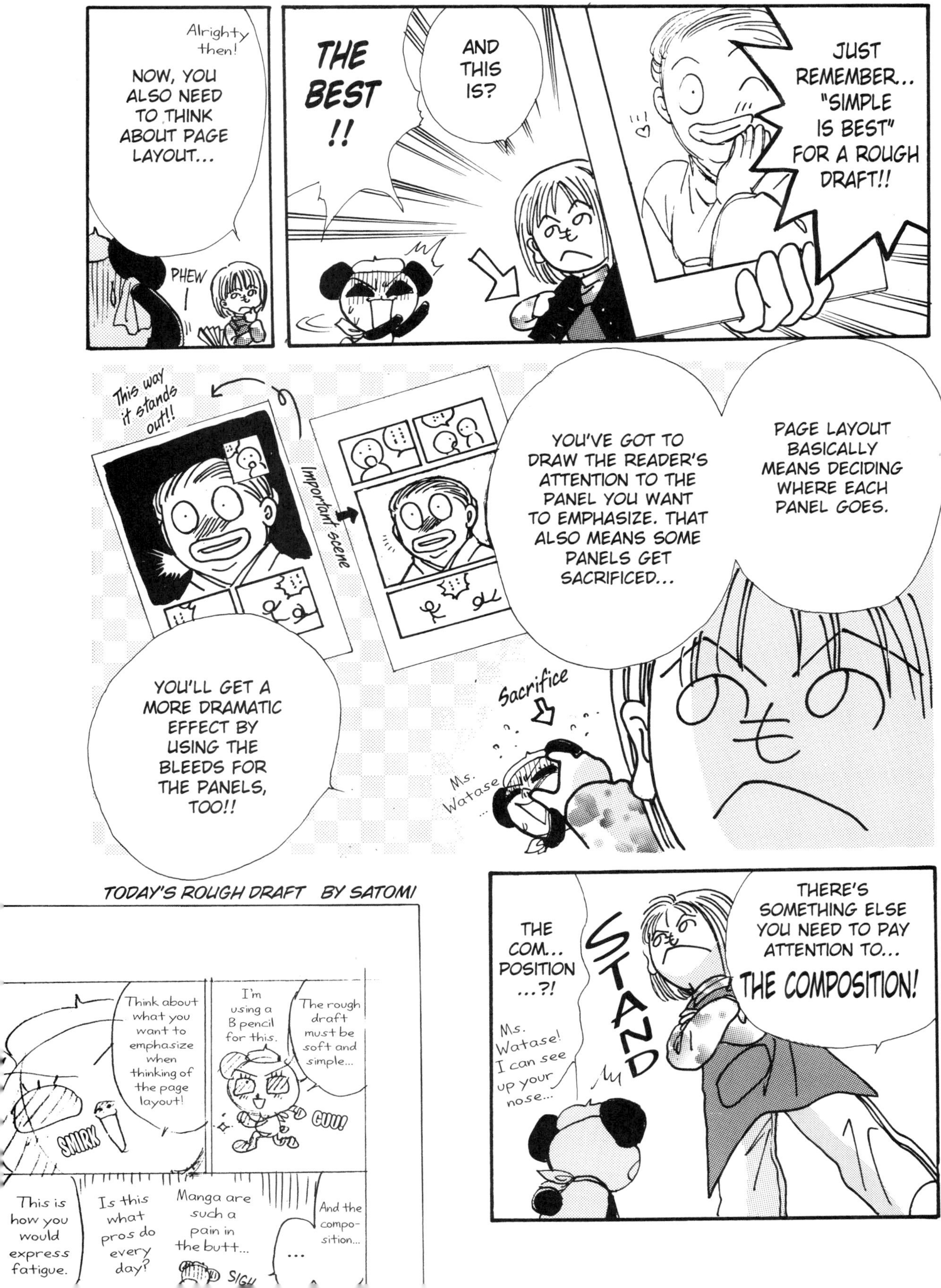
JUST REMEMBER... "SIMPLE IS BEST" FOR A ROUGH DRAFT!!
AND THIS IS?
THE BEST !!
Alrighty then!
NOW, YOU ALSO NEED TO THINK ABOUT PAGE LAYOUT...
PHEW
PAGE LAYOUT BASICALLY MEANS DECIDING WHERE EACH PANEL GOES.
YOU'VE GOT TO DRAW THE READER'S ATTENTION TO THE PANEL YOU WANT TO EMPHASIZE. THAT ALSO MEANS SOME PANELS GET SACRIFICED...
Important scene
This way it stands out!!
YOU'LL GET A MORE DRAMATIC EFFECT BY USING THE BLEEDS FOR THE PANELS, TOO!!
Sacrifice
Ms. Watase...
THERE'S SOMETHING ELSE YOU NEED TO PAY ATTENTION TO... THE COMPOSITION!
STAND
THE COM... POSITION ...?!
Ms. Watase! I can see up your nose...
TODAY'S ROUGH DRAFT BY SATOMI
The rough draft must be soft and simple...
I'm using a B pencil for this.
GUU!
Think about what you want to emphasize when thinking of the page layout!
SMIRK
And the composition...
...
Manga are such a pain in the butt...
SIGH
Is this what pros do every day?
This is how you would express fatigue.

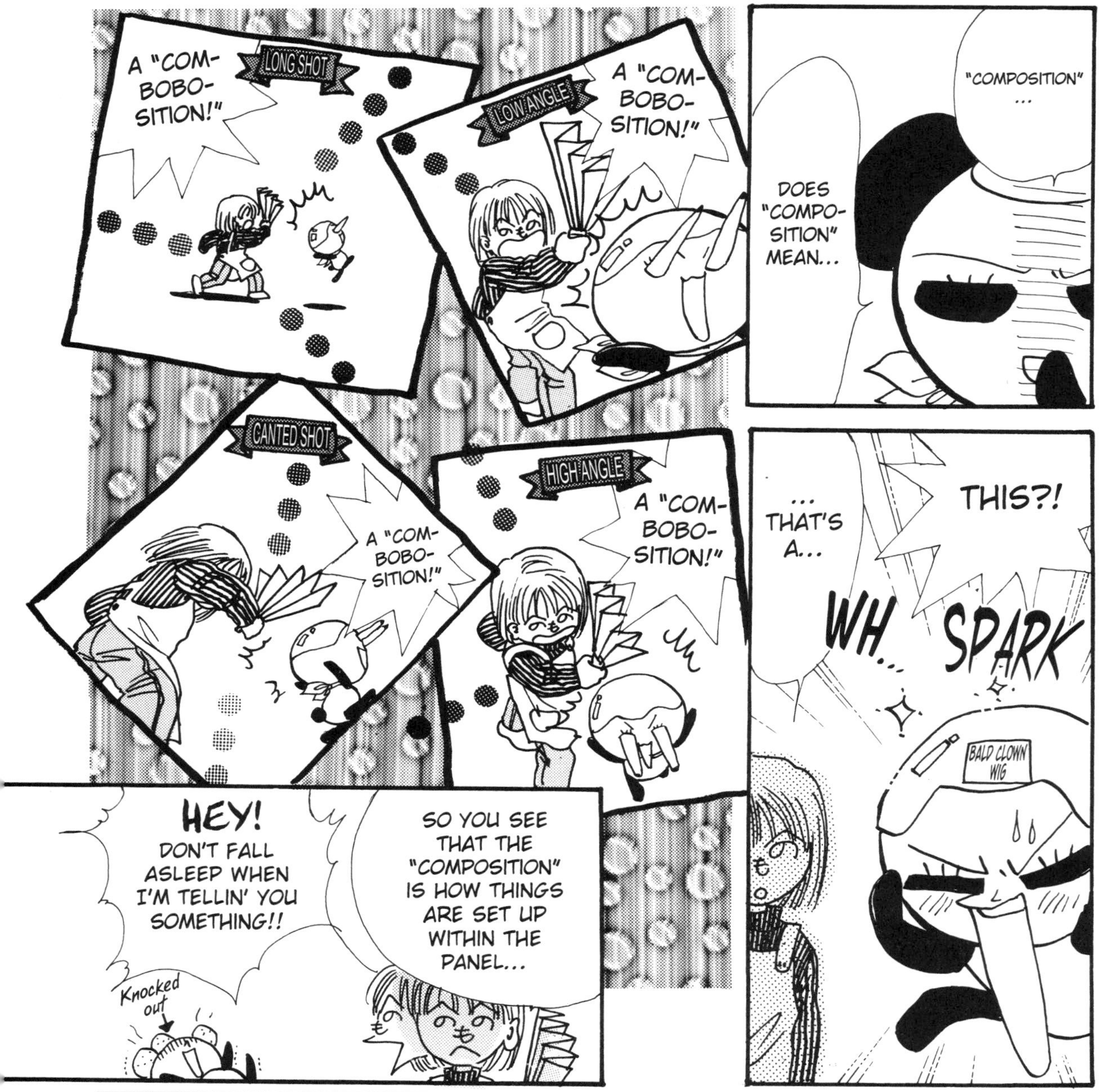
"COMPOSITION" ...
DOES "COMPOSITION" MEAN...
LOW ANGLE
A "COMBOBOSITION!"
LONG SHOT
A "COMBOBOSITION!"
... THAT'S A...
THIS?!
WH...
SPARK
BALD CLOWN WIG
HIGH ANGLE
A "COMBOBOSITION!"
CANTED SHOT
A "COMBOBOSITION!"
SO YOU SEE THAT THE "COMPOSITION" IS HOW THINGS ARE SET UP WITHIN THE PANEL...
HEY! DON'T FALL ASLEEP WHEN I'M TELLIN' YOU SOMETHING!!
Knocked out

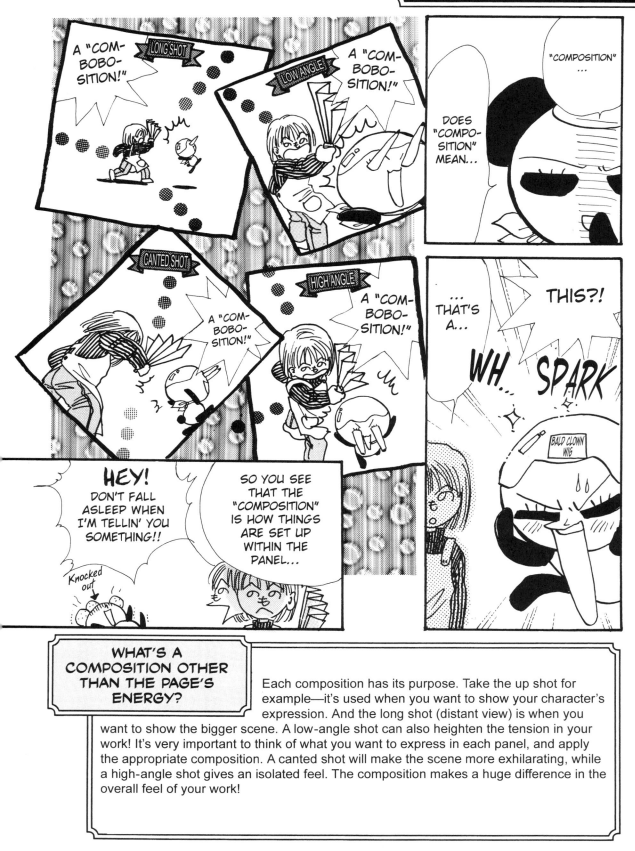

WHAT'S A COMPOSITION OTHER THAN THE PAGE'S ENERGY?

Each composition has its purpose. Take the up shot for example—it's used when you want to show your character's expression. And the long shot (distant view) is when you want to show the bigger scene. A low-angle shot can also heighten the tension in your work! It's very important to think of what you want to express in each panel, and apply the appropriate composition. A canted shot will make the scene more exhilarating, while a high-angle shot gives an isolated feel. The composition makes a huge difference in the overall feel of your work!

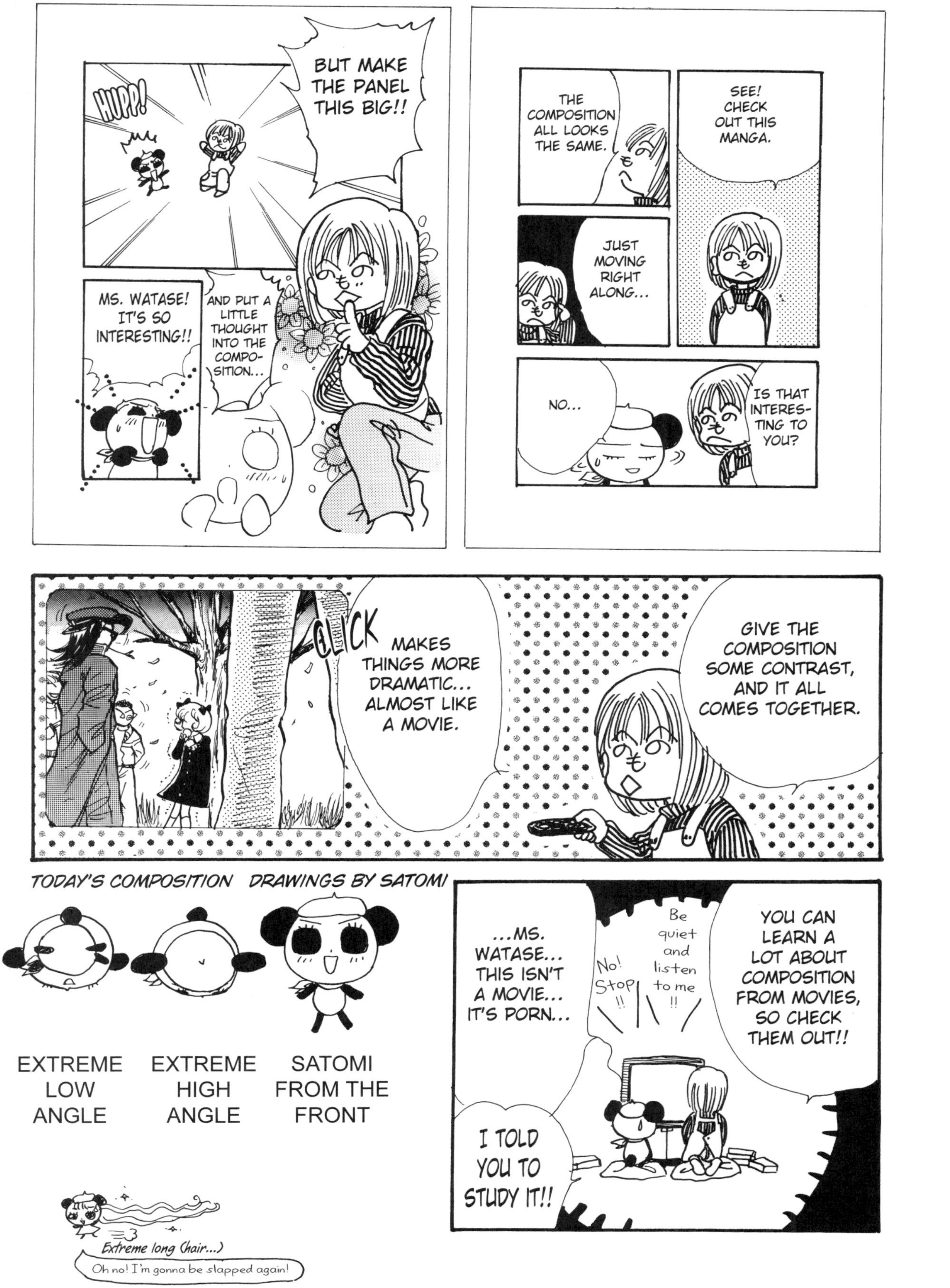
SEE! CHECK OUT THIS MANGA.
THE COMPOSITION ALL LOOKS THE SAME.
JUST MOVING RIGHT ALONG...
IS THAT INTERESTING TO YOU?
NO...
BUT MAKE THE PANEL THIS BIG!!
HUPP!
AND PUT A LITTLE THOUGHT INTO THE COMPOSITION...
MS. WATASE! IT'S SO INTERESTING!!
GIVE THE COMPOSITION SOME CONTRAST, AND IT ALL COMES TOGETHER.
MAKES THINGS MORE DRAMATIC... ALMOST LIKE A MOVIE.
CLICK
YOU CAN LEARN A LOT ABOUT COMPOSITION FROM MOVIES, SO CHECK THEM OUT!!
Be quiet and listen to me!!
No! Stop!!
...MS. WATASE... THIS ISN'T A MOVIE... IT'S PORN...
I TOLD YOU TO STUDY IT!!
TODAY'S COMPOSITION DRAWINGS BY SATOMI
EXTREME LOW ANGLE
EXTREME HIGH ANGLE
SATOMI FROM THE FRONT
Extreme long (hair...)
Oh no! I'm gonna be slapped again!

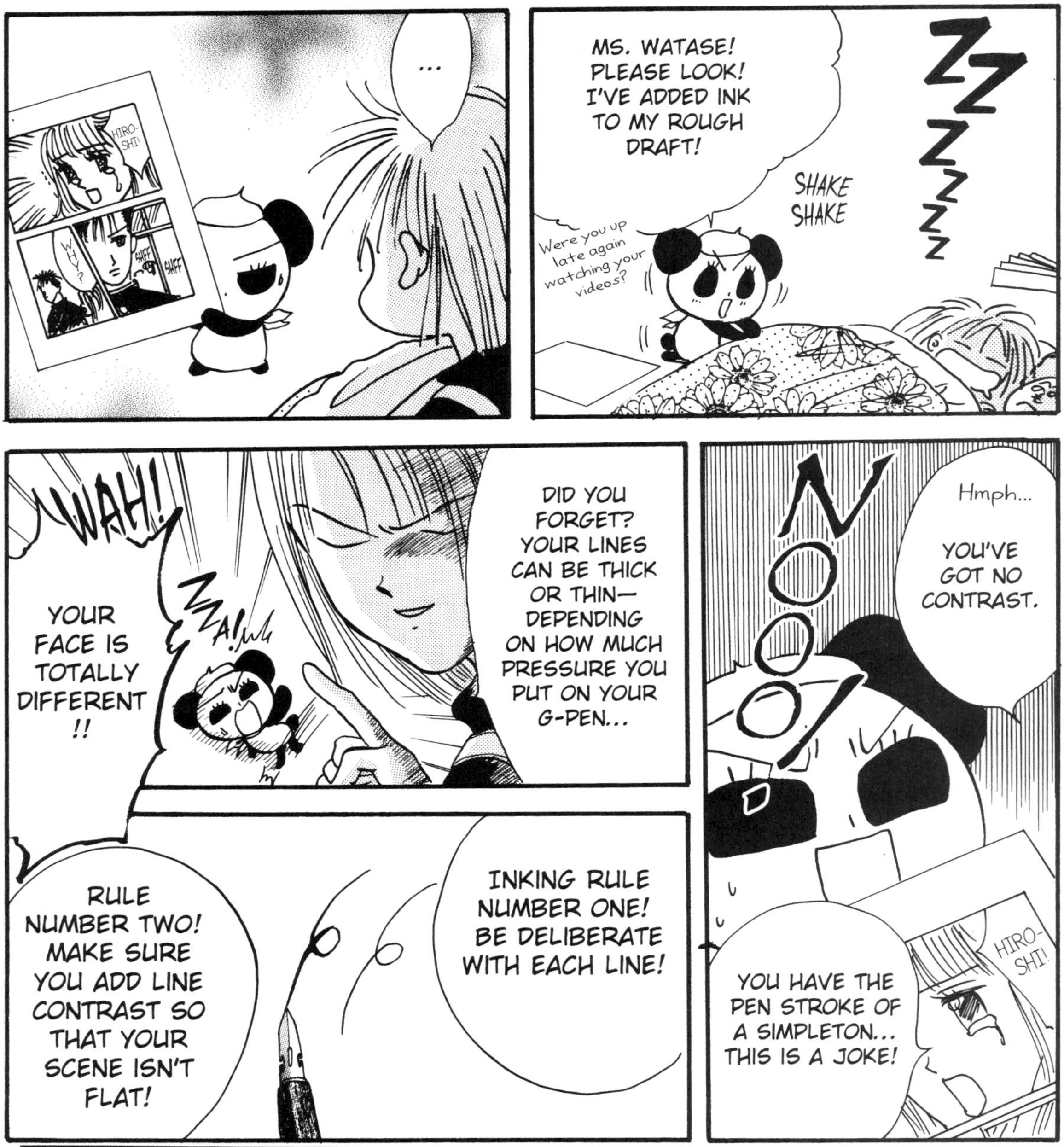
ZZZZZZ
MS. WATASE! PLEASE LOOK! I'VE ADDED INK TO MY ROUGH DRAFT!
SHAKE SHAKE
Were you up late again watching your videos?
...
HIRO-SHI!
WHY?
SNIFF SNIFF
Hmph...
YOU'VE GOT NO CONTRAST.
NOOOO!
HIRO-SHI!
YOU HAVE THE PEN STROKE OF A SIMPLETON... THIS IS A JOKE!
DID YOU FORGET? YOUR LINES CAN BE THICK OR THIN—DEPENDING ON HOW MUCH PRESSURE YOU PUT ON YOUR G-PEN...
WAH!
ZZA!
YOUR FACE IS TOTALLY DIFFERENT!!
INKING RULE NUMBER ONE! BE DELIBERATE WITH EACH LINE!
RULE NUMBER TWO! MAKE SURE YOU ADD LINE CONTRAST SO THAT YOUR SCENE ISN'T FLAT!

USE A PEN AT LEAST ONCE A DAY TO GET USED TO IT.

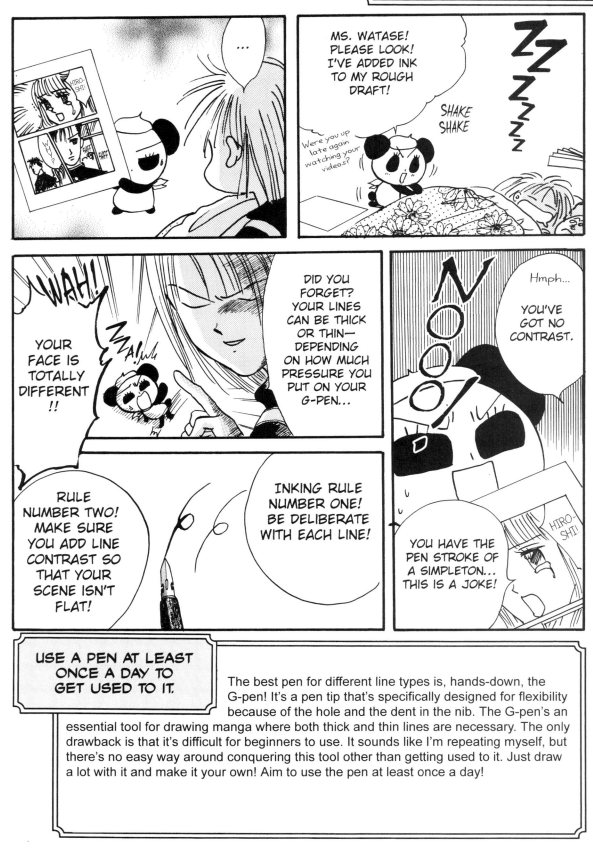

The best pen for different line types is, hands-down, the G-pen! It's a pen tip that's specifically designed for flexibility because of the hole and the dent in the nib. The G-pen's an essential tool for drawing manga where both thick and thin lines are necessary. The only drawback is that it's difficult for beginners to use. It sounds like I'm repeating myself, but there's no easy way around conquering this tool other than getting used to it. Just draw a lot with it and make it your own! Aim to use the pen at least once a day!

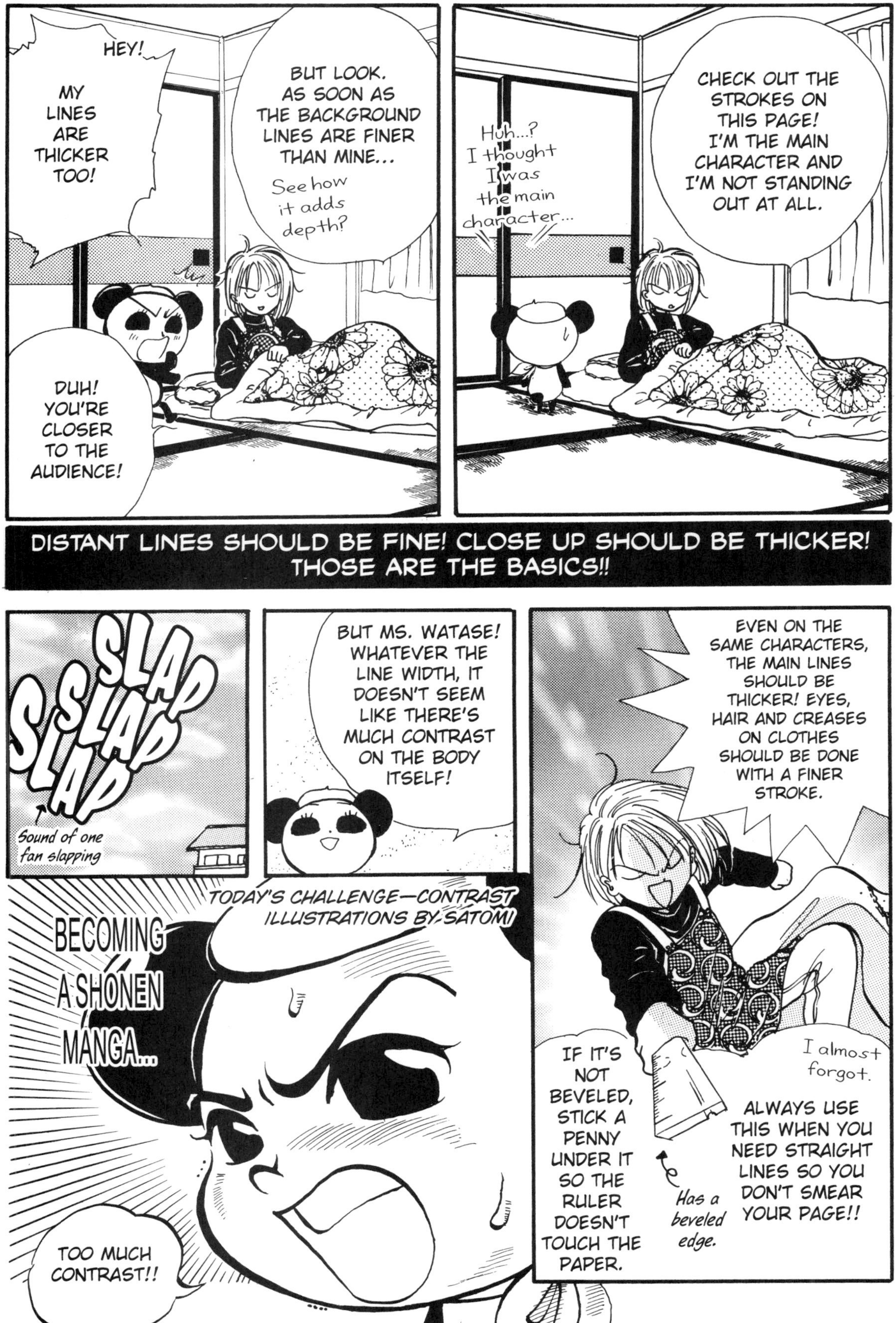
CHECK OUT THE STROKES ON THIS PAGE! I'M THE MAIN CHARACTER AND I'M NOT STANDING OUT AT ALL.
Huh...? I thought I was the main character...
BUT LOOK. AS SOON AS THE BACKGROUND LINES ARE FINER THAN MINE...
See how it adds depth?
HEY!
MY LINES ARE THICKER TOO!
DUH! YOU'RE CLOSER TO THE AUDIENCE!
DISTANT LINES SHOULD BE FINE! CLOSE UP SHOULD BE THICKER! THOSE ARE THE BASICS!!
EVEN ON THE SAME CHARACTERS, THE MAIN LINES SHOULD BE THICKER! EYES, HAIR AND CREASES ON CLOTHES SHOULD BE DONE WITH A FINER STROKE.
I almost forgot.
ALWAYS USE THIS WHEN YOU NEED STRAIGHT LINES SO YOU DON'T SMEAR YOUR PAGE!!
Has a beveled edge.
IF IT'S NOT BEVELED, STICK A PENNY UNDER IT SO THE RULER DOESN'T TOUCH THE PAPER.
BUT MS. WATASE! WHATEVER THE LINE WIDTH, IT DOESN'T SEEM LIKE THERE'S MUCH CONTRAST ON THE BODY ITSELF!
SLAP SLAP SLAP
Sound of one fan slapping
TODAY'S CHALLENGE—CONTRAST ILLUSTRATIONS BY SATOMI
BECOMING A SHŌNEN MANGA...
TOO MUCH CONTRAST!!

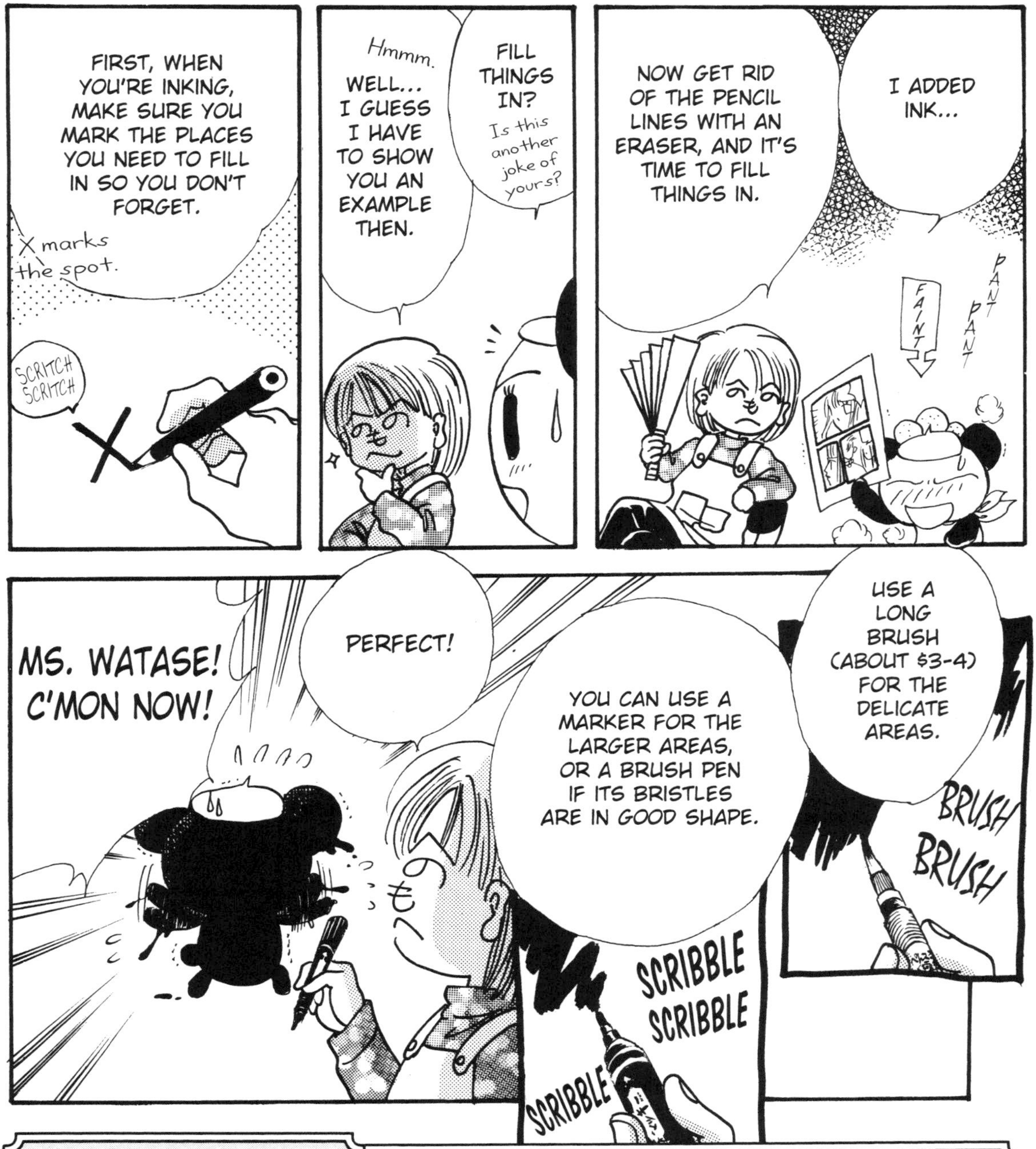
I ADDED INK...
NOW GET RID OF THE PENCIL LINES WITH AN ERASER, AND IT'S TIME TO FILL THINGS IN.
PANT PANT
FAINT
FILL THINGS IN?
Is this another joke of yours?
Hmmm.
WELL... I GUESS I HAVE TO SHOW YOU AN EXAMPLE THEN.
FIRST, WHEN YOU'RE INKING, MAKE SURE YOU MARK THE PLACES YOU NEED TO FILL IN SO YOU DON'T FORGET.
X marks the spot.
SCRITCH SCRITCH
USE A LONG BRUSH (ABOUT $3-4) FOR THE DELICATE AREAS.
BRUSH
BRUSH
YOU CAN USE A MARKER FOR THE LARGER AREAS, OR A BRUSH PEN IF ITS BRISTLES ARE IN GOOD SHAPE.
SCRIBBLE
SCRIBBLE
SCRIBBLE
PERFECT!
MS. WATASE! C'MON NOW!

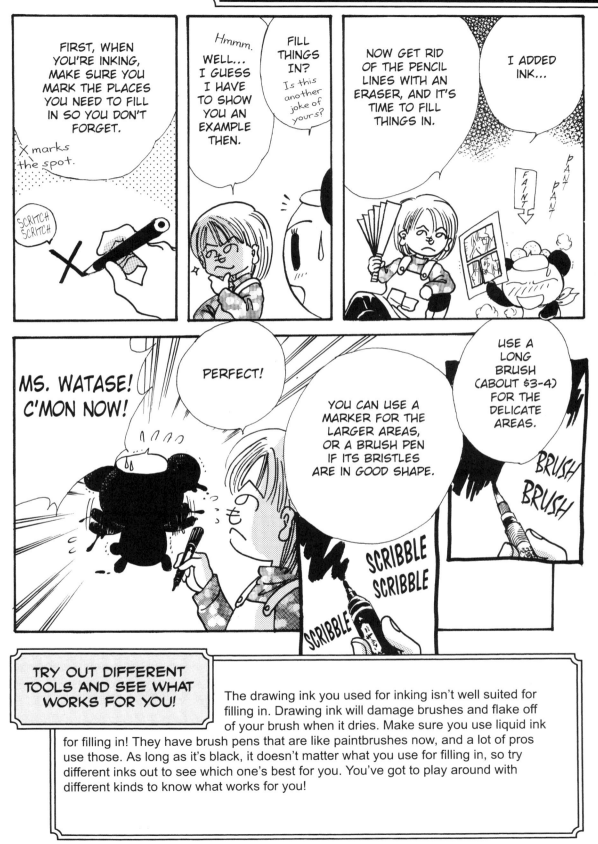

TRY OUT DIFFERENT TOOLS AND SEE WHAT WORKS FOR YOU!

The drawing ink you used for inking isn't well suited for filling in. Drawing ink will damage brushes and flake off of your brush when it dries. Make sure you use liquid ink for filling in! They have brush pens that are like paintbrushes now, and a lot of pros use those. As long as it's black, it doesn't matter what you use for filling in, so try different inks out to see which one's best for you. You've got to play around with different kinds to know what works for you!

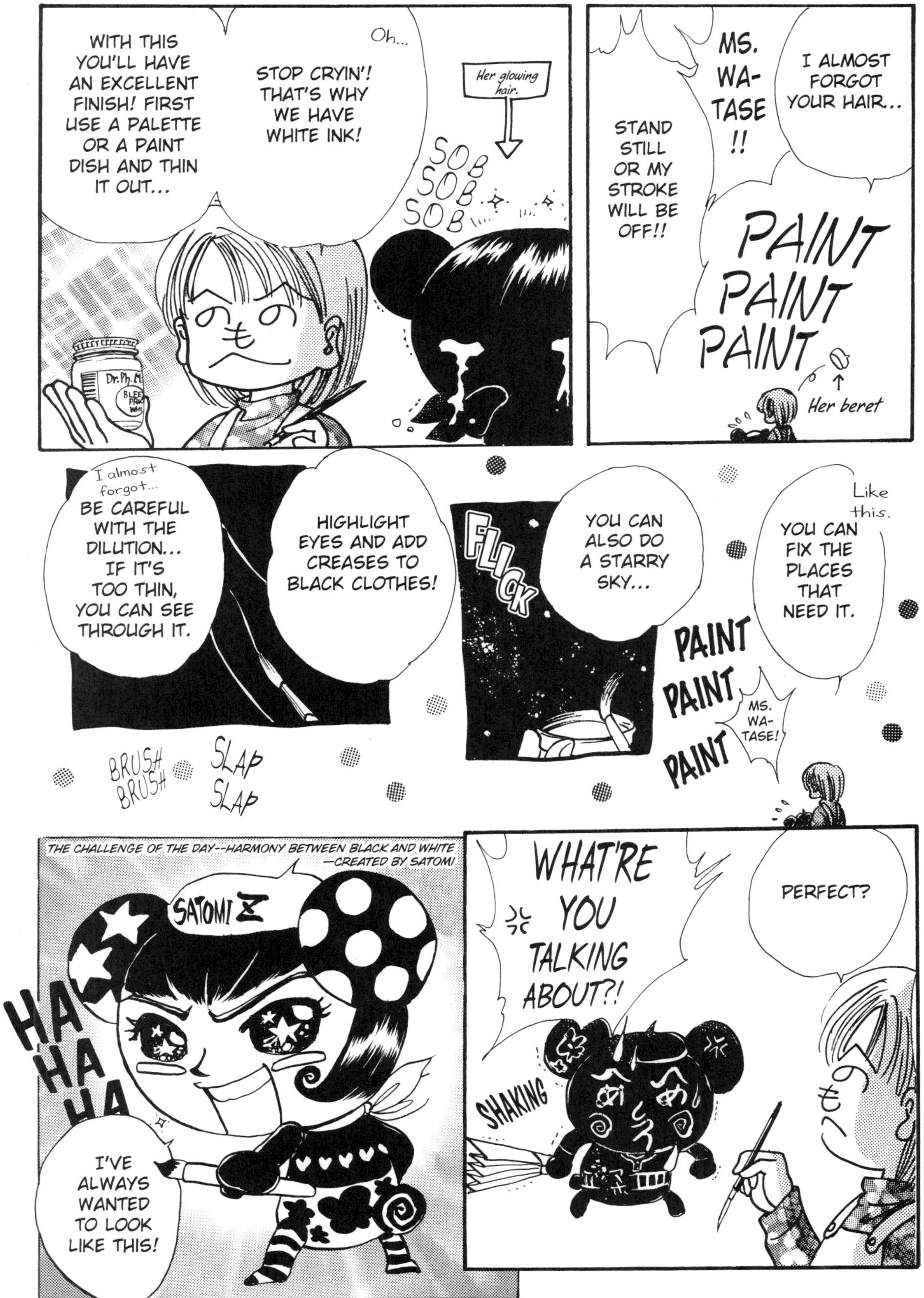
I ALMOST FORGOT YOUR HAIR...
MS. WA-TASE!!
STAND STILL OR MY STROKE WILL BE OFF!!
PAINT PAINT PAINT
Her beret
Her glowing hair.
Oh...
STOP CRYIN'! THAT'S WHY WE HAVE WHITE INK!
SOB SOB SOB
WITH THIS YOU'LL HAVE AN EXCELLENT FINISH! FIRST USE A PALETTE OR A PAINT DISH AND THIN IT OUT...
Like this.
YOU CAN FIX THE PLACES THAT NEED IT.
MS. WA-TASE!
PAINT PAINT PAINT
YOU CAN ALSO DO A STARRY SKY...
FLICK
HIGHLIGHT EYES AND ADD CREASES TO BLACK CLOTHES!
I almost forgot...
BE CAREFUL WITH THE DILUTION... IF IT'S TOO THIN, YOU CAN SEE THROUGH IT.
SLAP SLAP
BRUSH BRUSH
PERFECT?
WHAT'RE YOU TALKING ABOUT?!
SHAKING
THE CHALLENGE OF THE DAY--HARMONY BETWEEN BLACK AND WHITE —CREATED BY SATOMI
SATOMI Z
I'VE ALWAYS WANTED TO LOOK LIKE THIS!
HA HA HA

But still so uncool...

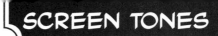

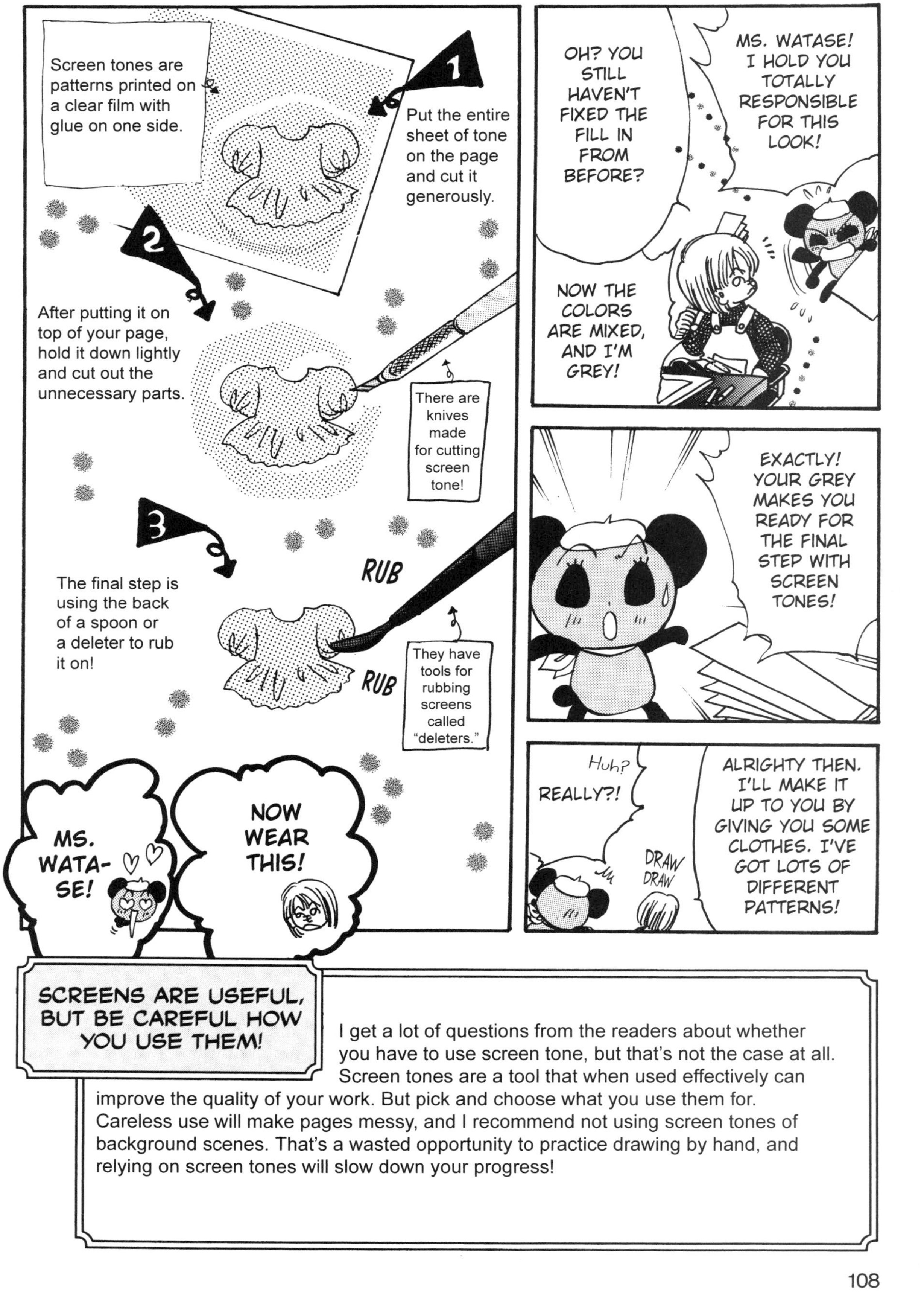
MS. WATASE! I HOLD YOU TOTALLY RESPONSIBLE FOR THIS LOOK!
OH? YOU STILL HAVEN'T FIXED THE FILL IN FROM BEFORE?
NOW THE COLORS ARE MIXED, AND I'M GREY!
EXACTLY! YOUR GREY MAKES YOU READY FOR THE FINAL STEP WITH SCREEN TONES!
ALRIGHTY THEN. I'LL MAKE IT UP TO YOU BY GIVING YOU SOME CLOTHES. I'VE GOT LOTS OF DIFFERENT PATTERNS!
Huh? REALLY?!
DRAW DRAW
Screen tones are patterns printed on a clear film with glue on one side.
1
Put the entire sheet of tone on the page and cut it generously.
2
After putting it on top of your page, hold it down lightly and cut out the unnecessary parts.
There are knives made for cutting screen tone!
3
The final step is using the back of a spoon or a deleter to rub it on!
RUB
RUB
They have tools for rubbing screens called "deleters."
NOW WEAR THIS!
MS. WATA-SE!

SCREENS ARE USEFUL, BUT BE CAREFUL HOW YOU USE THEM!

I get a lot of questions from the readers about whether you have to use screen tone, but that's not the case at all. Screen tones are a tool that when used effectively can improve the quality of your work. But pick and choose what you use them for. Careless use will make pages messy, and I recommend not using screen tones of background scenes. That's a wasted opportunity to practice drawing by hand, and relying on screen tones will slow down your progress!

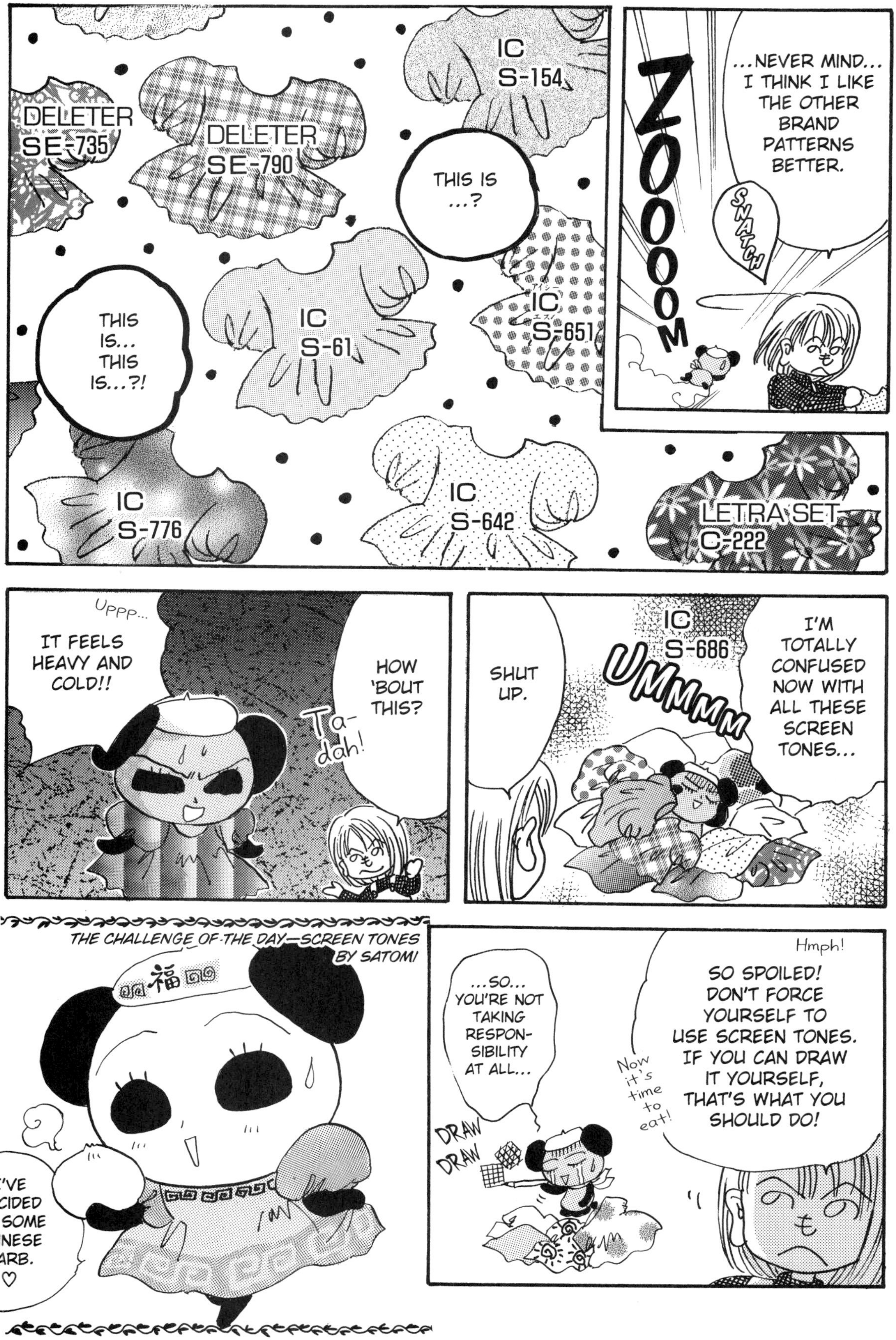
ZOOOOOOM
...NEVER MIND... I THINK I LIKE THE OTHER BRAND PATTERNS BETTER.
SNATCH
IC S-154
THIS IS ...?
DELETER SE-790
DELETER SE-735
IC S-651
IC S-61
THIS IS... THIS IS...?!
LETRA SET C-222
IC S-642
IC S-776
I'M TOTALLY CONFUSED NOW WITH ALL THESE SCREEN TONES...
IC S-686
UMMMMM
SHUT UP.
HOW 'BOUT THIS?
Ta-dah!
Uppp...
IT FEELS HEAVY AND COLD!!
Hmph!
SO SPOILED! DON'T FORCE YOURSELF TO USE SCREEN TONES. IF YOU CAN DRAW IT YOURSELF, THAT'S WHAT YOU SHOULD DO!
Now it's time to eat!
...SO... YOU'RE NOT TAKING RESPON-SIBILITY AT ALL...
DRAW DRAW
THE CHALLENGE OF THE DAY—SCREEN TONES BY SATOMI
福
I'VE DECIDED ON SOME CHINESE GARB. ♡

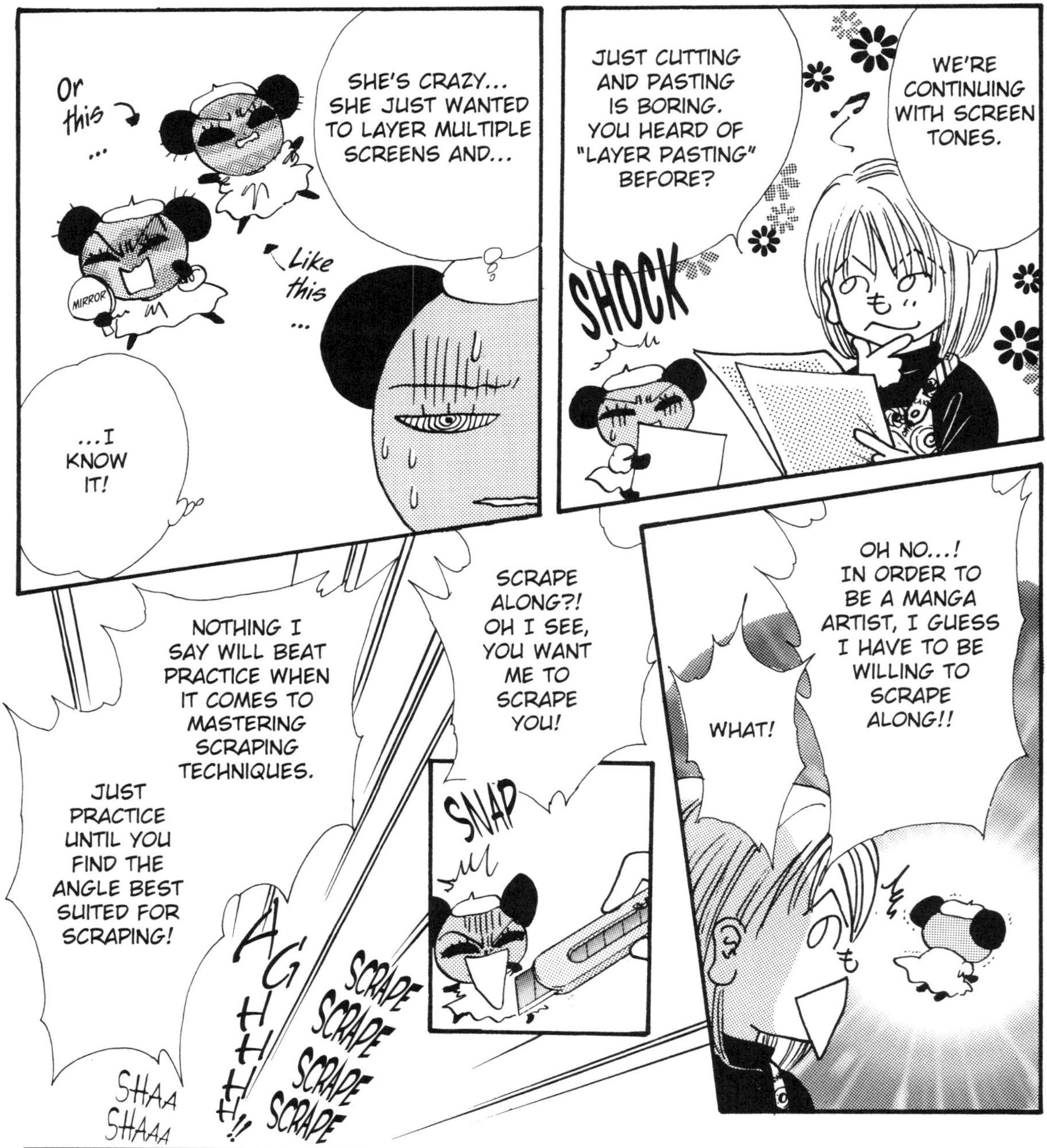
WE'RE CONTINUING WITH SCREEN TONES.
JUST CUTTING AND PASTING IS BORING. YOU HEARD OF "LAYER PASTING" BEFORE?
SHOCK
SHE'S CRAZY... SHE JUST WANTED TO LAYER MULTIPLE SCREENS AND...
Or this ...
Like this ...
MIRROR
...I KNOW IT!
OH NO...! IN ORDER TO BE A MANGA ARTIST, I GUESS I HAVE TO BE WILLING TO SCRAPE ALONG!!
WHAT!
SCRAPE ALONG?! OH I SEE, YOU WANT ME TO SCRAPE YOU!
SNAP
NOTHING I SAY WILL BEAT PRACTICE WHEN IT COMES TO MASTERING SCRAPING TECHNIQUES.
JUST PRACTICE UNTIL YOU FIND THE ANGLE BEST SUITED FOR SCRAPING!
AGHHHHH!!
SCRAPE SCRAPE SCRAPE SCRAPE
SHAA SHAAA

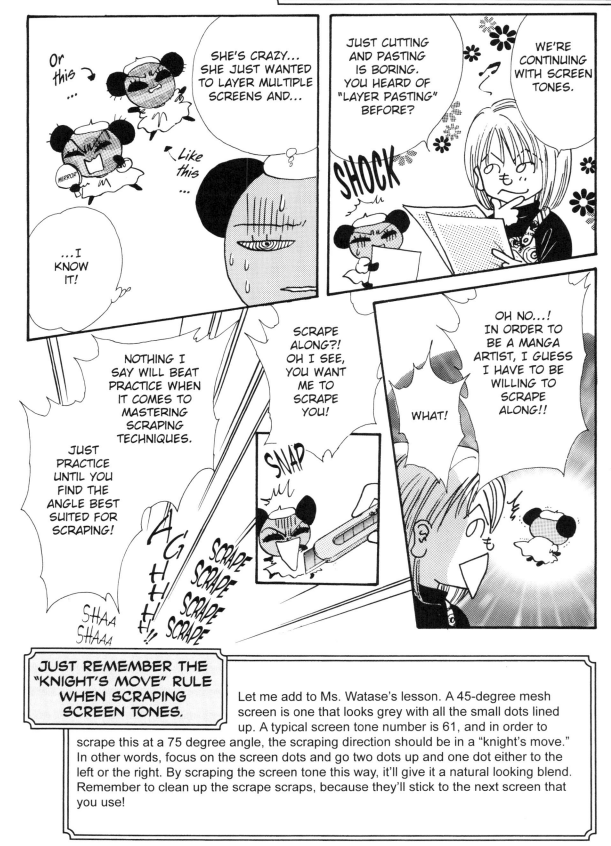

JUST REMEMBER THE "KNIGHT'S MOVE" RULE WHEN SCRAPING SCREEN TONES.

Let me add to Ms. Watase's lesson. A 45-degree mesh screen is one that looks grey with all the small dots lined up. A typical screen tone number is 61, and in order to scrape this at a 75 degree angle, the scraping direction should be in a "knight's move." In other words, focus on the screen dots and go two dots up and one dot either to the left or the right. By scraping the screen tone this way, it'll give it a natural looking blend. Remember to clean up the scrape scraps, because they'll stick to the next screen that you use!

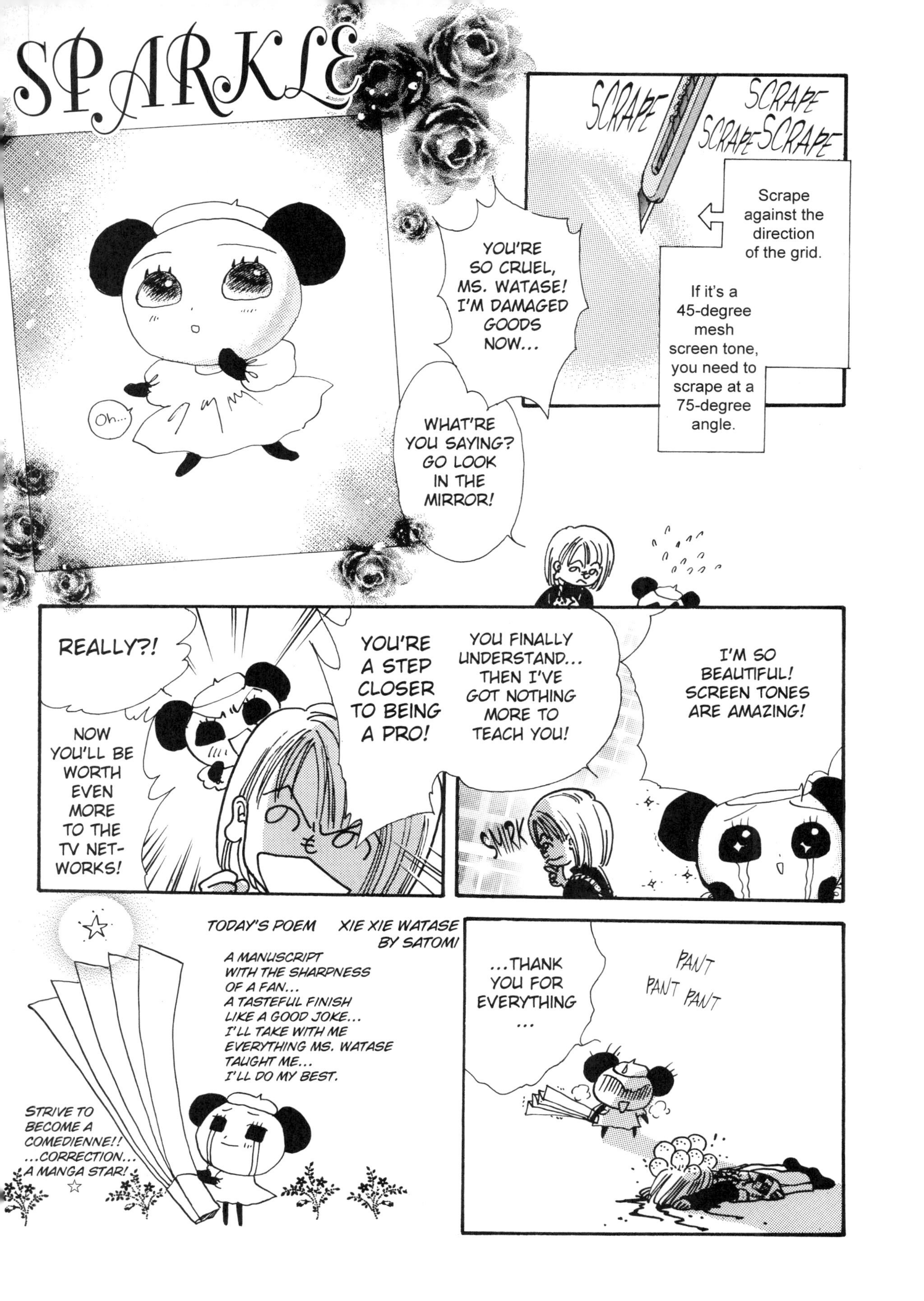
SCRAPE
SCRAPE
SCRAPE-SCRAPE
Scrape against the direction of the grid.
If it's a 45-degree mesh screen tone, you need to scrape at a 75-degree angle.
YOU'RE SO CRUEL, MS. WATASE! I'M DAMAGED GOODS NOW...
WHAT'RE YOU SAYING? GO LOOK IN THE MIRROR!
SPARKLE
Oh...
I'M SO BEAUTIFUL! SCREEN TONES ARE AMAZING!
SMIRK
YOU FINALLY UNDERSTAND... THEN I'VE GOT NOTHING MORE TO TEACH YOU!
YOU'RE A STEP CLOSER TO BEING A PRO!
REALLY?!
NOW YOU'LL BE WORTH EVEN MORE TO THE TV NET-WORKS!
...THANK YOU FOR EVERYTHING...
PANT
PANT PANT
TODAY'S POEM XIE XIE WATASE BY SATOMI
A MANUSCRIPT WITH THE SHARPNESS OF A FAN... A TASTEFUL FINISH LIKE A GOOD JOKE... I'LL TAKE WITH ME EVERYTHING MS. WATASE TAUGHT ME... I'LL DO MY BEST.
STRIVE TO BECOME A COMEDIENNE!! ...CORRECTION... A MANGA STAR! ☆

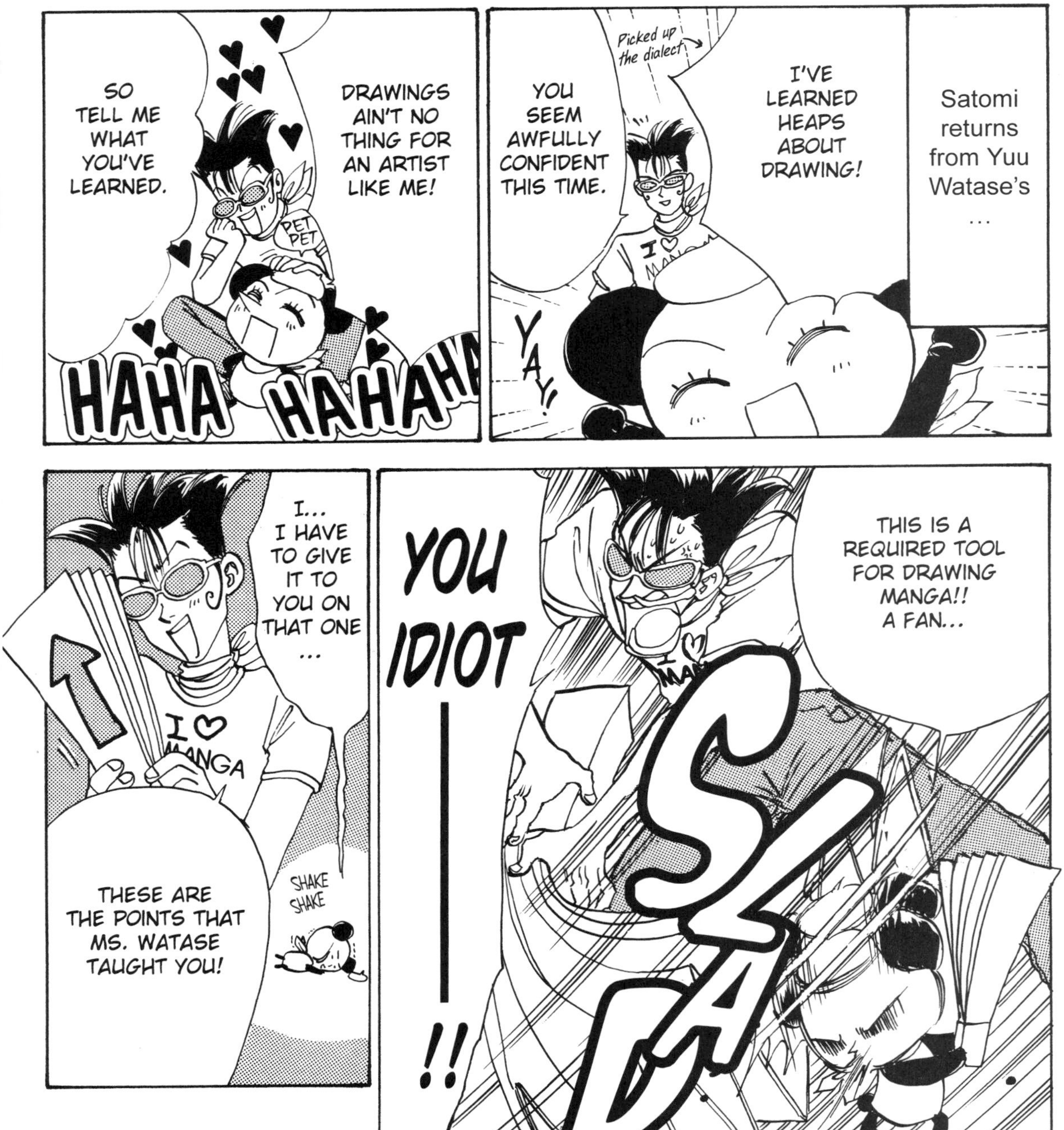
Satomi returns from Yuu Watase's ...
I'VE LEARNED HEAPS ABOUT DRAWING!
YOU SEEM AWFULLY CONFIDENT THIS TIME.
Picked up the dialect
YAY!!
DRAWINGS AIN'T NO THING FOR AN ARTIST LIKE ME!
SO TELL ME WHAT YOU'VE LEARNED.
PET PET
HAHA HAHAHA
THIS IS A REQUIRED TOOL FOR DRAWING MANGA!! A FAN...
YOU IDIOT—!!
SLAP
GIANT FAN
I... I HAVE TO GIVE IT TO YOU ON THAT ONE ...
I ♥ MANGA
THESE ARE THE POINTS THAT MS. WATASE TAUGHT YOU!
SHAKE SHAKE

CHALLENGE YOURSELF BY DRAWING THINGS YOU'RE NOT GOOD AT.

No matter how advanced a technique, the key to unlocking it is training. Practice makes perfect! If you don't draw because "you've never drawn it before" you'll never improve. You'll do better the second time than the first, no matter how uncomfortable you are with a certain drawing or effect. It'll also boost your confidence, so if you're going to take away anything from this, it should be a will to challenge yourself to encourage improvement!

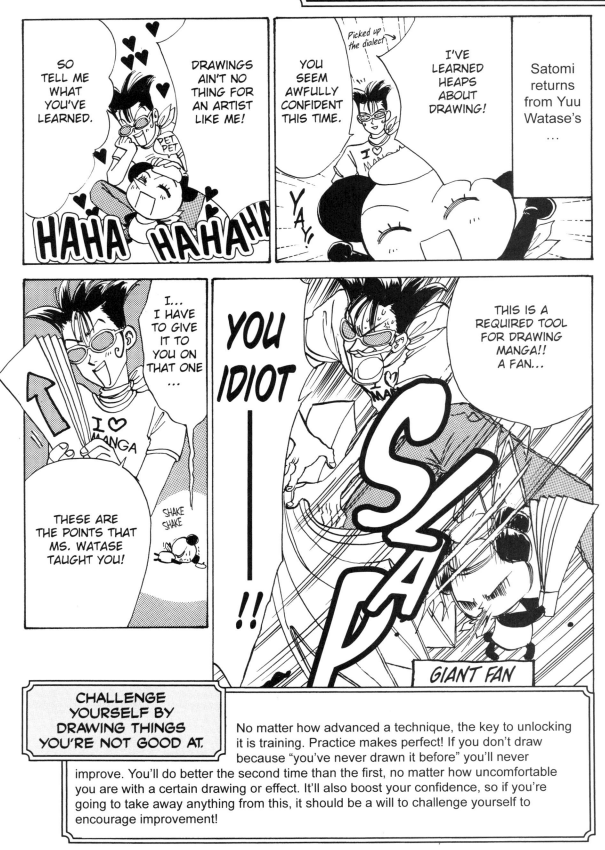

● THE FIVE POINTS OF DRAWING ●

- Keep the rough draft simple with a softer pencil.
- Make your work more dramatic with page layout and composition.
- Use pen strokes to add contrast to the page.
- Be deliberate with the finishing touches and pay attention to details!
- Use screen tones effectively, and don't forget to add your own twist.

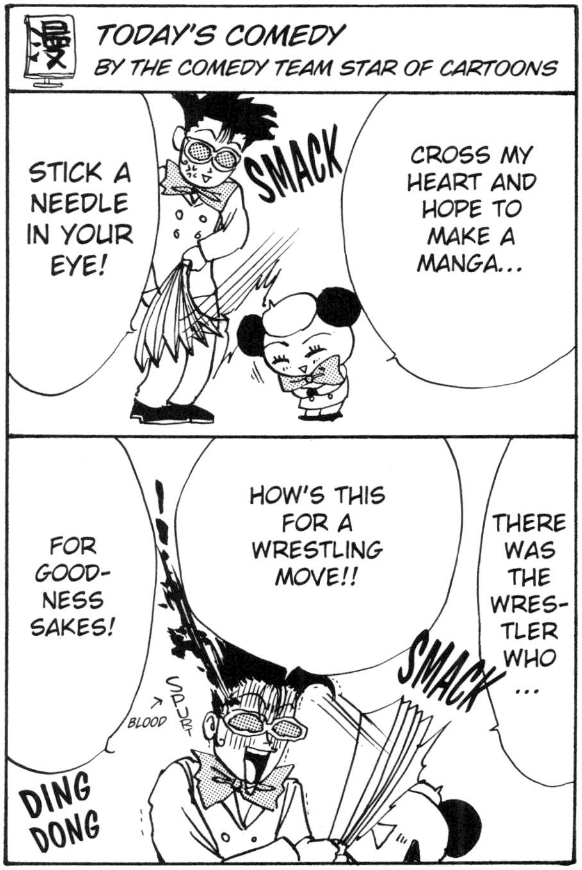
TODAY'S COMEDY
BY THE COMEDY TEAM STAR OF CARTOONS
CROSS MY HEART AND HOPE TO MAKE A MANGA...
SMACK
STICK A NEEDLE IN YOUR EYE!
THERE WAS THE WRES-TLER WHO ...
SMACK
HOW'S THIS FOR A WRESTLING MOVE!!
FOR GOOD-NESS SAKES!
SPURT
BLOOD
DING DONG

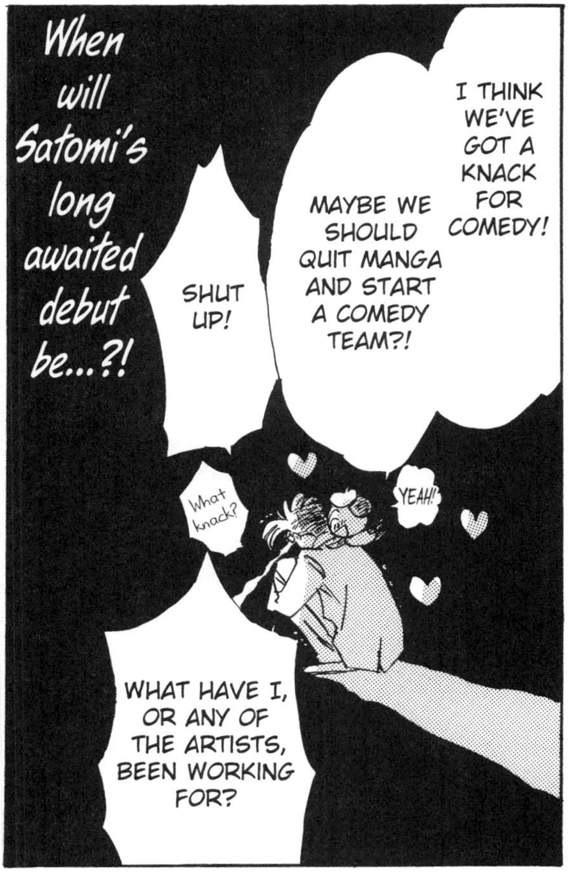
I THINK WE'VE GOT A KNACK FOR COMEDY!
MAYBE WE SHOULD QUIT MANGA AND START A COMEDY TEAM?!
SHUT UP!
When will Satomi's long awaited debut be...?!
YEAH!
What knack?
WHAT HAVE I, OR ANY OF THE ARTISTS, BEEN WORKING FOR?

Manga Star Presents!!

STEAL THIS FROM A PROFESSIONAL MANGA! Part 5

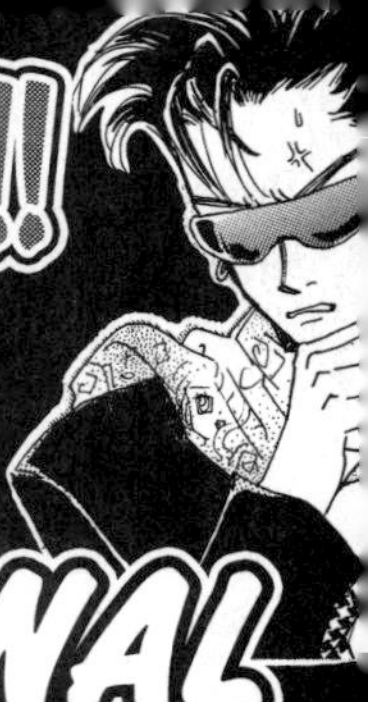

Sho-Comi's Yuu Watase uses her computer even for B&W pages! Here are some examples.

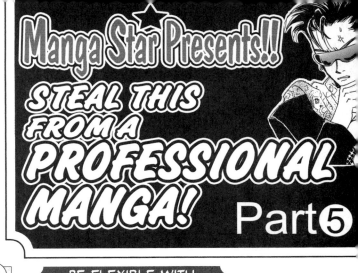

BE FLEXIBLE WITH WHICH TECHNIQUES YOU USE TO IMPROVE THE QUALITY OF YOUR WORK.

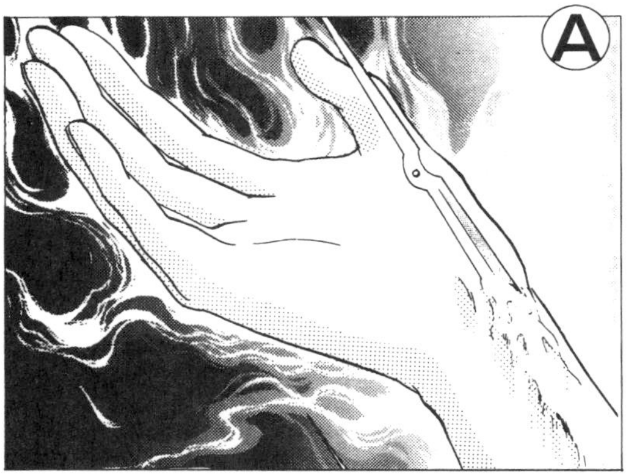
A

The techniques used on the background differ for all three panels shown on the left. If you noticed that on your own, pat yourself on the back for your knowledge and observation skills!

First, the effects seen on the hand in panel A... This effect is achieved by layering and scraping screen tones. But you might have guessed that already.

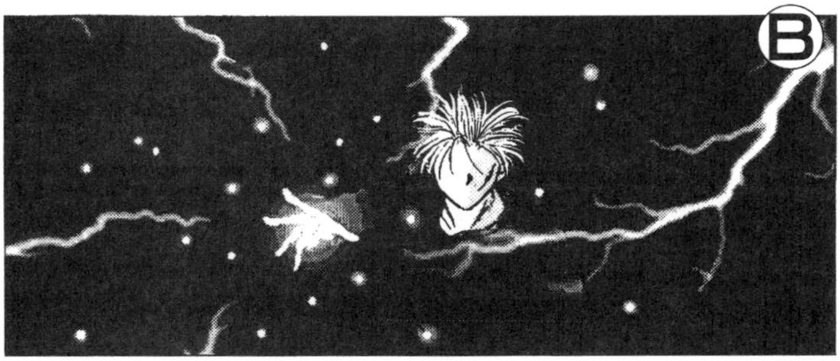
B

Now the background used in panel B... This can't be achieved through screen tones. How are they produced, you ask...? Well, using a computer, of course!! Scan an inked page onto the computer, digitally finish the background, and voila! Print out the finished panel and paste it on the page.

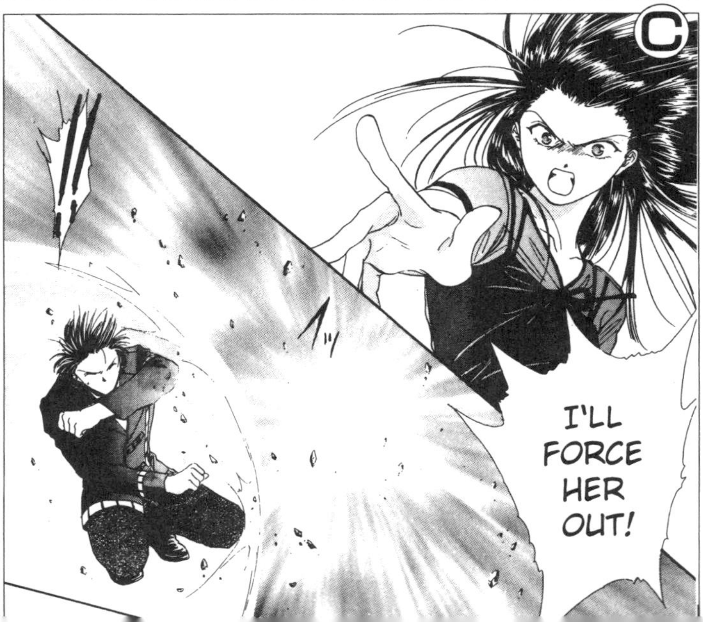
C
I'LL FORCE HER OUT!

So what about the blurred effect in C...? Screen tones are actually used for this.

They're all effective backgrounds, but some use existing screen tones while others are done on the computer. In order to increase the quality of your work, I can't emphasize enough how important it is to be flexible!

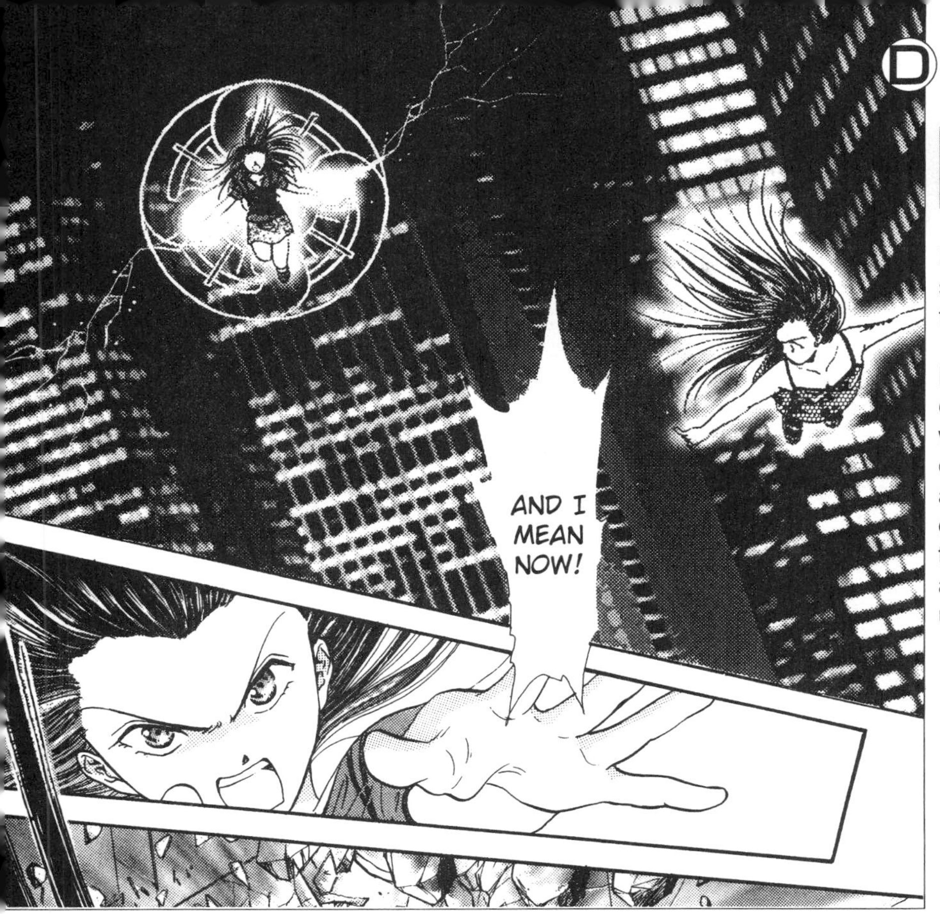
D
AND I MEAN NOW!

DIFFERENT COMPUTER FUNCTIONS... PART 1

Now let's take a look at some different drawings that used a computer.

Panel D is an example of a real picture that was scanned into the computer and used as a background. These effects are really hard to draw by hand, so it's an extremely effective use of the computer!

A FILTERED EFFECT CAN ONLY BE DONE ON THE COMPUTER.

Similar to panel D, panel E took a scanned picture and added a zoom filter. You can also blur or give a mosaic effect with the computer as well! The computer can do effects that are impossible by hand at the touch of the button. Make sure you really understand its advantage before you go out and use it, though.

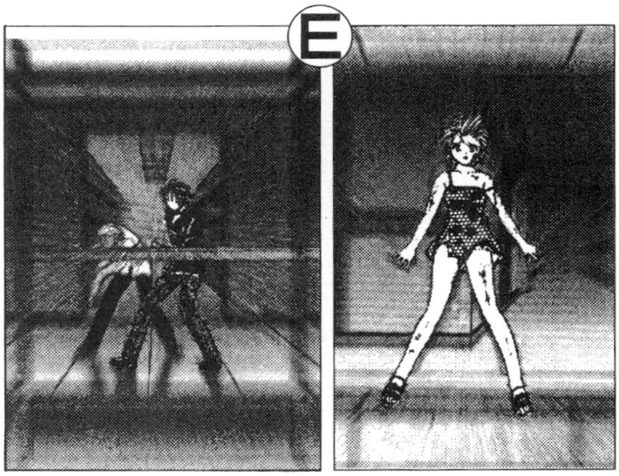
E

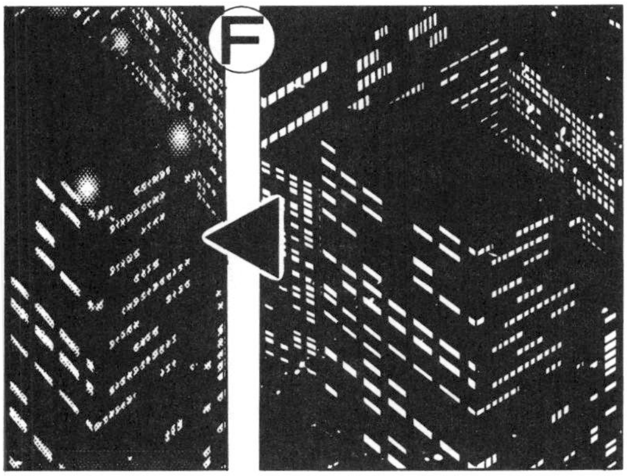
F

PUT A SCREEN TONE THROUGH THE COMPUTER.

Panel F is a really interesting effect. The image on the right is actually something that's sold as a screen tone, but instead of just cutting and pasting it, it's been scanned into the computer and the lights have been enhanced. An unrefined background quickly looks real. It's a good example of how effective it can be to use both the computer and screen tones.

CHAPTER 6: THE MIYUKI KITAGAWA EDITION

LET'S DRAW THE BACKGROUND!

Characters are important, but so is the background! Miyuki Kitagawa shows us her background drawing skills.

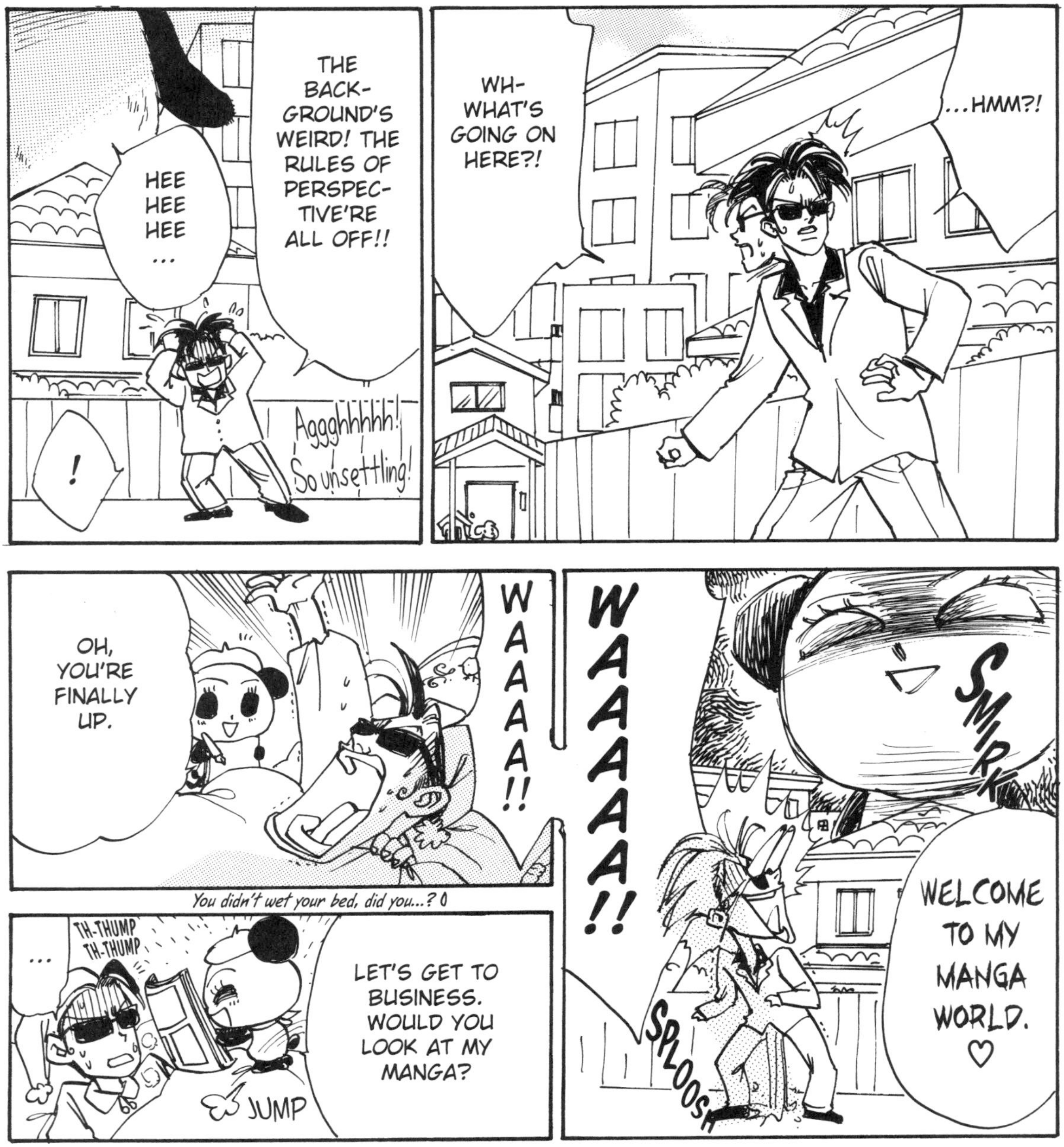

...HMM?!
WH- WHAT'S GOING ON HERE?!
THE BACKGROUND'S WEIRD! THE RULES OF PERSPECTIVE'RE ALL OFF!!
HEE HEE HEE ...
Aggghhhhh! So unsettling!
!
SMIRK
WAAAAAAA!!
WELCOME TO MY MANGA WORLD. ♡
SPLOOSH
WAAAAAA!!
OH, YOU'RE FINALLY UP.
You didn't wet your bed, did you...? ()
LET'S GET TO BUSINESS. WOULD YOU LOOK AT MY MANGA?
TH-THUMP TH-THUMP
...
JUMP

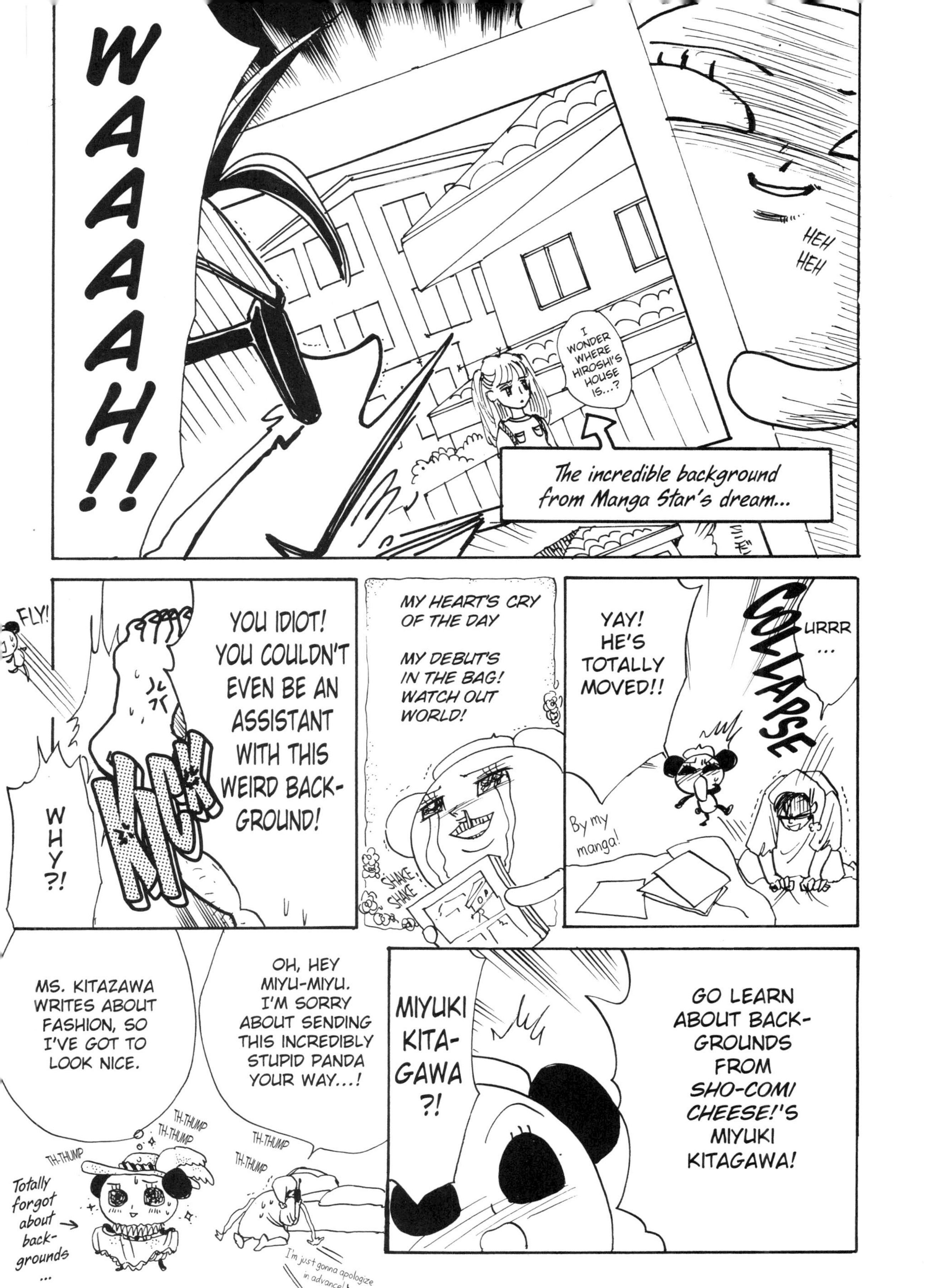
HEH HEH
I WONDER WHERE HIROSHI'S HOUSE IS...?
The incredible background from Manga Star's dream...
WAAAAAH!!
YAY! HE'S TOTALLY MOVED!!
URRR...
COLLAPSE
By my manga!
MY HEART'S CRY OF THE DAY
MY DEBUT'S IN THE BAG! WATCH OUT WORLD!
SHAKE SHAKE
YOU IDIOT! YOU COULDN'T EVEN BE AN ASSISTANT WITH THIS WEIRD BACK-GROUND!
FLY!
KICK
WHY?!
GO LEARN ABOUT BACK-GROUNDS FROM SHO-COMI CHEESE!'S MIYUKI KITAGAWA!
MIYUKI KITA-GAWA?!
OH, HEY MIYU-MIYU. I'M SORRY ABOUT SENDING THIS INCREDIBLY STUPID PANDA YOUR WAY...!
TH-THUMP
TH-THUMP
I'm just gonna apologize in advance!
MS. KITAZAWA WRITES ABOUT FASHION, SO I'VE GOT TO LOOK NICE.
TH-THUMP
TH-THUMP
TH-THUMP
Totally forgot about back-grounds...

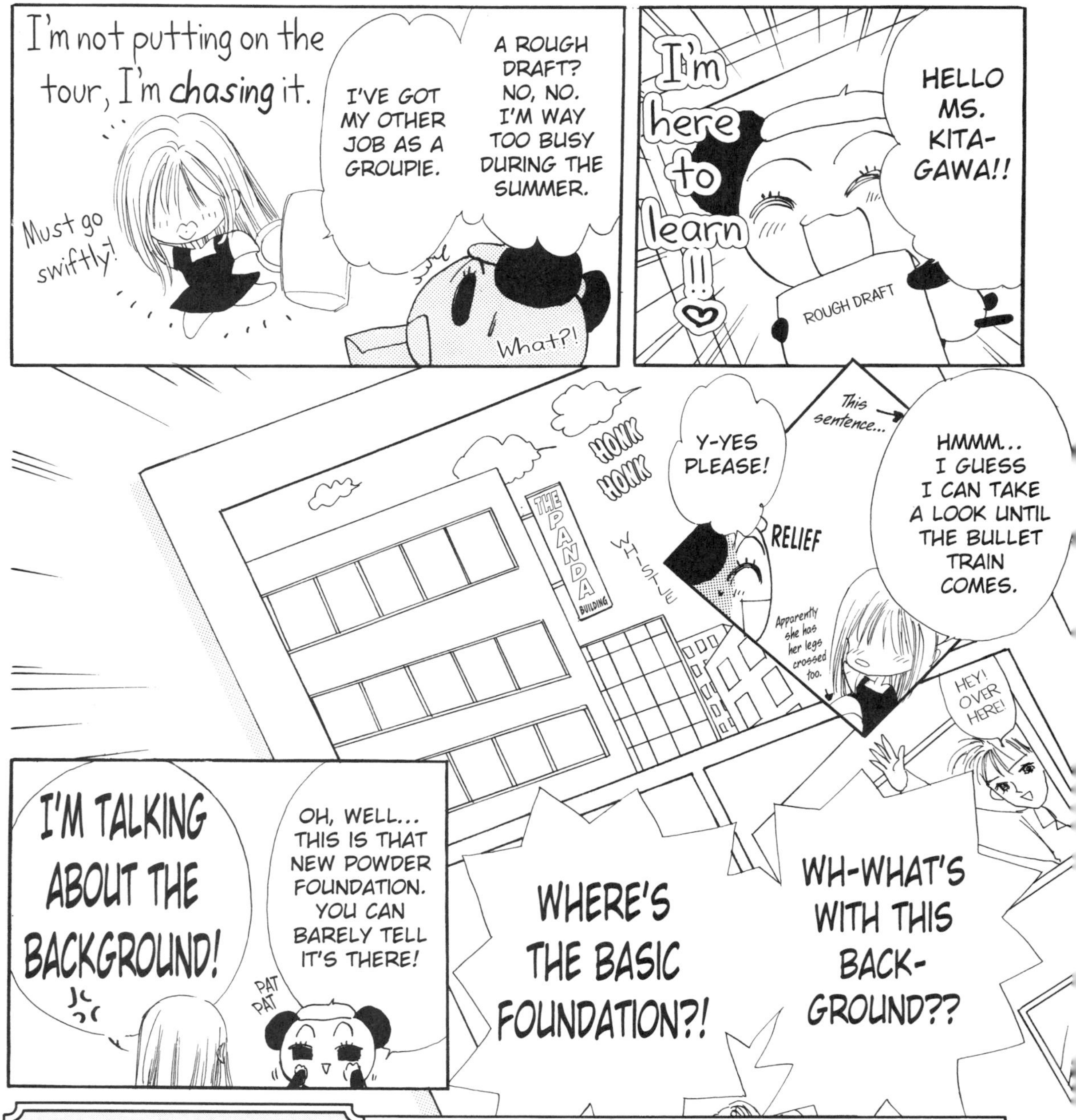
HELLO MS. KITA-GAWA!!
I'm here to learn!!
ROUGH DRAFT
A ROUGH DRAFT? NO, NO. I'M WAY TOO BUSY DURING THE SUMMER.
I'VE GOT MY OTHER JOB AS A GROUPIE.
I'm not putting on the tour, I'm chasing it.
Must go swiftly!
What?!
HMMM... I GUESS I CAN TAKE A LOOK UNTIL THE BULLET TRAIN COMES.
This sentence...
Y-YES PLEASE!
RELIEF
HONK HONK
THE PANDA BUILDING
WHISTLE
Apparently she has her legs crossed too.
HEY! OVER HERE!
WH-WHAT'S WITH THIS BACK-GROUND??
WHERE'S THE BASIC FOUNDATION?!
OH, WELL... THIS IS THAT NEW POWDER FOUNDATION. YOU CAN BARELY TELL IT'S THERE!
I'M TALKING ABOUT THE BACKGROUND!
PAT PAT

WHO'RE YOU DRAWING THE BACKGROUND FOR?! THE READERS!

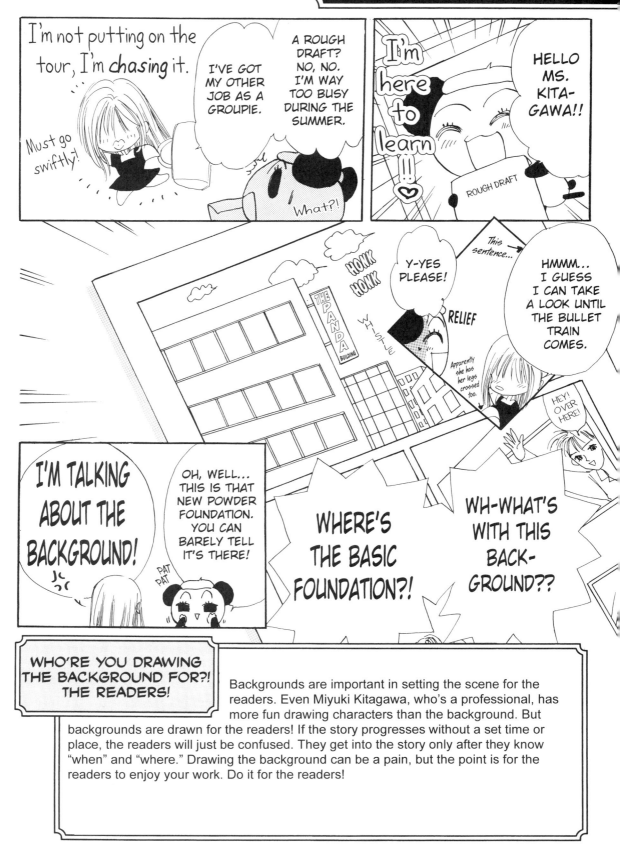

Backgrounds are important in setting the scene for the readers. Even Miyuki Kitagawa, who's a professional, has more fun drawing characters than the background. But backgrounds are drawn for the readers! If the story progresses without a set time or place, the readers will just be confused. They get into the story only after they know "when" and "where." Drawing the background can be a pain, but the point is for the readers to enjoy your work. Do it for the readers!

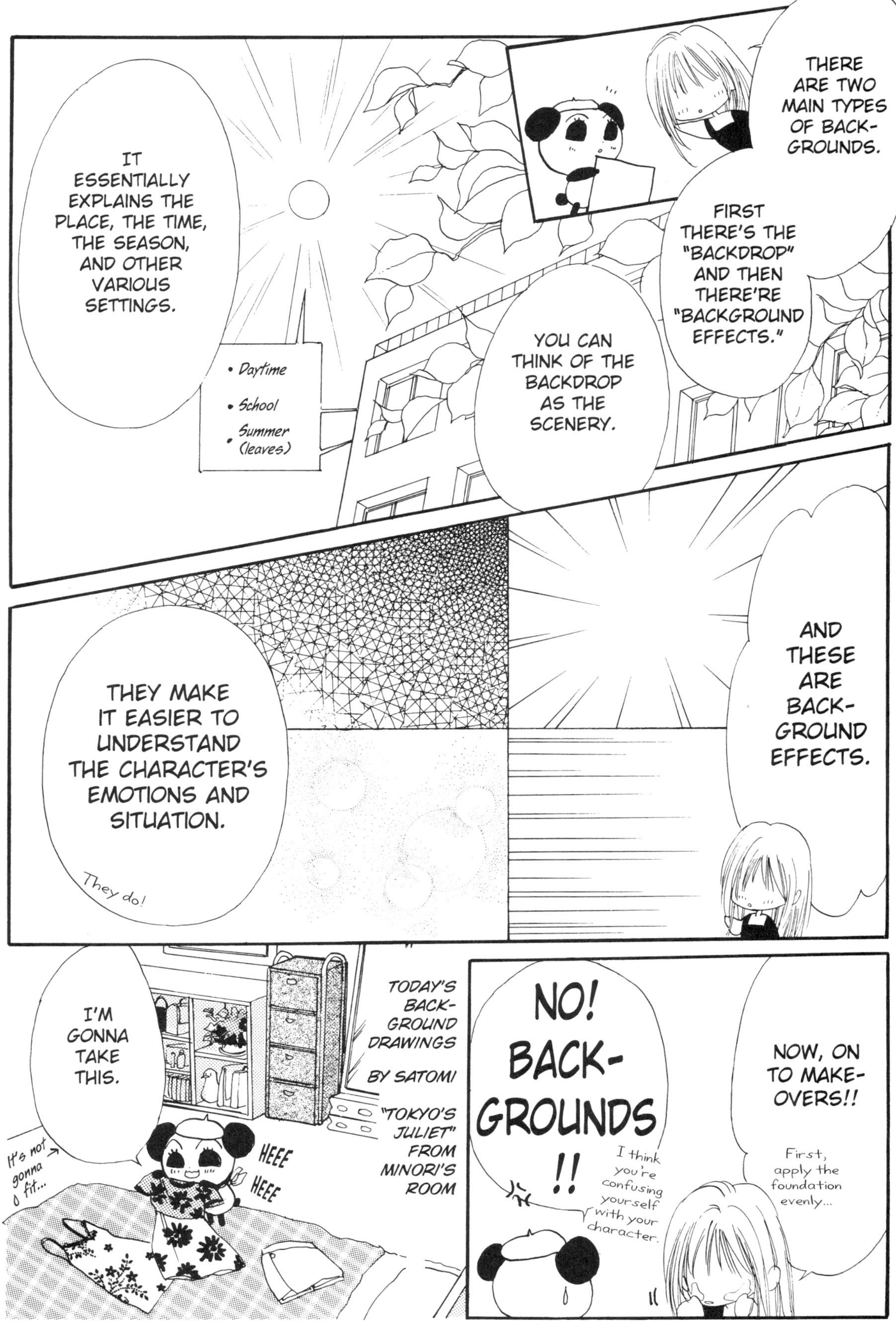
THERE ARE TWO MAIN TYPES OF BACK-GROUNDS.
FIRST THERE'S THE "BACKDROP" AND THEN THERE'RE "BACKGROUND EFFECTS."
YOU CAN THINK OF THE BACKDROP AS THE SCENERY.
IT ESSENTIALLY EXPLAINS THE PLACE, THE TIME, THE SEASON, AND OTHER VARIOUS SETTINGS.
• Daytime
• School
• Summer (leaves)
AND THESE ARE BACK-GROUND EFFECTS.
THEY MAKE IT EASIER TO UNDERSTAND THE CHARACTER'S EMOTIONS AND SITUATION.
They do!
NOW, ON TO MAKE-OVERS!!
First, apply the foundation evenly...
NO! BACK-GROUNDS!!
I think you're confusing yourself with your character.
TODAY'S BACK-GROUND DRAWINGS BY SATOMI "TOKYO'S JULIET" FROM MINORI'S ROOM
I'M GONNA TAKE THIS.
HEEE HEEE
It's not gonna fit...

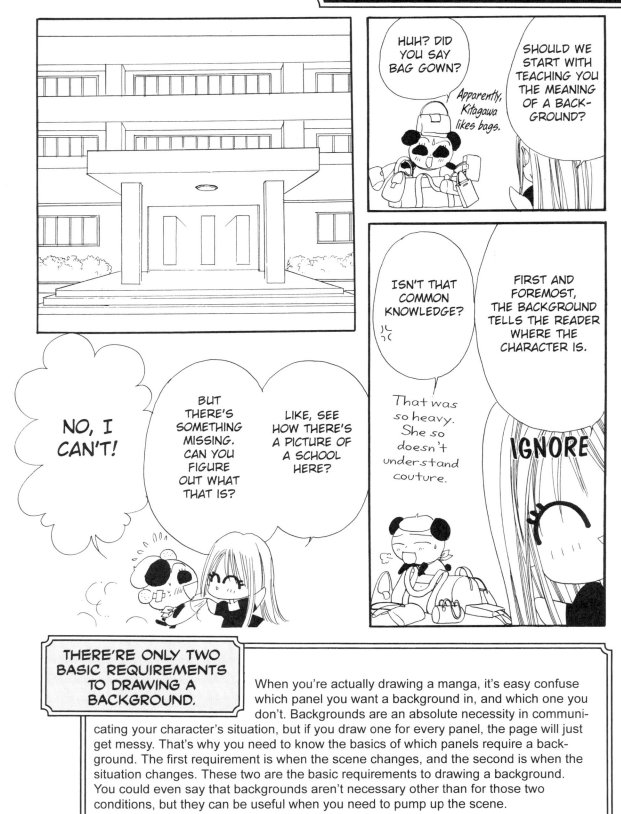

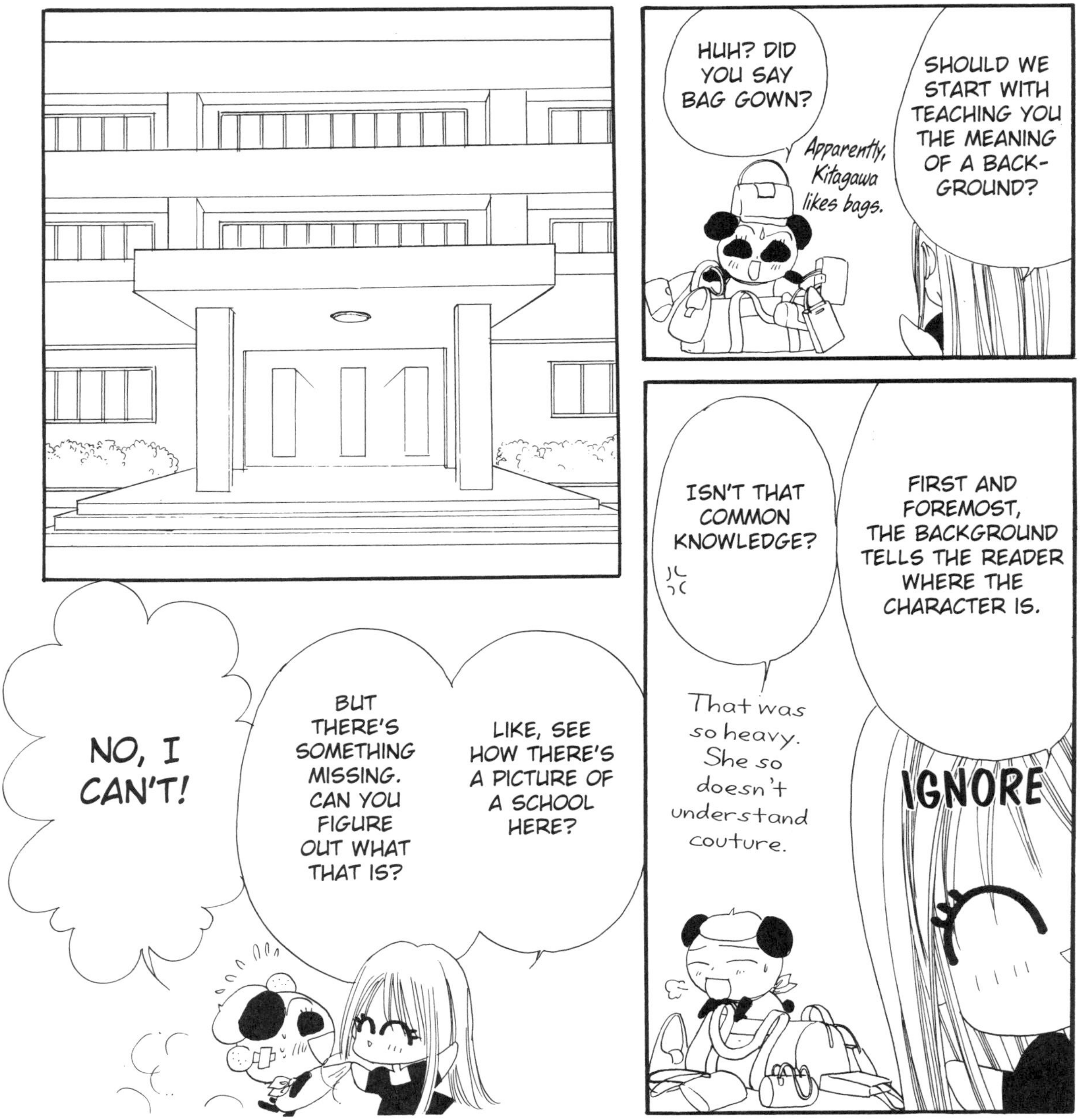
SHOULD WE START WITH TEACHING YOU THE MEANING OF A BACKGROUND?
HUH? DID YOU SAY BAG GOWN?
Apparently, Kitagawa likes bags.
FIRST AND FOREMOST, THE BACKGROUND TELLS THE READER WHERE THE CHARACTER IS.
ISN'T THAT COMMON KNOWLEDGE?
That was so heavy. She so doesn't understand couture.
IGNORE
LIKE, SEE HOW THERE'S A PICTURE OF A SCHOOL HERE?
BUT THERE'S SOMETHING MISSING. CAN YOU FIGURE OUT WHAT THAT IS?
NO, I CAN'T!

THERE'RE ONLY TWO BASIC REQUIREMENTS TO DRAWING A BACKGROUND.

When you're actually drawing a manga, it's easy confuse which panel you want a background in, and which one you don't. Backgrounds are an absolute necessity in communicating your character's situation, but if you draw one for every panel, the page will just get messy. That's why you need to know the basics of which panels require a background. The first requirement is when the scene changes, and the second is when the situation changes. These two are the basic requirements to drawing a background. You could even say that backgrounds aren't necessary other than for those two conditions, but they can be useful when you need to pump up the scene.

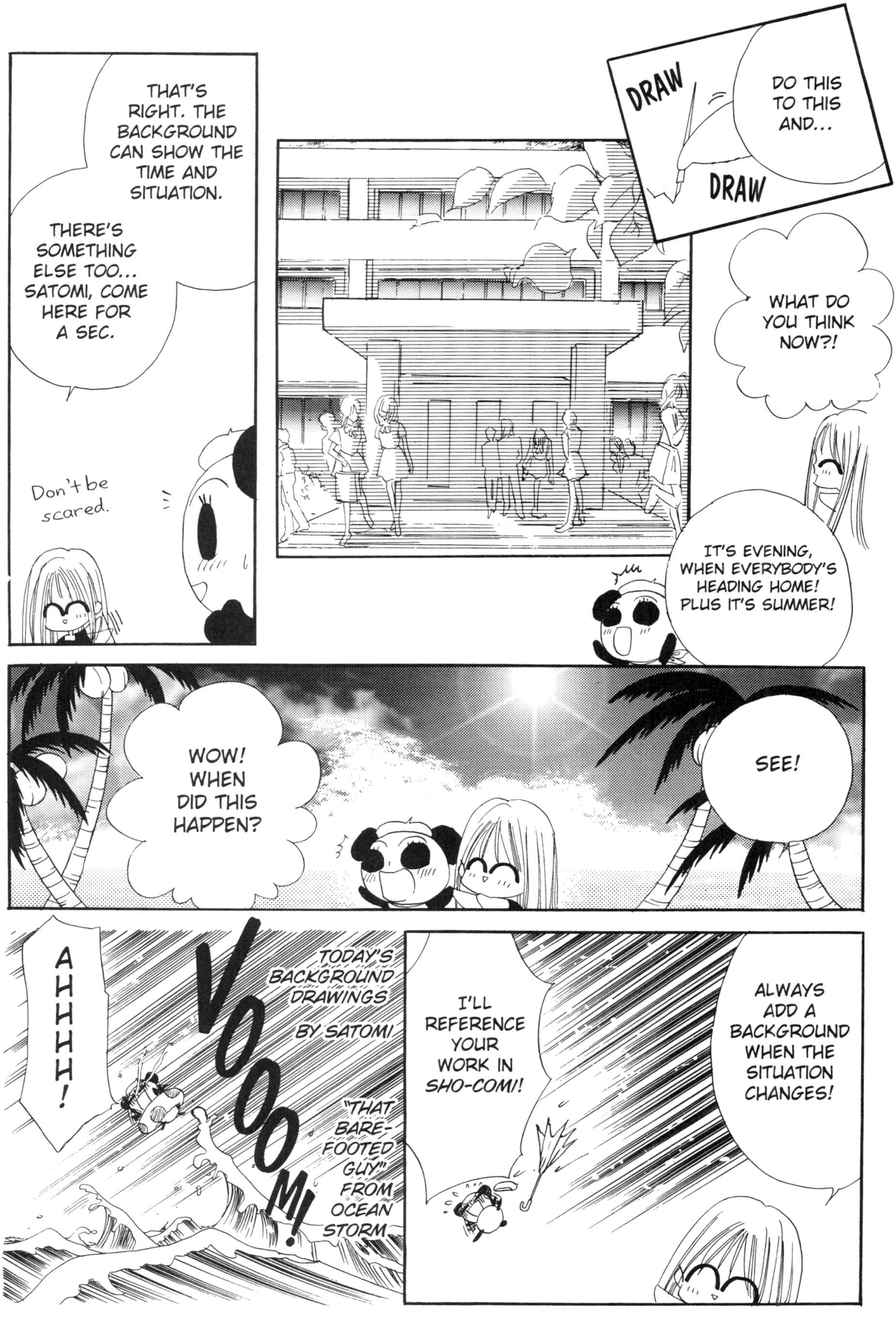
DRAW
DO THIS TO THIS AND...
DRAW
WHAT DO YOU THINK NOW?!
IT'S EVENING, WHEN EVERYBODY'S HEADING HOME! PLUS IT'S SUMMER!
THAT'S RIGHT. THE BACKGROUND CAN SHOW THE TIME AND SITUATION.
THERE'S SOMETHING ELSE TOO... SATOMI, COME HERE FOR A SEC.
Don't be scared.
SEE!
WOW! WHEN DID THIS HAPPEN?
ALWAYS ADD A BACKGROUND WHEN THE SITUATION CHANGES!
I'LL REFERENCE YOUR WORK IN SHO-COMI!
TODAY'S BACKGROUND DRAWINGS BY SATOMI "THAT BAREFOOTED GUY" FROM OCEAN STORM
VOOOOM!
AHHHH!

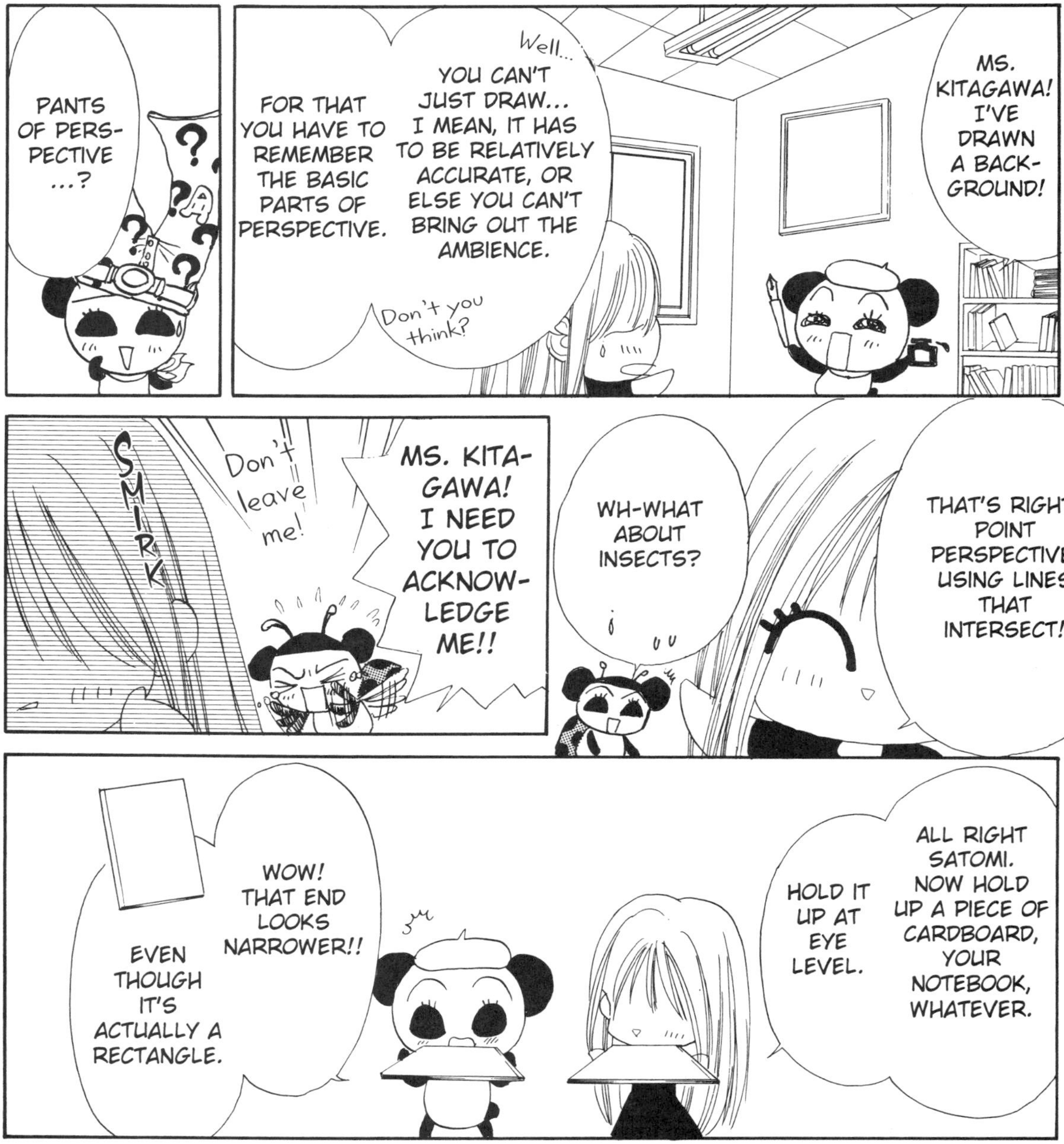
MS. KITAGAWA! I'VE DRAWN A BACKGROUND!
Well...
YOU CAN'T JUST DRAW... I MEAN, IT HAS TO BE RELATIVELY ACCURATE, OR ELSE YOU CAN'T BRING OUT THE AMBIENCE.
FOR THAT YOU HAVE TO REMEMBER THE BASIC PARTS OF PERSPECTIVE.
Don't you think?
PANTS OF PERSPECTIVE ...?
THAT'S RIGHT! POINT PERSPECTIVE, USING LINES THAT INTERSECT!
WH-WHAT ABOUT INSECTS?
MS. KITAGAWA! I NEED YOU TO ACKNOWLEDGE ME!!
Don't leave me!
SMIRK
ALL RIGHT SATOMI. NOW HOLD UP A PIECE OF CARDBOARD, YOUR NOTEBOOK, WHATEVER.
HOLD IT UP AT EYE LEVEL.
WOW! THAT END LOOKS NARROWER!!
EVEN THOUGH IT'S ACTUALLY A RECTANGLE.

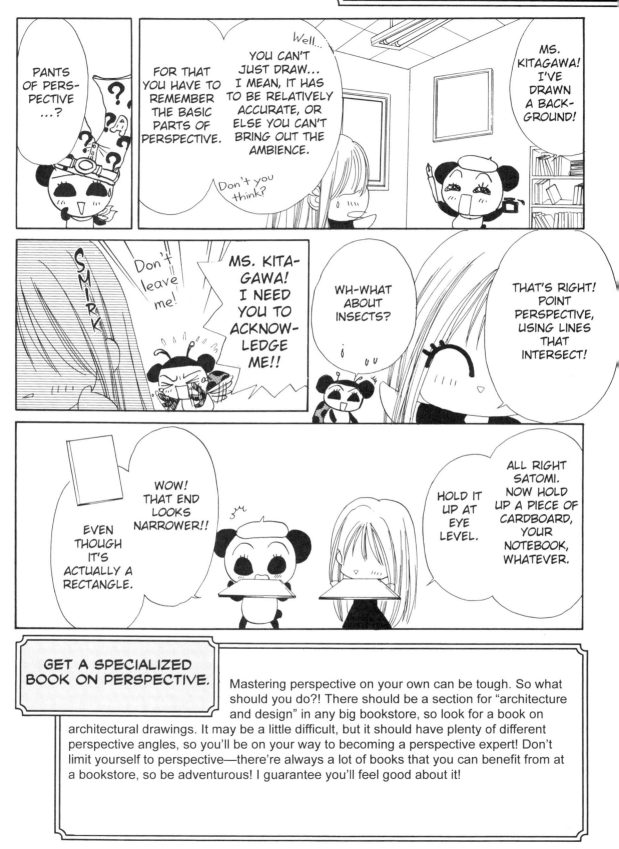

GET A SPECIALIZED BOOK ON PERSPECTIVE.

Mastering perspective on your own can be tough. So what should you do?! There should be a section for "architecture and design" in any big bookstore, so look for a book on architectural drawings. It may be a little difficult, but it should have plenty of different perspective angles, so you'll be on your way to becoming a perspective expert! Don't limit yourself to perspective—there're always a lot of books that you can benefit from at a bookstore, so be adventurous! I guarantee you'll feel good about it!

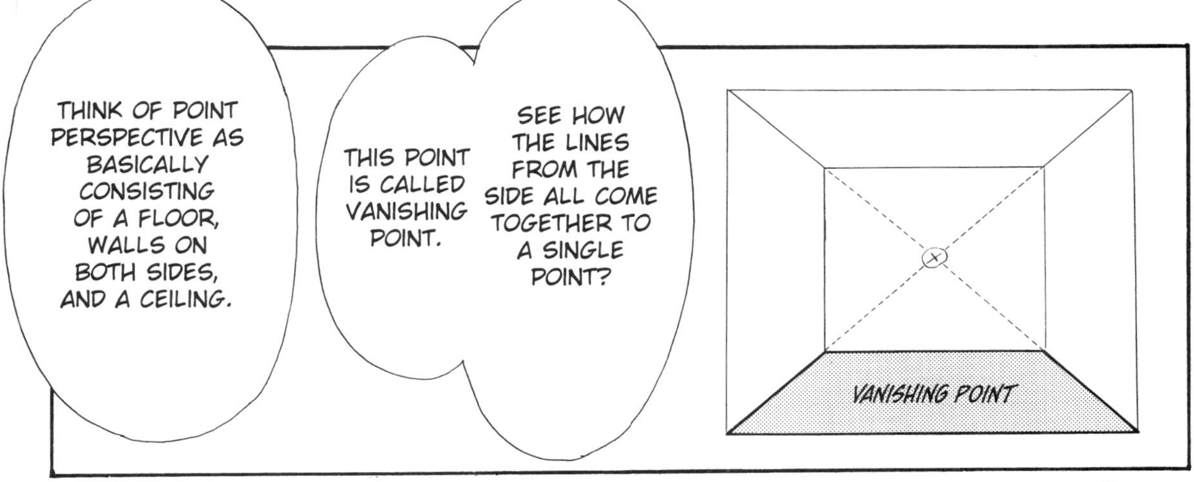
SEE HOW THE LINES FROM THE SIDE ALL COME TOGETHER TO A SINGLE POINT?
THIS POINT IS CALLED VANISHING POINT.
THINK OF POINT PERSPECTIVE AS BASICALLY CONSISTING OF A FLOOR, WALLS ON BOTH SIDES, AND A CEILING.
VANISHING POINT

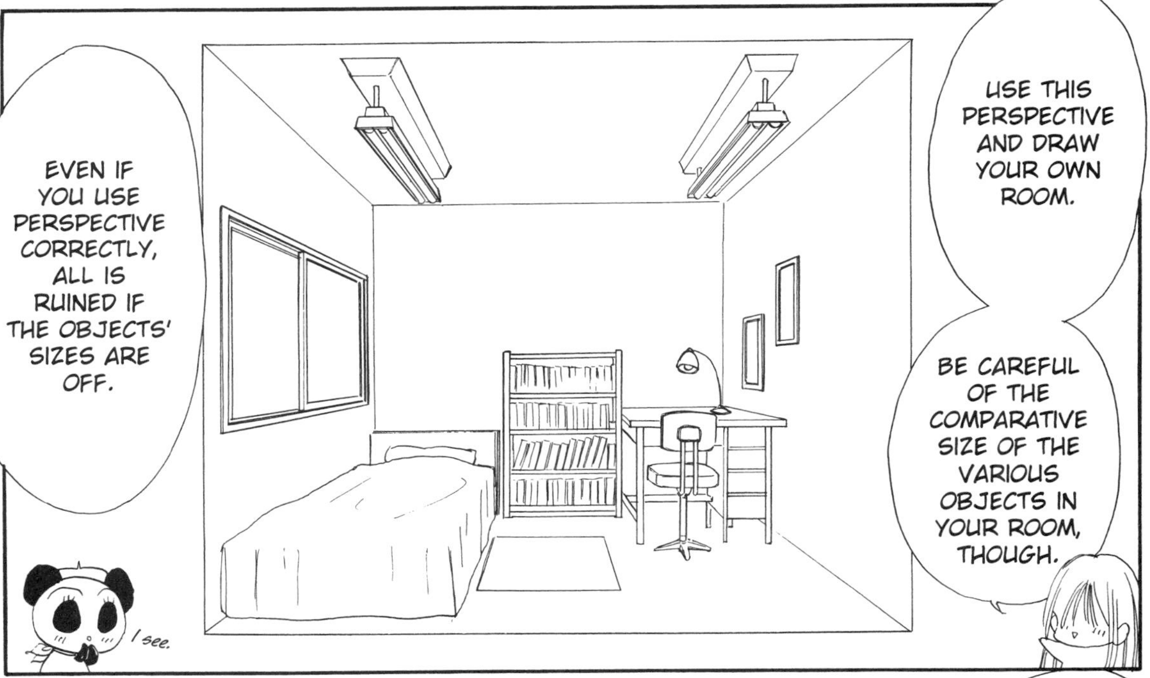
USE THIS PERSPECTIVE AND DRAW YOUR OWN ROOM.
BE CAREFUL OF THE COMPARATIVE SIZE OF THE VARIOUS OBJECTS IN YOUR ROOM, THOUGH.
EVEN IF YOU USE PERSPECTIVE CORRECTLY, ALL IS RUINED IF THE OBJECTS' SIZES ARE OFF.
I see.

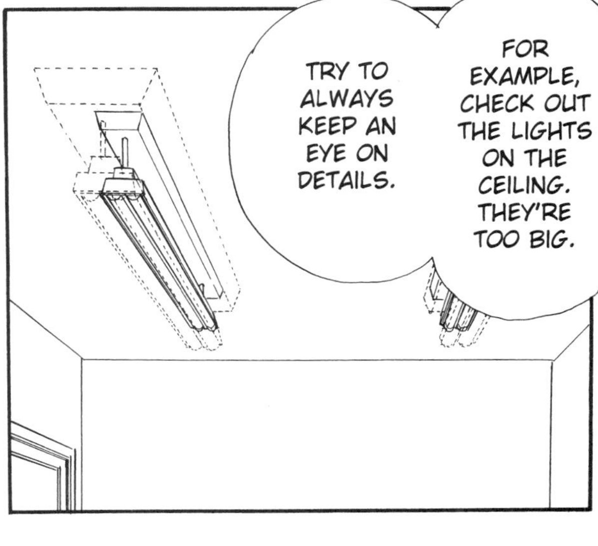
FOR EXAMPLE, CHECK OUT THE LIGHTS ON THE CEILING. THEY'RE TOO BIG.
TRY TO ALWAYS KEEP AN EYE ON DETAILS.

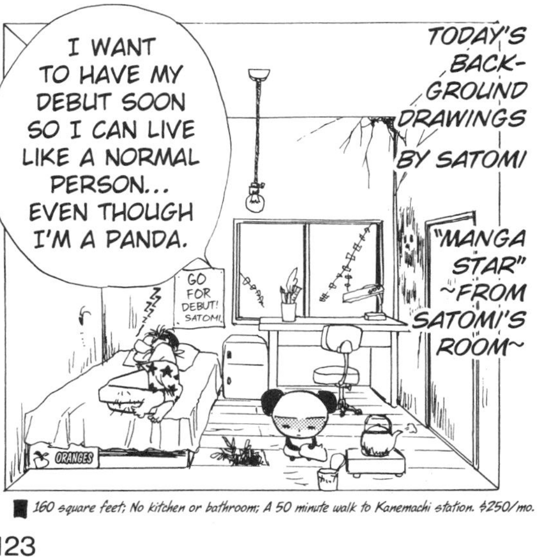
TODAY'S BACK-GROUND DRAWINGS BY SATOMI
I WANT TO HAVE MY DEBUT SOON SO I CAN LIVE LIKE A NORMAL PERSON... EVEN THOUGH I'M A PANDA.
"MANGA STAR" ~FROM SATOMI'S ROOM~
GO FOR DEBUT! SATOMI
ORANGES

■ 160 square feet; No kitchen or bathroom; A 50 minute walk to Kanemachi station. $250/mo.

TWO- AND THREE-POINT PERSPECTIVE

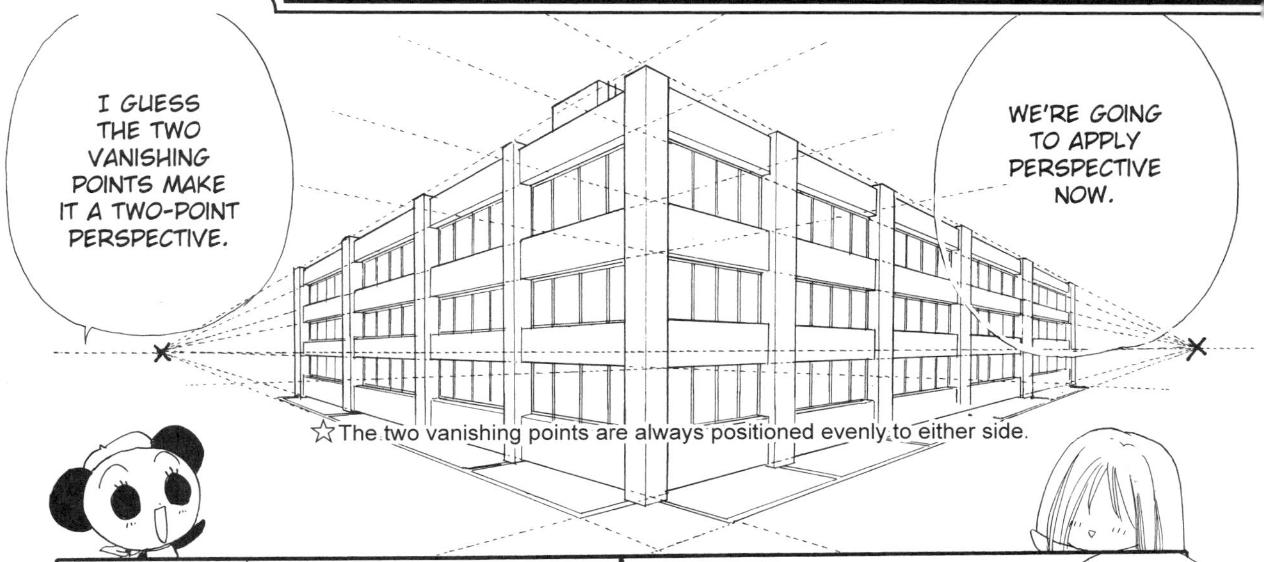
WE'RE GOING TO APPLY PERSPECTIVE NOW.
I GUESS THE TWO VANISHING POINTS MAKE IT A TWO-POINT PERSPECTIVE.

☆The two vanishing points are always positioned evenly to either side.

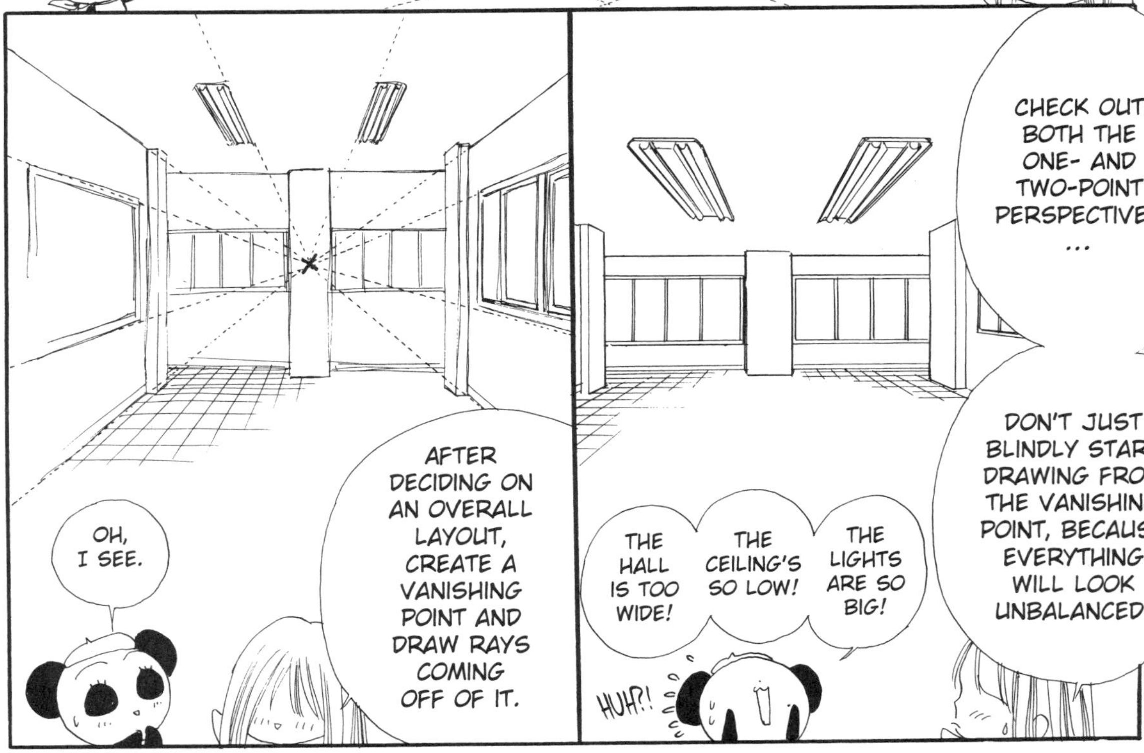
CHECK OUT BOTH THE ONE- AND TWO-POINT PERSPECTIVES ...
DON'T JUST BLINDLY START DRAWING FROM THE VANISHING POINT, BECAUSE EVERYTHING WILL LOOK UNBALANCED.
THE LIGHTS ARE SO BIG!
THE CEILING'S SO LOW!
THE HALL IS TOO WIDE!
HUH?!
AFTER DECIDING ON AN OVERALL LAYOUT, CREATE A VANISHING POINT AND DRAW RAYS COMING OFF OF IT.
OH, I SEE.

THE KEY TO DECIDING THE HEIGHT OF THE VANISHING POINT.

The vanishing point should always be adjusted to the height of the person looking directly at the scene. In other words, if the person is looking at a building from an elevated position, the vanishing point should be towards the top of the building, and if the person is closer to ground level, the vanishing point should be, too. By the way, if the vanishing point is placed at normal eye height (about 5 ft), the end product will come out looking very natural. If there's a character in the scene, the character's eye height, the horizon, and the skyline will all line up! Think about why this happens. Don't forget to use perspective for both the characters and the background!

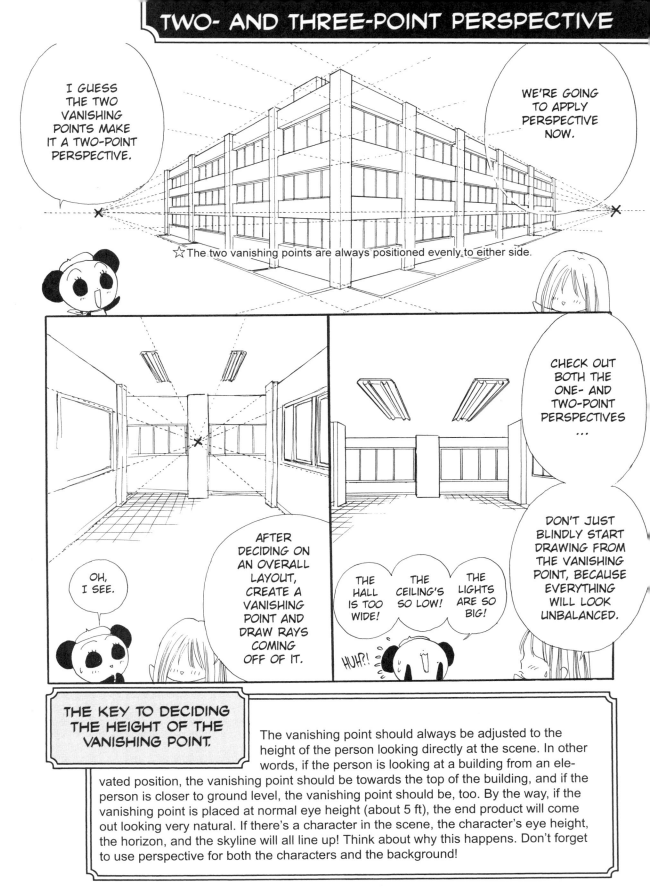

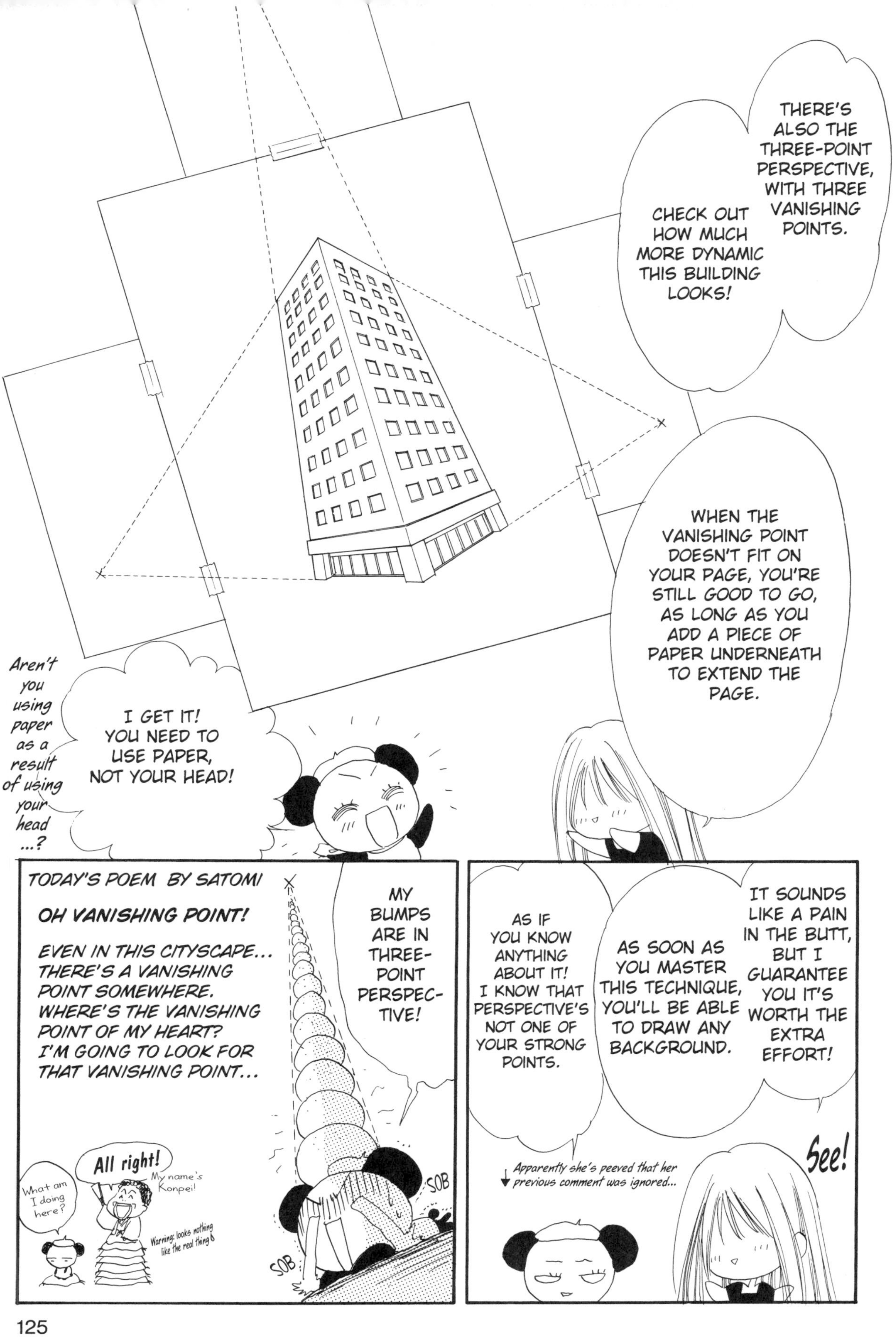

THERE'S ALSO THE THREE-POINT PERSPECTIVE, WITH THREE VANISHING POINTS.
CHECK OUT HOW MUCH MORE DYNAMIC THIS BUILDING LOOKS!
WHEN THE VANISHING POINT DOESN'T FIT ON YOUR PAGE, YOU'RE STILL GOOD TO GO, AS LONG AS YOU ADD A PIECE OF PAPER UNDERNEATH TO EXTEND THE PAGE.
I GET IT! YOU NEED TO USE PAPER, NOT YOUR HEAD!
Aren't you using paper as a result of using your head ...?
IT SOUNDS LIKE A PAIN IN THE BUTT, BUT I GUARANTEE YOU IT'S WORTH THE EXTRA EFFORT!
AS SOON AS YOU MASTER THIS TECHNIQUE, YOU'LL BE ABLE TO DRAW ANY BACKGROUND.
AS IF YOU KNOW ANYTHING ABOUT IT! I KNOW THAT PERSPECTIVE'S NOT ONE OF YOUR STRONG POINTS.
See!
Apparently she's peeved that her previous comment was ignored...
TODAY'S POEM BY SATOMI
OH VANISHING POINT!
EVEN IN THIS CITYSCAPE... THERE'S A VANISHING POINT SOMEWHERE. WHERE'S THE VANISHING POINT OF MY HEART? I'M GOING TO LOOK FOR THAT VANISHING POINT...
MY BUMPS ARE IN THREE-POINT PERSPEC-TIVE!
SOB
SOB
All right!
My name's Konpei!
What am I doing here?
Warning: looks nothing like the real thing

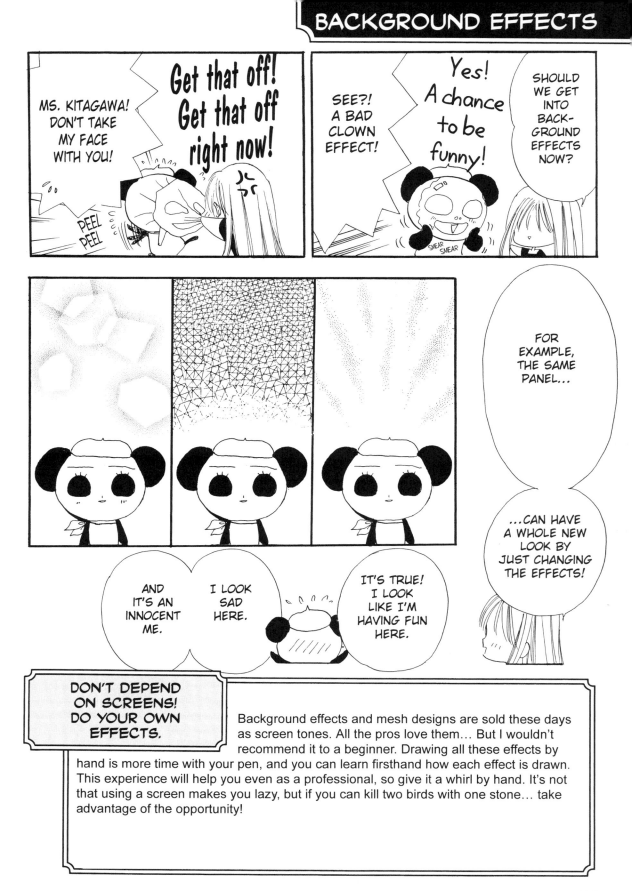

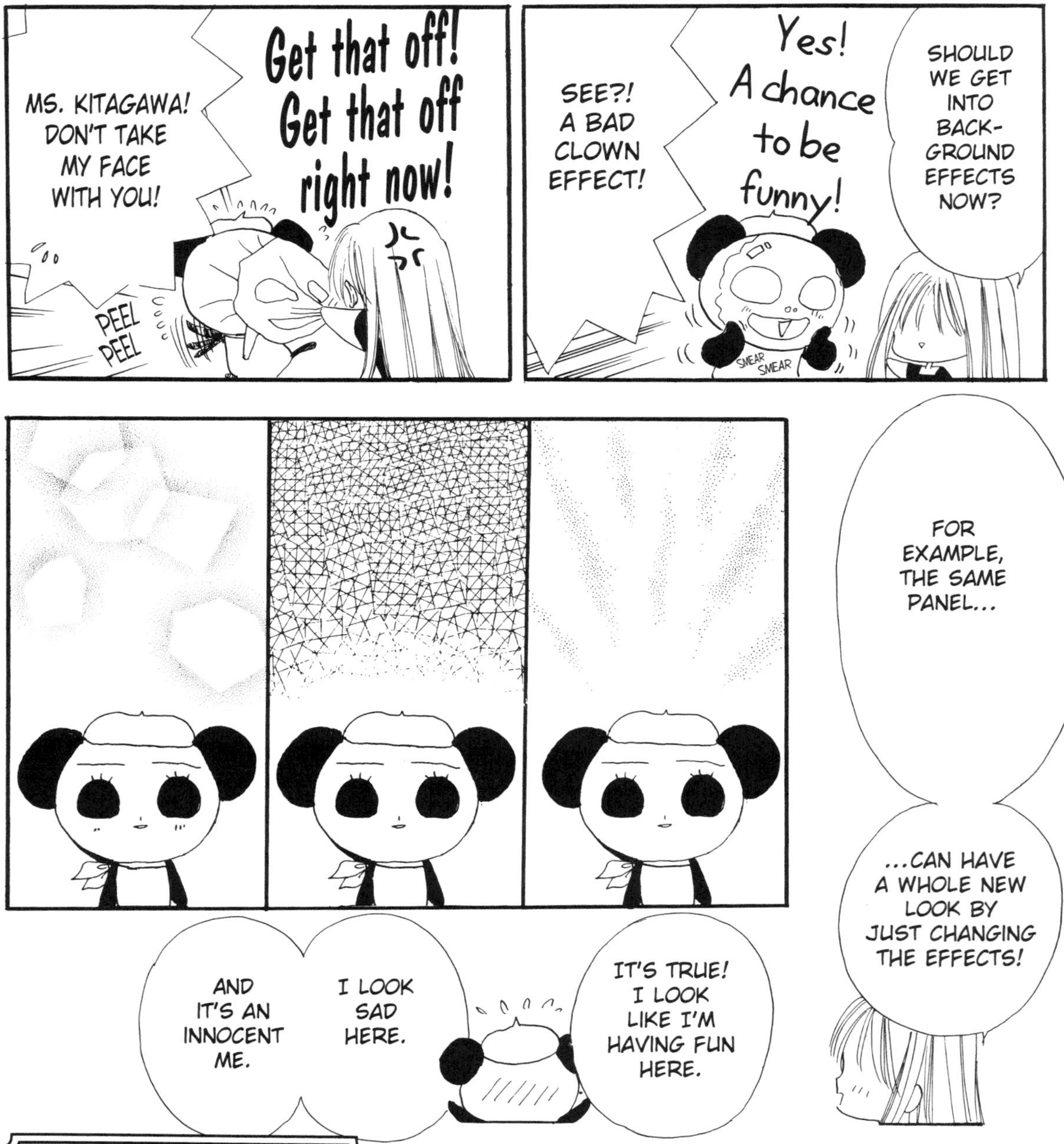
SHOULD WE GET INTO BACK-GROUND EFFECTS NOW?
Yes! A chance to be funny!
SEE?! A BAD CLOWN EFFECT!
SMEAR SMEAR
Get that off! Get that off right now!
MS. KITAGAWA! DON'T TAKE MY FACE WITH YOU!
PEEL PEEL
FOR EXAMPLE, THE SAME PANEL...
...CAN HAVE A WHOLE NEW LOOK BY JUST CHANGING THE EFFECTS!
IT'S TRUE! I LOOK LIKE I'M HAVING FUN HERE.
I LOOK SAD HERE.
AND IT'S AN INNOCENT ME.

DON'T DEPEND ON SCREENS! DO YOUR OWN EFFECTS.

Background effects and mesh designs are sold these days as screen tones. All the pros love them… But I wouldn't recommend it to a beginner. Drawing all these effects by hand is more time with your pen, and you can learn firsthand how each effect is drawn. This experience will help you even as a professional, so give it a whirl by hand. It's not that using a screen makes you lazy, but if you can kill two birds with one stone… take advantage of the opportunity!

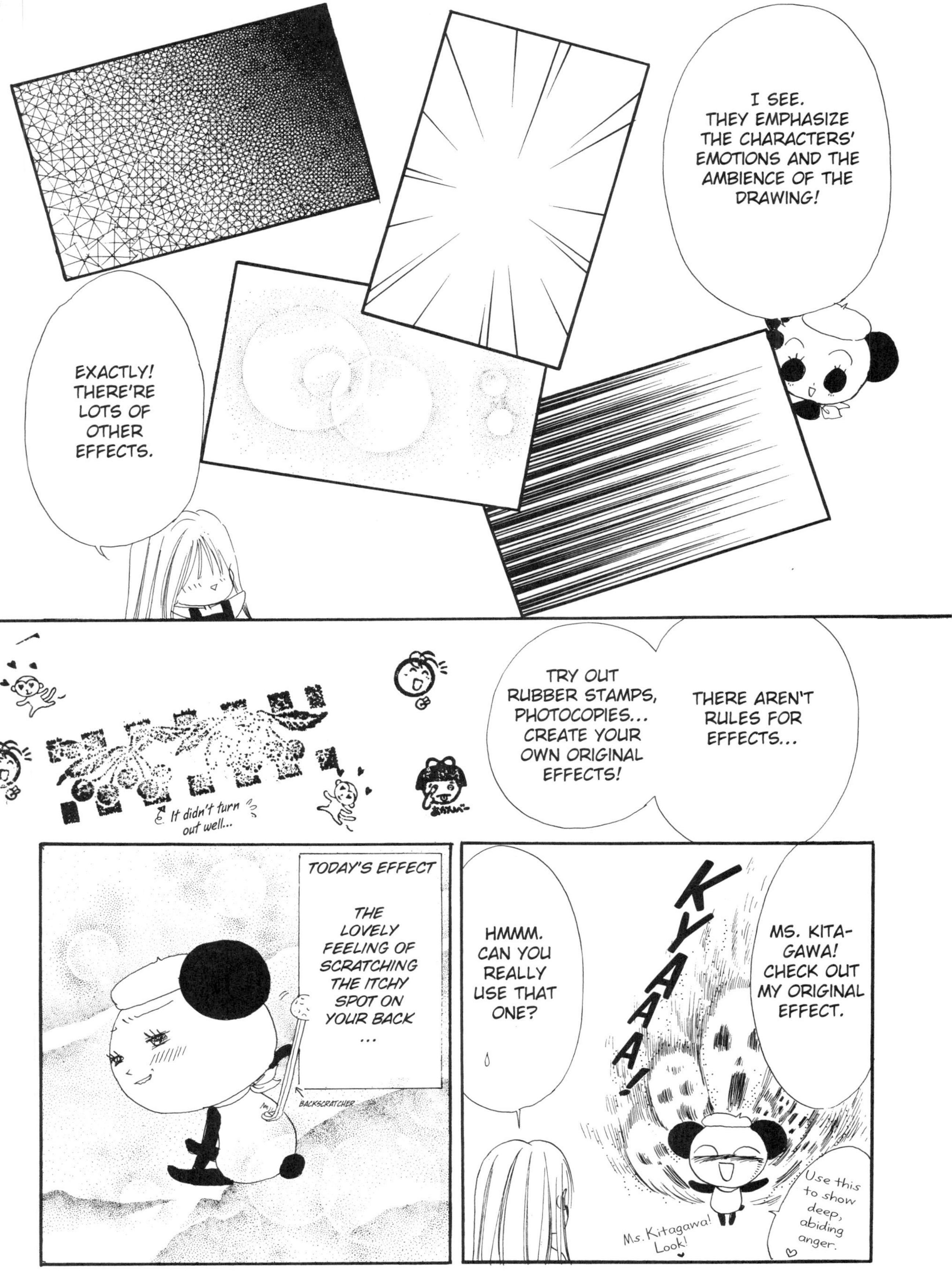
I SEE. THEY EMPHASIZE THE CHARACTERS' EMOTIONS AND THE AMBIENCE OF THE DRAWING!
EXACTLY! THERE'RE LOTS OF OTHER EFFECTS.
THERE AREN'T RULES FOR EFFECTS...
TRY OUT RUBBER STAMPS, PHOTOCOPIES... CREATE YOUR OWN ORIGINAL EFFECTS!
It didn't turn out well...
MS. KITA-GAWA! CHECK OUT MY ORIGINAL EFFECT.
KYAAAA!
HMMM. CAN YOU REALLY USE THAT ONE?
Use this to show deep, abiding anger.
Ms. Kitagawa! Look!
TODAY'S EFFECT
THE LOVELY FEELING OF SCRATCHING THE ITCHY SPOT ON YOUR BACK...
BACKSCRATCHER

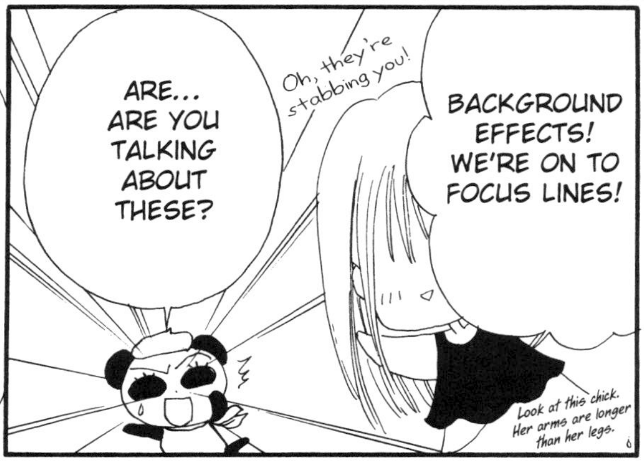
BACKGROUND EFFECTS! WE'RE ON TO FOCUS LINES!
Oh, they're stabbing you!
ARE... ARE YOU TALKING ABOUT THESE?
Look at this chick. Her arms are longer than her legs.

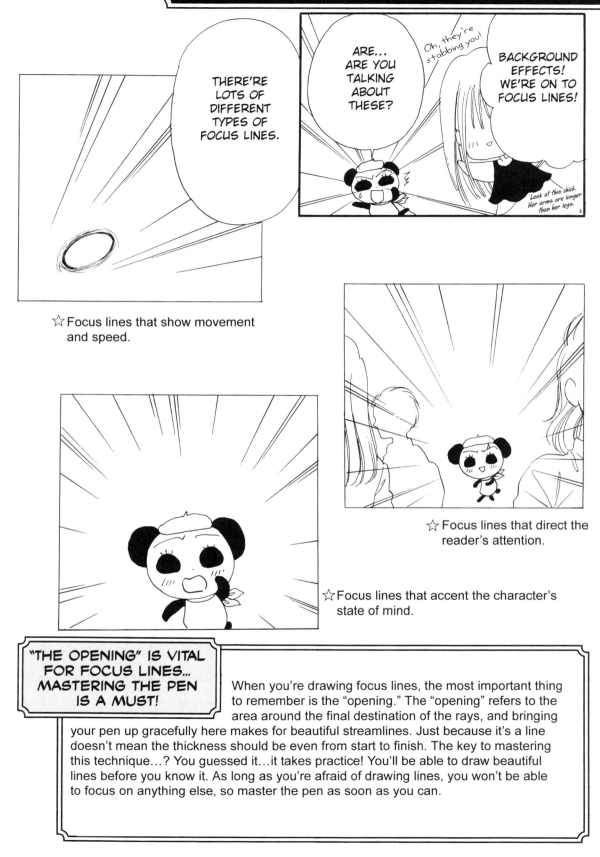

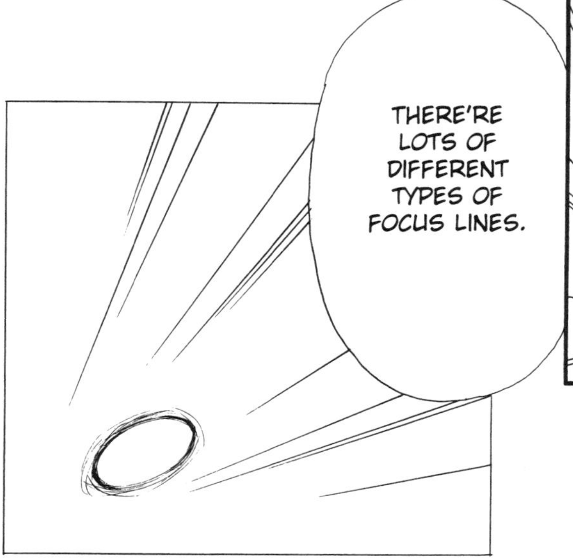
THERE'RE LOTS OF DIFFERENT TYPES OF FOCUS LINES.

☆Focus lines that show movement and speed.

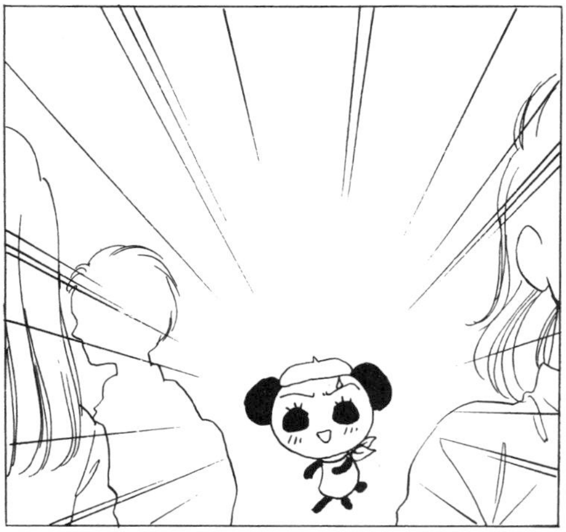

☆Focus lines that direct the reader's attention.

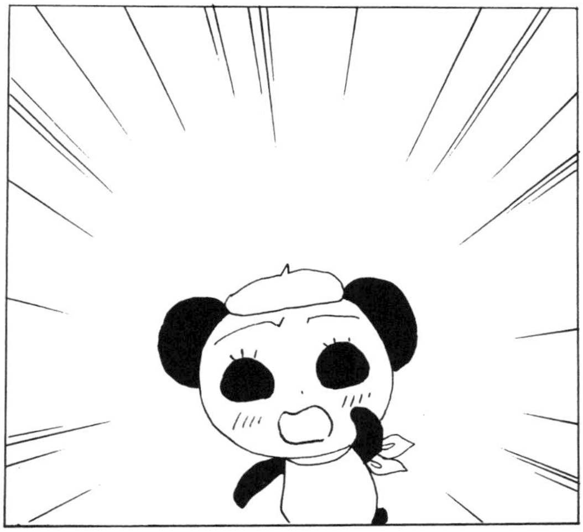

☆Focus lines that accent the character's state of mind.

"THE OPENING" IS VITAL FOR FOCUS LINES... MASTERING THE PEN IS A MUST!

When you're drawing focus lines, the most important thing to remember is the "opening." The "opening" refers to the area around the final destination of the rays, and bringing your pen up gracefully here makes for beautiful streamlines. Just because it's a line doesn't mean the thickness should be even from start to finish. The key to mastering this technique…? You guessed it…it takes practice! You'll be able to draw beautiful lines before you know it. As long as you're afraid of drawing lines, you won't be able to focus on anything else, so master the pen as soon as you can.

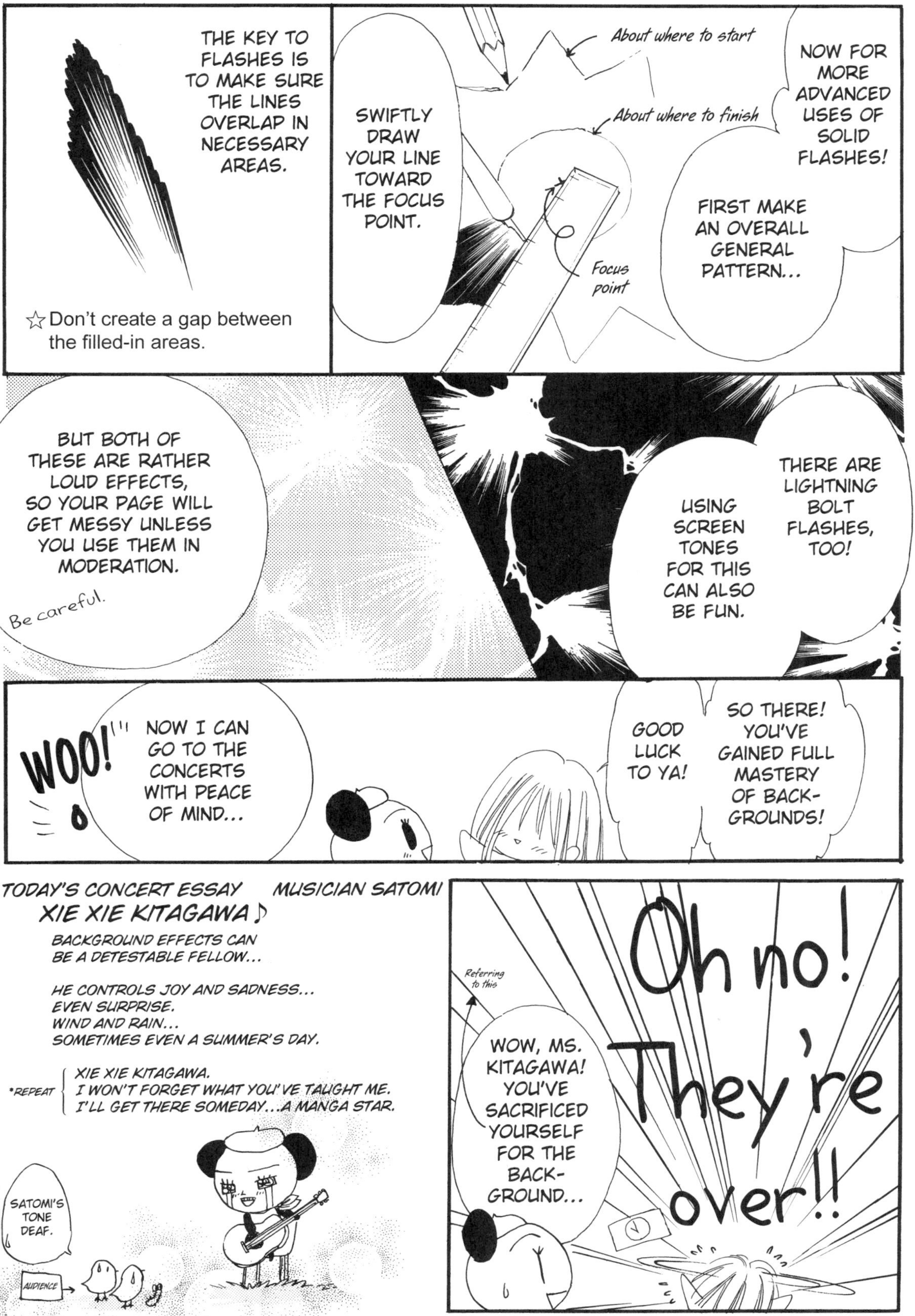
NOW FOR MORE ADVANCED USES OF SOLID FLASHES!
About where to start
FIRST MAKE AN OVERALL GENERAL PATTERN...
About where to finish
SWIFTLY DRAW YOUR LINE TOWARD THE FOCUS POINT.
Focus point
THE KEY TO FLASHES IS TO MAKE SURE THE LINES OVERLAP IN NECESSARY AREAS.
☆Don't create a gap between the filled-in areas.
THERE ARE LIGHTNING BOLT FLASHES, TOO!
USING SCREEN TONES FOR THIS CAN ALSO BE FUN.
BUT BOTH OF THESE ARE RATHER LOUD EFFECTS, SO YOUR PAGE WILL GET MESSY UNLESS YOU USE THEM IN MODERATION.
Be careful.
SO THERE! YOU'VE GAINED FULL MASTERY OF BACK-GROUNDS!
GOOD LUCK TO YA!
NOW I CAN GO TO THE CONCERTS WITH PEACE OF MIND...
WOO!
Oh no! They're over!!
WOW, MS. KITAGAWA! YOU'VE SACRIFICED YOURSELF FOR THE BACK-GROUND...
Referring to this
TODAY'S CONCERT ESSAY MUSICIAN SATOMI
XIE XIE KITAGAWA♪
BACKGROUND EFFECTS CAN BE A DETESTABLE FELLOW...
HE CONTROLS JOY AND SADNESS... EVEN SURPRISE. WIND AND RAIN... SOMETIMES EVEN A SUMMER'S DAY.
*REPEAT XIE XIE KITAGAWA. I WON'T FORGET WHAT YOU'VE TAUGHT ME. I'LL GET THERE SOMEDAY...A MANGA STAR.
SATOMI'S TONE DEAF.
AUDIENCE

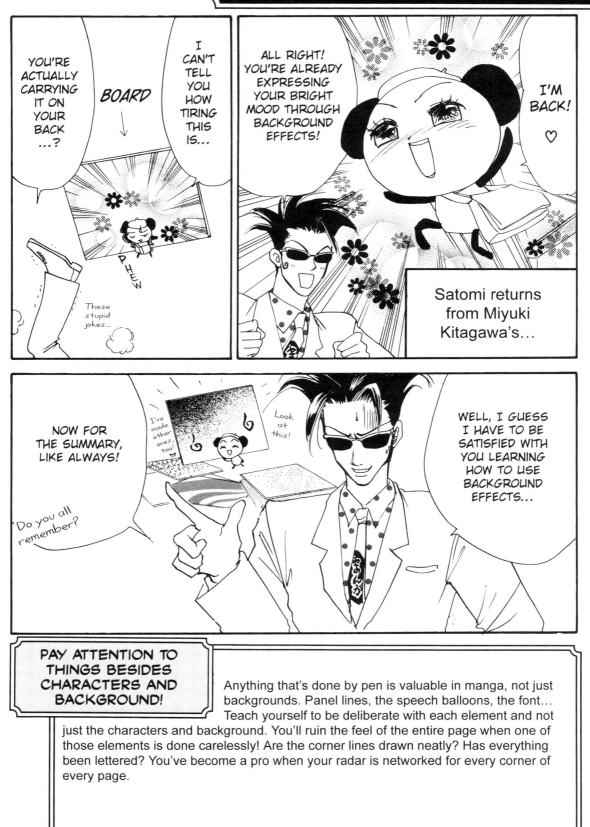

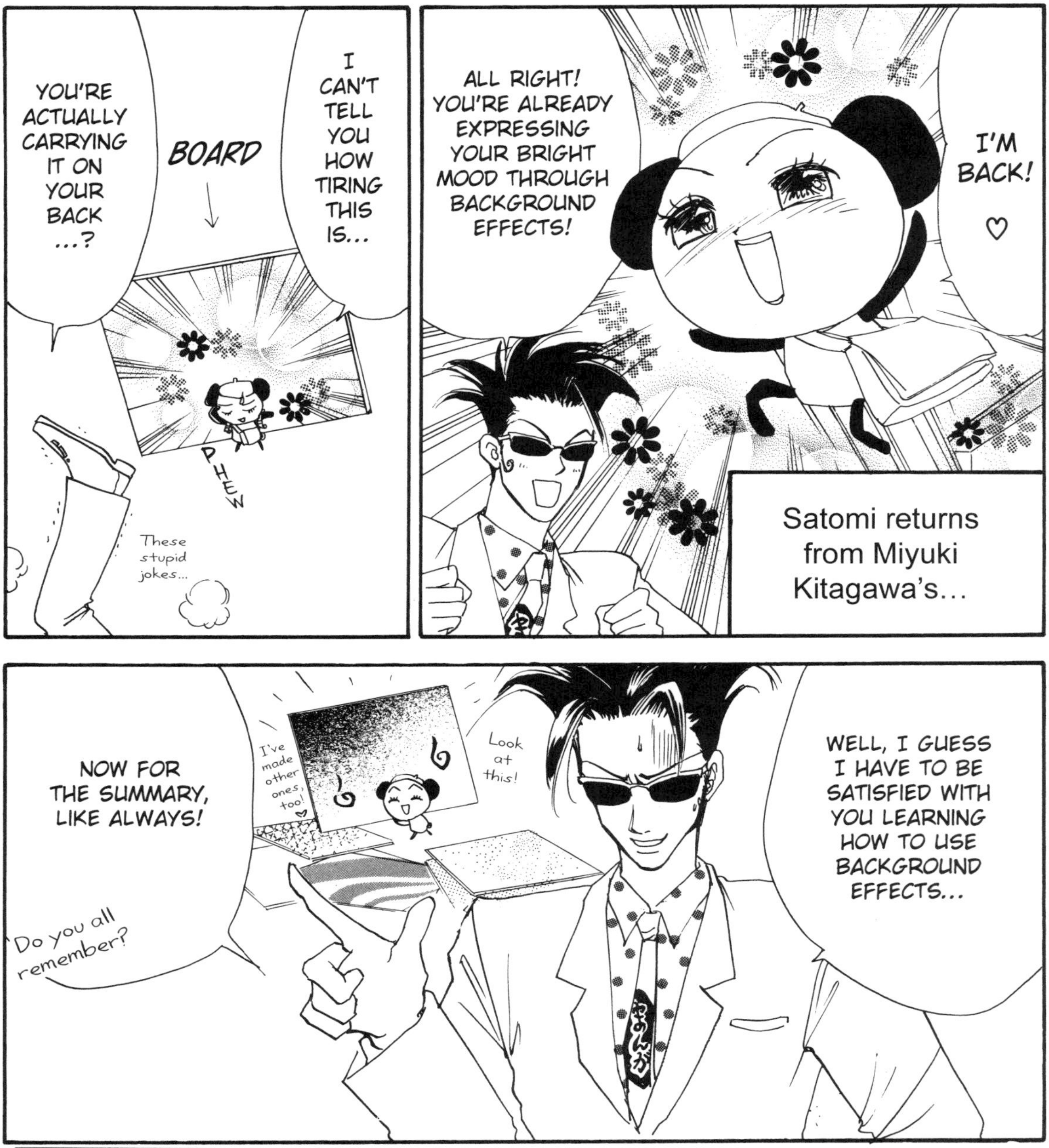
I'M BACK! ♡
ALL RIGHT! YOU'RE ALREADY EXPRESSING YOUR BRIGHT MOOD THROUGH BACKGROUND EFFECTS!
Satomi returns from Miyuki Kitagawa's…
I CAN'T TELL YOU HOW TIRING THIS IS…
BOARD
YOU'RE ACTUALLY CARRYING IT ON YOUR BACK …?
PHEW
These stupid jokes…
WELL, I GUESS I HAVE TO BE SATISFIED WITH YOU LEARNING HOW TO USE BACKGROUND EFFECTS…
Look at this!
I've made other ones, too! ♡
NOW FOR THE SUMMARY, LIKE ALWAYS!
Do you all remember?

PAY ATTENTION TO THINGS BESIDES CHARACTERS AND BACKGROUND!

Anything that's done by pen is valuable in manga, not just backgrounds. Panel lines, the speech balloons, the font… Teach yourself to be deliberate with each element and not just the characters and background. You'll ruin the feel of the entire page when one of those elements is done carelessly! Are the corner lines drawn neatly? Has everything been lettered? You've become a pro when your radar is networked for every corner of every page.

THE FIVE CARDINAL POINTS OF BACKGROUND EFFECTS

① There are two types of backgrounds—the "backdrop" and "background effects."

② Make sure you add a background when the scene changes.

③ Master perspective to draw accurate backgrounds.

④ Background effects accent the character's state of mind.

⑤ Overusing loud effects make the page messy.

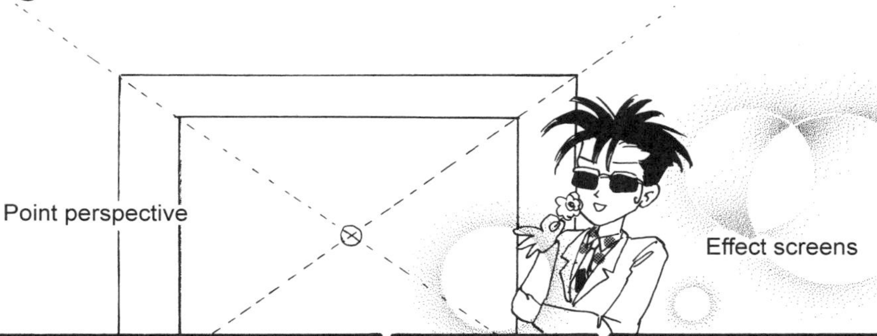
Point perspective
Effect screens

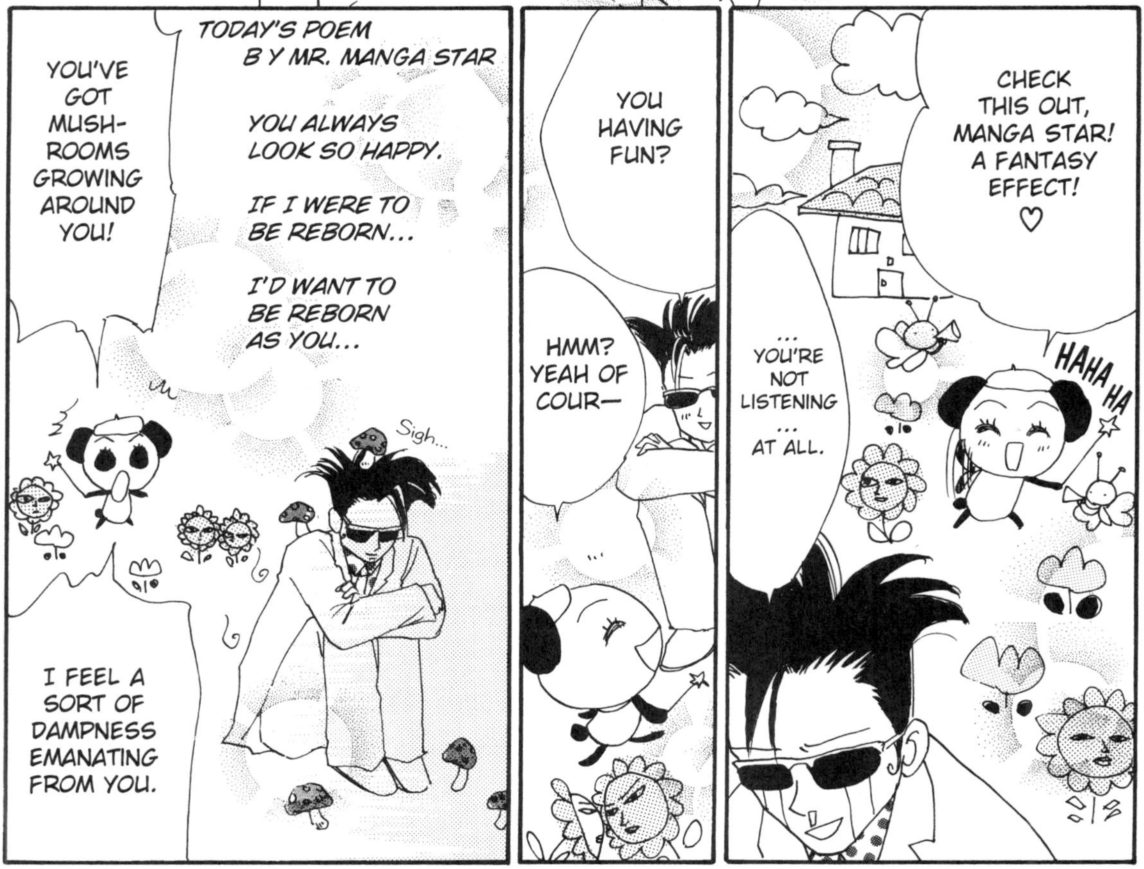
CHECK THIS OUT, MANGA STAR! A FANTASY EFFECT! ♡
HAHA HA
...YOU'RE NOT LISTENING ...AT ALL.
YOU HAVING FUN?
HMM? YEAH OF COUR—
...
TODAY'S POEM BY MR. MANGA STAR
YOU ALWAYS LOOK SO HAPPY.
IF I WERE TO BE REBORN...
I'D WANT TO BE REBORN AS YOU...
YOU'VE GOT MUSH-ROOMS GROWING AROUND YOU!
Sigh...
I FEEL A SORT OF DAMPNESS EMANATING FROM YOU.

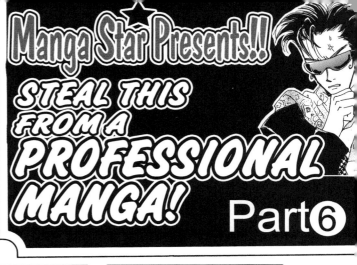

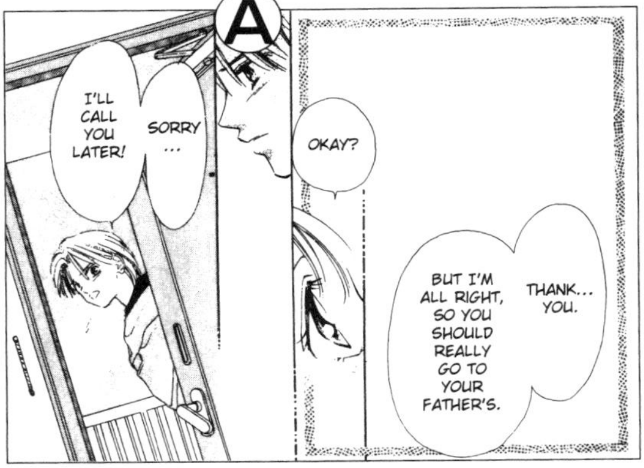

Manga Star Presents!! STEAL THIS FROM A PROFESSIONAL MANGA! Part 6

Miyuki Kitagawa is currently being featured in *Cheese*! Let's check out the variety of panel lines she uses on her pages.

A
OKAY?
THANK... YOU.
BUT I'M ALL RIGHT, SO YOU SHOULD REALLY GO TO YOUR FATHER'S.
SORRY ...
I'LL CALL YOU LATER!

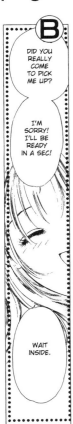

B
DID YOU REALLY COME TO PICK ME UP?
I'M SORRY! I'LL BE READY IN A SEC!
WAIT INSIDE.

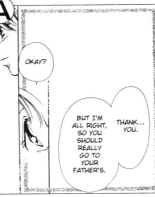

USE A SCREEN TO DRESS UP THE PANEL LINE.

It's just a panel line … But it's an important element in creating ambiance.
Miyuki Kitagawa is known for her fabulous page layouts, but her thoroughness, extending even to the panel lines, contributes to her reputation.

Here are some examples. Let's go over them together!
First let's look at A and B. The borderlines here are made out of screens that have been cut into strips.
It gives the page a warmer feel compared to a borderline that's simply been drawn with a ruler.

C
EITHER WAY, I SHOULD GET A GIFT FOR STARTING SCHOOL.
THAT'S WHY I'M LOOKING FOR A JOB.
BUT YOSHIKI'S OUT PARTYING WITH HIS FRIENDS TO CELEBRATE HIS ACCEPTANCE.
What a jerk.

And then there's C… The screen tone panel line has been enhanced with some roses and it's a trim-like border. No doubt, it's elegant!
But use with caution. Don't just use decorative panel lines at random. These panel lines can also make the page messy. Think of the overall spread and use them to make a point!

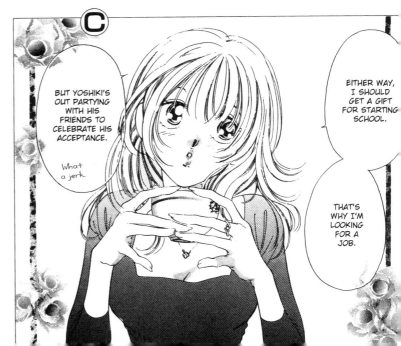

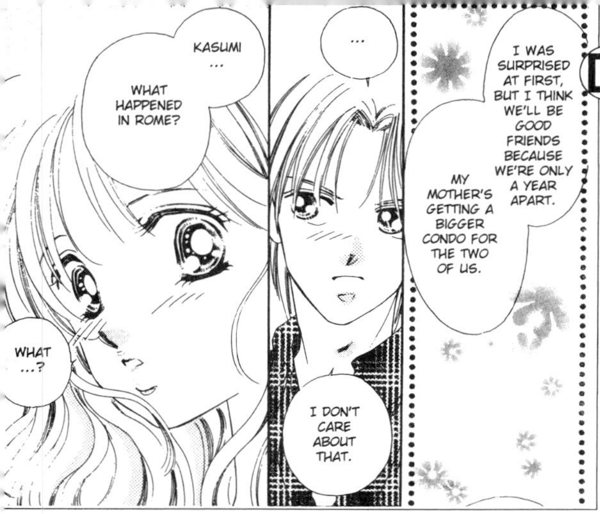
I WAS SURPRISED AT FIRST, BUT I THINK WE'LL BE GOOD FRIENDS BECAUSE WE'RE ONLY A YEAR APART.
MY MOTHER'S GETTING A BIGGER CONDO FOR THE TWO OF US.
D
...
I DON'T CARE ABOUT THAT.
KASUMI ...
WHAT HAPPENED IN ROME?
WHAT ...?

PANEL LINES AREN'T ALWAYS STRAIGHT.

Now check out the panel lines in D. The first panel's the same as the earlier example, but look at the third panel. This lacy border is also created by using a screen tone.
All the patterns that have been introduced so far were straight lines, but note that you can use different ones like this!

LET'S CHECK OUT OTHER VARIATIONS.

Now look at E. The screen tone used as a panel line in the bottom panel is used to frame the caption on the top panel.
See how much more it contributes to the overall feel of the entire page than a border drawn with a pen and ruler?!

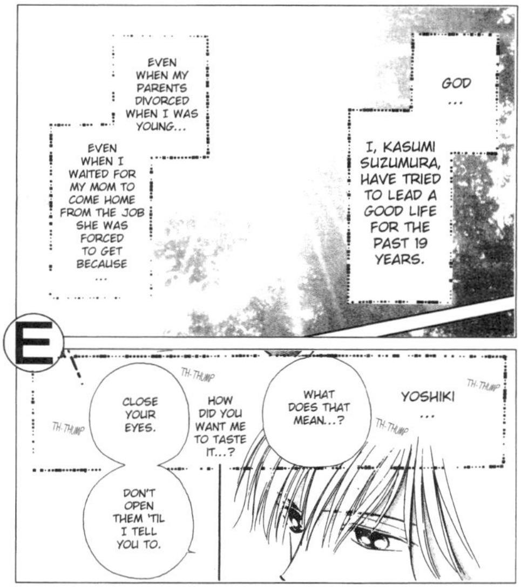
GOD ...
I, KASUMI SUZUMURA, HAVE TRIED TO LEAD A GOOD LIFE FOR THE PAST 19 YEARS.
EVEN WHEN MY PARENTS DIVORCED WHEN I WAS YOUNG...
EVEN WHEN I WAITED FOR MY MOM TO COME HOME FROM THE JOB SHE WAS FORCED TO GET BECAUSE ...
E
YOSHIKI ...
TH-THUMP
WHAT DOES THAT MEAN...?
TH-THUMP
HOW DID YOU WANT ME TO TASTE IT...?
TH-THUMP
CLOSE YOUR EYES.
DON'T OPEN THEM 'TIL I TELL YOU TO.
TH-THUMP

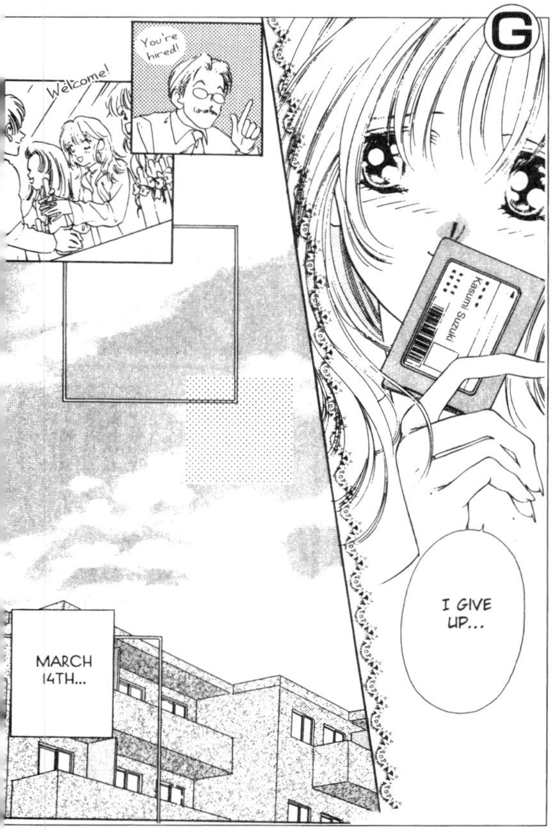
G
Kasumi Suzuki
I GIVE UP...
You're hired!
Welcome!
MARCH 14TH...

In F, the outline of the screen tone pasted over the entire panel works as the panel outline. How interesting!
It's difficult to successfully use this many patterns, but play around.
Lastly, G combines all the patterns we've introduced so far. You could say it's an expo of borderlines. Double lined borders can also be effective depending on the use.

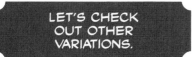

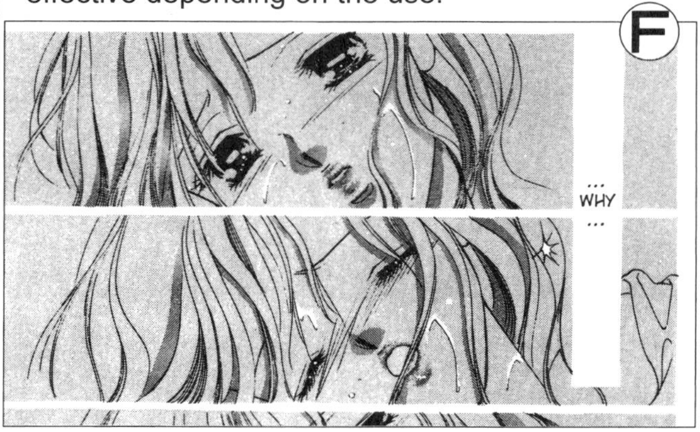
F
... WHY ...

CHAPTER 7: THE RIE TAKADA EDITION

LET'S ADD COLOR!

You don't need it for your submission, but it's a bridge that every pro must cross. Let's ask Rie Takada!

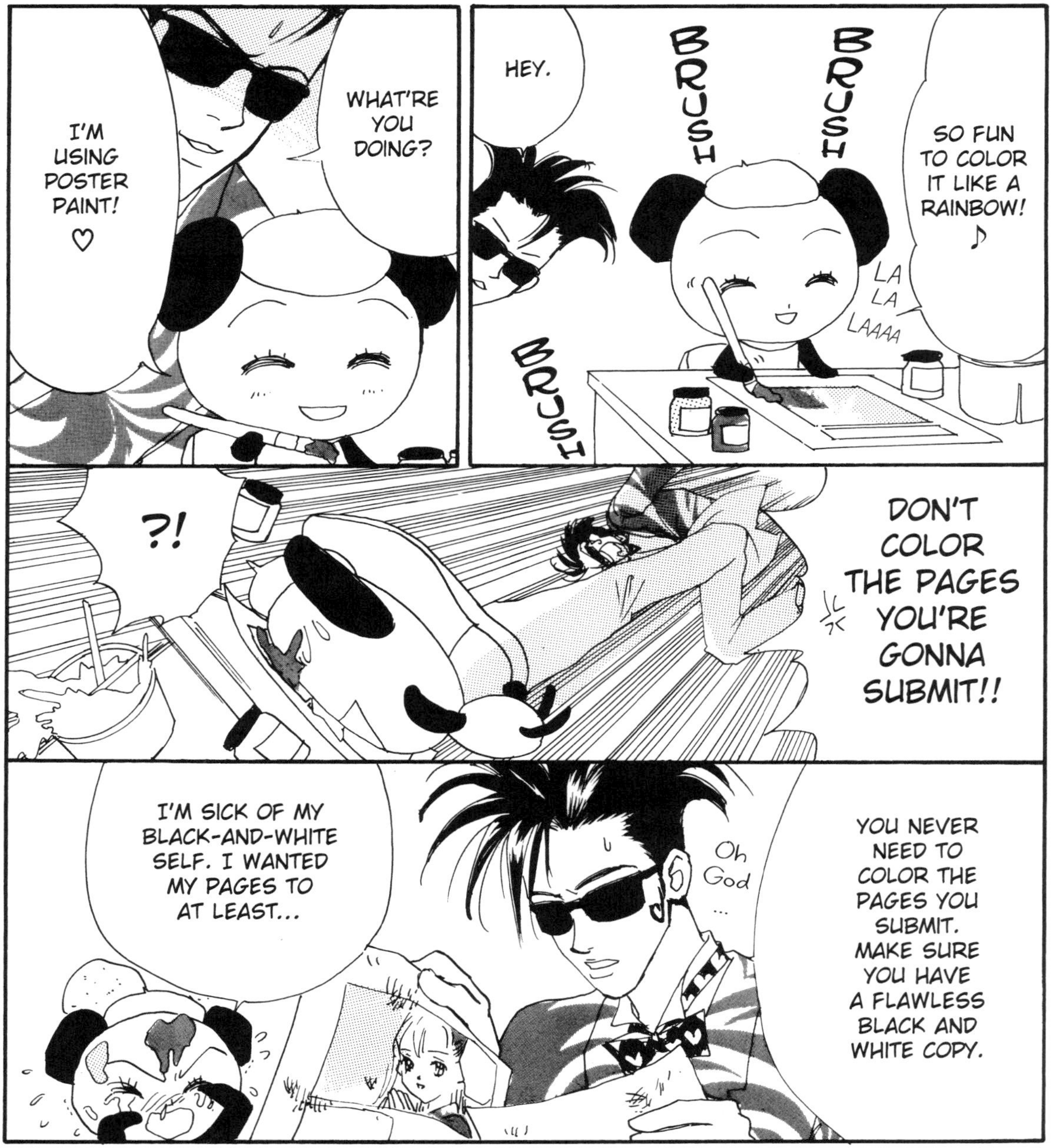

SO FUN TO COLOR IT LIKE A RAINBOW! ♪
BRUSH
BRUSH
HEY.
LA LA LAAAA
BRUSH
WHAT'RE YOU DOING?
I'M USING POSTER PAINT! ♡
DON'T COLOR THE PAGES YOU'RE GONNA SUBMIT!!
?!
YOU NEVER NEED TO COLOR THE PAGES YOU SUBMIT. MAKE SURE YOU HAVE A FLAWLESS BLACK AND WHITE COPY.
Oh God ...
I'M SICK OF MY BLACK-AND-WHITE SELF. I WANTED MY PAGES TO AT LEAST...

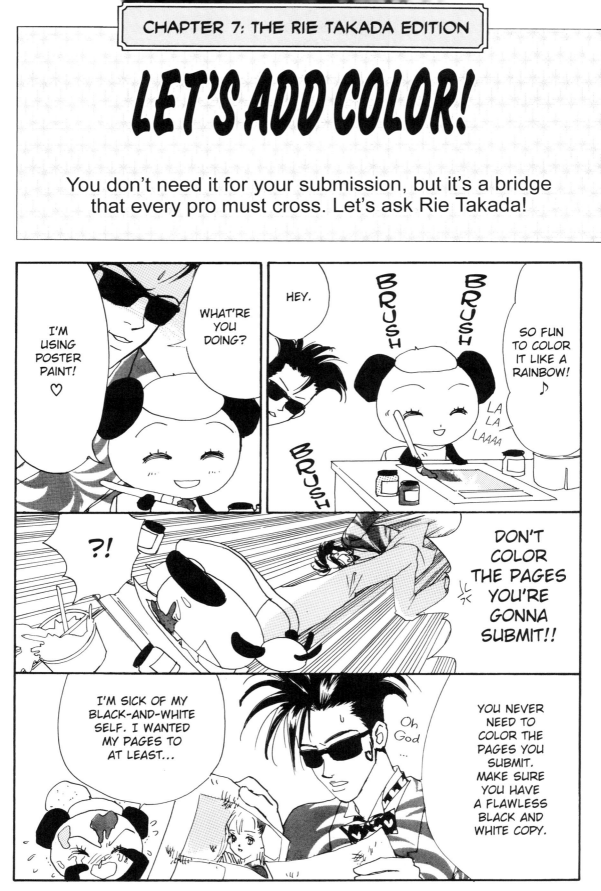

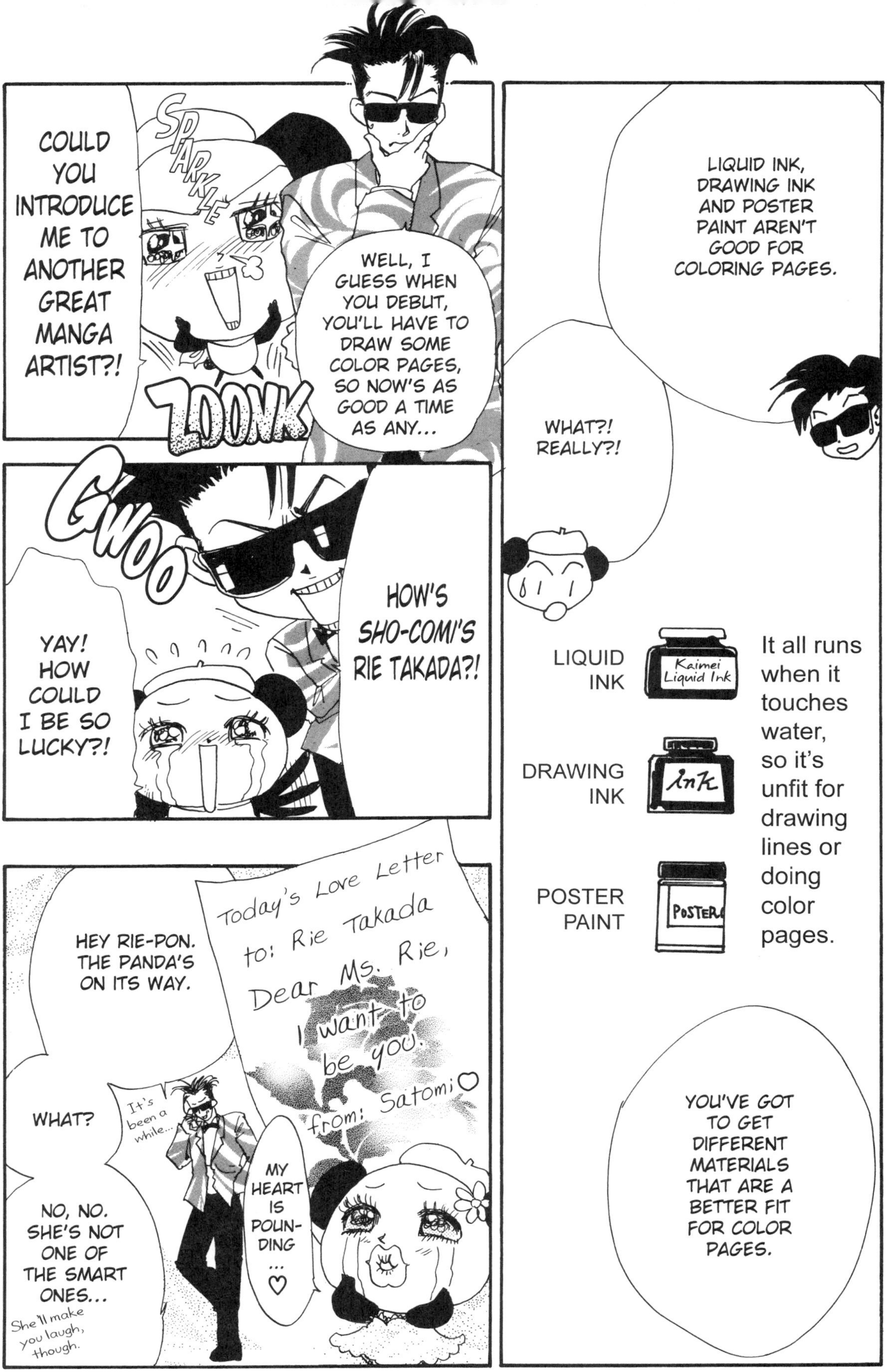
LIQUID INK, DRAWING INK AND POSTER PAINT AREN'T GOOD FOR COLORING PAGES.
WHAT?! REALLY?!
LIQUID INK
Kaimei Liquid Ink
DRAWING INK
Ink
POSTER PAINT
POSTER
It all runs when it touches water, so it's unfit for drawing lines or doing color pages.
YOU'VE GOT TO GET DIFFERENT MATERIALS THAT ARE A BETTER FIT FOR COLOR PAGES.
WELL, I GUESS WHEN YOU DEBUT, YOU'LL HAVE TO DRAW SOME COLOR PAGES, SO NOW'S AS GOOD A TIME AS ANY...
SPARKLE
COULD YOU INTRODUCE ME TO ANOTHER GREAT MANGA ARTIST?!
ZDONK
GWOO
HOW'S SHO-COMI'S RIE TAKADA?!
YAY! HOW COULD I BE SO LUCKY?!
Today's Love Letter
to: Rie Takada
Dear Ms. Rie,
I want to be you.
from: Satomi♡
HEY RIE-PON. THE PANDA'S ON ITS WAY.
MY HEART IS POUNDING... ♡
It's been a while...
WHAT?
NO, NO. SHE'S NOT ONE OF THE SMART ONES...
She'll make you laugh, though.

THE TOOLS FOR COLOR PAGES

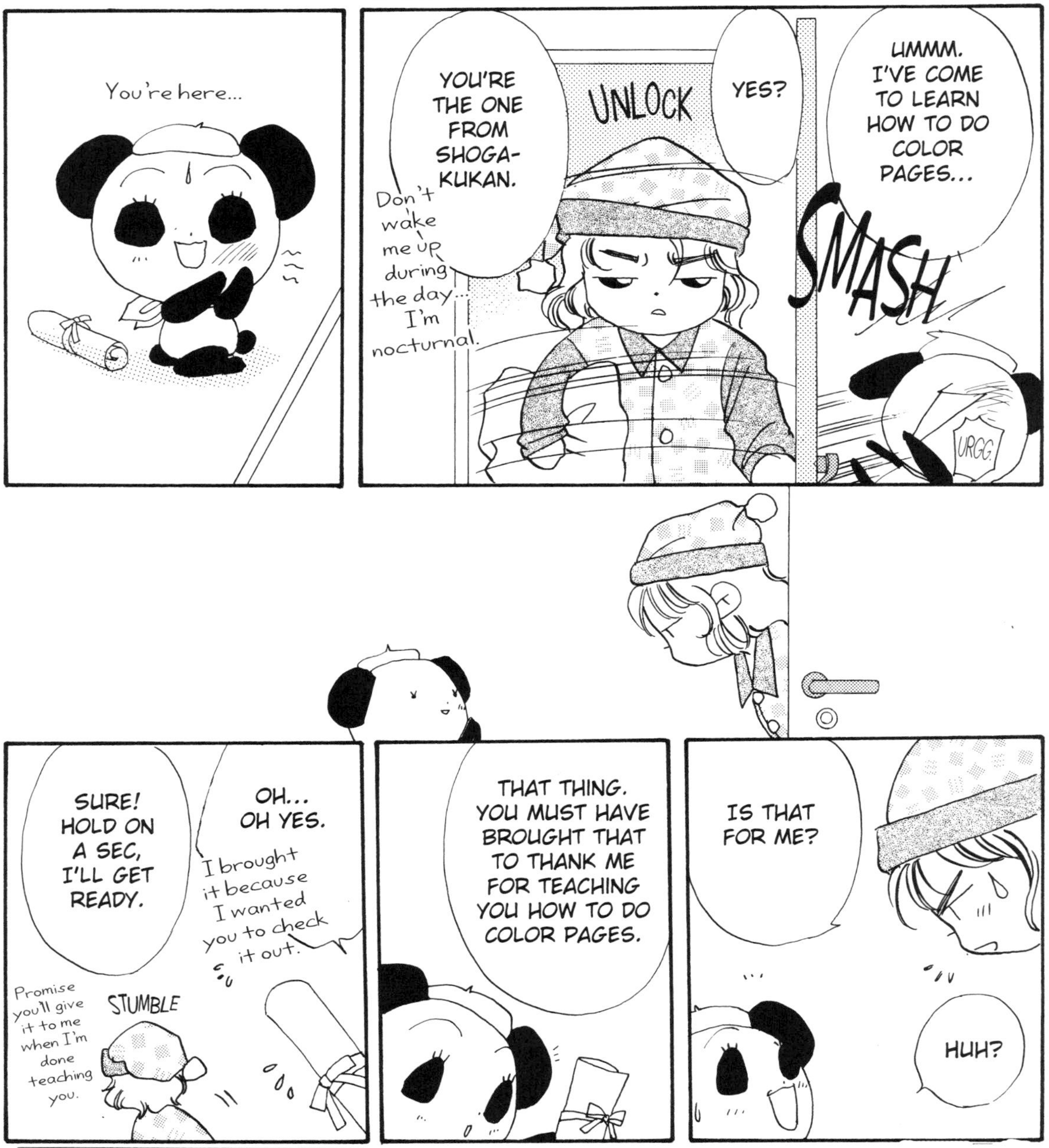
UMMM. I'VE COME TO LEARN HOW TO DO COLOR PAGES...
YES?
UNLOCK
SMASH
URGG.
YOU'RE THE ONE FROM SHOGA-KUKAN.
Don't wake me up during the day... I'm nocturnal.
You're here...
IS THAT FOR ME?
HUH?
THAT THING. YOU MUST HAVE BROUGHT THAT TO THANK ME FOR TEACHING YOU HOW TO DO COLOR PAGES.
OH... OH YES.
I brought it because I wanted you to check it out.
SURE! HOLD ON A SEC, I'LL GET READY.
STUMBLE
Promise you'll give it to me when I'm done teaching you.

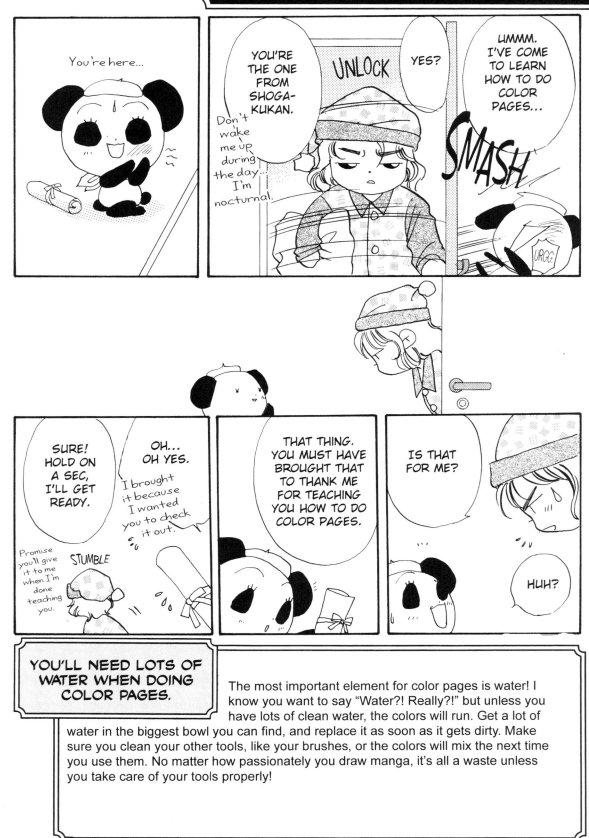

YOU'LL NEED LOTS OF WATER WHEN DOING COLOR PAGES.

The most important element for color pages is water! I know you want to say "Water?! Really?!" but unless you have lots of clean water, the colors will run. Get a lot of water in the biggest bowl you can find, and replace it as soon as it gets dirty. Make sure you clean your other tools, like your brushes, or the colors will mix the next time you use them. No matter how passionately you draw manga, it's all a waste unless you take care of your tools properly!

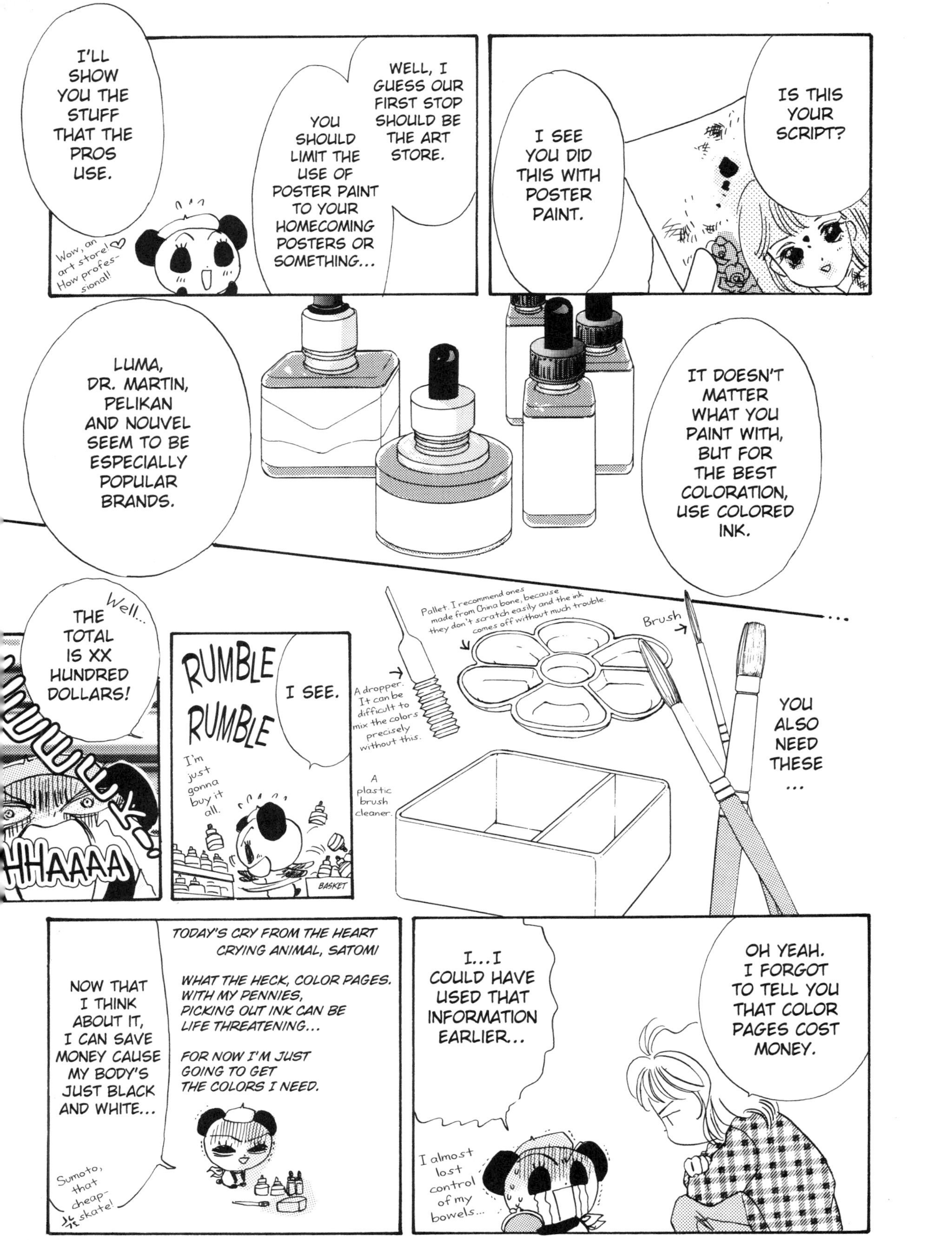
IS THIS YOUR SCRIPT?
I SEE YOU DID THIS WITH POSTER PAINT.
WELL, I GUESS OUR FIRST STOP SHOULD BE THE ART STORE.
YOU SHOULD LIMIT THE USE OF POSTER PAINT TO YOUR HOMECOMING POSTERS OR SOMETHING...
I'LL SHOW YOU THE STUFF THAT THE PROS USE.
Wow, an art store!♡ How profes-sional!
IT DOESN'T MATTER WHAT YOU PAINT WITH, BUT FOR THE BEST COLORATION, USE COLORED INK.
LUMA, DR. MARTIN, PELIKAN AND NOUVEL SEEM TO BE ESPECIALLY POPULAR BRANDS.
...
YOU ALSO NEED THESE...
Brush
Pallet. I recommend ones made from China bone, because they don't scratch easily and the ink comes off without much trouble.
A dropper. It can be difficult to mix the colors precisely without this.
A plastic brush cleaner.
I SEE.
RUMBLE RUMBLE
I'm just gonna buy it all.
BASKET
Well...
THE TOTAL IS XX HUNDRED DOLLARS!
HHAAAA
OH YEAH. I FORGOT TO TELL YOU THAT COLOR PAGES COST MONEY.
I...I COULD HAVE USED THAT INFORMATION EARLIER...
I almost lost control of my bowels...
TODAY'S CRY FROM THE HEART
CRYING ANIMAL, SATOMI
WHAT THE HECK, COLOR PAGES. WITH MY PENNIES, PICKING OUT INK CAN BE LIFE THREATENING...
FOR NOW I'M JUST GOING TO GET THE COLORS I NEED.
NOW THAT I THINK ABOUT IT, I CAN SAVE MONEY CAUSE MY BODY'S JUST BLACK AND WHITE...
Sumoto, that cheap-skate!

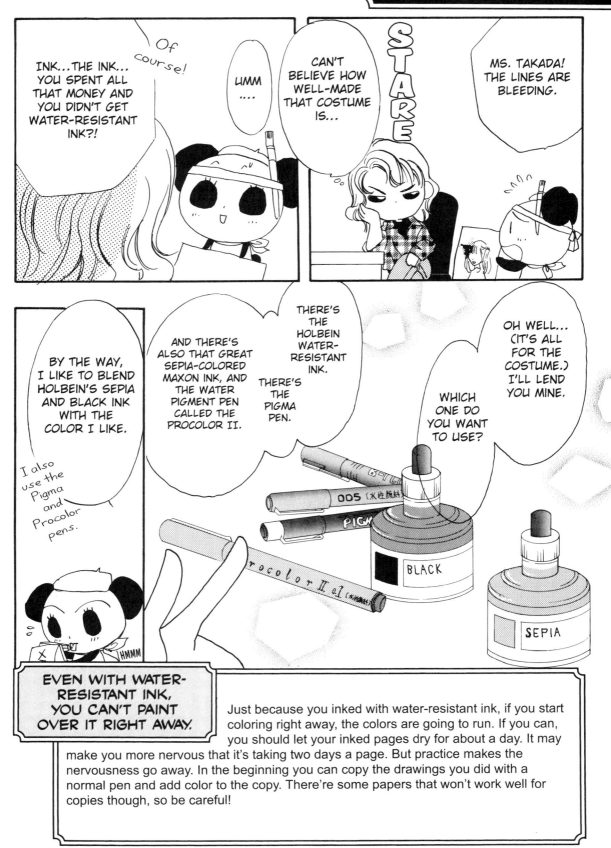

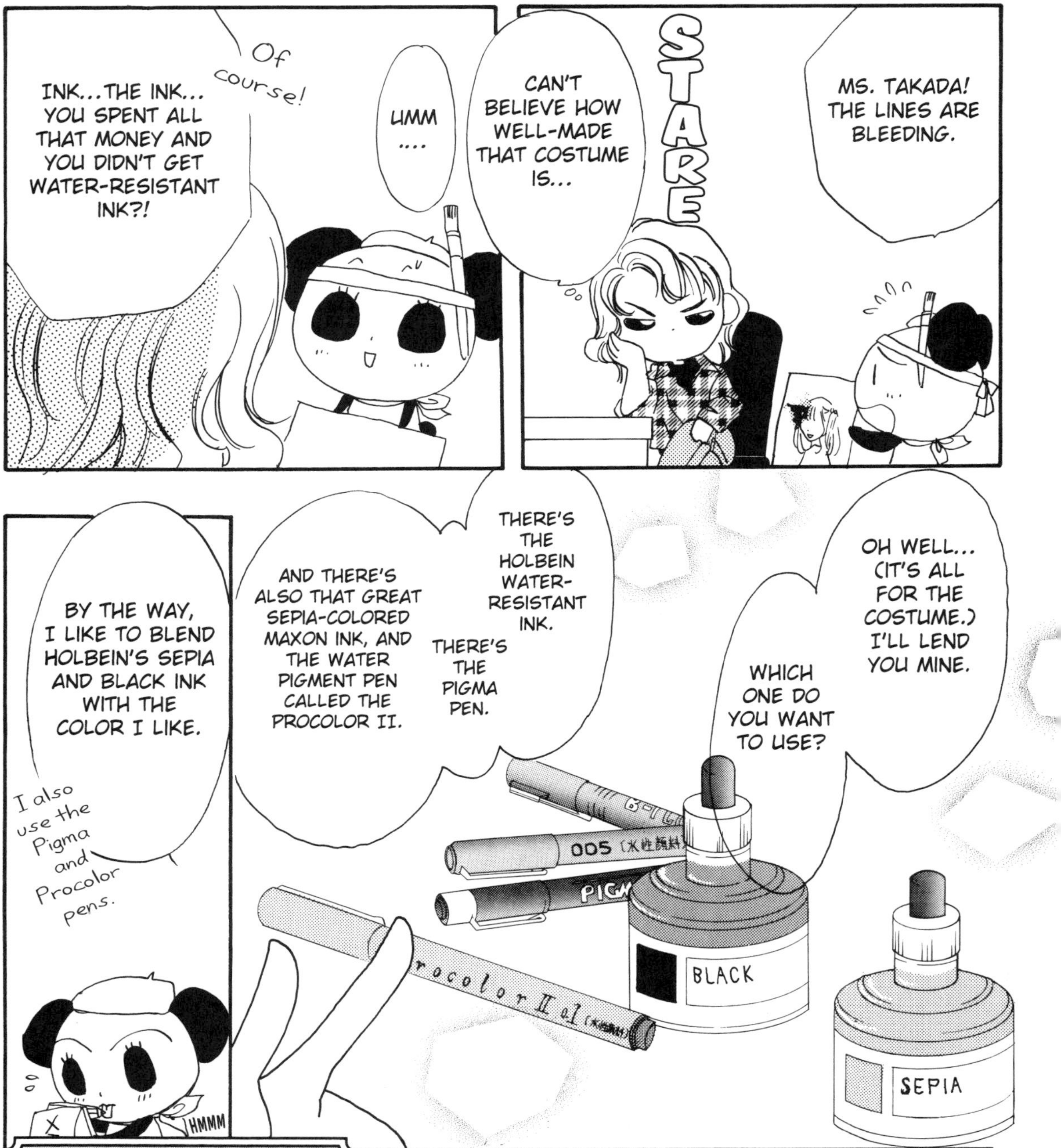
MS. TAKADA! THE LINES ARE BLEEDING.
STARE
CAN'T BELIEVE HOW WELL-MADE THAT COSTUME IS...
UMM ....
INK...THE INK... YOU SPENT ALL THAT MONEY AND YOU DIDN'T GET WATER-RESISTANT INK?!
Of course!
OH WELL... (IT'S ALL FOR THE COSTUME.) I'LL LEND YOU MINE.
WHICH ONE DO YOU WANT TO USE?
THERE'S THE HOLBEIN WATER-RESISTANT INK.
THERE'S THE PIGMA PEN.
AND THERE'S ALSO THAT GREAT SEPIA-COLORED MAXON INK, AND THE WATER PIGMENT PEN CALLED THE PROCOLOR II.
BY THE WAY, I LIKE TO BLEND HOLBEIN'S SEPIA AND BLACK INK WITH THE COLOR I LIKE.
I also use the Pigma and Procolor pens.
BLACK
SEPIA
HMMM

EVEN WITH WATER-RESISTANT INK, YOU CAN'T PAINT OVER IT RIGHT AWAY.

Just because you inked with water-resistant ink, if you start coloring right away, the colors are going to run. If you can, you should let your inked pages dry for about a day. It may make you more nervous that it's taking two days a page. But practice makes the nervousness go away. In the beginning you can copy the drawings you did with a normal pen and add color to the copy. There're some papers that won't work well for copies though, so be careful!

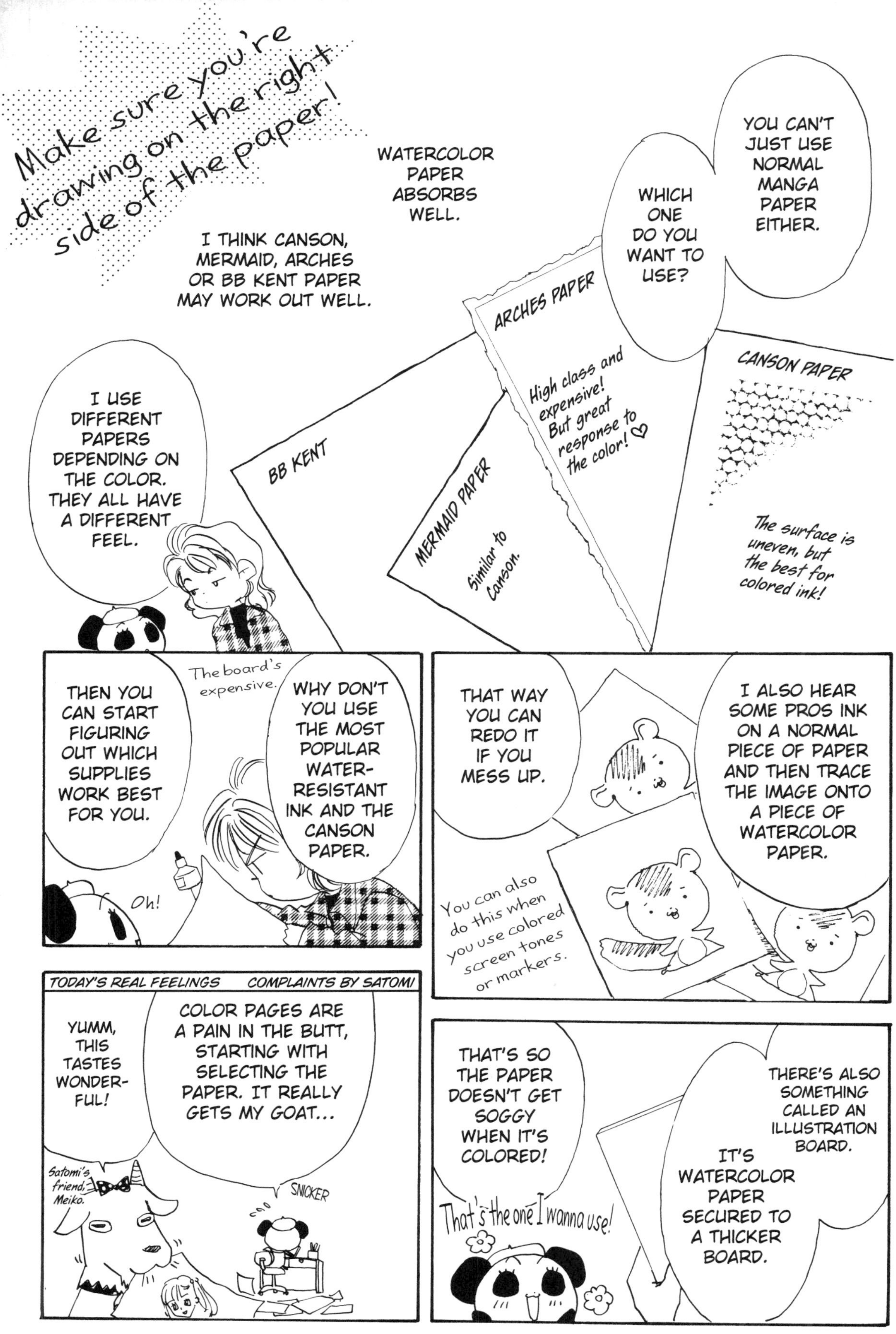
Make sure you're drawing on the right side of the paper!
YOU CAN'T JUST USE NORMAL MANGA PAPER EITHER.
WHICH ONE DO YOU WANT TO USE?
WATERCOLOR PAPER ABSORBS WELL.
I THINK CANSON, MERMAID, ARCHES OR BB KENT PAPER MAY WORK OUT WELL.
CANSON PAPER
The surface is uneven, but the best for colored ink!
ARCHES PAPER
High class and expensive! But great response to the color! ♡
MERMAID PAPER
Similar to Canson.
BB KENT
I USE DIFFERENT PAPERS DEPENDING ON THE COLOR. THEY ALL HAVE A DIFFERENT FEEL.
I ALSO HEAR SOME PROS INK ON A NORMAL PIECE OF PAPER AND THEN TRACE THE IMAGE ONTO A PIECE OF WATERCOLOR PAPER.
THAT WAY YOU CAN REDO IT IF YOU MESS UP.
You can also do this when you use colored screen tones or markers.
WHY DON'T YOU USE THE MOST POPULAR WATER-RESISTANT INK AND THE CANSON PAPER.
The board's expensive.
THEN YOU CAN START FIGURING OUT WHICH SUPPLIES WORK BEST FOR YOU.
Oh!
THERE'S ALSO SOMETHING CALLED AN ILLUSTRATION BOARD.
IT'S WATERCOLOR PAPER SECURED TO A THICKER BOARD.
THAT'S SO THE PAPER DOESN'T GET SOGGY WHEN IT'S COLORED!
That's the one I wanna use!
TODAY'S REAL FEELINGS COMPLAINTS BY SATOMI
COLOR PAGES ARE A PAIN IN THE BUTT, STARTING WITH SELECTING THE PAPER. IT REALLY GETS MY GOAT...
YUMM, THIS TASTES WONDER-FUL!
SNICKER
Satomi's friend, Meiko.

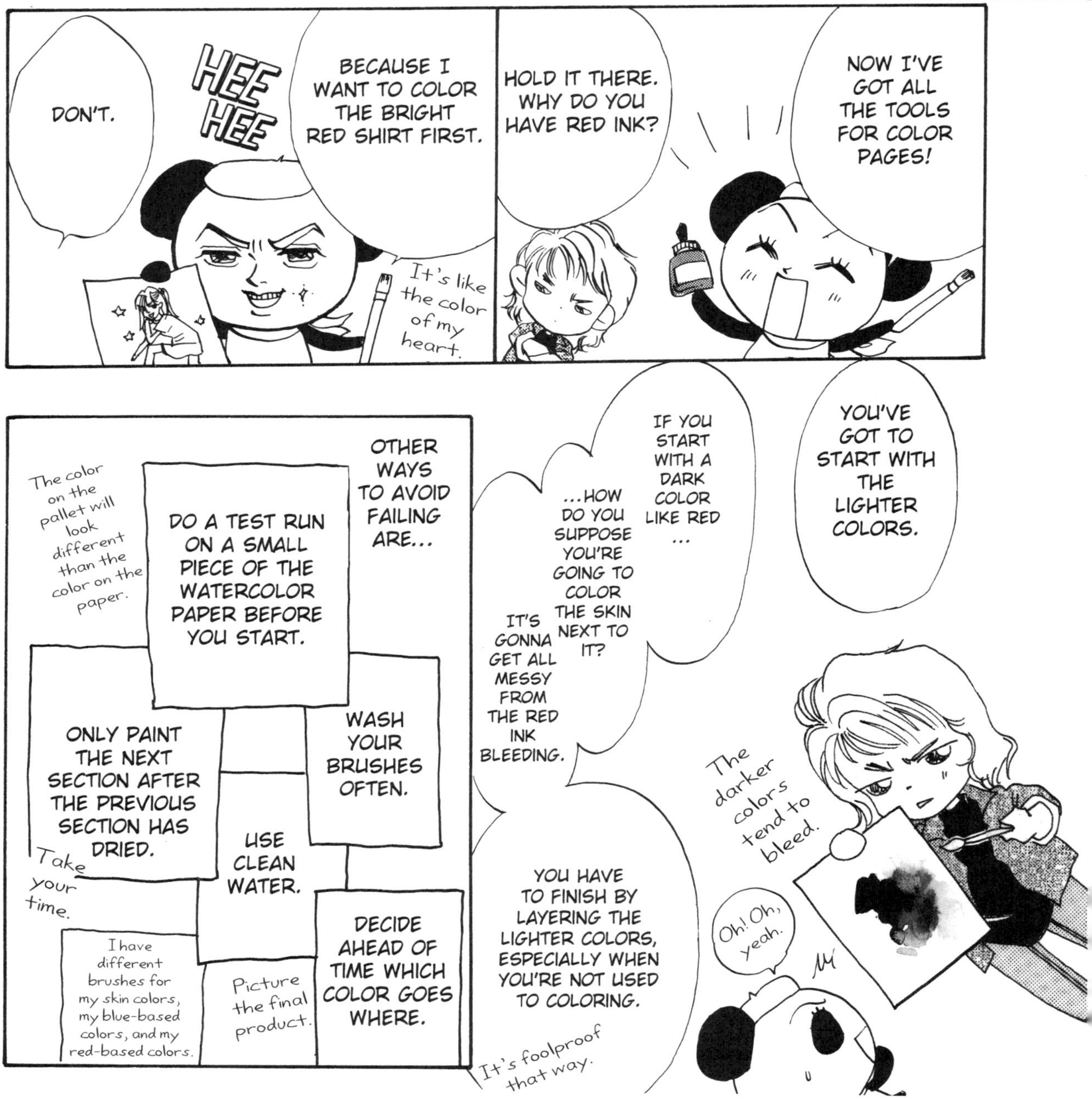
NOW I'VE GOT ALL THE TOOLS FOR COLOR PAGES!
HOLD IT THERE. WHY DO YOU HAVE RED INK?
BECAUSE I WANT TO COLOR THE BRIGHT RED SHIRT FIRST.
HEE HEE
DON'T.
It's like the color of my heart.
YOU'VE GOT TO START WITH THE LIGHTER COLORS.
IF YOU START WITH A DARK COLOR LIKE RED ...
...HOW DO YOU SUPPOSE YOU'RE GOING TO COLOR THE SKIN NEXT TO IT?
IT'S GONNA GET ALL MESSY FROM THE RED INK BLEEDING.
The darker colors tend to bleed.
YOU HAVE TO FINISH BY LAYERING THE LIGHTER COLORS, ESPECIALLY WHEN YOU'RE NOT USED TO COLORING.
Oh! Oh, yeah.
It's foolproof that way.
OTHER WAYS TO AVOID FAILING ARE...
DO A TEST RUN ON A SMALL PIECE OF THE WATERCOLOR PAPER BEFORE YOU START.
The color on the pallet will look different than the color on the paper.
WASH YOUR BRUSHES OFTEN.
ONLY PAINT THE NEXT SECTION AFTER THE PREVIOUS SECTION HAS DRIED.
Take your time.
USE CLEAN WATER.
DECIDE AHEAD OF TIME WHICH COLOR GOES WHERE.
Picture the final product.
I have different brushes for my skin colors, my blue-based colors, and my red-based colors.

THE KEY TO A BEAUTIFUL FINISH IS "LAYERING."

You can see from Yuu Watase's color page in the introduction that the bottom line in coloring is layering. Light colors, like skin tones, look better if you adjust not by using different colors, but by layering a single one. Use this method for effects, like highlights. Think of it as layering sheets of cellophane to make it darker. You can't tell if the light colors spill outside the lines a little, and this way there's less chance you'll mess up. You can kill two birds with one stone. Make sure you only color the next area next after the ink's dried. This is another basic rule.

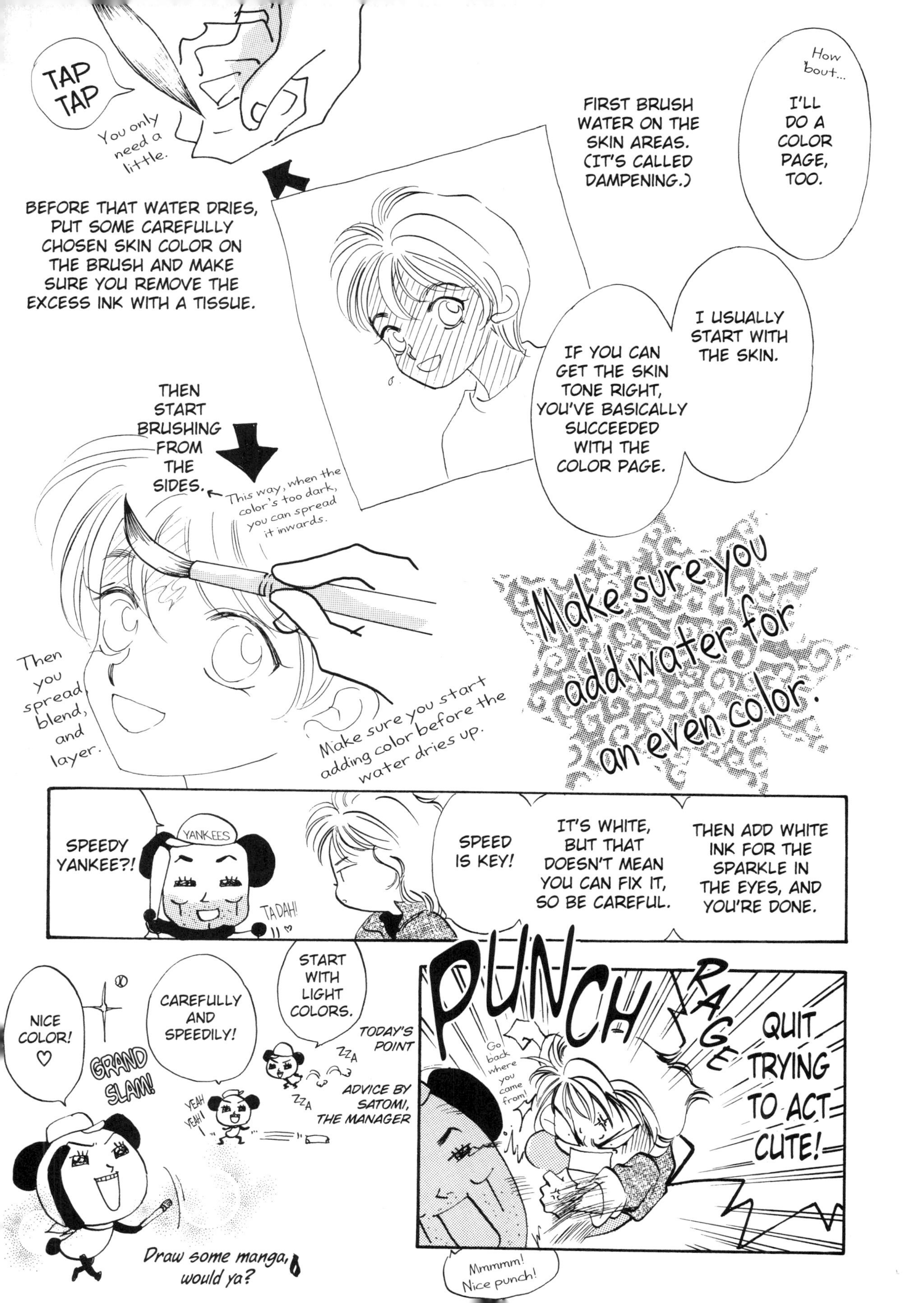

How 'bout...
I'LL DO A COLOR PAGE, TOO.
FIRST BRUSH WATER ON THE SKIN AREAS. (IT'S CALLED DAMPENING.)
TAP TAP
You only need a little.
BEFORE THAT WATER DRIES, PUT SOME CAREFULLY CHOSEN SKIN COLOR ON THE BRUSH AND MAKE SURE YOU REMOVE THE EXCESS INK WITH A TISSUE.
I USUALLY START WITH THE SKIN.
IF YOU CAN GET THE SKIN TONE RIGHT, YOU'VE BASICALLY SUCCEEDED WITH THE COLOR PAGE.
THEN START BRUSHING FROM THE SIDES.
This way, when the color's too dark, you can spread it inwards.
Make sure you add water for an even color.
Make sure you start adding color before the water dries up.
Then you spread, blend, and layer.
THEN ADD WHITE INK FOR THE SPARKLE IN THE EYES, AND YOU'RE DONE.
IT'S WHITE, BUT THAT DOESN'T MEAN YOU CAN FIX IT, SO BE CAREFUL.
SPEED IS KEY!
SPEEDY YANKEE?!
YANKEES
TADAH!
PUNCH
RAGE
QUIT TRYING TO ACT CUTE!
Go back where you came from!
Mmmmm! Nice punch!
START WITH LIGHT COLORS.
TODAY'S POINT
ADVICE BY SATOMI, THE MANAGER
ZZA
ZZA
CAREFULLY AND SPEEDILY!
YEAH YEAH!
NICE COLOR! ♡
GRAND SLAM!
Draw some manga, would ya?

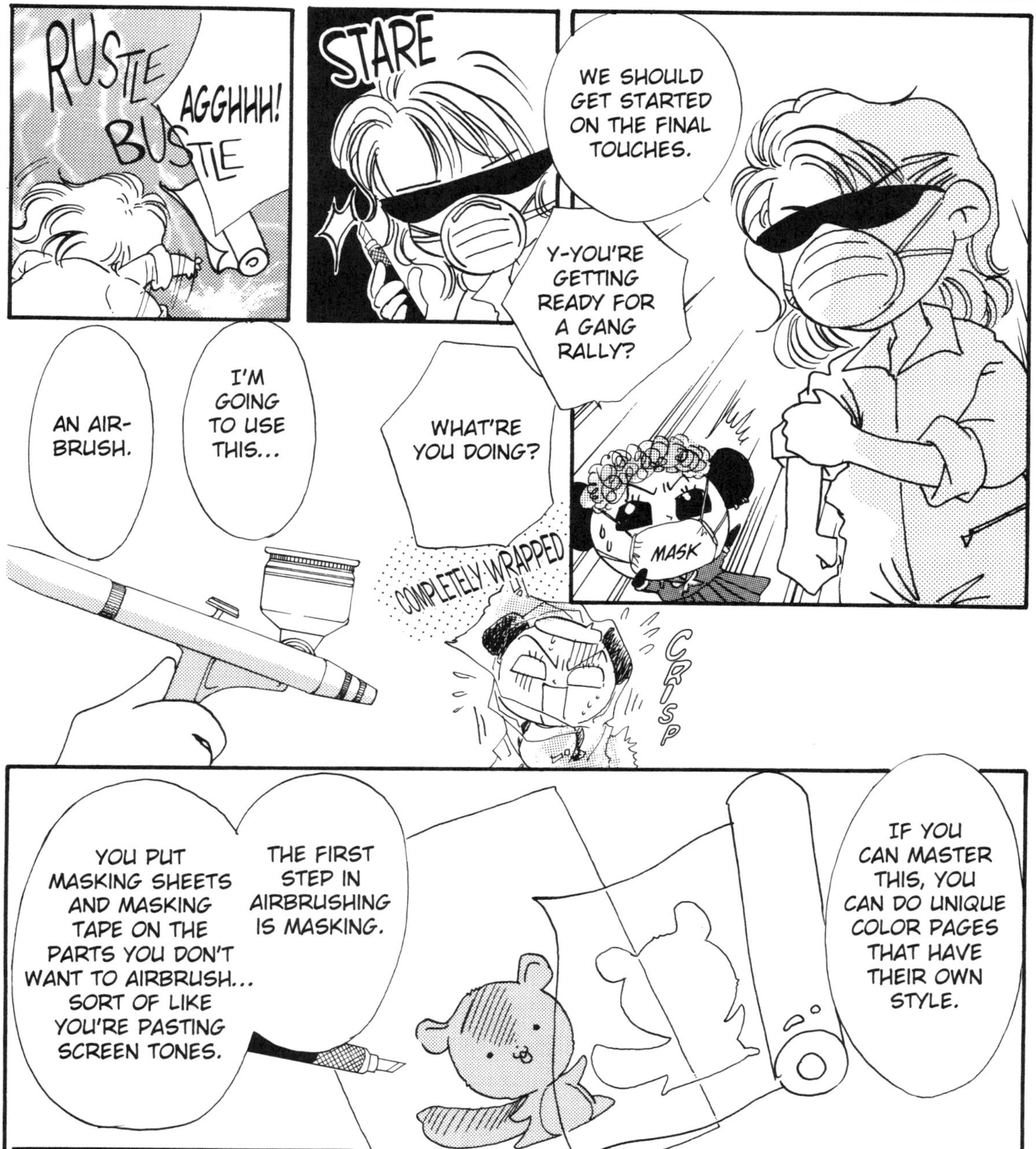
WE SHOULD GET STARTED ON THE FINAL TOUCHES.
Y-YOU'RE GETTING READY FOR A GANG RALLY?
MASK
STARE
RUSTLE BUSTLE
AGGHHH!
WHAT'RE YOU DOING?
COMPLETELY WRAPPED
CRISP
I'M GOING TO USE THIS...
AN AIR-BRUSH.
IF YOU CAN MASTER THIS, YOU CAN DO UNIQUE COLOR PAGES THAT HAVE THEIR OWN STYLE.
THE FIRST STEP IN AIRBRUSHING IS MASKING.
YOU PUT MASKING SHEETS AND MASKING TAPE ON THE PARTS YOU DON'T WANT TO AIRBRUSH... SORT OF LIKE YOU'RE PASTING SCREEN TONES.

USE A SIMPLE SPRAY INSTEAD OF AN EXPENSIVE AIRBRUSH.

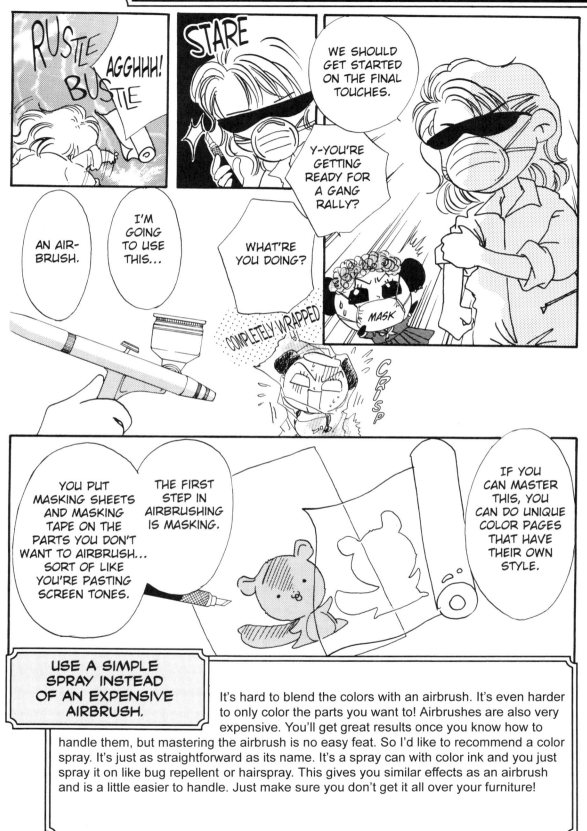

It's hard to blend the colors with an airbrush. It's even harder to only color the parts you want to! Airbrushes are also very expensive. You'll get great results once you know how to handle them, but mastering the airbrush is no easy feat. So I'd like to recommend a color spray. It's just as straightforward as its name. It's a spray can with color ink and you just spray it on like bug repellent or hairspray. This gives you similar effects as an airbrush and is a little easier to handle. Just make sure you don't get it all over your furniture!

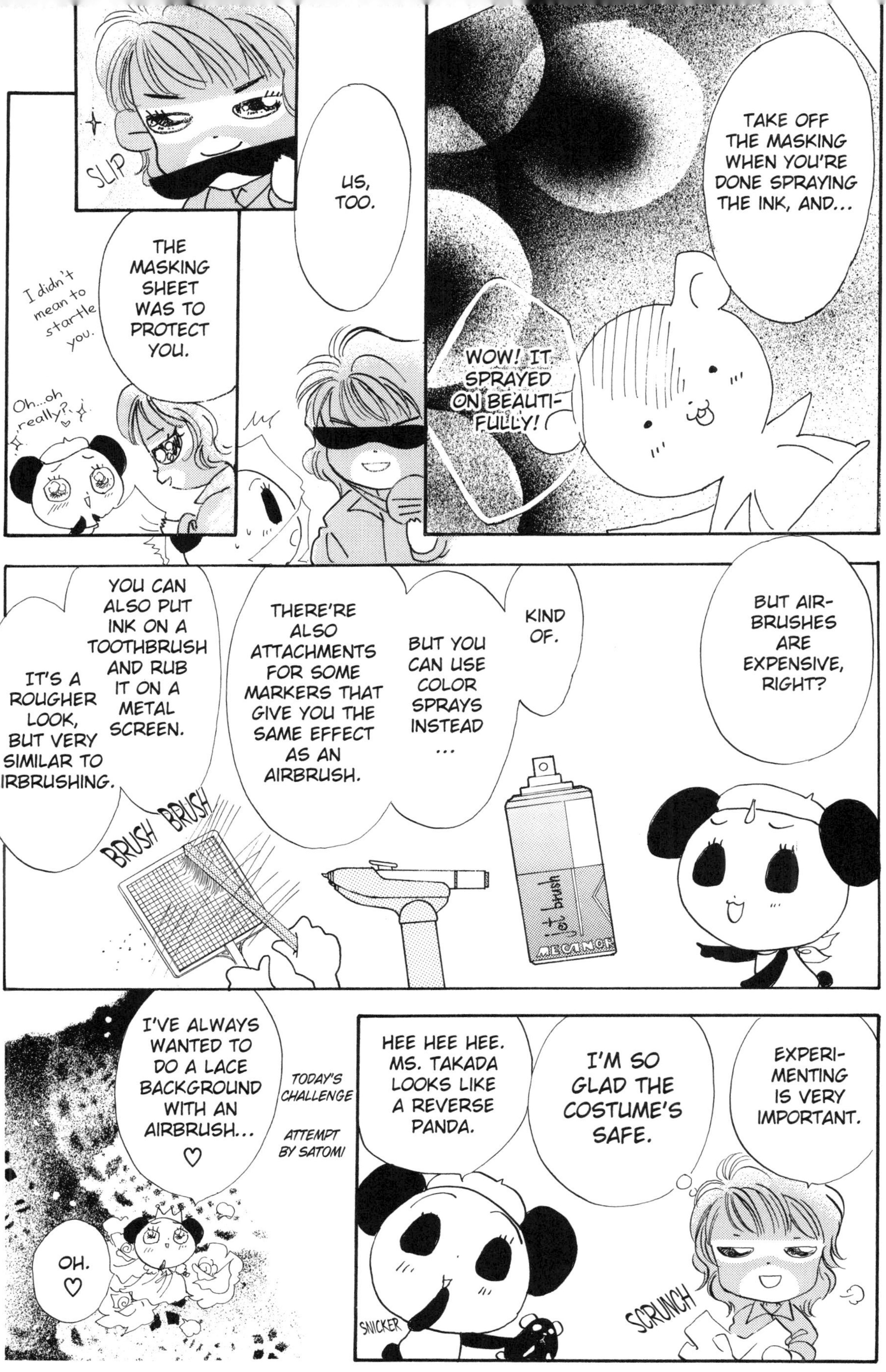
TAKE OFF THE MASKING WHEN YOU'RE DONE SPRAYING THE INK, AND...
WOW! IT SPRAYED ON BEAUTI-FULLY!
SLIP
US, TOO.
THE MASKING SHEET WAS TO PROTECT YOU.
I didn't mean to startle you.
Oh...oh really? ♡
BUT AIR-BRUSHES ARE EXPENSIVE, RIGHT?
KIND OF.
BUT YOU CAN USE COLOR SPRAYS INSTEAD...
THERE'RE ALSO ATTACHMENTS FOR SOME MARKERS THAT GIVE YOU THE SAME EFFECT AS AN AIRBRUSH.
YOU CAN ALSO PUT INK ON A TOOTHBRUSH AND RUB IT ON A METAL SCREEN.
IT'S A ROUGHER LOOK, BUT VERY SIMILAR TO AIRBRUSHING.
BRUSH BRUSH
EXPERI-MENTING IS VERY IMPORTANT.
I'M SO GLAD THE COSTUME'S SAFE.
HEE HEE HEE. MS. TAKADA LOOKS LIKE A REVERSE PANDA.
SCRUNCH
SNICKER
TODAY'S CHALLENGE
I'VE ALWAYS WANTED TO DO A LACE BACKGROUND WITH AN AIRBRUSH... ♡
ATTEMPT BY SATOMI
OH. ♡

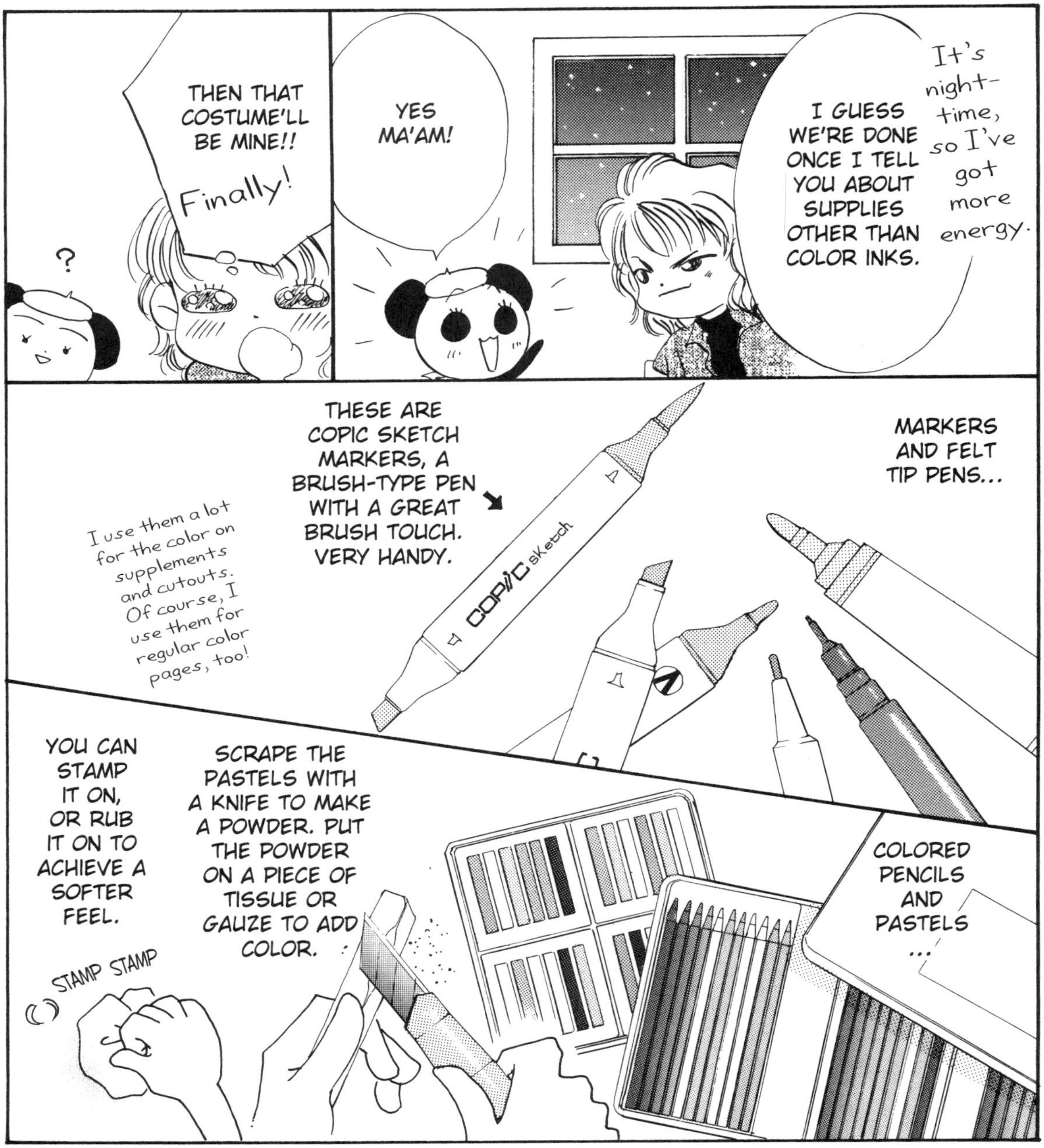
I GUESS WE'RE DONE ONCE I TELL YOU ABOUT SUPPLIES OTHER THAN COLOR INKS.
It's night-time, so I've got more energy.
YES MA'AM!
THEN THAT COSTUME'LL BE MINE!!
Finally!
?
MARKERS AND FELT TIP PENS...
THESE ARE COPIC SKETCH MARKERS, A BRUSH-TYPE PEN WITH A GREAT BRUSH TOUCH. VERY HANDY.
COPIC sketch
I use them a lot for the color on supplements and cutouts. Of course, I use them for regular color pages, too!
COLORED PENCILS AND PASTELS...
SCRAPE THE PASTELS WITH A KNIFE TO MAKE A POWDER. PUT THE POWDER ON A PIECE OF TISSUE OR GAUZE TO ADD COLOR.
YOU CAN STAMP IT ON, OR RUB IT ON TO ACHIEVE A SOFTER FEEL.
STAMP STAMP

USE DIFFERENT ART SUPPLIES AND LEARN THEIR EFFECTS.

There are a lot of different art supplies you can use for color pages. Of course, you can do most pages with just some colored ink, but you can also use opaque poster paint, acrylics, or gouache for a different look. If you use opaque colors for the entire page, it might look a little heavy, but using them for selected parts can add to the picture. It really comes down to your ideas! But you've got to know about the supplies to be able to use them. Just go around and try different ones.

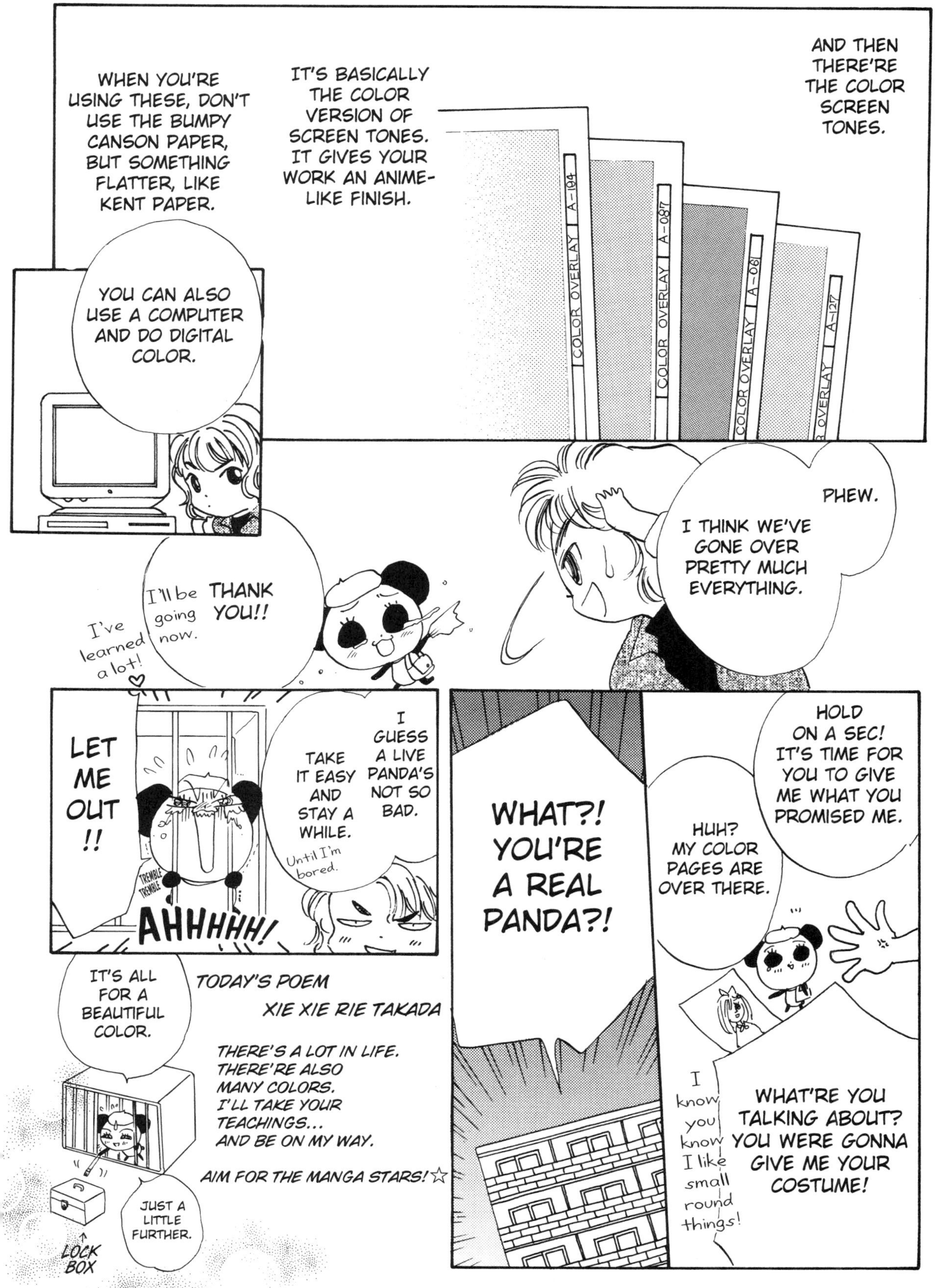
AND THEN THERE'RE THE COLOR SCREEN TONES.
IT'S BASICALLY THE COLOR VERSION OF SCREEN TONES. IT GIVES YOUR WORK AN ANIME-LIKE FINISH.
WHEN YOU'RE USING THESE, DON'T USE THE BUMPY CANSON PAPER, BUT SOMETHING FLATTER, LIKE KENT PAPER.
COLOR OVERLAY A-194
COLOR OVERLAY A-087
COLOR OVERLAY A-06
OVERLAY A-127
YOU CAN ALSO USE A COMPUTER AND DO DIGITAL COLOR.
PHEW.
I THINK WE'VE GONE OVER PRETTY MUCH EVERYTHING.
THANK YOU!!
I'll be going now.
I've learned a lot!
HOLD ON A SEC! IT'S TIME FOR YOU TO GIVE ME WHAT YOU PROMISED ME.
HUH? MY COLOR PAGES ARE OVER THERE.
WHAT?! YOU'RE A REAL PANDA?!
WHAT'RE YOU TALKING ABOUT? YOU WERE GONNA GIVE ME YOUR COSTUME!
I know you know I like small round things!
I GUESS A LIVE PANDA'S NOT SO BAD.
TAKE IT EASY AND STAY A WHILE.
Until I'm bored.
LET ME OUT!!
TREMBLE TREMBLE
AHHHHH!
TODAY'S POEM
XIE XIE RIE TAKADA
THERE'S A LOT IN LIFE.
THERE'RE ALSO MANY COLORS.
I'LL TAKE YOUR TEACHINGS...
AND BE ON MY WAY.
AIM FOR THE MANGA STARS!☆
IT'S ALL FOR A BEAUTIFUL COLOR.
JUST A LITTLE FURTHER.
LOCK BOX

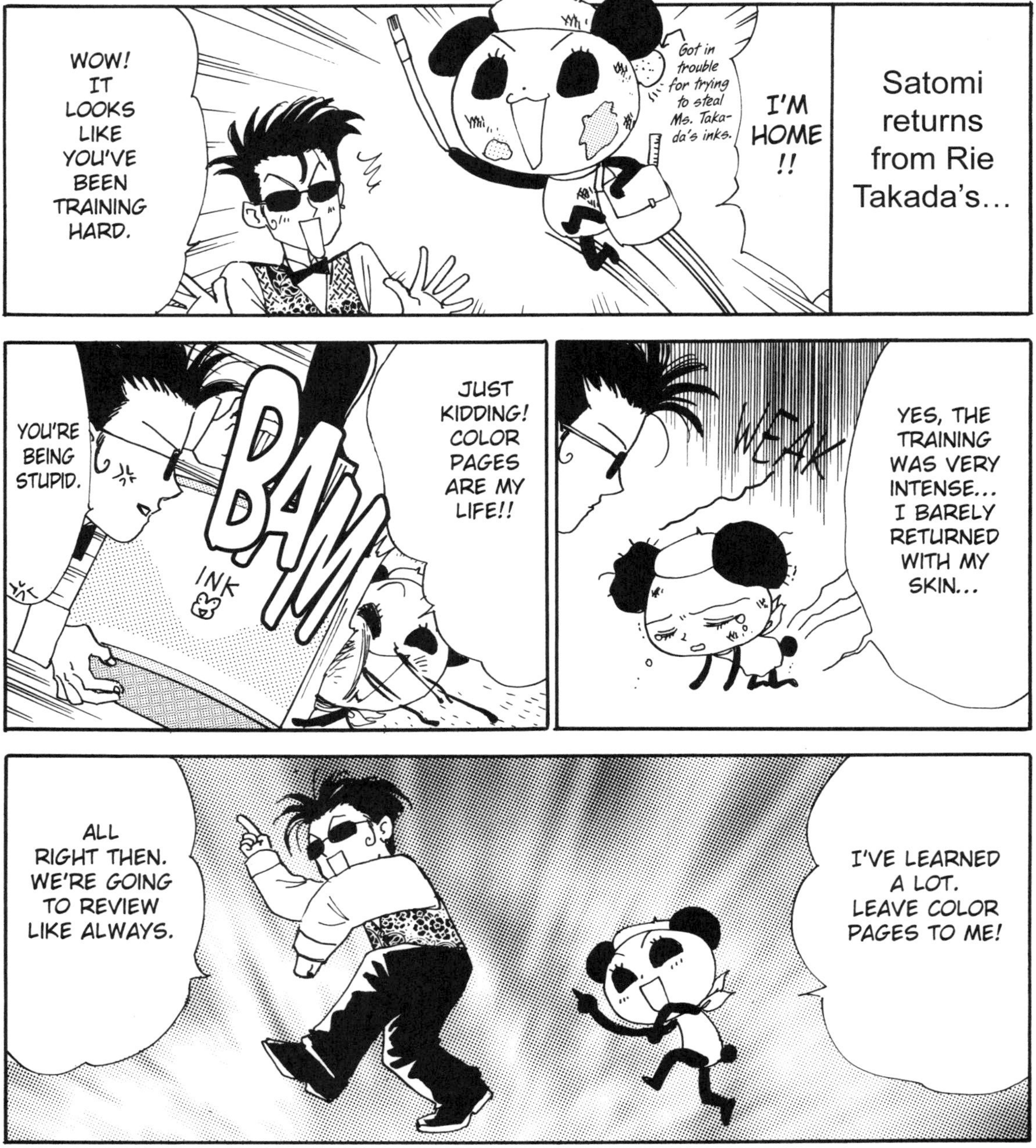
Satomi returns from Rie Takada's...
I'M HOME !!
Got in trouble for trying to steal Ms. Takada's inks.
WOW! IT LOOKS LIKE YOU'VE BEEN TRAINING HARD.
YES, THE TRAINING WAS VERY INTENSE... I BARELY RETURNED WITH MY SKIN...
WEAK
JUST KIDDING! COLOR PAGES ARE MY LIFE!!
BAM
INK
YOU'RE BEING STUPID.
I'VE LEARNED A LOT. LEAVE COLOR PAGES TO ME!
ALL RIGHT THEN. WE'RE GOING TO REVIEW LIKE ALWAYS.

CREATE A COLOR YOU CAN CALL YOUR OWN WITH COLORED INKS.

Colored inks come in many different colors, but more complex colors like skin tones aren't sold. All professionals save different colors like skin tones after they've made their own mixture. After mixing the ink, try layering it before you actually apply it to your page. When you come up with a color you like, make sure you remember that mixture. You could also make excess and store it in jars. Only mix 2-3 colors at a time. Mixing too many different colors just makes the colors run, so be careful!

●RIE TAKADA'S TEACHINGS THE FIVE RULES OF COLOR PAGES

1: Colored ink has the best coloration, so it is best for manga.

2: Use water resistant ink when inking, and use watercolor paper.

3: When adding color, start with the light colors and work your way to the dark ones.

4: Creativity makes for original effects!

5: Try out different art supplies and research on your own.

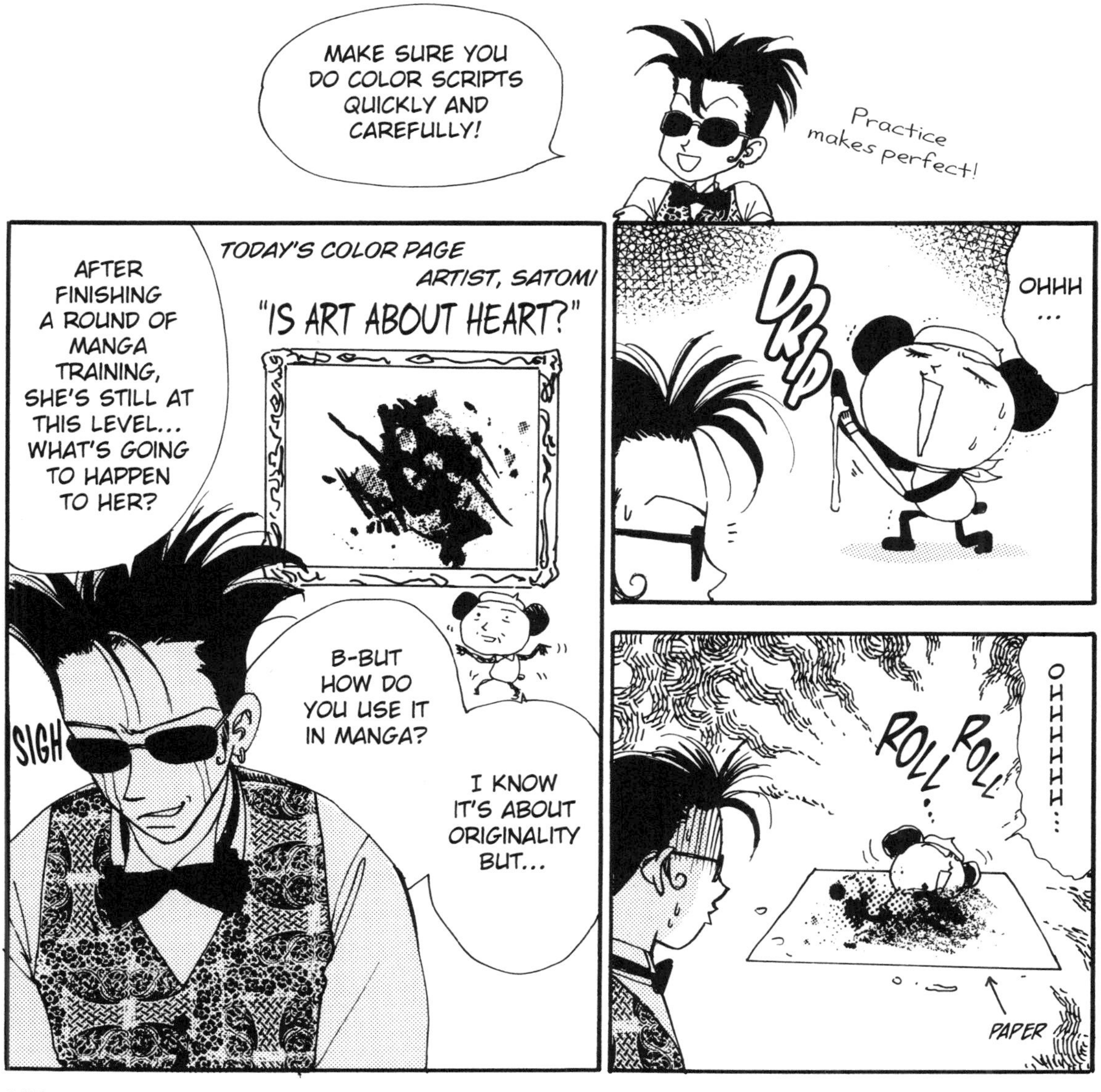
MAKE SURE YOU DO COLOR SCRIPTS QUICKLY AND CAREFULLY!
Practice makes perfect!
DRIP
OHHH...
ROLL ROLL
OHHHHHH...
PAPER
TODAY'S COLOR PAGE ARTIST, SATOMI
"IS ART ABOUT HEART?"
AFTER FINISHING A ROUND OF MANGA TRAINING, SHE'S STILL AT THIS LEVEL... WHAT'S GOING TO HAPPEN TO HER?
SIGH
B-BUT HOW DO YOU USE IT IN MANGA?
I KNOW IT'S ABOUT ORIGINALITY BUT...

The last entry is from *Sho-Comi's* Rie Takada! Look at the attention to detail in her drawing!

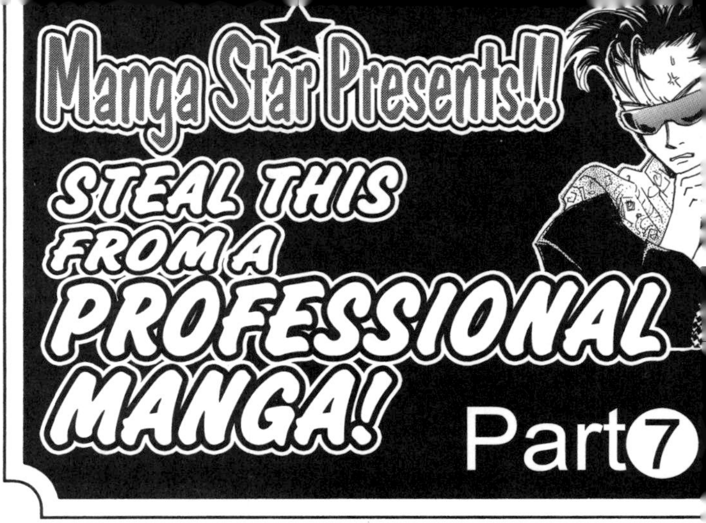
Manga Star Presents!!
STEAL THIS FROM A PROFESSIONAL MANGA!
Part 7

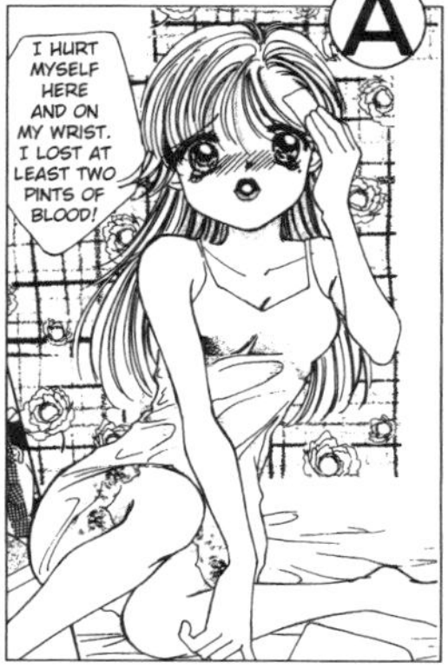
A
I HURT MYSELF HERE AND ON MY WRIST. I LOST AT LEAST TWO PINTS OF BLOOD!

CHECK OUT THE RELATIONSHIP BETWEEN BODY TYPE AND CLOTHES, AS WELL AS THE DIFFERENT TEXTURES.

The creases on the clothes people are wearing are very hard to draw. When you observe how the clothes are creased, you realize that both the material of the clothes and the person's body type affect them. Let's examine texture in depth.

First look at A. The shadows and part of the creases are drawn with stipples. Stippling was the most effective method of showing the delicacy of the thin underwear-like material.

Now compare the drawings in B, C and D. B and C are similar t-shirts, but the horizontal creases in B make it look fitted. The character's well-built physique is also accented. On the other hand, with the looser fitting t-shirt in C, the creases are vertical. You can also show the character's delicate body type.

Shirts like D usually fit loosely, so the creases should also have a softer feel.

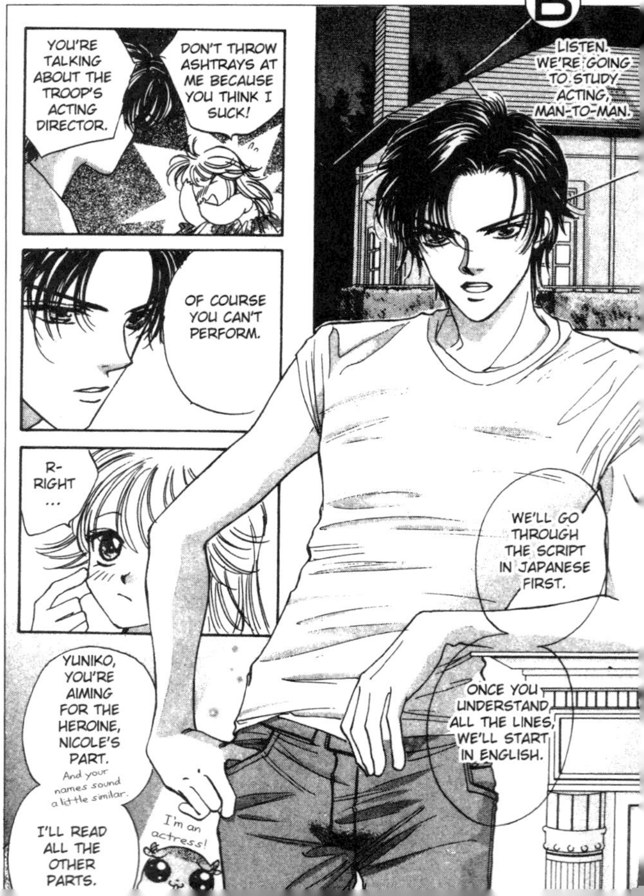
B
LISTEN. WE'RE GOING TO STUDY ACTING, MAN-TO-MAN.
WE'LL GO THROUGH THE SCRIPT IN JAPANESE FIRST.
ONCE YOU UNDERSTAND ALL THE LINES, WE'LL START IN ENGLISH.
YUNIKO, YOU'RE AIMING FOR THE HEROINE, NICOLE'S PART.
And your names sound a little similar.
I'LL READ ALL THE OTHER PARTS.
I'm an actress!
DON'T THROW ASHTRAYS AT ME BECAUSE YOU THINK I SUCK!
YOU'RE TALKING ABOUT THE TROOP'S ACTING DIRECTOR.
OF COURSE YOU CAN'T PERFORM.
R-RIGHT ...

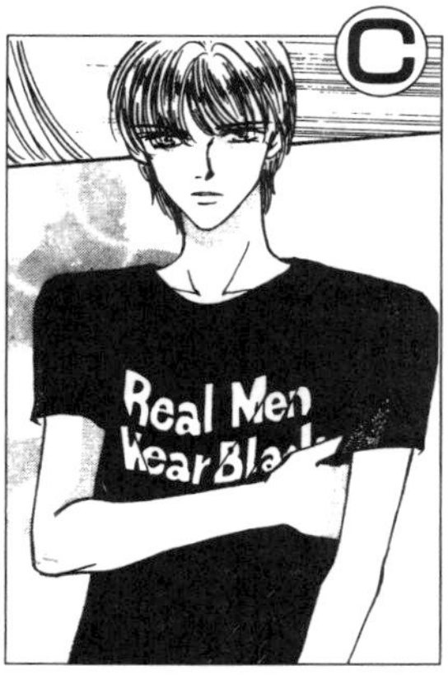
C
Real Men Wear Bla

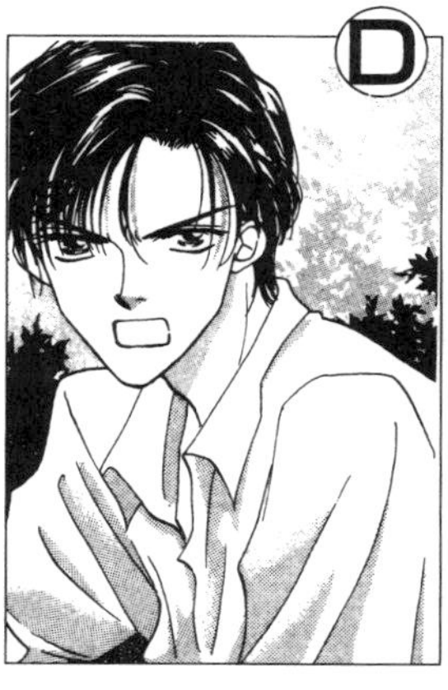
D

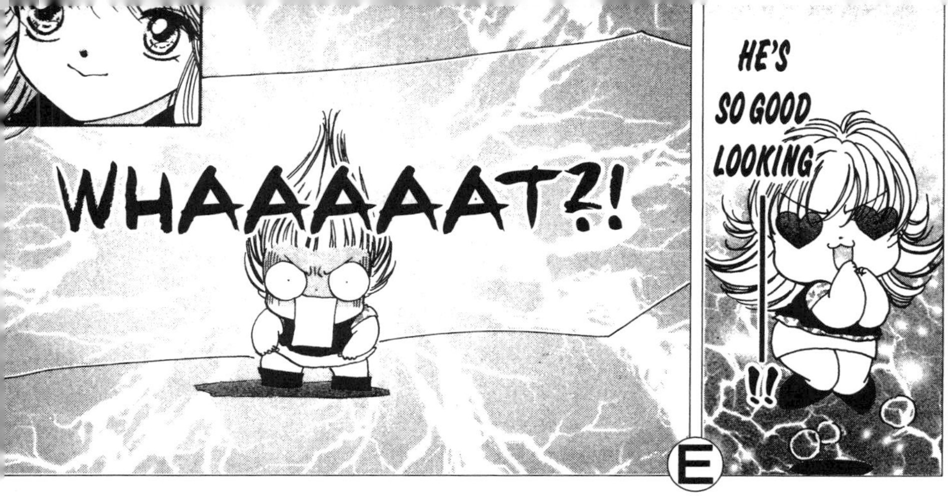
HE'S SO GOOD LOOKING
!!
WHAAAAAT?!

YOU CAN EXPRESS MOVEMENT AND EMOTION WITH HAIR.

Focus on the hair in all the panels shown on this page. The flow of hair shows movement and emotion.

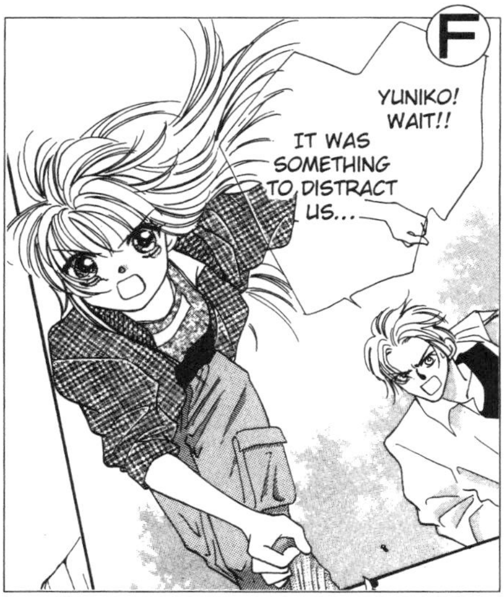
YUNIKO! WAIT!!
IT WAS SOMETHING TO DISTRACT US...

First check out E. In both cases, the character's emotions are supplemented by her hair. "He's so good looking" is expressed by her flipped hair, and her shock is shown through her raised hair. Exaggerated images need a lot of practice, so make sure you practice on a regular basis.

Next look at how the movement in F, G and H are expressed through the character's hair flow, especially the second panel in G. It only shows hair, but you can tell that the character has jumped out the window. Long hair is useful for expressing movement and emotion, and also for composition.

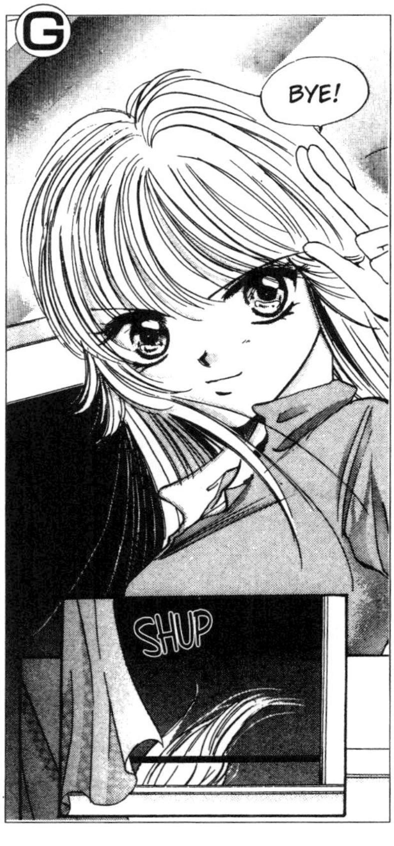
BYE!
SHUP

In F, her lingering hair makes the picture complete, and in the one panel in G, the hair across the character's face shows her unique state of mind. It also shows the wind blowing in from the window.

Long hair contributes to your work in more ways than one.

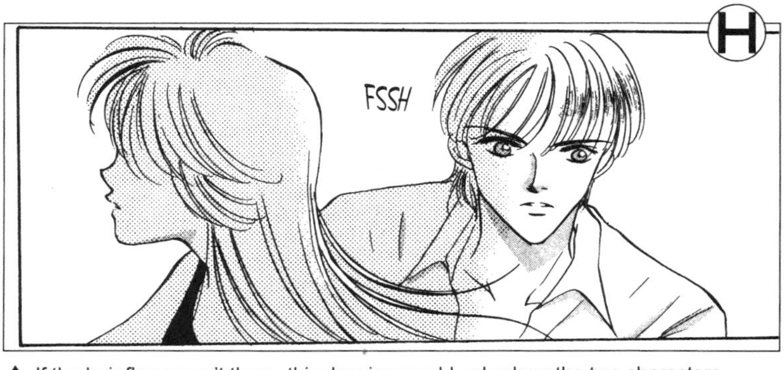
FSSH

▲ If the hair flow wasn't there, this drawing would only show the two characters standing, but by leaving her hair trailing behind her, it shows that they're passing by each other.

ADVANCED TECHNIQUES

Let's talk to *Ciao's* Yukako Iisaka about everything from layering screen tones to tricks using the computer!

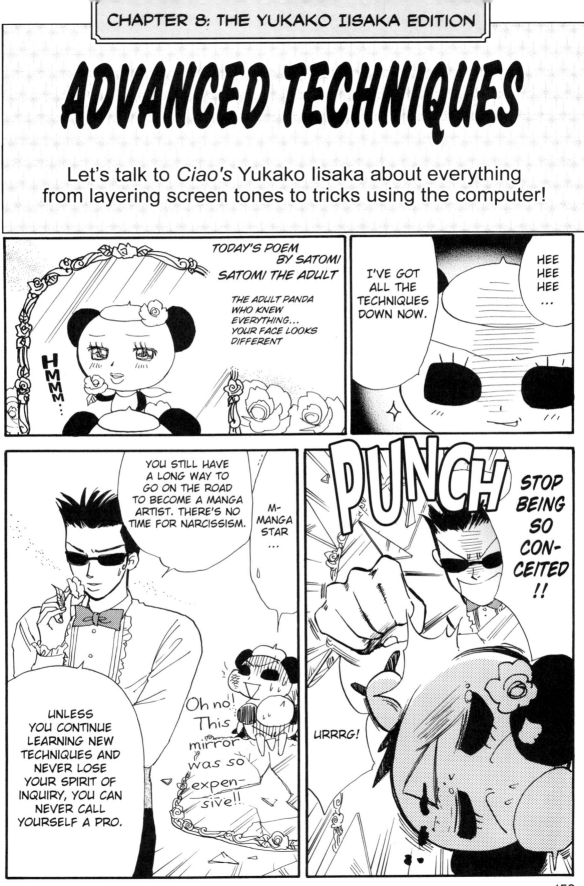

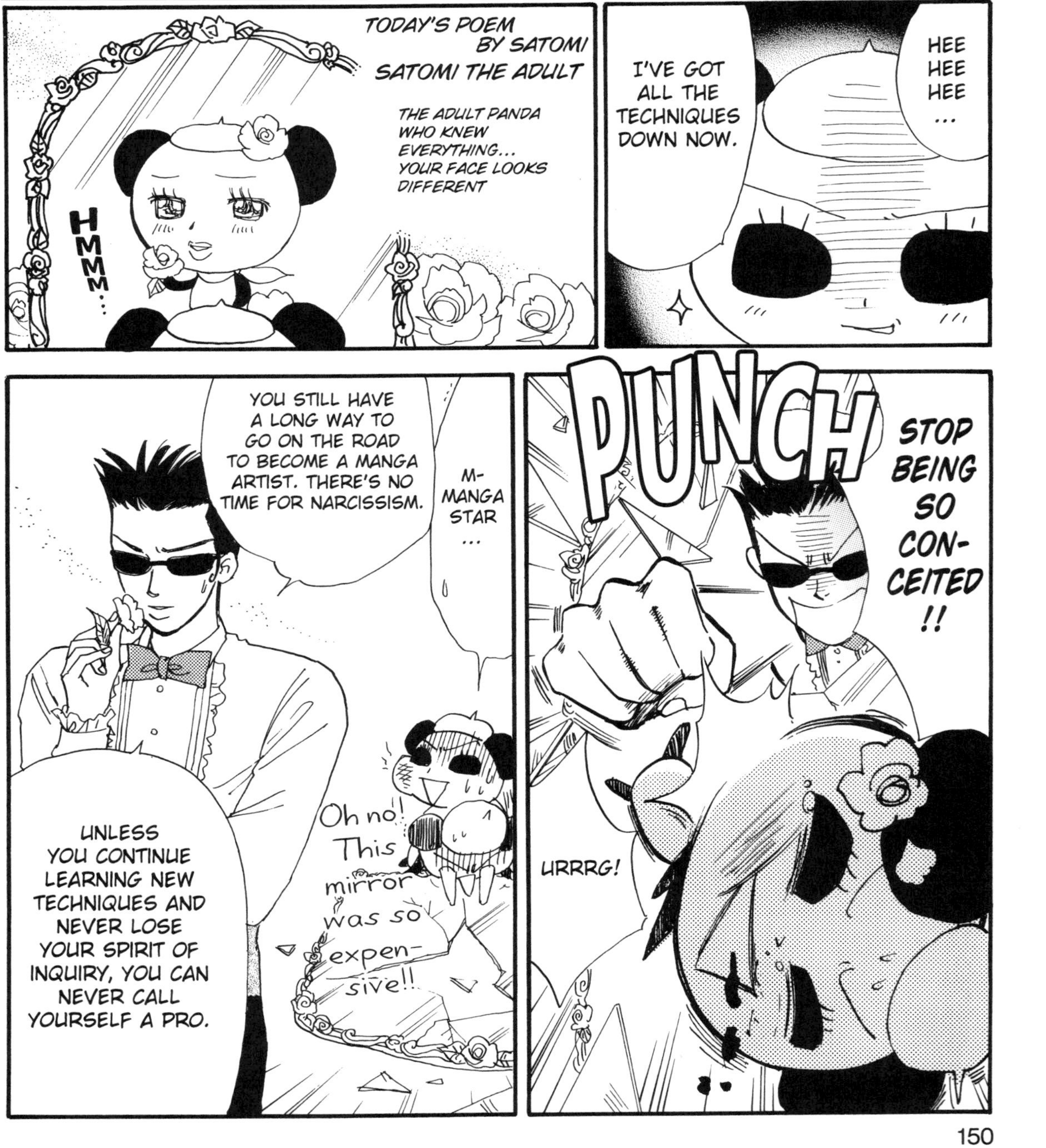
HEE HEE HEE ...
I'VE GOT ALL THE TECHNIQUES DOWN NOW.
TODAY'S POEM BY SATOMI
SATOMI THE ADULT
THE ADULT PANDA WHO KNEW EVERYTHING... YOUR FACE LOOKS DIFFERENT
HMMM...
PUNCH
STOP BEING SO CON-CEITED!!
URRRG!
YOU STILL HAVE A LONG WAY TO GO ON THE ROAD TO BECOME A MANGA ARTIST. THERE'S NO TIME FOR NARCISSISM.
M-MANGA STAR ...
Oh no! This mirror was so expen-sive!!
UNLESS YOU CONTINUE LEARNING NEW TECHNIQUES AND NEVER LOSE YOUR SPIRIT OF INQUIRY, YOU CAN NEVER CALL YOURSELF A PRO.

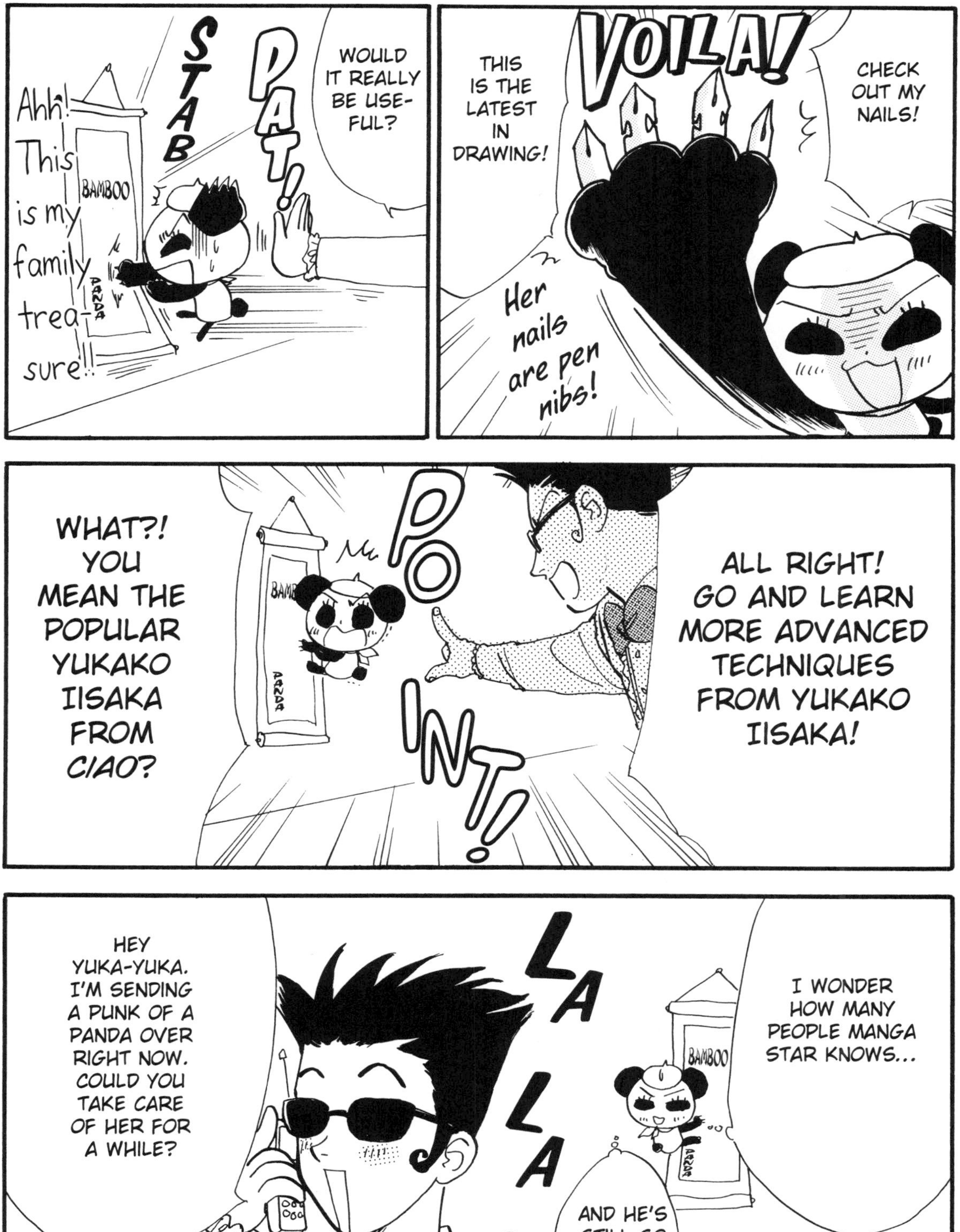
CHECK OUT MY NAILS!
VOILA!
THIS IS THE LATEST IN DRAWING!
Her nails are pen nibs!
WOULD IT REALLY BE USE-FUL?
PAT!
STAB
BAMBOO
PANDA
Ahh! This is my family trea-sure!!
ALL RIGHT! GO AND LEARN MORE ADVANCED TECHNIQUES FROM YUKAKO IISAKA!
POINT!
WHAT?! YOU MEAN THE POPULAR YUKAKO IISAKA FROM CIAO?
I WONDER HOW MANY PEOPLE MANGA STAR KNOWS...
AND HE'S STILL SO CREEPY WHEN HE TALKS.
LA LA LA
HEY YUKA-YUKA. I'M SENDING A PUNK OF A PANDA OVER RIGHT NOW. COULD YOU TAKE CARE OF HER FOR A WHILE?
LA

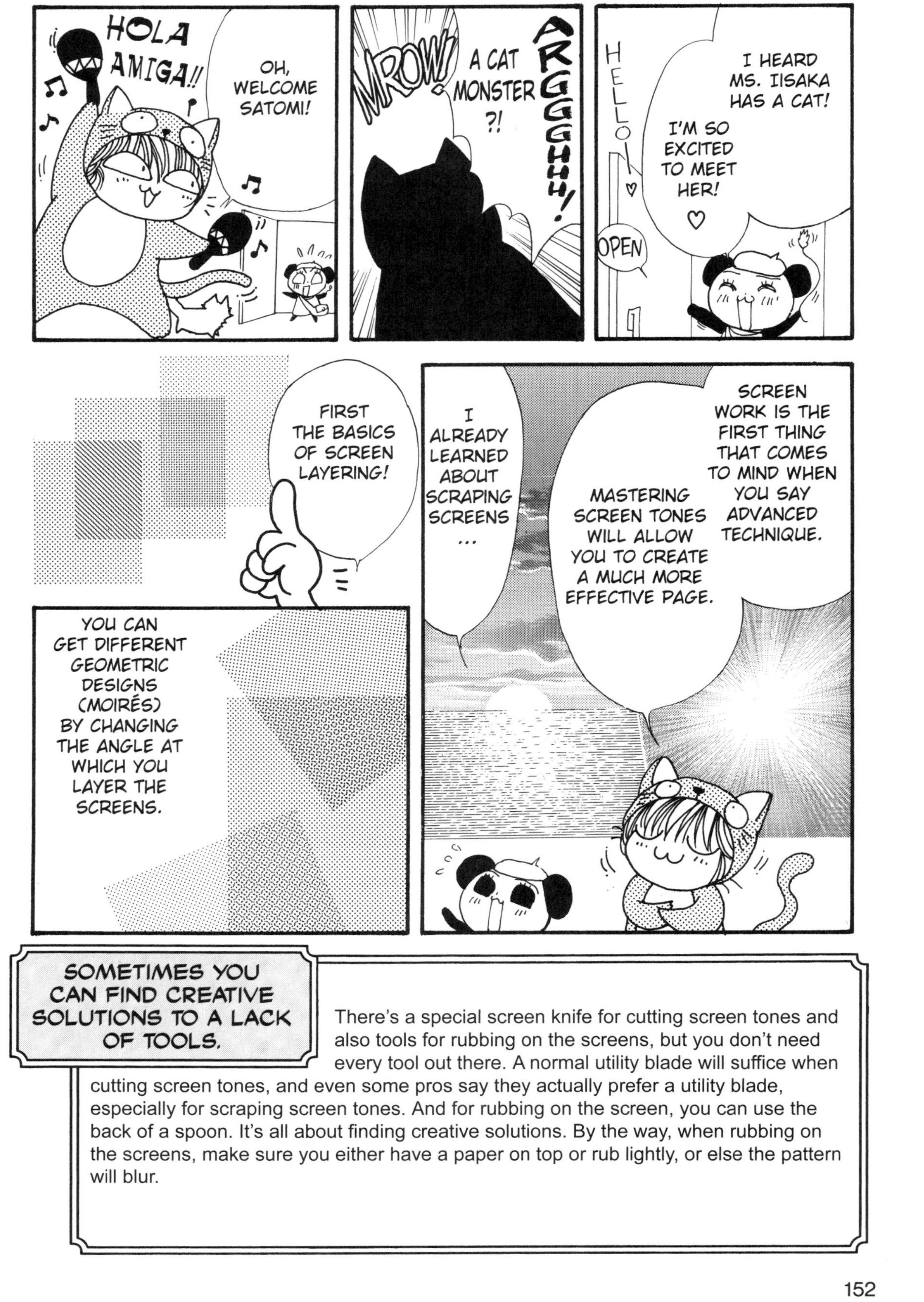
I HEARD MS. IISAKA HAS A CAT!
I'M SO EXCITED TO MEET HER! ♡
HELLO ♡
OPEN
ARGGGHHH!
A CAT MONSTER ?!
MROW!
OH, WELCOME SATOMI!
HOLA AMIGA!!
SCREEN WORK IS THE FIRST THING THAT COMES TO MIND WHEN YOU SAY ADVANCED TECHNIQUE.
MASTERING SCREEN TONES WILL ALLOW YOU TO CREATE A MUCH MORE EFFECTIVE PAGE.
I ALREADY LEARNED ABOUT SCRAPING SCREENS...
FIRST THE BASICS OF SCREEN LAYERING!
YOU CAN GET DIFFERENT GEOMETRIC DESIGNS (MOIRÉS) BY CHANGING THE ANGLE AT WHICH YOU LAYER THE SCREENS.

SOMETIMES YOU CAN FIND CREATIVE SOLUTIONS TO A LACK OF TOOLS.

There's a special screen knife for cutting screen tones and also tools for rubbing on the screens, but you don't need every tool out there. A normal utility blade will suffice when cutting screen tones, and even some pros say they actually prefer a utility blade, especially for scraping screen tones. And for rubbing on the screen, you can use the back of a spoon. It's all about finding creative solutions. By the way, when rubbing on the screens, make sure you either have a paper on top or rub lightly, or else the pattern will blur.

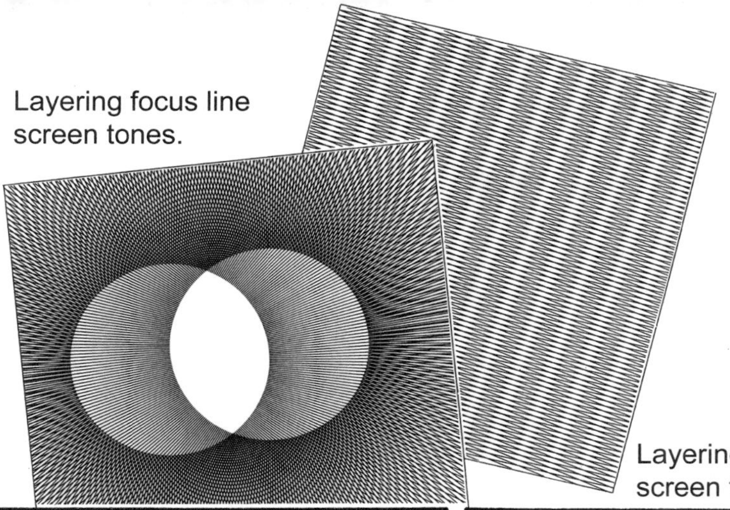
TRY LAYERING DIFFERENT TONES AT DIFFERENT ANGLES.
Layering focus line screen tones.
Layering diagonal line screen tones.
YOU CAN USE THIS TO YOUR ADVANTAGE BY CREATING NEW PATTERNS.

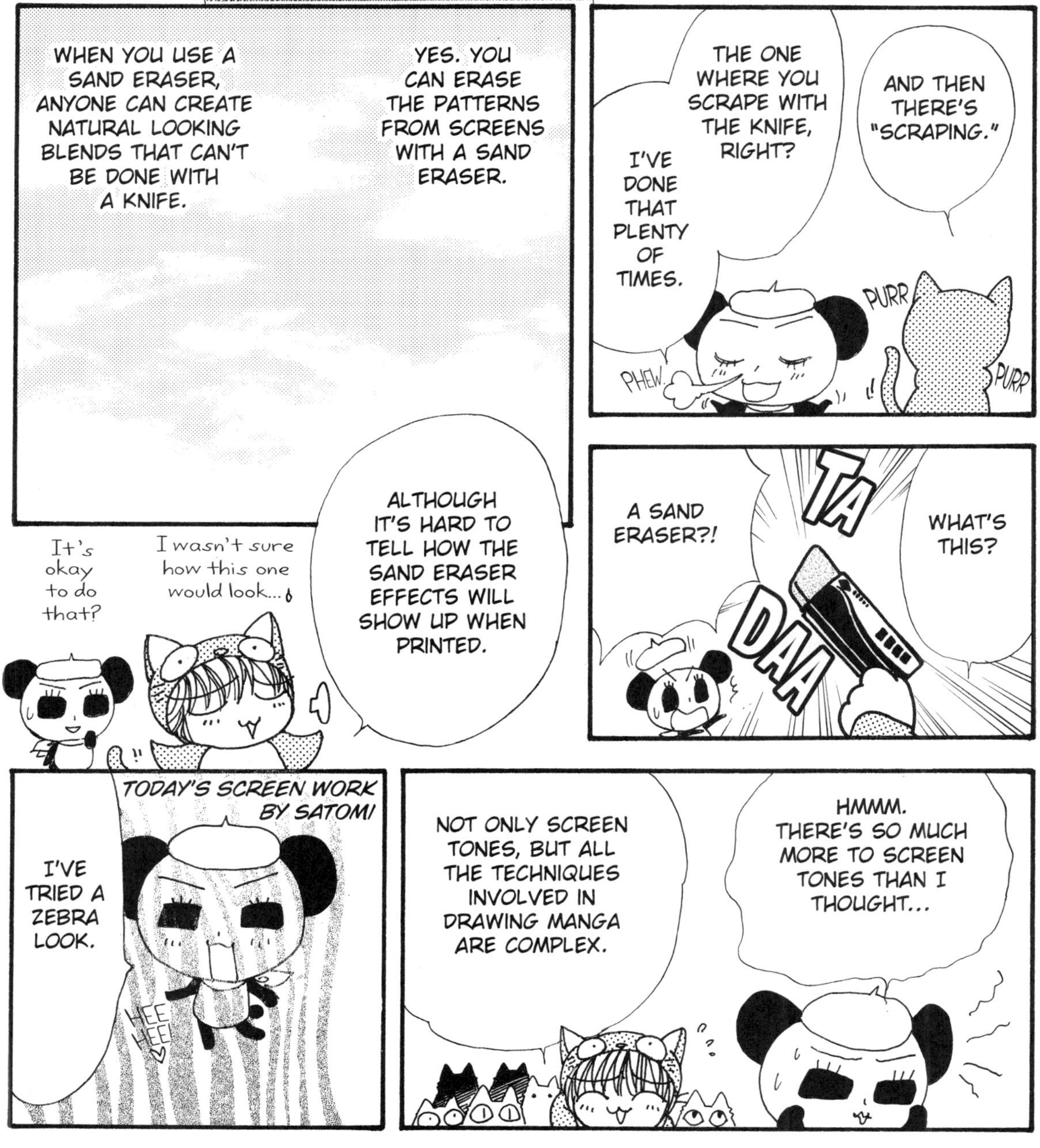
AND THEN THERE'S "SCRAPING."
THE ONE WHERE YOU SCRAPE WITH THE KNIFE, RIGHT?
I'VE DONE THAT PLENTY OF TIMES.
PURR
PURR
PHEW
YES. YOU CAN ERASE THE PATTERNS FROM SCREENS WITH A SAND ERASER.
WHEN YOU USE A SAND ERASER, ANYONE CAN CREATE NATURAL LOOKING BLENDS THAT CAN'T BE DONE WITH A KNIFE.
WHAT'S THIS?
TA
DAA
A SAND ERASER?!
ALTHOUGH IT'S HARD TO TELL HOW THE SAND ERASER EFFECTS WILL SHOW UP WHEN PRINTED.
I wasn't sure how this one would look...
It's okay to do that?
HMMM. THERE'S SO MUCH MORE TO SCREEN TONES THAN I THOUGHT...
NOT ONLY SCREEN TONES, BUT ALL THE TECHNIQUES INVOLVED IN DRAWING MANGA ARE COMPLEX.
TODAY'S SCREEN WORK BY SATOMI
I'VE TRIED A ZEBRA LOOK.
HEE HEE

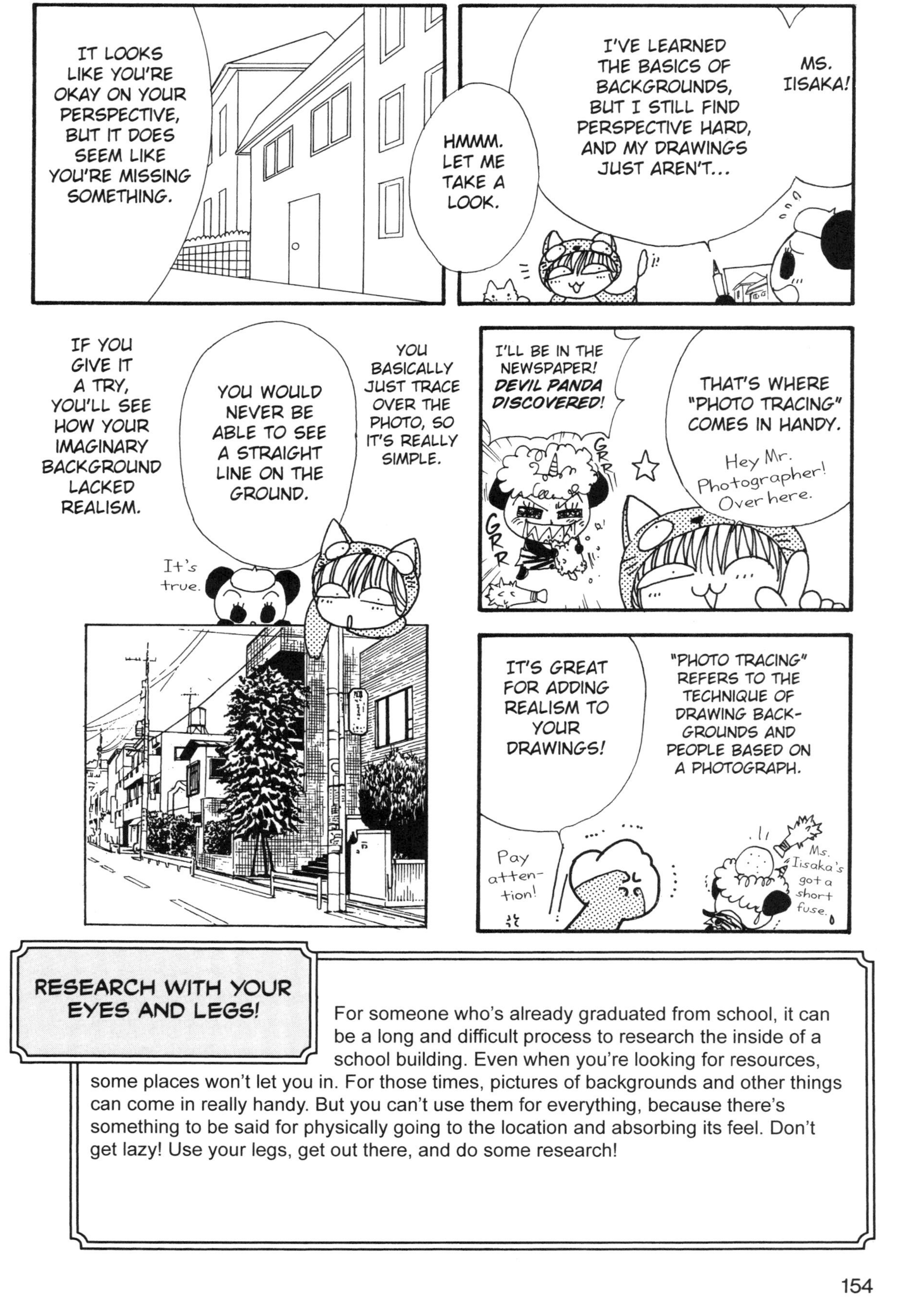
MS. IISAKA!
I'VE LEARNED THE BASICS OF BACKGROUNDS, BUT I STILL FIND PERSPECTIVE HARD, AND MY DRAWINGS JUST AREN'T...
HMMM. LET ME TAKE A LOOK.
IT LOOKS LIKE YOU'RE OKAY ON YOUR PERSPECTIVE, BUT IT DOES SEEM LIKE YOU'RE MISSING SOMETHING.
THAT'S WHERE "PHOTO TRACING" COMES IN HANDY.
Hey Mr. Photographer! Over here.
I'LL BE IN THE NEWSPAPER! ***DEVIL PANDA DISCOVERED!***
GRR
GRR
"PHOTO TRACING" REFERS TO THE TECHNIQUE OF DRAWING BACKGROUNDS AND PEOPLE BASED ON A PHOTOGRAPH.
IT'S GREAT FOR ADDING REALISM TO YOUR DRAWINGS!
Ms. Iisaka's got a short fuse.
Pay attention!
YOU BASICALLY JUST TRACE OVER THE PHOTO, SO IT'S REALLY SIMPLE.
YOU WOULD NEVER BE ABLE TO SEE A STRAIGHT LINE ON THE GROUND.
IF YOU GIVE IT A TRY, YOU'LL SEE HOW YOUR IMAGINARY BACKGROUND LACKED REALISM.
It's true.

RESEARCH WITH YOUR EYES AND LEGS!

For someone who's already graduated from school, it can be a long and difficult process to research the inside of a school building. Even when you're looking for resources, some places won't let you in. For those times, pictures of backgrounds and other things can come in really handy. But you can't use them for everything, because there's something to be said for physically going to the location and absorbing its feel. Don't get lazy! Use your legs, get out there, and do some research!

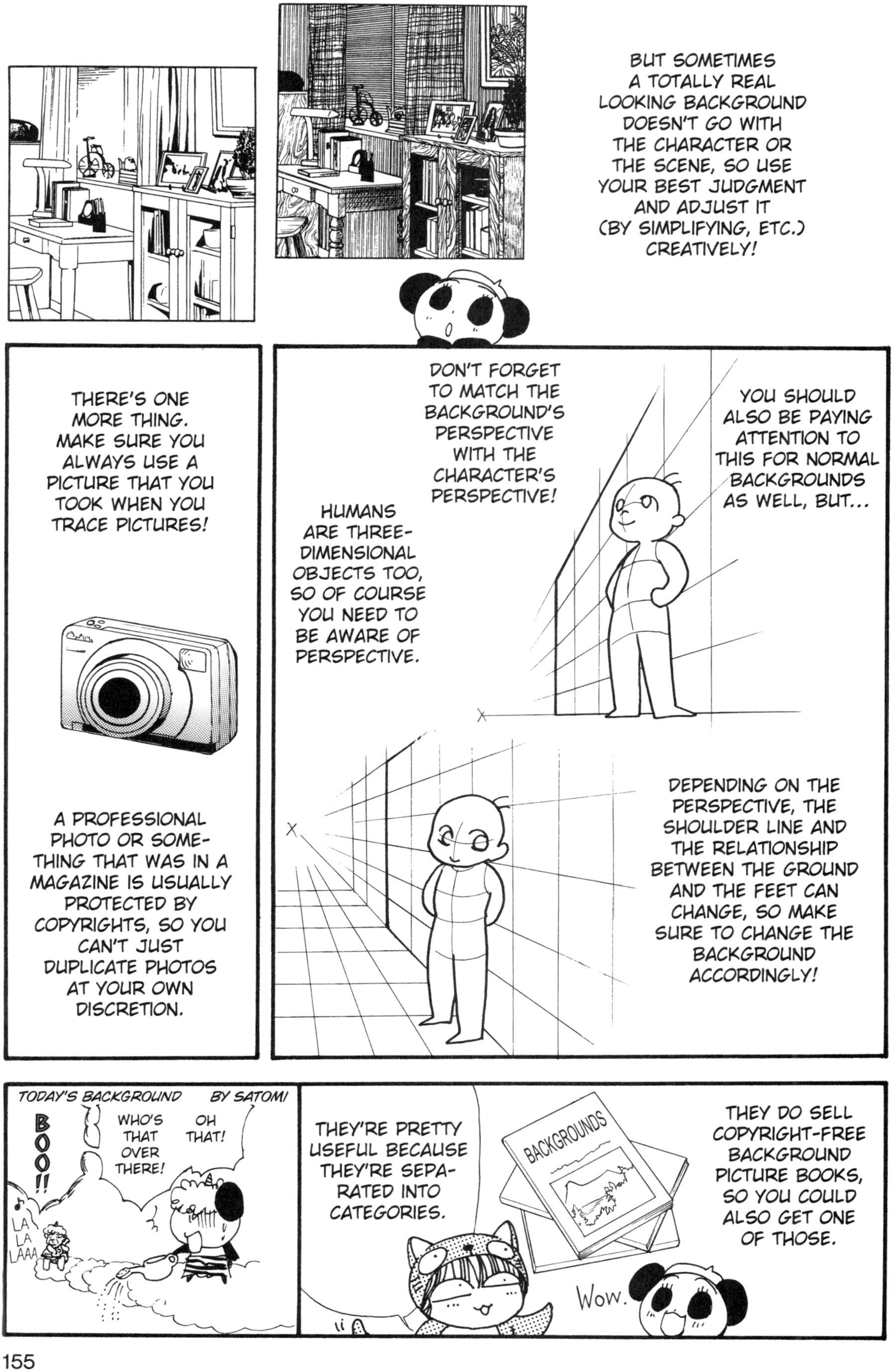

BUT SOMETIMES A TOTALLY REAL LOOKING BACKGROUND DOESN'T GO WITH THE CHARACTER OR THE SCENE, SO USE YOUR BEST JUDGMENT AND ADJUST IT (BY SIMPLIFYING, ETC.) CREATIVELY!
YOU SHOULD ALSO BE PAYING ATTENTION TO THIS FOR NORMAL BACKGROUNDS AS WELL, BUT...
DON'T FORGET TO MATCH THE BACKGROUND'S PERSPECTIVE WITH THE CHARACTER'S PERSPECTIVE!
HUMANS ARE THREE-DIMENSIONAL OBJECTS TOO, SO OF COURSE YOU NEED TO BE AWARE OF PERSPECTIVE.
DEPENDING ON THE PERSPECTIVE, THE SHOULDER LINE AND THE RELATIONSHIP BETWEEN THE GROUND AND THE FEET CAN CHANGE, SO MAKE SURE TO CHANGE THE BACKGROUND ACCORDINGLY!
THERE'S ONE MORE THING. MAKE SURE YOU ALWAYS USE A PICTURE THAT YOU TOOK WHEN YOU TRACE PICTURES!
A PROFESSIONAL PHOTO OR SOMETHING THAT WAS IN A MAGAZINE IS USUALLY PROTECTED BY COPYRIGHTS, SO YOU CAN'T JUST DUPLICATE PHOTOS AT YOUR OWN DISCRETION.
THEY DO SELL COPYRIGHT-FREE BACKGROUND PICTURE BOOKS, SO YOU COULD ALSO GET ONE OF THOSE.
BACKGROUNDS
WOW.
THEY'RE PRETTY USEFUL BECAUSE THEY'RE SEPARATED INTO CATEGORIES.
TODAY'S BACKGROUND BY SATOMI
OH THAT!
WHO'S THAT OVER THERE!
BOO!!
LA LA LAAA

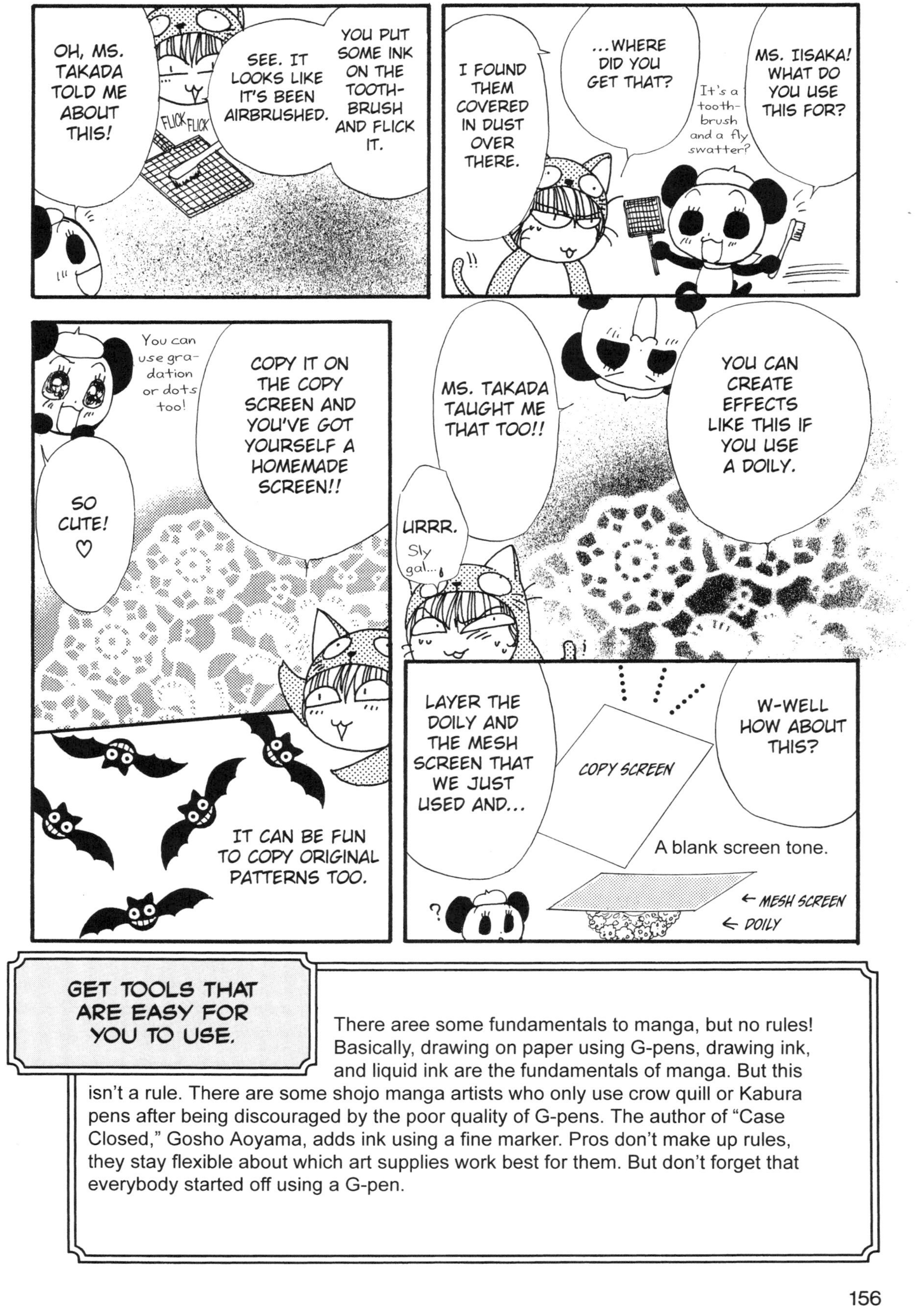
MS. ISAKA! WHAT DO YOU USE THIS FOR?
It's a toothbrush and a fly swatter?
...WHERE DID YOU GET THAT?
I FOUND THEM COVERED IN DUST OVER THERE.
YOU PUT SOME INK ON THE TOOTHBRUSH AND FLICK IT.
SEE. IT LOOKS LIKE IT'S BEEN AIRBRUSHED.
FLICK FLICK
OH, MS. TAKADA TOLD ME ABOUT THIS!
YOU CAN CREATE EFFECTS LIKE THIS IF YOU USE A DOILY.
MS. TAKADA TAUGHT ME THAT TOO!!
URRR.
Sly gal...
COPY IT ON THE COPY SCREEN AND YOU'VE GOT YOURSELF A HOMEMADE SCREEN!!
You can use gradation or dots too!
SO CUTE! ♡
W-WELL HOW ABOUT THIS?
LAYER THE DOILY AND THE MESH SCREEN THAT WE JUST USED AND...
COPY SCREEN
A blank screen tone.
← MESH SCREEN
← DOILY
IT CAN BE FUN TO COPY ORIGINAL PATTERNS TOO.

GET TOOLS THAT ARE EASY FOR YOU TO USE.

There aree some fundamentals to manga, but no rules! Basically, drawing on paper using G-pens, drawing ink, and liquid ink are the fundamentals of manga. But this isn't a rule. There are some shojo manga artists who only use crow quill or Kabura pens after being discouraged by the poor quality of G-pens. The author of "Case Closed," Gosho Aoyama, adds ink using a fine marker. Pros don't make up rules, they stay flexible about which art supplies work best for them. But don't forget that everybody started off using a G-pen.

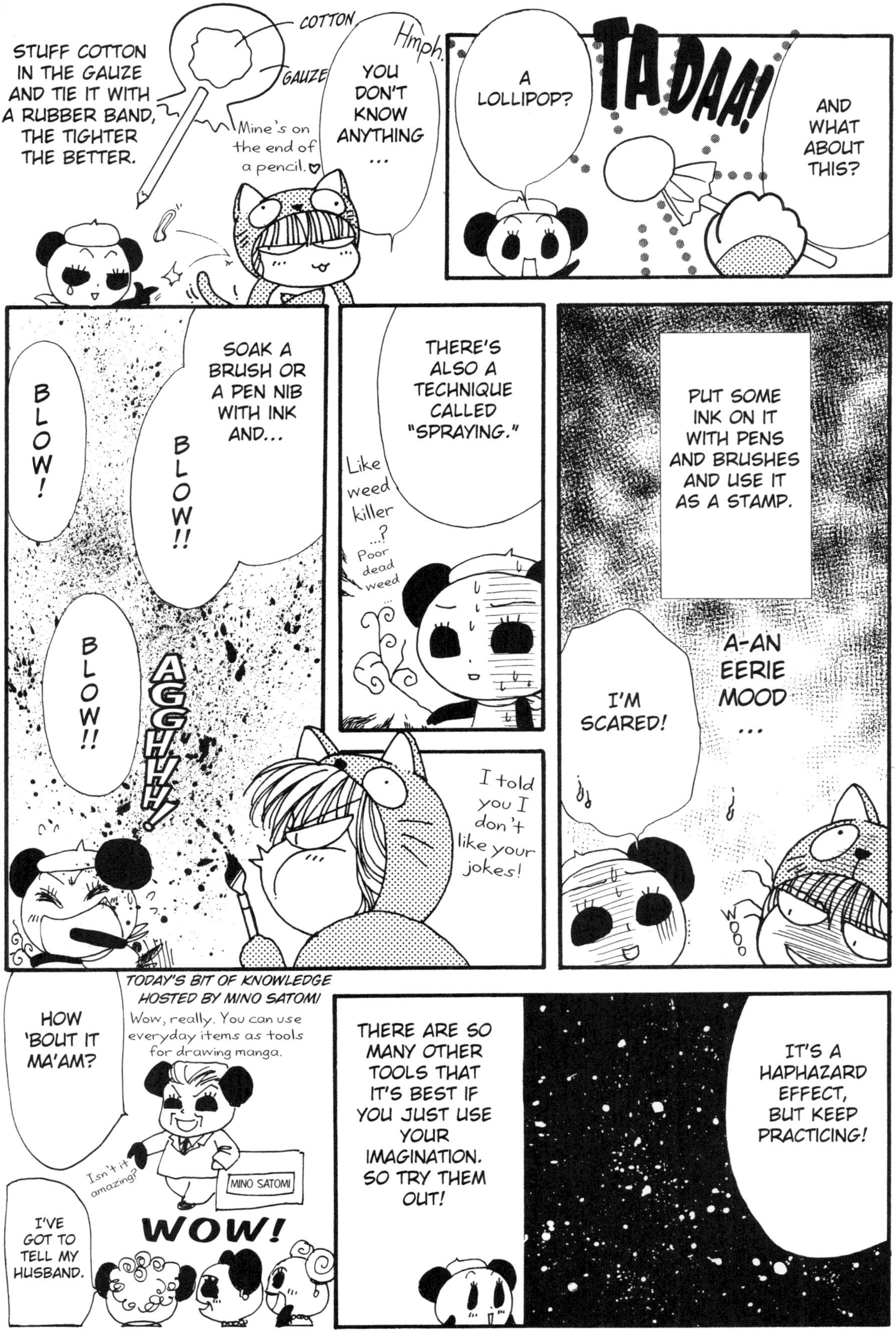
AND WHAT ABOUT THIS?
TA DAA!
A LOLLIPOP?
Hmph.
YOU DON'T KNOW ANYTHING ...
COTTON
GAUZE
STUFF COTTON IN THE GAUZE AND TIE IT WITH A RUBBER BAND, THE TIGHTER THE BETTER.
Mine's on the end of a pencil.♡
PUT SOME INK ON IT WITH PENS AND BRUSHES AND USE IT AS A STAMP.
A-AN EERIE MOOD ...
I'M SCARED!
WOOO
THERE'S ALSO A TECHNIQUE CALLED "SPRAYING."
Like weed killer ...?
Poor dead weed ...
I told you I don't like your jokes!
SOAK A BRUSH OR A PEN NIB WITH INK AND...
BLOW!!
BLOW!
BLOW!!
AGGHHHH!
IT'S A HAPHAZARD EFFECT, BUT KEEP PRACTICING!
THERE ARE SO MANY OTHER TOOLS THAT IT'S BEST IF YOU JUST USE YOUR IMAGINATION. SO TRY THEM OUT!
TODAY'S BIT OF KNOWLEDGE HOSTED BY MINO SATOMI
Wow, really. You can use everyday items as tools for drawing manga.
HOW 'BOUT IT MA'AM?
Isn't it amazing?
MINO SATOMI
WOW!
I'VE GOT TO TELL MY HUSBAND.

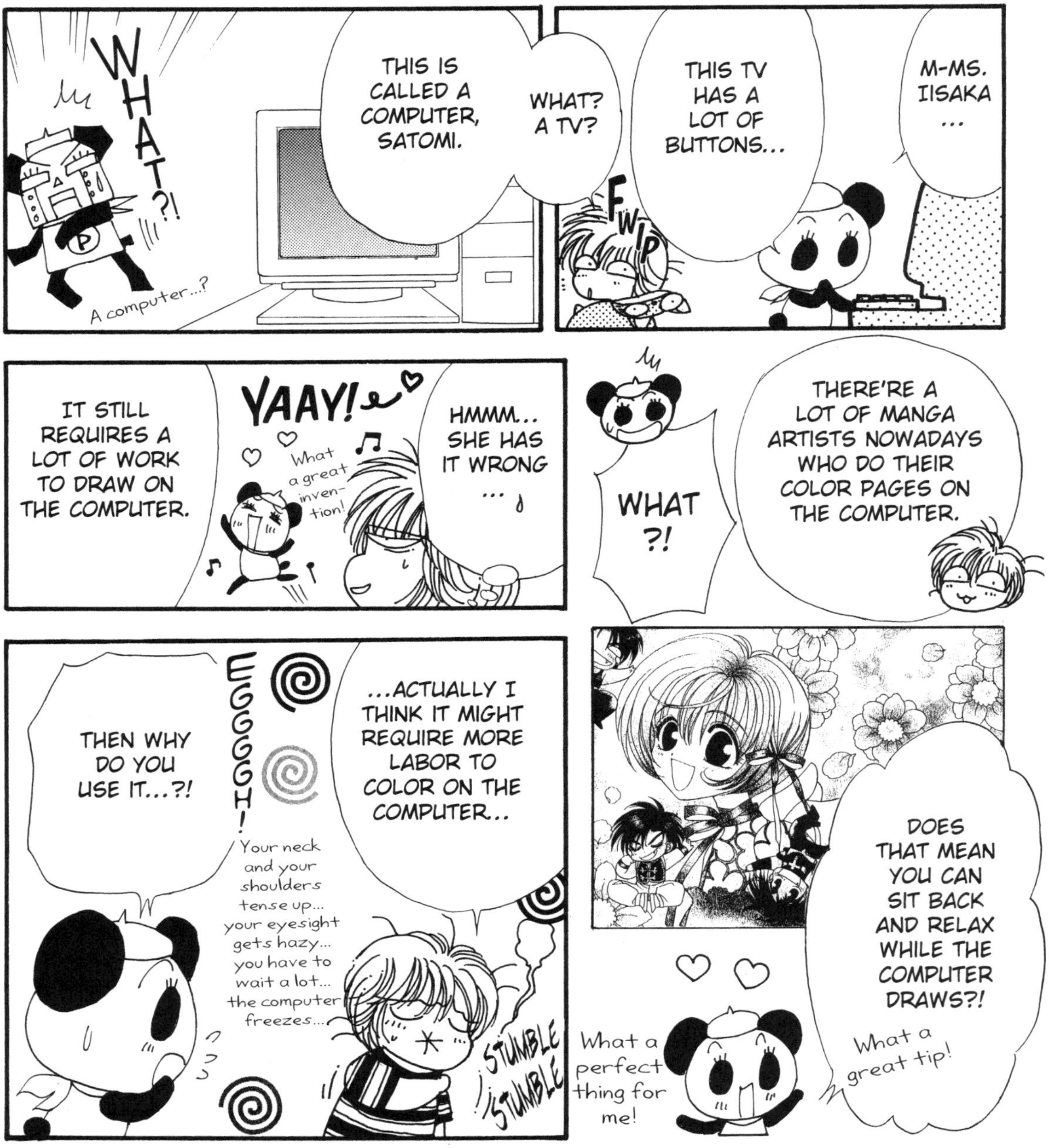
M-MS. IISAKA ...
THIS TV HAS A LOT OF BUTTONS...
FWIP
WHAT? A TV?
THIS IS CALLED A COMPUTER, SATOMI.
WHAT?!
A computer...?
THERE'RE A LOT OF MANGA ARTISTS NOWADAYS WHO DO THEIR COLOR PAGES ON THE COMPUTER.
WHAT ?!
HMMM... SHE HAS IT WRONG ...
YAAY!
What a great invention!
IT STILL REQUIRES A LOT OF WORK TO DRAW ON THE COMPUTER.
DOES THAT MEAN YOU CAN SIT BACK AND RELAX WHILE THE COMPUTER DRAWS?!
What a great tip!
What a perfect thing for me!
...ACTUALLY I THINK IT MIGHT REQUIRE MORE LABOR TO COLOR ON THE COMPUTER..
EGGGGH!
Your neck and your shoulders tense up... your eyesight gets hazy... you have to wait a lot... the computer freezes...
STUMBLE STUMBLE
THEN WHY DO YOU USE IT...?!

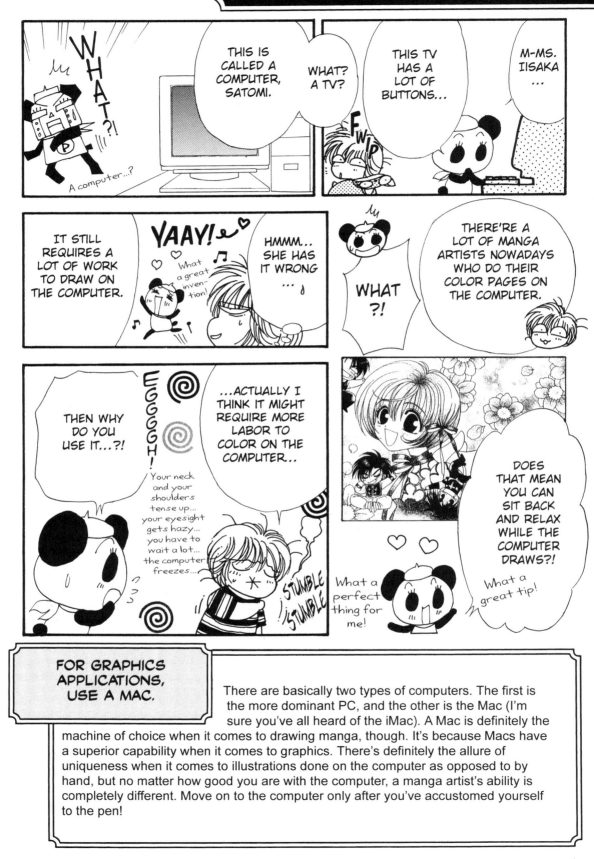

FOR GRAPHICS APPLICATIONS, USE A MAC.

There are basically two types of computers. The first is the more dominant PC, and the other is the Mac (I'm sure you've all heard of the iMac). A Mac is definitely the machine of choice when it comes to drawing manga, though. It's because Macs have a superior capability when it comes to graphics. There's definitely the allure of uniqueness when it comes to illustrations done on the computer as opposed to by hand, but no matter how good you are with the computer, a manga artist's ability is completely different. Move on to the computer only after you've accustomed yourself to the pen!

IT...IT'S ALL RIGHT SATOMI.

ALL BLACK

OH NO! MY DRAWING!!

I'M GONNA PRESS THIS ONE.

...Are you listening?

With a click of the...

IT'S BECAUSE I CAN DEPEND ON IT TO INCREASE THE QUALITY OF MY WORK...

YOU CAN CREATE OR DELETE THE UNEVENNESS FROM THE BRUSH SO EASILY ON THE COMPUTER.

MOST MANGA ARTISTS USE PHOTOSHOP, ILLUSTRATOR, OR PAINTER.

Free Transform

Mosaic

Ocean Ripple

DO THIS AND...

APPEAR

CLICK

IT'S FIXED!

Thank goodness.

EVEN IF YOU SCREW UP COLORING ON THE COMPUTER, YOU CAN DO IT OVER AS MANY TIMES AS YOU NEED.

I JUST HAVE TO GET THIS!!

THERE'RE A LOT OF SPECIAL EFFECTS THAT CAN ONLY BE DONE ON THE COMPUTER.

Really...

A record of the steps taken so far.

History	Actions
Illustration 1	
Open	
Magic Wand	
Airbrush	
Deselect	
Color	

WOW!

MY TRUE FEELINGS OF THE DAY BY SATOMI!

NO? — I WANT A COMPUTER!

BUT I HAVE NO MONEY.

SOMEONE GIVE ME SOME.

OF COURSE IT WOULD BE A FREE LOAN.

That would be my guess.

WHAAAA!!

$

$

I GUESS YOU'RE LOOKING AT ABOUT FIVE GRAND...

BUT IF YOU WANT TO DRAW MANGA ON THE COMPUTER, THERE'RE SOME BUSINESS INVESTMENTS YOU NEED TO MAKE...

COMPUTER DRAWING, PART 2

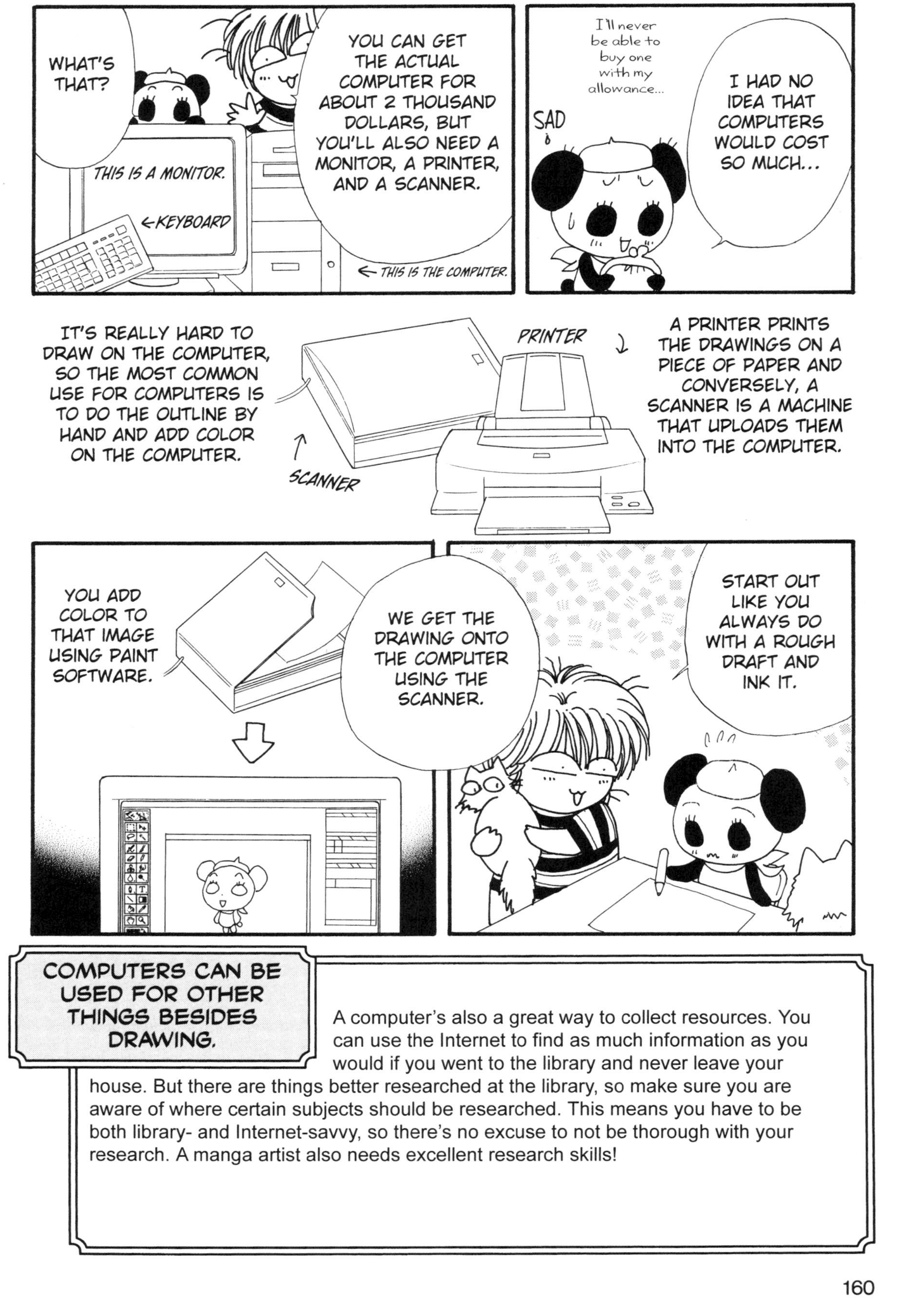
I HAD NO IDEA THAT COMPUTERS WOULD COST SO MUCH...
I'll never be able to buy one with my allowance...
SAD
YOU CAN GET THE ACTUAL COMPUTER FOR ABOUT 2 THOUSAND DOLLARS, BUT YOU'LL ALSO NEED A MONITOR, A PRINTER, AND A SCANNER.
WHAT'S THAT?
THIS IS A MONITOR.
←KEYBOARD
← THIS IS THE COMPUTER.
A PRINTER PRINTS THE DRAWINGS ON A PIECE OF PAPER AND CONVERSELY, A SCANNER IS A MACHINE THAT UPLOADS THEM INTO THE COMPUTER.
PRINTER
SCANNER
IT'S REALLY HARD TO DRAW ON THE COMPUTER, SO THE MOST COMMON USE FOR COMPUTERS IS TO DO THE OUTLINE BY HAND AND ADD COLOR ON THE COMPUTER.
START OUT LIKE YOU ALWAYS DO WITH A ROUGH DRAFT AND INK IT.
WE GET THE DRAWING ONTO THE COMPUTER USING THE SCANNER.
YOU ADD COLOR TO THAT IMAGE USING PAINT SOFTWARE.

COMPUTERS CAN BE USED FOR OTHER THINGS BESIDES DRAWING.

A computer's also a great way to collect resources. You can use the Internet to find as much information as you would if you went to the library and never leave your house. But there are things better researched at the library, so make sure you are aware of where certain subjects should be researched. This means you have to be both library- and Internet-savvy, so there's no excuse to not be thorough with your research. A manga artist also needs excellent research skills!

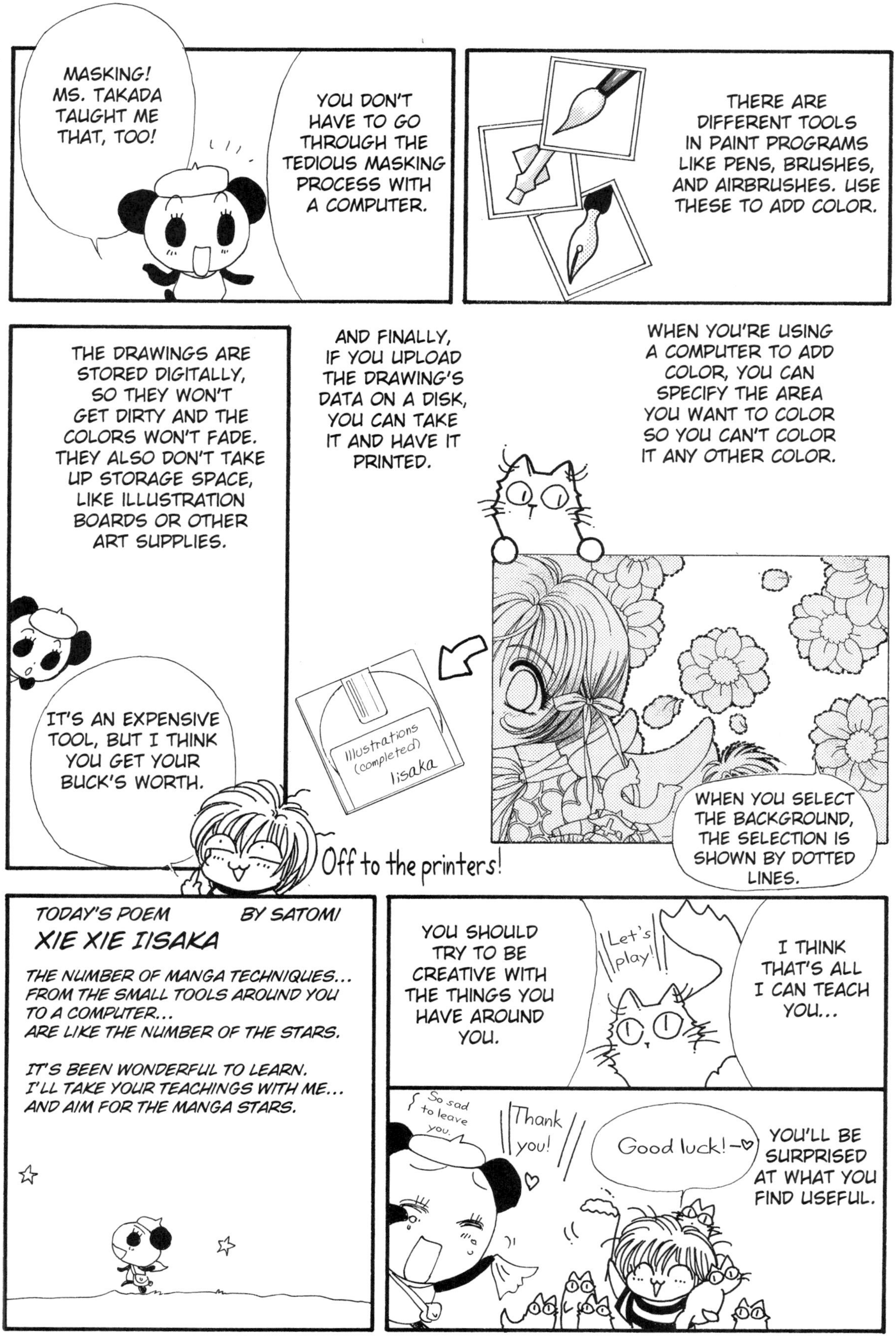

THERE ARE DIFFERENT TOOLS IN PAINT PROGRAMS LIKE PENS, BRUSHES, AND AIRBRUSHES. USE THESE TO ADD COLOR.
YOU DON'T HAVE TO GO THROUGH THE TEDIOUS MASKING PROCESS WITH A COMPUTER.
MASKING! MS. TAKADA TAUGHT ME THAT, TOO!
WHEN YOU'RE USING A COMPUTER TO ADD COLOR, YOU CAN SPECIFY THE AREA YOU WANT TO COLOR SO YOU CAN'T COLOR IT ANY OTHER COLOR.
WHEN YOU SELECT THE BACKGROUND, THE SELECTION IS SHOWN BY DOTTED LINES.
AND FINALLY, IF YOU UPLOAD THE DRAWING'S DATA ON A DISK, YOU CAN TAKE IT AND HAVE IT PRINTED.
Illustrations (completed) Iisaka
THE DRAWINGS ARE STORED DIGITALLY, SO THEY WON'T GET DIRTY AND THE COLORS WON'T FADE. THEY ALSO DON'T TAKE UP STORAGE SPACE, LIKE ILLUSTRATION BOARDS OR OTHER ART SUPPLIES.
IT'S AN EXPENSIVE TOOL, BUT I THINK YOU GET YOUR BUCK'S WORTH.
Off to the printers!
I THINK THAT'S ALL I CAN TEACH YOU...
Let's play!
YOU SHOULD TRY TO BE CREATIVE WITH THE THINGS YOU HAVE AROUND YOU.
YOU'LL BE SURPRISED AT WHAT YOU FIND USEFUL.
Good luck!—♡
Thank you!
So sad to leave you.
TODAY'S POEM BY SATOMI
XIE XIE IISAKA
THE NUMBER OF MANGA TECHNIQUES... FROM THE SMALL TOOLS AROUND YOU TO A COMPUTER... ARE LIKE THE NUMBER OF THE STARS.
IT'S BEEN WONDERFUL TO LEARN. I'LL TAKE YOUR TEACHINGS WITH ME... AND AIM FOR THE MANGA STARS.

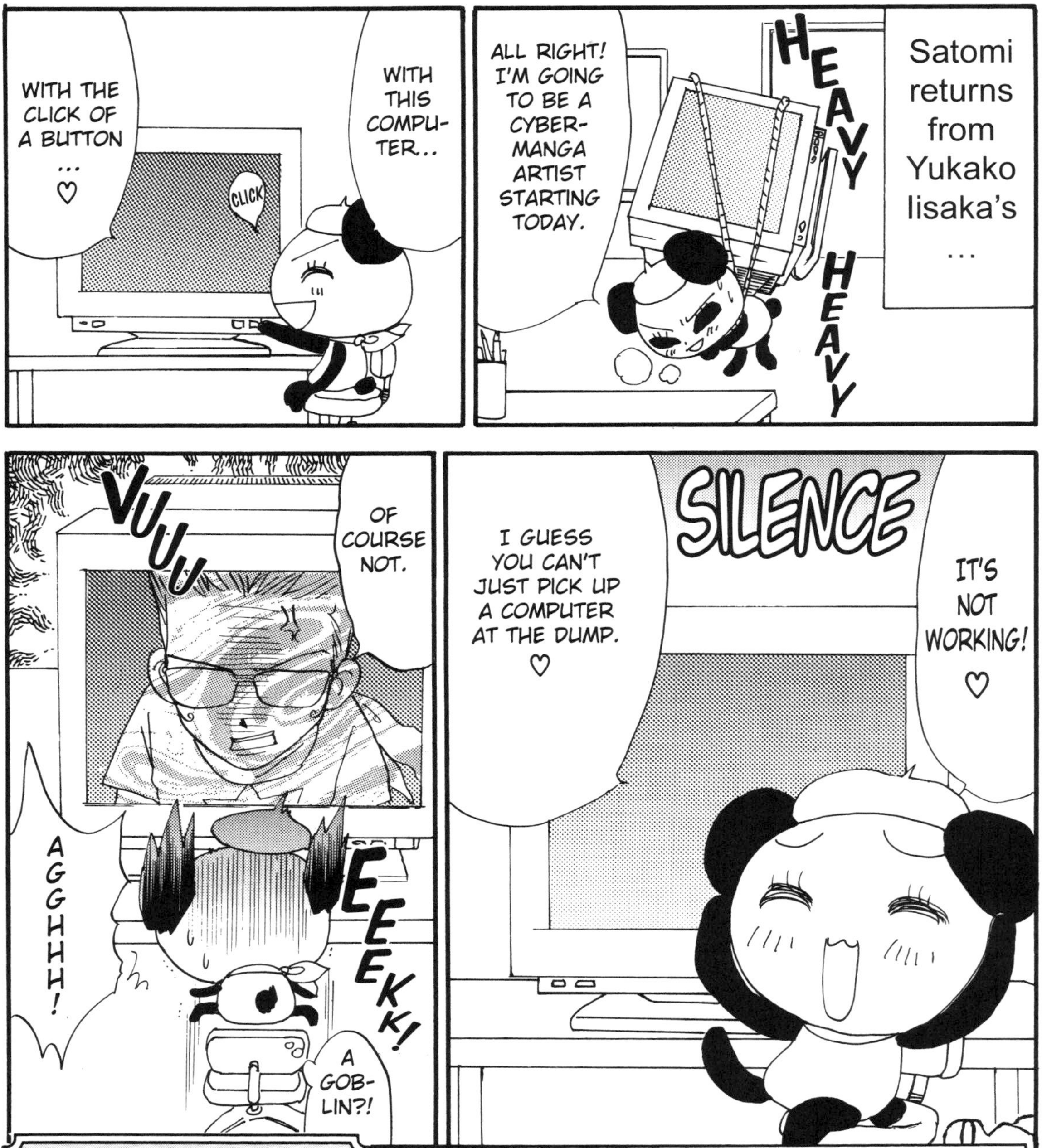
Satomi returns from Yukako Iisaka's …
HEAVY
HEAVY
ALL RIGHT! I'M GOING TO BE A CYBER-MANGA ARTIST STARTING TODAY.
WITH THIS COMPUTER…
WITH THE CLICK OF A BUTTON … ♡
CLICK
SILENCE
IT'S NOT WORKING! ♡
I GUESS YOU CAN'T JUST PICK UP A COMPUTER AT THE DUMP. ♡
VUUU
OF COURSE NOT.
EEEKK!
AGGHHH!
A GOB-LIN?!

WITHOUT THE FUNDAMENTALS, EVEN ADVANCED TECHNIQUES ARE WORTHLESS.

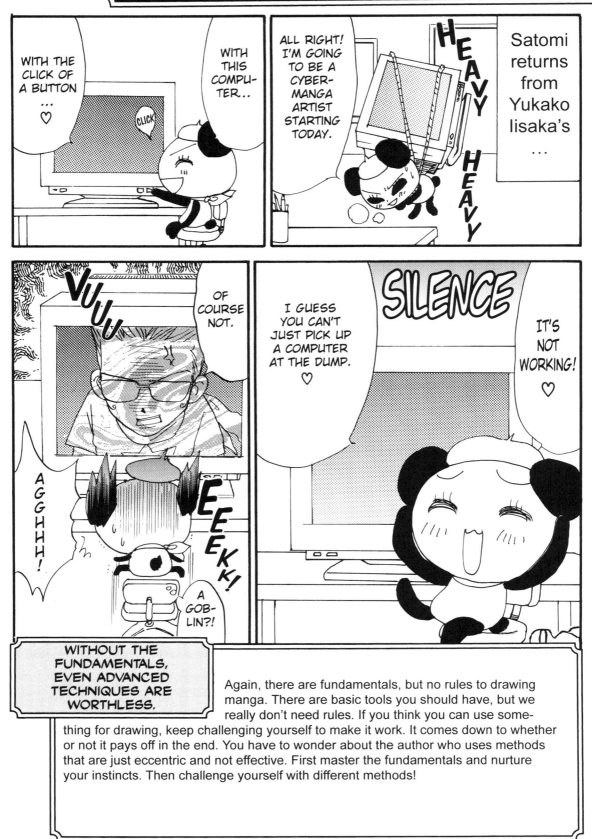

Again, there are fundamentals, but no rules to drawing manga. There are basic tools you should have, but we really don't need rules. If you think you can use something for drawing, keep challenging yourself to make it work. It comes down to whether or not it pays off in the end. You have to wonder about the author who uses methods that are just eccentric and not effective. First master the fundamentals and nurture your instincts. Then challenge yourself with different methods!

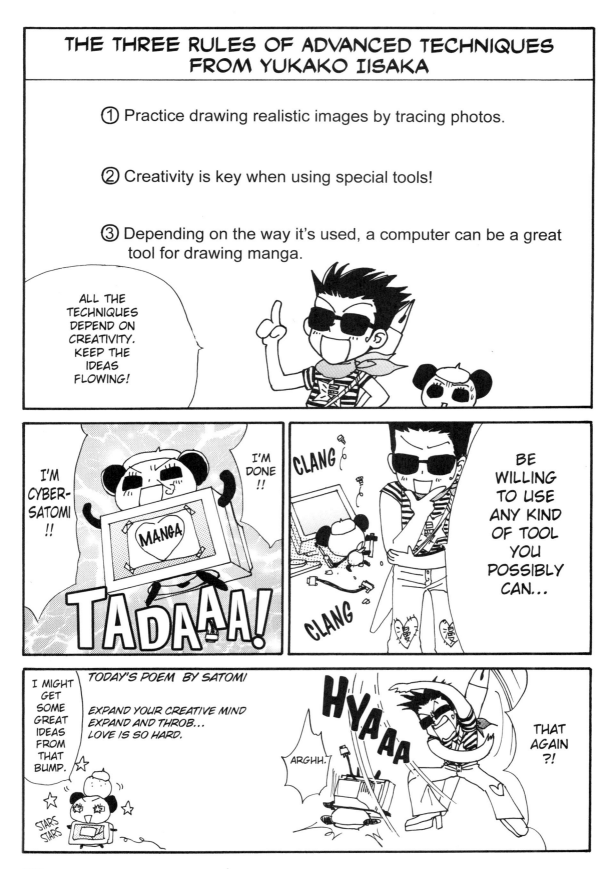

THE THREE RULES OF ADVANCED TECHNIQUES FROM YUKAKO IISAKA

① Practice drawing realistic images by tracing photos.

② Creativity is key when using special tools!

③ Depending on the way it's used, a computer can be a great tool for drawing manga.

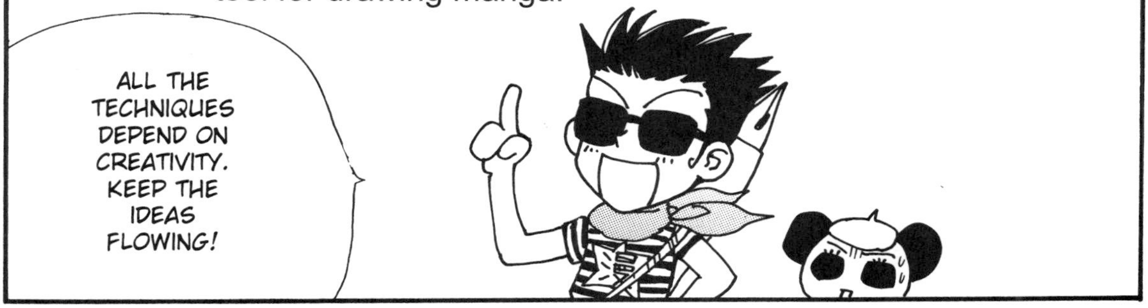
ALL THE TECHNIQUES DEPEND ON CREATIVITY. KEEP THE IDEAS FLOWING!

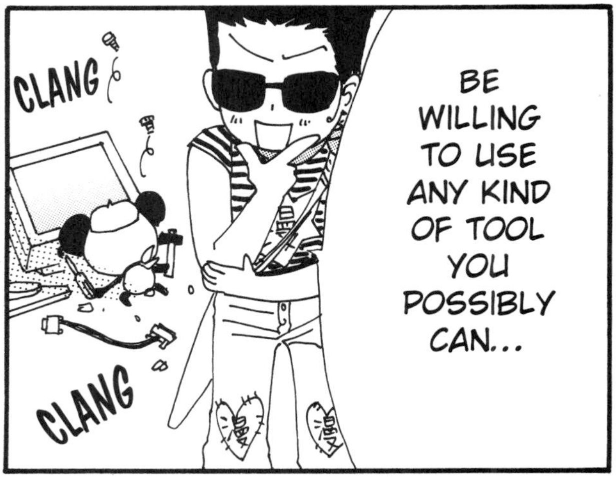
CLANG
BE WILLING TO USE ANY KIND OF TOOL YOU POSSIBLY CAN...
CLANG

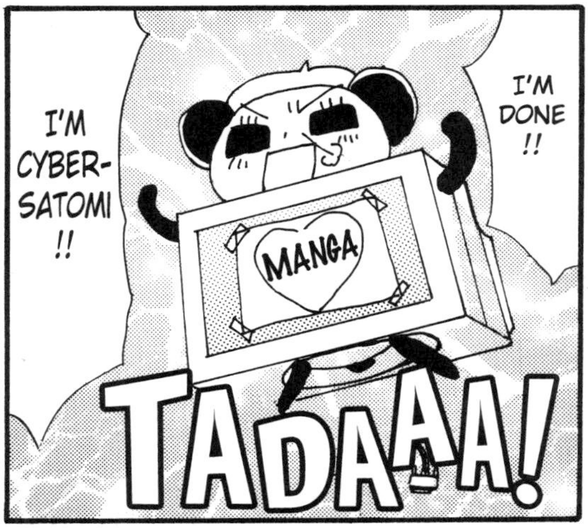
I'M DONE!!
I'M CYBER-SATOMI!!
MANGA
TADAAA!

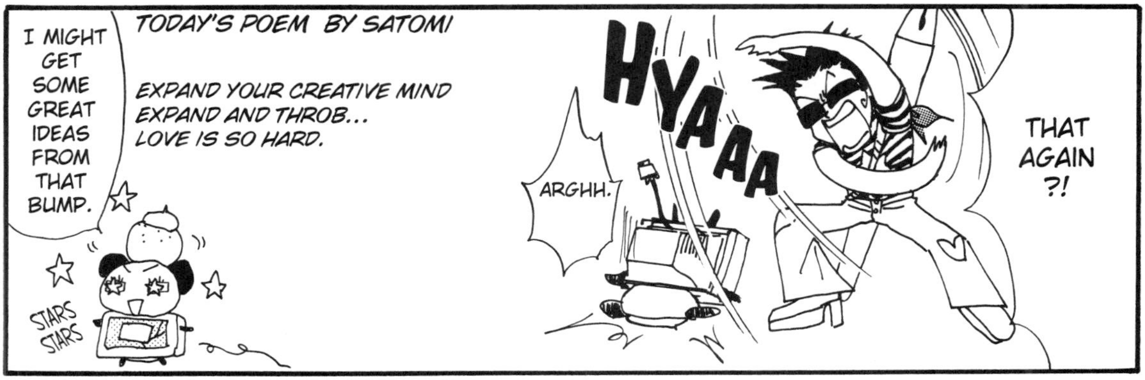
THAT AGAIN?!
HYAAAA
ARGHH.
TODAY'S POEM BY SATOMI
EXPAND YOUR CREATIVE MIND
EXPAND AND THROB...
LOVE IS SO HARD.
I MIGHT GET SOME GREAT IDEAS FROM THAT BUMP.
STARS STARS

THE IMPORTANCE OF THE FINAL TOUCHES!

You're nearing the completion of your manga and you're ready for the finishing touches. Let's get the recipe for great finishing touches from Mayu Shinjo.

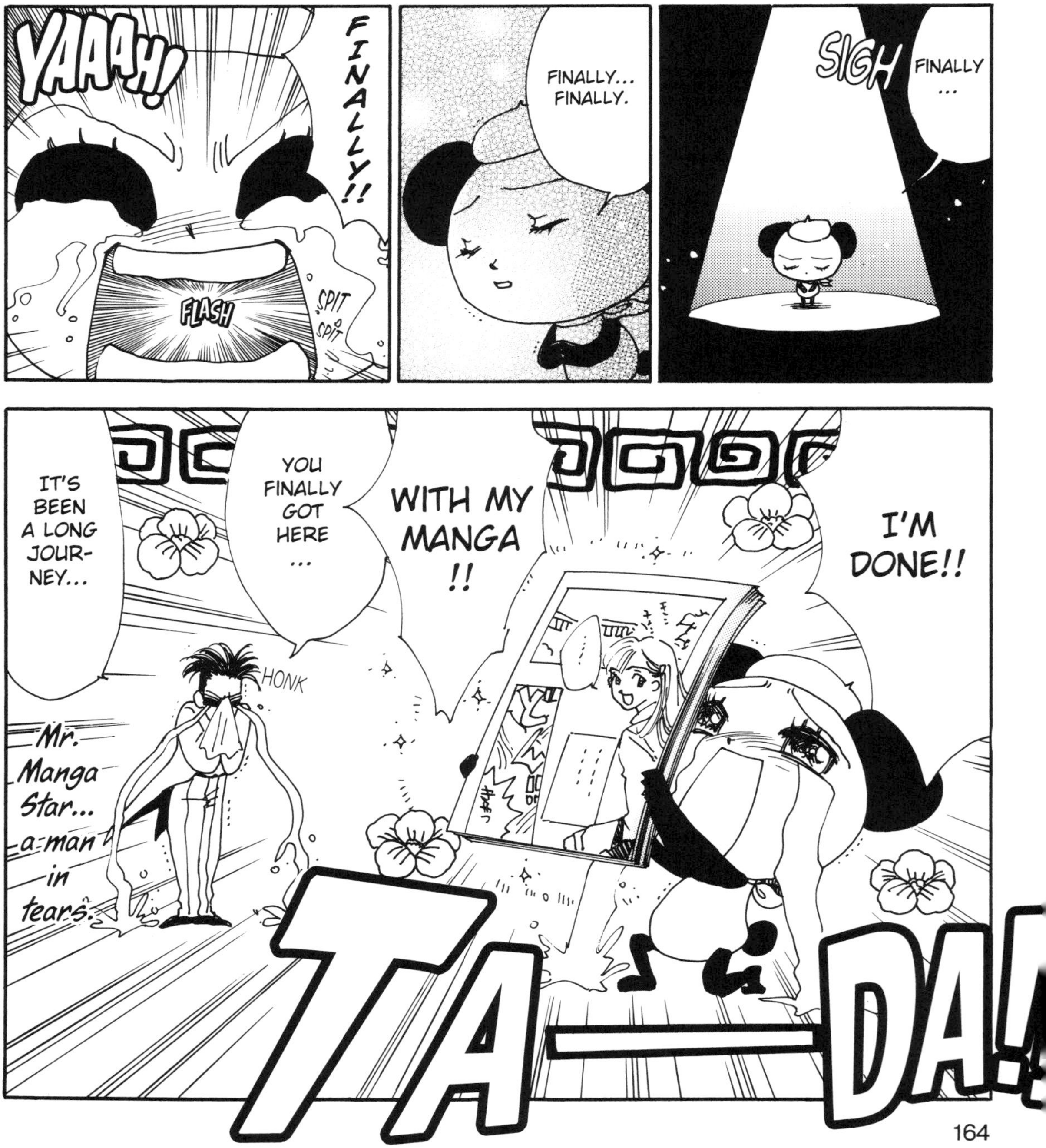
SIGH
FINALLY ...
FINALLY... FINALLY.
YAAAH!
FINALLY!!
FLASH
SPIT SPIT
I'M DONE!!
WITH MY MANGA !!
YOU FINALLY GOT HERE ...
IT'S BEEN A LONG JOURNEY...
HONK
Mr. Manga Star... a man in tears.
TA—DA!!

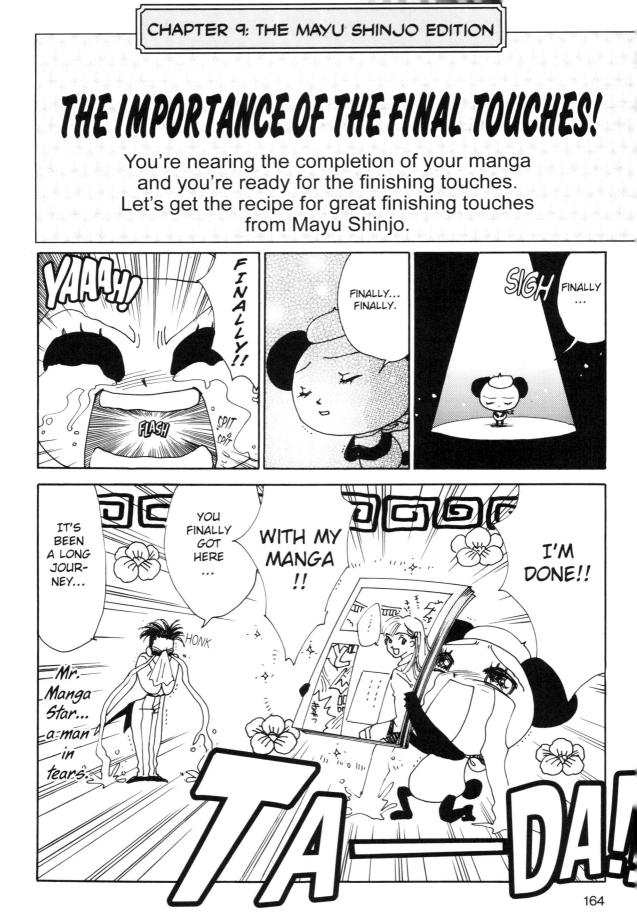

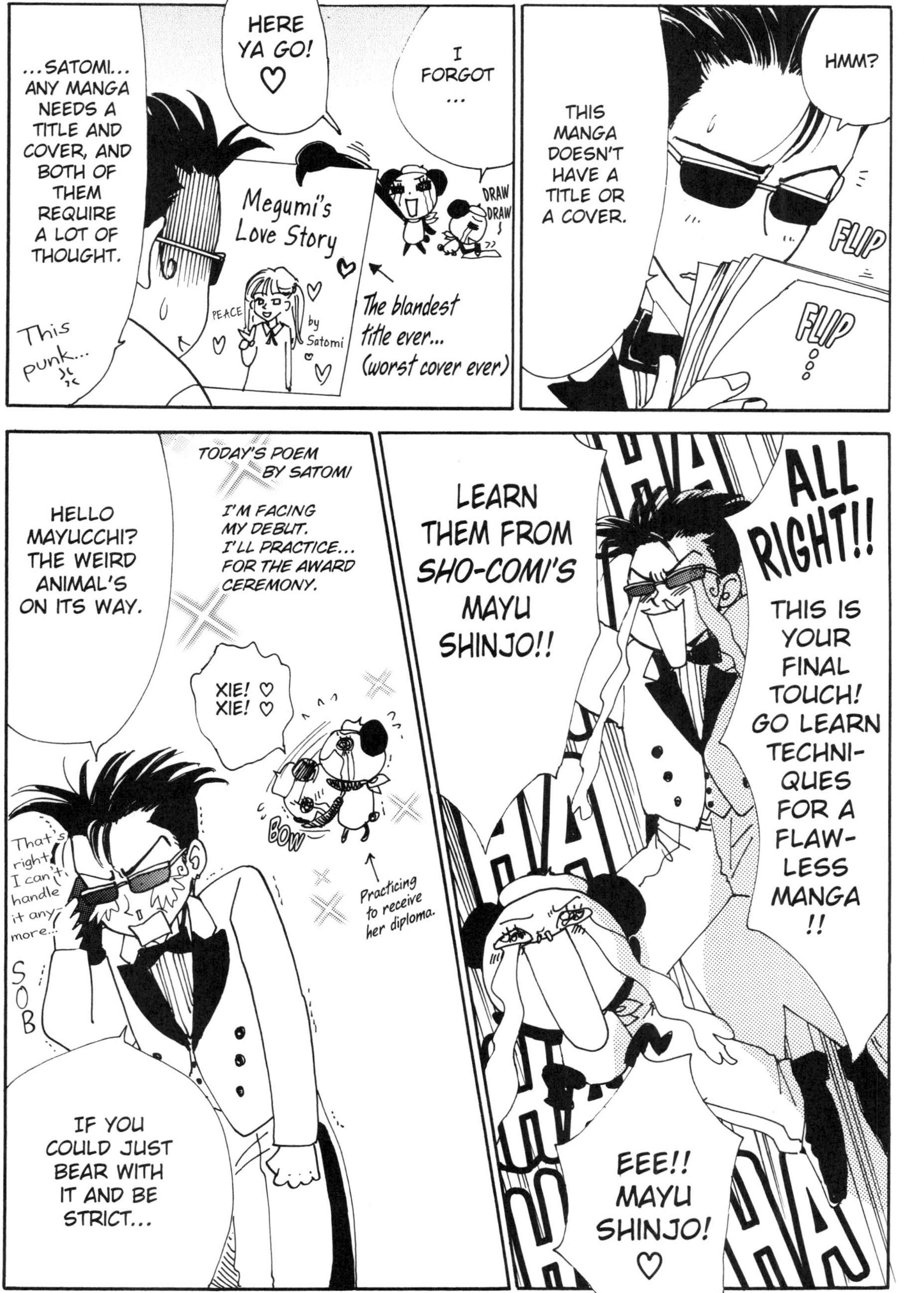
HMM?
THIS MANGA DOESN'T HAVE A TITLE OR A COVER.
FLIP
FLIP
I FORGOT ...
HERE YA GO! ♡
...SATOMI... ANY MANGA NEEDS A TITLE AND COVER, AND BOTH OF THEM REQUIRE A LOT OF THOUGHT.
DRAW DRAW
Megumi's Love Story
PEACE
by Satomi
The blandest title ever... (worst cover ever)
This punk...
ALL RIGHT!!
THIS IS YOUR FINAL TOUCH! GO LEARN TECHNIQUES FOR A FLAWLESS MANGA !!
LEARN THEM FROM SHO-COMI'S MAYU SHINJO!!
EEE!! MAYU SHINJO! ♡
TODAY'S POEM BY SATOMI
I'M FACING MY DEBUT. I'LL PRACTICE... FOR THE AWARD CEREMONY.
HELLO MAYUCCHI? THE WEIRD ANIMAL'S ON ITS WAY.
XIE! ♡ XIE! ♡
BOW
Practicing to receive her diploma.
That's right. I can't handle it anymore...
SOB
IF YOU COULD JUST BEAR WITH IT AND BE STRICT...

THE FINAL TOUCHES

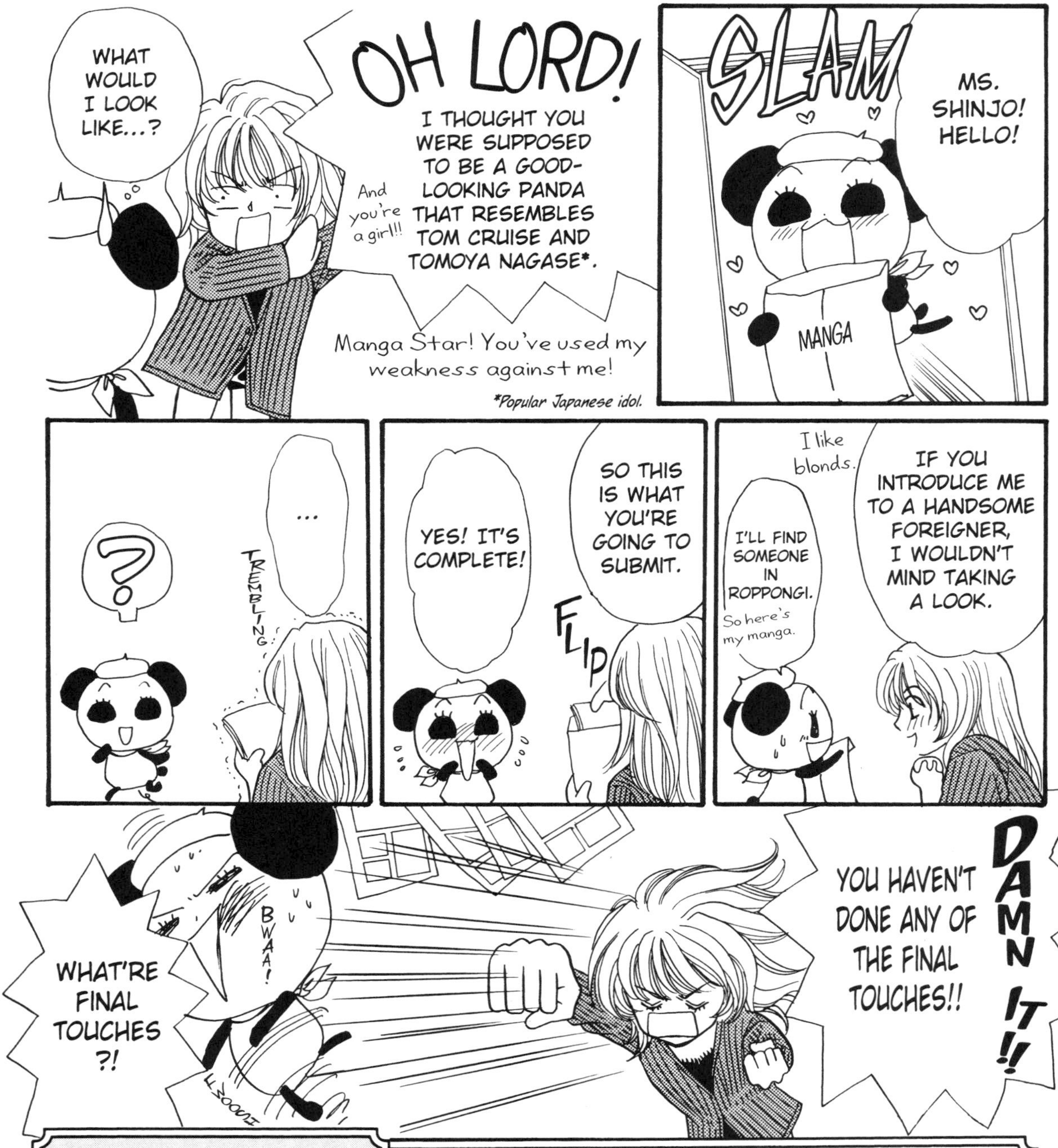
SLAM
MS. SHINJO! HELLO!
MANGA
OH LORD!
I THOUGHT YOU WERE SUPPOSED TO BE A GOOD-LOOKING PANDA THAT RESEMBLES TOM CRUISE AND TOMOYA NAGASE*.
And you're a girl!!
WHAT WOULD I LOOK LIKE...?
Manga Star! You've used my weakness against me!
*Popular Japanese idol.
I like blonds.
IF YOU INTRODUCE ME TO A HANDSOME FOREIGNER, I WOULDN'T MIND TAKING A LOOK.
I'LL FIND SOMEONE IN ROPPONGI.
So here's my manga.
SO THIS IS WHAT YOU'RE GOING TO SUBMIT.
YES! IT'S COMPLETE!
FLIP
...
TREMBLING
?
DAMN IT!!
YOU HAVEN'T DONE ANY OF THE FINAL TOUCHES!!
BWAA!
WHAT'RE FINAL TOUCHES?!

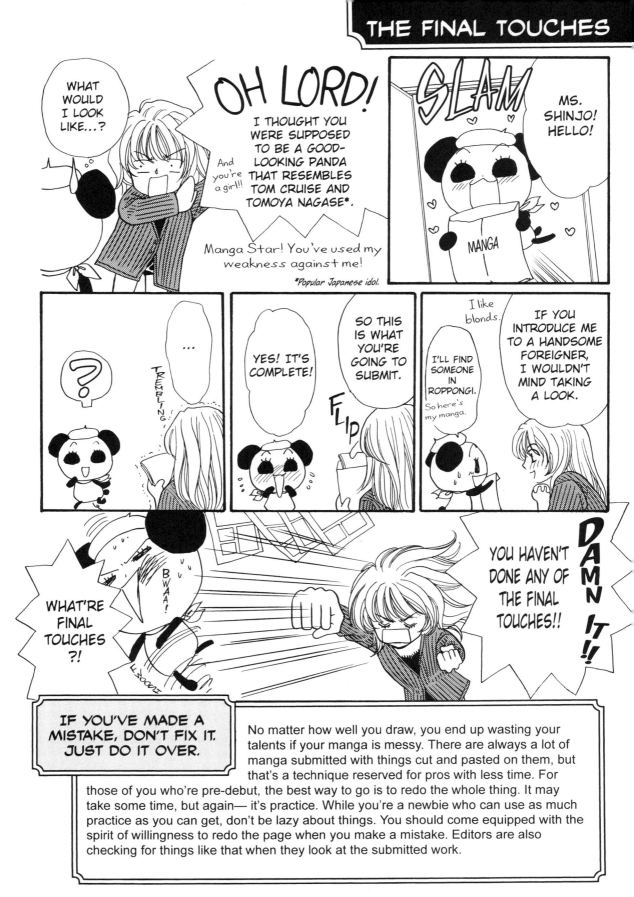

IF YOU'VE MADE A MISTAKE, DON'T FIX IT. JUST DO IT OVER.

No matter how well you draw, you end up wasting your talents if your manga is messy. There are always a lot of manga submitted with things cut and pasted on them, but that's a technique reserved for pros with less time. For those of you who're pre-debut, the best way to go is to redo the whole thing. It may take some time, but again— it's practice. While you're a newbie who can use as much practice as you can get, don't be lazy about things. You should come equipped with the spirit of willingness to redo the page when you make a mistake. Editors are also checking for things like that when they look at the submitted work.

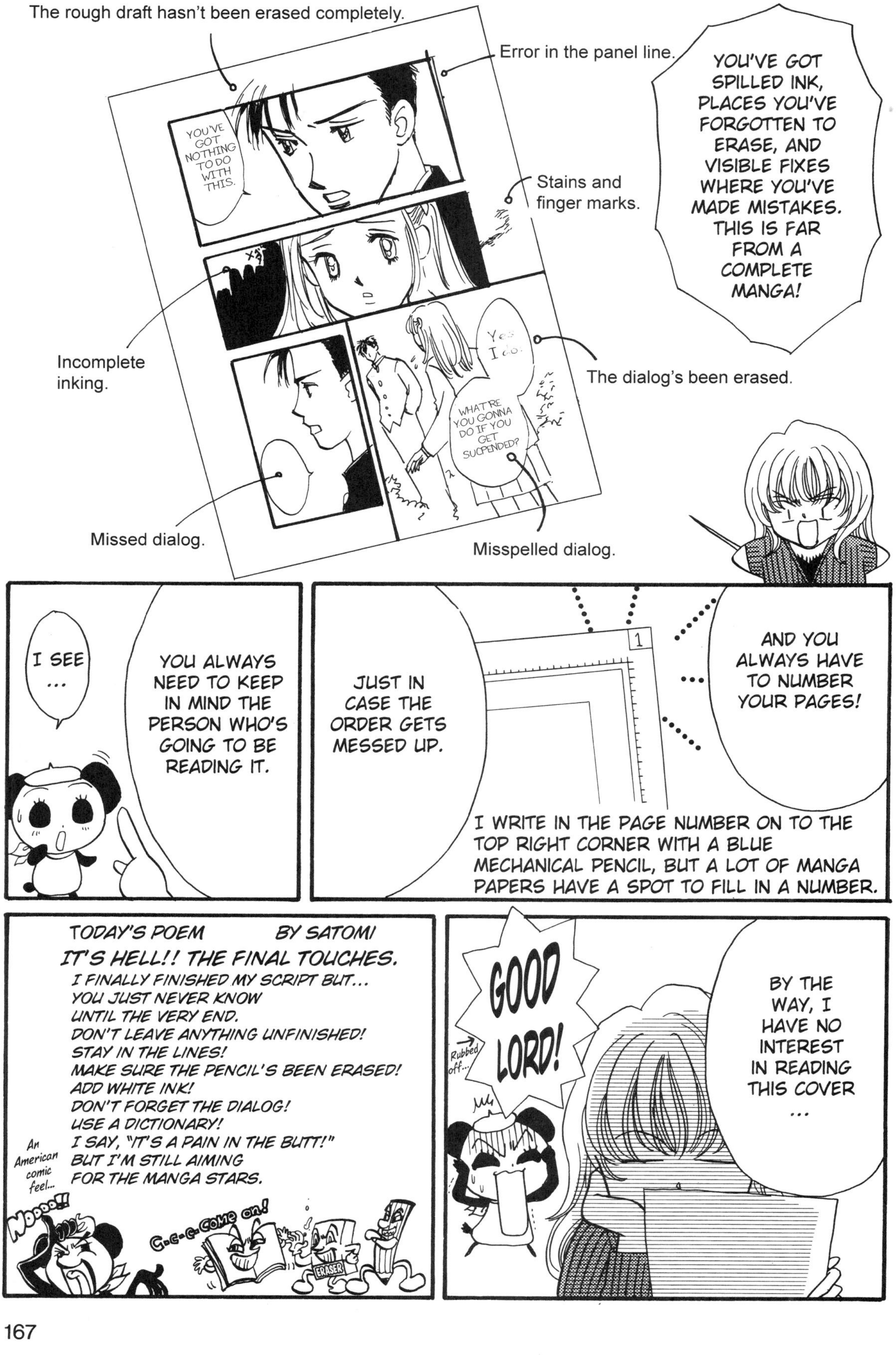
YOU'VE GOT SPILLED INK, PLACES YOU'VE FORGOTTEN TO ERASE, AND VISIBLE FIXES WHERE YOU'VE MADE MISTAKES. THIS IS FAR FROM A COMPLETE MANGA!
The rough draft hasn't been erased completely.
Error in the panel line.
YOU'VE GOT NOTHING TO DO WITH THIS.
Stains and finger marks.
Incomplete inking.
Yes I do.
The dialog's been erased.
WHAT'RE YOU GONNA DO IF YOU GET SUCPENDED?
Missed dialog.
Misspelled dialog.
AND YOU ALWAYS HAVE TO NUMBER YOUR PAGES!
1
JUST IN CASE THE ORDER GETS MESSED UP.
I WRITE IN THE PAGE NUMBER ON TO THE TOP RIGHT CORNER WITH A BLUE MECHANICAL PENCIL, BUT A LOT OF MANGA PAPERS HAVE A SPOT TO FILL IN A NUMBER.
YOU ALWAYS NEED TO KEEP IN MIND THE PERSON WHO'S GOING TO BE READING IT.
I SEE ...
BY THE WAY, I HAVE NO INTEREST IN READING THIS COVER ...
GOOD LORD!
Rubbed off...
TODAY'S POEM BY SATOMI
IT'S HELL!! THE FINAL TOUCHES.
I FINALLY FINISHED MY SCRIPT BUT...
YOU JUST NEVER KNOW
UNTIL THE VERY END.
DON'T LEAVE ANYTHING UNFINISHED!
STAY IN THE LINES!
MAKE SURE THE PENCIL'S BEEN ERASED!
ADD WHITE INK!
DON'T FORGET THE DIALOG!
USE A DICTIONARY!
I SAY, "IT'S A PAIN IN THE BUTT!"
BUT I'M STILL AIMING
FOR THE MANGA STARS.
An American comic feel...
Noooo!!
G-e-e-Come on!
ERASER

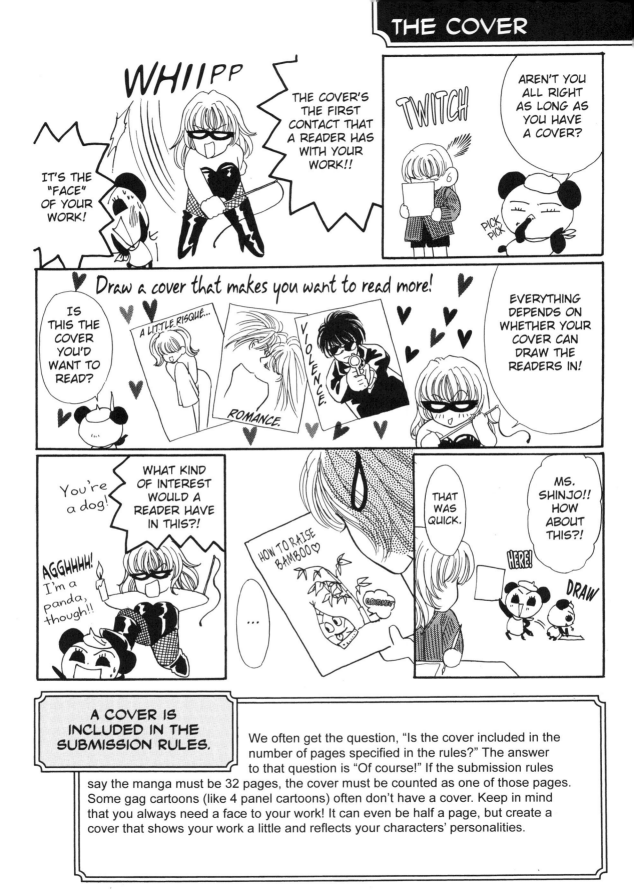

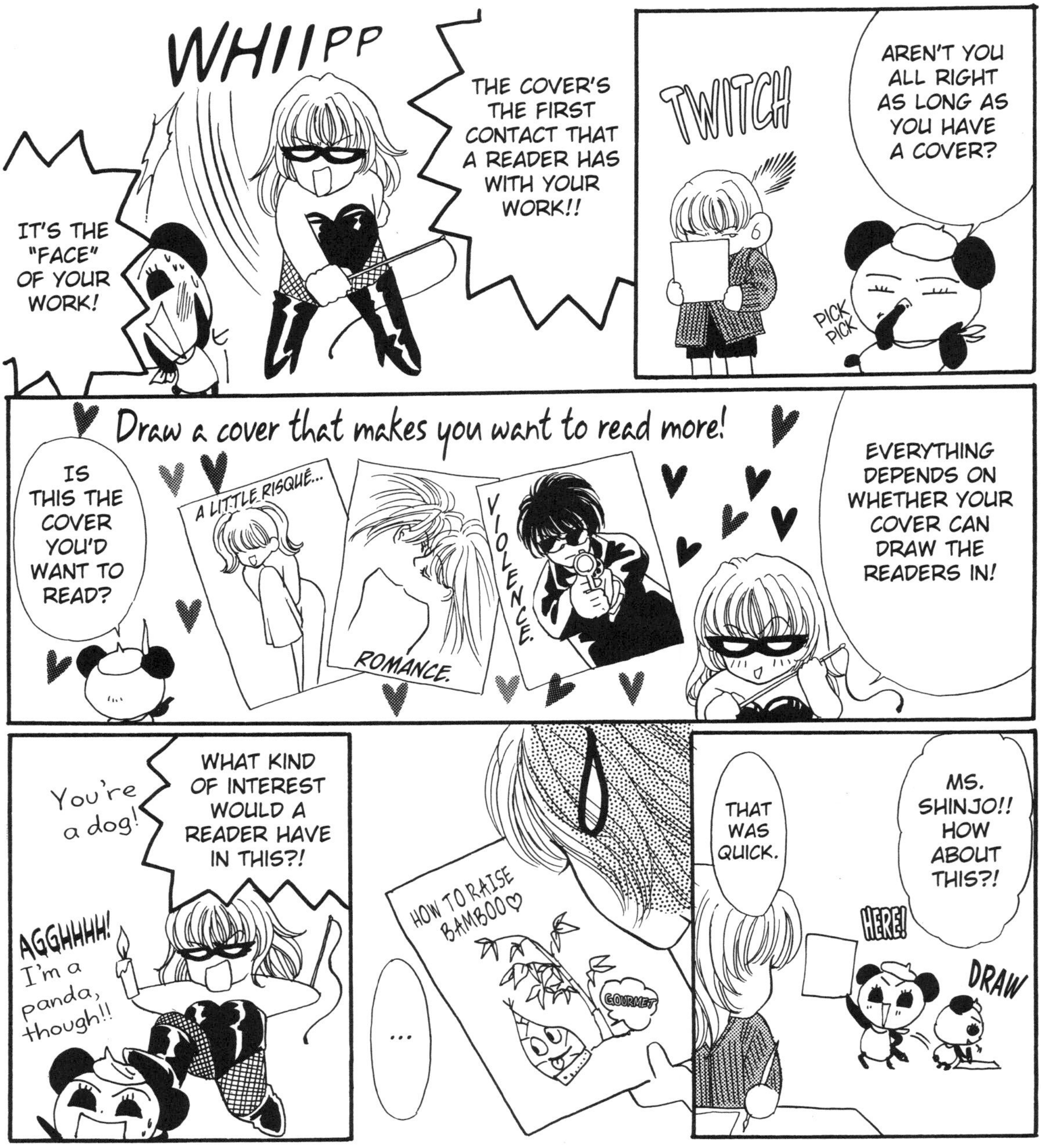
TWITCH
AREN'T YOU ALL RIGHT AS LONG AS YOU HAVE A COVER?
PICK PICK
WHIIPP
THE COVER'S THE FIRST CONTACT THAT A READER HAS WITH YOUR WORK!!
IT'S THE "FACE" OF YOUR WORK!
Draw a cover that makes you want to read more!
EVERYTHING DEPENDS ON WHETHER YOUR COVER CAN DRAW THE READERS IN!
VIOLENCE.
ROMANCE.
A LITTLE RISQUÉ...
IS THIS THE COVER YOU'D WANT TO READ?
MS. SHINJO!! HOW ABOUT THIS?!
THAT WAS QUICK.
HERE!
DRAW
HOW TO RAISE BAMBOO♡
GOURMET
...
WHAT KIND OF INTEREST WOULD A READER HAVE IN THIS?!
You're a dog!
AGGHHHH! I'm a panda, though!!

A COVER IS INCLUDED IN THE SUBMISSION RULES.

We often get the question, "Is the cover included in the number of pages specified in the rules?" The answer to that question is "Of course!" If the submission rules say the manga must be 32 pages, the cover must be counted as one of those pages. Some gag cartoons (like 4 panel cartoons) often don't have a cover. Keep in mind that you always need a face to your work! It can even be half a page, but create a cover that shows your work a little and reflects your characters' personalities.

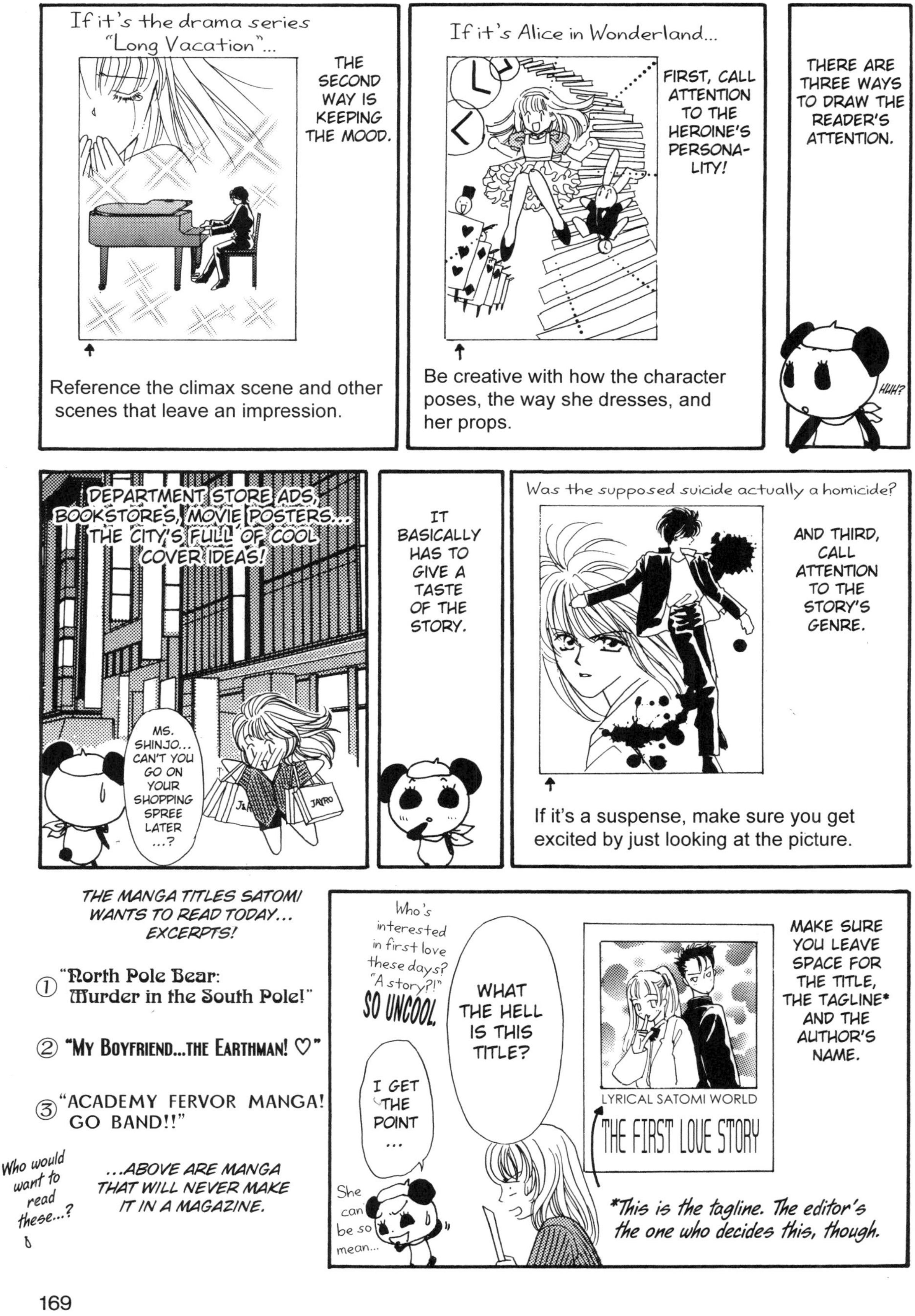
THERE ARE THREE WAYS TO DRAW THE READER'S ATTENTION.
HUH?
If it's Alice in Wonderland...
FIRST, CALL ATTENTION TO THE HEROINE'S PERSONA-LITY!
Be creative with how the character poses, the way she dresses, and her props.
If it's the drama series "Long Vacation"...
THE SECOND WAY IS KEEPING THE MOOD.
Reference the climax scene and other scenes that leave an impression.
Was the supposed suicide actually a homicide?
AND THIRD, CALL ATTENTION TO THE STORY'S GENRE.
If it's a suspense, make sure you get excited by just looking at the picture.
IT BASICALLY HAS TO GIVE A TASTE OF THE STORY.
DEPARTMENT STORE ADS, BOOKSTORES, MOVIE POSTERS... THE CITY'S FULL OF COOL COVER IDEAS!
JAYRO
MS. SHINJO... CAN'T YOU GO ON YOUR SHOPPING SPREE LATER ...?
MAKE SURE YOU LEAVE SPACE FOR THE TITLE, THE TAGLINE* AND THE AUTHOR'S NAME.
LYRICAL SATOMI WORLD
THE FIRST LOVE STORY
*This is the tagline. The editor's the one who decides this, though.
WHAT THE HELL IS THIS TITLE?
Who's interested in first love these days? "A story?!"
SO UNCOOL.
I GET THE POINT...
She can be so mean...
THE MANGA TITLES SATOMI WANTS TO READ TODAY... EXCERPTS!
① "North Pole Bear: Murder in the South Pole!"
② "My Boyfriend...the Earthman! ♡"
③ "ACADEMY FERVOR MANGA! GO BAND!!"
...ABOVE ARE MANGA THAT WILL NEVER MAKE IT IN A MAGAZINE.
Who would want to read these...?

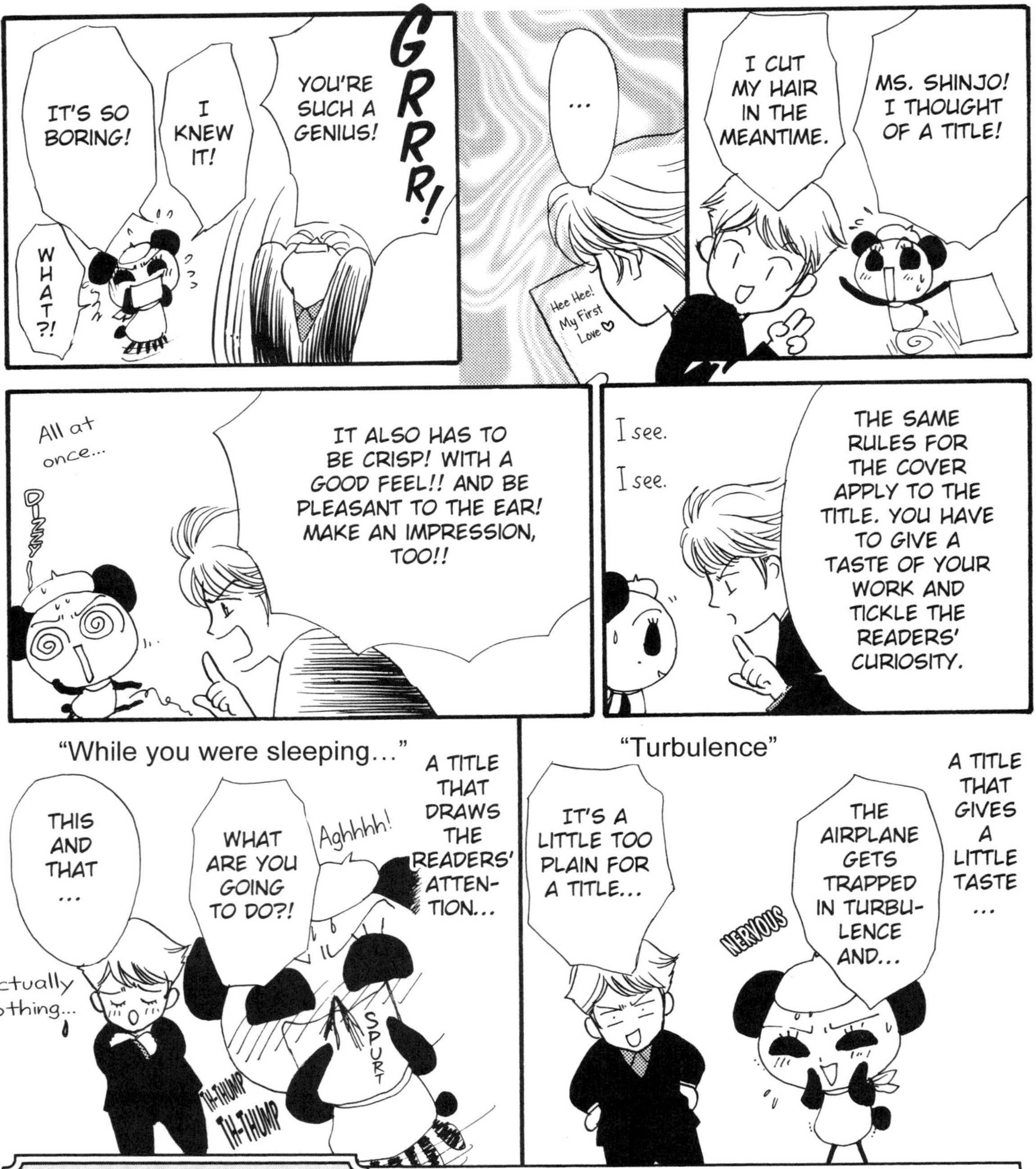
MS. SHINJO! I THOUGHT OF A TITLE!
I CUT MY HAIR IN THE MEANTIME.
...
Hee Hee! My First Love ♡
GRRR!
YOU'RE SUCH A GENIUS!
I KNEW IT!
IT'S SO BORING!
WHAT?!
THE SAME RULES FOR THE COVER APPLY TO THE TITLE. YOU HAVE TO GIVE A TASTE OF YOUR WORK AND TICKLE THE READERS' CURIOSITY.
I see.
I see.
IT ALSO HAS TO BE CRISP! WITH A GOOD FEEL!! AND BE PLEASANT TO THE EAR! MAKE AN IMPRESSION, TOO!!
All at once...
DIZZY~
"Turbulence"
A TITLE THAT GIVES A LITTLE TASTE...
THE AIRPLANE GETS TRAPPED IN TURBULENCE AND...
NERVOUS
IT'S A LITTLE TOO PLAIN FOR A TITLE...
"While you were sleeping..."
A TITLE THAT DRAWS THE READERS' ATTENTION...
Aghhhh!
WHAT ARE YOU GOING TO DO?!
THIS AND THAT...
Actually nothing...
SPURT
TH-THUMP
TH-THUMP

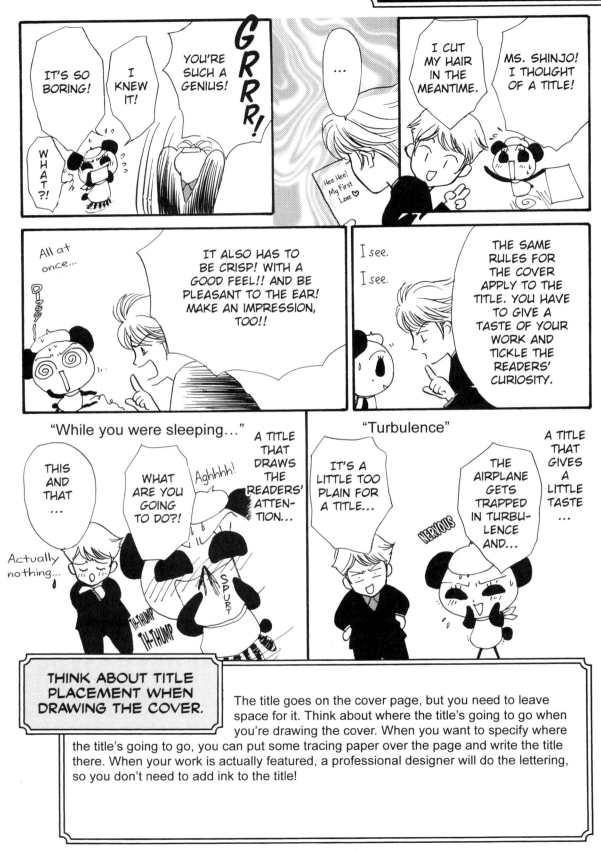

THINK ABOUT TITLE PLACEMENT WHEN DRAWING THE COVER.

The title goes on the cover page, but you need to leave space for it. Think about where the title's going to go when you're drawing the cover. When you want to specify where the title's going to go, you can put some tracing paper over the page and write the title there. When your work is actually featured, a professional designer will do the lettering, so you don't need to add ink to the title!

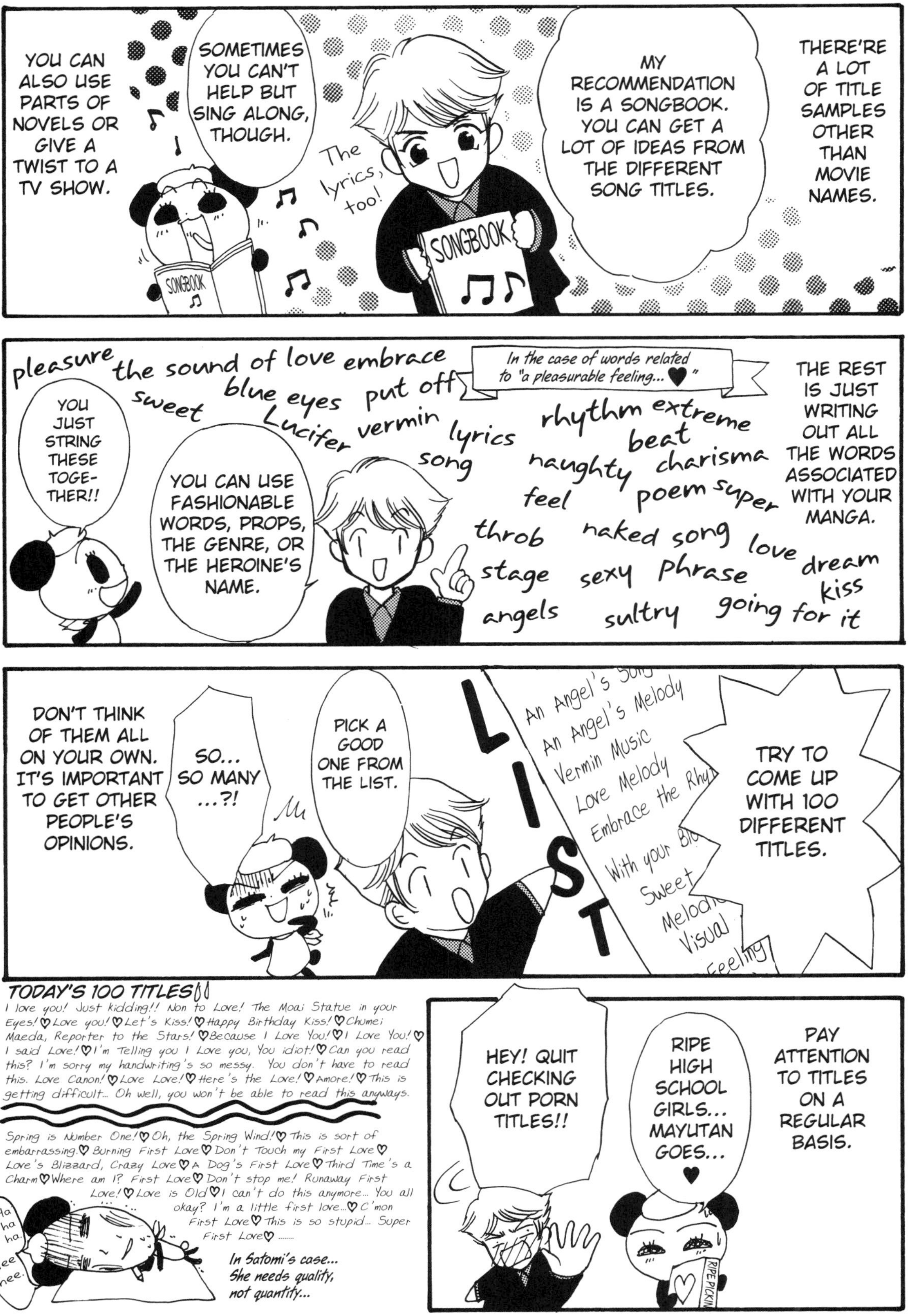
THERE'RE A LOT OF TITLE SAMPLES OTHER THAN MOVIE NAMES.
MY RECOMMENDATION IS A SONGBOOK. YOU CAN GET A LOT OF IDEAS FROM THE DIFFERENT SONG TITLES.
SONGBOOK
The lyrics, too!
SOMETIMES YOU CAN'T HELP BUT SING ALONG, THOUGH.
SONGBOOK
YOU CAN ALSO USE PARTS OF NOVELS OR GIVE A TWIST TO A TV SHOW.
THE REST IS JUST WRITING OUT ALL THE WORDS ASSOCIATED WITH YOUR MANGA.
In the case of words related to "a pleasurable feeling... ♥"
pleasure the sound of love embrace
blue eyes put off
sweet
Lucifer vermin lyrics rhythm extreme
beat
song naughty charisma
feel poem super
throb naked song love
stage sexy phrase dream
kiss
angels sultry going for it
YOU CAN USE FASHIONABLE WORDS, PROPS, THE GENRE, OR THE HEROINE'S NAME.
YOU JUST STRING THESE TOGE-THER!!
TRY TO COME UP WITH 100 DIFFERENT TITLES.
LIST
An Angel's Song
An Angel's Melody
Vermin Music
Love Melody
Embrace the Rhy
With your Bl
Sweet
Melodi
Visual
Feeling
PICK A GOOD ONE FROM THE LIST.
SO... SO MANY ...?!
DON'T THINK OF THEM ALL ON YOUR OWN. IT'S IMPORTANT TO GET OTHER PEOPLE'S OPINIONS.
PAY ATTENTION TO TITLES ON A REGULAR BASIS.
RIPE HIGH SCHOOL GIRLS... MAYUTAN GOES... ♥
RIPE PICKIN
HEY! QUIT CHECKING OUT PORN TITLES!!
TODAY'S 100 TITLES
I love you! Just kidding!! Non to Love! The Moai Statue in your Eyes! ♡ Love you! ♡ Let's Kiss! ♡ Happy Birthday Kiss! ♡ Chumei Maeda, Reporter to the Stars! ♡ Because I Love You! ♡ I Love You! ♡ I said Love! ♡ I'm Telling you I Love you, You idiot! ♡ Can you read this? I'm sorry my handwriting's so messy. You don't have to read this. Love Canon! ♡ Love Love! ♡ Here's the Love! ♡ Amore! ♡ This is getting difficult... Oh well, you won't be able to read this anyways.
Spring is Number One! ♡ Oh, the Spring Wind! ♡ This is sort of embarrassing. ♡ Burning First Love ♡ Don't Touch my First Love ♡ Love's Blizzard, Crazy Love ♡ A Dog's First Love ♡ Third Time's a Charm ♡ Where am I? First Love ♡ Don't stop me! Runaway First Love! ♡ Love is Old ♡ I can't do this anymore... You all okay? I'm a little first love... ♡ C'mon First Love ♡ This is so stupid... Super First Love ♡ ....
Ha ha ha
Hee hee
In Satomi's case... She needs quality, not quantity...

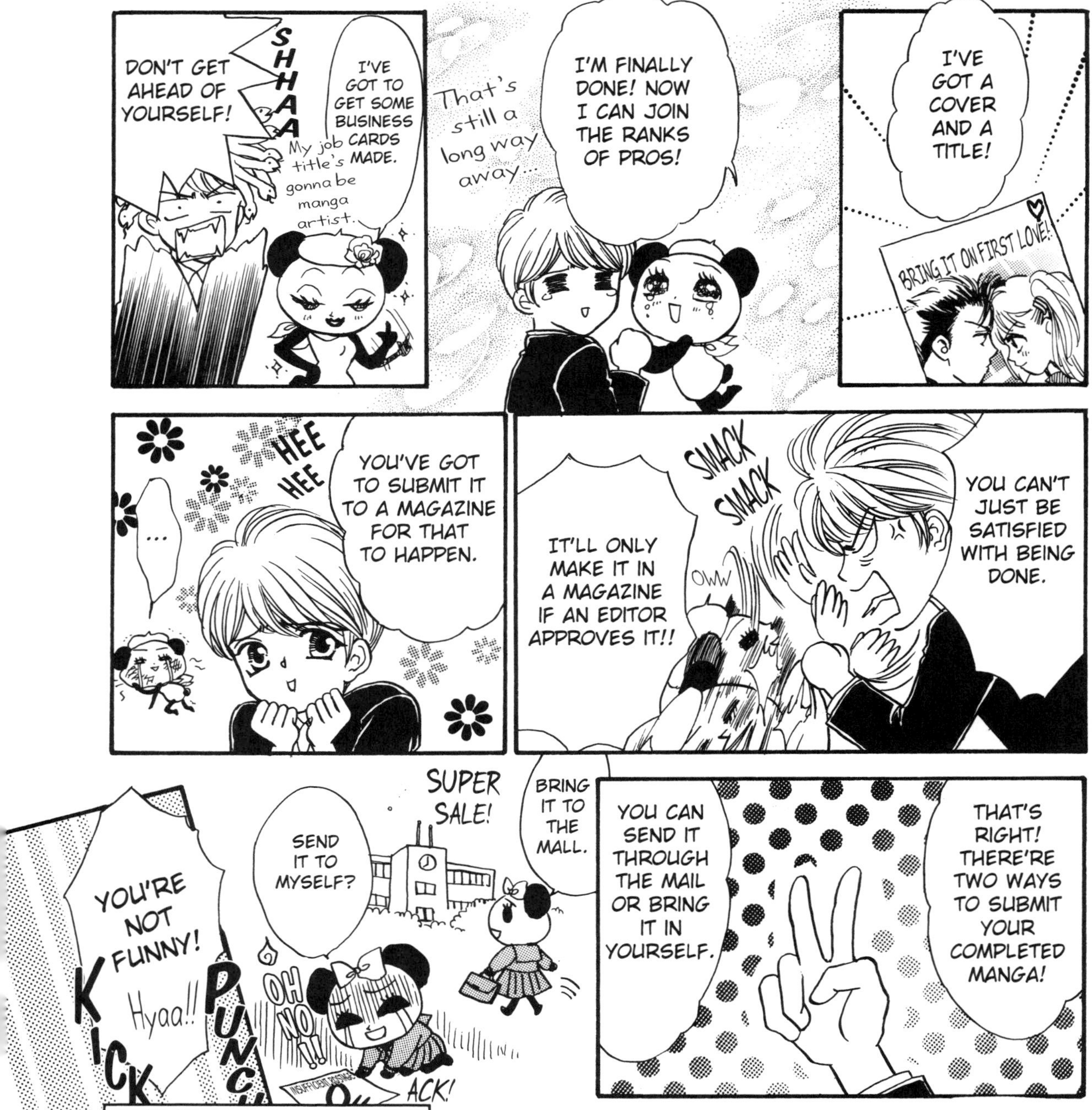
I'VE GOT A COVER AND A TITLE!
BRING IT ON FIRST LOVE!
I'M FINALLY DONE! NOW I CAN JOIN THE RANKS OF PROS!
That's still a long way away...
I'VE GOT TO GET SOME BUSINESS CARDS MADE.
My job title's gonna be manga artist.
SHHAA
DON'T GET AHEAD OF YOURSELF!
YOU CAN'T JUST BE SATISFIED WITH BEING DONE.
SMACK SMACK
IT'LL ONLY MAKE IT IN A MAGAZINE IF AN EDITOR APPROVES IT!!
OWW
YOU'VE GOT TO SUBMIT IT TO A MAGAZINE FOR THAT TO HAPPEN.
HEE HEE
...
THAT'S RIGHT! THERE'RE TWO WAYS TO SUBMIT YOUR COMPLETED MANGA!
YOU CAN SEND IT THROUGH THE MAIL OR BRING IT IN YOURSELF.
BRING IT TO THE MALL.
SUPER SALE!
SEND IT TO MYSELF?
OH NO!!
ACK!
YOU'RE NOT FUNNY!
Hyaa!!
KICK
PUNCH

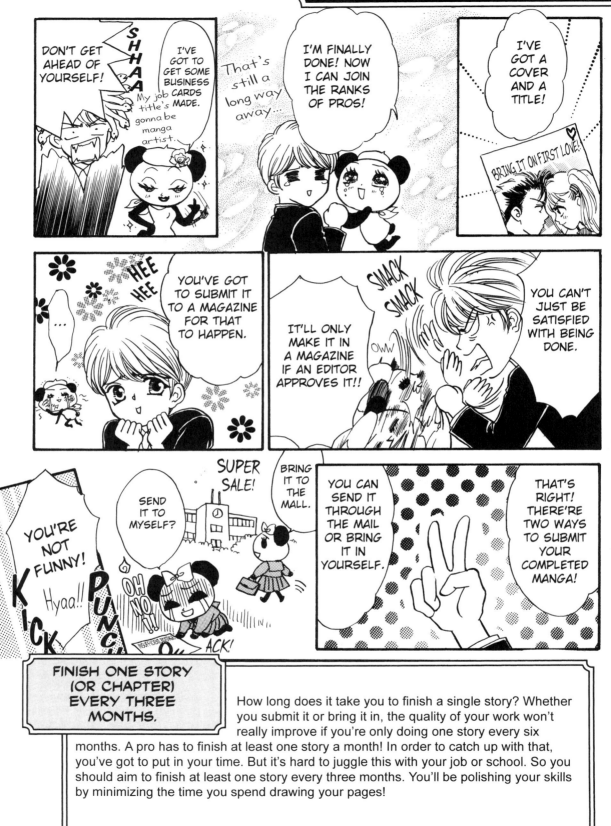

FINISH ONE STORY (OR CHAPTER) EVERY THREE MONTHS.

How long does it take you to finish a single story? Whether you submit it or bring it in, the quality of your work won't really improve if you're only doing one story every six months. A pro has to finish at least one story a month! In order to catch up with that, you've got to put in your time. But it's hard to juggle this with your job or school. So you should aim to finish at least one story every three months. You'll be polishing your skills by minimizing the time you spend drawing your pages!

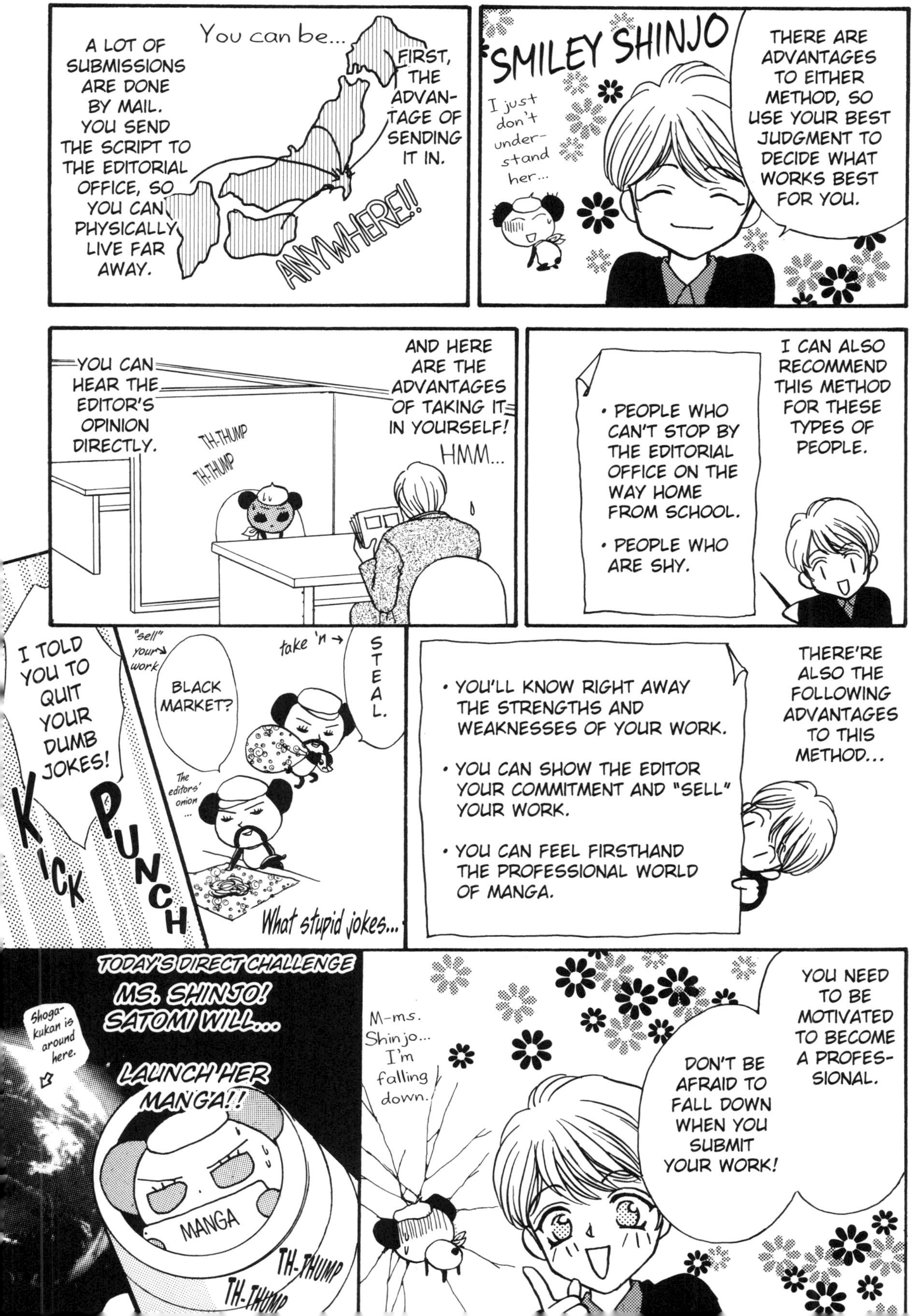
THERE ARE ADVANTAGES TO EITHER METHOD, SO USE YOUR BEST JUDGMENT TO DECIDE WHAT WORKS BEST FOR YOU.
SMILEY SHINJO
I just don't under-stand her...
FIRST, THE ADVAN-TAGE OF SENDING IT IN.
You can be...
A LOT OF SUBMISSIONS ARE DONE BY MAIL. YOU SEND THE SCRIPT TO THE EDITORIAL OFFICE, SO YOU CAN PHYSICALLY LIVE FAR AWAY.
ANYWHERE!!
I CAN ALSO RECOMMEND THIS METHOD FOR THESE TYPES OF PEOPLE.
• PEOPLE WHO CAN'T STOP BY THE EDITORIAL OFFICE ON THE WAY HOME FROM SCHOOL.
• PEOPLE WHO ARE SHY.
AND HERE ARE THE ADVANTAGES OF TAKING IT IN YOURSELF!
YOU CAN HEAR THE EDITOR'S OPINION DIRECTLY.
HMM...
TH-THUMP
TH-THUMP
THERE'RE ALSO THE FOLLOWING ADVANTAGES TO THIS METHOD...
• YOU'LL KNOW RIGHT AWAY THE STRENGTHS AND WEAKNESSES OF YOUR WORK.
• YOU CAN SHOW THE EDITOR YOUR COMMITMENT AND "SELL" YOUR WORK.
• YOU CAN FEEL FIRSTHAND THE PROFESSIONAL WORLD OF MANGA.
take 'n →
STEAL.
"sell" your work
BLACK MARKET?
I TOLD YOU TO QUIT YOUR DUMB JOKES!
The editors' onion ...
KICK
PUNCH
What stupid jokes...
YOU NEED TO BE MOTIVATED TO BECOME A PROFES-SIONAL.
DON'T BE AFRAID TO FALL DOWN WHEN YOU SUBMIT YOUR WORK!
M-ms. Shinjo... I'm falling down.
TODAY'S DIRECT CHALLENGE
MS. SHINJO! SATOMI WILL...
LAUNCH HER MANGA!!
Shoga-kukan is around here.
MANGA
TH-THUMP
TH-THUMP

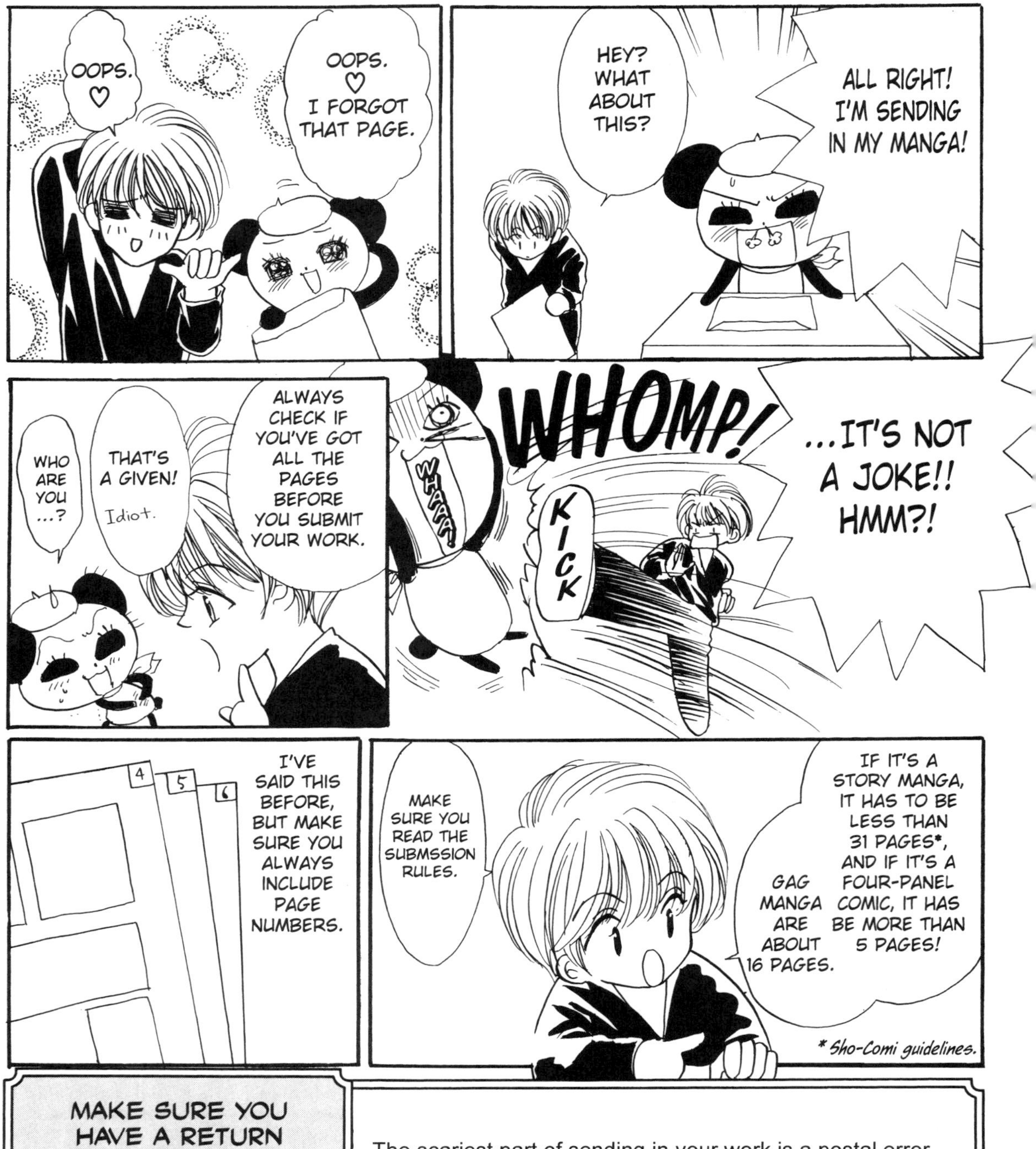
ALL RIGHT! I'M SENDING IN MY MANGA!
HEY? WHAT ABOUT THIS?
OOPS. ♡ I FORGOT THAT PAGE.
OOPS. ♡
...IT'S NOT A JOKE!! HMM?!
WHOMP!
WHAAA!
KICK
ALWAYS CHECK IF YOU'VE GOT ALL THE PAGES BEFORE YOU SUBMIT YOUR WORK.
THAT'S A GIVEN!
Idiot.
WHO ARE YOU ...?
IF IT'S A STORY MANGA, IT HAS TO BE LESS THAN 31 PAGES*, AND IF IT'S A FOUR-PANEL COMIC, IT HAS BE MORE THAN 5 PAGES!
GAG MANGA ARE ABOUT 16 PAGES.
MAKE SURE YOU READ THE SUBMSSION RULES.
* Sho-Comi guidelines.
I'VE SAID THIS BEFORE, BUT MAKE SURE YOU ALWAYS INCLUDE PAGE NUMBERS.
4
5
6

MAKE SURE YOU HAVE A RETURN ADDRESS.

The scariest part of sending in your work is a postal error. It would be an unbelievable loss to lose the work you've worked so hard on. Double check the address and make sure you put down a return address on the envelope. The most common mistake is sending in a manga intended for *Bessatsu Shojo Comics* to the editorial office for *Shojo Comics*. Just missing the *Bessatsu* will take your manga to the wrong place, so be careful! It might not be such a bad idea to send it registered mail or through a courier service.

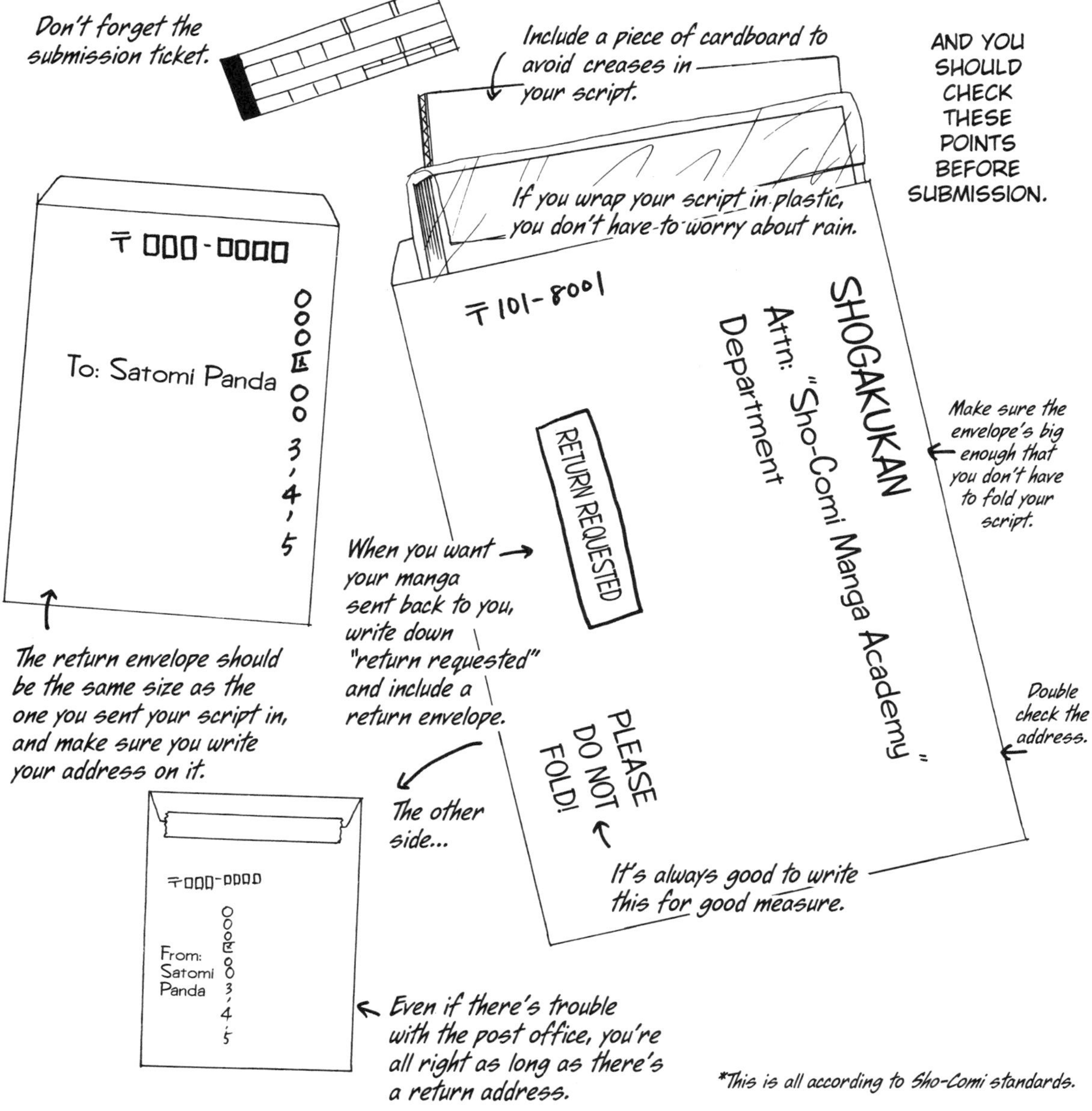
Don't forget the submission ticket.
Include a piece of cardboard to avoid creases in your script.
AND YOU SHOULD CHECK THESE POINTS BEFORE SUBMISSION.
If you wrap your script in plastic, you don't have to worry about rain.
〒 000-0000
000区00 3, 4, 5
To: Satomi Panda
〒101-8001
SHOGAKUKAN
Attn: "Sho-Comi Manga Academy" Department
RETURN REQUESTED
Make sure the envelope's big enough that you don't have to fold your script.
When you want your manga sent back to you, write down "return requested" and include a return envelope.
The return envelope should be the same size as the one you sent your script in, and make sure you write your address on it.
PLEASE DO NOT FOLD!
Double check the address.
The other side...
It's always good to write this for good measure.
〒000-0000
000区00 3, 4, 5
From: Satomi Panda
Even if there's trouble with the post office, you're all right as long as there's a return address.
*This is all according to Sho-Comi standards.

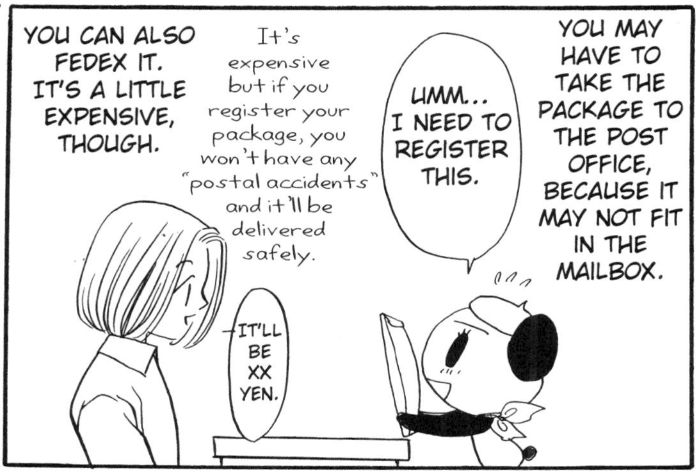
YOU MAY HAVE TO TAKE THE PACKAGE TO THE POST OFFICE, BECAUSE IT MAY NOT FIT IN THE MAILBOX.
UMM... I NEED TO REGISTER THIS.
It's expensive but if you register your package, you won't have any "postal accidents" and it'll be delivered safely.
YOU CAN ALSO FEDEX IT. IT'S A LITTLE EXPENSIVE, THOUGH.
IT'LL BE XX YEN.

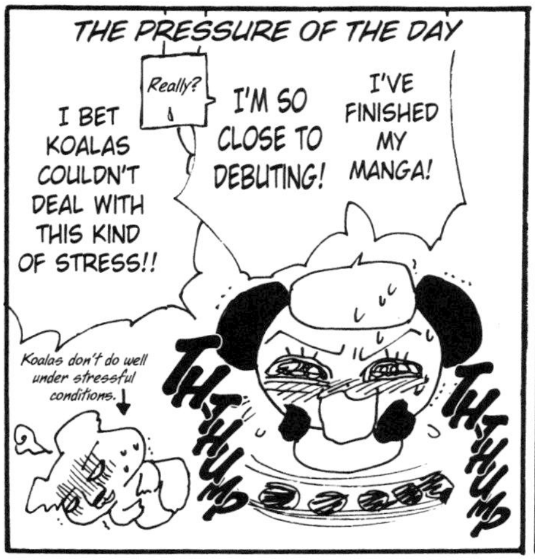
THE PRESSURE OF THE DAY
I'VE FINISHED MY MANGA!
I'M SO CLOSE TO DEBUTING!
Really?
I BET KOALAS COULDN'T DEAL WITH THIS KIND OF STRESS!!
THU-THUMP
THU-THUMP
Koalas don't do well under stressful conditions.

YOU NEED TO MAKE AN APPOINTMENT TO DO THAT.

The pushup bra's not working...

I'M GOING TO THE EDITORIAL OFFICE, OF COURSE!

HMPH

HOLD ON A SEC. WHERE'RE YOU GOING?

I'll be back soon!!

I'M BRINGING IN MY WORK SO I CAN SHOW THE EDITOR HOW PASSIONATE I AM.

There's usually someone there from 2 pm to about midnight.

SOMETIMES THERE'S NOBODY IN THE OFFICE ON WEEKENDS OR WEEKDAY MORNINGS, SO YOU SHOULD TRY TO CALL ON A WEEKDAY AFTERNOON.

SOB...

IT'S RUDE UNLESS YOU CALL BEFOREHAND AND ASK IF THE EDITOR HAS TIME!

YOU ALWAYS HAVE TO FILL IN A VISITOR CARD BEFORE YOU GO INTO THE SHOGAKUKAN BUILDING, AND YOU HAVE TO WRITE THE EDITOR'S NAME ON THAT.

YOU SHOULD ALWAYS TAKE DOWN THE NAME OF THE EDITOR YOU SPOKE TO!

Guest Registration Card

Name	Company name	
Address	Tel ( )	
Visiting party	Name	
Appointment(time)	No appointment	

CONSISTENCY IS KEY WHEN BRINGING IN YOUR MANGA.

It makes anyone nervous to bring in manga. The editors all know this, so you just have to go for it! You might forget everything that is said because you are so nervous, so make sure you bring a notepad. And don't be embarrassed to ask questions. It might be embarrassing at first, but you won't become a professional without knowing the answers! And make sure you're consistent in bringing in your manga. It'll be a good reference for them to see how much you've improved since your last manga, so you should bring it in at least twice.

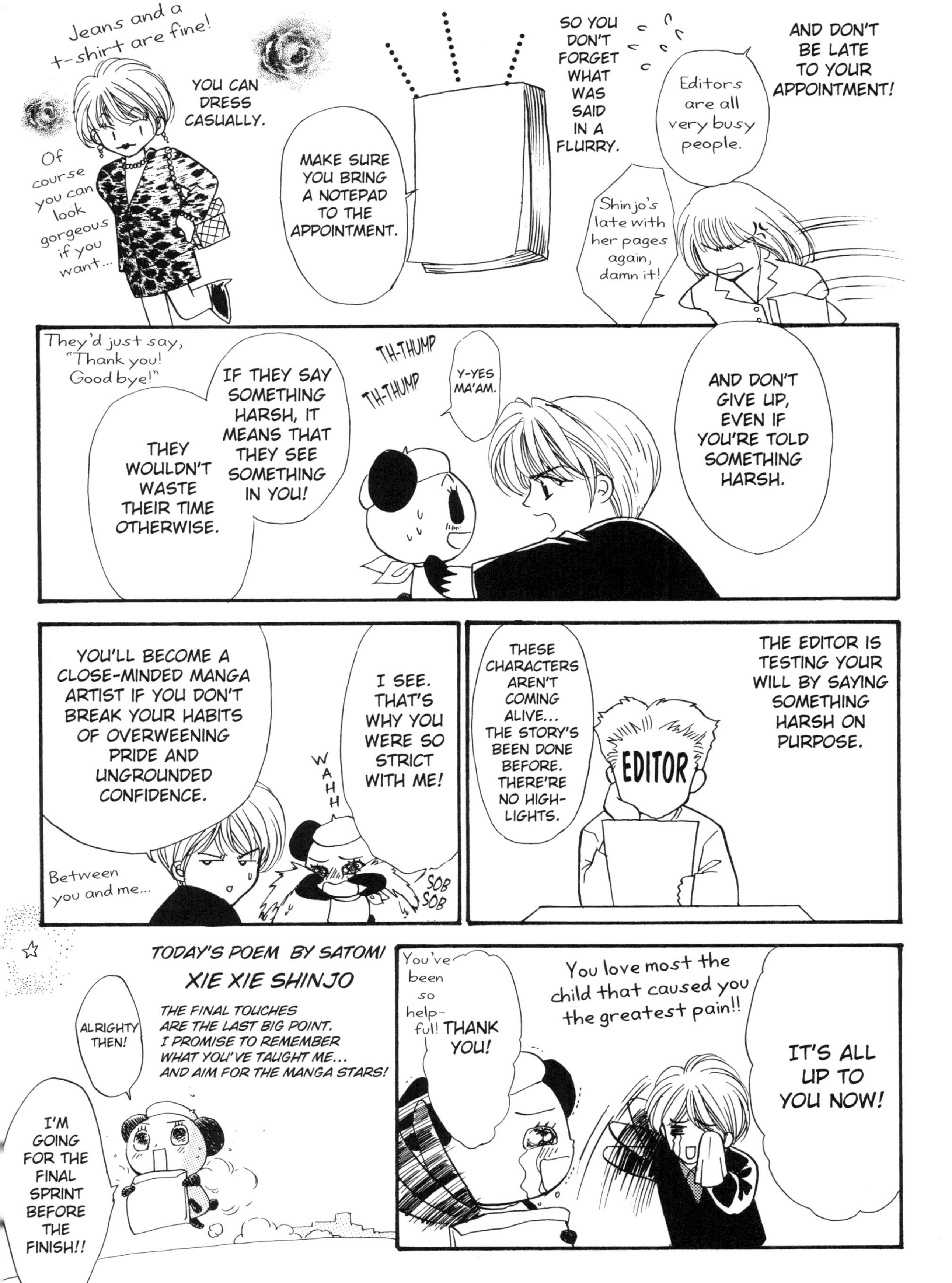
AND DON'T BE LATE TO YOUR APPOINTMENT!
Editors are all very busy people.
Shinjo's late with her pages again, damn it!
SO YOU DON'T FORGET WHAT WAS SAID IN A FLURRY.
MAKE SURE YOU BRING A NOTEPAD TO THE APPOINTMENT.
YOU CAN DRESS CASUALLY.
Jeans and a t-shirt are fine!
Of course you can look gorgeous if you want...
AND DON'T GIVE UP, EVEN IF YOU'RE TOLD SOMETHING HARSH.
Y-YES MA'AM.
TH-THUMP
TH-THUMP
IF THEY SAY SOMETHING HARSH, IT MEANS THAT THEY SEE SOMETHING IN YOU!
THEY WOULDN'T WASTE THEIR TIME OTHERWISE.
They'd just say, "Thank you! Good bye!"
THE EDITOR IS TESTING YOUR WILL BY SAYING SOMETHING HARSH ON PURPOSE.
THESE CHARACTERS AREN'T COMING ALIVE... THE STORY'S BEEN DONE BEFORE. THERE'RE NO HIGH-LIGHTS.
EDITOR
I SEE. THAT'S WHY YOU WERE SO STRICT WITH ME!
WAHH
SOB SOB
YOU'LL BECOME A CLOSE-MINDED MANGA ARTIST IF YOU DON'T BREAK YOUR HABITS OF OVERWEENING PRIDE AND UNGROUNDED CONFIDENCE.
Between you and me...
IT'S ALL UP TO YOU NOW!
You love most the child that caused you the greatest pain!!
THANK YOU!
You've been so help-ful!
TODAY'S POEM BY SATOMI
XIE XIE SHINJO
THE FINAL TOUCHES ARE THE LAST BIG POINT. I PROMISE TO REMEMBER WHAT YOU'VE TAUGHT ME... AND AIM FOR THE MANGA STARS!
ALRIGHTY THEN!
I'M GOING FOR THE FINAL SPRINT BEFORE THE FINISH!!

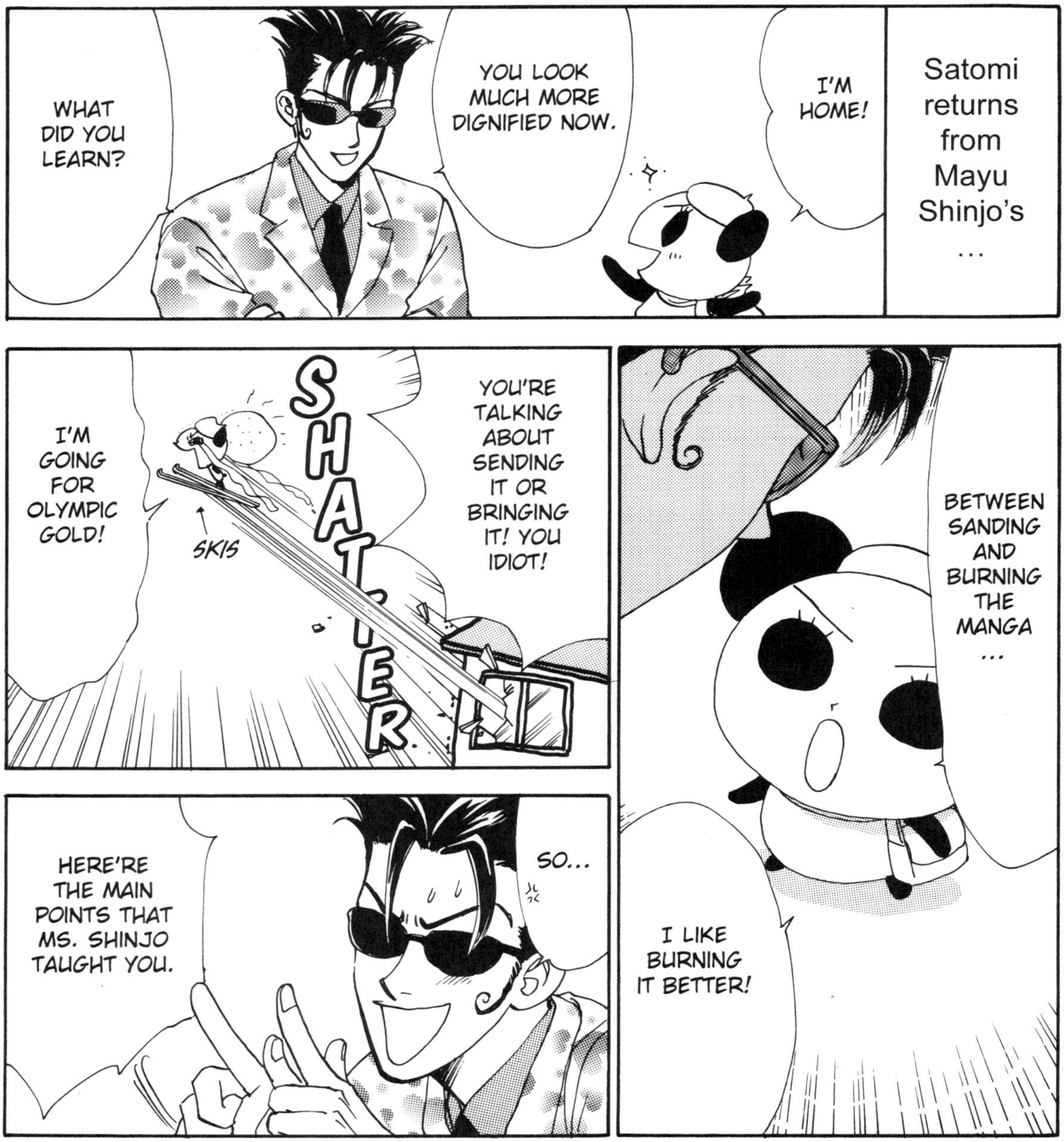
Satomi returns from Mayu Shinjo's ...
I'M HOME!
YOU LOOK MUCH MORE DIGNIFIED NOW.
WHAT DID YOU LEARN?
BETWEEN SANDING AND BURNING THE MANGA ...
I LIKE BURNING IT BETTER!
YOU'RE TALKING ABOUT SENDING IT OR BRINGING IT! YOU IDIOT!
SHATTER
I'M GOING FOR OLYMPIC GOLD!
SKIS
SO...
HERE'RE THE MAIN POINTS THAT MS. SHINJO TAUGHT YOU.

DON'T BE A HERMIT AND DRAW MANGA.

If there's one piece of advice to give you, the aspiring manga artist, it's this: Don't just spend all your time on manga! Of course, your drawing skills will improve the more you practice, but you also need to be social and really know the different trends out there. You won't know what's in at school or in town or what people want if you stay at home all the time. Make sure you have your radar on, or else you'll be coming up with outdated manga. It's important to read books and watch movies and try out different things!

THE FOUR MAIN POINTS FROM MAYU SHINJO

1: The cover is important because it's the face of your work!

2: Come up with a title that intrigues the readers.

3: Always follow the submission rules.

4: You can get direct feedback if you bring your manga in.

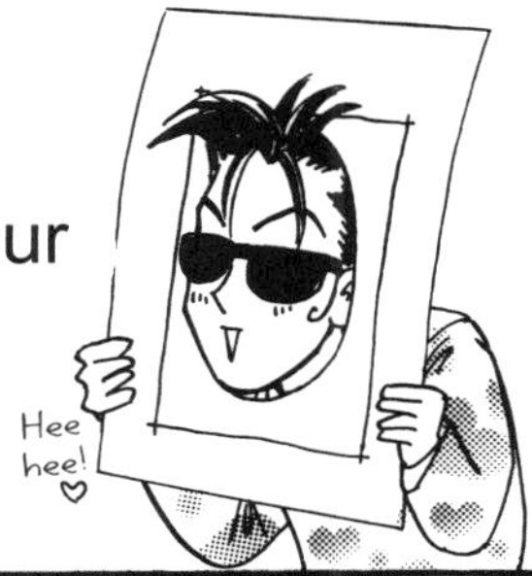

Hee hee!

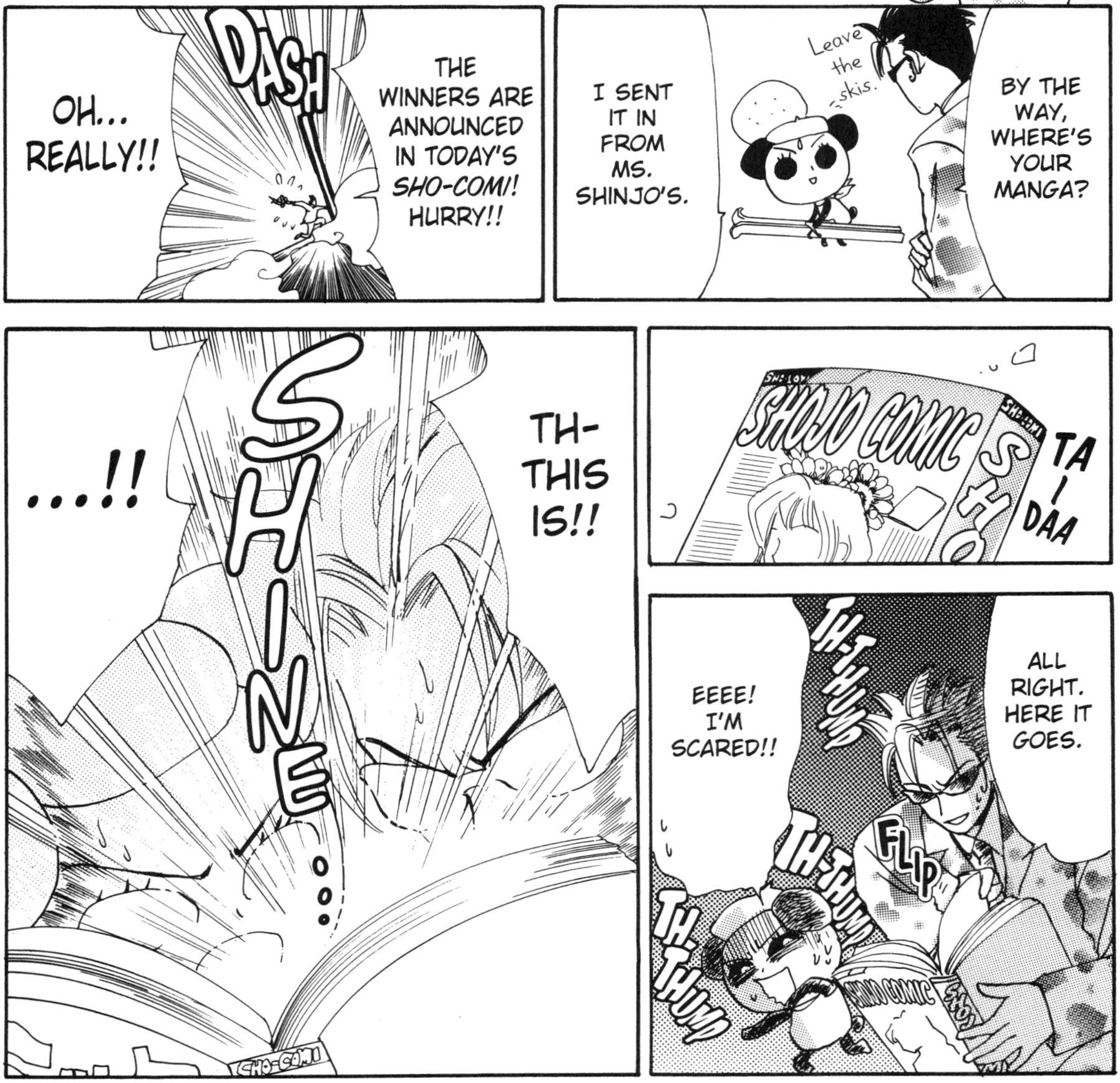

BY THE WAY, WHERE'S YOUR MANGA?
Leave the skis.
I SENT IT IN FROM MS. SHINJO'S.
THE WINNERS ARE ANNOUNCED IN TODAY'S SHO-COMI! HURRY!!
DASH
OH... REALLY!!
SHOJO COMIC
TA DAA
ALL RIGHT. HERE IT GOES.
EEEE! I'M SCARED!!
TH-THUMP
FLIP
TH-THUMP
TH-THUMP
SHOJO COMIC
TH-THIS IS!!
SHINE...
...!!
SHO-COMI

CHAPTER 10

AIM FOR THE MANGA STARS

Satomi's finally debuted! But there's still a long way to go on the road to the manga stars.

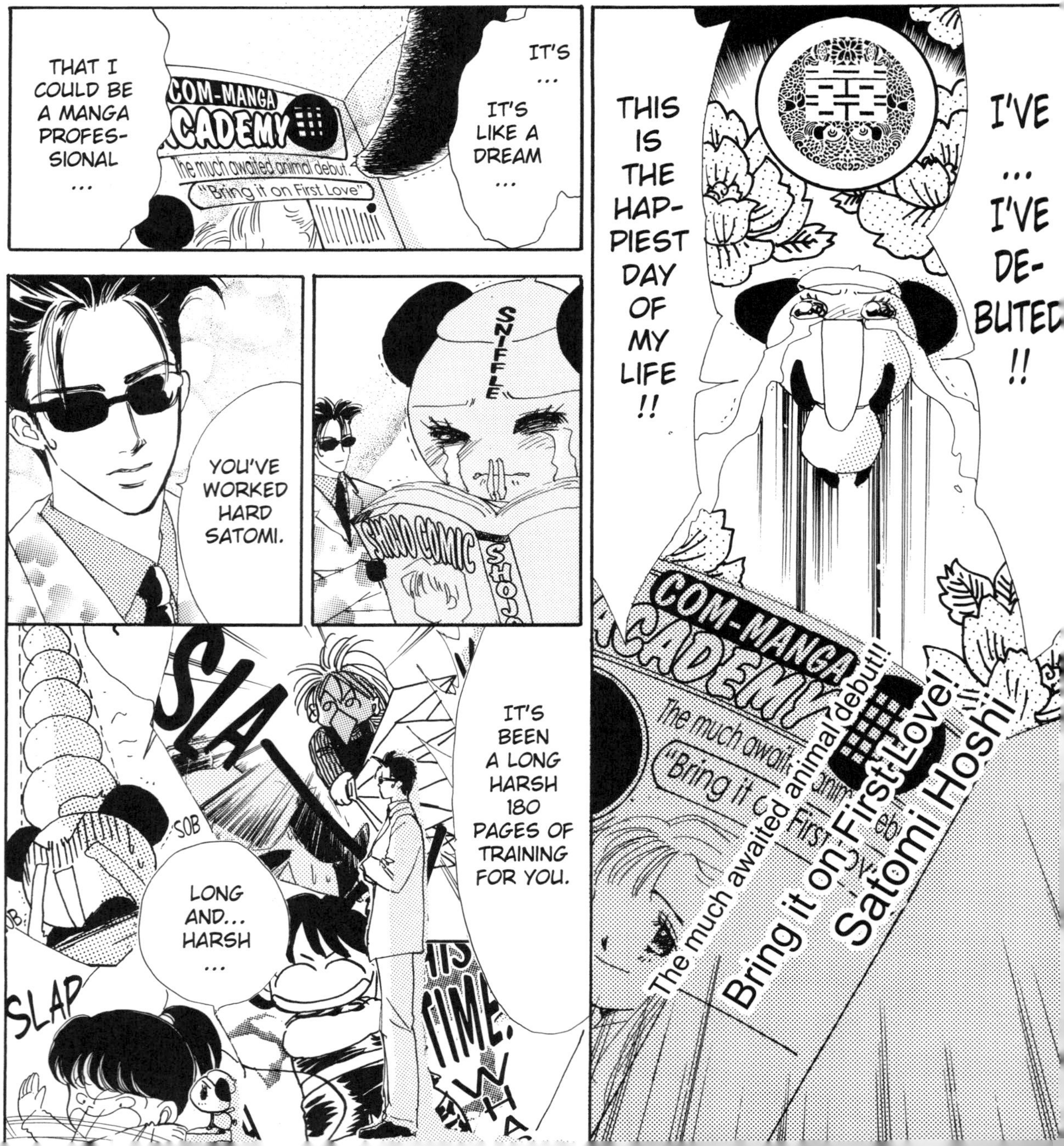
I'VE ... I'VE DE-BUTED !!
THIS IS THE HAP-PIEST DAY OF MY LIFE !!
COM-MANGA ACADEMY
The much awaited animal debut!!
Bring it on First Love!
Satomi Hoshi
IT'S ... IT'S LIKE A DREAM ...
THAT I COULD BE A MANGA PROFES-SIONAL ...
COM-MANGA ACADEMY
The much awaited animal debut.
"Bring it on First Love"
SNIFFLE
SHOJO COMIC
YOU'VE WORKED HARD SATOMI.
IT'S BEEN A LONG HARSH 180 PAGES OF TRAINING FOR YOU.
SLA
LONG AND... HARSH ...
SOB
SLAP

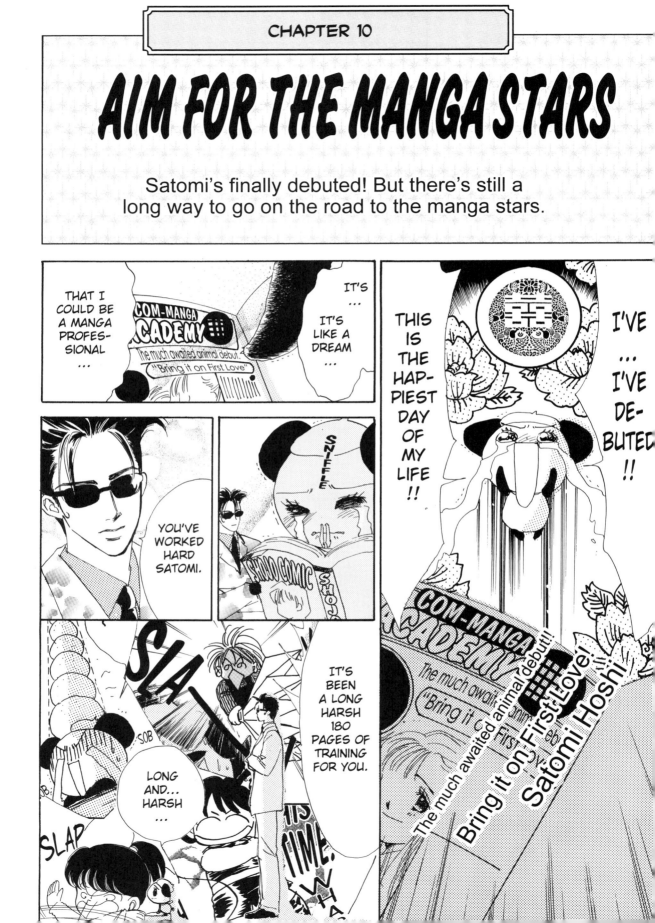

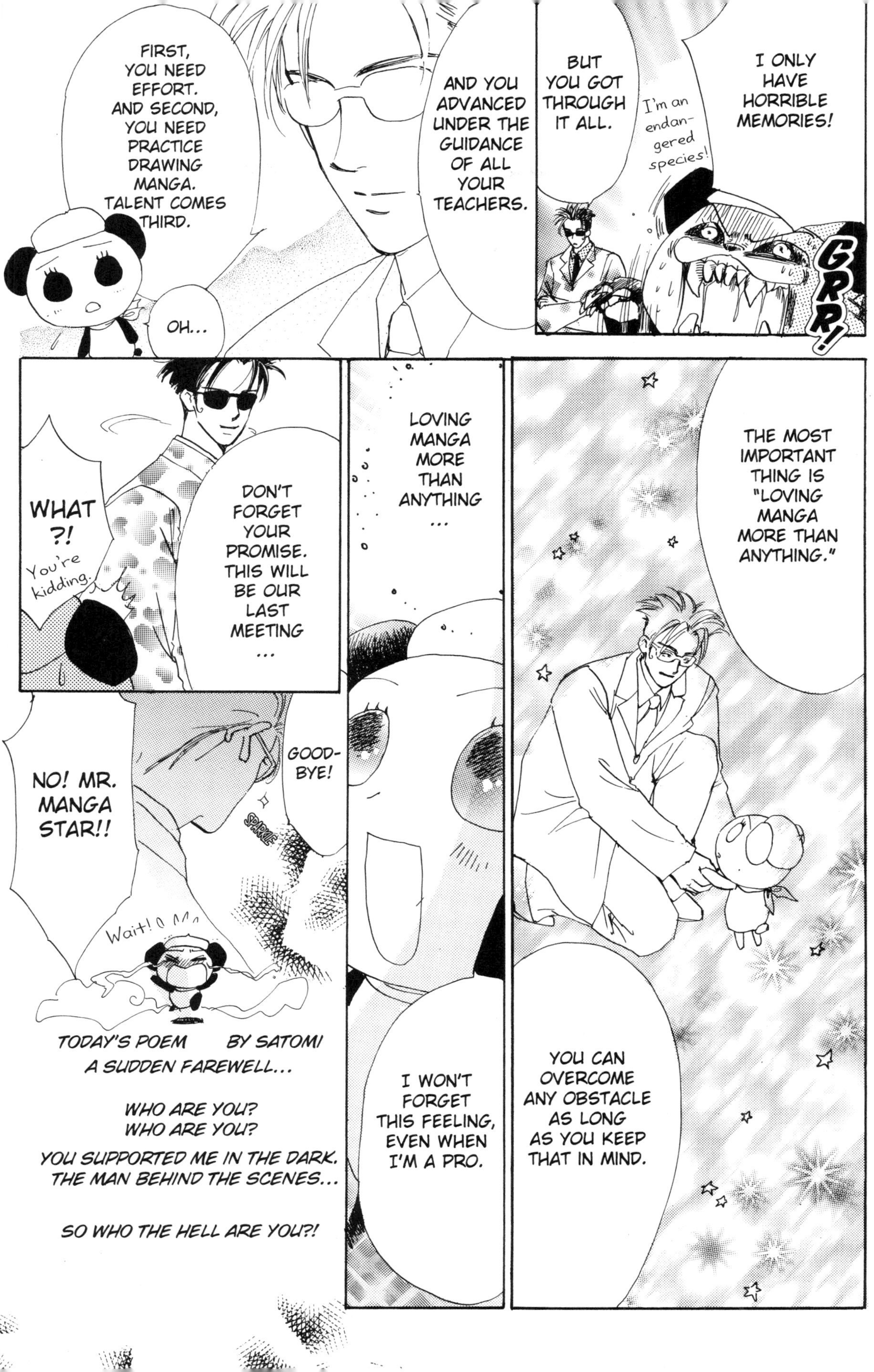
I ONLY HAVE HORRIBLE MEMORIES!
I'm an endangered species!
BUT YOU GOT THROUGH IT ALL.
GRR!
AND YOU ADVANCED UNDER THE GUIDANCE OF ALL YOUR TEACHERS.
FIRST, YOU NEED EFFORT. AND SECOND, YOU NEED PRACTICE DRAWING MANGA. TALENT COMES THIRD.
OH...
THE MOST IMPORTANT THING IS "LOVING MANGA MORE THAN ANYTHING."
YOU CAN OVERCOME ANY OBSTACLE AS LONG AS YOU KEEP THAT IN MIND.
LOVING MANGA MORE THAN ANYTHING...
I WON'T FORGET THIS FEELING, EVEN WHEN I'M A PRO.
DON'T FORGET YOUR PROMISE. THIS WILL BE OUR LAST MEETING...
WHAT?!
You're kidding.
GOOD-BYE!
SPARKLE
NO! MR. MANGA STAR!!
Wait!
TODAY'S POEM BY SATOMI
A SUDDEN FAREWELL...
WHO ARE YOU?
WHO ARE YOU?
YOU SUPPORTED ME IN THE DARK.
THE MAN BEHIND THE SCENES...
SO WHO THE HELL ARE YOU?!

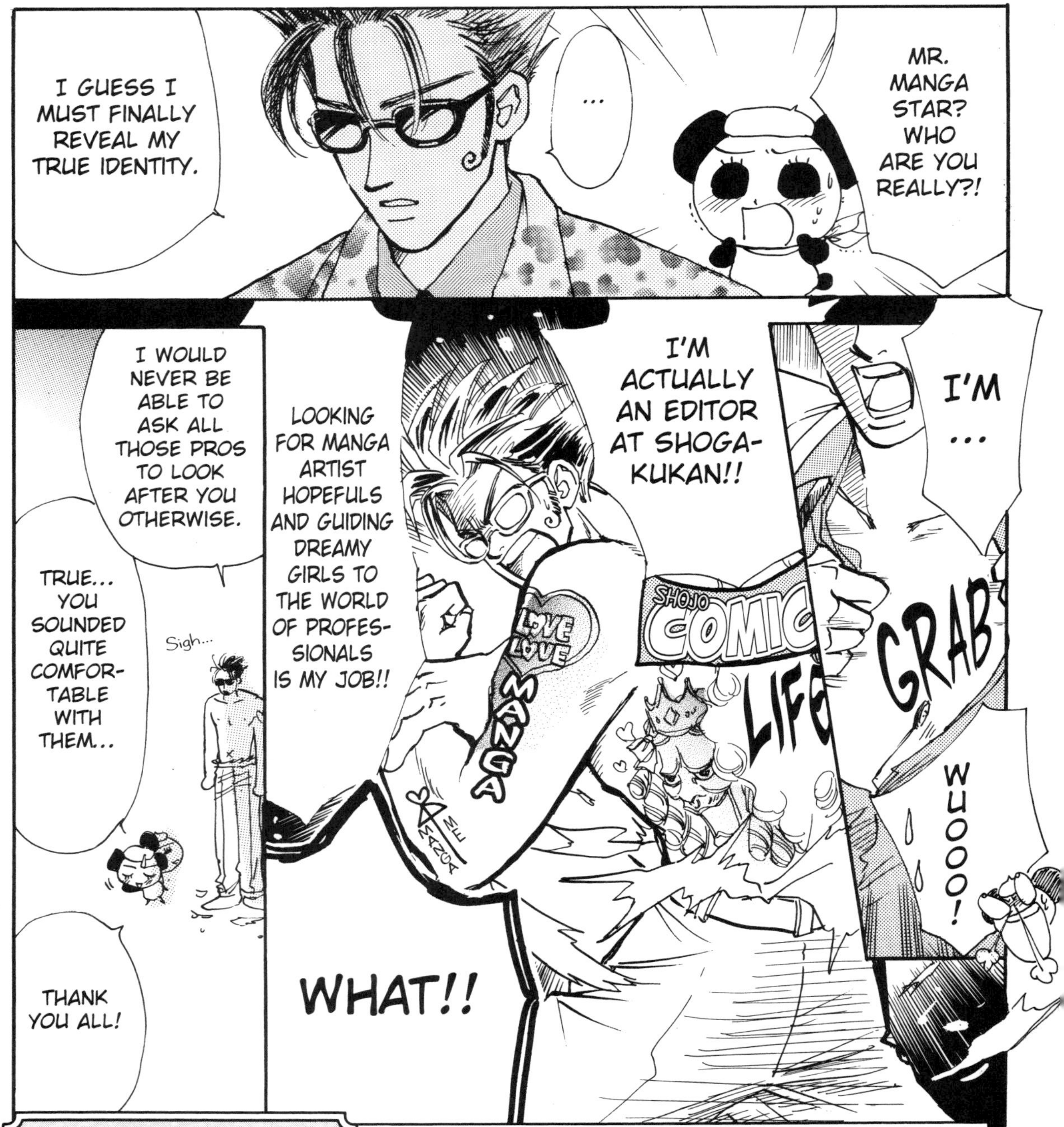
MR. MANGA STAR? WHO ARE YOU REALLY?!
...
I GUESS I MUST FINALLY REVEAL MY TRUE IDENTITY.
I'M ...
GRAB
WUOOOO!
I'M ACTUALLY AN EDITOR AT SHOGAKUKAN!!
SHOJO COMIC
LIFE
LOVE LOVE
MANGA
LOOKING FOR MANGA ARTIST HOPEFULS AND GUIDING DREAMY GIRLS TO THE WORLD OF PROFESSIONALS IS MY JOB!!
WHAT!!
I WOULD NEVER BE ABLE TO ASK ALL THOSE PROS TO LOOK AFTER YOU OTHERWISE.
TRUE... YOU SOUNDED QUITE COMFORTABLE WITH THEM...
Sigh...
THANK YOU ALL!

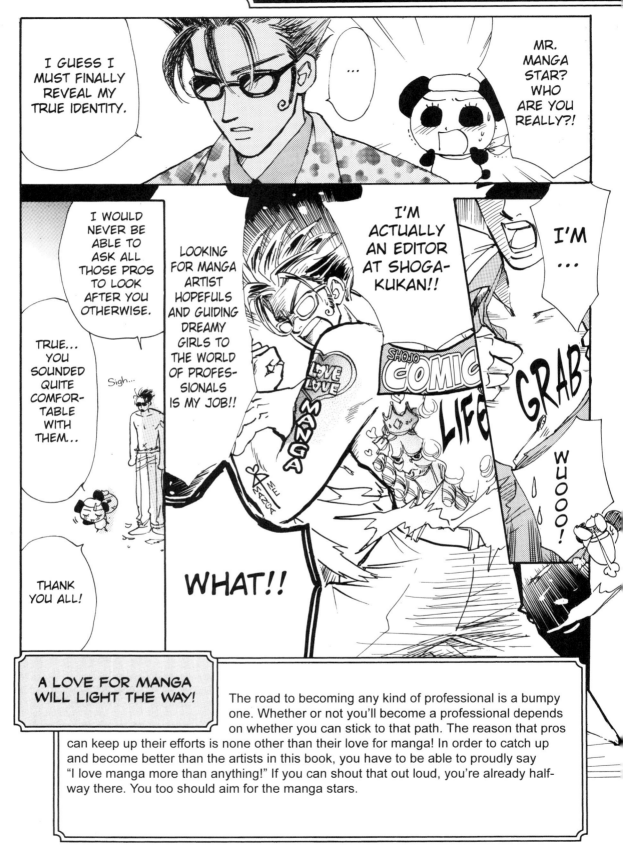

A LOVE FOR MANGA WILL LIGHT THE WAY!

The road to becoming any kind of professional is a bumpy one. Whether or not you'll become a professional depends on whether you can stick to that path. The reason that pros can keep up their efforts is none other than their love for manga! In order to catch up and become better than the artists in this book, you have to be able to proudly say "I love manga more than anything!" If you can shout that out loud, you're already half-way there. You too should aim for the manga stars.

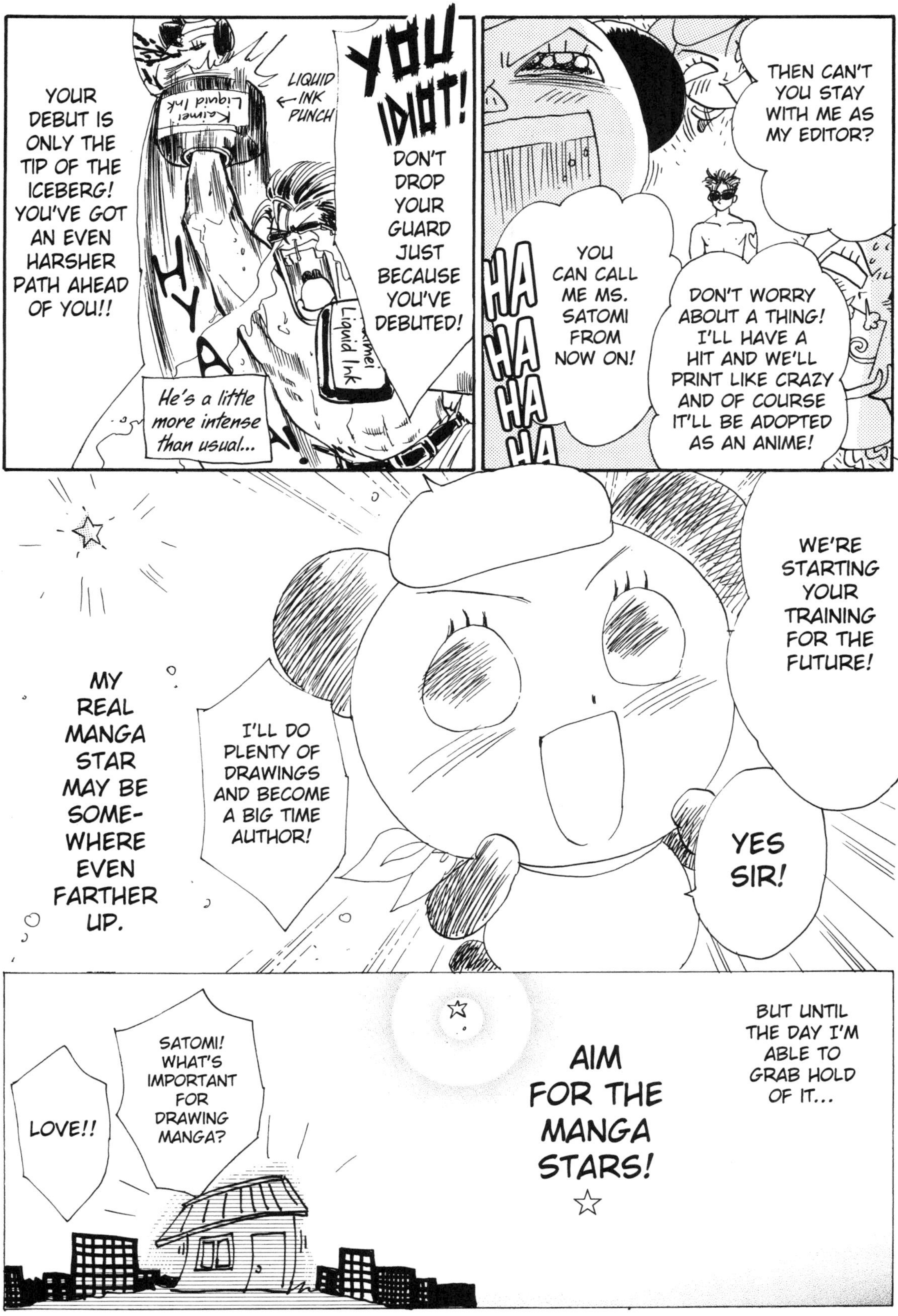
THEN CAN'T YOU STAY WITH ME AS MY EDITOR?
DON'T WORRY ABOUT A THING! I'LL HAVE A HIT AND WE'LL PRINT LIKE CRAZY AND OF COURSE IT'LL BE ADOPTED AS AN ANIME!
YOU CAN CALL ME MS. SATOMI FROM NOW ON!
HA HA HA HA HA
YOU IDIOT!
LIQUID INK PUNCH
Kaimei Liquid Ink
DON'T DROP YOUR GUARD JUST BECAUSE YOU'VE DEBUTED!
YOUR DEBUT IS ONLY THE TIP OF THE ICEBERG! YOU'VE GOT AN EVEN HARSHER PATH AHEAD OF YOU!!
He's a little more intense than usual...
WE'RE STARTING YOUR TRAINING FOR THE FUTURE!
YES SIR!
I'LL DO PLENTY OF DRAWINGS AND BECOME A BIG TIME AUTHOR!
MY REAL MANGA STAR MAY BE SOMEWHERE EVEN FARTHER UP.
BUT UNTIL THE DAY I'M ABLE TO GRAB HOLD OF IT...
AIM FOR THE MANGA STARS! ☆
SATOMI! WHAT'S IMPORTANT FOR DRAWING MANGA?
LOVE!!

SATOMI'S SUBMISSION DIARIES

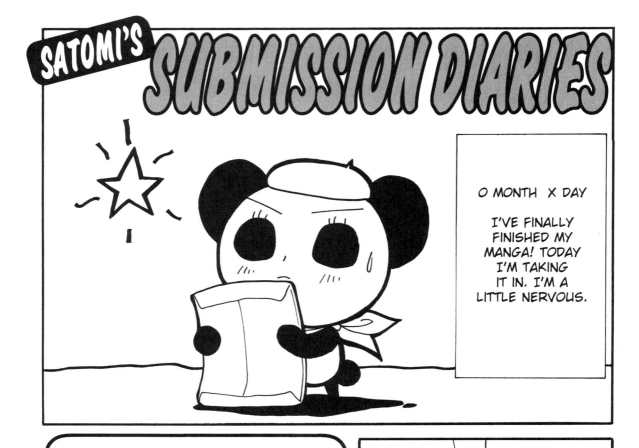

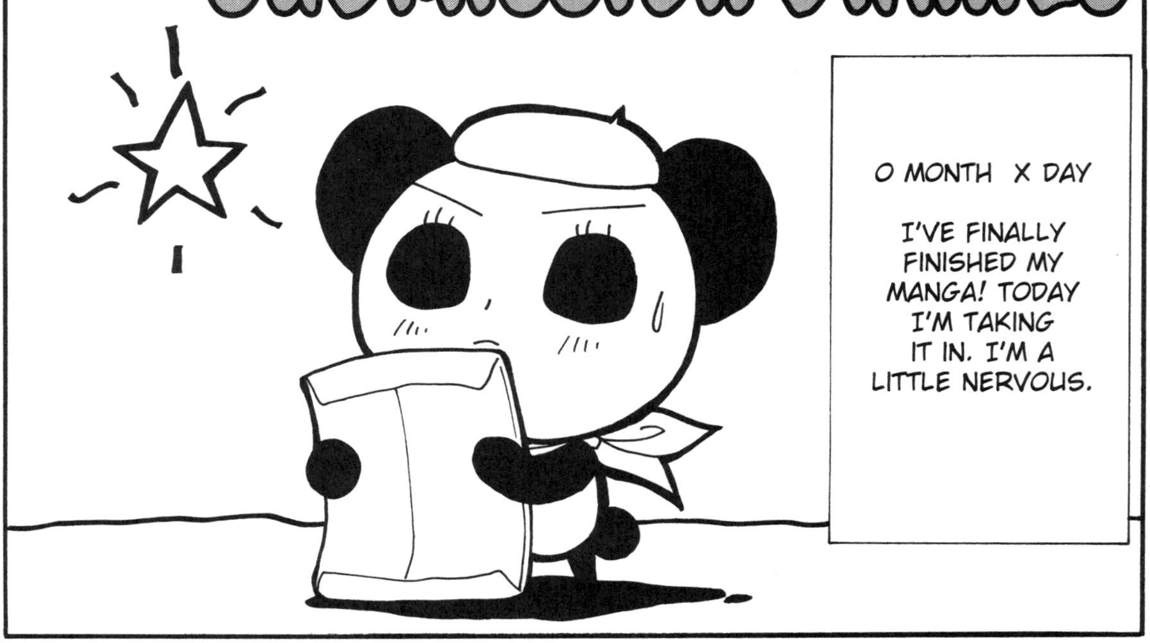
O MONTH X DAY
I'VE FINALLY FINISHED MY MANGA! TODAY I'M TAKING IT IN. I'M A LITTLE NERVOUS.

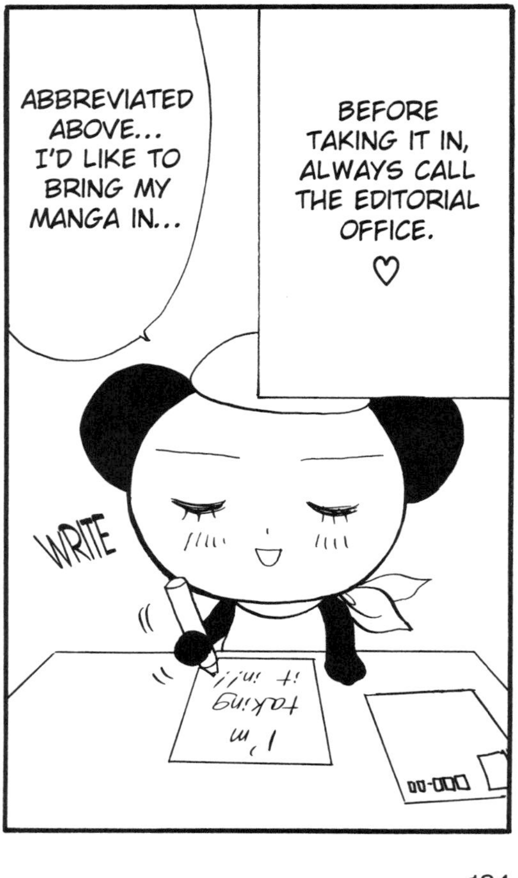
BEFORE TAKING IT IN, ALWAYS CALL THE EDITORIAL OFFICE. ♡
ABBREVIATED ABOVE... I'D LIKE TO BRING MY MANGA IN...
WRITE
I'm taking it in!!

YOU'RE A LITTLE OFF! MANGA STAR'S CRITIQUE CORNER

Wait a second!! Make sure you always call in your appointments. Give them 2 or 3 dates that you can go in and ask them what works best for them. Don't forget to take down the name of editor that you talked to on the phone. You'll have to write his/her name down when you go to Shogakukan!

Best of luck!!

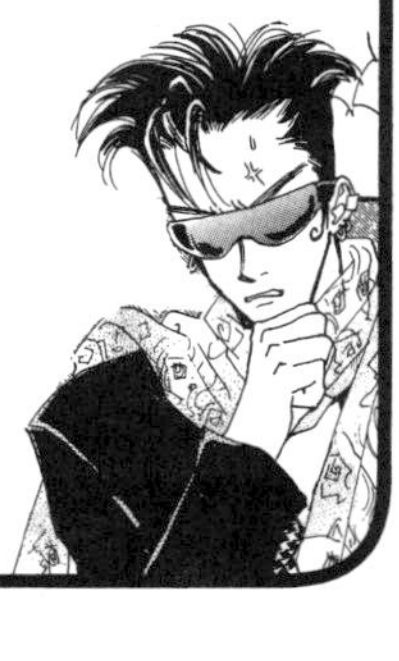

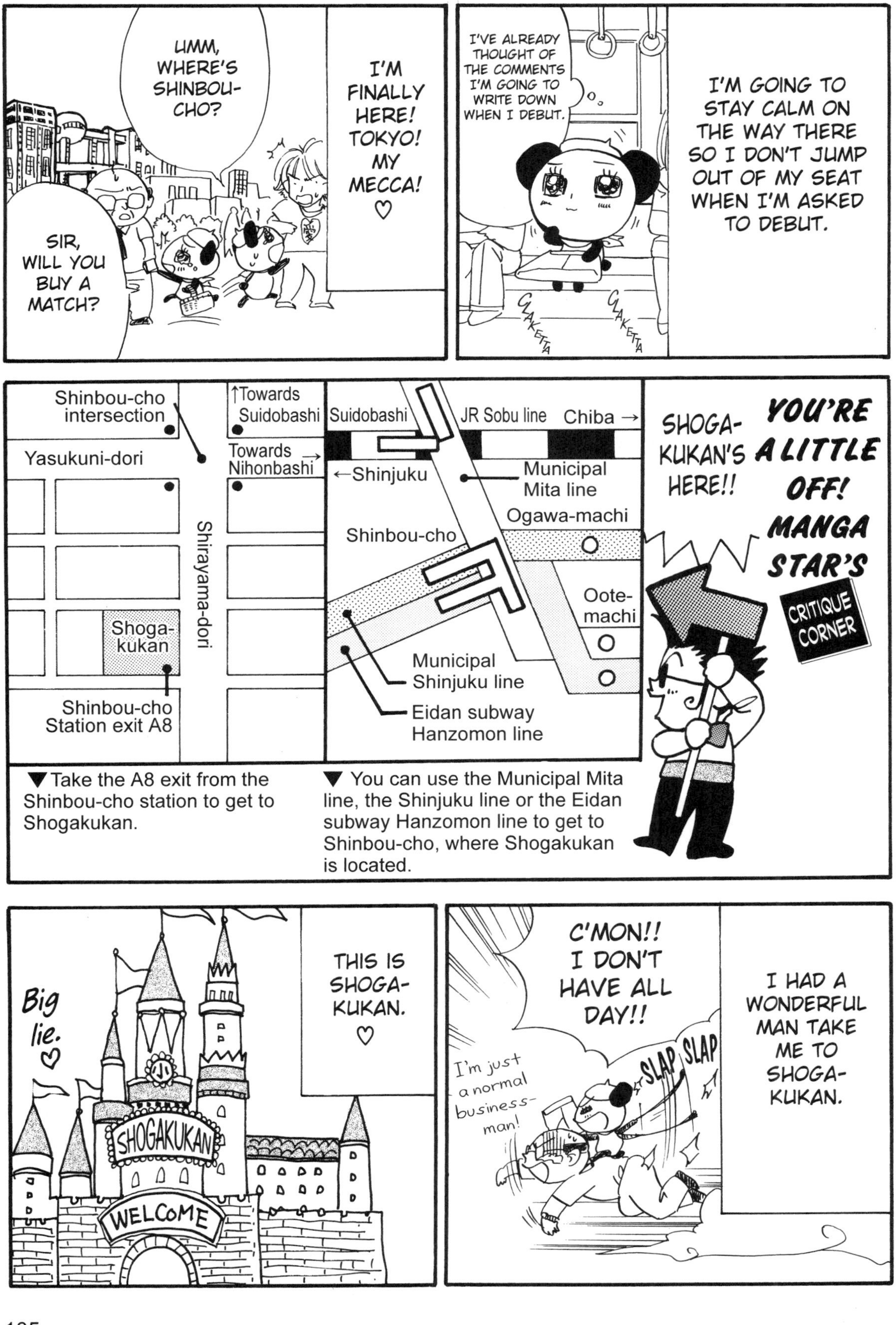
I'M GOING TO STAY CALM ON THE WAY THERE SO I DON'T JUMP OUT OF MY SEAT WHEN I'M ASKED TO DEBUT.
I'VE ALREADY THOUGHT OF THE COMMENTS I'M GOING TO WRITE DOWN WHEN I DEBUT.
CLAKETTA
CLAKETTA
I'M FINALLY HERE! TOKYO! MY MECCA! ♡
UMM, WHERE'S SHINBOU-CHO?
SIR, WILL YOU BUY A MATCH?
YOU'RE A LITTLE OFF! MANGA STAR'S
CRITIQUE CORNER
SHOGA-KUKAN'S HERE!!
Suidobashi
JR Sobu line
Chiba →
←Shinjuku
Municipal Mita line
Ogawa-machi
Shinbou-cho
Oote-machi
Municipal Shinjuku line
Eidan subway Hanzomon line
▼ You can use the Municipal Mita line, the Shinjuku line or the Eidan subway Hanzomon line to get to Shinbou-cho, where Shogakukan is located.
Shinbou-cho intersection
↑Towards Suidobashi
Towards Nihonbashi →
Yasukuni-dori
Shirayama-dori
Shoga-kukan
Shinbou-cho Station exit A8
▼ Take the A8 exit from the Shinbou-cho station to get to Shogakukan.
I HAD A WONDERFUL MAN TAKE ME TO SHOGA-KUKAN.
C'MON!! I DON'T HAVE ALL DAY!!
SLAP SLAP
I'm just a normal business-man!
THIS IS SHOGA-KUKAN. ♡
Big lie. ♡
SHOGAKUKAN
WELCOME

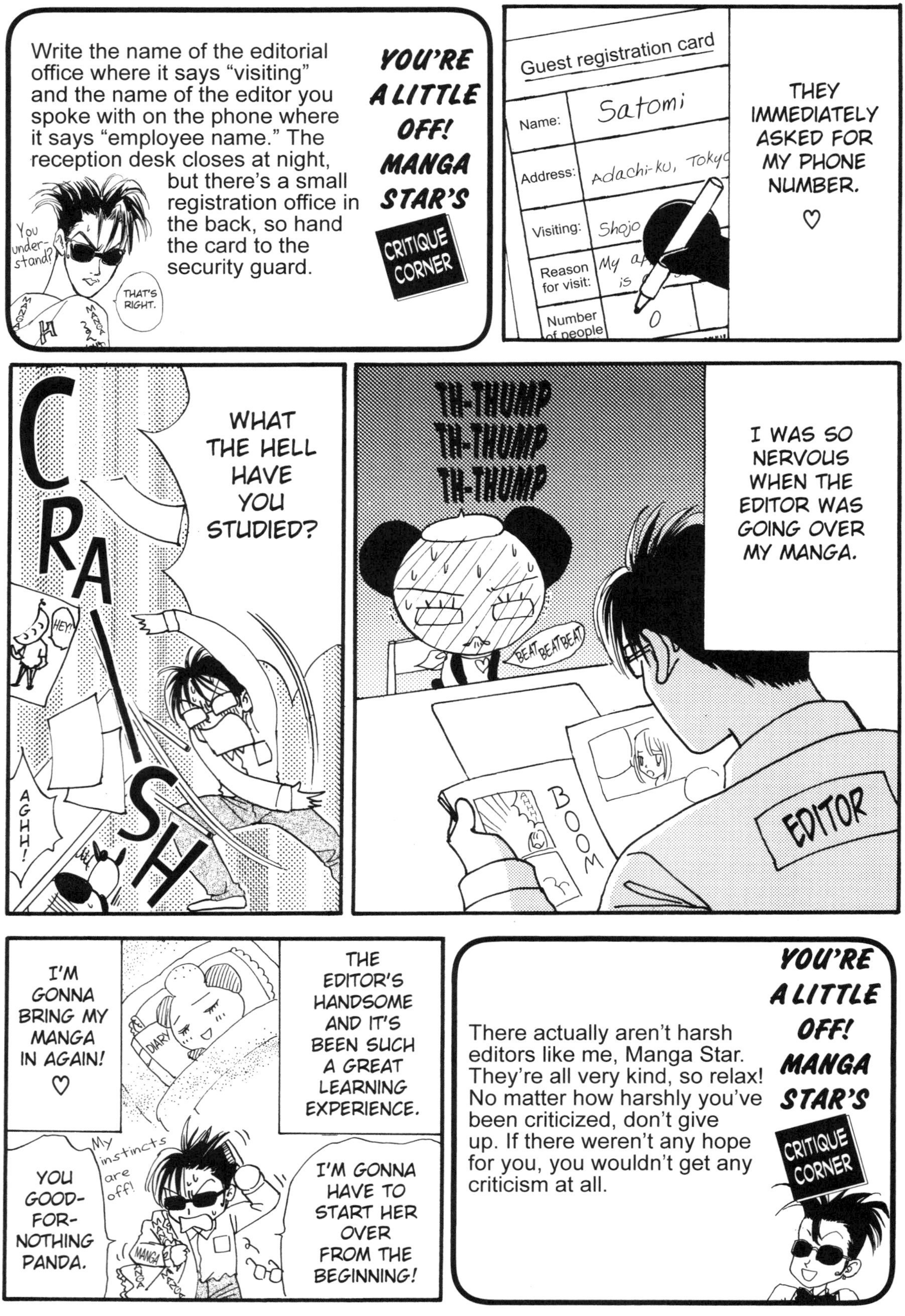
Guest registration card
Name:
Satomi
Address:
Adachi-ku, Toky
Visiting:
Shojo
Reason for visit:
Number of people
THEY IMMEDIATELY ASKED FOR MY PHONE NUMBER. ♡
YOU'RE A LITTLE OFF! MANGA STAR'S
CRITIQUE CORNER
Write the name of the editorial office where it says "visiting" and the name of the editor you spoke with on the phone where it says "employee name." The reception desk closes at night, but there's a small registration office in the back, so hand the card to the security guard.
You understand?
THAT'S RIGHT.
I WAS SO NERVOUS WHEN THE EDITOR WAS GOING OVER MY MANGA.
TH-THUMP TH-THUMP TH-THUMP
BEAT BEAT BEAT
BOOM
EDITOR
WHAT THE HELL HAVE YOU STUDIED?
CRASH
HEY!
AGHH!
YOU'RE A LITTLE OFF! MANGA STAR'S
CRITIQUE CORNER
There actually aren't harsh editors like me, Manga Star. They're all very kind, so relax! No matter how harshly you've been criticized, don't give up. If there weren't any hope for you, you wouldn't get any criticism at all.
THE EDITOR'S HANDSOME AND IT'S BEEN SUCH A GREAT LEARNING EXPERIENCE.
I'M GONNA BRING MY MANGA IN AGAIN! ♡
DIARY
I'M GONNA HAVE TO START HER OVER FROM THE BEGINNING!
My instincts are off!
YOU GOOD-FOR-NOTHING PANDA.

Important Information!

Invaluable Data for Shojo Manga Artists

Which tools is that artist using? We surveyed all our popular featured manga artists and came up with an incredible database!

What do you use for your...

1: Pencil **2:** Paper **3:** Pen nib **4:** Pen holder **5:** Drawing ink **6:** Eraser **7:** Fill ink **8:** Fill brush **9:** White ink **10:** White ink brush **11:** Screen tone **12:** Ruler **13:** Curve template **14:** Color method **15:** Coloring brush **16:** Paper for color pages **17:** Work station **18:** Other special tools

circle-type 600P. It's a circle cutter and you can move the blade end.

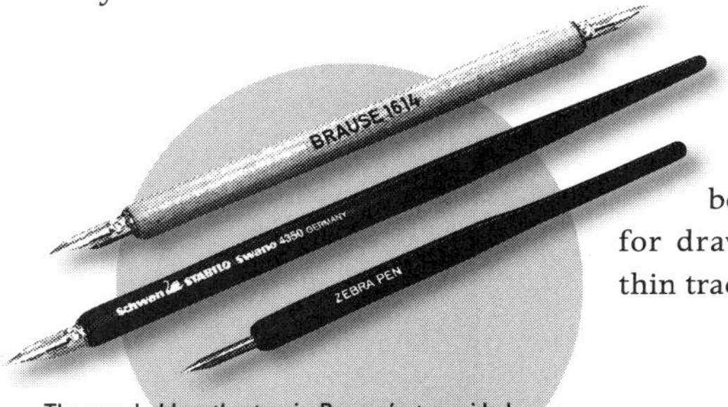
BRAUSE 1614
ZEBRA PEN

The pen holder—the top is Brause's two-sided pen holder followed by Stabilo's wooden pen holder and Zebra's crow quill pen holder. The crow quill pen holders are different depending on the manufacturer, so be careful. We recommend wooden ones for user friendliness.

Shoko Akira—Sekai ha Kitto Kimi no Mono (Betsucomi)

1: A 0.5 mm mechanical pencil with HB and light blue lead. **2:** IC Manga paper, 100 lb. 3: Zebra G and crow quill pen. I use the G-pen for most of the characters and the crow quill pen for the background and details. **4:** A wooden one. I don't know the manufacturer. **5:** Kaimei Liquid Ink. **6:** AIR-IN **7:** Kaimei Liquid Ink **8:** A long thin brush. **9:** Dr. Martin's BP white ink **10:** A normal long thin brush. **11:** IC Comic and Design screen tones. **12:** 30 cm **13:** Probably Staedtler set of three. **14:** Dr. Martin. **15:** I have about five, but the one I use the most is the one that elementary school kids use a lot;

I use Illustrator, Photoshop and Painter as my software. **15:** I use two medium-fine brushes, one thick one and about two thin ones. **16:** I only use Crescent boards. **17:** I use a tilted table for drawing and the Fuji Color's thin tracing light box.

Wakuni Akisato—Shocking Pink Sky (Betsucomi)

1: Mitsubishi Uni's H leaded pencil. **2:** IC Manga paper, 100 lb. **3:** Main lines are done with the Zebra G, and hair, face and background are done with the Zebra crow quill pen. **4:** I use a normal G-pen holder. **5:** MAXON's COMIC INK. **6:** MONO **7:** I use a PILOT brush pen, Pentel's brush pen and COPiC's multi-liner brush. **10:** Too's Tamage brush2. **11:** I use J-tones, Deleter and IC for gradation and designs. I also use Letra set 61, 71, 81 and 1211 as well as IC 41. **12:** 24 cm one for backgrounds and a 30 cm for borders. **13:** Staedtler set of three. **14:** Dr. Martin, but Holbein for the eyes and hair. I use MAXON Comic Ink's sepia color for the main lines. **15:** I use coloring brush #1. **16:** I use BB Kent's rougher paper. **17:** I put a plastic B3 board on a 30 degree angled desk. **18:** LT cutter's

Start Here

Miki Aihara – Hot Gimmick (Betsucomi)

1: 0.5 mechanical pencil. (lead B) **2:** IC Manga paper, 100 lb. **3:** Zebra G, School, Nikko crow quill pen. I use the G, School and Nikko crow quill pen for people, and the Zebra crow quill pen for backgrounds. **4:** I don't have any in particular. I just try different ones they have at the store. **5:** I'm a loyal Kaimei fan. **6**: I use MONO. **7:** I use Kaimei and Prockey, etc. **8:** A long thin brush. **9:** I use Dr. Martin's BP (bleed proof) for delicate parts along with Misnon. **10:** I just use a normal long thin brush. **11:** I use IC

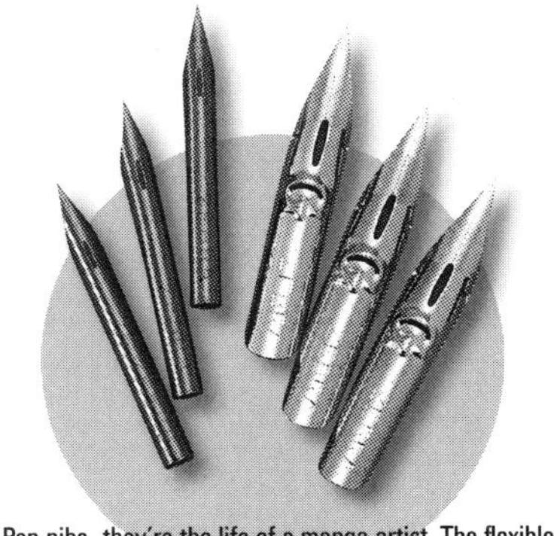

Pen nibs—they're the life of a manga artist. The flexible G-pens are on the right and the delicate crow quill pens are on the left. They're both made by Zebra.

screen tones and comic screen tones, design screens, Deleter, J-tones, and MAXONs. I use IC 60 and 939 often. **12:** 30 and 50 cm. **13:** Staedtler set of three and various others. **14:** Dr. Martin Ink. But I've also been using Mac these days.

Pentel's neo-sable brush. **16:** BB Kent, Canson paper and Crescent board 310. **17:** I put down a magazine and add an angle with cartons.

Hinako Ashibara–MiSS (Betsucomi)

1: A pencil with F lead. (I use a HB 0.5 mm mechanical pencil for backgrounds.) **2:** IC Manga paper, 100 lb. **3:** Zebra G and Nikko's crow quill pen. (I do the face, the background and accessories with a crow quill pen.) **4:** I don't know who the manufacturer is. (Single-ended with a circular cross-section.) The crow quill penholder is made by Nikko. **5:** Pilot drawing ink. **6:** MONO. **7:** Markers and Pilot's drawing ink. **8:** A long thin brush and Pentel's brush pen. **9:** Dr. Martin's BP white ink, but I get almost everything done with

ink
PILOT

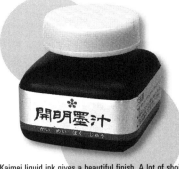

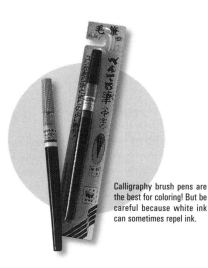

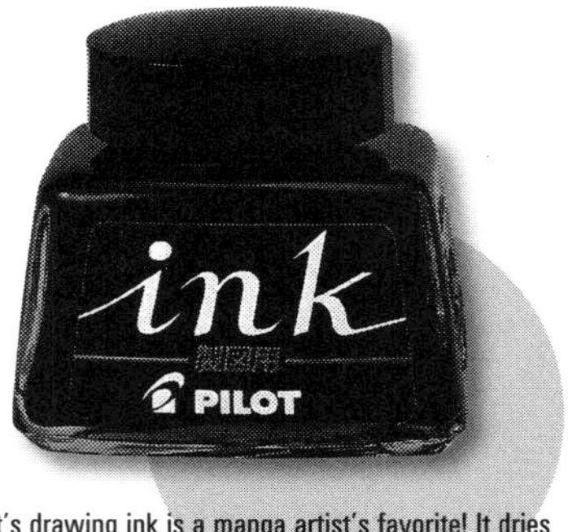

Pilot's drawing ink is a manga artist's favorite! It dries quickly but it's not very water resistant so it doesn't work well for color scripts.

Pentel's correction fluid. **11:** Mainly IC 10, 30, 00, 61 and 154. But I also mix it up with screens from Design, Deleter, Letra and MAXON. **12:** 15 and 30 cm. **13:** Staedtler set of three. **14:** Mainly colored inks (Dr. Martin), but I also sometimes use watercolors, acrylics, color sprays, colored pencils and screen tones. **15:** I have two or three that I use for the most part, but the one I use the most is the thinnest long brush. **16:** Canson board. **17:** I do the rough draft and screen tones on an angled tracing light box and for

開明墨汁
かい めい ぼく じゅう

Kaimei liquid ink gives a beautiful finish. A lot of shojo manga artists use liquid ink for inking.

inking, I prop a board on a magazine and do it there.

Yuna Anisaki–LUV ~Ai toka, koi toka (Sho-Comi)

1: When my hand's feeling good I use a 0.5 mm mechanical pencil with B or 2B lead. When my hand's tired... I use a normal pencil. Uni's 2B because it's soft. **2:** IC Manga paper, 100 lb. **3:** Zebra crow quill pen; I have three stages that pens go through. Brand new. A little used, slightly thicker lines. Well used, really thick lines, garbage. Those are the three pens I use. **4:** Zebra's wooden holder **5:** Kaimei liquid ink. My assistants use Kaimei's drawing ink, which apparently dries quicker so it's a better fit for hasty work and heavy sweaters. **6:** I use the plastic eraser they sell at the convenience store. I also would never do a rough draft without a kneaded eraser. **7:** I do hair and shiny coloring with Pentel's brush pen, the one that has a sponge-like tip. I also use thick felt pens and markers. **8:** Pentel's brush pen. When I want a brush feel (bristly) I use Pentel's brush pen with the light blue cap. **9:** I alternate between white ink by Dr. Martin and Misnon (red label, blue label and FLO-II), depending on my mood. Misnon's white ink repels the ink from brush pens though, so I use Dr. Martin for those pages.

10: I use Shirokatsura's thinnest one. **11:** The ones I use the most are Deleter's SE 0, 30, 40, 50 and 56. I usually buy whatever I can get my hands on, though. Sometimes I make originals with copy sheets. **12:** I use a 45 cm one for rough drafts and panel lines and a 20 cm one for inking. **13:** The biggest one in the Staedtler set of three. **14:** I use water with water-based color markers and whatever else is handy. Oh, and I use Holbein's black or grey for the main lines. **15:** I use a big long thin brush and mid-sized brushes that say "Seisen" on it. **16:** I use Muse's Canson board and Watson paper. **17:** I put a tracing board on my lap and sit on a legless chair. **18:** My assistants have taught me things like, "you should use a pencil and an eraser by the same manufacturer" and "putting a tone on a template and using the needle part of a compass lets you cut the tone circularly." I'm still learning...

Yukako Iizuka–Luna ☾ Lunatic (Ciao)

1: I use a mechanical 0.3 mm B leaded pencil. **2:** Art Color's script paper, 10 lb. **3:** Zebra G and crow quill pen; I use the G-pen for the character's main lines and the crow quill pen for the hair, eyes, and background. **4:** I break cheap plastic penholders for my G-pens

Calligraphy brush pens are the best for coloring! But be careful because white ink can sometimes repel ink.

← *Read this way*

5: Pilot drawing ink. 6: MONO. **7:** Pentel's postcard brush pen. **9:** Dr. Martin's BP white ink and Pentel's correction fluid. **10:** A long thin brush. **11:** IC, J-tones, Deleter, MAXON comic patterns, but I mainly use IC 61. **12:** 20 cm. **14:** Dr. Martin. **15:** A small round brush, a medium and large flat brush; a total of three brushes. **16:** Canson board. **17:** I stack magazines and create an incline.

Miyuki Oobayashi–Kirakira Labyrinth (Ciao)

1: 0.5 mm mechanical pencil with B/HB lead. **2:** IC Manga paper, 100 lb. **3:** Zebra crow quill pen (the hard one). **4:** I put duct tape on when I need it to be bigger. **5:** liquid ink. **6:** MONO; my assistant uses Staedtler. (Apparently MONO's too soft for erasing the entire page.) **7:** Pentel's brush pen. **9:** COPiC's Opaque White. **10:** A long thin brush that costs about $10. **11:** IC, Deleter, MAXON, J-tones etc. I use Letra's Comic tone C4 and C1 a lot. **12:** A 30 cm ruler for the panel lines and a 15 cm one for the backgrounds and flash effects. **13:** I use three of ORAPRS's No. E108s. **14:** Mainly Dr. Martin and Luma colored inks; I use COPiC for contrast and the details. I also use Sakura's waterproof red and their ballpoint pens as well. And soft pastels. I use Liquitex's white for highlighting and to even out the page a little. I sometimes use a white spray and brushes made by COPiC. **15:** Medium-sized long brush for designing; I got mine at Sekaido. **16:** Rough-textured BB Kent paper. **17:** I normally do my work at my desk but sometimes on a tracing light box. **18:** Sometimes I add mesh with a copy machine. I play around a lot. I also use copy screens.

17: A desk that can be angled... not the kind that costs hundreds of dollars, the build-it-yourself kind. **18:** I use weak adhesive tape instead of masking tape. I also use it to keep the page aligned.

Yasue Imai–Tenshi na Yatsura (Ciao)

1: 0.5 mm mechanical pencil with HB lead **2:** IC Manga paper, 100 lb. **3:** Zebra G and crow quill pen; the G-pen is generally used for the characters and the crow quill pen is for details and backgrounds. **4:** Tachikawa. **5:** Pilot drawing ink and Kaimei liquid ink. **6:** AIR-IN from PLUS. **7:** Pentel's brush pens, Sakura Micron 0.5-1.0 pens and Mackee pens. **9:** Mainly Misnon and Dr. Martin's BP white ink. **11:** IC **12:** 30 and 20 cm. **14:** Dr. Martin and acrylics; Specialized paint for airbrushing. **15:** I usually use three different sizes and a flat brush for backgrounds. **16:** Mermaid. **18:** I draw on a normal table.

Saki Oota–Kimi wa Boku no Mono (Cheese!)

1: 0.3 mm mechanical pencil with B or HB lead. **2:** IC Manga paper, 100 lb. **3:** Zebra crow quill pen (for all the main lines).

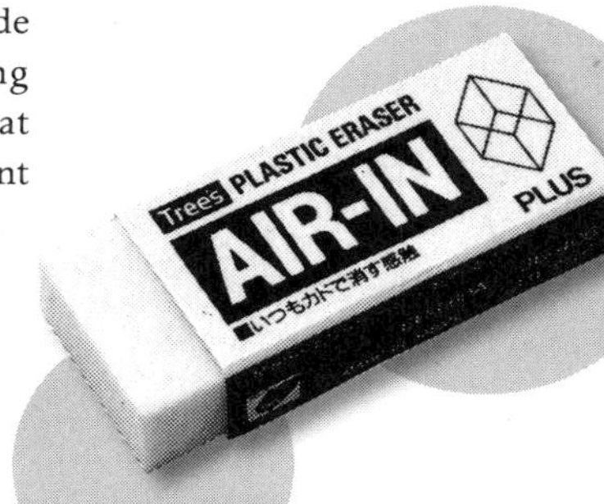
Trees PLASTIC ERASER
AIR-IN
PLUS
An eraser that many manga artists love to use. AIR-IN from PLUS is easy to use and erases well.

and use a holder for crow quill pens made by Zebra. **5:** Kaimei liquid ink. **6:** MONO's light eraser. **7:** I use a Kabura pen with two Kuretake brush pens. **9:** For corrections, I use Misnon and Dr. Martin's BP white ink (details like eyes). **10:** I use a thin sable brush. **11:** IC, Letra, Deleter, J-tones and original screens. **12:** 10-60 cm. **13:** Pantall's vortex template. **14:** I do most of my coloring on the computer, but sometimes I use COPiC markers. **16:** I use Art Color's 100 lb paper for my pictorial cuts. **17:** I stack magazines under my tracing light box so that I can draw on an angled surface.

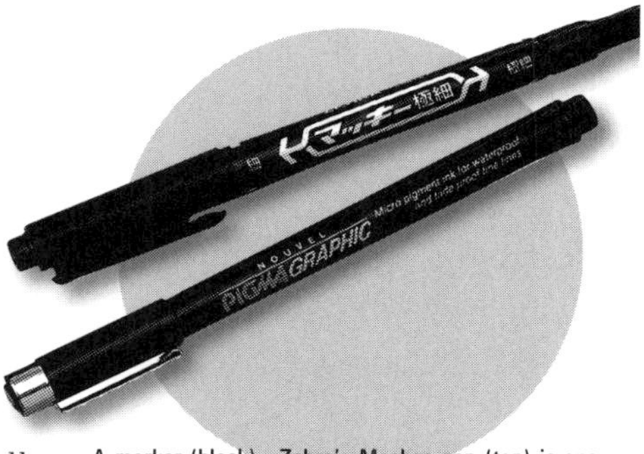
PIGMA GRAPHIC
A marker (black)– Zebra's Mackee pen (top) is one of the main oil-based pens and Sakura Color's Pigma (bottom) is an extra fine water-based marker.

Kaneyoshi Izumi–Doubt!! (Betsucomi)

1: 0.5 mm mechanical pencil (softer lead like HB). **2:** Art Color and professional Kent paper. **3:** Nikko's School crow quill pen; I use worn-down ones for characters and new ones for details. **5:** Kaimei liquid ink. **9:** Correction liquid; I basically don't use much because it gets messy. **12:** A 36 cm ruler, because a 30 cm one isn't long enough for the panel lines. **13:** I hardly use them. I use templates. **14:** COPiC, Dr. Martin and Art Pencil; Sometimes I mix acrylics with Dr. Martin, but I wouldn't recommend it. **16:** I use illustration boards because they're the cheapest.

← Read this way

Miyuki Kitagawa–Tsumi ni Nureta Futari (Cheese!)

1: 0.5 mm mechanical pencil with B or light blue lead. **2:** Art Color, 100 lb. **3:** Nikko's round pen for both characters and background. **5:** Kaimei liquid ink, Sumino hana. **6:** MONO's No Dust. **7:** Mackee. **8:** Pentel's brush pens. **9:** I use Dr. Martin's BP white ink for details along with Misnon. **10:** A long thin brush. **11:** IC, Letra, Deleter and J-tones; I usually use Letra for shadows. **12:** 30 cm. **13:** Staedtler set of three **14:** Dr. Martin and Holbein for the facial outline. **15:** I use about four brushes that vary in size and a flat brush for the background. **16:** Muse's Canson boards. **17:** I put a sketchbook on top of stacked magazines to create an angle.

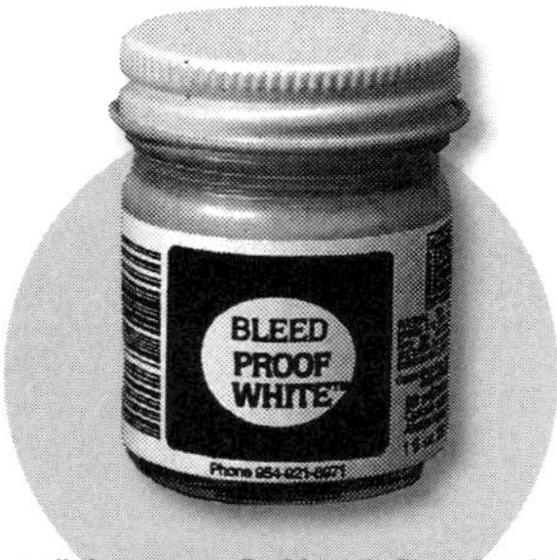
BLEED
PROOF
WHITE

Almost all the pros use Dr. Martin's Bleed Proof White Ink. It's smooth and easy to use!

(I consistently use 51 of them.) **12:** 30 cm. **13:** Staedtler set of three. **14:** Dr. Martin's colored ink and COPiC markers. **15:** About three of them that vary in size. **16:** Canson boards. **17:** I use cartons to give an angle after stacking magazines.

Yuuki Obata–Sukikirai Suki (Betsucomi)

1: 0.5 mm mechanical pencil with B lead. **2:** Art Color script paper. **3:** Zebra G to outline people's faces and the Zebra crow quill pen for hair, eyes and background. **4:** Brause's double end penholder with round cross section. **5:** I use both Kaimei liquid ink and Pilot drawing ink. **6:** MONO (the bigger one). **7:** Kaimei liquid ink **8:** I put Kaimei liquid ink on brush pens that have run out of ink. It's nice that there's a cap and you don't have to wash it each time. **9:** Pentel's correction fluid and white Milky pens for details. **11:** I use Comic screen tones #1 for brighter shadows and I use Design 40 for darker ones. **14:** Dr. Martin, but I add water to water-based markers for contrasting skin tones, pinks, and oranges. **16:** Canson boards and Kent boards. **17:** I put a dictionary under an already angled tracing light box to angle it even more.

Kazumi Ooya–Yume Chu (Betsucomi)

1: 0.5 mm mechanical pencil with HB lead. **2:** KMK Kent, 100 lb or IC Manga paper. **3:** I use Zebra's school pen for the main lines and the Zebra crow quill pen for the face and the hair. **4:** Something that's cushioned with a bigger grip. **5:** Pilot drawing ink. **6:** MONO. **7:** Pentel's brush pen (for coloring hair) and Uni's POSCA markers. **9:** Misnon. **11:** The Letra set (1208, 1212 etc.), Deleter, IC (60s and 80s), Design; I think I use over 100 of them. **12:** A ruled 30 cm ruler. **13:** Rotring's three-piece set and templates. **14:** Dr. Martin and COPiC. **15:** I use a medium-fine brush for almost everything. **16:** BB Kent board (natural fine texture). **17:** I place a board on a thick book to give it an angle and draw on that.

Aya Oda–Magic Tower Pass (Sho-Comi)

1: 0.5 mm mechanical pencil etc. **2:** 100 lb manga paper. **3:** A crow quill pen. **5:** liquid ink. **6:** I use anything. **7:** Brush pens etc. **12:** 45 cm. **13:** Staedtler set of three. **14:** Colored inks etc. **15:** 2-3 thin to thick brushes. **16:** Canson paper.

Chie Shinohara–Sorawa Akai Kawa no Hotori (Sho-Comi)

1: 0.3 mm mechanical pencil with 2B lead. **2:** 110 High quality paper; I special order them with borderlines. **3:** I only use the Nume pen from Tachikawa except when I use the Zebra crow quill pen for backgrounds. **4:** Caran d'Ache 114. (If anyone knows of a place in Japan where they sell these, please let me know.) **5:** liquid ink. **6:** Dust Free by PLUS. **7:** Pentel's brush pens. **9:** Dr. Martin's BP white ink.

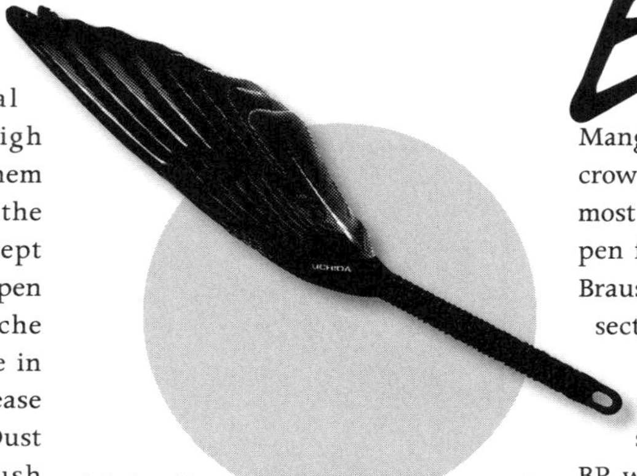

A feathered broom can be very useful. You can get rid of eraser and screen scraps without ruining your page.

Eriko Ono–Kocchi Muite!! Miiko (Ciao)

1: 0.5 mm mechanical pencil with B lead. **2:** IC Manga paper, 100 lb. **3:** Zebra G and crow quill pens. (I use the G-pen for most of the characters and the round pen for details and background.) **4:** Brause's double end penholder; cross section is round. **5:** Kaimei drawing sol. **6:** AIR-IN by PLUS. **7:** Kaimei liquid ink. **8:** Too's script brush. **9:** I use Luma's BP white ink for details as well as Misnon. **11:** IC and the Letra set.

Masami Takeuchi–+1 (Plus one) (Sho-Comi)

1: 0.5 mm mechanical pencil with B lead. **2:** IC Manga paper, 100 lb. **3:** Zebra G and crow quill pen; the G-pen is for thick lines and I do everything else with the crow quill pen. **4:** I use a wooden penholder for my G-pen and a plastic one for my crow quill pen. **5:** Kaimei liquid ink. **6:** MONO's No Dust. **7:** Pentel's brush pen. **9:** SAM COMIC WHITE. **11:** I use IC 61 & 21 the most and the rest is sort of random. **12:** A 40 and 20 cm one. **13:** Rotring's three-piece set. **14:** I use Holbein's grey ink for lines and Dr. Martin for coloring. **15:** I use four different long brushes that are separated by color. **16:** The thicker Canson boards. **17:** The Lightin Hero. (I close it when I'm not working.) **18:** (You may know this already but...) I burn off the oil on the pen nibs.

These are the most popular three-piece curve template sets. You've pretty much got everything covered here. Make sure you get one that's beveled!

Yumi Tamura–BOX Kei! (Betsucomi)

1: 0.5 mm mechanical pencil with B lead (Adds a soft grip on a short and light one). I also use blue lead for selecting the tone. **2:** I have AH Kent 110 lb cut for me at the store. **3:** Zebra G and crow quill pens; I use the G-pen for the facial outlines and other thicker lines and the crow quill pen for finer lines

sketchbook. **17:** An angled tracing light box or on top of a cutting board.

Mayu Shinjo–Sensual Phrase (Sho-Comi)

1: 0.3 mm mechanical pencil with B lead. **2:** IC's Manga paper. **3:** I use a G-pen for my characters and the Zebra crow quill pen for the background and details. **4:** A versatile penholder (wooden). **5:** Kaimei liquid ink. **6:** AIR-IN. **7:** Pentel's brush pens (fine). **8:** Zebra's brush pens (small) and Pentel's brush pen (fine). **9:** I use Dr. Martin's BP white ink for correcting filled areas and Misnon for correcting lines. **11:** I use Letra's 1212 and 1211 for skin tones. For creases in clothes I usually use IC 51. **12:** I use a 36 cm ruler for borderlines and a 15 cm one for backgrounds. **13:** Staedtler set of three. **14:** Mainly COPiC markers, and I usually mix Dr. Martin's colored inks for skin tones. I've been using my Mac lately though. **15:** I usually have three brushes that vary in size. I also separate them by color, too. **16:** Canson Kent fine 1 mm boards. **17:** I think normal desks are too soft so I have a thick piece of glass on top of mine. I don't angle it but adjust myself with my seat.

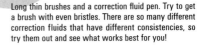

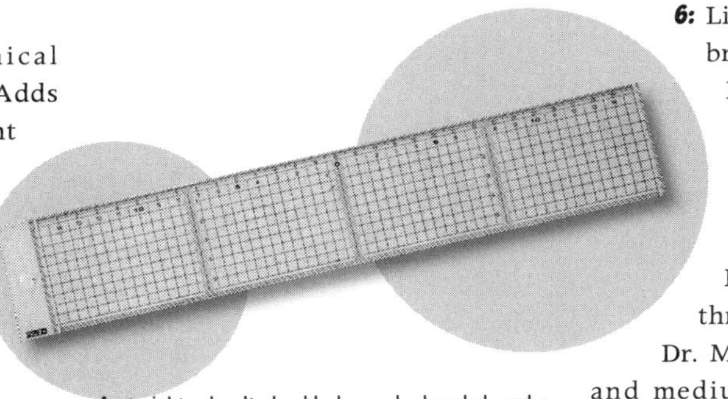

A straight ruler. It should always be beveled, and a ruled one is even handier!

10: I usually use a long thin brush. **11:** Letra and IC; mainly 61, 50 and 40. I use different manufacturers for patterns though. **12:** 30 cm. **13:** Staedtler set of three. **14:** Mainly Dr. Martin's colored ink. **15:** I usually use three brushes that vary in size. **16:** BB Kent's extra fin e or Canson paper; both only boards. **17:** I write on an angled tracing light box.

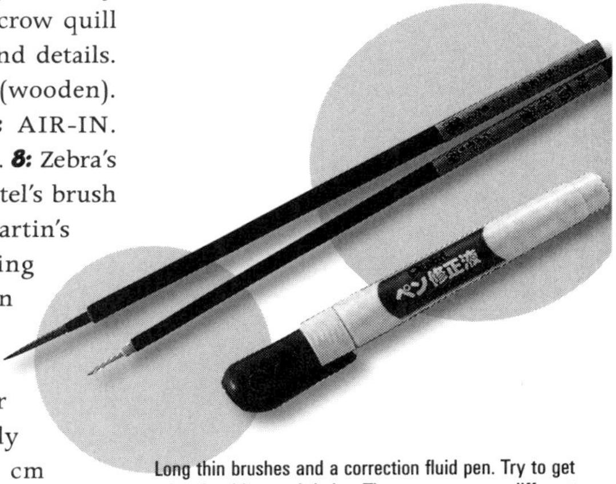

Long thin brushes and a correction fluid pen. Try to get a brush with even bristles. There are so many different correction fluids that have different consistencies, so try them out and see what works best for you!

Masumi Shimizu–Prism Heart (Ciao)

1: 0.5 mm mechanical pencil with B lead. **2:** Art Color's Manga script paper. **3:** Zebra G and crow quill pen. The G-pen is used for the character's main lines and the crow quill pen is used for hair, face, and background. **4:** Zebra penholders. (I particularly like the wooden ones because they're light.) **5:** Pilot drawing ink. **6:** Light by MONO. **7:** Pentel's brush pens. **9:** Dr. Martin's BP white ink and extra fine correction fluid. **10:** Shirokatsura's fine sable brush. **11:** I use anything. **12:** 45 and 18 cm. **13:** Staedtler set of three. **14:** Colored ink from Dr. Martin and Luma. **15:** Fine and medium-sized long brushes. **16:** Canson boards and Arches two-piece set (large and small). **14:** I use colored ink (Dr. Martin) for everything. I use water resistant black Holbein ink for the characters' main lines, though. **15:** Three middle-fine brushes (I use them separately depending on the color groups; red, pink, yellow, brown, blue and green). I use a larger brush (though almost everything is done with an airbrush and sometimes pastels) for the background. **16:** Canson paper. **18:** It's not anything rare, but I use a toothbrush for starry effects.

after fiddling with them on the computer and copy machine. It's all right for some of the color page to be three-dimensional, so sometimes I raise the surface with some modeling paste. It's fun to put stickers on or add some beads or pins!

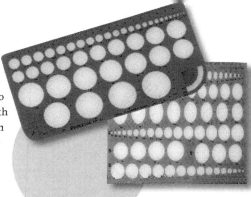

In addition to the curve templates, circle and oval templates are necessary tools for drawing curves. There aren't many that are beveled though, so be careful when you use them!

Yumi Tsukirino–Pi Pi Pi ★Adventure (Ciao)

1: 0.5 mm mechanical pencil with 2B lead. **2:** IC Manga paper, 100 lb. **3:** I use a G-pen for the character's main parts, but a crow quill pen for the character's hair, eyes, background and effects. **4:** Brause's double end penholder with a round cross section. **5:** Pilot drawing ink. **6:** MONO. **7:** A brush pen (for narrow parts) and a marker (for bigger parts). **8:** Pentel's brush pen. **9:** I use Dr. Martin's BP white ink for the drawing but MONO's white tape for the text. **11:** I use Comic tone C-1~4 for a mesh effect and IC screens for patterns. I use Deleter for flashes. **12:** 30 and 15 cm. **13:** UEDA SHOJI's like the face, hair and effects. **4:** I use the Zebra's double end holder for my G-pen (the cross section is a hexagon) and a Zebra penholder for my crow quill pen. **5:** Kaimei liquid ink. **6:** MONO. **7:** I use Kaimei liquid ink with a brush and some markers as well. **8:** A long thin brush. **9:** Mainly Dr. Martin's BP white ink but sometimes I use Misnon and POSCA white and white ink that come in tape form. **10:** A very thin long brush. **11:** I use the Letra set screen tones the most (1212 and 61). I also use IC, Deleter and Design screens. I usually buy all the new ones that come out. **12:** Normally I use a 30 cm ruler but I also have a 50 cm one. **13:** LINEX's three-piece set; I only use the big one for the most part. **14:** I use water resistant Holbein ink for lines or the black, sepia or grey color from Marvel. I use Luma or Dr. Martin colored inks for coloring but I use color screens, pastels and COPiC markers depending on the look I'm going for. But lately, I've been using Photoshop on my Mac a lot. **15:** Mainly three or four varying sized brushes as well as an airbrush. **16:** I have Classico Fabriano paper (fine) cut into boards for me. I also use Canson boards (with color) too. **17:** I create an angled surface with cartons and magazines. **18:** Recently, I've been having fun pasting copies of pictures and such, done on copy film (something like a screen tone)

AUTOMATIC DIRECTION GUIDE PEN KNIFE

A design knife, also referred to as a screen tone knife. It's great for cutting screens, but some pros prefer a normal utility blade.

Kaoru Tsuge–Unfinished Sonata (Sho-Comi)

1: 0.3 mechanical pencil with B lead. **2:** IC's Manga paper, 100 lb. **3:** Zebra G and crow quill pen. (The crow quill pen is used for the face, hair and background. The G-pen is used for main lines and hair in close-ups.) **5:** Pilot certification ink. **6:** MONO. **7:** Pentel's brush pen and Zebra's soft small brush pen for hair. **9:** I use a correction pen made by Uni. **11:** IC 937, Comic screen 1, Deleter 40 & 30. **12:** 36 cm. **14:** Everything Dr. Martin **15:** One mid-sized brush. **16:** Canson boards. **17:** I stack magazines and angle my sketchbook.

DELETER
J-TONE
IC SCREEN
S-5004

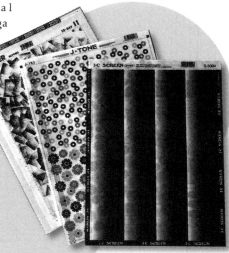

Screen tones are printed on a clear film that has glue on one side. You cut these with a knife and paste it on your script. They have screen tones for different effects now, but try to do it by hand while you're still new at this.

crow quill pen for the details and background. **4:** Brause's double-ended penholder with a circular cross section. **5:** Kaimei liquid ink. **7:** Brush pens and markers. **8:** I use everything from a long thin brush to a flat brush, markers, brush pens... anything really. **9:** I use Dr. Martin's BP white ink for the details as well as Misnon. **10:** A normal long thin brush. **11:** IC, Deleter, the Letra set; I especially use IC 40, SE 20, 30 and 50. **12:** 36-45 cm. **13:** Rotring's three-piece set; I also use other brands because I often lose or break them. **14:** Colored ink (Dr. Martin). **15:** I mainly use three brushes that vary in size, and sometimes a flat brush for the background. **16:** Canson or BB Kent (rough). **17:** I use an angled tracing light box.

Natsuko Hamaguchi–Daten (Betsucomi)

1: 0.5 mm mechanical pencil with 2B lead. **2:** Deleter's manga paper type C, 100 lb. **3:** Zebra G (main lines) and the Zebra crow quill pen (face, hair and background etc.). **4:** I have 2-3 G and crow quill pens with different nibs that are either new or have been used a lot. **5:** Liquid ink. **6:** I think the regular MONO eraser is the best. **7:** I drain the ink from Pentel's brush pens and use them with liquid ink. **9:** Dr. Martin or Luma's BP white ink. **10:** I think the

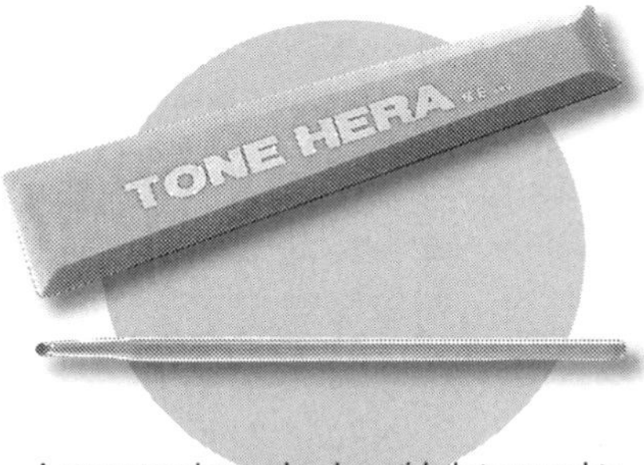
TONE HERA

A screen tone hera and a glass stick that are used to paste the screen on. Also used to rub it, though you could also use the back of a spoon.

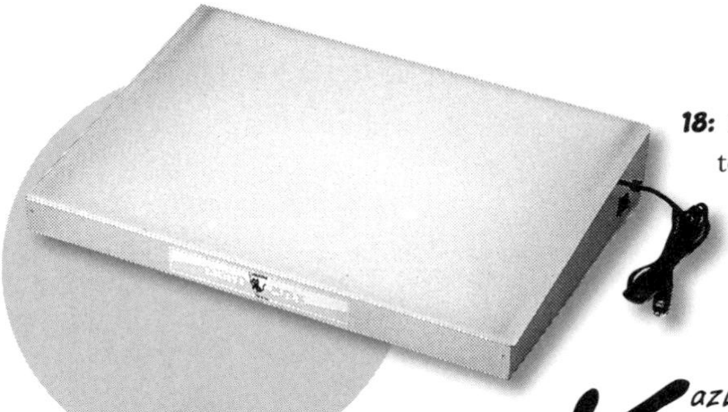

A tracing light box; the ones with an angle are sometimes called dress boards. They have a fluorescent light inside making it easier to trace.

Rin Natsumi–Sanagi to Oosma (Sho-Comi)

1: Usually a 0.5 mm mechanical pencil (B) and 0.3 mm (HB) for the details. **2:** Deleter paper, 100 lb. **3:** Zebra G and crow quill pen; I use the G-pen to outline faces but depending on the size of the drawing, I might do the entire thing with a crow quill pen. **5:** Kaimei drawing sol. **6:** I think MONO's the best! **7:** I always color the hair with a brush pen; either Zebra or Pilot. **8:** A brush pen; if it runs out of ink sometimes I put ink on it and use it... **9:** If I'm erasing large areas, I use Pentel's fine tip but for more detailed areas, I use Dr. Martin's BP white ink. **11:** I mainly use IC and Deleter, especially Deleter 0 and 31. **12:** I use a 50 cm ruler for dividing the panels and the background, but usually a 15 cm one suffices. **13:** I like the templates better. **14:** Colored ink (Dr. Martin and Luma). **15:** Sometimes I only use one, but I know that's not proper form. **16:** I mostly use boards...Canson and sketchbooks. **17:** A normal desk, kotatsu, or on my knees.

Yuri Hasebe–My Darling ♥ Lion (Cheese!)

1: 0.5 mm HB or 0.3 mm B mechanical pencil. **2:** IC Manga paper, 120 lb. **3:** Zebra G and crow quill pen; I use the G-pen for the characters in general and the

◄ *Read this way*

18: I use a makeup brush to brush off my screen tone scraps.

Kazuko Tomidokoro–Raibaru wa Cute Boy (Ciao)

1: 0.5 mm mechanical pencil with HB lead. **2:** IC Manga paper, 80 or 100 lb. **3:** Zebra G and crow quill pen; I even do the details on my characters with a G-pen and do the background and effects with the crow quill pen. **4:** Brause's double-ended penholder with a round cross section. **5:** Pilot drawing ink. **6:** MONO. **7:** I use two (both large and fine) Kuretake pens and markers. **9:** I use the white Sakura poster paint and Misnon. **10:** A long thin brush. **11:** IC and Deleter; mainly 41, 61 and the throw net types. **12:** 30 and 36 cm. **13:** Staedtler's set of three. **14:** I use colored ink for skin (Dr. Martin) and use Luma for pink tones. I also use Sakura's matte and Turner's transparent watercolors. The Turner paint I use is Transvert. **15:** I use a medium-sized Holbein and a long thin brush. I usually stick with the Holbein brush, though. I use the long thin brush for white ink. I use a bigger brush when I'm painting a bigger area. **16:** I'm not very picky. Sometimes I use a sketchbook sold at the stationery store or art store. **17:** I do my work on a tilted tracing light box. **18:** A kneaded eraser is a must. You can lighten up areas or erase something lightly. Sometimes when you need to redo the rough draft it's easier when you can see your old rough draft. You can also collect the scraps from the screen and normal erasers. Another useful tool is a pen-type sand eraser. You can use it when you need to redo something. Sometimes the ink doesn't go on well on the Misnon, so I always have this eraser handy. You can erase ink lines and print. I use an American brand eraser.

Nanako Matsumoto–Akuma no Youna Anata (Cheese!) & Hayabusa no Joe (Bestucomi)

1: 0.5 mm mechanical pencil with HB lead. **2:** Sekaido Manga paper, 100 lb. **3:** I use Rotring's Art Pen Graph (EF) and Rotring's 0.1 mm for the main lines. For details (like the face) I use the Zebra crow quill pen and the Zebra school pen for hair. **4:** MAXON pen holder No. 3 (crow quill pens) and Schwan Stabilo Swano 4350 (school pens). **5:** Pilot drawing ink. **7:** Zebra brush pens etc. **9:** Dr. Martin's BP white ink. **12:** IC and Deleter etc.; I use Deleter SE40 for shadows. **13:** 30 and 40 cm. **15:** I do skin with Dr. Martin. I also use Nouvel design markers and color screen tones (Deleter). **17:** Sekaido Kent paper (the thickest one). **18:** I usually work at the table, and when I'm doing color pages I work on an angled tracing light box.

Setona Mizushiro–Allegro Agitato (Betsucomi)

1: 0.5 mm mechanical pencil with HB lead. **2:** IC Manga paper, 100 lb. **3:** Zebra crow quill pen, brush pen (hard tip) and ballpoint pens; I use Rotring 0.18 for the background. **5:** Pilot certification ink. **6:** MONO's Light. **7:** Kuretake Twin brush pen, Zebra Mackee and Uni's POSCA. small brush pen (hard tips). **8:** Pilot's small brush pen (hard tip) and long thin brushes (small, medium and large). **9:** White poster paint **10:** A small thin brush. **11:** IC screen tones, IC Elter, Deleter, the Letra set (31, 33, 41-43, 51-53, 61-64, 82, 84). **12:** 40, 30, 20 and 10 cm and about a 30 cm triangular ruler; I think the ones that are ruled in 5-10 mm increments are the easiest to use. **13:** I have a six-piece set from an unknown manufacturer and one that I got at the $1 store. **14:** I use COPiC's sepia for the main lines and Winsor & Newton colored inks. I mix the inks to get a skin color. I arbitrarily use poster paints, gouaches, acrylics, colored pencils, Coupy pencils and colored pens. **15:** I mainly use about five medium-sized brushes, two medium-sized flat brushes, and two long thin brushes. Sometimes I use a paste brush for the background. **16:** I mainly use KMK's Kent boards, but I've used oil-painting paper once before. **17:** I put something that'll work as a platform on my desk and a plywood board to give it an angle. **18:** Maybe a spray pump that lets you use water-based pens as an airbrush? (refer to illustration). I think it cost about $5 but it's light, it doesn't require maintenance and it's cheap. I don't use it very often though.

CARMINE
PRUSSIAN BLUE
HOLBEIN DRAWING INK

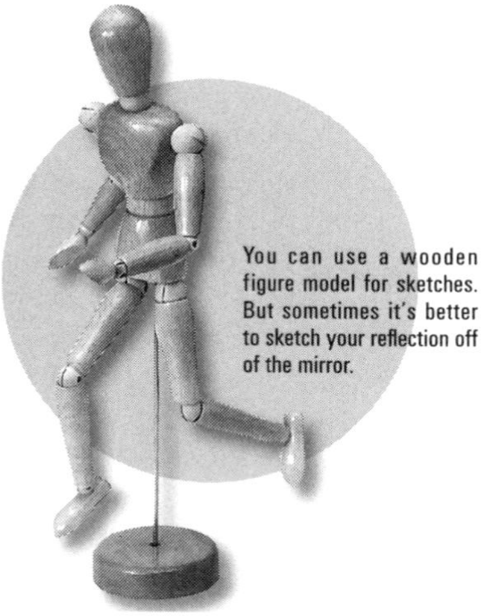

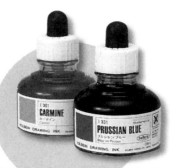

Colored inks. These are Holbein, but they're water resistant, so we recommend using the sepia or black for inking.

You can use a wooden figure model for sketches. But sometimes it's better to sketch your reflection off of the mirror.

You put the pen here.
Made of rubber.

thinnest long brush works the best. **11:** Mainly Deleter; I usually use SE 40/41 for the character's shadows. **12:** I use a 37 cm ruler for creating the panels and Staedtler's 20 cm one for everything else. **13:** Rotring's three-piece set. **14:** Mainly colored ink (Dr. Martin, Luma, Winsor & Newton, Brilliant Watercolor). Also colored pencils, and for the main lines I use a water resistant colored ink (sepia). **15:** I use varying sizes of Tokyo Namura's nylon round brush. **16:** Kent paper for color pages. Now I'm using Canson's Fontenay watercolor paper (fine) and I really like it. As long as it takes the ink well, I'm not particular about the paper that I use, though. **17:** I stack books and use a board canvas as my drawing board. **18:** I use a cookbook stand (*refer to illustration)

to hold the books I'm referencing. My assistant uses paper tape (the kind you can peel) for picking up screen tone scraps.

Mitsuru Fujii–Amai Sutoresu (Betsucomi)

1: 0.5 mm mechanical pencil with HB or B lead. If I'm doing scenery or architecture, I use blue lead. **2:** Art Color Manga paper, 100 lb... **3:** Zebra G and crow quill pen, spoon nibs; I'm not particular about my school pens though. G-pen=people, main lines, solid flashes; crow quill pen=hair, stipples, focus lines; spoon pen=focus lines, solid flashes; school pen=net effects, ropes; I use a 1 mm drawing pen (water-based or pigment ink). **4:** I like wooden ones. **5:** Sumi ink; I dilute it a little with a mister. **7:** Sumi ink, oil-based markers, Pilot's

← *Read this way*

9: Correction pens and Milky pens. **11:** IC and Deleter; I use IC 30 and 50 the most. **12:** 20 and 40 cm ones. **13:** It's made by Rotring. It's very old and it says, "made in West Germany." **14:** Dr. Martin, but lately I've been using my computer for the most part, and I use Photoshop and Painter. **15:** I use three brushes that vary in size and a flat brush, but like I mentioned before most of it is done on the computer... **16:** Arches, but ...you know the rest. **17:** A normal table. **18:** Original screen tones I made on my Mac.

Kaho Miyasaka–Binetsu Shojo (Sho-Comi)

1: 0.3 mm mechanical pencil with H lead. **2:** Deleter's professional C type, 100 lb. **3:** Zebra school pens (main lines) and Zebra crow quill pens (hair, face); sometimes I only use one of them for the whole thing... **4:** Brause's double-ended penholder with a circular cross section. **5:** Pilot drawing ink. **6:** PLUS AIR-IN. **7:** Pentel brush pens and COPiC liner pens. **9:** Dr. Martin's pen-white and Pentel's correction pen. **11:** The Letra set, IC, Deleter, MAXON and Design screen tones. I mainly use Letra 1211 and IC 61, as well as the gradations. **12:** 40 cm. **13:** Staedtler's set of three. **14:** Luma, Dr. Martin and COPiC. **15:** Mainly 3-5 brushes, and I separate them by color tones. **16:** Classico Fabriano paper and Crescent boards; Arches types. **17:** I use an A2 sized angled tracing light box.

Yukino Miyawaki–1/2 Weddings (Ciao)

1: 0.5 mm mechanical pencil with HB and F lead. **2:** IC, 100 lb and Art Color, 100 lb manga paper. **3:** I use Zebra

POSE CATALOGUE

A background photo book is a must for any manga artist! They contain pictures of different buildings and backgrounds. There are also photo books of different poses, but they don't get used as much as the background collection.

G for the character's outline and the Zebra crow quill pen for details, backgrounds and effects. **4:** I break Beaver penholders so they're smaller for my G-pens and I use Yanoha and Zebra for my crow quill pens. **5:** Sumi no Sei. **6:** MONO's Light and AIR-IN HARD. **7:** I use Kuretake Manga black ink for big areas, and for everything else I use markers and brush pens. **8:** I use two Kuretake brush pens and both large and small Zebra brush pens. **9:** BP white ink from Luma and Dr. Martin, as well as IC comic super white. I also use Misnon. **10:** A normal Shirakatsura brush. **11:** I use a lot of different screens from different manufacturers. **12:** A 36 cm ruler for longer areas and a 20 cm one for shorter needs. **13:** Staedtler's two-piece set. **14:** I use Dr. Martin and Luma for my colored inks and sometimes COPiC markers for the details. **15:** I use coloring brushes of varying sizes and a Shirakatsura big brush. **16:** I switch between Canson, BB Kent, and Baron Kent papers depending on the drawing and the materials I'm using. **17:** I work on an angled tracing light box.

Taeko Watanabe–Kaze Hikaru (Bestucomi)

1: 0.5 mm mechanical pencil with 2B lead. **2:** High quality blank paper, 100 lb. **3:** Zebra G and crow quill pen; I use the G-pen for the characters in general and the crow quill pen for details and backgrounds. **4:** I use an extra big wooden penholder with a rubber grip. **5:** I use two kinds of liquid ink for the main lines and effects. **6:** PLUS AIR-IN. **7:** Pentel brush pens. **8:** Pentel extra fine and medium-sized brush pens. **9:** Misnon; When I'm doing colored scripts I use Dr. Martin's BP white ink. **10:** A long thin brush. **11:** The Letra set and IC screens along with ones by other manufacturers; I mainly use Letra 51 and 62. **12:** 30 cm. **13:** Staedtler's three piece set. **14:** Mainly Dr.

IC COLOR OVERLAY
MAXON
IC 102

A color screen tone is used just like a normal screen tone. It gives the page an anime pop.

Martin colored inks and some Luma. **15:** I usually use three brushes that vary in size. **16:** BB Kent (fine) and Canson. I mainly stick with the boards. **17:** I use a desktop drawing board with an opaque acrylic board on top. I put a light underneath so it works like a tracing light box. **18:** A hybrid mechanical pencil that alternates between a pencil and a 2 mm eraser, a mechanical pencil with blue lead, mechanical eraser, reusable tape (as a temporary joint for script protectors and point papers).

INDEX

A

Acrylics   144
Airbrush   15, 142, 143, 156, 161

B

Background   5, 94, 108, 114, 115-131, 154, 155
Bleeds   88, 89, 99, 101
Bringing in manga   172-174, 176-179
Brush cleaner   9, 137
Brushes   6, 9, 11, 13, 15, 106, 136, 137, 140, 141
Brush pens   98, 106, 188

C

Characters   26, 28, 29, 37-54, 56-58, 60, 68, 74-76, 80, 85, 94, 118, 130
Circle templates   192
Climax   65, 87
Close-ups   30, 54, 73, 102
Colored inks   8, 137, 144, 146, 149, 194
Colored pencils   12, 144
Colored screen tones   145, 195
Colored manga paper   139
Colored pages   8-14, 134-147, 158
Coloring   6, 106, 108
Color sprays   142, 143
Computers   14-16, 114, 115, 150, 158-163
Composition   2, 54, 70, 74, 85, 101-103, 113, 149, 172
Contrast   3, 30, 72, 73, 86, 87, 92, 102-105, 113
COPiC   10, 11, 144
Copy screen tones   156
Counterparts   46, 47, 50, 51, 52, 53
Cover   165, 168-170, 172, 179
Crow quill nib pens   4, 5, 20, 98, 156, 187
Curve templates   191
Cut and paste   168

D

Different panel shapes   86, 87
Design   24, 25, 26, 30, 31, 35
Details   148, 149
Drama   48, 50, 103, 113
Drawing ink   21, 98, 106, 135, 156, 188

E

Effects   5, 27, 72, 119, 126, 127, 128, 129, 130, 131
Energy   66, 67, 79, 92
Episodes   6, 41, 61, 62, 63, 65, 67-71, 79
Erasers   3, 5, 8, 100, 106, 108
Exaggeration   46, 37, 149, 155
Expressions   16, 25, 26, 28, 30, 32, 35, 37, 46, 54, 102

F

Feather duster	190
Final touches	6, 113, 164-168, 180
Focus lines	128

G

Genre	60, 61, 71, 169
Gouache	144
G-pens	4, 20, 98, 104, 156, 187

H

Head shots	30
Highlights	12, 13, 107

I

Illustration boards	139
Ink	3, 4, 5, 8, 9, 98, 138, 140, 141
Inking	3, 4, 5, 8, 100, 104, 106, 114, 138, 139, 149, 156
Introduction	52

K

Kabura pens	156
Knives	7, 144, 152, 153, 192

L

Light blue pencils	7
Light box	8, 193
Lines	42, 46, 70, 77, 78, 80-82, 84, 93, 133
Liquid ink	4, 21, 106, 135, 156, 188
Long shots	73, 102
Long thin brushes	6, 13, 106, 191

M

Macs	14, 15, 16, 158
Main character	28, 32, 44-54, 58, 61, 63-66, 71, 82, 83, 95, 169
Magic markers	106
Margin	88, 89
Markers (black)	3, 6, 156, 188
Markers (colored)	144
Masking	15, 16, 142, 143, 161
Mechanical pencils	8
Mesh	126
Monologues	82, 83, 93

O

Opening	128
Oval template	192

P

Page layout	55, 100, 101, 113
Page turning effect	88-91, 93
Panel division	86, 93
Panel Lines	3, 130, 132, 133

Paper	8, 21, 98, 99
Pastels	144
Pencils	3, 8, 84, 100, 113
Pen holder	20
Pen nibs	20, 104, 187
Pens	20, 84, 98, 100, 104, 128, 130, 133, 138
Pen touch	104, 105, 113
Perspective	116, 122-125, 131,154, 155
Photo tracing	154, 163
Plot	2, 67-71, 74, 75, 78
Point perspective	122, 123
Poster paint	135, 137, 144
Presentation	90-93
Props	60, 61, 71

R

Reproduction	30
Rivals	48, 49, 50, 51
Rough drafts	2, 3, 8, 12, 76, 99-101, 104, 160
Rulers	3, 132, 191

S

Sand eraser	7, 153
Scraping screens	7, 110, 111, 152, 153
Screen tones	6, 7, 54, 72, 73, 108-111, 113-115, 126, 132, 133, 150, 152, 156, 192
Screen tone knife	108, 152, 192
Setting	41-43, 50, 53, 60, 62
Side characters	48, 49, 50, 51, 52, 53
Solid flash	7, 128, 129
Spread	55, 86, 88, 93
Speech balloons	37, 81, 84-86, 93, 130
Story	51, 54, 56, 57, 58, 59, 60-69, 70, 75, 83, 92
Storyboard	2, 62, 70, 76-78, 80, 81, 86, 88, 91, 93-95
Story flow	66, 67, 71
Structure	75, 76, 79, 88, 90-92, 94, 95
Submission	172-179, 178, 179
Subtitles	82

T

Text	37, 130
Theme	58, 59, 62, 67-71
Three point perspective	124, 125
Timing	55, 77, 78, 79, 93
Tissue	4, 9
Title	165, 169, 170, 171, 172, 179
Tracing paper	172
Two point perspective	124

W

Water resistant ink	8, 138, 139, 149
White ink	6, 12, 13, 106-108, 140, 141, 190

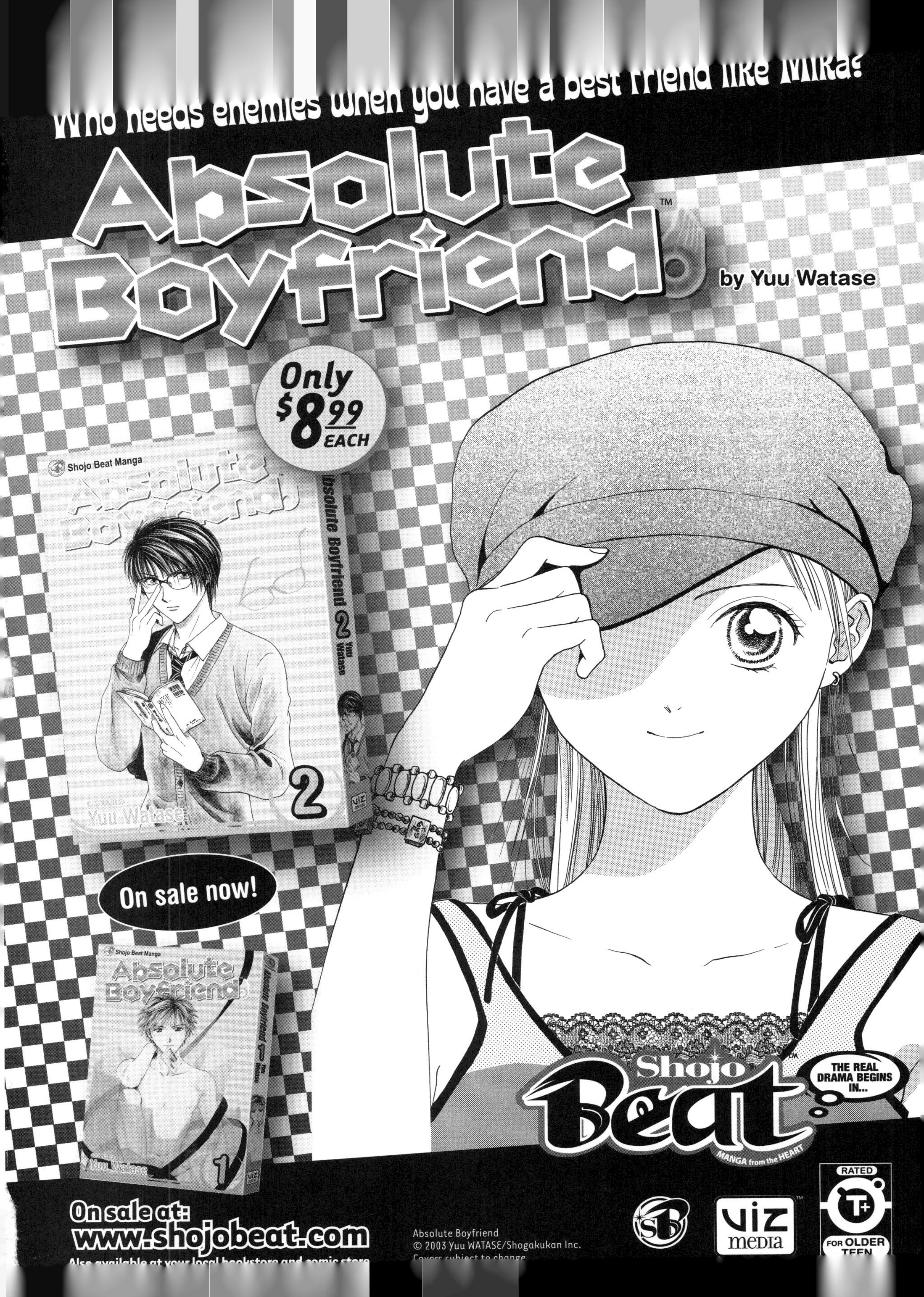
Who needs enemies when you have a best friend like Mika?
Absolute Boyfriend™
by Yuu Watase
Only $8.99 EACH
Shojo Beat Manga
Absolute Boyfriend
Absolute Boyfriend 2 Yuu Watase
Yuu Watase
2
On sale now!
Shojo Beat Manga
Absolute Boyfriend
Absolute Boyfriend 1 Yuu Watase
Yuu Watase
1
Shojo Beat
MANGA from the HEART
THE REAL DRAMA BEGINS IN...
On sale at:
www.shojobeat.com
Also available at your local bookstore and comic store
Absolute Boyfriend
© 2003 Yuu WATASE/Shogakukan Inc.
Covers subject to change.
viz media
RATED T+ FOR OLDER TEEN

Shojo Beat's

Manga Artist Academy

The Shojo Beat Profiles Edition

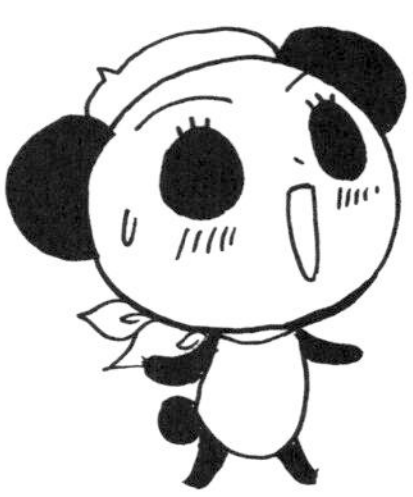

Concept by Hiroyuki Iizuka
Art by Amu Sumoto, et al
English Translation & Adaptation/Mai Ihara
Touch-up Art & Lettering/James Gaubatz
Design/Courtney Utt
Editor/Pancha Diaz

Managing Editors/Masumi Washington & Megan Bates
VP & Editor in Chief/ Yumi Hoashi
Sr. Director of Acquisitions/Rika Inouye
Sr. VP of Marketing/Liza Coppola
Executive VP of Sales & Marketing/John Easum
Publisher/Hyoe Narita

Printed in the U.S.A.

Published by VIZ Media, LLC.
P.O. Box 77010
San Francisco, CA 94107

Shojo Beat Profiles Edition
10 9 8 7 6 5 4 3 2 1
First printing, October 2006

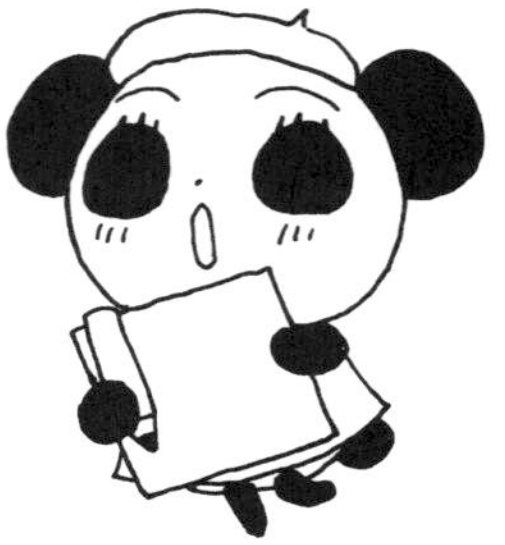

www.viz.com